g. c.
9838.

GARDA SÍOCHÁ

GW00761068

NOT TO BE REMOVED
FROM LIBRARY

IRISH LAW REPORTS MONTHLY INDEX, 1976–1990

Editor
BART D. DALY, BCL, *Barrister-at-Law*

Editorial advisors
RAYMOND BYRNE, *Barrister-at-Law*
TONY KERR, *Barrister-at-Law*

Editorial Board
THE HON. MR JUSTICE BRIAN WALSH
JENNEFER ASTON, *Librarian*
SIR JAMES COMYN
BRENDAN T. BYRNE, *Attorney*
MARCUS BERESFORD, *Solicitor*
BRUCE ST JOHN BLAKE, *Solicitor*
FRANK CLARKE, *Barrister-at-Law*
RODERICK H. MURPHY, *Barrister-at-Law*
PATRICK MacENTEE, SC
THE HON. MR JUSTICE HUGH J. O'FLAHERTY
JAMES O'REILLY, *Barrister-at-Law*
YVONNE SCANNELL, *Lecturer in law*

Administrator
MICHAEL ADAMS

IRISH LAW
REPORTS MONTHLY
INDEX, 1976–1990

Julitta Clancy

THE ROUND HALL PRESS
DUBLIN

This book was typeset by
Seton Music Graphics, Bantry, for
The Round Hall Press, Kill Lane, Blackrock, Co. Dublin

© THE ROUND HALL PRESS LIMITED 1993

All rights reserved. No part of this publication may be
reproduced, stored in any retrieval system, transmitted in any
form, or by any means, electronic, mechanical, photocopying,
recording, or otherwise, without the prior permission of the publishers.

A catalogue record for this book
is available from the British Library

ISBN 0–947686–82–7

Printed in Ireland by
Colour Books Ltd, Dublin.

Contents

NOT TO BE REMOVED
FROM LIBRARY

List of Judges

THE SUPREME COURT

The Hon. Brian C. Walsh	16 December 1961	–	23 March 1990
The Hon. Seamus Henchy	2 October 1972	–	16 October 1988
The Hon. Frank Griffin	3 January 1973	–	
The Hon. Thomas F. O'Higgins, Chief Justice	29 October 1974	–	15 January 1985
The Hon. John Kenny	21 October 1975	–	24 April 1982
The Hon. Weldon Roycroft Parke	16 January 1976	–	18 February 1981
The Hon. Anthony J. Hederman Supreme Court	29 June 1981	–	
The Hon. Niall McCarthy	1 November 1982	–	
The Hon. Thomas A. Finlay. Chief Justice	16 January 1985	–	
The Hon. Hugh J. O'Flaherty	26 March 1990	–	

THE HIGH COURT

The Hon. George Murnaghan	31 December 1953	–	4 July 1979
The Hon. Seán de Buitléir	3 October 1966	–	6 July 1980
The Hon. Thomas A. Finlay	10 October 1972	–	15 January 1985
	(President from 17 December 1974)		
The Hon. John Gannon	3 January 1973	–	5 December 1990
The Hon. Weldon Roycroft Parke	6 November 1974	–	15 January 1976
The Hon. Liam Hamilton	29 October 1974	–	15 January 1985
	(President, 16 January 1985 –)		
The Hon. Thomas A. Doyle	17 December 1974	–	14 June 1984
The Hon. James McMahon	21 October 1975	–	5 January 1986
The Hon. Herbert R. McWilliam	16 January 1976	–	12 February 1985
The Hon. Declan Costello	20 May 1977	–	
The Hon. James D'Arcy	24 June 1977	–	4 April 1987
The Hon. Ronan C. Keane	13 July 1979	–	
The Hon. Donal Barrington	27 September 1979	–	31 August 1989

The Hon. William R. Ellis	27 September 1979	– 10 December 1983
The Hon. Mella Carroll	6 October 1980	–
The Hon. Roderick J. O'Hanlon	20 March 1981	–
The Hon. Edward M. Walsh	18 December 1981	– 2 November 1982
The Hon. Francis D. Murphy	4 March 1982	–
The Hon. Henry D. Barron	4 March 1982	–
The Hon. Kevin Lynch	23 January 1984	–
The Hon. Seamus F. Egan	2 July 1984	–
The Hon. Justice Robert Barr	28 January 1985	–
The Hon. Gerard J. W. Lardner	6 March 1985	–
The Hon. John Blayney	20 January 1986	–
The Hon. J. J. Patrick MacKenzie	10 February 1986	–
The Hon. Richard P. Johnson	19 January 1987	–
The Hon. Vivian Lavan	20 September 1989	–
The Hon. Frederick R. Morris	20 December 1990	–

List of Reporters

Bruce Antoniotti
Richard Barrett
Eilis Barry
Bernard Barton
Rosario Boyle
Raymond Byrne
Eamon Cahill
Niamh Cahill
Anthony M. Collins
Caroline Costello
Michael Counihan
Noel Davitt
Hilary Delany
Hayes Dockrell
Christopher Doyle
Henry Downing
Marjorie Farrelly
Kenneth Ferguson
Margo Ford
Paul Gardiner
Maurice Hearne
Samuel Hussey
Michael P. Kane
David Kennedy
Tony Kerr
Noreen Mackey

Olivia Meagher
Charles Meenan
Patrick Mooney
Joan More-O'Ferrall
Shane Murphy
Yvonne Murphy
Shane Murray
Michael MacGrath
Eileen McAuley
Sunniva McDonagh
Finbarr McElligott
Damian McHugh
Margaret Nerney
Charles O'Conor
Michael O'Higgins
Michael P. O'Kane
Séamus Ó Tuathail
Jennifer Payne
Stephen Pye
David Riordan
June Sheehan
John Trainor
Greta Walsh
Anne Watkin
Marie Whelan

Cases Reported

Armstrong, Hamilton v	HC	[1984]	306
Army Pensions Board, State (Williams) v	SC	[1983]	331
Army Pensions Board, Williams v	HC	[1981]	379
Asahi Synthetic Fibres, Murphy v	HC	[1986]	24
Ashmark Ltd (No.1), In re	HC	[1990]	330
Ashmark Ltd (No.2), In re	HC	[1990]	455
Assicurazioni Generali SPA, Chariot Inns Ltd v	SC	[1981]	173
Athlone Urban District Council v Gavin	SC	[1986]	277
Atkins v Atkins	HC	[1976–7]	62
Attorney General v Gilliland see People (AG) v Gilliland			
Attorney General v Leaf Ltd	HC	[1982]	441
Attorney General v Palmer Products Ltd see Attorney General v Leaf Ltd			
Attorney General v Paperlink Ltd	HC	[1984]	373
Attorney General v Sheehy	HC	[1989]	303
Attorney General v Sun Alliance and London Insurances Ltd	SC	[1985]	522
Attorney General (ex rel McGarry) v Sligo County Council	SC	[1989]	768
Attorney General (ex rel McGarry) v Sligo County Council (No.2)	SC	[1989]	785
Attorney General (ex rel Martin) v Dublin Corporation	SC	[1983]	254
Attorney General (ex rel SPUC) v Open Door Counselling	HC	[1987]	477
Attorney General (ex rel SPUC) v Open Door Counselling	SC	[1989]	19
Attorney General, Aughey v	HC	[1986]	206
Attorney General, Aughey v	SC	[1989]	87
Attorney General, Blake v	SC	[1981]	34
Attorney General, Brennan v	HC	[1983]	449
Attorney General, Brennan v	SC	[1984]	355
Attorney General, Cafolla v	HC &SC	[1986]	177
Attorney General, Cashman v	HC	[1990]	200
Attorney General, Curtis v	HC	[1986]	428
Attorney General, Dillane v	SC	[1980]	167
Attorney General, Draper v	HC&SC	[1984]	643
Attorney General, McCann v	HC	[1983]	67
Attorney General, Madigan v	HC&SC	[1986]	136
Attorney General, Murray and Murray v	HC	[1985]	542
Attorney General, O'G (T) v	HC	[1985]	61
Attorney General, PMPS Ltd v	SC	[1984]	88
Attorney General, Rederij Kennemerland BV v	HC&SC	[1989]	821
Attorney General, Representative Church Body v	HC	[1989]	177
Attorney General, Shannon v	HC&SC	[1985]	449
Attorney General, Sunshine Radio Productions v	HC	[1984]	170
Attorney General, Tormey v	HC	[1984]	657
Attorney General, Tormey v	SC	[1985]	375
Attorney General for England and Wales v Brandon Book Publishers	HC	[1987]	135
Aughey v Attorney General and Ireland	HC	[1986]	206
Aughey v Attorney General	SC	[1989]	87
Avenue Properties Ltd v Farrell Homes Ltd	HC	[1982]	21
B (L) v B (H)	HC	[1980]	257
B (R), S (A) v	HC	[1984]	66
Bairead v Maxwells of Donegal Ltd	HC	[1986]	508
Baker v Cohn-Vossen, In re estate of Mieth	HC	[1986]	175
Bakht v Medical Council	SC	[1990]	840
Balkan Tours Ltd v Minister for Communications	HC	[1988]	101
Ballagh, State (Lynch) v	SC	[1987]	65
Ballybay Meat Exports Ltd v Monaghan County Council	HC	[1990]	864

Bord Telecom Éireann, Murphy v	HC	[1986] 483
Bord Telecom Éireann, Murphy v	ECJ&HC	[1989] 53
Bord Uchtála (An), C (K) v; In re JH (an infant)	HC&SC	[1985] 302
Bord Uchtála (An), C (K) v; In re JH (an infant)(No.2)	HC	[1986] 65
Bord Uchtála (An), H (A) and H (M) v	HC	[1984] 237
Bord Uchtála (An), M (J) and M (G) v	SC	[1988] 203
Bord Uchtála (An), McC v	HC	[1982] 159
Bourke (DH) & Son Ltd, Caulfield v	HC	[1980] 223
Bourke (G and J & F) Ltd, Carroll Group Distributors Ltd v	HC	[1990] 285
Bouzagou v Sgt Fitzgibbon Street Garda Station see State (Bouzagou) v Sgt Fitzgibbon St Garda Station		
Bowes v Fitzpatrick see State (Bowes) v Fitzpatrick		
Bowes v Motor Insurers' Bureau of Ireland	SC	[1990] 59
Boyce v McBride	SC	[1987] 95
Boylan v Northern Bank Ltd	HC	[1976–7] 287
Boyle v Allen	CC	[1979] 281
Boyle v General Medical Services (Payments) Board see State (Boyle) v General Medical Services (Payments) Board		
Boyle v Governor of the Military Detention Barracks see State (Boyle) v Governor of Curragh Military Detention Barracks		
Boyle v Neylon see State (Boyle) v Neylon		
Bradbury Ltd v Duffy and Whelan	HC	[1979] 51
Brady v Beckmann Instruments (Galway) Inc	SC	[1986] 361
Brady v Donegal County Council	HC&SC	[1989] 282
Brady v Irish National Insurance Co Ltd	HC&SC	[1986] 669
Brandon Book Publishers, AG for England and Wales v	HC	[1987] 135
Bray UDC, Freeney v	HC	[1982] 29
Breathnach (Inspector of Taxes) v McCann	HC	[1984] 679
Breen v Keane	CC	[1981] 279
Breen, Kelly v	HC	[1978] 63
Brennan v Attorney General	HC	[1983] 449
Brennan v Attorney General	SC	[1984] 355
Brennan v Kelly	HC	[1988] 306
Brennan v Mahon see State (Brennan) v Mahon		
Brennan v Savage Smyth & Co. Ltd	SC	[1982] 223
Bristol Myers Co, Beecham Group Ltd v	SC	[1983] 500
Brittain Group Sales Ltd, British Leyland Exports v	HC	[1982] 359
British Leyland Exports Ltd v Brittain Group Sales Ltd	HC	[1982] 359
British Railways Board, Waterford Harbour Commissioners v	SC	[1979] 296
Brogan, Monaghan County Council v	HC	[1987] 564
Brophy, Desmond & Boyle v	HC	[1986] 547
Browne v An Bord Pleanála	HC	[1989] 865
Browne, Cooney v	HC&SC	[1985] 673
Browne, Cooney v	HC	[1986] 444
Browne (Inspector of Taxes), Stephen Court Ltd v	HC	[1984] 231
Bubble Up Co. Inc, The Seven Up Co. v	HC	[1990] 204
Buckingham International Holdings Ltd, Kutchera v	HC	[1988] 1
Buckingham International Holdings Ltd, Kutchera v	SC	[1988] 501
Budget Travel Ltd, Mitchell v	SC	[1990] 739
Bula Ltd v Crowley	SC	[1990] 756
Bula Ltd v Tara Mines	HC	[1988] 149
Bula Ltd v Tara Mines (Injunction proceedings)	HC	[1988] 157
Buncrana Urban District Council, McNamee v	HC&SC	[1984] 77
Bunyan v United Dominions Trust (Irl) Ltd	EAT	[1982] 404
Burke v Garvey (Garda Commissioner) see State (Burke) v Garvey		
Burke, O'hUallachain v	HC	[1988] 693

Coogan, SPUC (Ireland) Ltd v	HC	[1989]	526
Coogan, SPUC (Ireland) Ltd v	SC	[1990]	70
Cooke (an infant) v Walsh	HC	[1983]	429
Cooke (an infant) v Walsh	SC	[1984]	208
Cooke v Walsh	SC	[1989]	322
Cooney v Browne	HC	[1986]	444
Cooney v Browne	HC&SC	[1985]	673
Cooney, State (Lynch) v	HC	[1982]	190
Cooney, State (Lynch) v	SC	[1983]	89
Co-Operative Molasses Traders Ltd, Cremer v	HC&SC	[1985]	564
Córas Iompair Éireann v Carroll	HC	[1983]	173
Córas Iompair Éireann v Carroll	SC	[1986]	312
Cork Corporation v O'Connell	SC	[1982]	505
Cork County Council, Crown Chemical Company (Irl) v	HC	[1984]	555
Cork Prison, Governor of see Governor of Cork Prison			
Corran Construction Co. v Bank of Ireland Finance Ltd	HC	[1976–7]	175
Corrigan v Crofton	HC	[1985]	189
Corrigan, DPP v	HC	[1980]	145
Corrigan, DPP v	HC	[1987]	575
Cosgrove v Ireland	HC	[1982]	48
Costello v Bofin see State (Costello) v Bofin			
Costello v DPP	HC	[1983]	489
Costello v DPP	SC	[1984]	413
Costello, Minister for Labour v	HC	[1989]	485
Costello (John) Ltd, Irish Shell and BP Ltd v	SC	[1981]	66
Costello (John) Ltd, Irish Shell and BP Ltd v	SC	[1985]	554
Cotter v Ahern	HC	[1976–7]	248
Courtney v Minister for the Marine	HC	[1989]	605
Coveney v Special Criminal Court see State (Coveney) v Special Criminal Court			
Coyle v Central Trust Investment Society Ltd	HC	[1978]	211
Coyle, Whitecross Potatoes Ltd v	HC	[1978]	31
Creedon v Criminal Injuries Compensation Tribunal see State (Creedon) v Criminal Injuries Compensation Tribunal			
Creedon v Dublin Corporation	SC	[1983]	339
Creen v Drinan	HC	[1983]	82
Cremer (Peter) GMbh v Co-operative Molasses Traders Ltd	HC&SC	[1985]	564
Criminal Injuries Compensation Tribunal, Hill v	HC	[1990]	36
Criminal Injuries Compensation Tribunal, State (Creedon) v	SC	[1989]	104
Criminal Injuries Compensation Tribunal, State (Hayes) v	HC	[1982]	210
Crodaun Homes Ltd v Kildare County Council	SC	[1983]	1
Crofton, Corrigan v	HC	[1985]	189
Cronin v Lunham Bros Ltd	HC	[1986]	415
Cronin v Youghal Carpets (Yarns) Ltd	HC&SC	[1985]	666
Crothers v Kelly see State (Crothers) v Kelly			
Crotty v An Taoiseach	HC&SC	[1987]	400
Crotty v An Taoiseach	HC	[1990]	617
Crowley v Allied Irish Banks Ltd	SC	[1988]	225
Crowley v Flynn	HC	[1983]	513
Crowley v McVeigh	HC	[1990]	220
Crowley v Northern Bank Finance Corporation Ltd	HC	[1978]	219
Crowley, Bula Ltd v	SC	[1990]	756
Crowley, Rafferty v	HC	[1984]	350
Crown Chemical Co. (Ireland) Ltd v Cork County Council	HC	[1984]	555
Cuddy v Mangan see State (Cuddy) v Mangan			
Cullen v Toibin	HC&SC	[1984]	577

Hannigan v Clifford	SC	[1990]	65
Hanrahan v Merck Sharp & Dohme (Ireland) Ltd	SC	[1988]	629
Harding Investments Ltd, McCabe v	SC	[1984]	105
Harris v Wren	HC	[1984]	120
Harris and Victor Stud Co, Williams v	SC	[1980]	237
Harte v Fanning and Mahon	HC	[1988]	70
Harte v Fanning	HC	[1988]	75
Hartery v Welltrade (Middle East) Ltd	HC	[1978]	38
Hartnett, O'Sullivan v	HC	[1981]	469
Hartnett, O'Sullivan v	SC	[1983]	79
Harvey v Minister for Social Welfare	SC	[1990]	185
Haverty v An Bord Pleanála see State (Haverty) v An Bord Pleanála			
Hayes v Criminal Injuries Compensation Tribunal see State (Hayes) v			
Criminal Injuries Compensation Tribunal			
Hayes v Ireland	HC	[1987]	651
Hazylake Fashions Ltd v Bank of Ireland	HC	[1989]	698
Health, Minister for see Minister for Health			
Health Education Bureau, Gallaher (Dublin) Ltd v	HC	[1982]	240
Healy v MacGillicuddy, In the goods of Kavanagh	HC	[1978]	175
Healy, DPP v	SC	[1990]	313
Healy, Stanbridge v	HC	[1985]	290
Heaney v Minister for Finance	HC	[1986]	164
Hearne, Burns v; In re Noyek (A) & Sons Ltd	HC	[1987]	508
Hearne, Burns v; In re Noyek (A) & Sons Ltd	SC	[1989]	155
Hearne, Doyle v	SC	[1988]	318
Hearne, Kennedy v	HC	[1988]	52
Hearne, Kennedy v	SC	[1988]	531
Hedigan, Galvin Estates Ltd v	HC	[1985]	295
Hegarty v O'Loughran	HC	[1987]	603
Hegarty v O'Loghran	SC	[1990]	403
Hegarty, Wall v	HC	[1980]	124
Heneghan v Western Regional Fisheries Board	HC	[1986]	225
Henley Forklift (Ireland) Ltd v Lansing Bagnall & Co Ltd	SC	[1979]	257
Hennessy, Murphy v	HC	[1985]	100
Hesketh Investments Ltd, In re	HC	[1984]	134
Hetherton, Lynch v	HC	[1990]	857
Hibernian Transport Co Ltd, In re	HC	[1990]	42
Hibernian Transport Companies Ltd, In re	HC	[1984]	583
Hickey and Co. Ltd v Roches Stores Ltd	HC	[1980]	107
Higgins v Reid see State (Higgins) v Reid			
Hill v Criminal Injuries Compensation Tribunal	HC	[1990]	36
Hillary v Sweeney, In re Sweeney	HC	[1976–7]	88
Hoey, People (DPP) v	SC	[1988]	666
Hogan (deceased), In re	HC	[1980]	24
Hogan v Carroll see State (Hogan) v Carroll			
Hogan v Minister for Justice	HC	[1976–7]	184
Hogan v St Kevins Co	HC	[1987]	17
Hogan, Kellystown Co v	SC	[1985]	200
Holiday Motor Inns Ltd v Dublin County Council	HC	[1976–7]	343
Holloway v Belenos Publications Ltd	HC	[1987]	790
Holloway v Belenos Publications Ltd	HC	[1988]	685
Holly, DPP (Hanley) v	HC	[1984]	149
Holohan v Donohoe	SC	[1986]	250
Hong Kong and Shanghai Banking Corporation, Parkes & Sons Ltd v	HC	[1990]	341
Horans Hotel, Sweeney v	SC	[1987]	240
Horgan v Deasy	HC	[1979]	71

Hortensius Ltd v Bishop	HC	[1989]	294
Hosford v John Murphy & Sons Ltd	HC	[1988]	300
Housing (Private Rented Dwellings) Bill 1981, In re	SC	[1983]	246
Howley, People (DPP) v	SC	[1989]	629
Hughes v Neylon *see* State (Hughes) v Neylon			
Hughes v O'Hanrahan *see* State (Hughes) v O'Hanrahan			
Hughes v O'Rourke & Ors	SC	[1986]	538
Hughes, O'Sullivan v	HC	[1986]	555
Hughes, Rahinstown Estates Co. v	HC	[1987]	599
Hughes Dairy Ltd, Kennedy v	SC	[1989]	117
Hummingbird Ltd, Mara v	HC&SC	[1982]	421
Hunting Lodges Ltd, In re	HC	[1985]	75
Hussey v Irish Land Commission *see* State (Hussey) v Irish Land Commission			
Hussey, White v	HC	[1989]	109
Hutton v Philippi	EAT	[1982]	578
Hyland v Minister for Social Welfare	HC	[1989]	196
Hyland v Minister for Social Welfare	SC	[1990]	213
Hynes Ltd v O'Malley Property Ltd	SC	[1989]	619
Hynes-O'Sullivan v O'Driscoll	SC	[1989]	349
I (P) v Ireland	SC	[1989]	810
IBM Ireland Ltd v Employment Appeals Tribunal *see* State (IBM Ireland Ltd) v Employment Appeals Tribunal			
IBM Ireland Ltd v Feeney	CC	[1983]	50
ICI *see* Insurance Corporation of Ireland			
ITT World Directories Inc v Controller of Patents	SC	[1985]	30
Incorporated Law Society of Ireland v Minister for Justice	HC	[1978]	112
Incorporated Law Society of Ireland v Minister for Justice	HC	[1987]	42
Incorporated Law Society of Ireland, Gilmer v	HC	[1989]	590
Incorporated Law Society of Ireland, MacGabhann v	HC	[1989]	854
Incorporated Law Society of Ireland, Trustee Savings Banks v	HC	[1988]	541
Incorporated Law Society of Ireland, Trustee Savings Bank v	SC	[1989]	665
Independent Newspapers Ltd, Barrett v	SC	[1986]	601
Independent Newspapers Ltd, Fitzpatrick v	HC	[1988]	707
Independent Newspapers Ltd, State (DPP) v	HC	[1985]	183
Industrial Development Authority, MCB (Galway) Ltd v	SC	[1981]	58
Industrial Yarns Ltd v Greene	HC	[1984]	15
Industrie Buitoni Perugina SPA v Dowdall O'Mahoney & Co	HC	[1978]	116
Industry, Minister for *see* Minister for Industry and Energy			
Inspector of Taxes v Kiernan	HC	[1981]	157
Inspector of Taxes v Kiernan	SC	[1982]	13
Inspector of Taxes v Lunham Bros Ltd *see* Cronin v Lunham Bros Ltd			
Inspector of Taxes v McCann *see* Breathnach v McCann			
Inspector of Taxes v Maxwells Ltd *see* Bairead v Maxwells of Donegal Ltd			
Inspector of Taxes v Youghal Carpets *see* Cronin v Youghal Carpets			
Inspector of Taxes, Insulation Products Ltd v	CC	[1984]	610
Inspector of Taxes, Kellystown Co v	SC	[1985]	200
Inspector of Taxes, Knockhall Piggeries v	HC	[1985]	655
Inspector of Taxes, McCann Ltd v	HC	[1986]	239
Inspector of Taxes, Mogul of Ireland Ltd v	HC	[1979]	75
Inspector of Taxes, Stephen Court Ltd v	HC	[1984]	231
Inspector of Taxes' Association v Minister for Public Service	SC	[1986]	296
Insulation Products Ltd v Inspector of Taxes	CC	[1984]	610
Insurance Corporation of Ireland, International Commercial Bank v	HC& SC	[1989]	788

Irish Land Commission, State (Hussey) v	HC	[1983]	407
Irish Life Assurance Co. Ltd, Lift Manufacturers Ltd v	HC	[1979]	277
Irish National Insurance Co., Brady v	HC&SC	[1986]	669
Irish Nursery and Landscape Co. Ltd, Kelly v	SC	[1981]	433
Irish Permanent Building Society v Caldwell	HC	[1979]	273
Irish Permanent Building Society v Caldwell	HC	[1981]	242
Irish Permanent Building Society v O'Sullivan	HC	[1990]	598
Irish Permanent Building Society v Registrar of Building Societies	HC	[1979]	273
Irish Permanent Building Society v Registrar of Building Societies	HC	[1981]	242
Irish Permanent Building Society, Director of Consumer Affairs v	HC	[1990]	743
Irish Pharmaceutical Union v Employment Appeals Tribunal *see* State (Irish Pharmaceutical Union) v Employment Appeals Tribunal			
Irish Shell and BP Ltd v Costello (John) Ltd	SC	[1981]	66
Irish Shell and BP Ltd v Costello (John) Ltd	SC	[1985]	554
Irish Shell Ltd v Elm Motors Ltd	HC	[1982]	519
Irish Shell Ltd v Elm Motors Ltd	SC	[1984]	595
Irish Shipping Ltd (in liquidation), In re	HC	[1986]	518
Irish Transport & General Workers' Union, Rodgers v	HC	[1978]	51
Irish Trust Bank Ltd v Central Bank of Ireland	HC	[1976–7]	50
Ivory v Ski-Line Ltd	HC	[1989]	433
J (JS), RSJ v	HC	[1982]	263
Jacob (PE) & Co. Ltd, Fortune v	SC	[1976–7]	277
Jacob International Ltd v O'Cleirigh	SC	[1985]	651
Jaggers Restaurant Ltd v Ahearne	SC	[1988]	553
Jervis St Hospital see Governors of Jervis St Hospital			
Joe Walsh Tours Ltd, Director of Consumer Affairs v	SC	[1985]	273
Johnson v Longleat Properties (Dublin) Ltd	HC	[1976–7]	93
Johnson, DPP v	HC	[1988]	747
Johnson, McCarthy v	SC	[1989]	706
Johnson, State (Litzouw) v	HC	[1981]	273
Johnson & Johnson (Ireland) Ltd v C P Security Ltd	HC	[1986]	559
Johnston v Langheld, In re Bonnet	HC	[1983]	359
Jordan v Commissioner of An Garda Siochána *see* State (Jordan) v Commissioner of An Garda Siochána			
Joyce v Circuit Court Judge for Western Circuit	HC	[1987]	316
Joyce, DPP v	SC	[1985]	206
Judge v DPP	HC	[1984]	224
Justice, Minister for *see* Minister for Justice			
K (M) v McC (F)	HC	[1982]	277
K v W	SC	[1990]	121
K v W (No.2)	HC	[1990]	791
K, N v	HC&SC	[1986]	75
Kane v Governor of Mountjoy Prison	HC&SC	[1988]	724
Kavanagh (deceased), In re; Healy v MacGillicudy	HC	[1978]	175
Kavanagh v Centreline Ltd & Ors	HC	[1987]	306
Kavanagh, Parsons v	HC	[1990]	560
Keane, Breen v	CC	[1981]	279
Keane, Maguire v	SC	[1986]	235
Kearney v Minister for Justice	HC	[1987]	52
Keating v Bank of Ireland	HC	[1983]	295
Keating v Governor of Mountjoy Prison	SC	[1990]	850
Keating v New Ireland Assurance Co	SC	[1990]	110

Keating, DPP v	HC	[1989]	561
Keegan and Lysaght v Stardust Compensation Tribunal *see* State			
(Keegan) v Stardust Victims Compensation Tribunal			
Keenan, PMPA Insurance Co Ltd v	SC	[1985]	173
Keenan Brothers Ltd, In re	HC	[1985]	254
Keenan Brothers Ltd, In re	SC	[1985]	641
Keeney v O'Malley *see* State (Keeney) v O'Malley			
Kehoe, DPP v	CCA	[1983]	237
Kehoe, People (DPP) v	CCA	[1986]	690
Kelleher, State (McEldowney) v	HC	[1982]	568
Kelleher, State (McEldowney) v	SC	[1985]	10
Kelleher, State (Williams) v *see* State (Williams) v			
DPP and Kelleher			
Kelly and Deighan, In re	HC&SC	[1984]	424
Kelly v Board of Governors of St Laurence's Hospital	SC	[1989]	437
Kelly v Board of Governors of St Laurence's Hospital and Staunton	SC	[1989]	877
Kelly v Boland	HC	[1989]	373
Kelly v Breen	HC	[1978]	63
Kelly v Ireland	HC	[1986]	318
Kelly v Irish Nursery and Landscape Co Ltd	SC	[1981]	433
Kelly, Brennan v	HC	[1988]	306
Kelly, DPP v	SC	[1983]	271
Kelly, DPP v	CCA	[1989]	370
Kelly, Guardian Builders Ltd v	HC	[1981]	127
Kelly, People (DPP) v	SC	[1982]	1
Kelly, State (Crothers) v	HC	[1978]	167
Kelly, State (Rollinson) v	HC	[1982]	249
Kelly, State (Rollinson) v	SC	[1984]	625
Kelly's Carpetdrome Ltd, In re; Byrne v UDT Bank	HC	[1984]	418
Kellystown Co v Hogan (Inspector of Taxes)	SC	[1985]	200
Kelso, DPP v	SCC	[1984]	329
Kennedy v Hearne	HC	[1988]	52
Kennedy v Hearne	SC	[1988]	531
Kennedy v Hughes Dairy Ltd	SC	[1989]	117
Kennedy and Arnold v Ireland	HC	[1988]	472
Kennedy v Wrenne	HC	[1981]	81
Kennedy, State (O'Donoghue) v	HC	[1979]	109
Kenny v Quinn	CC	[1981]	385
Kenny, People (DPP) v	SC	[1990]	569
Kent, Siebel v	HC	[1976–7]	127
Kent County Council v C S	HC	[1984]	292
Kerrane, Knockhall Piggeries v	HC	[1985]	655
Kerry Co-Operative Creameries v An Bord Bainne	HC	[1990]	664
Kerry Co-Operative Creameries, Cadbury Ireland Ltd v	HC	[1982]	77
Kerry County Council, Ahern v	HC	[1988]	392
Kerry County Council, McMahon v	HC	[1981]	419
Kerry County Council, O'Connor v	HC	[1988]	660
Kershaw v Eastern Health Board see State (Kershaw) v			
Eastern Health Board			
Kett v Shannon	SC	[1987]	364
Kiernan, Inspector of Taxes v	HC	[1981]	157
Kiernan, Inspector of Taxes v	SC	[1982]	13
Kildare County Council v McKone Estates Ltd	HC	[1984]	313
Kildare County Council, Crodaun Homes Ltd v	SC	[1983]	1
Kildare County Council, McKone Estates Ltd v	HC	[1984]	313
Kilkenny County Council, Walsh v	HC	[1978]	1

McCaud v Governor of Mountjoy Prison *see* State (McCaud) v
Governor of Mountjoy Prison
McClafferty, McMahon v   HC   [1990]   32
McColgan v DPP *see* State (McColgan) v DPP and Clifford
McConnell (AF & GW) Co. Ltd, Furlong v   HC   [1990]   48
McCooey, White v   HC   [1976–7] 72
McCord v Electricity Supply Board   SC   [1980] 153
McCormack v Curran *see* State (McCormack) v Curran
McCormack, Chemical Bank v   HC   [1983] 350
McCormick v Cameo Investments Ltd   HC   [1978] 191
McCoy v Dun Laoghaire Corporation *see* State (McCoy) v
Dun Laoghaire Corporation
McCutcheon, DPP v   HC   [1986] 433
MacDaibheid v Carroll   HC   [1978]   14
MacDaibheid v Carroll   HC   [1982] 430
McDaid v Sheehy   HC   [1989] 342
McDermot, Irish Agricultural Wholesale Society Ltd v   HC   [1982] 457
McDermott v Minister for Social Welfare   ECJ   [1987] 324
McDermott, McGrath v   HC   [1988] 181
McDermott, McGrath v   SC   [1988] 647
McDonagh v Barry *see* State (McDonagh) v Barry
McDonagh v Sheerin *see* State (McDonagh) v Sheerin
McDonagh and Joyce, Coffey v   HC   [1979] 243
McDonald v Galvin   HC   [1976–7] 41
McDonald, DPP (Long) v   SC   [1983] 223
McEldowney v Kelleher *see* State (McEldowney) v Kelleher
McElhinney v DPP   SC   [1989] 411
McElligott & Sons Ltd, In re   HC   [1985] 210
MacEnroe v Allied Irish Banks Ltd   SC   [1980] 171
McEntee, Reilly v   HC   [1984] 572
MacEoin Kelly Associates, O'Toole (Jack) & Co.v   SC   [1987] 269
Macey Ltd v Tylers Ltd   HC   [1978]   82
McF v G   HC   [1983] 228
McFadden v Governor of Mountjoy Prison *see* State (McFadden) v
Governor of Mountjoy Prison
MacGabhann v Incorporated Law Society of Ireland   HC   [1989] 854
McGarry v Sligo County Council *see* Attorney General (McGarry)
v Sligo County Council
MacGillicudy, Healy v   HC   [1978] 175
McGimpsey v Ireland   HC   [1989] 209
McGimpsey v Ireland   SC   [1990] 440
McGirl v McArdle   HC   [1989] 495
McGivern (Frank) Ltd, Fitzpatrick v   HC   [1976–7] 239
McGlinchey v Governor of Portlaoise Prison *see* State (McGlinchey)
v Governor of Portlaoise Prison
McGlinchey v Wren   SC   [1983] 169
McGovern v Governors and Guardians of Jervis St Hospital SC   [1981] 197
McGowan v Gannon   HC   [1983] 516
McGowan v Wren   HC   [1988] 744
McGrail v Ruane   HC   [1989] 498
McGrath v Commissioner of An Garda Siochána   HC   [1990]   5
McGrath v Commissioner of An Garda Siochána   SC   [1990] 817
McGrath v McDermott   HC   [1988] 181
McGrath v McDermott   SC   [1988] 647
McGrath v Murphy *see* Director of Public Prosecutions
(McGrath) v Murphy

Nagle v Flynn *see* Director of Public Prosecutions (Nagle) v Flynn

Nalty, Daniel Morrissey & Sons Ltd v	HC	[1976-7] 269
Nangle, DPP v	HC	[1984] 171
National Ice and Cold Storage, Western Meats v	HC	[1982] 99
National Maternity Hospital, Dunne v	SC	[1989] 735
Neilan, State (O'Leary) v	HC	[1984] 35
Neilan, State (Wilson) v	HC	[1987] 118
Neville & Sons Ltd v Guardian Builders Ltd	HC	[1990] 601
New Ireland Assurance Co, Keating v	SC	[1990] 110
Neylon, State (Bloomfield) v	HC	[1985] 602
Neylon, State (Boyle) v	HC	[1986] 337
Neylon, State (Boyle) v	SC	[1987] 535
Neylon, State (Hughes) v	HC	[1982] 108
Neylon, State (Multiprint Label Systems Ltd) v	HC	[1984] 545
19th Ltd, In re	HC	[1989] 652
Nolan, Savage v	HC	[1978] 151
Northampton County Council v ABF	HC	[1982] 164
North Western Health Board v Martyn	LC	[1982] 584
North Western Health Board v Martyn	HC	[1985] 226
North Western Health Board v Martyn	SC	[1988] 519
North Western Health Board, O'Dowd v	SC	[1983] 186
Northern Bank Finance Corporation Ltd, Crowley v	HC	[1978] 219
Northern Bank Finance Corporation Ltd, Cully v	HC	[1984] 683
Northern Bank Finance Corporation Ltd v Quinn and		
Achates Investment Co	HC	[1979] 221
Northern Bank Ltd v Duffy	HC	[1981] 308
Northern Bank Ltd v Edwards	SC	[1986] 167
Northern Bank Ltd, Boylan v	HC	[1976-7] 287
Nova Media Services Ltd v Minister for Posts & Telegraphs	HC	[1984] 161
Noyek (A) & Sons Ltd, In re; Burns v Hearne	HC	[1987] 508
Noyek (A) & Sons Ltd, In re; Burns v Hearne	SC	[1989] 155

OHS Ltd v Green Property Co. Ltd	HC	[1986] 451
Oakthorpe Holdings Ltd, In re; Walsh v Registrar of Companies	HC	[1989] 62
O'B v O'B	SC	[1984] 1
O'B v W	SC	[1982] 234
O'B, O'B v	SC	[1984] 1
O'Brien v Bord na Móna	SC	[1983] 314
O'Brien v Ireland	HC	[1990] 466
O'Brien v Stoutt, In the goods of Walker	HC	[1982] 327
O'Brien v Stoutt, In the goods of Walker	SC	[1985] 86
O'Brien v White-Spunner	HC	[1979] 240
O'Brien, Collins v	HC	[1981] 328
O'Broin v Ruane	HC	[1989] 732
O'C v D (PC)	HC&SC	[1985] 123
O'Callaghan v Commissioners of Public Works	HC	[1983] 391
O'Callaghan v Commissioners of Public Works	SC	[1985] 364
O'Callaghan v Hamilton Leasing (Ireland) Ltd	HC	[1984] 146
Ó Cléirigh, Jacob International Ltd v	SC	[1985] 651
Ó Colmain, Murray v	SC	[1981] 137
O'Conail v Shakleton	SC	[1982] 451
O'Connell v Fawsitt *see* State (O'Connell) v Fawsitt		
O'Connell, Cairnduff v	SC	[1986] 465
O'Connell, Cork Corporation v	SC	[1982] 505

Ó Connlain, Belvedere Estates Ltd v	SC	[1990]	100
O'Connor v DPP	HC	[1987]	723
O'Connor v Kerry County Council	HC	[1988]	660
O'Connor v McCarthy	HC	[1982]	201
O'Connor v Mooney & Co Ltd	HC	[1982]	373
O'Connor v O'Connor	HC	[1978]	247
O'Connor, Allibert SA v	HC	[1982]	40
O'Connor, DPP v	SC	[1985]	333
O'Connor, O'Connor v	HC	[1978]	247
Ó Culacháin v Charles McCann Ltd	HC	[1986]	229
Ó Culacháin, Carroll Industries plc v	HC	[1989]	552
Ó Culacháin, Hammond Lane Metal Co Ltd v	HC	[1990]	249
Ó Culacháin, Irish Agricultural Machinery Ltd v	SC	[1989]	478
O'D v O'D	HC	[1976–7]	142
O'Daly v Gulf Oil Terminals (Ireland) Ltd	HC	[1983]	163
O'Dare v Sheehy see State (O'Dare) v Sheehy			
O'Dea, Ellis v	SC	[1990]	87
Ó Domhnaill v Merrick	SC	[1985]	40
O'Donnell v Begley	HC	[1987]	105
O'Donnell, Mulhall v	HC	[1989]	367
O'Donnell, State (Gartlan) v	HC	[1986]	588
O'Donoghue v Kennedy see State (O'Donoghue) v Kennedy			
O'Dowd v North Western Health Board	SC	[1983]	186
O'Driscoll v Governor of Cork Prison	HC	[1989]	239
O'Driscoll, Hynes-O'Sullivan v	SC	[1989]	349
O'Flynn v An Bord Gais Éireann	HC	[1982]	324
O'Flynn v Mid-Western Health Board	HC	[1990]	149
O'Friel v St Michael's Hospital	EAT	1982	260
O'G (T) v Attorney General & Anor	HC	[1985]	61
O'H (A) (otherwise F) v F (P)	HC	[1986]	489
O'H (N) v R (G)	HC	[1986]	563
O'Hagan v Delap see State (O'Hagan) v Delap			
O'Hanrahan, Maguire v	HC	[1988]	243
O'Hanrahan, State (Hughes) v	SC	[1986]	218
O'Hara v Flint	SC	[1979]	156
Ó hArgain (Inspector of Taxes) v Beechpark Estates Ltd	HC	[1979]	57
O'hUallachain v Burke	HC	[1988]	693
O'Keeffe v McMenamin see State (O'Keeffe) v McMenamin			
O'Kelly v Darragh	HC	[1988]	309
O'Leary v Neilan see State (O'Leary) v Neilan			
O'Loughlin v Teeling	HC	[1988]	617
O'Loughran, Hegarty v	HC	[1987]	603
O'Loughran, Hegarty v	SC	[1990]	403
Olympia Productions Ltd v Olympia Theatres Ltd	HC	[1981]	424
Olympic Amusements (Bundoran) Ltd, DPP v	SC	[1987]	320
O'Mahony v Biggs	SC	[1983]	223
O'Mahony v Melia	HC	[1990]	14
O'Mahony, People (DPP) v	SC	[1986]	244
O'Malley v An Taoiseach	HC	[1990]	460
O'Malley, Comerford v	HC	[1987]	595
O'Malley, State (Keeney) v	HC	[1986]	31
O'Malley Property Ltd, Hynes Ltd v	SC	[1989]	619
Ó Maoldomhnaigh, McNally v	HC	[1989]	688
Ó Monacháin v An Taoiseach	HC&SC	[1986]	660
O'Mullane v Riordan	HC	[1978]	73
O'Neill v Beaumont Hospital Board	HC&SC	[1990]	419

O'Neill v Butler	HC	[1979]	243
O'Neill v Clare County Council	HC	[1983]	141
O'Neill v DPP	HC	[1989]	881
O'Neill v Ryan, Ryan Air Ltd	HC	[1990]	140
O'Neill, Byrne v	SC	[1979]	47
O'Neill, McCarthy v	SC	[1981]	443
O'Neill, Roberts v	HC	[1981]	403
O'Neill, Roberts v	SC	[1983]	206
O'Neill (Charles) & Co Ltd, Adidas v	SC	[1983]	112
O'Neill (Charles) & Co Ltd, Three Stripe International v	HC	[1989]	124
Open Door Counselling, Attorney General (ex rel SPUC) v	HC	[1987]	477
Open Door Counselling, Attorney General (ex rel SPUC) v	SC	[1989]	19
O'R, Revenue Commissioners v	SC	[1984]	406
O'Regan v Plunkett see State (O'Regan) v Plunkett			
O'Reilly and Judge v DPP	HC	[1984]	224
O'Reilly v Limerick Corporation	HC	[1989]	81
O'Reilly v Minister for the Environment	HC	[1987]	290
O'Reilly, Camillo v	SC	[1988]	738
O'Reilly, Gillick v	HC	[1984]	402
O'Reilly, Macken v	SC	[1979]	79
O'Reilly, Revenue Commissioners v	HC	[1983]	34
O'Reilly, Revenue Commissioners v	SC	[1984]	406
Ó Riain (Inspector of Taxes), Mogul of Ireland Ltd v	HC	[1979]	75
O'Riordan, Dublin County Council v	HC	[1986]	104
Ormond (an infant) v Ireland	HC	[1988]	490
Orr (John) Ltd v Orr	HC	[1987]	702
O'Rourke v Grittar	HC	[1990]	877
O'Rourke v Martin see State (O'Rourke) v Martin			
O'Rourke v Talbot (Ireland) Ltd	HC	[1984]	587
O'Rourke, Hughes v	SC	[1986]	538
O'Shea v DPP	HC&SC	[1989]	309
O'Shea, Damen and Zonen v	HC	[1976–7]	275
O'Shea, People (DPP) v (No.1)	SC	[1983]	549
O'Shea, People (DPP) v (No.2)	SC	[1983]	592
Osheku v Ireland & Ors	HC	[1987]	330
O'Sullivan v Dunne	HC	[1988]	80
O'Sullivan v Hartnett	HC	[1981]	469
O'Sullivan v Hartnett	SC	[1983]	79
O'Sullivan (an infant) v Hughes	HC	[1986]	555
O'Sullivan, Irish Permanent Building Society v	HC	[1990]	601
O'Toole, DPP v	HC	[1983]	41
O'Toole, Minister for Labour v	SC	[1990]	180
O'Toole (Jack) Ltd v MacEoin Kelly Associates	SC	[1987]	269
Overend, Park Hall School Ltd v	HC	[1987]	345
Owenabue Ltd v Dublin County Council	HC	[1982]	150
P (E) v C (M)	HC	[1985]	34
P (C) v P (D)	HC	[1983]	380
P (H) v P (W)	HC	[1985]	527
P (D), P (C) v	HC	[1983]	380
P (W), P (H) v	HC	[1985]	527
PMPA Insurance Co. Ltd, In re	HC	[1986]	524
PMPA Insurance Co. Ltd, In re	SC	[1988]	109
PMPA Insurance Co. Ltd v Fifteen Insurance Officials	LC	[1982]	367
PMPA Insurance Co. Ltd v Keenan	HC&SC	[1985]	173

Pierce, Dowd v	CC	[1984]	653
Pigs and Bacon Commission v McCarren & Co.	SC	[1981]	237
Pine Valley Developments Ltd v Dublin County Council *see* State			
(Pine Valley Developments Ltd) v Dublin County Council			
Pine Valley Developments Ltd v Minister for Environment	HC&SC	[1987]	747
Pletzer v Magee *see* State (Pletzer) v Magee			
Plunkett, Irish Commercial Society Ltd v	HC	[1986]	624
Plunkett, Irish Commercial Society Ltd v	SC	[1987]	504
Plunkett, Irish Commercial Society Ltd v	HC	[1989]	461
Plunkett, State (O'Regan) v	HC	[1984]	347
Pobjoy, Purcell v	HC	[1990]	835
Pok Sun Shum v Ireland & Ors	HC	[1986]	593
Polymark (Ireland) Ltd v Labour Court *see* State (Polymark)			
v Labour Court			
Portion Foods Ltd v Minister for Agriculture	HC	[1981]	161
Portland Estates (Limerick) Ltd v Limerick Corporation	SC	[1980]	77
Portlaoise Prison, Governor of *see* Governor of Portlaoise Prison			
Post Office Workers Union v Minister for Labour	HC	[1981]	355
Posts and Telegraphs, Minister for *see* Minister for Posts and Telegraphs			
Power v Conroy	HC	[1980]	31
Power v Moran *see* State (Power) v Moran			
Power, Flynn v	HC	[1985]	336
Powers Supermarkets Ltd, In re application of	HC	[1981]	270
Powerscourt Estates v Gallagher	HC	[1984]	123
Powerscourt Shopping Centre Ltd, FG Sweeney Ltd v	HC	[1985]	442
Practice Direction (Guardianship of Infants Act 1964, Family Law			
(Maintenance of Spouses and Children Act 1976, Family Law			
Protection of Spouses and Children) Act 1981	HC	[1984]	148
Practice Notice: Acceptance of Sums Paid into Court in Satisfaction		[1983]	376
Practice Notice: Transfer of Jury Actions		[1983]	428
Practice Notice: Withdrawal of Actions		[1983]	376
Prendergast (W J) & Sons Ltd v Carlow County Council	SC	[1990]	749
President of the Circuit Court, Walsh v	HC&SC	[1989]	325
Prison Service Credit Union Ltd v Registrar of Friendly Societies	HC	[1987]	367
Private Motorists Protection Association *see* PMPA (*above*)			
Private Motorists Provident Society *see* PMPS (*above*)			
Prunty, People (DPP) v	CCA	[1986]	716
Public Lighting Services, SEE Co. Ltd v	SC	[1987]	255
Public Lighting Services, SEE Co. Ltd v	SC	[1988]	677
Public Service, Minister for *see* Minister for Public Service			
Purcell v Pobjoy	HC	[1990]	835
Purcell, Bank of Ireland v	HC	[1988]	480
Purcell, Bank of Ireland v	SC	[1990]	106
Quigley, Western Health Board v	HC	[1982]	390
Quill, Skibbereen UDC v	HC	[1986]	170
Quilligan and O'Reilly, People (DPP) v	CCC&SC	[1987]	606
Quilligan and O'Reilly, People (DPP) v (No.2)	SC	[1989]	245
Quinn v Quality Homes Ltd	HC	[1976–7]	314
Quinn v Wren	HC&SC	[1985]	410
Quinn, Kenny v	CC	[1981]	385
Quinn and Achates Investment Co., Northern Bank			
Finance Corp. Ltd v	HC	[1979]	221
Quinnsworth Ltd, Sinnott v	SC	[1984]	523
Quirke v Bord Luthcleas na hÉireann	HC	[1989]	129

Quirke v Folio Homes Ltd	SC	[1988]	496
Quitmann Products Ltd, Fried Krup Huttenwerke v	HC	[1982]	551
R v R	HC	[1979]	1
R (E) v R (J)	HC	[1981]	125
R (J) v R (J)	HC	[1979]	236
R (G), O'H (N) v	HC	[1986]	563
R (J), R (E) v	HC	[1981]	125
R (J), R (J) v	HC	[1979]	236
R Ltd, In re	SC	[1989]	757
Rabbette v Mayo County Council	HC	[1984]	156
Racing Board, McCann v, *see* McCann v Attorney General			
Radio Telefís Éireann v Magill TV Guide Ltd	HC	[1990]	534
Rafferty v Crowley	HC	[1984]	350
Rafferty v C A Parsons	SC	[1987]	98
Rahinstown Estates Co. v Hughes (Inspector of Taxes)	HC	[1987]	599
Rainey v Delap	HC&SC	[1988]	620
Rajan v Minister for Industry and Commerce *see* State (Rajan) v Minister for Industry and Commerce			
Ranks (Ireland) Ltd, In re	HC	[1988]	751
Ranks (Ireland) Ltd, Fleming v	HC	[1983]	541
Raso, Dublin Corporation v	HC	[1976–7]	139
Rattigan, Dunne v	CC	[1981]	365
Reddy v Bates	SC	[1984]	197
Rederij Kennemerland BV v Attorney General	HC&SC	[1989]	821
Reen v Bank of Ireland Finance Ltd	HC	[1983]	507
Registrar General of Births and Deaths, AS v RB and	HC	[1984]	66
Registrar General of Marriages, FML and Al v	HC	[1984]	667
Registrar of Building Societies, Ireland Benefit Building Society v	HC	[1981]	73
Registrar of Building Societies, Irish Permanent Building Society v	HC	[1979]	273
Registrar of Building Societies, Irish Permanent Building Society v	HC	[1981]	242
Registrar of Companies, Walsh v; In re Oakthorpe Holdings Ltd	HC	[1989]	62
Registrar of Friendly Societies, Prison Service Credit Union Ltd v	HC	[1987]	367
Registrar of Titles, State (Philpott) v	HC	[1986]	499
Reid v Limerick Corporation	HC	[1984]	366
Reid v Limerick Corporation	SC	[1987]	83
Reid, State (Higgins) v	HC	[1983]	310
Reilly v McEntee	HC	[1984]	572
Reno Engrais et Produits Chemiques SA v Irish Agricultural Wholesale Society Ltd	HC	[1976–7]	179
Representative Church Body v Attorney General	HC	[1989]	177
Revenue Commissioners v Donnelly	SC	[1983]	329
Revenue Commissioners v Kirkhope Shaw	HC	[1982]	433
Revenue Commissioners v O'R and McG	SC	[1984]	406
Revenue Commissioners v O'Reilly and McG	HC	[1983]	34
Revenue Commissioners, Dunne v	HC	[1982]	438
Revenue Commissioners, E(A) v	CC	[1984]	301
Revenue Commissioners, Maye v	HC	[1986]	377
Revenue Commissioners, Pandion Haliaetus Ltd v	HC	[1988]	419
Revenue Commissioners, Royal Trust Co (Irl) Ltd v	HC	[1982]	459
Revenue Commissioners, Spain v	HC	[1980]	21
Revenue Commissioners, State (Melbarien Enterprises Ltd) v	HC	[1986]	476
Revenue Commissioners, Warnock v	HC	[1986]	37
Revenue Commissioners, Weekes v	HC	[1989]	165
Reynolds v Waters	HC	[1982]	335
Rhatigan v Textiles y Confecciones Europeas SA	HC	[1989]	659
Rhatigan v Textiles y Confecciones Europeas SA	SC	[1990]	825

Richardson v Governor of Mountjoy Prison *see* State (Richardson) v
   Governor of Mountjoy Prison

Riordan, In re	HC	[1981]	2
Riordan's Travel Ltd v Acres & Co. Ltd	HC	[1979]	3
Roadstone Ltd, Stafford v	HC	[1980]	1
Roberts v O'Neill	HC	[1981]	403
Roberts v O'Neill	SC	[1983]	206
Robinson v Chariot Inns Ltd	HC	[1986]	621
Roche v Peilow	SC	[1986]	189
Roche, DPP v	SC	[1989]	39
Roche, State (Clarke) v	HC	[1986]	565
Roche, State (Clarke) v	SC	[1987]	309
Roches Stores (Dublin) Ltd, Hickey & Co. Ltd v	HC	[1980]	107
Rodgers v Irish Transport & General Workers' Union	HC	[1978]	51
Roe, State (Slattery) v	HC	[1986]	511

Rogers v Galvin *see* State (Rogers) v Galvin

Rogers v Louth County Council	SC	[1981]	144
Rohan Construction Ltd v Antigen Ltd	HC	[1989]	783
Rohan Construction Ltd v ICI	HC	[1986]	419
Rohan Construction Ltd v ICI	SC	[1988]	373

Rollinson v Kelly *see* State (Rollinson) v Kelly

Rooney v Connolly	SC	[1987]	768
Roper v Ward	HC	[1981]	408
Roper, McInerney Properties Ltd v	HC	[1979]	119
Ross Co Ltd v Swan	HC	[1981]	416
Rosses Point Hotel v Commissioner of Valuation	HC	[1987]	512
Rothwell, Halpin v	HC	[1984]	613
Roughan, McCarter & Co. Ltd v	HC	[1986]	447
Rowan v Rowan	HC	[1988]	65
Rowan v Rowan	SC	[1989]	625
Royal Liver Trustees Ltd, Tempany v	HC	[1984]	273
Royal Trust Co. Ltd v Revenue Commissioners	HC	[1982]	459
Ruane, Butler v	SC	[1989]	159
Ruane, Flynn v	HC	[1989]	690
Ruane, McGrail v	HC	[1989]	498
Ruane, O'Broin v	HC	[1989]	732
Ruane, Singh v	HC	[1990]	62
Ruane, State (Collins) v	HC	[1984]	443
Ruane, State (Collins) v	SC	[1985]	349
Ruane, State (Daly) v	HC	[1988]	117
Ruane, State (DPP) v	SC	[1985]	349
Russell v Fanning	HC	[1986]	401
Russell v Fanning	SC	[1988]	333
Russell v Governor of Portlaoise Prison	HC	[1986]	401
Ruth (Pat) Ltd, In re	HC	[1981]	51
Rutledge, In the goods of;Hanly v Finnerty	HC	[1981]	198
Ryan v DPP	HC	[1989]	466
Ryan v Ireland	SC	[1989]	544
Ryan, Doyle v	CC	[1981]	374
Ryan, DPP v	SC	[1989]	333
Ryan and Ryan Air Ltd, O'Neill v	HC	[1990]	140
Ryan, Travers v	HC	[1985]	343
Ryan (WH) Ltd, Carey v	SC	[1982]	121
S (S) (an infant), In re; Kent Co Council v CS	HC	[1984]	292

Subject Matter

ABANDONMENT OF TRIAL
Criminal trial
Delay

Proposed retrial—Whether prejudice arising—Constitution of Ireland 1937, Articles 38.1, 40.3. **O'Connor v DPP** [1987] 723, HC.

ABATTOIR
Intensification of use

Whether material change of use requiring planning permission. *See* PLANNING (Enforcement—Section 27 application—Intensification of use—Premises used as abattoir).

Licence
Refusal

County council refusing licence—Plaintiff instituting proceedings to order council to grant licence—Mandatory injunction sought—Public Health—Town Improvement Clauses Act 1847, ss. 125–131—Slaughter of Animals Act 1935. **Doupe v Limerick Co Council** [1981] 456, HC.

ABORTION
Information
Clinic

Non-directive counselling with regard to abortion in England—Whether in breach of right to life of unborn—Right of communication—Conflict with right to life of unborn—Jurisdiction of Courts. **Attorney General (SPUC) v Open Door Counselling** [1987] 477, HC; [1989] 19, SC.

Publication

Students' groups—Publication of information about abortion clinics outside the State—Whether right to give such information under European Community law—Constitution of Ireland 1937, Article 40.3.3. **Society for the Protection of Unborn Children (Ireland) Ltd v Grogan** [1990] 350, SC.

Whether constitutional right

Whether right to information about availability of a service of abortion outside the State. **Attorney General (SPUC) v Open Door Counselling** [1987] 477, HC; [1989] 19, SC.

Non-directive counselling
Clinic

Whether such activity unlawful having regard to the Constitution—Whether such activity amounts to a conspiracy to corrupt public morals. **Attorney General (SPUC) v Open Door Counselling** [1987] 477, HC

Right to life of unborn
Constitutional right

Enforcement—Locus standi—Whether Attorney General had exclusive right to enforce Article 40.3.3. **Society for the Protection of Unborn Children (Ireland) Ltd v Coogan** [1989] 526, HC; [1990] 70, SC.

ABSOLUTE ORDER
Certiorari. *See* CERTIORARI. (Absolute order).
Habeas corpus. *See* HABEAS CORPUS (Procedure—Absolute order made in first instance).

ABUSE OF DOMINANT POSITION
European Community competition law. *See* EUROPEAN COMMUNITY (Competition—Abuse of dominant position).

ABUSE OF PROCESS
Delay in bringing proceedings
Infant plaintiff

Proceedings instituted on behalf of infant sixteen years after cause of action accrued—Whether delay unreasonable—Whether an abuse of the process of the courts—Statute of Limitations 1957, s. 49—Convention for the Protection of Human Rights and Fundamental Freedoms (1950) Art 6(1). **O'Domhnaill v Merrick** [1985] 40, SC.

Estoppel *per rem judicatam*
Civil action for damages for assault

Criminal proceedings involving same issue finding no assault took place—Whether plaintiff estopped from bringing civil proceedings—Whether defendants estopped from denying plaintiff's ability to bring civil proceedings—Defendants not party to criminal prosecution—Additional evidence sufficient to overcome plea to estoppel. **Kelly v Ireland** [1986] 318, HC.

Extradition
State acquiescing in orders refusing extradition

Subsequent attempt to extradite person in identical circumstances—Whether State precluded from denying person relief identical to that previously obtained—Equality of treatment—Constitution of Ireland 1937, Art 40.1—Extradition Act 1965, s. 50(2). **McMahon v Leahy** [1985] 422, SC.

Injunction application
Constitutional action

Presumption of constitutionality—Fair question to be tried—Balance of convenience—Whether abuse of process of court—Forum shopping—Domestic legislation to ratify international treaty—Injunction sought to prevent deposit of deeds of ratification—Effect of potential embarrassment for government if injunction granted—European Communities (Amendment) Act 1986. **Crotty v An Taoiseach** [1987] 400, HC, SC.

Malicious abuse
Tort

Claim for damages for malicious abuse of the process of the courts—Whether such action lay in respect of instituting a civil action—Ingredients of such tort—Meaning of malice—Proof of damage—Cause of loss. **Dorene Ltd v Suedes (Ireland) Ltd** [1982] 126, HC.

Planning
Challenge to validity of decision

Residents' association challenging decision to grant planning permission—Developers seeking to have proceedings dismissed—Whether proceedings frivolous or vexatious. **Cavern Systems Ltd v Clontarf Residents' Association** [1984] 24, HC.

Planning
Unauthorised change of use

Duplicitous use of mandamus procedure to obtain order compelling the planning authority to grant planning permission. **Cork Corporation v O'Connell** [1982] 505, SC.

Tort
Malicious abuse

Claim for damages. *See* Malicious abuse (*above*).

ACCESS TO COURTS, RIGHT OF. *See* CONSTITUTION (Personal rights—Access to courts).

ACCIDENT
Compensation
Fatal injury
Criminal injuries compensation. *See* MALICIOUS INJURIES (Fatal injury).

Industrial injury
Employer's liability insurance—Contract—Interpretation. *See* INSURANCE (Contract—Interpretation—Employer's liability insurance).

Motor insurance
Scheme of compulsory insurance under Road Traffic Acts—Whether court's duty to safeguard position of third parties irrespective of contractual arrangements made between insurers and insured. *See* MOTOR INSURANCE (Compulsory insurance scheme).

Employer's liability. *See* NEGLIGENCE (Employer—Accident at work).

Highway
Injury to pedestrian
Difference in road levels. *See* NEGLIGENCE (Highway—Highway authority—Injury to pedestrian).

Occupier's liability. *See* NEGLIGENCE (Occupier).

Personal injuries
Damages. See DAMAGES (Personal injuries).

Road traffic accident. *See* ROAD TRAFFIC ACCIDENTS.

ACCOUNT
Bank account. *See* BANK (Account).

ACCOUNTANT
Disclosure of information
Revenue
Notice served by Revenue Commissioners requiring information—Whether notice *ultra vires*—Whether unduly burdensome and oppressive—Finance Act 1974, s. 59. **Warnock v Revenue Commissioners** [1986] 37, HC.

Legal costs accountant. *See* COSTS (Taxation—Legal costs accountant).

Negligence
Duty of care
Third party—Preparation of accounts—Third party investing in company for whom accountant acted as auditor—Whether auditor owing duty of care to third party—Whether auditor in breach of duty—Whether accounting standards as to audits complied with—Whether negligent—Whether accounts prepared by auditor resulted in misleading impression in third party. **Kelly v Boland** (Trading as Haughey Boland & Co) [1989] 373, HC.

ACCUSED
Access to solicitor
Right of access to solicitor while in detention. See ARREST (Access to solicitor).

Acquittal
Appeal against acquittal. See CRIMINAL LAW (Acquittal—Appeal).

Arrest
Legality. See ARREST (Legality).

Bail. *See* CRIMINAL LAW (Bail).

ACCUSED *continued*
Character
Evidence
Unruly character—Young person—Whether evidence of unruly character must be tested by cross-examination—Natural justice—Children's Act 1908, s. 102(3). **State (O'Donoghue) v Kennedy** [1979] 109, HC.

Conviction. *See* CRIMINAL LAW (Conviction).

Defence
Murder
Diminished responsibility. *See* CRIMINAL LAW (Defence—Insanity or diminished responsibility).

Detention
Legality. See ARREST (Detention—Legality).

Dwelling
Inviolability
Constitutional right—Arrest—Legality—Arrest made inside accused's home—Whether gardai empowered to enter a private dwelling without permission of occupant. *See* ARREST (Legality—Place of arrest—Dwelling of citizen).

Constitutional right—Criminal investigation—Forcible entry of accused's home—Search warrant—Invalidity—Evidence—Admissibility. **People (DPP) v Kenny** [1990] 569, SC.

Identification
Identification parade
Objection to participation—Admissibility of evidence—Requirement as to direction of jury. **People (DPP) v Marley** [1985] 17, CCA.

Legal aid. *See* CRIMINAL LAW (Legal aid).

Media coverage
Complaints
Criminal contempt—*Ex parte* application by accused—Taoiseach receiving letter from accused—Taoiseach authorising publication in the national press—Photograph of accused published—Whether prima facie case of criminal contempt established. **In re Malcolm MacArthur** [1983] 355, HC.

Misdescription
Medical certificate
Road traffic offence—Whether accused the person named on the certificate—Whether sufficient evidence—Case stated. **DPP v McPartland** [1983] 411, HC.

Physical restraint
Whether constitutes arrest. See ARREST (Restraint).

Preliminary examination
Cross-examination of witness
Whether accused person has right of cross-examination at preliminary stage. **State (Sherry) v Wine** [1985] 196, SC.

Inspection of exhibits
Whether accused person entitled to inspect exhibits to be produced at trial. **State (Pletzer) v Magee** [1986] 441, HC.

Statement
Admissibility in evidence. See CRIMINAL LAW (Evidence—Statement by accused).

Surveillance
Overt surveillance. See ARREST (Legality—Surveillance—Overt surveillance).

ACCUSED *continued*

Trial. *See* CONSTITUTION (Trial of offences); CRIMINAL LAW (Trial).

Right to fair trial
Delay—Whether such as to prejudice accused's right to fair trial. *See* CRIMINAL LAW (Trial—Delay).

ACQUISITION OF LAND *See* COMPULSORY PURCHASE.

ACQUISITION NOTICE

Open spaces. *See* PLANNING (Acquisition notice).

ACQUITTAL

Appeal against acquittal. *See* CRIMINAL LAW (Acquittal—Appeal).

Autrefois acquit
Whether the quashing of an order amounts to an acquittal
Grounds for granting an order of certiorari. *See* CRIMINAL LAW (Autrefois acquit).

ACTION

Abuse of process. *See* ABUSE OF PROCESS.

Cause

Accrual. *See* LIMITATIONS OF ACTIONS (Accrual of cause of action).

Estoppel. *See* ESTOPPEL (Res judicata—Cause of action estoppel).

Several causes of action
Damages for personal injuries—Two distinct and separate causes of action—Plaintiff seeking to join unrelated defendants. *See* PRACTICE (Trial—Several causes of action).

Survival
Death of respondent—Whether claim should proceed against the personal representatives—Unfair dismissal claim—Death of employer—Civil Liability Act 1961, s. 8(1)—Succession Act 1965, s. 8—Unfair Dismissals Act 1977, ss. 1, 15. **Hutton v Philippi** [1982] 578, EAT.

Compromise

Authority of legal adviser
Consent order—Authority not in writing—Denial by plaintiffs that action settled—Validity of order. **Barrett v W J Lenehan & Co Ltd** [1981] 206, HC.

Mistake
Action commenced against two defendants—Plaintiff's counsel entering into settlement agreement with second defendant without adverting to the question of the first defendant's costs—Whether unilateral mistake rendering agreement a nullity. **Reen v Bank of Ireland Finance Ltd** [1983] 507, HC.

Severability of clauses
Whether defendants entitled to rescind agreement. **Taylor v Smyth** [1990] 377, HC.

Solicitor
Duty of care—Agreement—Option—Failure to exercise by solicitor on behalf of client—Failure to notify client. *See* SOLICITOR (Negligence—Duty of care—Compromise of action).

Whether prudent
Conflicting expert evidence—Large claim—Settlement reducing amount considerably. **Rohan Construction Ltd v Insurance Corp of Ireland** [1986] 419, HC.

Costs. *See* COSTS.

Damages. *See* DAMAGES.

ACTION *continued*

Date listed for hearing

Personal injuries claim

Damages awarded less than lodgment—Question as to costs—Whether action first listed for hearing only when it appeared in a list of cases to be heard on a specified date— RSC 1986, O 22 rr 1(2), 46. **Donohue v Dillon** [1988] 654, HC.

Delay

Dismissal for want of prosecution. See PRACTICE (Dismissal for want of prosecution).

Infant plaintiff

Delivery of statement of claim—Proceedings instituted on behalf of infant sixteen years after cause of action accrued. *See* Delay (Action—Infant plaintiff).

Dismissal for want of prosecution. *See* PRACTICE (Dismissal for want of prosecution).

Frivolous or vexatious

Motion to strike out. See PRACTICE (Frivolous or vexatious action).

Limitation. *See* LIMITATIONS OF ACTIONS.

Locus standi to maintain. *See* LOCUS STANDI.

Motion to strike out. *See* PRACTICE (Frivolous or vexatious action—Motion to strike out).

Parties. *See* PRACTICE (Parties).

Pleadings. *See* PRACTICE (Pleadings).

Possession

Landlord. See LANDLORD AND TENANT (Ejectment—Notice to quit).

Recovery of land. See LAND (Action for possession).

Trespass. See TRESPASS (Ejectment—Action for possession).

Relator proceedings. *See* PRACTICE (Relator proceedings).

Security for costs. *See* COSTS (Security for costs).

Service out of the jurisdiction. *See* PRACTICE (Service out of jurisdiction).

Settlement. *See* Compromise (*above*).

Stay of proceedings. *See* PRACTICE (Stay of action).

Trial. *See* PRACTICE (Trial).

Vexatious. *See* PRACTICE (Frivolous or vexatious action).

Want of prosecution. *See* PRACTICE (Dismissal for want of prosecution).

ADJOURNMENT

Inquest

Jurisdiction of coroner. See INQUEST (Adjournment).

District Court hearing

Discretion of District Justice to adjourn or refuse to adjourn

Whether properly exercised. **State (Pheasantry Ltd) v Donnelly** [1982] 512, HC.

Refusal to adjourn to hear additional witnesses—Whether exercise of discretion within jurisdiction—Extent of review on certiorari. **State (Daly) v Ruane** [1988] 117, HC.

Habeas corpus inquiry

Constitutionality of procedure

Whether an adjournment upon a return date warranted under the provision of Article 40—Constitution of Ireland 1937, Article 40.4. **State (Whelan) v Governor of Mountjoy Prison** [1983] 52, HC.

ADJOURNMENT *continued*
Trial
Criminal trial
District Court—Defendant requesting adjournment to obtain legal representation and a witness—Whether refusal to grant adjournment breach of natural justice. **Flynn v Ruane** [1989] 690, HC.

ADMINISTRATION OF COMPANY *See* COMPANY (Administration).

ADMINSTRATION OF ESTATES *See* SUCCESSION (Administration).

ADMINISTRATION OF JUSTICE
Constitution. *See* CONSTITUTION (Administration of justice).

Contempt of court. *See* CONTEMPT OF COURT.

ADMINISTRATIVE ACTION
Judicial review. *See* JUDICIAL REVIEW.

ADMINISTRATIVE CIRCULAR
Validity
Social welfare
Fuel allowances—Departmental circular excluding persons on short term social welfare—Whether ultra vires Minister for Social Welfare—Whether decision based on guidelines in circular valid—Social Welfare (Supplementary Welfare Allowances) Regulations 1977, art 6. **State (Kershaw) v Eastern Health Board** [1985] 235, HC.

ADMINISTRATIVE TRIBUNAL
Decision
Judicial review. *See* TRIBUNAL (Decision).

ADMINISTRATIVE SCHEME
Validity
Constitution
Scheme implementing EC Council directive—Compensatory payments to persons farming in disadvantaged areas. *See* CONSTITUTION (Administrative scheme—Validity).

ADMISSIBILITY OF EVIDENCE
Civil action. *See* EVIDENCE (Admissibility).

Criminal trial. *See* CRIMINAL LAW (Evidence—Admissibility).

ADMISSION BY ACCUSED
Admissibility in evidence. *See* CRIMINAL LAW (Evidence—Statement of accused).

ADOPTION
Consent
Dispensing with
Child placed for adoption—Consent form signed by mother—Subsequent delay—Allegation that mother pressurised to consent—Institution of proceedings by adoptive parents for order dispensing with the mother's consent—Whether consent freely given—Whether in child's best interests to remain with adoptive parents. **McF v G & G** [1983] 228, HC.

Infant placed for adoption—Parents' subsequent marriage legitimising infant—Natural mother witholding consent to adoption—Whether consent to be dispensed with—Adoption Act 1974, s. 3. In re J H (otherwise R), an Infant; **K.C. v An Bord Uchtála** [1985] 302, HC, SC.

Infant placed for adoption—Parents' subsequent marriage legitimising infant—Natural mother witholding consent to adoption—Whether consent to be dispensed with—

ADOPTION
Consent
Dispensing with continued

Whether father deemed to have consented to placement of infant for adoption—Welfare of child—Constitution of Ireland 1937, Articles 41, 42—Guardianship of Infants Act 1964, ss. 2, 3—Adoption Act 1974, s. 3. In re J H (otherwise R), an Infant (No. 2): **K C v An Bord Uchtála** [1986] 65, HC.

Placement of child with foster parents—Consent to adoption signed by mother—Mother subsequently changing her mind and wanting to withdraw consent—Application for order dispensing with consent of mother—Whether mother agreed to place the child for adoption—Whether in the child's best interest to remain with adoptive parents—Adoption Act 1974, s. 3. **McC v An Bord Uchtála** [1982] 159, HC.

Full and free consent

Validity of agreement to place child for adoption—Whether consent of mother free and fully informed—Finding of fact by trial judge that consent not free and informed—Whether such finding could be disturbed on appeal—Adoption Act 1974, s. 3. In re M: **J M and G M v An Bord Uchtála** [1988] 203, SC.

Eligibility to adopt
Exclusion

Widower—Infant placed for adoption—Final consent signed—Death of prospective adoptive mother before adoption order made—Legislation providing that, whereas a widow could obtain the adoption order, widower could not—Whether such provision constitutionally valid—Constitution of Ireland 1937, Articles 40.1, 40.2.1—Adoption Act 1952, s. 13(1)—Adoption Act 1974, s. 5(1). **T O'G v Attorney General** [1985] 61, HC.

Legislation
Bill

Validity—Bill permitting adoption where parents have totally abandoned all parental rights—Whether Bill amounted to an attack upon the family—Whether inalienable and imprescriptible rights can be lawfully curtailed—Constitution of Ireland 1937, Articles 26, 40, 41, 42, 43, 44. In re Adoption (No. 2) Bill 1987 [1989] 266, SC.

Natural father
Application for guardianship. See Child (Guardianship and custody—Natural father's application).

Placement
Location

Mother consenting to put child up for adoption—Fosterage arranged—Foster parents seeking order of custody—Mother wanting child placed for adoption outside the county in which she was residing—Foster parents living short distance from the mother—Mother applying for an order of habeas corpus—Welfare of infant—Constitution of Ireland 1937, Article 40.4.2—Guardianship of Infants Act 1964, s. 3. **State (M G) v A H and M H: A H v An Bord Uchtála** [1984] 237, HC.

Practice
Discovery

Prospective parents applying for an order dispensing with consent of mother—Prospective parents seeking discovery of certain documents—Claim of privilege—Whether in best interests of child to disclose—Whether adoption society entitled to rely on s. 8—Adoption Act 1976, s. 8. s. **M v G M** [1985] 186, HC.

Rights of father and child
Parents lawfully married

Child placed in care—Father wrongfully removing child from foreign jurisdiction—Claim for return of child—If order granted child would be legally adopted—Such development not permissible under Irish law—Whether aliens entitled to the protection

ADOPTION
Rights of father and child
Parents lawfully married continued
of the Constitution—Constitution of Ireland 1937, Article 41. **Northampton Co Council v F and F** [1982] 164, HC.

Welfare of child
Dispensing with consent. See CONSENT—Dispensing with *(above).*

Location of placement. See PLACEMENT—Location *(above).*

ADULTERY
Divorce *a mensa et thoro*
Whether subsequent misconduct revives adultery and cruelty previously condoned. **B L v M L** [1989] 528, HC.

ADVANCE RULINGS
Revenue Commissioners. *See* REVENUE (Advance rulings).

ADVERSE POSSESSION
Administration of estates
Administrator seeking to recover possession of land
Limitation period—Statute of Limitations 1957, s. 45, as amended by Succesion Act 1965, s. 126—Operative date of s. 126—Applicability to claim of a personal representative to recover assets of deceased. **Drohan v Drohan** [1981] 472, HC.

Joint tenants
Next-of-kin of deceased owner remaining in possession
Whether interest of other next-of-kin defeated by adverse possession—Whether shares of those excluded from possession acquired as joint tenants or as tenants in common—Administration of Estates Act 1959, ss. 13, 22—Succession Act 1965, s. 125(1). **Maher v Maher** [1987] 582, HC.

Occupation with approval and consent of owner
Occupation continuing to the exclusion of the owner—Nature of occupation—Whether as a result of a licence or a tenancy at will—Whether owner's title extinguished—Statute of Limitations 1957, ss. 13(2), 17(1), 18, 24, 51(1), **Bellew v Bellew** [1983] 128, SC.

ADVERTISEMENT
Building society
Meaning of 'annual percentage rate of charge'. *See* BUILDING SOCIETY (Advertising).

Planning application
Compliance with regulations. See PLANNING (Application—Advertisement).

Retail prices regulation
Prohibition on advertising goods at cost less than "net invoice price"
Whether meaning of prohibition clear. *See* RESTRICTIVE PRACTICES (Prices regulation).

Unauthorised development
Advertisement hoardings
Application for order restraining continuing development—Works representing considerable improvement to the appearance of the premises—Appeal—Whether court power to direct removal. **Dublin Corporation v Maiden Poster Sites** [1983] 48, HC.

ADVICE
Negligence. *See* NEGLIGENCE (Advice or information).

AFFIDAVIT
Discovery
Format. See DISCOVERY (Affidavit—Format).

AFFIDAVIT *continued*
Evidence
Admissibility
Objection to introduction of evidence at trial without prior notice—Case involving constitutional rights of citizen—Whether principles of ordinary litigation ought to be waived—RSC 1962, O 39 r 1. **Shannon v Attorney General** [1985] 449, HC.

AFFILIATION ORDER
Jurisdiction of High Court
Whether mother may institute proceedings in High Court
Legislation conferring jurisdiction on High Court, but contemplating the making of rules as to relevant procedures to be followed—No such rules of Court made—Whether High Court inherent jurisdiction to operate the provisions—Bastardy (Ireland) Act 1863—Illegitimate Children (Affiliation Orders) Act 1930, s. 2(1)—Courts of Justice Act 1924, ss. 22, 36(ix), 84—Courts (Supplemental Provisions Act 1961, s. 14(2)—Courts Act 1871, s. 19(1)—Family Law (Maintenance of Spouses and Children) Act 1976, s. 28—RSC 1962, O 111—District Court Rules 1948, r 30—District Court Rules (No. 2) 1962. In re O'B; **O'B v W** [1982] 234, SC.

AGE LIMIT
Appointment to post
Upper age limit
Whether discriminatory to married women. *See* EMPLOYMENT (Equality of treatment—Access to employment—Age limit for entry to post).

AGENCY
Agreement
Auctioneer
Auction cancelled—Vendor subsequently selling premises by private treaty—Whether auctioneer entitled to fees. **Daniel Morrissey and Sons Ltd v Nalty** [1976–7] 269, HC.

Construction
Privity—Option to renew agreement Termination of agency—Agent claiming privity with party to separate agreement—Whether separate agreement to be considered as single agreement—Whether agency terminated on reasonable notice. **Henley Forklift v Lansing Bagnall** [1979] 257, SC.

Sole selling agent
Whether principal entitled to refuse to pay commission where sale completed without assistance of agent—Whether agent acting solely in connection with sale—Whether agency arose only in future on happening of certain events—Whether intention of parties to be taken from documents only—Whether term to be implied into agreement—Whether consistent with expressed intention of parties. **G F Galvin (Estates) Ltd v Hedigan** [1985] 295, HC.

Auctioneer. *See* AUCTIONEER.

Authority of agent
Ostensible authority
Whether principal made representation to third party—Whether agency in existence—Third party given use of motor vehicle by employee of owner—Third party involved in motor accident—Third party negligent—Whether owner liable. **Kett v Shannon** [1987] 364, SC.

Sale of land
Oral agreement—Statute of Frauds 1695, s. 2. **Guardian Builders Ltd v Kelly** [1981] 127, HC.

Solicitor
Settlement of action—Settlement not in writing—Consent not drawn up—Denial by plaintiffs that action settled. **Barrett v W J Lenehan & Co Ltd** [1981] 206, HC.

AGENCY
Authority of agent *continued*
Vicarious liability
Third party given use of motor vehicle by employee of owner—Third party involved in motor accident—Third party negligent—Whether agency in existence—Whether owner liable. **Kett v Shannon** [1987] 364, SC.

Existence
Contract
Sale of land—Failure to complete—Vendor's action for specific performance—Purchaser claiming representative capacity—Purchaser failing to establish such capacity. **The Dublin Laundry Company Ltd (In Liquidation) v Clarke** [1989] 29, HC.

AGGRAVATED DAMAGES. *See* DAMAGES (Aggravated damages).
AGREEMENT
Agency. *See* AGENCY (Agreement).

Mistake
Whether mistake making agreement a nullity. See MISTAKE (Agreement).

Trade union
Collective agreement. See TRADE UNION (Collective agreement).

AGRICULTURAL LAND
Valuation
Statute
Constitutional validity—Valuation carried out between 1852 and 1866—No revaluation ever taking place—Valuation determining the extent of liability in respect of certain taxes, and the extent of eligibility for certain benefits—Whether an unjust attack on property rights—Valuation (Ireland) Act 1852, ss. 5, 11, 32, 33, 34—Constitution of Ireland 1937, Articles 40.1, 40.3, 43—Local Government Act 1946, ss. 11, 12. **Brennan v Attorney General** [1983] 449, HC; [1984] 355, SC.

AGRICULTURE
Cattle. *See* ANIMALS (Cattle).

Common agricultural policy
Export of cereals
Carousel fraud—Payment of monetary compensation amounts—Dispute as to whom payable—Irregularities in forms and declarations—Whether statements made *bona fide*—Claim for interest payable on amounts remaining unpaid—Whether money payable under statute—European Communities (Common Agricultural Policy) (Market Intervention) Regulations 1973—European Council Regulation 729/1970, Article 8—European Council Regulation 974/1978, Article 2A—European Commission Regulation 1380/1975, Articles 10, 14, 16. **Irish Grain Board Ltd v Minister for Agriculture** [1981] 10, HC.

Intervention scheme
Company liquidation—Company owing a sum for monetary compensation levies—Company owed a sum for monetary compensation payments on farm levies—Intervention agent claiming a right of set off—Whether claims exist in the same right—Whether intervention agent acting as agent for the importing State—Council Regulations 25/62, 729/70 articles 2, 3, 4, 974/71 article 2(a). **Continental Irish Meat Ltd v Minister for Agriculture** [1983] 503, HC.

Monetary compensation amounts—Description of goods on import-export documentation between EEC states to which MCA's are referrable—Council Regulation 974/71—Commission Regulation 1380/75. **Portion Foods Ltd v Minister for Agriculture** [1981] 161, HC.

Levy on livestock. See Export levy on livestock (*below*).

AGRICULTURE *continued*
Contract
Breach

Supply of potatoes to UK—Whether contract void for illegality—Onus of proof—Sale of Goods Act 1893, s. 51. **Whitecross Potatoes (International) Ltd v Coyle** [1978] 31, HC.

Mistake

Supply of seed potatoes—Crop failure—Whether contract rendered void—Whether implied obligations remaining. **Western Potato Co-Operative Ltd v Durnan** [1985] 5, CC.

Co-operatives
Competition

Application of European Community competition rules to the activities of farmers' co-operatives—Whether exemption available under Council Regulation 2662EEC—Jurisdiction of Irish courts to apply such Council Regulation—Treaty of Rome, Articles 38, 39, 42, 85, 86—Council Regulation 26/62/EEC, arts 1 and 2. **Kerry Co-Operative Creameries v An Bord Bainne** [1990] 664, HC.

Dairy farming
Milk quotas. See MILK QUOTAS (*below*).

Disadvantaged areas
Compensatory payments to persons farming in disadvantaged areas

European Council directive—Implementation by administrative scheme—Validity—Payment limited to applicants whose income together with that of their spouses did not exceed a specific figure—Whether breach of constitutional pledge to guard the institution of marriage—Whether condition necessitated by membership of European Community—Council Directive 75/268/EEC—Constitution of Ireland 1937, Articles 29.4.3, 41. **Greene v Minister for Agriculture** [1990] 364, HC.

Diseases of animals
Animal disease eradication scheme

Whether payments made on ex gratia basis—Non-statutory scheme—Whether conditions of scheme amounted to promise on conditions—Whether conditions complied with—Diseases of Animals Act 1966. **McKerring v Minister for Agriculture** [1989] 82, HC.

Export levy on livestock
European Community

Excise duty—Whether measure having effect equivalent to customs duty—Common organisation of the markets—Whether duty unreasonable—Imposition of Duties (No. 239) Agricultural Produce (Cattle and Milk) Order 1979—Agricultural Produce (Cattle and Milk) Regulations 1979. **Doyle v An Taoiseach** [1986] 693, HC.

Grazing of land
Letting of land for grazing

Contract—Construction—Public auction—Letting made on the eleven months system—Letting commenced on 23rd March 1979—Price agreed—No written or oral term as to date of termination. **Collins v O'Brien** [1981] 328, HC.

Land
Valuation. See AGRICULTURAL LAND (Valuation).

Levy orders
Recovery of levies due

Statutory levy—Bonus scheme paid to bacon exporters by plaintiffs—Bonus scheme financed from levies—Part of levies scheme condemned by Court of Justice of European Community—Severability of levy orders—Pigs and Bacon (Amendment) Act 1939, ss. 34, 38. **Pigs and Bacon Commission v McCarren & Co** [1981] 237, SC.

Milk levy
Regulations giving effect to EC milk levy

Such regulations having retrospective effect—Whether unjust—Whether unjustified

AGRICULTURE
Milk Levy
Regulations giving effect to EC milk levy continued

attack on property rights—Council Regulations 804/84, 856/84, 857/84—Commission Regulation 1371/84—European Communities (Milk Levy) Regulations 1985, reg 4, 12—Constitution of Ireland 1937, Articles 29.4.3—40.3.2, 43. **Lawlor v Minister for Agriculture** [1988] 400, HC.

Milk quotas
European Community

'Mulder Regulations'—Interpretation—Whether qualifying gallonage required to be produced on original holding—Principles of non-discrimination, proportionality and legal certainty—Council Regulation 857/84/EEC, art 3a—Council Regulation 764/89/EEC. **O'Brien v Ireland** [1990] 466, HC.

Revenue
Income tax

Exemption—Animal husbandry—Partnership—Fattening of pigs in purpose-built housing—Whether farming—Whether exempt from taxation—Whether trade or profession—Finance Act 1974, s. 13(1), (3)—Finance Act 1969, s. 18(1). **Knockhall Piggeries v Kerrane** (Inspector of Taxes) [1985] 655, HC.

AIDING AND ABETTING *See* CRIMINAL LAW (Aiding and abetting).

ALIEN
Constitutional rights
Entitlement

Child born of lawfully married parents who were citizens of, and domiciled in, a foreign jurisdiction—Wrongful removal of infant from the foreign jurisdiction—Claim for return of child for adoption—Such development not permissible under Irish law—Whether aliens entitled to the protection of the Constitution—Constitution of Ireland 1937, Article 41.1.2. **Northampton Co Council v A B F** [1982] 164, HC.

Citizenship—Discrimination—Statute—Validity—Male alien marrying Irish citizen—Application for certificate of naturalisation—Different provisions for female aliens marrying Irish citizens—Whether diversity of arrangements amounts to discrimination—Whether plaintiff capable of asserting constitutional rights—Natural justice—Constitution of Ireland 1937, Articles 9, 40—Irish Nationality and Citizenship Act 1956, ss. 8, 15–16. **Somjee v Minister for Justice** [1981] 324, HC.

Fair procedures—Unlawful detention—Extradition—Alien brought before District Court on foot of English warrant—Order for delivery at point of departure—Whether valid—Procedures antedating the making of the order—Whether unfair—Entitlement of prosecutor to fair procedures—Habeas corpus—Constitution of Ireland 1937, Article 40—Extradition Act 1965, ss. 43, 45, 47, 50. **State (McFadden) v Governor of Mountjoy Prison** (No. 1) [1981] 113, HC.

Family

Deportation order—Male alien married to Irish citizen. **Pok Sun Shum v Ireland** [1986] 593, HC.

Whether a family consisting of alien parents and children who are Irish citizens has the right to reside in the State—Exigencies of the common good—Whether justifiable interference with rights of family—Constitutional rights of children—When power to expel aliens may be exercised—Fair procedures—Constitution of Ireland 1937, Articles 40, 41, 42—Aliens Act 1935—Aliens Order 1946. **Fajujonu v Minister for Justice** [1990] 234, SC.

Deportation order
Alien marrying before order took effect

Extension to permission to stay—Whether order in conflict with rights of family—Whether aliens entitled to benefit of provisions of Constitution relating to family—

ALIEN
Deportation order
Alien marrying before order took effect continued

Whether order must comply with natural justice—Aliens Order 1946—Aliens (Amendment) Order 1975—Aliens Act 1935—Irish Nationality and Citizenship Act 1956, ss. 15, 16—Constitution of Ireland 1937, Articles 41, 42. **Pok Sun Shum v Ireland** [1986] 593, HC.

Male alien married to Irish citizen

Infant of the marriage—Alien overstaying and breaching permission to stay—Plaintiffs seeking to restrain alien's deportation—Whether deportation order would infringe plaintiff's constitutional rights—Effect of marriage—Constitution of Ireland 1937, Arts 9, 40, 41, 42—Aliens Act 1935, ss. 4, 5, 12—Irish Nationality and Citizenship Act 1956, ss. 8, 16—Aliens Order 1935, reg 13—Aliens (Amendment) Order 1975. **Osheku v Ireland** [1987] 330, HC.

Landing permission
Refusal

Habeas corpus—Applicant not holding Irish visa—Married to Irish citizen—Previous residence with family in State—Evidence of domestic problems—Constitution—Family—Whether decision of immigration officer bona fide—Whether domestic problems to be considered in refusing leave to stay—Aliens Order 1946, Art 5(4)—Aliens (Amendment) Order 1975, Art 3. **State (Bouzagou) v Station Sergeant Fitzgibbon Street** [1986] 98, HC.

Habeas corpus—Discretion of immigration officer—Opinion that aliens ulikely to benefit from study of English in the State—Whether discretion validly exercised—Aliens (Amendment) Order 1975, Art 3(2)—Aliens (Amendment) Order 1985, Sixth Schedule. **State (Kugan) v Station Sergeant Fitzgibbon Street** [1986] 95, HC.

Settlement permission
Refusal

Fair procedures—Male alien married to Irish citizen—Aliens Registration Office refusing to permit alien to settle in the State—Permission granted for fourteen days only—Whether endorsement on alien's passport the exercise of statutory powers without fair procedures—Entitlement to fair procedures—Whether denial of wife's constitutional rights to the company and society of her spouse—Constitution of Ireland 1937, Articles 40 3, 41 1—Aliens (Amendment) Order 1975, reg 3. **Abdelkefi v Minister for Justice** [1984] 138, HC.

Voting rights
Dáil Éireann elections

Bill conferring right to vote on British citizens—Whether Bill repugnant to the Constitution—Whether constitutional provisions exclude aliens from voting rights—Constitution of Ireland 1937, Arts 6, 12 2 1, 12 2 2, 12 4 1, 16 1 1, 16 1 2, 16 7, 26, 47—Electoral Act 1963, ss. 5(1), 51(1), 70(1). In re Electoral (Amendment) Bill 1983 [1984] 539, SC.

ALIMONY *See* FAMILY LAW (Maintenance—Alimony).

ALLOWANCE
Capital allowances. *See* REVENUE (Income tax—Capital allowances).

Fuel allowance. *See* SOCIAL WELFARE (Supplementary welfare allowance—Fuel allowance).

AMUSEMENT HALLS
Licensing
Slot machines. See GAMING AND LOTTERIES (Gaming licence).

ANCIENT MONUMENT *See* NATIONAL MONUMENT.

ANGLO-IRISH AGREEMENT 1985
Constitutional challenge to validity. *See* CONSTITUTION (International relations—Treaty—Anglo-Irish Agreement).

ANIMALS
Cattle
Livestock export levy. See AGRICULTURE (Export levy on livestock).

Poisoning
> Cattle wandering onto cemetery—Cattle poisoned by eating yew leaves—Wall between pastureland and cemetery damaged—Whether local authority negligent or in breach of statutory duty in not having wall repaired—Public Health (Ireland) Act 1878, ss. 181, 185, 193, 234. **Walsh v Kilkenny Co Council** [1978] 1, HC.

Straying onto highway
> Driver colliding with cattle—Liability of owner or keeper for damage caused. *See* Negligence—Straying onto main road (*below*).

Disease eradication scheme
Whether payments made on ex gratia basis
> Whether conditions of scheme amounted to promise on conditions. *See* AGRICULTURE (Diseases of animals).

Dog
Guard dog
> Scienter—Liability of owner for injuries caused. *See* NEGLIGENCE—Liability of owner (*below*).

Horses
Showjumping
> Rule-making body—Prohibition on use of non-Irish horses by Irish showjumpers in international competitions—Whether unreasonable restraint of trade. *See* RESTRAINT OF TRADE (Reasonableness—Public policy—Equestrian rule-making body).

Injury or death
Factory emissions
> Onus of proof. *See* NUISANCE (Emissions from factory).

Poisoning
> Cattle wandering into cemetery—Cattle poisoned by eating yew leaves. *See* Cattle—Poisoning (*above*).

Negligence
Liability of owner
> Personal injuries caused by animal—Guard dog—Scienter—Propensity to attack—Whether owner strictly liable—Whether defence to show that its escape was caused by the wrongful act of a third party. **Kavanagh v Centreline Ltd** [1987] 306, HC.

Straying onto main road
> Liability of owner or keeper—Cattle—Driver colliding with cattle which had strayed onto main road—Whether cattle constituted a public nuisance—Whether defendants negligent—Whether under a duty to prevent cattle straying onto public road. **Gillick v O'Reilly** [1984] 402, HC.

Straying onto highway
Liability of owner or keeper for damage caused. See NEGLIGENCE—Straying onto main road (*above*).

ANNULMENT
Marriage. *See* MARRIAGE (Nullity).

APARTHEID
Injunction to restrain sporting links with a country where apartheid is practised. *See* INJUNCTION (Sporting activity—Irish Rugby Football Union tour of South Africa).

APPEAL

Acquittal. *See* CRIMINAL LAW (Acquittal—Appeal).

Case stated. *See* CASE STATED.

Central Criminal Court
Jurisdiction of Supreme Court. See SUPREME COURT (Jurisdiction—Appeal—Central Criminal Court).

Circuit Court
Jurisdiction. See CIRCUIT COURT (Jurisdiction—Appeal—Criminal appeal).

Corporation tax
Questions of law. See REVENUE (Corporation tax—Appeal).

Criminal appeal. *See* CRIMINAL LAW (Appeal).

Damages award. *See* DAMAGES (Appeal).

Jurisdiction of Supreme Court
Whether Supreme Court may substitute its own assessment of damages for those made by a jury in the High Court. **Holohan v Donoghue** [1986] 250, SC.

Employment Appeals Tribunal determination
Appeal to Circuit Court
Whether further right of appeal lay to High Court. *See* HIGH COURT (Jurisdiction—Appeal—Circuit Court decision—Appeal from Employment Appeals Tribunal determination).

Extension of time
Appeal from High Court to Supreme Court
Whether Supreme Court has same powers as High Court to extend time for appeal—RSC 1962, O 58 r 8, O 108 r 70, O 111, r 1. **Hughes v O'Rourke** [1986] 538, SC.

Generally. *See* PRACTICE (Appeal).

High Court
Jurisdiction. See HIGH COURT (Jurisdiction—Appeal).

Labour Court determination
Jurisdiction of High Court. See HIGH COURT (Jurisdiction—Appeal—Labour Court determination).

Time for taking. See Time for taking—Appeal from Labour Court determination (*below*).

Malicious injuries
Compensation application
Application dismissed on appeal by High Court—Whether substantive appeal lies to Supreme Court. *See* SUPREME COURT (Jurisdiction—Appeal—Malicious injuries).

Occupier's liability
Jurisdiction of Supreme Court
Case tried in High Court on basis of duty owed to licensee—Whether appropriate for Supreme Court to decide case on basis of a different duty. **Rooney v Connolly** [1987] 768, SC.

Patent appeal
Decision of Controller
Appeal to the High Court—Whether further right of appeal to the Supreme Court. *See* SUPREME COURT (Jurisdiction—Appeal—Patent appeal).

Planning decision. *See* PLANNING (Appeal).

Sentence
Jurisdiction of Circuit Court. See CIRCUIT COURT (Practice—Criminal appeal—Appeal against sentence).

APPEAL *continued*
Supreme Court
Findings of fact
Whether disturbable on appeal. *See* SUPREME COURT (Appeal—Evidence—Findings of fact).

Function of Court
Primary and secondary facts—Whether Supreme Court empowered to reach different conclusions to those of trial court in relation to inferences from primary facts. **Hanrahan & Ors v Merck Sharp & Dohme** [1988] 629, SC.

Grounds of appeal
New arguments—Whether appropriate to address issue. *See* SUPREME COURT (Appeal—Grounds—New arguments).

Jurisdiction. See SUPREME COURT (Jurisdiction—Appeal).

Time for taking
Appeal from Labour Court determination
Whether appeal out of time—Health Act 1970, s. 18—Employment Equality Act 1977, ss. 2(c), 3, 12(3), 20, 21(4), 22, 24(2). **North Western Health Board v Martyn** [1985] 226, HC.

Unfair dismissal. *See* EMPLOYMENT (Unfair dismissal).

APPLICATION
Planning permission. *See* PLANNING (Application).

APPOINTMENT
Arbitrator. *See* ARBITRATION (Appointment of arbitrator).

Teacher. *See* EDUCATION (Teacher—Appointment).

AQUACULTURE
Designated area
Ministerial order
Objections—Inquiry—Appeal to High Court—Whether order be set aside. *See* FISHERIES (Aquaculture).

ARBITRATION
Agreement
Cessation
Revocation of authority of arbitrator—Allegations of fraud raised by party opposing stay of action—Discretion of court to refuse stay—Arbitration Act 1954, ss. 12, 39—Arbitration Act 1980, s. 5—Insurance (No. 2) Act 1983. **Administratia Asigurarilor de Stat v Insurance Corporation of Ireland plc** (Under Administration) [1990] 159, HC.

Appointment of arbitrator
Whether appointment precipitate
Local government—Public health—Application for permission to connect a sewer—No formal dispute to the claim for connection—Property arbitrator appointed—Whether developers precipitate—Whether excessive delay—Public Health (Ireland) Act 1878, ss. 24, 216, 217. **Kildare County Council v McKone Estates Ltd** [1984] 313, HC.

Award
Enforcement
Building contract—Dispute referred to arbitration—Award made but payment not forthcoming—Application for liberty to enforce the award—Whether arbitrator guilty of misconduct—Arbitration Act 1954, s. 41. **Grangeford Structures Ltd (in liquidation) v SH Ltd** [1988] 129, HC.

ARBITRATION
Award
Enforcement continued

Foreign award—New York Convention—Whether arbitral procedure in accordance with agreement of parties to contract—Ambiguity of documentation—Whether court has jurisdiction to investigate facts on which defence to enforcement based—Matters appropriate for consideration as defence to enforcement—Arbitration Act 1980 ss. 2, 6(1), 9(2), Schedule. **Cremer GmbH & Co v Co-operative Molasses Traders Ltd** [1985] 564, HC, SC.

Finality

Drainage scheme—Claim for compensation—Measure of compensation—Principles to be applied—Whether competent for arbitrator to state a case in relation to a final award. Arbitration Act 1954, s. 35(1). **Commissioners of Public Works in Ireland v Flood** [1980] 38, HC.

Setting aside

Building contract—Dispute referred to arbitration—Award—Application for an order to set aside award—Arbitrator refusing to state a case—Whether misconduct—Arbitration Act 1954, ss. 35(1), 36(1), 38(1). **Stillorgan Orchard Ltd v McLoughlin & Harvey Ltd** [1978] 128, HC.

Building contract
Award

Enforcement—Dispute referred to arbitration—Award made but payment not forthcoming—Application for liberty to enforce the award—Whether arbitrator guilty of misconduct. **Grangeford Structures Ltd (in liquidation) v S.H. Ltd** [1988] 129, HC.

Dispute referred to arbitration—Application for an order to set aside award—Arbitrator refusing to state a case—Whether misconduct—Arbitration Act 1954, ss. 35(1), 36(1), 38(1). **Stillorgan Orchard Ltd v McLoughlin & Harvey Ltd** [1978] 128, HC.

Interpretation

Architect's certificate—Architect issuing final certificate for payment—Contractor subsequently making claim for additional payments—Whether contractor barred from pursuing these claims—Interpretation of building contract—General conditions. **P Elliott & Co Ltd v Minister for Education** [1987] 710, HC, SC.

Case stated
Compensation claim

Drainage scheme—Appointment of arbitrator—Whether competent for arbitrator to state a case in relation to a final award. Arbitration Act 1954, s. 35(1). **Commissioners of Public Works in Ireland v Flood** [1980] 38, HC.

Discretion of arbitrator and court

Parties agreeing to be bound by auditor's certificate—Reference to arbitration—Arbitrator refusing case stated—Whether court should direct arbitrator to state case—Whether special circumstances preclude court making direction—Whether real and substantial issue between parties—Arbitration Act 1954, s. 35(1). **Hogan v St Kevin's Co** [1987] 17, HC.

Jurisdiction of High Court

Lease—Terms—Construction—Rent review clause—Function of High Court. **Hynes Ltd v O'Malley Property Ltd** [1989] 619, SC.

Refusal

Whether misconduct. *See* Misconduct—Arbitrator—Building contract—Dispute referred to arbitration (*below*).

Compulsory acquisition of land
Compensation. See COMPULSORY PURCHASE (Compensation—Assessment).

ARBITRATION
Compulsory acquisition of land *continued*
Valuation

Dispute as to value—Valuation going to arbitration—Arbitrator stating case to High Court—Power of court to remit—Arbitration Act 1954, s. 36. **Meenaghan v Dublin County Council** [1984] 616, HC.

Drainage scheme
Compensation

Measure of compensation—Principles to be applied—Arterial Drainage Act 1945, ss. 15(2)(b), 17—Arbitration Act 1954, s. 35(1). **Commissioners of Public Works in Ireland v Flood** [1980] 38, HC.

Lease
Option to furnish fee simple

Price calculation as if rent were a ground rent—Whether option enforceable—Whether refusal of county registrar to deal with matter subject to arbitration—Arbitration Act 1954, s. 18—Landlord and Tenant (Ground Rents) Act 1967, ss. 17, 22. **Carr v Phelan** [1976–7] 149, HC.

Misconduct
Arbitrator

Building contract—Dispute referred to arbitration—Award—Application for an order to set aside award—Arbitrator refusing to state a case—Whether misconduct—Arbitration Act 1954, ss. 35(1), 36(1), 38(1). **Stillorgan Orchard Ltd v McLoughlin & Harvey Ltd** [1978] 128, HC.

Dispute referred to arbitration—Award made but payment not forthcoming—Application for liberty to enforce the award—Whether arbitrator guilty of misconduct—Arbitration Act 1954, s. 41. **Grangeford Structures Ltd** (in liquidation) **v SH Ltd** [1988] 129, HC.

Whether misconduct established—Whether objection made to arbitrator's conduct at time of arbitration—Whether parties entitled to complain later—Whether arbitrator took all matters between parties into account—Whether court would exercise discretion to extend leave for appealing to court—RSC 1962, O 56, r 4. **Childers Heights Housing Ltd v Molderings** [1987] 47, HC.

Planning decisions
Compensation. See PLANNING (Compensation).

Practice
Absence of party

Whether hearing may take place in the absence of a party to an arbitration—Grounds on which an award may be made—Arbitration Act 1954, s. 19(1). **Grangeford Structures Ltd v SH Ltd** [1990] 277, SC.

Stay on proceedings. See Stay on proceedings (*below*).

Stay on proceedings
Discretion of court to refuse

Fraud alleged by party opposing stay—Contracts of reinsurance—Arbitration clause—Whether clause operative when serious and complex issues of law involving allegations of fraud raised—Application to revoke authority of arbitrator—Arbitration Act 1954, ss. 12, 39—Arbitration Act 1980, s. 5—Insurance (No. 2) Act 1983. **Adminstratia Asigurarilor de Stat v Insurance Corporation of Ireland plc** [1990] 159, HC.

Notice of motion served

Agreement to strike out motion and allow extended time for the filing of defence—Subject matter of claim being a matter agreed to be referred to arbitration—Application to stay proceedings—Whether seeking of consent for extension of time "a step in the

ARBITRATION
Stay on proceedings
Notice of motion served continued
proceedings"—Arbitration Act 1980, s. 5. **O'Flynn v An Bord Gais Éireann** [1982] 324, HC.

Power to stay proceedings
Whether any court before which an action has been commenced may stay proceedings or whether such power is exclusively vested in the High Court—Arbitration Act 1954, ss. 2, 12(1)—Arbitration Act 1980 s. 5(1). **Mitchell v Budget Travel Ltd** [1990] 739, SC.

Time limit
Agreement to refer disputes to arbitration
Time limit—Whether undue hardship caused by refusal to extend time—Arbitration Act 1954, ss. 3(1), 42, 45. **Walsh v Shield Insurance Co Ltd** [1976–7] 218, HC.

ARCHITECT
Certificate
Building contract. See BUILDING CONTRACT (Architect—Certificate).

Negligence
Contribution
Building defects—Certificate—Engineer's certificate as to structural stability—Architect's certificate based on such certificate—Whether builder or architect negligent—Contribution as between defendants—Damages. **Quinn v Quality Homes Ltd** [1976–7] 314, HC.

Foreseeability—Accident—Plaintiff falling from roof—Institution of proceedings against occupier—Occupier joining architects as third party—Trial judge finding occupier liable but holding that architect pay 30% contribution in respect of the damages payable—Appeal against the findings in respect of contribution—Whether architects concurrent wrongdoers—Whether architects could reasonably have foreseen this accident—Civil Liability Act 1961, ss. 22, 29. **Crowley v Allied Irish Banks** [1988] 225, SC.

ARMY *See* DEFENCE FORCES.

ARREARS OF TAX *See* REVENUE (Income tax—Arrears of tax).

ARREST
Access to solicitor
Right of access to solicitor while in detention
Whether delay by Gardai in permitting access by solicitor to client constituted a denial of right of access—Whether right of reasonable access to solicitor was a constitutional right—Constitution of Ireland 1937, Article 40.3. **DPP v Healy** [1990] 313, SC.

Whether arises as a constitutional right
Constitution of Ireland 1937, Article 40.3—Criminal Justice Act 1984, s. 4. **People (DPP) v Conroy** [1988] 4, CCA, SC.

Detention
Detention in successive garda stations. See Legality—Statutory power—Offences Against the State Acts—Whether detention in successive garda stations permitted (*below*).

Extension of period of detention
Legality—Evidence—Admissibility—Incriminating statement—Garda Superintendent authorising detention now dead—Whether Superintendent's suspicion that accused had committed a scheduled offence need be expressly proved—Offences Against the State Act 1939, s. 30. **People (DPP) v Byrne** [1989] 613, SC.

Statutory power—Extension of period of detention under statute—Whether required to be in writing—Format of document extending period of detention—Offences Against the State Act 1939, s. 30(3). **People (DPP) v Kehoe** [1986] 690, CCA.

ARREST
Detention *continued*
Legality
Detention in garda station—Whether lawful—Whether detained person free to leave—Whether under arrest—Whether detained for purpose of questioning—Whether detained person entitled to leave—Onus of proof. **People (DPP) v Coffey** [1987] 727, CCA.

Habeas corpus inquiry. *See* HABEAS CORPUS.

Legality
Arrest without warrant
Road traffic offence—Drunken driving—Arrest taking place in driver's driveway—Whether garda trespassing—Whether arrest lawful if garda effecting it a trespasser—Constitution of Ireland 1937, Article 40.5—Road Traffic Act 1961, s. 49(2), (3), (6)—Road Traffic (Amendment) Act 1978, ss. 10, 13. **DPP v Corrigan** [1987] 575, HC.

Road traffic offence—Drunken driving—Breathalyser test—Case stated—Whether opinion of garda justified arrest without warrant—Road Traffic Act 1961, s. 49—Road Traffic (Amendment) Act 1978, ss. 10, 12. **DPP v Gilmore** [1981] 102, SC.

Constitutional right Infringement
Arrest made inside accused's house—No invitation to enter—Whether gardai empowered to enter a private dwelling without permission of occupant. *See* Place of arrest—Dwelling of citizen (*below*).

Arrest made to ensure applicant be available for extradition—Whether misuse of arrest powers amounts to conscious and deliberate violation of constitutional rights—Whether alien entitled to basic fairness of procedures—Constitution of Ireland 1937, Article 40.3.1, 40.4.2—Extradition Act 1965, Part II—Offences Against the State Act 1939, s. 30. **Trimbole v Governor of Mountjoy Prison** [1985] 465, HC, SC.

Detention in garda station
Whether lawful—Whether detained person free to leave—Whether under arrest. *See* Detention—Legality (*above*).

Extradition request
No extradition treaty—Order extending application of Extradition Act—Arrest under s. 30 of Offences against the State Act 1939—Arrest made to ensure applicant be available for detention under Part II—Whether misuse of arrest powers amounts to conscious and deliberate violation of constitutional rights—Constitution of Ireland 1937, Articles 40.3.1, 40.4.2—Extradition Act 1965, Part II. **Trimbole v Governor of Mountjoy Prison** [1985] 465, HC, SC.

Motive
Arrest under statutory power—Emergency Powers Act—Arrest in respect of scheduled offence—Questioning in respect of non-scheduled offence—Whether arrest lawful—Whether arrest effected for spurious purpose unconnected with offence authorised by statutory power—Whether sufficient reasons and explanation given for arrest—Emergency Powers Act 1976, s. 2. **People (DPP) v Towson** [1978] 122, CCA.

Arrest under statutory power—Offences Against the State Acts—Arrest in respect of scheduled offence—Questioning in respect of non-scheduled offence—Whether arrest lawful—Whether colourable device—Whether exclusion of murder as scheduled offence anomalous—Offences against the State Act 1939, s. 30. **State (Bowes) v Fitzpatrick** [1978] ILRM 195, HC.

Arrest under statutory power—Offences against the State Acts—Arrest in respect of scheduled offence—Questioning in respect of non-scheduled offence—Non-scheduled offence more serious—Whether arrest lawful—Whether arrest merely colourable device—Purpose of statute—Whether applicable to subversive and non-subversive crime—Interpretation—Long title. **People (DPP) v Quilligan** [1987] 606, CCC, SC.

ARREST
  Legality
   Motive continued
     Arrest under statutory power—Offences Against the State Acts—Arrest in respect of scheduled offence—Questioning in relation to non-scheduled offence—Non-scheduled offence more serious—Whether arrest lawful—Whether colourable device—Purpose of statute—Whether applicable to subversive and non-subversive crime. **People (DPP) v Walsh** [1988] 137, CCC, SC.

     Arrest under statutory power—Offences Against the State Acts—Arrest in respect of scheduled offence—Questioning in respect of non-scheduled offence—Predominant motive for arrest—Whether colourable device—Validity of extension order for detention for further 24 hour period—Offences Against the State Act 1939, s. 30. **People (DPP) v Howley** [1989] 629, SC.

   Place of arrest
     Driveway—Driver suspected of having committed road traffic offence—Arrest without warrant—Whether garda trespasser. *See* Legality—Arrest without warrant (*above*).

     Dwelling of citizen—Road traffic offences—Arrest made inside accused's home—No invitation to enter—Whether absence of order to leave could be construed as implied invitation—Whether gardai empowered to enter a private dwelling without permission of occupant—Whether arrest illegal—Constitution of Ireland 1937, Article 40.5—Courts (Supplemental Provisions) Act 1961, s. 52—Road Traffic Act 1961, ss. 49(4), 107. **DPP v Gaffney** [1986] 657, HC; [1988] 39, SC.

   Road traffic offences (generally). See ROAD TRAFFIC OFFENCES (Arrest).

   Statutory power
     Emergency Powers Act—Motive—Arrest in respect of scheduled offence—Questioning in respect of non-scheduled offence—Whether arrest lawful. *See* Legality—Motive—Arrest under statutory power—Emergency Powers Act (*above*).

     Offences Against the State Acts—Extradition request—No extradition treaty—Order extending application of Extradition Act—Arrest made to ensure applicant be available to detention under Part II—Whether misuse of arrest powers amounts to conscious and deliberate violation of constitutional rights. *See* Legality—Extradition request—No extradition treaty—Order extending application of Extradition Act (*above*).

     Offences Against the State Acts—Motive—Arrest in respect of scheduled offence—Questioning in respect of non-scheduled offence—Whether arrest lawful. *See* Legality—Motive—Arrest under statutory power—Offences Against the State Acts (*above*).

     Offences Against the State Acts—Suspicion—Whether suspicion of arresting officer required—Whether suspicion of other person, communicated to arresting officer, sufficient—Offences Against the State Act 1939, s. 30. **People (DPP) v McCaffrey** [1986] 687, CCA.

     Offences Against the State Acts—Whether detention in successive garda stations permitted—Conviction based on incriminating statements made while in police custody—Whether certain statements, made in circumstances in which there was not an exact compliance with the Judge's Rules, should be excluded—Whether direction to authorise continued detention valid—Courts of Justice Act 1924, s. 29—Interpretation Act 1937, s. 11 (c)—Offences against the State Act 1939, ss. 30(3), 30(4), 52. **DPP v Kelly** [1983] 271, SC.

   Surveillance
     Overt surveillance—Manner and purpose—Whether amounts to continuing detention—Whether amounts to unlawful harassment—Extradition warrants—Whether garda authority in executing warrant more restricted than authority to detect crime—Constitution of Ireland 1937, Article 40.4—Conspiracy and Protection of Property Act 1875—Offences Against the State Act 1939, s. 30. **Kane v Governor of Mountjoy Prison** [1988] 724, HC, SC.

ARREST *continued*
Motive. *See* Legality—Motive (*above*).

Re-arrest
Indictable offence
No evidence offered—Charges struck out—Accused re-arrested on same charges—Application for prohibition to prevent preliminary examination by District Justice—Whether District Court order amounted to an acquittal—Criminal Justice Act 1967, s. 8(5). **State (Hogan) v Carroll** [1981] 25, SC.

Released prisoner
Temporary release scheme—Breach of condition—Order for re-arrest—Failure to make arrest until after expiry of prisoner's sentence—Whether subsequent imprisonment lawful—Criminal Justice Act 1960, s. 2. **Cunningham v Governor of Mountjoy Prison** [1987] 33, HC.

Reasonable use of force
False imprisonment
Garda in scuffle with young person—Whether acting in the course of duty—Whether reasonable force used. **Dowman v Ireland** [1986] 111, HC.

Restraint
Whether constitutes arrest
Whether subsequent arrest pursuant to statute required release of arrested person to be valid—Offences Against the State Act 1939, s. 30. **People (DPP) v Kehoe** [1986] 690, CCA.

Warrant. *See* CRIMINAL LAW (Arrest warrant).

Absence. See Legality—Arrest without warrant (*above*).

ARSON *See* MALICIOUS INJURIES (Fire).

ARTERIAL DRAINAGE
Entry on and interference with lands
Arbitration
Measure of compensation—Principles to be applied—Whether separate headings of award required—Set off against gross amount for benefit of landowner—Arterial Drainage Act 1945, ss. 15(2) (b) 17. **Commissioners of Public Works in Ireland v Flood** [1980] 38.

ASBESTOS WASTE
Disposal
Planning permission granted for use of site for disposal of asbestos waste
Appeal. *See* PLANNING (Appeal—Grant of permission—Use of site for disposal of asbestos waste).

ASSETS
Company. *See* COMPANY (Assets).

ASSOCIATION
Freedom of association. *See* CONSTITUTION (Personal rights—Freedom of association).

ATHLETICS
Club to promote athletic sport
Income tax exemption
Whether *bona fide* club. *See* REVENUE (Income tax—Exemption—Club to promote athletic or amateur games or sports).

Suspension of athlete
Failure to undergo dope test
Natural justice. See Natural and Constitutional Justice (Athletic body).

ATTACHMENT
Contempt of court
Civil contempt

Committal—Jurisdiction of court—Deliberate disobedience of court order—No serious effort to purge contempt—Nature of Court's jurisdiction—Whether defendants be committed to prison—Prohibition of Forcible Entry and Occupation Act, 1971. **Ross Co Ltd v Swan** [1981] 416, HC.

ATTORNEY GENERAL
Costs awarded against Attorney General
Interest

Constitutional issue—Defendant unsuccessful in High Court—Defendant succeeding in Supreme Court on appeal—Supreme Court awarding costs against Attorney General—Whether interest should run only from date of taxation of costs—Debtors (Ireland) Act 1840, s. 27—RSC, O 42 r 15. **Cooke v Attorney General** [1989] 322, SC.

Declaratory relief
Matters of public right

Whether obtainable only at the suit of the Attorney General—Challenge to administrative decision—Building society registration—Locus standi of plaintiffs—Anomalous nature of Attorney General's position—One of defendants having sought and received Attorney General's advice in relation to the matter in dispute. **Irish Permanent Building Society v Cauldwell** (Registrar of Building Societies) [1981] 242, HC.

Fiat
Injunction granted

Undertaking to abide by any order as to damages—Whether fiat extends to undertaking. *See* PRACTICE (Relator proceedings—Role of Attorney General—Whether Attorney General liable in respect of plaintiff's loss).

Refusal

Action to establish public right of way—Whether decision of Attorney General subject to review by the courts—Whether action maintainable in absence of fiat of Attorney General. **Dunne v Rattigan** [1981] 365, CC.

Declaratory relief—Matter of public right—Whether relief obtainable only at suit of Attorney General. *See* Declaratory relief—Matters of public right (*above*).

Guardian of public rights
Injunctive relief

Company operating in breach of a statutory monopoly—Attorney General, acting as guardian of public rights, seeking an injunction—Whether proceedings misconceived. **Attorney General v Paperlink Ltd** [1984] 373, HC.

Statutory order made by Minister for Industry and Energy—Application for an injunction to require observance of the scheme established by the order—Whether Attorney General appropriate person to assert and defend the public interest allegedly violated— Ministers and Secretaries Act 1924. **Campus Oil Ltd v Minister for Industry and Energy** [1984] 45, HC.

Jurisdiction
Power to end private prosecutions

Whether such power devolved on the Attorney General after 1922—Constitution of Ireland 1937, Art 30.3—Ministers and Secretaries Act 1924, s. 6(1)—Prosecution of Offences Act 1974, s. 3. **State (Collins) v Ruane** [1984] 443, HC; [1985] 349, SC.

Relator action
Generally. See PRACTICE (Relator proceedings).

AUCTION
Sale of land
Licensed premises
Agent for vendor bidding—Whether contract rendered illegal—Sale of Land by Auction Act 1867, s. 3. **Airlie v Fallon** [1976–7] 1, HC.

AUCTIONEER
Contract
Fees
Auction cancelled—Vendor subsequently selling premises by private treaty—Whether auctioneer entitled to fees. Daniel Morrissey and Sons Ltd v Nalty [1976–7] 269, HC.

Sole selling agent
Whether principal entitled to refuse to pay commission where sale completed without assistance of agent. **G F Galvin Estates Ltd v Hedigan** [1985] 295, HC.

Duty of care
Advice or information
Building society agent acting as auctioneer. *See* Negligence—Advice or information (*below*).

Pre-contractual representation—Representation made to plaintiff's brother—Plaintiff relying on representation—Plaintiff entering into agreement to purchase certain property—Property found unsuitable for use as residence—Property sold at a loss—Whether duty of care owed to plaintiff by auctioneer—Whether breach of duty of care—Whether negligent misrepresentation. **Stafford v Mahony** [1980] 53, HC.

Inspection of property
Auctioneer inspecting dwelling on behalf of housing authority—Failure to discover serious defects—Whether duty of care owed to purchaser—Standard of care—Ordinary skill and competence. **Ward v McMaster** [1986] 43, HC.

Negligence
Advice or information
Building society agent acting as auctioneer—Advice to prospective purchasers—Purchasers relying on advice and purchasing house—Defects subsequently discovered—Liability of building society in respect of negligent advice given by agent acting as auctioneer. **Irish Permanent Building Society v O'Sullivan and Collins** [1990] 598, HC.

AUDITOR
Negligence
Duty of care owed to third party
Preparation of accounts—Third party investing in company for whom accountant acted as auditor. *See* ACCOUNTANT (Negligence—Duty of care—Third party).

AUTHOR
Copyright. *See* COPYRIGHT.

AUTHORISED OFFICERS
Appointment
Evidence
Sufficiency—Certificate. *See* MINISTER (Authorised officers—Appointment—Evidence—Sufficiency).

Consumer protection legislation
Authorisation required to indicate the matters in respect of which the officer may act—Whether provision satisfied by a recital in the authorisation of the powers which he is authorised to exercise—Consumer Information Act 1978, s. 16. **Director of Consumer Affairs v Joe Walsh Tours Ltd** [1985] 273, SC.

AUTHORITY
Agent. *See* AGENCY (Authority of agent).

AUTREFOIS ACQUIT. *See* CRIMINAL LAW (Autrefois acquit).

AVOIDANCE OF TAX
Capital gains tax. *See* REVENUE (Capital gains tax—Avoidance).

Income tax. *See* REVENUE (Income tax—Avoidance).

AWARD
Arbitration. *See* ARBITRATION (Award).

Damages. *See* DAMAGES (Award).

BAIL
Admittance of persons to bail
Power of peace commissioner
> Constitution—Validity—Administration of justice—Whether statutory conferral of power on peace commissioner invalid—Constitution of Ireland 1937, Article 34.1—Criminal Justice Act 1951, s. 15—Criminal Justice Act 1984, s. 26. **O'Mahoney v Melia** [1990] 14, HC.

Convicted prisoner
Lawful sentence of imprisonment
> Prosecutor obtaining conditional order of certiorari—Prosecutor also granted bail—Grant of bail unwarranted. State **(Dunne) v Martin** [1982] 18, SC.

Extradition cases
Test applicable
> Whether different from that pertaining in domestic criminal matters—Likelihood of prisoner's being available for extradition. People **(Attorney General) v Gilliland** [1986] 357, SC.

Objection by DPP
Grounds of objection. See CRIMINAL LAW (Bail—Objection).

Station bail. See CRIMINAL LAW (Bail—Station bail).

BAILMENT
Supermarket store
Customer
> Relationship of customer to goods between selection and completion of purchase—Whether bailment, licence or custody—Defendant leaving supermarket without paying for goods—Whether defendant guilty of larceny—Larceny Act 1916, ss. 1, 2. **DPP v Morrissey** [1982] 487, HC.

Title
Bailee denying bailor's title
> Whether implied term as to title excluded—Estoppel—Whether bailee entitled to claim rights of third party. **Webb v Ireland** [1988] 565, HC, SC.

BALANCE OF CONVENIENCE *See* INJUNCTION (Interlocutory—Balance of convenience).

BANK
Account
Disclosure of information. See Disclosure of information (*below*).

BANK

Account *continued*

Freezing of money in bank account

Offences Against the State Acts—Minister empowered to freeze moneys in a bank account and cause them to be paid into the High Court—Whether such power amounts to confiscation of property—Whether such powers permissible delimitation of property rights—Constitution of Ireland 1937, Articles 40 3 2, 43—Offences Against the State Act 1939, ss. 18, 19, 20, 22—Offences Against the State (Amendment) Act 1985, ss. 2, 3, 4, 5. **Clancy v Ireland** [1989] 670, HC.

Inspection

Jurisdiction of High Court to make order for inspection with extra-territorial effect—Bankers' Books Evidence Act 1879, s. 7—Bankers' Books Evidence (Amendment) Act 1959, s. 2. Chemical **Bank v McCormack** [1983] 350, HC.

Advice or information

Duty of care. See Duty of care—Advice or information (*below*).

Central Bank

Privilege of officers

Subpoena *sub duces tecum* issued requiring officer of Central Bank to produce documents—Oath of secrecy—Statutory privilege—Central Bank Act 1942, ss. 6(1), 31. **Cully v Northern Bank Finance Corporation Ltd** [1984] 683, HC.

Deposit

Fraudulent misappropriation

Foreign company—Money lodged to account—Claim that this money consisted of funds fraudulently misappropriated—Whether sufficient inference of fraud—Obligations of receiving bank—Whether required to repay the funds actually advanced. **Banco Ambrosiano v Ansbacher & Co** [1987] 669, HC, SC.

Deposit of title deeds

Equitable mortgage

Family home. *See* FAMILY LAW (Property—Family home—Equitable mortgage).

Whether bank entitled to claim lien over deeds—Whether bank took possession of deeds in course of banking business—Deeds taken as security for loan. **In re Farm Fresh Frozen Foods Ltd** [1980] 131, HC.

Disclosure of information

Central Bank

Oath of secrecy. *See* Central Bank—Privilege of officers (*above*).

Particulars sought by Revenue Commissioners

Exemption from disclosure—Scope of exemption—Whether transactions carried out in ordinary course of banking business—Income tax—Avoidance—Transfer of assets abroad in such a manner as to retain the power to enjoy the income thereof—Finance Act 1974, s. 59. **Royal Trust Co Ltd v Revenue Commissioners** [1982] 459, HC.

Taxpayer's account—Whether condition precedent fulfilled—Extent of information which bank may be required to furnish—Whether such details include payment into and withdrawals from an account—Bankers' Books Evidence Act 1959—Income Tax Act 1967, ss. 169, 172, 174—Finance Act 1983, s. 16. **O'C v D** [1985] 123, HC, SC.

Discounting of foreign bills

Duty of care. See Duty of care—discounting of foreign bills (*below*).

Duty of care

Advice or information

Customer of bank involved in business with relative making payment by cheque to customer—Customer allowed to maintain account beyond overdraft—Relative's business collapsing—Customer previously requesting advice and information from bank on

BANK
Duty of care
Advice or information continued
relative's creditworthiness—Whether bank encouraged customer to continue dealings with relative—Customer's business collapsing—Whether bank liable. **Towey v Ulster Bank Ltd** [1987] 142, HC.

Collecting banker
Failure to take steps necessary to protect interests of its customer—Duty to exercise diligence in collecting payment on foot of cheques lodged for collection. **Towey v Ulster Bank Ltd** [1987] 142, HC.

Contractual duty to exercise care and skill
Cheques—Payment—Duty to make enquiry in appropriate circumstances—Company's cheques signed by authorised signatories—Fraudulent dealings—Whether bank within its mandate in paying cheques. **MacEnroe v Allied Irish Banks Ltd** [1980] 171, SC.

Discounting of foreign bills
Mistaken operation of procedure by bank—Correction of procedures—Whether bank liable in negligence for economic loss suffered by plaintiff—Whether negligent mis-statement—Whether breach of duty of care. **Hazylake Fashions Ltd v Bank of Ireland** [1989] 698, HC.

Guarantor
Company debts—Change of ownership and variation of company's banking arrangements—Opening of new account—Whether guarantor thereby discharged from his obligations—Whether bank failed to alert guarantor as to fraudulent dealings—Whether bank negligent in paying cheques. *See* Guarantee—Contract (*below*).

Guarantee
Charge to bank to secure loan to company
Associated company acting as surety—Directors also guaranteeing loan and charging property—Default in repayments—Proceedings against corporate surety—Decree for possession of property—Appeal to Supreme Court pending—Proceedings also instituted against directors—Whether bank entitled to exercise its rights to possession of director's property until they have exercised their rights against the principal debtor and co-surety—Whether doctrine of marshalling applicable. **Lombard and Ulster Banking Ltd v Murray** [1987] 522, HC.

Contract
Company debts guaranteed by majority shareholder and managing director—Change of ownership and management and variation of the company's banking arrangements—Opening of new account—Agreement with bank that money in new account would not be set off against debt or interest due on other accounts—Whether material change in contract—Whether guarantor discharged from his obligations—Whether rule in *Clayton's Case* applicable—Whether bank negligent. **MacEnroe v Allied Irish Banks Ltd** [1980] 171, SC.

Industrial and provident society
Society engaged in business of banking
Deposits—Legislation enacted prohibiting such societies from accepting or holding deposits—Whether legislation invalid—Whether unjust attack on property rights of shareholders. *See* INDUSTRIAL AND PROVIDENT SOCIETY (Shareholder—Property rights).

Winding up—Duty of care—Minister—Depositor lodging money with industrial and provident society—Society subsequently going into liquidation—Depositor receiving a dividend of only part of sum lodged—Whether Minister owed duty of care. *See* INDUSTRIAL AND PROVIDENT SOCIETY (Winding up—Duty of care—Minister).

BANK *continued*
Lien
Deposit of title deeds
Equitable mortgage—Whether bank entitled to claim lien over deeds. *See* Deposit of title deeds (*above*).

Negligence. *See* Duty of care (above).

Trustee savings bank. *See* TRUSTEE SAVINGS BANKS.

Winding up
Industrial and provident society in business of banking
Duty of care—Minister. *See* INDUSTRIAL AND PROVIDENT SOCIETY (Winding up—Duty of care—Minister).

BANKRUPTCY
Adjudication
Entitlement to lessee's interest in property
Property subject to legal proceedings—Proceedings compromised—Sum of money paid to bankrupt's estate—Disposal of said sum—Whether valid charge on the money—Landlord and Tenant Acts 1931–1958. **In re Dolan** [1981] 155, HC.

Company
Winding up
Application of bankruptcy rules. *See* COMPANY (Winding up—Fraudulent preference—Application of bankruptcy rules).

BARRING ORDER
See FAMILY LAW (Barring order).

BARRISTER
Appearance
Presumption that counsel and solicitor appear on express instruction of the client—**L'Henryenat v Ireland** [1984] 249, SC.

Books
Expenditure on purchase
Capital allowance—Expenditure on law reports and legal textbooks—Whether "plant" qualifying for allowances—Income Tax Act 1967, s. 241—Finance Act 1971, s. 26. **Breathnach v McCann** [1984] 679, HC.

Fees
Taxation of costs. *See* COSTS (Taxation—Counsel's fees).

BENEFICIAL INTEREST
House
Matrimonial property
Wife seeking declaration of interest. *See* FAMILY LAW (Property—Beneficial interest).

Unmarried couple—Purchase of house—Conveyance solely in man's name—Whether resulting trust to be inferred. *See* TRUST (Resulting trust—Unmarried couple).

BENJAMIN ORDER
See SUCCESSION (Administration of estates—Ascertainment of next-of-kin).

BEQUEST
Will
Charitable gifts
Cy-pres. *See* CHARITY (Cy-pres).

Construction. See WILL (Construction).

BETTING
  See BOOKMAKER.

BIAS
  Tribunal
    Dismissal
      Validity—Predisposition to dismiss—Whether such affects validity of dismissal. **McGrath v Maynooth College** [1979] 166, SC.

BIGAMY
  See CRIMINAL LAW (Bigamy).

BILL
  Constitutional validity
    Article 26 references. See CONSTITUTION (Bill).

BILL OF EXCHANGE
  Cheque. *See* CHEQUE.

  Discounting of foreign bills
    Duty of care
      Bank. *See* BANK (Duty of care—Discounting of foreign bills).

BILL OF SALE
  Contract for sale of goods
    Retention of title clause
      Whether clause effective to reserve title—Whether a bill of sale of stock—Whether valid—Agricultural Credit Act 1978, s. 36—Bills of Sale (Ireland) Act 1879, s. 3—Sale of Goods Act 1893, ss. 1, 17. **Somers v James Allen (Ireland) Ltd** [1984] 437, HC; [1985] 624, SC.

BIRTH
  Registration
    Paternity of child
      Evidence admissible to prove paternity—Evidence of wife that child not the child of the marriage—Whether admissible. *See* CHILD (Paternity).

BIRTH CONTROL
  Contraceptives
    Unlawful sale
      Authority of gardai to enter premises. *See* CRIMINAL LAW (Health offences—Family planning).

BLOOD
  Specimen
    Driving while drunk
      See ROAD TRAFFIC OFFENCES (Drunken driving—Blood specimen).

BODILY INTEGRITY, RIGHT TO.
  See CONSTITUTION (Personal rights—Bodily integrity).

BOG LAND
  Compulsory purchase powers
    Bord na Mona. See TURF DEVELOPMENT (Compulsory purchase powers).

BOOKMAKER
Course betting permit
Revocation
Validity—Constitution—Whether Racing Board administering justice—Fair procedures—Natural justice—Racing Board and Racecourses Act 1945, s. 24—Constitution of Ireland 1937, Articles 37, 40. **McCann v Attorney General and the Racing Board** [1983] 67, HC.

Offence
Betting duty regulations
Infringement—Failure to forward returns to Collector of Customs and Excise—Whether obligation to make returns within specified time—Whether failure to do so gives rise to a separate offence in respect of each individual bet—Whether single or multiple offences—Whether offences of minor character triable summarily—Finance Act 1926, ss. 25(2), 42, 43—Betting Act 1931, ss. 6, 15—Betting Duty (Certified Returns) Regulations 1934, regs 27, 29. State **(Rollinson) v Kelly** [1982] 249, HC.

Infringement—Whether single or multiple offences—Whether offences of minor character triable summarily—Finance Act 1926, s. 25(2)—Betting Duty (Certified Returns) Regulations 1934. State **(Rollinson) v Kelly** [1982] 249, HC; [1984] 625, SC.

Infringement—Whether minor offence capable of being tried summarily—Constitution of Ireland 1937, Article 38 2—Finance Act 1926, ss. 24, 25—Betting Duty (Certified Returns) Regulations 1934, regs 8, 18, 23, 29. **Charlton v Ireland** [1984] 39, HC.

Infringement—Penalty—Whether court has jurisdiction to mitigate penalty—Statute—Interpretation—Excise Management Act 1827—Finance Act 1926, s. 25(2)—Criminal Justice Act 1951, s. 8—Finance Act 1982, ss. 69(1)(b), 70. **DPP v Gray** [1987] 4, SC.

Register of bookmaking offices
Certificate
Application to Garda Superintendent for certificate that premises suitable for registration—Objection to grant of certificate—Certificate refused—Appeal to District Court—Statute providing that objector not entitled to be heard nor to adduce evidence in opposition to appeal—Whether denial of such rights constituted an impermissible interference with the jurisdiction of the courts—Constitution—Validity of statute—Betting Act 1931, s. 13(5)(a)—Constitution of Ireland 1937, Articles 6, 34. **Cashman v Clifford** [1990] 200, HC.

BOOKS
Expenditure on purchase
Barrister
Capital allowances—Whether "plant". *See* REVENUE (Income tax—Capital allowances—Plant—Books).

BORD NA MÓNA
Compulsory purchase powers
Bog land
Whether power of judicial nature—Natural justice. *See* COMPULSORY PURCHASE (Fair procedures—Natural justice—Bog land—Power to compulsorily acquire bogland).

BORD PLEANÁLA *See* PLANNING.

BRAIN DAMAGE
Damages
Assessment. See DAMAGES (Personal injuries—Brain damage).

Industrial accident
Father of family suffering brain damage
Whether employer owed duty of care to victim's children not to deprive them of the

BRAIN DAMAGE
Industrial accident
Father of family suffering brain damage continued
> non-pecuniary benefits derived from parent-child relationships. *See* CONSTITUTION (Family—Rights—Extent of guarantee).

BREACH OF CONFIDENCE
Publication
Application to restrain. See CONFIDENTIALITY (Breach—Publication).

BREACH OF CONTRACT
Building contract. *See* BUILDING CONTRACT (Breach).

Damages. *See* DAMAGES (Breach of contract).

Generally. See CONTRACT (Breach).

Inducement to commit breach. *See* TORT (Inducement to commit breach of contract).

Sale of goods
Whether contract void for illegality
> Onus of proof—Sale of Goods Act 1893, s. 51. **Whitecross Potatoes (Int.) Ltd v Coyle** [1978] 31, HC.

Sale of land. *See* SALE OF LAND (Contract—Breach).

Standard form agreement
Electricity supply
> Whether customer in breach of agreement—Whether supply may be disconnected without notice. *See* CONTRACT (Breach—Standard form agreement).

BREACH OF COVENANT
Lease
See LANDLORD AND TENANT (Breach of covenant).

Forfeiture. See LANDLORD AND TENANT (Forfeiture).

BREACH OF INJUNCTION
Contempt of court
Deliberate disobedience of High Court order
> Trade union members—Power to commit to prison—Alternative remedy. **Ross Co Ltd (In receivership) v Swan** [1981] 416, HC.

BREACH OF STATUTORY DUTY *See* STATUTORY DUTY.

BREAD
Consumer subsidy on retail price
Breach of agreement
> Whether subsidy may be recouped. *See* CONTRACT (Breach—Consumer subsidy agreement).

BREWERY
Rating
Tanks and vessels
> Whether rateable—Whether machinery. *See* RATING AND VALUATION (Exemption—Machinery—Brewery).

BRIDGE
Railway bridge
Derailment of train
> Vertical clearance between road surface and underside of bridge less than prescribed statutory dimension. *See* RAILWAY BRIDGE.

BROADCASTING
Copyright
Infringement
Diffusion service—Transmission of foreign TV broadcasts containing musical works of foreign authors—Whether infringement of copyright—Whether broadcasts to be treated as being first made within the State. Performing **Rights Society Ltd v Marlin Communal Aerials Ltd** [1982] 269, SC.

TV and radio programme schedules—Whether a compilation and a literary work in which copyright subsisted—Copyright Act 1963, ss. 2(1), 8(1). **Radio Telefis Eireann v Magill TV Guide Ltd** [1990] 534, HC.

Election broadcast
Ministerial order
Judicial review—Order preventing access by Provisional Sinn Fein candidates to radio and television to promote their electoral campaign—Whether violation of the provisions of the Constitution—Whether Minister's opinion that the broadcasting would be likely to promote, or incite to crime, reviewable by the courts—Constitution of Ireland 1937, Article 40.6.1—Broadcasting Authority Act 1960, s. 31(1)—Broadcasting Authority (Amendment) Act 1976, s. 16. State **(Lynch) v Cooney** [1982] 190, HC; [1983] 89, SC.

Radio broadcasting station
Unlicensed possession and use of apparatus for wireless telegraphy
Apparatus seized—Challenge to constitutionality of relevant provisions of Act—Whether seizure procedure inconsistent with guarantee of fair procedures—Application for a mandatory injunction requiring return of apparatus—Wireless Telegraphy Act 1926. ss. 3, 5, 8, 12. **Nova Media Services Ltd v Minister for Posts and Telegraphs** [1984] 161, HC.

Apparatus seized—Application for a mandatory injunction requiring return of apparatus. **Sunshine Radio Productions Ltd v Attorney General** [1984] 170, HC.

Schedules
Infringement of copyright. See Copyright—Infringement—TV and radio programme schedules (*above*).

BROKER
Insurance broker
Duty of care. See INSURANCE (Broker—Duty of care).

BRUSSELS CONVENTION ON JURISDICTION AND ENFORCEMENT OF JUDGMENTS
See JUDGMENT (Enforcement—Brussels Convention).

BUILDER
Duty of care. *See* NEGLIGENCE (Builder—Duty of care).

BUILDING
Defects
Breach of contract. See BUILDING CONTRACT (Breach—Defects).

Negligence. See NEGLIGENCE (Defective premises).

Demolition
Damage to adjoining premises
Demolition work causing damage to plaintiff's premises—Whether work carried out negligently—Work being carried out by independent contractor—Whether defendant vicariously liable. **Boylan v Northern Bank Ltd** [1976–7] 287, HC.

BUILDING

Demolition *continued*

Loss of premises

Damages—Assessment—Foreseeability. *See* DAMAGES (Loss of premises).

Non-compliance with planning conditions

Whether High Court has jurisdiction to order demolition. *See* PLANNING (Conditions—Non-compliance).

Development

Planning control. See PLANNING.

Historic interest

Preservation

Effectiveness of planning legislation. *See* PLANNING (Enforcement—Section 27 application—Breach of conditions—Building of historic interest).

Rating and valuation. *See* RATING AND VALUATION.

Repair

Breach of covenant in lease. See LANDLORD AND TENANT (Breach of covenant—Repair).

BUILDING COMPANY

Liquidation

Booking deposits

Purchaser's lien—Whether a person who has paid a booking deposit but entered into no contract with the builder is entitled to a purchaser's lien or to rank as a secured creditor in the liquidation of the building company. In re Barrett Apartments Ltd [1985] 679, SC.

BUILDING CONTRACT

Arbitration

Award

Application for an order to set aside award—Arbitrator refusing to state a case—Whether misconduct—Arbitration Act 1954, ss. 35(1), 36(1), 38(1). **Stillorgan Orchard Ltd v McLoughlin & Harvey Ltd** [1978] 128, HC.

Enforcement—Award made but payment not forthcoming—Application for liberty to enforce the award—Whether arbitrator guilty of misconduct—Arbitration Act 1954, s. 41. **Grangeford Structures Ltd (In liquidation) v SH Ltd** [1988] 129, HC.

Architect

Certificate

Final certificate issued—Contractor subsequently making claim for additional payments—Whether contractor barred from pursuing these claims—Interpretation of building contract—General conditions. **P Elliott & Co Ltd v Minister for Education** [1987] 710, HC, SC.

Interim certificate—Payment on foot of interim certificate—Summary judgment—Whether defendant entitled to set off. *See* Practice—Set off (*below*).

Negligence

Certificate—Engineer's certificate as to structural stability—Architect's certificate based on such certificate—Building defects—Whether builder or architect negligent—Contribution as between defendants—Damages. **Quinn v Quality Homes Ltd** [1976–7] 314, HC.

Breach

Defects

Damages—Assessment—Whether purchaser entitled to loss in letting value or loss of interest on capital. **Fitzpatrick v Frank McGivern Ltd** [1976–7] 239, HC.

BUILDING CONTRACT
Breach
Defects continued

Damages—Assessment—Alleged defects in workmanship and materials—Repairs deferred while liability disputed—Rescission in accordance with commercial good sense—Date by reference to which damages should be assessed—Plaintiff's financial stringency. **Corrigan v Crofon** [1985] 189, HC.

Date of accrual of right of action. *See* LIMITATION OF ACTIONS (Defective premises).

Exclusion clause—Further clause that purchaser not deprived of his common law rights—Claim for damages for remedying defects and for diminution in value—Whether caught by exclusion clause—Whether purchaser entitled to damages for inconvenience and loss of engagement. **Johnson v Longleat Properties** (Dublin) Ltd [1976–7] 93, HC.

Completion
Investigation of title

Negligence—Solicitor—Building contract followed by lease—Stage payments—Building company—Charge by deposit of title deeds created—Investigation not made until after completion of building and making of payments—Building company going into liquidation. **Roche v Peilow** [1986] 189, SC.

Exclusion clause
Scope

Claim for damages for remedying defects and for diminution in value—Whether caught by exclusion clause—Whether purchaser entitled to damages for inconvenience and loss of engagement—Further clause that purchaser not deprived of his common law rights. **Johnson v Longleat Properties (Dublin) Ltd** [1976–7] 93, HC.

Interpretation
General conditions

Architect issuing final certificate for payment—Contractor subsequently making claim for additional payments—Whether contractor barred from pursuing these claims. **P Elliott & Co Ltd v Minister for Education** [1987] 710, HC, SC.

Practice
Set off

RIAI standard form building contract, 1966 edition—Whether provisions of same inconsistent with right of set off—Summary judgment. **John Sisk and Son Ltd v Lawter Products BV** [1976–7] 204, HC.

Specific performance
Whether specific performance lies

Sub-contractor—Nomination of alternative sub-contractor—Application for interlocutory injunction—Balance of convenience—Whether prejudice likely to result. **Lift Manufacturers v Irish Life Assurance Co** [1979] 277, HC.

BUILDING SOCIETY
Advertising
Control by Registrar

Society virtually dormant—Cooption of new directors who were also directors of another industrial and provident society—No evidence of intention to advance loans—Society dependent on a single depositor—Refusal by Registrar of permission to advertise or solicit for deposits or subscriptions for shares—Whether financial policy of society in the interests of the orderly and proper regulation of building society business—Building Societies Act 1976, s. 19. **Ireland Benefit Building Society v Cauldwell** [1981] 73, HC.

Meaning of "annual percentage rate of charge"

Whether cost of house insurance and mortgage protection insurance included—Consumer Information Act 1978, ss. 11, 12—Consumer Information (Consumer Credit)

BUILDING SOCIETY
Advertising
Meaning of "annual percentage rate of charge" continued
Order 1987, Art 3. **Director of Consumer Affairs v Irish Permanent Building Society** [1990] 743, HC.

Agency
Negligent advice
Liability of building society—Building society agent acting as auctioneer—Negligent advice to potential purchasers—Purchasers relying on advice—Defects subsequently discovered—Liability of building society in respect of agent acting as an auctioneer. **Irish Permanent Building Society v O'Sullivan and Collins** [1990] 598, HC.

Prior mortgage
Charge to secure apportioned rent
Whether society precluded from lending money on such premises—Whether such charge a "prior mortgage"—Building Societies Act 1976, s. 80. **Rafferty v Crowley** [1984] 350, HC.

Registration
Certificate of registration
Whether null and void—Injunction sought to restrain society from carrying on business—Refusal of Attorney General to lend his name to relator proceedings—Locus standi of plaintiff—Scope of declaratory relief—Whether society registrable—Name and rules of society—Whether mistake of law meant Registrar had acted outside his jurisdiction—Building Societies Acts 1836 and 1976—RSC 1962, O 19, r 8. **Irish Permanent Building Society v Cauldwell** [1981] 242, HC.

BUNREACHT
Cúirteanna
Úsáid sa cháirt
An tAcht Cúirteanna Breithiánais 1924, alt 71—Forlóirí—'Sa mhéid gur féidir é agus gach ní a bhaineann leis an scéal d'áireamh'—Ceartas Aiceanta. **Ó Monacháin v An Taoiseach** [1986] 660.

BURGLARY
Malicious injury claim
Whether crime against property
Test applicable. *See* CRIMINAL LAW (Larceny—Burglary).

BURIAL GROUND
Cattle wandering onto cemetery
Cattle poisoned by eating yew leaves
Wall between pastureland and cemetery damaged—Whether local authority negligent or in breach of statutory duty in not having wall repaired—Public Health (Ireland) Act 1878, ss. 181, 185, 193, 234. **Walsh v Kilkenny Co Council** [1978] 1, HC.

Location
Proximity to dwelling-house
Churchyard attached to religious denomination—Minister's approval—Whether burial ground can be located within 100 yards of a dwelling-house without owner's consent— Public Health (Ireland) Act 1878, ss. 160, 174—Local Government (Sanitary Services) Act 1948, s. 44. **McCarthy v Johnson** [1989] 706, SC.

BYE-LAWS
Breach
Parking bye-laws
Statutory authority for regulations. *See* ROAD TRAFFIC OFFENCES (Parking).

BYE-LAWS *continued*
Validity
Casual trading
Proposal to designate land as casual trading area subject to conditions—Whether decision perverse—Whether draft bye-laws *ultra vires* Casual Trading Act 1980. **Comerford v O'Malley** [1987] 595, HC.

CANAL
Lack of maintenance
Flooding
Nuisance—Whether commissioners' duty to maintain canal—Whether commissioners negligent—Whether plaintiff contributorily negligent—Damages—Wexford Harbour Embankment Act 1852, ss. 25, 26, 45. **Stelzer v Wexford North Slob Commissioners** [1988] 279, HC.

CANNABIS
Possession
Offence. See CRIMINAL LAW (Misuse of drugs—Controlled drugs—Cannabis resin).

CAPACITY
Marriage
Nullity proceedings. See MARRIAGE (Nullity—Capacity).

Testator
Will
Validity. *See* WILL (Validity—Capacity of testator).

CAPITAL ALLOWANCES
Income tax. *See* REVENUE (Income tax—Capital allowances).

CAPITAL GAINS TAX *See* REVENUE (Capital Gains Tax).

CAR *See* MOTOR VEHICLE.

CARAVANS *See* TEMPORARY DWELLINGS.

CARE
Child
Health board
Fit person order. *See* CHILD (Care—Health board—Fit person order).

Place of safety order. *See* CHILD (Care—Health board—Place of safety order).

Wardship. See CHILD (Ward of court).

Duty of care. *See* NEGLIGENCE (Duty of care).

CASE STATED
Acquittal
Appeal against acquittal
Whether DPP had validly invoked the jurisdiction of the High Court—Whether possible to state case against acquittal. **DPP v Nangle** [1984] 171, HC.

Arbitrator
Case stated on point of law. See ARBITRATION (Practice—Case stated).

Charge
Public mischief
Whether offence known to common law. **DPP (Vizzard) v Carew** [1981] 91, HC.

CASE STATED *continued*
Circuit Court
Jurisdiction

Delegated legislation—Whether ultra vires—Jurisdiction of Circuit Court to decide question of regulations being *ultra vires*—Scheme of compulsory motor insurance—Whether Court's duty to safeguard the position of third parties—Road Traffic Act 1961, s. 56—Road Traffic (Compulsory Insurance) Regulations 1962—Courts of Justice Act 1947, s. 16. **Greaney v Scully** [1981] 340, SC.

Consultative case stated from Circuit Court to Supreme Court—Evidence not completed in Circuit Court—Whether case stated lies in those circumstances—Courts of Justice Act 1947, s. 16. **Doyle v Hearne** [1988] 318, SC.

Arbitration—Lease—Rent review clause—Interpretation. **Hynes Ltd v O'Malley Property Ltd** [1989] 619, SC.

Practice
Interpretation of statutory provisions

Whether reference must be on basis of particular circumstances arising. **O'Neill v Butler** [1979] 243, HC.

Service

Not possible to serve respondent with notice of appeal and copy of case stated—Whether service on solicitor, who acted in the District Court proceedings on behalf of the respondent, sufficient—Summary Jurisdiction Act 1857, s. 2. **Crowley v McVeigh** [1990] 220, HC.

Time limit

District Justice signing case stated after expiration of six month period—Whether High Court jurisdiction to hear appeal—District Court Rules 1955, r 17. **McMahon v McClafferty** [1990] 32, HC.

Revenue
Income tax

Appeal Commissioner's findings—Extent of judicial review of findings of fact by Appeal Commissioner—Nature of case stated—Income Tax Act 1967, s. 1, Schedule D—Finance (Miscellaneous Provisions) Act 1968, s. 17. **Mara v Hummingbird Ltd** [1982] 421, HC, SC.

Road traffic offences
Driving without insurance

Jurisdiction of Circuit Court to decide question of regulations being *ultra vires*—Road Traffic (Compulsory Insurance) Regulations 1962—Road Traffic Act 1961, s. 56—Courts of Justice Act 1947, s. 16. **Greaney v Scully** [1981] 340, SC.

Supreme Court
Jurisdiction

Case stated from High Court—Landlord and tenant—Compensation award—Appeal—Function of Supreme Court in answering case stated. **Aherne v Southern Metropole Hotel** [1989] 693, SC.

Case stated under Article 40.4.3 of the Constitution—Extradition—Order extending Part II of the 1965 Act to the USA—Whether such order a 'law' within the meaning of Article 40.4.3, so as to allow High Court to state a case to the Supreme Court—Whether 'one judgment' rule applied—Constitution of Ireland 1937, Articles 15.2.1, 29.5.2, 34.4.5, 40.4.3—Extradition Act 1965, ss. 4, 8(1)—Extradition Act 1965 (Part II) Order 1984. **State (Gilliland) v Governor of Mountjoy Prison** [1987] 278, SC.

NOT TO BE REMOVED
FROM LIBRARY

CASUAL TRADING
Bye-laws
Validity
Proposal to designate land as casual trading area subject to conditions—Whether decision perverse—Jurisdiction of Circuit Court on appeal from Urban District Council resolution. **Comerford v O'Malley** [1987] 595, HC.

Market right
Franchise to carry on market and fair
Failure to hold market or fair—Legislation regulating carrying on of markets and fairs by licence—Whether franchise survived legislation even though not in use—Statute—Interpretation—Casual Trading Act 1980, ss. 1, 2(2)(h), 3, 5, 9—Interpretation Act 1937, s. 11(a). **Skibbereen UDC v Quill** [1986] 170, HC.

Street trading offences. *See* ROAD TRAFFIC OFFENCES (Street trading).

CATTLE
Livestock export levy
European Community. See AGRICULTURE (Export levy on livestock).

Poisoning
Cattle wandering onto cemetery
Poisoned by eating yew leaves—Wall between pastureland and cemetery damaged—Liability of local authority. *See* ANIMALS (Cattle—Poisoning).

Straying onto main road
Liability of owner or keeper for damage caused. See ANIMALS (Negligence—Straying onto main road).

CAUSE
Action
Estoppel. See ESTOPPEL (Res judicata—Cause of action estoppel).

Generally. See ACTION (Cause).

Certiorari
Time limit for showing cause. See CERTIORARI (Cause).

CEMETERY. *See* BURIAL GROUND.

CENTRAL BANK
Privilege
Oath of secrecy
Subpoena duces tecum issued requiring officer of Central Bank to produce documents—Statutory privilege—Central Bank Act 1942, ss. 6(1), 31. **Cully v Northern Bank Finance Corporation Ltd** [1984] 683, HC.

CENTRAL CRIMINAL COURT
Not guilty verdict
Appeal
Whether open to DPP to appeal against acquittal—Extent of Supreme Court's appellate jurisdiction—Constitution of Ireland 1937, Articles 34.4.3, 38.5—Courts of Justice Act 1924, ss. 31, 63. **People (DPP) v O'Shea** [1983] 549, SC.

CERTIFICATE
Architect. *See* BUILDING CONTRACT (Architect—Certificate).

Company charge
Registration. See COMPANY (Charge—Registration—Certificate of Registrar).

CERTIFICATE *continued*
Evidence
Appointment
Authorised officers—Whether certificate that officer had been appointed sufficient evidence of fact of appointment. **Minister for Agriculture v Cleary** [1988] 294, HC.

Tax clearance. *See* REVENUE (Tax clearance certificate).

CERTIORARI
Absolute order
Absolute order made in first instance
Jurisdiction—RSC O 84, rr 9, 57. **State (Aherne) v Governor of Limerick Prison** [1983] 17, SC.

Validity—Circumstances in which absolute order may be made at first instance—Natural justice—*Audi alteram partem*—Constitution of Ireland 1937, Article 40—Habeas Corpus (Ireland) Act—RSC O 84, rr 2 and 9—Fisheries (Consolidation) Acts 1959 to 1978. In re Zwann [1981] 333, SC.

Absolute order set aside on appeal
Order made by judge when *functus officio* affirming valid conviction. **State (Dunne) v Martin** [1982] 18, SC.

Matters to be considered
Planning permission—Mistake—Genuine mistake—Cause shown by respondents—Matters to be considered in granting absolute order of certiorari—Local Government (Planning and Development) Act 1963, s. 26. **State (Toft) v Galway Corporation** [1981] 439, SC.

Alternative remedy
Appeal by way of case stated
District Court conviction—Whether certiorari appropriate remedy. **Gill v Connellan** [1988] 448, HC.

Whether restrictive on certiorari proceedings
Planning. **State (Abenglen Properties Ltd) v Dublin Corporation** [1981] 54, HC; [1982] 590, SC.

Appeal committee
Conduct of proceedings
No cross-examination of witnesses Compliance with requirements of natural justice. **State (Boyle) v General Medical Services (Payment) Board** [1981] 14, HC.

Army Pensions Board
Natural justice
Widow applying for pension—Applicant not permitted to attend hearing and give oral evidence—Decision refusing application—Refusal to reveal material upon which decision based—Decision set aside on certiorari. **State (Williams) v Army Pensions Board** [1981] 379, HC; [1983] 331, SC.

Availability of remedy
Generally. See JUDICIAL REVIEW (Availability of relief).

Cause
Time limit for showing cause
Extension of period made ex parte—High Court judge refusing to hear prosecutor—Whether prosecutor to be heard on application for extension of period for showing cause—Delay by prosecutor in appealing against refusal to hear his arguments—Whether prejudice caused to prosecutor. **State (Hughes) v O'Hanrahan** [1986] 218, SC.

Compensation tribunal
Award
Criminal Injuries Compensation Tribunal. *See* Criminal Injuries Compensation Tribunal (*below*).

CERTIORARI
Compensation tribunal
Award continued

Ex gratia award for compensation in respect of nervous shock suffered by prosecutor's wife—No such award made to prosecutor—Whether decision to be quashed—Appropriate test—Whether decision fundamentally at variance with reason and common sense. **State (Keegan) v Stardust Victims Compensation Tribunal** [1987] 202, HC, SC.

Constitutionality of legislation
Challenge

Whether open to prosecutor, on an application for certiorari, to challenge the constitutionality of legislation—Constitution of Ireland 1937, Article 34—Street and House-to-House Collections Act 1962, s. 13(4). **State (McEldowney) v Kelleher and Attorney General** [1982] 568, HC; [1985] 10, SC.

Whether certiorari an appropriate procedure for challenging the validity of legislation—Constitution of Ireland 1937, Article 40.6.1—Broadcasting Authority Act 1960, s. 31(1)—Broadcasting Authority (Amendment) Act 1976, s. 16. **State (Lynch) v Cooney** [1982] 190, HC; [1983] 89, SC.

Conviction
Appeal

Circuit Court appeal—Certificate of conviction not correctly recording the orders spoken by the judge. **State (O'Dare) v Sheehy** [1984] 99, HC.

Sentence increased—Order of certiorari quashing order of appellate court—Appeal. RSC O 84, rr 9, 57. **State (Aherne) v Governor of Limerick Prison** [1983] 17, SC.

Discretion to refuse remedy

Adequacy of alternative relief. **State (Wilson) v Neilan** [1987] 118, HC.

District Court

Fair procedures—Accused not represented at trial—Conviction set aside—District Justice acting in excess of jurisdiction. **State (Collins) v Ruane** [1984] 443, HC; [1985] 349, SC.

Interruptions by judge—Whether conviction made within jurisdiction—Alternative remedy of appeal by way of case stated—Whether certiorari appropriate remedy. **Gill v Connellan** [1988] 448, HC.

Plea of guilty—Legal aid denied—Charges not stated to accused in open court—Application for certiorari to quash conviction—Whether District Court orders good on their face—Whether orders made without or in excess of jurisdiction. **State (McDonagh) v Barry** [1983] 525, HC.

Plea of guilty—Voluntary nature of plea—Constitution—Natural justice—Leave to argue upon grounds not raised in the application—Whether fact that prosecutrix has appealed to Circuit Court is of itself a reason for refusing certiorari—Factors guiding court in exercise of its discretion—Whether prosecutrix has established that District Court order should be quashed—Conditional order discharged. **State (Glover) v McCarthy** [1981] 47, HC.

Road traffic offence—Whether District Justice had jurisdiction to reopen case and hear additional evidence for prosecution in absence of applicant's counsel—Applicant's counsel specifically excused from attending—Natural justice—RSC 1986, O 84 r 27(4), (6). **Dawson v Hamill** [1990] 257, HC.

Scheduled offence—Driving without insurance—Validity of conviction before ten day period to produce certificate has elapsed—Criminal Justice Act 1951, s. 2. **State (McDonagh) v Sheerin** [1981] 149, HC.

Scheduled offence—Summary trial only with consent of accused—Prosecutor tried summarily and convicted on two charges—Failure to inform prosecutor of his right to

CERTIORARI
Conviction
District Court continued

trial by jury—No objection to being tried summarily—Whether District Justice acted without jurisdiction—Criminal Justice Act 1951, s. 2—Offences Against the State Act 1939, s. 45 (2)—Offences against the State (Scheduled Offences) Order 1972. **State (McDonagh) v Sheerin** [1981] 149, HC.

Summons issued by District Court clerk—Supreme Court holding that the issue of a summons was a judicial act—Application to quash conviction out of time—Whether extension be granted—RSC 1986, O 84, r 21. **White v Hussey** [1989] 109, HC.

Road traffic offence

Accused not receiving copy of certificate of analysis until justi before the trial—Whether District Court order be quashed—Natural justice. **State (O'Regan) v Plunkett** [1984] 347, HC.

Time limit

Challenge to conviction—Application to quash conviction out of time—Whether extension be granted. *See* Time limit—Extension—Challenge to conviction (*below*).

Coroner
Adjournment of inquest

Natural justice. *See* INQUEST (Adjournment).

Criminal Injuries Compensation Tribunal
Award

Calculation of compensation—Whether decision of Tribunal at variance with reason and commonsense. **Hill v Criminal Injuries Compensation Tribunal** [1990] 36, HC.

Fatal injury attributable to crime of violence—Whether decision of Tribunal subject to judicial review—Whether Tribunal entitled to reduce the gross loss suffered by the value of social welfare benefits payable—Whether Tribunal acted contrary to natural justice—Criminal Injuries Compensation Scheme 1974, paras 1, 2, 3, 4, 6, 15, 16, 25, 26. **State (Hayes) v Criminal Injuries Compensation Tribunal** [1982] 210, HC.

Delay
Application to quash sentence

Out of time—Whether delay in seeking order a ground for refusal—Whether order issues *ex debito justitiae*. **State (Gleeson) v Martin** [1985] 577, HC.

Discretion

Prison—Temporary release scheme—Revocation of temporary release order—Whether contrary to rules of natural justice—Prisons (Temporary Release) Rules 1960, r 6. **State (Murphy) v Governor of St Patrick's Institution** [1982] 475, HC.

Lack of candour

Whether disentitling prosecutor to relief—Whether delay excessive—Whether certiorari would have any effect. **State (Furey) v Minister for Defence** [1988] 89, SC.

Preliminary examination

Technical flaws—Discretion of court. **State (Pletzer) v Magee** [1986] 441, HC.

Time limit

Extension. *See* Time limit—Extension (*below*).

Whether evidence explaining delay

Whether applicant had any merits—Alternative remedy available—Whether issue decided at ex parte hearing—RSC 1986, O 84, r 21(1). **Solan v DPP and Wine** [1989] 491, HC.

Discretion of court
Factors guiding court in exercise of its discretion. **State (Litzouw) v Johnson** [1981] 273, HC.

CERTIORARI *continued*
District Court order
Error
Whether error made within jurisdiction—Renewal of publican's licence. **In re Riordan** [1981] 2, HC.

District Court proceedings
Constitutional argument against statute
Appeal pending to Circuit Court—Whether certiorari available. **State (Pheasantry Ltd) v Donnelly** [1982] 512, HC.

Employment
Dismissal
Garda probationer—Dismissal for not being likely to become efficient and well-conducted guard—Previous breaches of discipline as basis for dismissal—Pending inquiry into breach of discipline discontinued—Natural justice—Garda Síochána (Disciplinary) Regulations 1945, arts 8, 9. **State (Burke) v Garvey** [1979] 232, SC.

Employment Appeals Tribunal determination
Unfair dismissal claim
Failure by employer to deliver notice of appearance—Tribunal refusing to hear employer—Whether violation of natural and constitutional justice—Whether error within jurisdiction—Redundancy Appeals Tribunal Regulations 1968, reg 23—Unfair Dismissals (Claims and Appeals) Regulations 1977, regs 5, 9, 10—Maternity Protection (Disputes and Appeals) Regulations 1981, reg 15—Unfair Dismissals Act 1977, ss. 8, 9, 10. **Halal Meat Packers (Ballyhaunis) Ltd v Employment Appeals Tribunal** [1990] 293, HC.

Whether determination bad on its face—Whether certiorari be granted—Whether more appropriate to appeal to Circuit Court—Unfair Dismissals Act 1977, s. 10(4). **Mythen v Employment Appeals Tribunal** [1989] 844, HC.

Garda Síochána
Conciliation and Arbitration scheme
Chairman's decision—Grounds of review—Whether decision irrational or unreasonable—Doctrine of legitimate expectation—Promissory estoppel—Whether ministerial statement made in Dáil Éireann may be relied on by plaintiff—Constitution of Ireland 1937, Article 15.1—Garda Síochána Act 1924, s. 13—Garda Síochána Act 1977, s. 1—Police Forces Amalgamation Act 1925, ss. 8(1), 12, 14. **Garda Representative Association v Ireland** [1989] 1, HC.

Discipline
Inquiry—Discontinuance—Garda Commissioner directing that a new inquiry be held into some allegations—Whether appointment of new board of inquiry be quashed—Garda Síochána (Discipline) Regulations 1971. **McGowan v Wren** [1988] 744, HC.

Inquiry—Reference to appeal board—Board deciding it had no jurisdiction—Whether jurisdictional error. **State (Sheehan) v McMahon** [1976–7] 305, HC, SC.

Grounds for granting
Distinction between a proceeding commenced without jurisdiction and one validly commenced during which jurisdiction is exceeded. **State (Keeney) v O'Malley** [1986] 31, HC.

Health board
General medical services scheme
Complaints of abuse of scheme—Referral of matter to Minister—Failure to inform fully of nature of complaint—Whether referral *ultra vires*—Health Act 1970, s. 58. **O'Flynn v Mid-Western Health Board** [1990] 149, HC.

Health services
Free general medical services
Participation by applicant in 'choice of doctor scheme'—Conditions of participation—

CERTIORARI
Health services
Free general medical services continued

Provision for investigation where rate of attendance excessive—Power to disallow fees—Hearing—Refusal to allow cross-examination—Whether principles of natural justice disregarded—Whether regulations *ultra vires*—Constitution of Ireland 1937, Art 40.3—Health Acts 1970 and 1972—Health Service Regulations 1972. **State (Boyle) v General Medical Services (Payment) Board** [1981] 14, HC.

Inquest
Adjournment. See INQUEST (Adjournment).

Suicide verdict

Natural justice. *See* INQUEST (Verdict—Suicide).

Jurisdiction
District Court conviction

Interruptions by judge—Whether conviction made within jurisdiction—Alternative remedy of appeal by way of case stated—Whether certiorari appropriate remedy. **Gill v Connellan** [1988] 448, HC.

Tribunal

Decision—Whether subject to judicial review—Natural justice—Criminal Injuries Compensation Scheme. **State (Hayes) v Criminal Injuries Compensation Tribunal** [1982] 210, HC.

Labour Court determination
Application to quash

Whether error of law as to jurisdiction—Employment Equality Act 1977, ss. 19, 20. **State (Aer Lingus Teo) v Labour Court** [1987] 373, HC, SC.

Natural justice

Infringement—Whether employer entitled as a right to have determination quashed—Extent of court's discretion—Whether order necessary for the protection of the employer's legal rights. **State (Polymark (Irl) Ltd) v Labour Court** [1987] 357, HC.

Refusal to entertain appeal from recommendation of equality officer

Whether correct. **Aer Rianta v Labour Court** [1990] 193, HC.

Land Commission
Procedures

Natural and constitutional justice—Land Act 1965, ss. 12, 45. **State (Hussey) v Irish Land Commission** [1983] 407, HC.

Landlord and tenant
Local authority tenant

Notice to quit—District Court hearing—Tenant not represented—Tenant not invited to give evidence—Whether hearing in breach of natural justice—Housing Act 1966, s. 62. **State (Crothers) v Kelly** [1978] 167, HC.

Notice to quit—No explanation given nor complaint brought to tenant's attention—Requests for explanation unanswered—District Court order for possession—Appeal to Circuit Court—Whether a reason for refusing to make absolute a conditional order of certiorari—Factors guiding a court in the exercise of its discretion—Landlord and Tenant Law Amendment (Ireland) Act 1860, ss. 86, 87, 88—Housing Act 1966, ss. 62, 118. **State (Litzouw) v Johnson** [1981] 273, HC.

Local authority
Gaming licence

Application for licence refused by District Court—Local authority rescinding resolution allowing gaming—Whether decision of local authority *ultra vires* by reason of bad

CERTIORARI
Local authority
Gaming licence continued
faith—Whether unconstitutional invasion of judicial process—Whether resolution made as a result of bias or interest—Whether made in disregard of the essentials of justice—Presumption that administrative decision made within jurisdiction. **State (Divito) v Arklow UDC** [1986] 123, SC.

Medical Council
Failure to register applicant
Applicant qualified as a doctor outside jurisdiction—Whether council should be compelled to register applicant—Whether council could be compelled to make and issue rules specifying courses of training and exams—Whether compensation payable for loss of livelihood by reason of failure of council to register applicant—Medical Practitioners Act 1955, ss. 3 and 6—Medical Practitioners Act 1978, ss. 6, 26, 27, 28, 29. **Bakht v Medical Council** [1990] 840, SC.

Ministerial decision
Broadcasting
Order preventing access by Provisional Sinn Fein candidates to promote their electoral campaign—Whether violation of the provisions of the Constitution—Constitution of Ireland 1937, Article 40.6.1—Broadcasting Authority Act 1960, s. 31(1)—Broadcasting Authority (Amendment) Act 1976, s. 16. **State (Lynch) v Cooney** [1982] 190, HC; [1983] 89, SC.

Discretion
Estoppel—Legitimate expectation—Exercise of statutory discretion—Appointment of teacher—Whether Minister estopped from exercising discretion to refuse to appoint applicant as teacher—Whether applicant had legitimate expectation that she would be appointed—Whether Minister could exercise discretion to appoint applicant to a position other than that applied for—Vocational Education Act 1930, ss. 23, 30. **Devitt v The Minister for Education** [1989] 639, HC.

Patent office
Refusal of increments to examiners
Arrears of work—Controller promulgating policy of accelerated acceptance of patent specifications—Refusal of increment to examiners failing to implement this policy—Whether orders of certiorari and mandamus be granted. **State (Rajan) v Minister for Industry and Commerce** [1988] 231, HC.

Planning
Application to quash decision
Existence of adequate alternative remedy—Whether error appearing on the face of the record—Discretion—Whether certiorari should issue *ex debito justitiae*—Nature of certiorari proceedings—Local Government (Planning and Development) Act 1963, s. 26 (4). **State (Abenglen Properties Ltd) v Dublin** Corporation [1981] 54, HC; [1982] 590, SC.

Enforcement notice
Application to quash—Exempted development claim—No application made to Bord Pleanála for ruling—Whether certiorari be granted—Local Government (Planning and Development) Act 1963, s. 31. **O'Connor v Kerry Co Council** [1988] 660, HC.

Grant of permission
Planning permission given to company seeking a change of user from dwellinghouse to amusement centre—Mistake in name of company causing grant of planning permission to a non-existent company—Genuine mistake—Cause shown by respondents—Jurisdiction of planning authority—Matters to be considered in granting absolute order of certiorari—Local Government (Planning and Development) Act 1963, s. 26. **State (Toft) v Galway Corporation** [1981] 439, SC.

CERTIORARI

Planning *continued*

Refusal of permission

Notification of refusal—Adequacy of notification. **State (Sweeney) v Minister for Environment** [1979] 35, HC.

Practice and procedure

Absolute order made in first instance. See Absolute order—Absolute order made in first instance (*above*).

Delay. See Delay (*above*).

Time limit—Extension. *See* Time limit—Extension (*below*).

Prison

Temporary release

Revocation—Fair procedures—Releasee charged with an offence—Whether sufficient reason for revocation—Criminal Justice Act 1960, ss. 2, 4, 6, 7—Prisoners (Temporary Release) Rules 1960, rr 3(2), 5, 6, 7. **State (Murphy) v Governor of St Patrick's Institution** [1982] 475, HC; [1985] 141, SC.

School

Board of Management

Admission of students—Criteria applied—Whether subject to judicial review. **O hUallachain v Burke** [1988] 693, HC.

Discipline

Natural justice—Suspension and expulsion—Whether failure to interview pupil expelled rendered expulsion invalid—Whether legal representation required at hearing—Whether draft article of management of school consistent with requirements of natural justice. **State (Smullen) v Duffy** [1980] 46, HC.

Scope of remedy

Extent of review. **State (Daly) v Ruane** [1988] 117, HC.

Sentence

Accused already serving sentence

Aggregate sentences exceeding 12 months—Whether District Justice acted in excess of jurisdiction. **State (Payne) v Clifford** [1985] 70, HC.

Social welfare

Decision of appeals officer

Refusal of old age pension—Whether decision bad in law —Whether error within jurisdiction—Social Welfare Act 1952, s. 43. **State (Power) v Moran** [1976–7] 20, HC.

Fuel allowance

Department circular excluding persons on short term social welfare from scheme—Whether circular *ultra vires* the Minister. **State (Kershaw) v Eastern Health Board** [1985] 235, HC.

Statute

Validity

Constitution—Whether issue of validity of enactment properly determined in certiorari proceedings. *See* Constitutionality of legislation (*above*).

Summons

Sufficiency

Whether open to prosecutor to challenge sufficiency of summons—Prosecutor acquiescing in adjournments of his case. **State (O'Leary) v Neilan** [1984] 35, HC.

Time limit

Extension

Challenge to conviction—Application to quash conviction out of time—Whether

CERTIORARI
Time limit
Extension continued
> extension be granted—Discretion of court—Matters to be considered—Interests of people of Ireland—RSC 1986, O 84, r 21. **White v Hussey** [1989] 109, HC.

> Conditional order not served in time—Application for extension of the time for service—Whether order automatically discharged—Statutory time limit for challenging decision of An Bord Pleanála having expired—Local Government (Planning and Development) Act 1963, s. 82(3A)—RSC 1962, O 108, r 7. **State (Flynn & O'Flaherty Ltd) v Dublin Corporation** [1983] 125, HC.

> Service of statement of opposition and affidavit—*Ex parte* application by respondent for extension of time limit—Whether application contrary to Supreme Court Rules—RSC 1986, O 52 r 2, O 84 rr 4, 22(4), O 112 rr 7, 8. **Butler v Ruane** [1989] 159, SC.

> Time limit for showing cause. *See* Cause—Time limit for showing cause (*above*).

Trial
Cross-examination
> Objection by prosecution—Whether justice erred in acceding to objection—Whether error within jurisdiction—Road Traffic (Amendment) Act 1978. **O'Broin v Ruane** [1989] 732, HC.

Interruptions by judge
> Scope of inquiry into whether lower court acted within its jurisdiction—Conduct of trial—Natural justice—Whether conduct of trial went to jurisdiction. **Gill v Connellan** [1988] 448, HC.

CHARACTER OF ACCUSED
Evidence. *See* CRIMINAL LAW (Evidence—Character).

CHARGE
Criminal charge. *See* CRIMINAL LAW (Charge)

Equitable mortgage
Deposit of title deeds
> Banker's lien. *See* BANK (Deposit of title deeds).

> Family home. *See* FAMILY LAW (Property—Family home—Equitable mortgage).

Generally. *See* COMPANY (Charge).

Land. *See* REAL PROPERTY (Incumbrance—Charge).

Mortgage. *See* MORTGAGE .

Prior mortgage. *See* MORTGAGE (Prior mortgage).

Retention of title clause. *See* SALE OF GOODS (Retention of title clause).

CHARITY
Cy-près
Charitable gift
> Will trusts—Collection of books—Collection no longer used as envisaged by bequest—Other requirements no longer fulfilled—Application for cy-près order—Whether permissible to alter the original purposes of charitable gift—Irish Church Act 1869—Charities Act 1961, s. 47. **Representative Church Body v Attorney General** [1989] 177, HC.

Whether applicable
> Gift to body which did not exist either at date of the making of will or at death of testatrix—Whether gift lapsed—Gift over—Whether gift over must also lapse—Whether cy-près doctrine applicable. In re Prescott: **Purcell v Pobjoy** [1990] 835, HC.

CHARITY *continued*
House to house collection. *See* STREET AND HOUSE TO HOUSE COLLECTIONS.

Rates
Exemption
> Educational institution—Whether of a public nature and used exclusively for public purposes. *See* RATING AND VALUATION (Exemption—Charitable or public purposes).

CHATTEL
Lost or mislaid chattels
Treasure trove
> Chattel found in land—Finder trespassing—Rights of ownership and possession as between landowner and finder—Chattel part of ancient hoard—Treasure trove—Whether finder entitled to reward—Promissory estoppel—Legitimate expectation—Reasonable reward—Factors to be taken into consideration—National Monuments Act 1930, ss. 8, 14(1), 26. **Webb v Ireland** [1988] 565, HC, SC.

Personal chattels
Passing of property
> Retention of title—Power to take possession. *See* SALE OF GOODS (Retention of title clause—Passing of property).

Real property
Charge
> Extent of property mortgaged—Reciever attempting to claim proceeds of sale of chattels—Chattels not part of property charged. *See* REAL PROPERTY (Incumbrance—Charge—Deed of charge).

CHEQUE
Conditional or unconditional payment
Discharge of debt
> Cheque drawn by creditor in favour of debtor and endorsed back to creditor—Cheque referred to drawer—Whether cheque accepted as unconditional payment of defendant's indebtedness. **Private Motorists' Provident Society Ltd v Moore** [1988] 526, HC.

Payment
Duty of care
> Bank—Contractual duty to exercise care and skill—Duty to make enquiry in appropriate circumstances—Fraudulent dealings in company account—Whether bank negligent in paying cheques. *See* BANK (Duty of care—Contractual duty to exercise care and skill).

Winding up of company
> Cheques drawn prior to presentation of petition—Cheques paid subsequently—Whether monies paid prior to the commencement of the winding up. *See* COMPANY (Winding up—disposition of property—Cheques drawn by company prior to presentation of petition).

CHILD
Adoption. *See* ADOPTION.

Affiliation. *See* AFFILIATION ORDER.

Care
Health board
> Fit person order—Child committed to care of health board as 'fit person'—Validity—Constitution—Habeas corpus application—Nature of District Court order—Whether fair procedures—Whether child should be returned to custody of parents—Children Act 1908. **State (D and D) v G** [1990] 10, SC.

CHILD
Care
Health board continued
Fit person order—Child committed to care of health board as "fit person"—
Validity—Whether health board 'fit person'—Contents of 'fit person' order—Children
Act 1908, ss. 21, 23(1), 24(1), 38, 58—Health Act 1970, ss. 5, 66(2)—Interpretation Act
1937, s. 11(c). **State (D and D) v G and Midland Health Board** (No 2) [1990] 130, SC.

Place of safety order—Inquiry into legality of detention—Whether fair procedures
observed—Whether failure to bring case before District Court within a reasonable
time—Whether failure to give parent adequate information about detention of children
within a reasonable time—Children Act 1908, ss. 20, 24—Summary Jurisdiction Rules
1909, rules 6, 12. **State (F) v Superintendent, B Garda Station** [1990] 243, HC.

Place of safety order—Welfare of child—Inquiry into legality of detention—Whether
'place of safety' order may be made pursuant to s. 24 of the Children Act 1908 when
child has already been taken to a place of safety pursuant to s. 20—Search—Whether
the need for the search authorised by s. 24 is fundamental to the exercise of the
jurisdiction of the District Court—Time for issuing of "fit person" summons—Children
Act 1908, ss. 20, 24. **M F v Superintendent of Ballymun Garda Station** [1990] 243, HC;
[1990] 767, SC.

Industrial school. See Detention—Industrial school (*below*).

Wardship. See Ward of court (*below*).

Custody
Father
English court ordering that infant be placed in the custody of a county council—
Father removing infant from jurisdiction—Father an Irish citizen domiciled in England—
Council seeking an order of habeas corpus—Legality of infant's detention. *See*
Custody—Removal from jurisdiction—Father (*below*).

Foster parents
Mother consenting to put child up for adoption—Fosterage arranged—Foster parents
seeking order of custody—Mother wanting child placed for adoption outside the county
in which she was residing—Foster parents living short distance from the mother—
Mother applying for an order of habeas corpus—Welfare of infant—Constitution of
Ireland 1937, Article 40 4 2—Guardianship of Infants Act 1964, s. 3. **State (M G) v A
H and M H** [1984] 237, HC.

Guardianship. See Guardianship and custody (*below*).

Health board
Fit person order. *See* Care—Health board—Fit person order (*above*).

Place of safety order. *See* Care—Health board—Place of safety order (*above*).

Removal from jurisdiction
Father—English Court ordering that infant be placed in the custody of a county
council—Father removing infant from jurisdiction of English courts—Father being an
Irish citizen domiciled in England—Council seeking an order of habeas corpus—Legality
of infant's detention—Whether father and infant entitled to be regarded as family—
Constitution of Ireland 1937, Articles 40, 41, 42. **Kent Co Council v CS** [1984] 292.

Wife—Application by wife for passports for children—Passports issued despite husband's
objections—Removal of children from jurisdiction by wife—Whether infringement of
husband's constitutional and statutory rights—Extent of relief husband entitled to
obtain—Ministers and Secretaries Act 1924, s. 1—Adoption Act 1952, s. 40—Guardianship of Infants Act 1964, ss. 6, 10, 11—Constitution of Ireland 1937, Articles 40, 41,
42. **Cosgrove v Ireland** [1982] 48, HC.

CHILD
Custody
Removal from jurisdiction
Wife—Entry of child's name on wife's passport—Forged consent of husband—Removal of child from jurisdiction by wife—Mandamus—Effectiveness of order. **P I v Ireland** [1989] 810, SC.

Separation of parents
Husband seeking custody of the children—Domicile of the parties—Whether husband abandoned Irish domicile of origin—Factors to be taken into account in awarding custody—Whether age a weighty factor—Guardianship of Infants Act 1964. **J W v M W** [1978] 119, HC.

Welfare of child
Both parents considered suitable—Whether children of tender years should remain in custody of mother—Guardianship of Infants Act 1964, s. 3. **O'D v O'D** [1976–7] 142, HC.

Detention
Industrial school
Parents unable to provide for support—District Court order that child be sent to industrial school—Father consenting to said order—Father subsequently seeking return of child—Constitution—Validity—Minister refusing to order child's release—Whether provisions unconstitutional—Constitution of Ireland 1937, Articles 40, 42—Children Act 1908, s. 58—Children Act 1941, s. 10. In Re Doyle, An Infant: **State (Doyle) v Minister for Education and the Attorney General** [1989] 277, SC.

Fit person order. *See* Care—Health board—Fit person order (*above*).

Fosterage. *See* Custody—Foster parents (*above*).

Guardianship and custody
Natural father's application
Extent of applicant's rights—Test to be applied—Whether welfare of child the first and paramount consideration—Guardianship of Infants Act 1964, s. 6A—Status of Children Act 1987, s. 12. **K v W** [1990] 121, SC.

Child in custody of prospective adopters—Welfare of child. **K v W** (No 2) [1990] 791.

Removal of children from jurisdiction by wife
Passports issued despite husband's objections—Entitlement of husband to damages. *See* Custody—Removal from jurisdiction—Wife (*above*).

Illegitimate child
Succession rights. See ILLEGITIMATE CHILD (Succession rights—Intestacy).

Paternity
Affiliation. See AFFILLIATION ORDER.

Evidence admissible to prove paternity
Evidence of wife that child not the child of the marriage—Whether admissible—Rule in *Russell v Russell*—Whether part of the common law of Ireland—Whether incompatible with the provisions of the Constitution—Constitutional entitlements to fair procedures—Obligations of the Registrar of Births and Deaths—Constitution of Ireland 1937, Articles 34.1, 38.1, 40.3.5—Registration of Births and Deaths (Ireland) Act 1863—Births and Deaths Registration Act (Ireland) 1880, s. 7—Guardianship of Infants Act 1964, ss. 6(4), 11(4). **A s. v R B and W s.** [1984] 66, HC.

Personal injuries
Damages
Brain damage. *See* DAMAGES (Personal injuries—Brain damage—Infant).

Occupier's liability. See NEGLIGENCE (Occupier—Licensee—Church—Infant licensee).

CHILD *continued*

Place of safety order. *See* Care—Health board—Place of safety order (*above*).

Removal from jurisdiction. *See* Custody—Removal from jurisdiction (*above*).

Ward of court

Foreign judgment

Committal of children into care of local authority in England—Removal by parents to Ireland—Enquiry into detention of children by health board—Health board action taken at request of English authority—Search warrant—Whether warrant executed within jurisdiction—Whether District Court order made within jurisdiction—Recognition of validity of English Court order—Comity of courts—Constitution of Ireland 1937, Article 40.4.2—Children Act 1908, s. 24. **Saunders v Mid-Western Health Board** [1989] 229, HC.

Young offender. *See* CRIMINAL LAW (Young offender).

CHOICE OF LAW *See* PRIVATE INTERNATIONAL LAW.

CHURCH

Churchyard

Location

Proposal to use land close to dwellinghouse as cemetery—Whether consent of owner of dwellinghouse required. *See* BURIAL GROUND (Location).

Negligence

Personal injuries

Infant plaintiff suffering extensive burns after her sleeve caught fire whilst lighting a candle on a candelabra—Whether concealed danger—Whether defendant negligent—Whether damages awarded excessive. **Rooney v Connolly** [1987] 768, SC.

CHURCH ANNULMENT

Annulment of first marriage

Husband marrying again before obtaining civil annulment of first marriage

First marriage voidable—Whether second marriage valid. **F M L v Registrar General of Marriages** [1984] 667, HC.

Effect on civil claim

Psychiatric illness

Inability to form and sustain normal marriage relationship—Respondent obtaining nullity decree from ecclesiastical court—Whether relevant to the determination of civil court. **DC (Otherwise DW) v DW** [1987] 58, HC.

Relevance

Whether application for church annulment relevant to judicial determination of validity of marriage—Need for law reform regarding nullity—Matrimonial Causes and Marriage Law (Ireland) Amendment Act 1870, s. 13. **N (otherwise K) v K** [1986] 75, HC, SC.

Grounds recognised

Effect on civil claim

Impotence—Failure to inseminate—Whether ground recognised by ecclesiastical courts—Matrimonial Causes and Marriage Law (Ireland) Amendment Act 1870, s. 13. **M M (otherwise G) v P M** [1986] 515, HC.

CIRCUIT COURT

Jurisdiction

Appeal

Criminal appeal—Sentence—Power of Circuit Court judge to increase sentences. **State (O'Rourke) v Martin** [1984] ILRM 333, HC.

CIRCUIT COURT
Jurisdiction
Appeal continued

Criminal appeal—Regulations—Whether ultra vires—Jurisdiction of Circuit Court to decide question of regulations being ultra vires when hearing a criminal appeal—Whether Circuit Court judge has jurisdiction to state a case on the point—Compulsory motor insurance regulations—Whether Court's duty to safeguard the position of third parties—Road Traffic Act 1961, s. 56—Road Traffic (Compulsory Insurance) Regulations 1962—Courts of Justice Act 1947, s. 16. **Greaney v Scully** [1981] 340, SC.

Criminal appeal—Appeal against conviction—Whether Circuit Judge power to increase sentence—Procedure adopted in challenging Circuit Court order—Habeas corpus application—Whether well founded—Whether, despite increase in sentence, prisoner still held in accordance with law—Constitution of Ireland 1937, Art 40.4.2—Petty Sessions Act 1851, s. 24—Courts of Justice Act 1924, ss. 51, 85, 91—Courts of Justice Act 1928, s. 18—Courts (Establishment and Constitution) Act 1961, s. 5—Courts (Supplemental Provisions) Act 1961, ss. 22(3), 22(5)(a), 48, 50. **State (Aherne) v Governor of Limerick Prison** [1983] 17, SC.

Case stated

Consultative case stated from Circuit Court to Supreme Court—Evidence not completed in Circuit Court—Whether case stated lies in those circumstances—Courts of Justice Act 1947, s. 16. **Doyle v Hearne** [1988] 318, SC.

Equity

Whether court having jurisdiction to issue injunction to enforce statutory provisions—Submission to jurisdiction—Right to transfer case to High Court. **Parsons v Kavanagh** [1990] 560, HC.

Landlord and tenant

Jurisdiction of Circuit Court to fix rent—Whether jurisdiction to fix inflationary rent—Whether contrary to public policy—Landlord and Tenant Act 1931. **McGovern v Governors of Jervis St Hospital** [1981] 197, SC.

Trial

Transfer of criminal trial—Indictable offence—Accused sent for trial at next sitting in Monaghan—Courthouse destroyed by fire—All business listed transferred to Cavan—Whether infringement of accused's rights—Powers of President of Circuit Court—Whether accused person has right to be tried by jury drawn from any particular locality—Courts of Justice Act 1947, s. 10—Courts (Supplemental Provisions) Act 1961, ss. 25, 26—Criminal Procedure Act 1967, s. 8—Juries Act 1967 –District Court (Criminal Procedure Act 1967) Rules. **State (Hughes) v Neylon** [1982] 108, HC.

Transfer of criminal trial—Statute providing for the transfer of the trial of a person from the Circuit Court before which he is triable to the Dublin Circuit Court—Whether Dublin Circuit Court jurisdiction to try the case—Statute—Validity—Constitution of Ireland 1937, Article 34.3.4—Courts (Establishment and Constitution) Act 1961, s. 4(1)—Courts (Supplemental Provisions) Act 1961, s. 25—Courts Act 1981, s. 31. **State (Boyle) v Neylon** [1986] 337, HC; [1987] 535, SC.

Practice
Criminal appeal

Appeal against sentence—Misuse of drugs—Change of circumstances of offender—Whether Circuit Court obliged to take account of change in devising regime of rehabilitation rather than punishment—Misuse of Drugs Act 1977, s. 28(2). **State (Slattery) v Roe** [1986] 511, HC.

Stay of action

Road traffic accident—Two actions—Separate courts—One party commencing proceedings in Circuit Court claiming damages for his car—Other party issuing proceedings

CIRCUIT COURT
Practice
Stay of action
in High Court claiming damages for personal injuries—Circuit Court case coming on for hearing before High Court action was heard—Application to have Circuit Court proceedings stayed—Courts of Justice Act 1924, s. 94—Civil Liability Act 1961, ss. 34(1), 37(1)—Courts Act 1971, s. 6—Circuit Court Rules, O 30, r 11. **Murphy v Hennessy** [1985] 100, HC.

CIRCUMSTANTIAL EVIDENCE
Murder. *See* CRIMINAL LAW (Evidence—Circumstantial—Murder)

CITIZENSHIP *See also* ALIEN.
Irish citizenship
Discrimination
Sexes—Entitlement of alien male married to Irish citizen—Irish Nationality and Citizenship Act 1956, ss. 8, 15, 16—Constitution of Ireland 1937, Articles 9, 40. **Somjee v Minister for Justice** [1981] 324, HC.

CIVIL ACTION. *See* ACTION.

CIVIL CONTEMPT. *See* CONTEMPT OF COURT (Civil contempt).

CIVIL LEGAL AID *See* LEGAL AID.

CIVIL SERVICE
Dismissal
Office holder
Probationer—Natural justice—Termination of services—Whether reasons required—Whether reasons be disclosed—Civil Service Regulation Act 1956, ss. 5, 7—Civil Service Regulation (Amendment) Act 1958, s. 3. **State (Daly) v Minister for Agriculture** [1988] 173, HC.

Staff association
Recognition
New staff association seeking recognition from Minister for the Public Service—Refusal of recognition—Nature of decision—Whether administrative or judicial—Whether refusal of recognition supported by evidence before Minister—Judicial review—Administrative act—Civil Service Regulation Act 1956, s. 17. **Inspector of Taxes Association v Minister for the Public Service** [1986] 296, SC.

Suspension
Refusal to obey order
Application for injunction restoring plaintiffs to their position—Whether suspension in breach of natural justice—Whether suspension a breach of the constitutional right to earn a livelihood—Whether injunction be granted—Civil Service Regulation Act 1956, s. 13. **Yeates v Minister for Posts and Telegraphs** [1978] 22, HC.

CLINIC
Family planning
Abortion information
Non-directive counselling—Whether breach of right to life of unborn. *See* ABORTION (Information—Clinic).

CLUB
Income tax
Exemption
Whether legitimate avoidance of payment of tax—Funds provided by one person—Total control in two trustees—Whether bona fide club—Whether established for sole

CLUB
Income tax
Exemption continued
purpose of 'promoting sport'—Whether two persons can constitute a 'body of persons'—Income Tax Act 1967, ss. 1(1), 349. **Revenue Commissioners v O'Reilly** [1983] 34, HC; [1984] 406, SC.

Renewal of licence
Club being a limited company
Whether supply of exciseable liquor under the control of the members—Registration of Clubs (Ireland) Act 1904, s. 4. **In re Parnell GAA Club Ltd** [1984] 246, HC.

COERCION *See* DURESS; UNDUE INFLUENCE.

COHABITATION
Widow's pension
Disqualification on ground of cohabitation
Meaning thereof. *See* SOCIAL WELFARE (Pensions—Widow's contributory pension).

COLD STORAGE FACILITIES
Failure to produce goods on demand
Conditions of trade
Exemption clause. *See* CONTRACT (Exemption clause—Conditions of trade—Cold storage facilities—Failure to produce goods on demand).

COLLECTIVE AGREEMENT. *See* TRADE UNION (Collective agreement).

COMMISSIONERS OF PUBLIC WORKS
Arterial drainage
Entry on and interference with lands
Measure of compensation. *See* ARTERIAL DRAINAGE.

National monument
Preservation order. *See* NATIONAL MONUMENT (Preservation order).

COMMITTAL
Contempt of court. *See* CONTEMPT OF COURT (Civil contempt—Committal).

COMMON AGRICULTURAL POLICY
European Community. *See* AGRICULTURE (Common agricultural policy).

COMMON INFORMER
District Court prosecution
Right of DPP to intervene
Prosecution brought by Garda as common informer—DPP directing that charge be withdrawn—District Justice entertaining case—Application to quash conviction—Whether DPP power to intervene—Constitution of Ireland 1937, Article 30.3—Minister and Secretaries Act 1924, s. 6(1)—Criminal Justice Administration Act 1924—Prosecution of Offences Act 1974, s. 3. **State (DPP) v Ruane** [1984] 443, HC; [1985] 349, SC.

COMMUNICATE, RIGHT TO. *See* CONSTITUTION (Personal rights—Communication).

COMPANY
Action
Security for costs
Limited company. *See* COSTS (Security for costs—Company—Limited company).

Liquidation. *See* COSTS (Security for costs—Company—Liquidation).

COMPANY *continued*

Administration

Remuneration of administrator

Insurance company—Administrator appointed receiver and manager of the property and assets of a body connected with the insurance company—Administrator's appointment ceasing upon appointment of liquidator—Administrator retaining certain funds to defray expenses—Whether certain items of expenditure be paid out of the retained funds—Insurance (No 2) Act 1983, ss. 1, 2(2), (3), 3(1)(a), (4)(a), 4. In re PMPA Insurance Co Ltd [1986] 524, HC; [1988] 109, SC.

Agreement

Execution

Requirement of writing—Initialling of agreement—Whether sufficient compliance with requirement—Companies Act 1963, s. 38. **Henley Forklift (Ireland) Ltd v Lansing Bagnall** [1979] 257, SC.

Articles of association

Construction. See Memorandum and articles of association (below).

Assets

Aggregation

Winding up. *See* Winding up—Assets—Aggregation (*below*).

Distribution

Winding up. *See* Winding up—Assets—Distribution (*below*).

Injunction restraining removal or disposal

Mareva injunction—Trade dispute—Whether jurisdiction to grant such an injunction—Balance of convenience—Supreme Court of Judicature (Ireland) Act 1877, s. 28(8). **Fleming v Ranks (Ireland) Ltd** [1983] 541, HC.

Winding up

Money paid by mistake to company prior to liquidation—Whether constituting assets of company subsequent to liquidation. *See* Winding up—Assets—Money paid by mistake to company prior to liquidation (*below*).

Auditor

Negligence

Duty of care owed to third party—Preparation of accounts—Third party investing in company for whom accountant acted as auditor—Whether auditor owing duty of care to third party. *See* ACCOUNTANT (Negligence—Duty of care—Third party).

Charge

Fixed or floating

Book debts—Charge and debenture expressed to be fixed charge—Company obliged to pay monies received from debtors into designated bank account—Restrictions placed on company's dealings with such monies—Whether instrument as a whole indicated intention to create fixed charge—Whether charge in reality a floating security—Companies Act 1963, ss. 285, 288. **In re Keenan Brothers Ltd** [1985] 254, HC; 641, SC.

Prior mortgage

Liquidation—Debenture granted subject to rights of a prior mortgagee—Particulars registered—Failure to register particulars of earlier mortgage—Mortgagee obtaining order extending time for registration—Sale of property—Whether debenture holder priority over mortgagee—Companies Act 1963, ss. 99, 106, 316. **Spain v McCann:** In re Clarets Ltd [1978] 215, HC.

Registration

Certificate of Registrar—Conclusiveness—Liquidation—Right to enforce security—Validity of mortgage—Mortgage not registered within twelve days of creation—Mortgage subsequently registered—Whether certificate of registration conclusive evidence that

COMPANY
Charge
Registration continued
requirements complied with—Companies Act 1963, ss. 99, 104. **Lombard and Ulster Banking Ireland Ltd v Amurec Ltd** [1976–7] 222, HC.

Failure to register—Whether time for registration should be extended—Whether usual saver for rights of intervening creditors should be omitted—Companies Act 1963, ss. 99, 106. In re Farm Fresh Frozen Foods Ltd [1980] 131, HC.

Yachts—Whether charge of yachts requires registration to be enforceable—Whether yacht a ship for the purpose of company law—Companies Act, 1963, s. 99—Bills of Sale (Ireland) Act 1879, s. 4. **Barber v Burke** [1980] 186, SC.

Retention of title clause. See SALE OF GOODS (Retention of title clause).

Validity
Fraudulent preference—Whether charge void as being fraudulent preference. *See* Winding up—Fraudulent preference (*below*).

Winding up. *See* Winding up—Charge—Validity (*below*).

Compulsory winding up. *See* Winding up (*below*).

Corporation tax. *See* REVENUE (Corporation tax).

Deed
Validity
Mortgage—Involvement in development project—Execution of mortgage—Validity challenged—Whether valid directors' meeting to approve contents of mortgage—Whether mortgagee entitled to believe meeting properly constituted. **Ulster Investment Bank Ltd v Euro Estates Ltd** [1982] 57, HC.

Director
Guarantee of company debts
Charging of property—Associated company also acting as guarantor—Defaults in repayment—Institution of proceedings against corporate surety and against directors. *See* Guarantee—Charge to bank to secure loan for company (*below*).

Liability for default of company
Development company—Failure to complete development—Insolvency—Planning authority seeking injunction to compel company to complete housing development and comply with terms and conditions of planning permission—Whether directors of company personally liable for default of development company—Local Government (Planning and Development) Act 1976, s. 27—Companies Act 1963, ss. 131, 148. **Dun Laoghaire Corporation v Parkhill Developments Ltd** [1989] 235, HC.

Winding up
Liquidator seeking to impose personal responsibility on directors of company—Whether entitled to use the transcript of evidence on oath taken from the directors in the course of their examinations in the winding up proceedings—Companies Act 1963, ss. 245(4), 297, 298. **In re Aluminium Fabricators Ltd** [1984] 399, HC.

Fraudulent preference
Charge
Validity. *See* Winding up—Fraudulent preference (*below*).

Fraudulent trading
Debts
Winding up. *See* Winding up—Fraudulent trading (*below*).

COMPANY *continued*
Guarantee
Charge to bank to secure loan for company

Associated company acting as surety—Directors also guaranteeing loan—Default in repayments—Proceedings against corporate surety—Proceedings also instituted against directors—Whether doctrine of marshalling applicable. **Lombard and Ulster Banking Ltd v Murray** [1987] 522, HC.

Majority shareholder and managing director acting as guarantor

Change of ownership and management—Variation of company's banking arrangements—Opening of new account—Agreement that money in new account would not be set off against debts—Whether material change in contract—Whether guarantor discharged from his obligations. **MacEnroe v Allied Irish Banks Ltd** [1980] 171, SC.

Receivership

Whether receiver owes duty of care to guarantor. *See* Receivership—Duty of care—Receiver (*below*).

Incorporation
Building society

Whether incidents of incorporation attach to building societies—Whether society registerable—Building Societies Act 1976. **Irish Permanent Building Society v Cauldwell** [1981] 242, HC.

Insurance company
Administration

Remuneration of administrator. *See* Administration—Remuneration of administrator—Insurance company (*above*).

Liquidation. *See* Winding up (*below*).

Liquidator
Remuneration. See Winding up—Liquidator—Remuneration (*below*).

Memorandum and articles of association
Construction

Winding up—Validity of resolutions passed by the company purporting to give shares in company's assets to non-members—Companies Act 1963, s. 280. **Roper v Ward** [1981] 408, HC.

Minority
Oppression. See Oppression of minority (*below*).

Oppression of minority
Acquisition of shares

Dissenting shareholder—Whether acquisition unfair—Whether acquisition oppressive—Whether company advancing money for the purchase of its own shares—Whether the making by directors of an unsatisfactory decision in the context of the business of a company constitutes oppression—Companies Act 1963, ss. 60, 204. **McCormick v Cameo Investments Ltd** [1978] 191, HC.

Hearing of s. 205 petition in camera

Whether circumstances existed which would justify such order—Companies Act 1963, s. 205. **In re R Ltd** [1989] 757, SC.

Meetings and accounts

Whether affairs of the company being exercised in an oppressive manner in respect of minority shareholder—Numerous breaches of statutory obligations as to meetings and accounts—Failure of directors to respond to requests for information—Company divesting itself of all its assets and liabilities—Whether minority shareholder dealt with fairly—Whether oppression made out—Companies Act 1963, s. 205. **In re Clubman Shirts Ltd** [1983] 323, HC.

COMPANY *continued*

Transfer of shares

Director transferring shares and receiving two cheques—One being for face value of shares paid by another director, other being severance payments paid by company—Whether company giving financial assistance for the purchase of shares—Whether affairs of company exercised in an oppressive manner—Winding up—Whether in the interests of the members—Companies Act 1963, ss. 60, 186, 191, 205, 213. **In re Greenore Trading Co Ltd** [1980] 94, HC.

Winding up petition

Whether order for winding up appropriate—Whether alternative remedy appropriate—Discretion of court. *See* Winding up—Whether just and equitable—Oppression (*below*).

Payment of money by mistake

Money paid by mistake to company prior to liquidation

Whether constituting assets of company subsequent to liquidation. *See* Winding up—Assets—Money paid by mistake to company prior to liquidation (*below*).

Persona

Legal entity distinct from that of shareholder

Licensing Acts—Company applying for certificate of transfer of publican's on-licence—Company having only two shareholders—Such shareholders being sole directors of the company—Such persons having previous convictions for licensing offences—Whether such convictions be recorded on the licence applied for—Intoxicating Liquor Act 1927, s. 30—Interpretation Act 1937, s. 11(c). **In re Hesketh Investments Ltd** [1984] 134, HC.

Veil of incorporation

Parent company and subsidiaries—Planning application—Application for one subsidiary—Land registered in name of another subsidiary—Purchase notice to planning authority made by subsidiary not being the registered owner—Whether purchase notice valid—Whether veil of incorporation should be lifted. **State (McInerney & Co Ltd) v Dublin Co Council** [1985] 513, HC.

Planning permission granted to director of company—Breach of conditions—Enforcement order—Prior order in existence against company—Whether appropriate to make order against director—Whether veil of incorporation be lifted—Local Government (Planning and Development) Act 1976, s. 27. **Dublin Co Council v O'Riordan** [1986] 104, HC.

Powers

Exercise—Ultra vires. See Ultra vires (*below*).

Preferential debts

Winding up. See Winding up—Priority of creditors—Preferential debts (*below*).

Property

Retention of title clause

Contract for sale of goods. *See* SALE OF GOODS (Retention of title clause).

Receivership

Duty of care

Receiver—Guarantor and sundry creditors seeking information concerning purchase price of the assets—Whether guarantor entitled to the information—Whether sale be restrained—Whether receiver owes duty of care to guarantor. **McGowan v Gannon** [1983] 516, HC.

Equitable assignment of assets

Policy of insurance—Benefits stated to be payable to company—Whether intention to pay benefits to employees—Whether company holding benefits in trust for beneficiaries. **McCann v Irish Board Mills** [1980] 216, HC.

COMPANY

Receivership *continued*

Information to guarantor

Whether guarantor entitled to information on proposed purchase price of the assets—Whether receiver owes duty of care to guarantor. **McGowan v Gannon** [1983] 516, HC.

Priority of creditors

Customs and excise duty—Company importing goods for processing and exporting them for sale—Exemption from duty—Appointment of receiver—Receiver selling goods on the home market—Whether full duty now payable—Whether duty payable in priority to the other creditors—Customs Consolidation Act 1876, s. 177—Finance Act 1932, ss. 38, 45—European Communities (Customs) Regulations 1972, reg 11. **Spain v Revenue Commissioners** [1980] 21, HC.

Sale of goods—Retention of title clause. *See* SALE OF GOODS (Retention of title clause—Receivership).

Property

Retention of title clause—Contract for sale of goods. *See* SALE OF GOODS (Retention of title clause—Receivership).

Revenue

Corporation tax. See REVENUE (Corporation tax).

Tax clearance certificate

Requirement with tenders for government contracts—Refusal by Revenue Commissioners—Whether Revenue Commissioners can have regard to tax default of previous "connected" company. *See* REVENUE (Tax clearance certificate).

Security for costs. *See* COSTS (Security for costs—Company).

Shareholders agreement

Negative term

Breach—Appointment of executives—Injunction to restrain the granting of a service agreement—Principles applicable—Balance of convenience. **TMG Group Ltd v Al Babtain Holding and Construction Co Ltd** [1982] 349, HC.

Shares

Acquisition

Dissenting shareholder—Whether acquisition unfair—Whether acquisition oppressive—Whether company advancing money for the purpose of its own shares—Companies Act 1963, ss. 60, 204. **McCormick v Cameo Investments Ltd** [1978] 191, HC.

Issue

Technical irregularity. *See* Winding up—Issue of shares—Technical irregularity—Whether petitioner acquiesced in the arrangement (*below*).

Ultra vires

Notice

Guarantee and mortgage by company of third party debt—Transaction *ultra vires* company—Creditor failing to understand effect of memorandum and articles—Whether creditor had actual note of guarantee being ultra vires—Subsequent resolution empowering company to execute guarantee—Whether retrospective—Whether company estopped from relying on ultra vires nature of guarantee—Estoppel in pais—Companies Act 1963, ss. 7, 8(1), 10(1). Northern Bank **Finance Corporation Ltd v Quinn** [1979] 221, HC.

Winding up

Action

Security for costs. *See* COSTS (Security for costs—Company—Liquidation).

Application of bankruptcy rules. See Winding up—Fraudulent preference—Application of bankruptcy rules to winding up of insolvent companies (*below*).

COMPANY
  Winding up *continued*
   Assets

Aggregation—*Lis pendens*—Registration—Effect of proceedings establishing equitable interest in property on mortgage executed subsequent to registration of *lis pendens*— Whether equitable interest entitled to priority over mortgagee's interest—Whether mortgage valid. **In re Kelly's Carpetdrome Ltd: Byrne v UDT Bank Ltd** [1984] 418, HC.

Distribution—Constitution—Articles and memorandum—Whether company precluded by its constitution from distributing profits among its members—Meaning of company for corporation profits tax purposes—Nature of what is distributed to members in a winding up—Meaning of profits—Finance Act 1932, s. 47—Finance Act 1954, s. 21— Companies Act 1963, s. 275. **Wilson v Dunnes Stores** (Cork) Ltd [1982] 444, HC.

Distribution—Recreation club for employees and former employees—Company limited by guarantee—Decision to sell company's property and distribute the proceeds— Application to court by liquidator pursuant to s. 280 of Companies Act 1963—Construction of memorandum and articles of association—Whether associate members entitled to share in the distribution of the assets—Resolution purporting to give shares to those who were not members—Whether valid or effective—Companies Act 1963, s. 280. **Roper v Ward** [1981] 408, HC.

Set off—Money paid by mistake to company prior to liquidation—Whether constituting assets of company subsequent to liquidation—Whether subject to right of set-off— Whether company holding money as trustee—Purpose of constructive trust—Estoppel— Whether arising—Whether person acted to his detriment. **In re Irish Shipping Ltd** [1986] 518, HC.

   Charge

Validity—Application for directions—Validity of mortgage and debenture—Whether right of subrogation arose—Whether guarantee extended to whole debt—Construction of document creating guarantee and suretyship. **In re the 19th Ltd (In Liquidation), Industrial Credit Corporation plc, Notice Party** [1989] 652, HC.

Validity—Certificate of Registrar—Conclusiveness—Validity of mortgage—Mortgage not registered within twelve days of creation—Mortgage subsequently registered— Whether certificate of registration conclusive evidence that requirements complied with—Companies Act 1963, ss. 99, 104. **Lombard and Ulster Banking Ireland Ltd v Amurec Ltd** [1976–7] 222, HC.

Validity—Company creating a floating charge within twelve months before the commencement of the winding up—Whether company solvent immediately after creation of the charge—Companies Act 1963, s. 288. **Crowley v Northern Bank Finance** [1978] 219, HC.

Validity—Fraudulent preference -Charge registered one month before winding up— Whether charge void as being fraudulent preference—Companies Act 1963, s. 286. **Corran v Bank of Ireland Finance Ltd** [1976-7] 175, HC.

   Compulsory winding up

Petition by creditor—Claim that company indebted to petitioning creditor—Company disputing petitioner's entitlement—Whether winding up proceedings should be brought where petitioner is aware that company has a substantial and reasonable defence. **In re Pageboy Couriers Ltd** [1983] 510, HC.

   Corporation profits tax

Liability —Whether taxpayer is corporate body precluded by its constitution from distributing profits among its members—Meaning of company for corporation profits tax purposes—Meaning of profits—Nature of what is distributed in a winding up— Finance Act 1932, s. 47—Finance Act 1954, s. 21—Companies Act 1963, s. 275. **Wilson v Dunnes Stores Ltd** [1982] 444, HC.

COMPANY
Winding up *continued*
Costs

Costs properly incurred in winding up—Whether fees of legal costs accountant constitute same—Companies Act 1963, s. 281. **In re Castle Brand Ltd** [1990] 97, HC.

Deposit interest

Liability to tax—Whether deposit interest earned by money in the hands of the liquidator liable to tax—Whether tax payable a 'necessary' disbursement'—Whether tax payable ranks as a preferential payment or as an unsecured debt—Companies Act 1963, ss. 244, 285—Finance Act 1983, s. 56—Winding Up Rules 1966, r 129. **In re Hibernian Transport Co Ltd** [1984] 583, HC.

Liability to tax—Voluntary winding up—Corporation tax payable in respect of interest earned by monies kept on deposit by liquidator during winding up—Whether such a tax constituted a charge properly incurred in the winding up—Companies Act 1963, s. 281. In re A Noyek & Sons Ltd: **Burns v Hearne** [1987] 508, HC; [1989] 155, SC.

Disclaimer of onerous property

Application to disclaim a lease—Whether lease "onerous"—Position of guarantors—Whether the disclaimer would end the liability of the guarantors—Companies Act 1963, s. 290. **Tempany v Royal Liver Trustees Ltd, in re Farm Machinery Distributors Ltd** [1984] 273, HC.

Hiring contract—Power to disclaim—Whether properly burdened with onerous covenant—High Court order giving liberty to disclaim—Effect of section—Whether other party to the contract entitled to prove for the injury sustained—Measure of damages—Companies Act 1963, s. 290(1), (3), (9). **In re Ranks (Ireland) Ltd** [1988] 751, HC.

Disposition of property

Bank account overdrawn—Lodgments subsequent to petition—Nature of lodgments—Whether 'disposition'—Application for direction—Whether 'special circumstances'—Notice—Companies Act 1963, s. 218. **In re Pat Ruth Ltd** [1981] 51, HC.

Disposition of property made after commencement of winding up—Whether court should validate payment—Principles to be applied—Companies Act 1963, ss. 218, 220(2). **In re Ashmark Ltd** (No 1) [1990] 330, HC.

Cheques drawn by company prior to presentation of petition—Cheques paid subsequently—Whether monies paid prior to the commencement of the winding up—Whether court should validate payment—Bills of Exchange Act 1882, ss. 3(1), 53, 73—Companies Act 1963, ss. 218, 220(2). **In re Ashmark Ltd (No 2); Ashmark Ltd v Nitra Ltd** [1990] 455, HC.

Examination

Evidence—Whether evidence may be used in proceedings against third parties—Security for costs—Whether court may set aside order in proceedings after holding of examination—Companies Act 1963, s. 245(4). **Irish Commercial Society v Plunkett** [1986] 624, HC.

Fraudulent preference

Application of bankruptcy rules to winding up of insolvent companies—Whether the giving of security by a third party to a creditor of an insolvent company where the payment would constitute a fraudulent preference if made by the company amounts to a fraudulent preference—Whether a disposition by an insolvent company of its assets is per se *ultra vires*—Companies Act 1963, s. 284. **John C Parkes & Sons Ltd v Hong Kong and Shanghai Banking Corporation** [1990] 341, HC.

Charge registered one month before winding up—Whether charge void as being fraudulent preference—Companies Act 1963, s. 286. **Corran v Bank of Ireland Finance Ltd** [1976–7] 175, HC.

COMPANY

Winding up *continued*

Debts—Whether transaction constituted carrying on business—Whether fraudulent intent proved in each of participants—Test for determining extent of liability of participants—Companies Act, 1963, s. 297. **In re Hunting Lodges Ltd** [1985] 75, HC.

Limited liability company—Payment made by insolvent company—Action by liquidator—Fraudulent preference alleged—Application for security for costs—Principles to be applied—Companies Act 1963, ss. 281, 285, 286, 290. **Comhlucht Paipear Riomhaireachta Teo v Úarás na Gaeltachta** [1990] 266, SC.

Liquidator seeking to aggregate the assets of various companies—One company applying for security for costs—Conduct of person in actual control—Whether to be taken into account—Whether *prima facie* evidence of fraudulent preference—Companies Act 1963, s. 390. **Irish Commercial Society Ltd (in liquidation) v Plunkett** [1989] 461, HC.

Industrial and provident society

Minister—duty of care—Whether owing duty of care to depositor. **McMahon v Ireland** [1988] 610, HC.

Interest on debts

Realisation of assets—Monies placed on deposit and earning interest—Surplus arising due to lengthy liquidation—Whether creditors entitled to be paid interest in priority to shareholders' claim to residue—Rate at which interest should be paid—Irish Bankrupt and Insolvent Act 1857, s. 304—Companies Act 1963, ss. 283, 284—Bankruptcy Act 1988, ss. 4, 86. In re Hibernian Transport Co Ltd: **Shell International Petroleum Company Ltd v Gordon** [1990] 42, HC.

Issue of shares

Technical irregularity—Whether petitioner acquiesced in the arrangement—Estoppel in pais—Whether affairs of company exercised in an oppressive manner—Whether winding up in the interests of the members—Companies Act 1963, ss. 205, 213. In re Greenore Trading Co Ltd [1980] 94, HC.

Lease

Forfeiture clause in lease—Relief against forfeiture—Conveyancing Acts 1881-1892. **MCB (Galway) Ltd (in liquidation) v Industrial Development Authority.** [1981] 58, SC.

Necessary disbursements

Deposit interest—Liability to tax—Whether deposit interest earned by money in the hands of the liquidator liable to tax—Whether tax payable a 'necessary' disbursement. *See* Winding up—Deposit interest—Liability to tax (*above*).

Preferential payments

Deposit interest—Liability to tax—Whether tax payable ranks as a preferential payment or as an unsecured debt. *See* Winding up—Deposit interest—Liability to tax (*above*).

Priority of creditors

Equitable interest—Whether equitable interest entitled to priority over mortgagee's interest. In re Kelly's Carpetdrome Ltd: **Byrne v UDT Bank Ltd** [1984] 418, HC.

Interest on debts—Realisation of assets—Monies placed on deposit and earning interest—Surplus arising due to lengthy liquidation—Whether creditors entitled to be paid interest in priority to shareholders' claim to residue. *See* Winding up—Interest on debts (*above*).

Prior mortgage—Debenture granted subject to rights of a prior mortgagee—Particulars registered—Failure to register particulars of earlier mortgage—Mortgagee obtaining order extending time for registration—Sale of property—Whether debenture holder priority over mortgagee—Companies Act 1963, ss. 99, 106, 316. **Spain v McCann**: In re Clarets Ltd [1978] 215, HC.

COMPANY
Winding up *continued*

Preferential debts—Wages due to employees—Such wages having preferential status—Employment contributions under social welfare legislation in respect of such wages due—Whether 'employer's contribution' having similar preferential status—Companies Act 1963, s. 285(2)(e)—Social Welfare (Consolidation) Act 1981, ss. 9(1)(a), 10(1)(b). In re Castlemahon Poultry Products Ltd [1987] 222, SC.

Proceedings

Liquidator seeking to impose personal responsibility on directors of company—Whether entitled to use the transcript of evidence on oath taken from the directors in the course of their examinations in the winding up proceedings—Companies Act 1963, ss. 245(4), 297, 298. **In re Aluminium Fabricators Ltd** [1984] 399, HC.

Property

Retention of title clause—Contract for sale of goods—*Generally. See* SALE OF GOODS (Retention of title clause).

Retention of title clause—Contract for sale of goods—Plant—No express provision in agreement of sale empowering suppliers to repossess in the event of default—Whether such term to be implied and whether purchasing company to bear cost of removal of plant—Whether charge created by retention of title clause—Companies Act 1963, s. 99. **In re Galway Concrete Ltd.** [1983] 402, HC.

Remuneration of liquidator

Liquidator making application for interim payment of fees—Inquiry by examiner—Examiner's report coming before the court—Liquidator not afforded an opportunity to submit evidence establishing the necessity of the work undertaken—Court ruling against liquidator—Appeal to Supreme Court—Whether liquidator entitled to remuneration—Companies Act 1963, s. 228—RSC O 74, r 47. **In re Merchant Banking Ltd** [1987] 260, SC.

Right to enforce security

Validity of mortgage—Mortgage not registered within twelve days of creation—Mortgage subsequently registered—Whether certificate of registration conclusive evidence that requirements complied with—Companies Act 1963, ss. 99, 104. **Lombard and Ulster Banking Ireland Ltd v Amurec Ltd** [1976–7] 222, HC.

Sale of properties

Capital gains tax—Liquidator selling property and incurring liability for capital gains tax—Whether tax payable 'an expense incurred in the realisation of an asset'—Whether tax payable 'a necessary disbursement' of the liquidator—Companies Act 1963, s. 285 (2)—Capital Gains Tax Act 1975, Schedule 4, Clause 15—Corporation Tax Act 1976, ss. 6(2), 13(5)—Winding Up Rules, O 74 r 129. **In re Van Hool McArdle Ltd** [1982] 340, HC.

Corporation tax—Liability incurred for corporation tax—Whether such tax an expense incurred in the realisation of an asset—Whether such tax a necessary disbursement of the liquidator—Companies Act 1963, s. 285 (2)(ii)—Winding up Rules O 77, r 129—Capital Gains Tax Act 1975. **Revenue Commissioners v Donnelly** [1983] 329, SC.

Sale by liquidator of mortgaged lands with mortgagee's consent—What portion of court fees to be borne by mortgagee—Set-off of mutual debts and credits—Mortgagee's claim to interest on mortgage debt—Whether interest to be compounded at quarterly or monthly intervals—Whether claim allowable for interest accruing after date of liquidation—Application of bankruptcy rules to winding up of insolvent companies—Whether mortgagee entitled to refuse to release charge pending adjudication of claims against purchase price—Irish Bankrupt and Insolvent Act 1857, s. 251—Companies Act 1963, s. 284—Supreme Court and High Court (Fees) Order 1984. **In re McCairns (PMPA) plc (in liquidation)** [1989] 501, HC.

COMPANY
Winding up *continued*
Secured creditor
Lien—Purchaser—Building company—Prospective purchasers paying 'booking deposits'—Whether a person who has paid a 'booking deposit' but entered into no contract with the builder is entitled to a purchaser's lien or to rank as a secured creditor in the liquidation of the building company. **In re Barrett Apartments Ltd** [1985] 679, HC, SC.

Unsecured debts
Deposit interest—Liability to tax—Whether tax payable ranks as a preferential payment or as an unsecured debt. *See* Winding up—Deposit interest—Liability to tax (*above*).

Voluntary winding up
Failure to make declarations of solvency or hold creditors meeting—Whether court having power to annul resolution to wind up or extend time for creditors meeting—Companies Act 1963, ss. 234, 280(1). In re Oakthorpe Holdings Ltd: **Walsh v The Registrar of Companies** [1989] 62, HC.

Preferential payments—Deposit interest—Liability to tax—Whether such tax constituted a charge properly incurred in the winding up—Companies Act 1963, s. 281. In re Noyek (A) & Sons Ltd: **Burns v Hearne** [1987] 508, HC; [1989] 155, SC.

Whether just and equitable
Company with two directors—Test applicable—Whether administration of company practicable—Whether oral hearing required—Whether petitioner guilty of misconduct disentitling relief—Companies Act 1963, s. 213(f). **In re Vehicle Buildings and Insulations Ltd** [1986] 239, HC.

Oppression—Company conducted in informal manner—Equivalent to partnership—Three directors equal owners—One director claiming oppression—Whether order for winding up appropriate—Whether alternative remedy appropriate—Discretion of court—Whether activities complained of brought basis of informal arrangements to end—Companies Act 1963, ss. 205, 213, 215. **In re Murph's Restaurant Ltd** [1979] 141, HC.

COMPENSATION
Compulsory acquisition. *See* COMPULSORY PURCHASE (Compensation).

Criminal injuries. *See* MALICIOUS INJURIES.

Disturbance. *See* LANDLORD AND TENANT (Compensation for disturbance).

Garda Síochána
Fatal injury. See GARDA SÍOCHÁNA (Compensation—Fatal injury).

Planning. *See* PLANNING (Compensation).

Redundancy. *See* EMPLOYMENT (Redundancy—Compensation).

Sale of land
Misdescription. See SALE OF LAND (Misdescription).

Unfair dismissal. *See* EMPLOYMENT (Unfair Dismissal—Compensation).

COMPETITION LAW
European Community. *See* EUROPEAN COMMUNITY (Competition).

RESTRAINT OF TRADE *See* RESTRAINT OF TRADE

RESTRICTIVE PRACTICES *See* RESTRICTIVE PRACTICES

COMPILATION
Infringement of copyright. *See* COPYRIGHT (Infringement—Compilation).

COMPLAINT. *See* CRIMINAL LAW (Complaint).

COMPROMISE OF ACTION *See* ACTION (Compromise).

COMPULSORY PURCHASE
Bog land
Power to compulsorily acquire bog land
Bord na Mona—Whether power of judicial nature. *See* Fair procedures—Natural justice—Bog land—Power to compulsorily acquire bogland (*below*).

Compensation
Assessment
Local authority—Housing Act—Factors to which arbitrator had regard—Acquisition of Land (Assessment of Compensation) Act 1919, s. 2—Local Government (Planning and Development) Act 1963, s. 69—Housing Act 1966, s. 84(1). **Holiday Motor Inns Ltd v Dublin County Council** [1976–7] 343, HC.

Valuation—Dispute as to value—Valuation going to arbitration—Factors to be taken into account—Sewerage facilities—Arbitrator stating case to High Court—Public Health (Ireland) Acxt 1878, ss. 23, 24—Acquisition of Land (Assessment of Compensation) Act 1919, s. 2—Local Government (Planning and Development) Act 1963, ss. 55, 56, 69. **Meenaghan v Dublin County Council** [1984] 616, HC.

Valuation—Date—Local authority purchase—Property at valuation date subject to rent control—Whether subsequent declaration of invalidity of rent control legislation operates retrospectively to affect the assessment of compensation—Acquisition of Land (Assessment of Compensation) Act 1919, s. 2. **Reid v Limerick Corporation** [1984] 366, HC; [1987] 83, SC.

Local authority—Compulsory purchase order—Subject land designated on the county development plan—Whether designation amounts to reservation for a particular purpose—Whether, in the event of housing development taking place, sanitary authority would refuse a connection for sewerage—Public Health (Ireland) Act 1878, s. 23—Acquisition of Land (Assessment of Compensation) Act 1919, s. 2—Local Government (Planning and Development) Act 1963, ss. 55, 56(1)(b)(i), 69, 4th Schedule, Rule 11. **Dublin County Council v Shortt** [1982] 117, HC; [1983] 377, SC.

Mitigation of loss
Realignment of road necessitating acquisition of adjacent business—Claimant, in order to mitigate loss, acquiring alternative premises prior to the service of notice—Whether acquiring authority liable to compensate claimant for losses occasioned before service—Assessment of compensation for disturbance—Whether identical with damages for breach of contract or for tort—Acquisition of Land (Assessment of Compensation) Act 1919, s. 2—Housing Act 1969, s. 84. **Gunning v Dublin Corporation** [1983] 56, HC.

Fair procedures
Natural justice
Bog land—Power to compulsorily acquire bogland—Whether power of judicial nature—Whether procedures adopted in breach of natural justice—Distinction between procedures in relation to the decision to acquire and procedures in relation to the assessment of fair compensation—Constitution of Ireland 1937, Articles 40.3, 43—Turf Development Act 1946, ss. 17, 28, 30–6. **O'Brien v Bord na Mona** [1983] 314, SC.

Documents—Discovery—Land Commission acquisition—Objectors' application for sight of certain documents refused—Whether procedure adopted fair and in accordance with principles of natural justice—Land Act 1965, ss. 12, 45. **State (Hussey) v Irish Land Commission** [1983] 407, HC.

Land Acts
Objection
Locus standi—Prospective purchaser—Sale of land—Whether prospective purchaser

COMPULSORY PURCHASE
Land Acts
Objection continued
has standing to object to compulsory acquisition of land—Land Act 1923, s. 40(6). **State (Callaghan) v Irish Land Commission** [1978] 201, SC.

Purchase price
Price fixed at sum payable in Land Bonds equal in nominal value to the sum fixed— Whether the statutory provisions enabling the price to be paid in such a way instead of cash ceased to be part of the law on the coming into force of the Constitution— Whether provision inconsistent with Articles 40 or 43—Constitution of Ireland 1937, Articles 40 3, 43, 50—Land Act 1923, ss. 3, 25—Land Bond Act 1934, ss. 2, 4 (3)— Land Act 1950, ss. 5 (1) 27. **Dreher v Irish Land Commission** [1984] 94, SC.

Sale of land
Notice of inspection subsequent to agreement for sale—Land Commission consenting to registration of purchaser as owner—Whether sufficient to enable completion of sale— Land Act 1965, s. 13. **Horgan v Deasy** [1979] 71, HC.

Condition of sale that contract dependent on Land Commission approval—Whether prospective purchaser has standing to object to compulsory acquisition of land—Land Act 1923, s. 40(6). **State (Callaghan) v Irish Land Commission** [1978] 201, SC.

Vesting
Building ground excepted from scheme of general vesting—Applicatin by tenant to have Land Commission acquire landlord's interest—Whether acquisition in the interest of the country—Land Act 1923, s. 24—Land Act 1939, s. 40(1). In re estate of soden [1985] 685, SC.

Local authority
Assessment of Compensation
Valuation date—Property rent controlled at valuation date—Subsequent declaration of unconstitutionality of rent control legislation—Whether declaration operates retro-spectively in assessment of compensation. *See* Compensation—Assessment—Valuation— Date (*above*).

Housing authority
Planning application refused in view of compulsory purchase order on land—Effect of order—Whether a mere change of ownership—Whether order made in compliance with housing legislation—Housing Act 1966, s. 55—Local Government (Planning and Development) Act 1963, s. 26. State (Sweeney) v Minister for Environment [1979] 35, HC.

Residential and recreational development. *See* Powers—Local authority—Residential and recreational development—County council also planning authority (*below*).

Powers
Bord na Móna
Power to compulsorily acquire bogland—Whether power of judicial nature—Absence of right of appeal—Whether statutory provisions invalid—Whether procedures adopted in breach of natural justice. *See* Fair procedures—Natural justice—Bog land—Power to compulsorily acquire bog land (*above*).

Local authority
Residential and recreational development—County council also planning authority— Whether council can only acquire lands for recreational purposes in its capacity as planning authority—Local Government (Ireland) Act 1898, s. 10—Local Government (No 2) Act 1960, ss. 10, 11—Local Government (Planning and Development) Act 1963, s. 2—Housing Act 1966, s. 2. **Leinster Importing Co Ltd v Dublin Co Council** [1984] 605, HC.

CONCURRENT WRONGDOERS. *See* NEGLIGENCE (Concurrent wrongdoers).

CONDITION
Contract
 Sale of land. See SALE OF LAND (Contract—Condition).

 Waiver. See CONTRACT (Condition—Waiver).

Planning permission. *See* PLANNING (Conditions).

Will
 Construction. See WILL (Construction—Condition).

CONDUCT
Estoppel. *See* ESTOPPEL (Conduct).

CONFESSION
Accused
 Admissibilty in evidence. See CRIMINAL LAW (Evidence—Admission). *See also* CRIMINAL LAW (Evidence—Statement of accused).

CONFIDENTIALITY
Breach
 Publication
  Book written by deceased member of British intelligence service—Application to restrain publication in Ireland—Constitution—Freedom of expression—Confidentiality—Whether different criteria applied to government information—Constitution of Ireland 1937, Article 40.6.1. **Attorney General for England and Wales v Brandon Book Publishers Ltd** [1987] 135, HC.

Confidential documents
 Discovery—Privilege. *See* DISCOVERY (Privilege).

Disclosure of information. *See* DISCLOSURE OF INFORMATION.

CONFLICT OF LAWS See PRIVATE INTERNATIONAL LAW.

CONSECUTIVE SENTENCE See CRIMINAL LAW (Sentence—Consecutive sentence).

CONSENT
Adoption. *See* ADOPTION (Consent).

Marriage
 Nullity proceedings. See MARRIAGE (Nullity—Duress).

CONSPIRACY
Inducement of breach of contract
 Employment contract
  Plaintiff offered position as principal of a primary school—Pressure exerted on manager to cancel appointment—Appointment subsequently cancelled—Whether manager in breach of contract—Whether defendants induced such breach—Whether defendants engaged in an actionable conspiracy. **Cotter v Ahern** [1976–7] 248, HC.

Offence
 Conspiracy to corrupt public morals
  Whether established—Non-directive counselling regarding abortion. **Attorney General (SPUC) v Open Door Counselling** [1987] 477, HC.

CONSTITUTION
Access to courts. *See* Personal rights—Access to courts (*below*).

Access to solicitor. *See* Personal rights—Access to solicitor (*below*).

CONSTITUTION *continued*

Adaptation of enactments. *See* Continuance of laws—Adaptation of enactments (*below*).

Administration of justice

Courts. See Courts (*below*).

Director of Public Prosecutions

Criminal law—Preliminary examination—District Justice discharging accused—DPP directing that accused be sent forward for trial in Circuit Court in respect of the same charges—Whether provisions under which DPP purported to act constitutionally valid—Whether invasion into the judicial domain. *See* DIRECTOR OF PUBLIC PROSECUTIONS (Powers—Validity—Power to send person forward for trial).

Power to direct trial in Special Criminal Court. *See* DIRECTOR OF PUBLIC PROSECUTIONS (Powers—Validity—Power to direct trial in Special Criminal Court—Whether power unconstitutional).

Trial on indictment—Preliminary examination—Substitution by DPP of new counts—Whether invasion of judicial domain—Whether procedure unfair or discriminatory. *See* DIRECTOR OF PUBLIC PROSECUTIONS (Powers—Validity—Trial on indictment—Preliminary examination—DPP substituting new counts).

Trial on indictment—Preliminary examination—DPP inserting additional counts—Whether invasion of judicial domain. *See* DIRECTOR OF PUBLIC PROSECUTIONS (Powers—Validity—Trial on indictment—Preliminary examination—DPP inserting additional counts).

Judicial power

Interference—Betting—Register of bookmaking offices—Application to Garda Superintendent for certificate that premises suitable for registration—Objection to grant of certificate—Certificate refused—Appeal to District Court—Statute providing that objector not entitled to be heard nor to adduce evidence in opposition to appeal—Whether denial of such rights constituted an impermissible interference with the jurisdiction of the courts—Betting Act 1931, s. 13(5)(a)—Constitution of Ireland 1937, Articles 6, 34. **Cashman v Clifford** [1990] 200, HC.

Interference—Street and house-to-house collection—Opinion of Garda superintendent that proceeds of collection would benefit an unlawful organisation—Appeal to District Court—Review of opinion excluded—Whether appeal procedure constitutionally invalid—Whether unwarranted invasion of the judicial power—Whether open to prosecutor, on an application for certiorari, to challenge the constitutionality of legislation—Constitution of Ireland 1937, Article 34—Street and House-to-House Collections Act 1962, s. 13(4). **State (McEldowney) v Kelleher and Attorney General** [1982] 568, HC; [1985] 10, S

Peace commissioner

Admittance of persons to bail—Whether administration of justice—Whether conferral of such power on peace commissioner invalid—Constitution of Ireland 1937, Article 34 1—Criminal Justice Act 1951, s. 15—Criminal Justice Act 1984, s. 26. **O'Mahony v Melia** [1990] 14, HC.

Peace commissioner signing summons—Whether invalid as being an exercise of judicial power—Whether defect cured by attendance in court—Constitution of Ireland 1937, Article 34 4 3. **Joyce v Circuit Court Judge for Western Circuit** [1987] 316, HC.

Racing Board

Licensed bookmaker—Revocation of course betting permit—Whether invalid—Whether Racing Board administering justice—Entitlement to fair procedures—Whether hearing contrary to natural justice—Locus standi—Constitution of Ireland 1937, Articles 37, 40.3—Racing Board and Racecourse Act 1945, s. 24. **McCann v Attorney General and Racing Board** [1983] 67, HC.

CONSTITUTION
Administration of justice *continued*
Revenue Commissioners
Enforcement procedure—Default provisions—Computer-based programme—Payment due received before enforcement notice issued—Whether procedure involved the administration of justice—Whether operated unfairly—Statute—Validity—Whether publication of enforcement notice a libel—Whether Collector General exercising judicial function—Constitution of Ireland 1937, Articles 34, 40.3—Finance Act 1968, s. 7—Income Tax Act 1967, s. 131(1), 485. **Kennedy v Hearne** [1988] 52; [1988] 531, SC.

Administrative scheme
Validity
Scheme implementing EC Council directive—Agriculture—Compensatory payments to persons farming in disadvantaged areas—Payment limited to applicants whose income together with that of their spouses did not exceed a specific figure—Whether breach of constitutional pledge to guard the institution of marriage—Whether condition necessitated by membership of European Community—Council Directive 75/268/EEC—Constitution of Ireland 1937, Articles 29 4 3, 41. **Greene v Minister for Agriculture** [1990] 364, HC.

Adoption. *See* Family—Child—Adoption (*below*).

Aliens
Whether aliens entitled to benefit from provisions of Constitution. See ALIEN (Constitutional rights).

Certificate of naturalisation
Discrimination—Sexes. *See* Irish Nationality and citizenship—Discrimination—Sexes (*below*).

Attorney General
Power to end private prosecutions
Whether such power devolved on the Attorney General after 1922— Constitution of Ireland 1937, Art 30 3—Ministers and Secretaries Act 1924, s. 6(1)—Prosecution of Offences Act 1974, s. 3. **State (Collins) v Ruane** [1984] 443, HC; [1985] 349, SC.

Bill
Validity
Adoption—Bill permitting adoption where parents have totally abandoned all parental rights—Whether Bill amounted to an attack upon the family—Whether inalienable and imprescriptible rights can be lawfully curtailed—Constitution of Ireland 1937, Articles 26, 40, 41, 42, 43, 44. **In re Adoption (No 2) Bill 1987** [1989] 266, SC.

Elections—Dáil Éireann—Bill conferring rights to vote on British citizens—Whether Bill repugnant to the Constitution—Whether constitutional provisions exclude aliens from voting rights—Constitution of Ireland 1937, Articles 6, 12 2 1 and 2, 12 4 1, 16 1 1 and 2, 16 7 26, 47—Electoral Act 1963, ss. 5(1), 51(1), 70(1). **In re Electoral (Amendment) Bill 1983** [1984] 539, SC.

Landlord and Tenant—Bill affecting rent and security of tenure—Landlords receiving an amount of rent substantially less than the market rent—Whether unjust attack on their property rights—Constitution of Ireland 1937, Articles 26, 40 3 2. **In Re Housing (Private Rented Dwellings) Bill 1981** [1983] 246, SC.

Bodily integrity, right to. *See* Personal rights—Bodily integrity (*below*).

Child. *See* Family—Child (*below*).

Citizenship. *See* Irish nationality and citizenship (*below*).

Communicate, right to. *See* Personal rights—Communication (*below*).

CONSTITUTION *continued*
Continuance of laws
Adaptation of enactments
Enactment of Parliament of Great Britain and Ireland—Provision of ferry service—Suspension of service by decision of English government—Whether decision having extra-territorial effect—Whether statutory obligations suspended by Oireachtas—Constitution of Saorstat Eireann 1922, Article 73—Constitution of Ireland, 1937, Article 50—Adaptation of Enactments Act 1922, s. 5. **Waterford Harbour Commissioners v British Railways** [1979] 296, SC.

Precedent
Whether High Court bound to follow pre-Treaty English decisions—Effect of Article 50—Constitution of Ireland 1937, Article 50—**Irish Shell Ltd v Elm Motors Ltd** [1984] 595, SC.

Courts
Access to court. See Personal rights—Access to court (*below*).

Administration of justice
Exception—Limited powers and functions of a judicial nature. *See* Administration of justice (*above*).

Justice to be administered in public—Circumstances which justify hearing other than in public—Statutory provision and denial of justice—Whether circumstances existed on a s. 205 application—Courts (Supplemental Provisions) Act 1961, s. 45—Companies Act 1963, s. 205—Constitution of Ireland 1937, Article 34. **In re R Ltd** [1989] 757, SC.

Scope of jurisdiction—Whether jurisdiction to adjudicate on manner in which public resources are administered by other organs of State—Separation of powers—Whether court jurisdiction to entertain a claim for damages for alleged breach of constitutional duty by State—Distributive and commutative justice—Housing—Travelling community—Whether housing authority under statutory duty to provide serviced halting sites for members of travelling community—Whether State under a constitutional duty to provide such sites—Constitution of Ireland 1937—Housing Act 1966, ss. 53, 54, 56, 58, 60, 111. **O'Reilly v Limerick Corporation** [1989] 181, HC.

Irish language
Use of Irish in court—Whether Justice obliged to hear case in Irish without assistance of interpreter— Natural justice—Courts of Justice Act 1924, s. 71—Constitution of Ireland 1937, Article 8. **Ó Monacháin v An Taoiseach** [1986] 660, SC.

Judicial independence
District Court—Sole and exclusive authority to control and supervise conduct of proceedings within limits of jurisdiction. **Clune v DPP** [1981] 17, HC.

Criminal law—Trial—Special Criminal Court—Members appointed and removable at will by Government—Whether court independent—Whether court required by Constitution to be independent of Government—Whether exercise of Government powers must conform to constitutional justice—Offences Against the State Act 1939, s. 39(2), (4)—Constitution of Ireland 1937, Articles 34, 35, 38.3, 38.6. **Eccles v Ireland** [1986] 343, SC.

Jurisdiction
Circuit Court—Criminal jurisdiction—Transfer of trial—Statute providing for the transfer of the trial of a person from the Circuit Court before which he is triable to the Dublin Circuit Court—Whether Dublin Circuit Court jurisdiction to try the case—Statute—Validity—Constitution of Ireland 1937, Article 34 3 4—Courts (Establishment and Constitution) Act 1961, s. 4(1)—Courts (Supplemental Provisions) Act 1961, s. 25—Courts Act 1981, s. 31. **State (Boyle) v Neylon** [1986] 337, HC; [1987] 535, SC.

District Court—Accused detained pursuant to statutory power—Whether remand order made by district justice valid—Whether District Court can embark on constitutional

CONSTITUTION
Courts
Jurisdiction continued

inquiry as to validity of detention—Whether unwarrantable and unlawful usurpation of the constitutional role of the High Court—Constitution of Ireland 1937, Article 40.4. 2—Criminal Justice Act 1984, s. 4. **Keating v Governor of Mountjoy Prison** [1990] 850, SC.

District Court—Sole and exclusive authority of District Justice to control and supervise conduct of proceedings within limits of jurisdiction—Conditional order of prohibition granted prohibiting hearing of indictable offences without copies of the statements of evidence being furnished—Application for absolute order—Quia timet—Jurisdiction of High Court—Presumption that District Justice will act in accordance with principles of natural justice and fairness—Criminal Justice Act 1951—Criminal Procedure Act 1967. **Clune v DPP** [1981] 17, HC.

Supreme Court—Appellate jurisdiction—Appeal against acquittal—Charge on indictment before Central Criminal Court—Jury, at the direction of the judge, recording verdict of not guilty—Whether open to Director of Public Prosecutions to bring an appeal against such verdict—Extent of Supreme Court's appellate jurisdiction—Plea of autrefois acquit explained—Constitution of Ireland 1937, Arts 34 3 1, 34 4 3, 38 1, 38 5, 38 6—Courts of Justice Act 1924, ss. 31, 63—Courts (Supplemental Provisions) Act 1961, ss. 11(1), 48—Criminal Procedure Act 1967, s. 34(1). **People (DPP) v O'Shea** [1983] 549, SC.

Supreme Court—Appellate jurisdiction—Damages—Assessment—Whether Supreme Court may substitute its own assessment of damages for those made by a jury in the High Court—Constitution of Ireland 1937, Article 34 4 3—Courts of Justice Act 1924, s. 96. **Holohan v Donoghue** [1986] 250, SC.

Transfer of trial—Accused sent forward for trial to Dublin Circuit Court—Accused seeking trial in High Court (Central Criminal Court)—Prohibition on transfer—Whether statutory provisions prohibiting transfer repugnant to Constitution—Whether withdrawing jurisdiction from High Court expressly conferred by Constitution—Constitution of Ireland 1937, Articles 34.2, 34.3, 36.iii—Courts Act 1964, s. 4—Courts Act 1981, s. 32(1). **Tormey v Attorney General** [1984] 657, HC; [1985] 375, SC.

Criminal law
Evidence

Unconstitutionally obtained evidence—Statements by accused while in unlawful detention—Admissibility—Whether conscious and deliberate violation of constitutional rights of accused—Constitution of Ireland 1937, Article 34 4 3—Courts (Establishment and Constitution) Act 1961, s. 3—Courts (Supplementary Provisions) Act 1961, s. 12—Courts of Justice Act 1924, ss. 29, 31. **DPP v Lynch** [1981] 389, SC.

Unconstitutionally obtained evidence—Whether evidence obtained in breach of constitutional rights is inadmissible—Circumstances where such evidence may be admitted—Rationale for exclusionary rule. **People (DPP) v Kenny** [1990] 569, SC.

Prosecution of offences

Private prosecution—Whether Attorney General or DPP had power to end private prosecution—Prosecution brought by Garda as common informer—Constitution of Ireland 1937, Art 30 3—Ministers and Secretaries Act 1924, s. 6(1)—Prosecution of Offences Act 1974, s. 3. **State (Collins) v Ruane** [1984] 443, HC; [1985] 349, SC.

Powers of DPP—Validity. *See* DIRECTOR OF PUBLIC PROSECUTIONS (Powers—Validity).

Revenue legislation

Payment of penalties in default of income tax returns—Whether penalties imposition or punishment—Whether criminal matter—Constitution of Ireland 1937, Article 34—Income Tax Act 1967, s. 500. **McLoughlin v Tuite** [1986] 304, HC.

CONSTITUTION
Criminal law *continued*
Trial of offences. See Trial of offences (*below*).

Criminal procedure
District Court
Jurisdiction—Accused detained pursuant to statutory power—Whether remand order made by district justice valid—Whether District Court can embark on constitutional inquiry as to validity of detention. *See* Courts—Jurisdiction—District Court (*above*).

Special Criminal Court
DPP directing trial in Special Criminal Court—Whether power unconstitutional—Opinion of DPP that ordinary courts inadequate—Whether reviewable by the courts—Offences Against the State Act 1939, ss. 47, 48—Prosecution of Offences Act 1974, s. 3. **O'Reilly and Judge v DPP** [1984] 224, HC.

Dáil Éireann
Dissolution
Injunction—Whether Courts can prevent the Taoiseach from advising the President to dissolve Dáil Éireann—Duty of Oireachtas to revise Dáil consituencies—Constitution of Ireland 1937, Articles 13 2 1, 13 2 2, 13 8 1, 16 3 1, 16 2. **O'Malley v An Taoiseach** [1990] 461, HC.

Elections
Ballot papers—Alphabetical listing of candidates—Statute—Validity—Challenge to the alphabetical listing of election candidates required by statute—Alleged distortion in voting patterns in favour of candidates at head of ballot paper—Whether the system constitutes a reasonable regulation of elections to Dáil Éireann—Constitution of Ireland 1937, Articles 16, 40.1, 40.3. **O'Reilly v Minister for Environment** [1987] 290, HC.

Bill conferring rights to vote on British citizens—Whether Bill repugnant to the Constitution. *See* Bill—Validity—Elections (*above*).

Right to vote—Physically incapacitated citizens—Statute—Validity—Whether absence of facilities for enabling such citizens to exercise franchise frustrating the right to vote—Whether provision of postal voting for certain classes of voters arbitrary—Whether extension of postal voting would lead to increased risk of abuse—Constitution of Ireland 1937, Articles 16 1 2, 16 7, 40 1, 40 3—Electoral Act 1963, ss. 5, 22, 26. **Draper v Attorney General** [1984] 643, HC, SC.

Dwelling
Inviolability. See Personal rights—Inviolability of dwelling (*below*).

Education
Industrial school
District Court order that child be sent to industrial school—Father consenting to said order—Father subsequently seeking return of child—Minister refusing to order child's release—Whether provisions unconstitutional—Constitution of Ireland 1937, Articles 40, 42—Children Act 1908, s. 58—Children Act 1941, s. 10. In Re Doyle, An Infant: **State (Doyle) v Minister for Education and the Attorney General** [1989] 277, SC.

Right to free primary education
Interference with this right—Claim for damages—Whether such claim a claim in tort—Assessment of damages—Constitution of Ireland 1937, Article 42 2—Trade Disputes Act 1906, s. 4. **Hayes v Ireland** [1987] 651, HC.

Equality
Adoption
Exclusion—Widower—Infant placed for adoption—Prospective mother dying before adoption order made—Statutory provision excluding widower from obtaining adoption

CONSTITUTION
Equality
Adoption continued
order—Whether arbitrary discrimination—Statute—Validity—Constitution of Ireland 1937, Articles 40 1, 40 2 1—Adoption Act 1952, s. 13(1)—Adoption Act 1974, s. 5(1). **O'G v Attorney General** [1985] 61, HC.

Criminal law
Conviction in special criminal court—Disqualification—Whether discriminatory—Constitution of Ireland 1937, Article 40 1—Offences Against the State Act 1939, s. 34. **People (DPP) v Quilligan** [1987] 606, CCC, SC.

Extradition—State acquiescing in orders refusing extradition—Subsequent attempt to extradite person in respect of identical circumstances—Whether State precluded from denying person relief identical to that previously obtained—Whether attempt to extradite an abuse of the processes of the courts—Constitution of Ireland 1937, Arts 15 4 1, 40 1—Extradition Act 1965, s. 50(2). **McMahon v Leahy** [1985] 432, SC.

Irish nationality and citizenship
Discrimination—Sexes—Statute—Validity—Male alien marrying Irish citizen—Different provisions for female aliens marrying Irish citizens—Whether diversity of arrangements amounts to discrimination. *See* Irish Nationality and Citizenship—Discrimination—Sexes (*below*).

Planning appeal
Requirement of lodgment of deposit—Whether arbitrary discrimination—Hearing—Whether oral hearing required—Fair procedures—Statute—Validity—Constitution of Ireland 1937, Articles 40 1, 40 3—Local Government (Planning and Development) Act 1976, ss. 15, 16, 18. **Finnegan v An Bord Pleanála** [1979] 134, HC, SC.

Prize bonds
Whether inflation has rendered the statutory prize bond competition unfair—Whether injustice resulted—Finance (Miscellaneous Provisions) Act 1956—Constitution of Ireland 1937, Articles 34, 40.1. **Heaney v Minister for Finance** [1986] 164, HC.

Succession rights
Illegitimate child—Intestacy—Deceased's illegitimate daughter claiming share of the estate—Whether illegitimate child 'issue' of the deceased—Whether statutory discrimination between child born inside and outside marriage invalid—Constitution of Ireland 1937, Articles 40.1 and 3, 43 1.2—Succession Act 1965, ss. 67, 69, 110. **In re Walker: O'Brien v s.** [1982] 327, HC; [1985] 86, SC.

European Community membership
Directive
Implementation—Administrative scheme—Validity. *See* Administrative scheme—Validity—Scheme implementing EC Council directive (*above*).

Constitutional provision permitting membership of Community
Nature and extent of permission—Provision prohibiting invocation of constitutional provisions to invalidate steps necessitated by membership—Amendment of original treaties specified in constitutional provision—Whether necessitated by membership—Whether within scope of original treaties. **Crotty v An Taoiseach** [1987] 400, HC, SC.

Treaty
Government intending to ratify treaty—Obligations to engage in foreign policy co-operation—Whether limiting ability to engage in independent foreign policy making—Whether in conflict with sovereignty of Irish State and People—Whether consistent with Constitution—Constitution of Ireland 1937, Articles 1, 5, 6, 28, 29 4 1, 29 4 3—Single European Act [Treaty] Title III, Article 30. **Crotty v An Taoiseach** [1987] 400, HC, SC.

CONSTITUTION *continued*
Extradition
Constitutional rights
Apprehension of breach—Probability of being subjected to torture and degrading treatment. *See* EXTRADITION (Constitutional rights—Probability of being subjected to assault, torture and degrading treatment).

Procedure
Statute—Validity—Whether extradition arrangements safeguard personal rights of citizen—Whether procedures in courts of Northern Ireland meet minimum standards applicable in this State—Presumption of constitutionality—Constitution of Ireland 1937, Article 34.1—Extradition Act 1965, Part III. **Shannon v Attorney General** [1985] 449, HC, SC.

Treaty
Validity. *See* International relations—Treaty—Extradition (*below*).

Fair procedures
Broadcasting
Statute—Validity—Unlicensed possession and use of apparatus for wireless telegraphy—Apparatus seized—Whether seizure procedure inconsistent with guarantee of fair procedures. *See* BROADCASTING (Radio Station—Unlicensed possession and use of apparatus for wireless telegraphy).

Criminal Law
Charges relating to stolen car—Judicial review—Evidence—Preservation—Duty of Gardai to preserve evidence material to guilt or innocence—Garda disposal of vehicle—Whether prejudice arising—Whether injunction to restrain prosecution of said charges be granted. **Murphy v DPP** [1989] 71, HC.

Child
Paternity—Evidence—Admissibility—Evidence of wife that child not the child of the marriage—Whether admissible—Rule in Russell v Russell—Whether incompatible with the provisions of the Constitution—Entitlement to fair procedures. *See* CHILD (Paternity—Evidence).

Defence forces
Dismissal—Natural justice—Certiorari—Delay—Lack of candour—Whether disentitling to relief. **State (Furey) v Minister for Justice** [1988] 89, SC.

Extradition
Statutory scheme for production of documents—Whether entitlement to production of sworn informations on which warrant based—Whether such production a requirement of the right to fair procedures—Constitution of Ireland 1937, Articles 4, 29.4.1—Extradition Act 1965, ss. 54(1), 55. **Ellis v O'Dea** [1990] 87, SC.

Fisheries
Arrest of foreign fishing vessel—Detention order made—Vessel released upon provision of security—Whether requirement to give security amounted to a requirement to give bail—If so, whether such bail oppressive—Whether contrary to fair procedures—Statute—Validity—Major or minor offence—Constitution of Ireland 1937, Articles 38 1, 40 3—Fisheries Consolidation Act 1959, ss. 221, 222(A), 232, 235(2)(a) and (b)—Fisheries Amendment Act 1978, ss. 2(2), 5, 7, 14. **L'Henryenat v Ireland** [1984] 249, HC, SC.

Garda Síochána
Discipline—Investigation—Allegation that conflict of evidence required investigations into separate breaches of discipline—Natural justice—Invalid inquiry—Whether plaintiff entitled to costs and expenses of his representation and attendance at the inquiry—Constitution of Ireland 1937, Article 40.1—Garda Síochána (Discipline) Regulations 1971, reg 8. **McHugh v Commissioner of the Gárda Síochána** [1985] 606, HC; [1987] 181, SC.

CONSTITUTION
Fair procedures
Garda Síochána continued

Discipline—Special inquiry—Details of alleged breach of discipline not disclosed—Constitution of Ireland 1937, Article 40—Garda Síochána Act 1924, ss. 4(2), 5—Garda Síochána (Discipline) Regulations 1971, reg 34. **Hogan v Minister for Justice** [1976–7] 184, HC.

Housing

Corporation tenant—Notice to quit—No explanation given nor complaint brought to tenant's attention—Requests for explanation unanswered—District Court order for possession—Appeal—Landlord and Tenant Law (Amendment) Act 1860, ss. 86, 87, 88—Housing Act 1966, ss. 62, 118. **State (Litzouw) v Johnson** [1981] 273, HC.

Trade union

Meeting—Resolution for the introduction of a compulsory retirement scheme—Resolution passed—Plaintiff not present when vote taken—Whether resolution valid—Whether natural justice infringed—Whether infringement of plaintiff's right to work—Constitution of Ireland 1937, Articles 40 3 1, 45. **Rodgers v ITGWU, HC.**

Trial

Delay—Trial abandoned—Proposed re-trial—Whether prejudice arising—Whether interlocutory injunction to restrain said trial be granted—Constitution of Ireland 1937, Articles 38 1, 40 3. **O'Connor v DPP** [1987] 723, HC.

Family
Aliens

Whether aliens entitled to benefit from provisions of Constitution relating to family. *See* Family—Rights—Aliens (*below*).

Child

Adoption—Bill—Validity. *See* Bill—Validity—Adoption (*above*).

Adoption—Infant placed for adoption—Natural parents' subsequent marriage legitimising infant—Natural mother witholding consent to adoption—Whether consent to be dispensed with—Welfare of child within family to be presumed unless exceptional circumstances arise—Constitution of Ireland 1937, Articles 41, 42— Guardianship of Infants Act 1964, ss. 2, 3. **In re J H (otherwise R) an infant; K C v An Bord Uchtala** [1985] 302, HC, SC; [1986] 65, HC.

Adoption—Statute—Validity—Equality—Statutory provision excluding widower from obtaining adoption order. *See* Equality—Adoption (*above*).

Care—Fit person order—Child committed to care of Health Board as 'fit person'—Habeas corpus application—Whether child should be returned to custody of parents. *See* CHILD (Care—Health board—Fit person order).

Care—Place of safety order—Inquiry into legality of detention—Whether fair procedures observed. *See* CHILD (Care—Health board—Place of safety order).

Paternity—Evidence—Admissibility—Evidence of wife that child not the child of the marriage—Rule in Russell v Russell—Whether inconsistent with guarantee of fair procedures. *See* CHILD (Paternity—Evidence).

Removal from jurisdiction—Application by wife for passports for children—Passports issued despite husband's objections—Whether infringement of husband's constitutional and statutory rights—Extent of relief husband entitled to obtain. *See* CHILD (Custody—Removal from jurisdiction—Wife).

Removal from jurisdiction—Child born of lawfully married parents who were citizens of and domiciled abroad—Claim for return—If order granted child would be legally adopted—Such development not permissible under Irish law. *See* CHILD (Custody—

CONSTITUTION
Family
Child continued

Removal from jurisdiction—Child born of lawfully married parents who were citizens of and domiciled abroad).

Removal from jurisdiction—Father removing infant from jurisdiction of English courts—Father being an Irish citizen domiciled in England—English county council seeking order of habeas corpus—Legality of infant's detention—Whether father and infant entitled to be regarded as a "family"—Constitution of Ireland 1937, Articles 40, 41, 42. **Kent Co Council v C s.** [1984] 292.

Marriage. See Marriage (*below*).

Rights

Aliens—Whether a family consisting of alien parents and children who are Irish citizens has the right to reside in the State—When power to expel aliens may be exercised—Exigencies of the common good—Whether justifiable interference with rights of family—Constitutional rights of children—Fair procedures—Constitution of Ireland 1937, Articles 40, 41, 42—Aliens Act 1935—Aliens Order 1946. **Fajujonu v Minister for Justice** [1990] 234, SC.

Aliens—Whether aliens entitled to the protection of the Constitution—Child—Custody—Wrongful removal of infant from foreign jurisdiction. *See* CHILD (Custody—Removal from jurisdiction—Child born of lawfully married parents who were citizens of and domiciled abroad—Wrongful removal of infant from foreign jurisdiction).

Extent of guarantee—Whether negligent act of private person infringes the constitutional rights of the family—Industrial accident—Father of family suffering brain damage—Whether employer owed duty of care to victim's children not to deprive them of the non-pecuniary benefits derived from parent-child relationships—Education of children—Whether defendants' carelessness infringed the plaintiffs' constitutional rights—Constitution of Ireland 1937, Articles 41, 42. **Hosford v John Murphy & Sons Ltd** [1988] 300, HC.

Father convicted prisoner—Effect of imprisonment on rights of family—Right to communicate—Inquiry into lawfulness of detention—Constitution of Ireland 1937, Article 40.4.2. **State (Gallagher) v Governor of Portlaoise Prison** [1987] 45, HC.

Infringement—Damages—Non-pecuniary benefits deriving from parent-child relationship— Whether recoverable at common law—Industrial accident—Victim suffering brain damage—Whether employer owed duty of care to victim's children. *See* Family—Rights—Extent of guarantee (*above*).

Freedom of association. *See* Personal rights—Freedom of association (*below*).

Freedom of expression. *See* Personal rights—Freedom of expression (*below*).

Habeas corpus
Inquiry into legality of detention. See HABEAS CORPUS.

Housing
Travelling community

Whether housing authority under statutory duty to provide serviced halting sites for members of travelling community—Whether State under a constitutional duty to provide such sites—Whether court jurisdiction to entertain a claim for damages for alleged breach of constitutional duty by State—Constitution of Ireland 1937– Housing Act 1966, ss. 53, 54, 56, 58, 60, 111. **O'Reilly v Limerick Corporation** [1989] 181, HC.

Injunction
Right to travel

Injunction to restrain sporting links with a country where apartheid is practised—

CONSTITUTION
Injunction
Right to travel continued

Irish Rugby Football Union tour of South Africa—Use of word "Irish" or association with Ireland by touring party—Players' and officials' right to travel. **Lennon v Ganly** [1981] 84, HC.

International relations
European Community membership. See European Community membership (*above*).

Generally recognised principles of international law

Extradition—Whether extradition arrangements which fail to exempt from extradition where person may be discriminated against in respect of race, religion or nationality in violation of Constitution—Whether establishment of prima facie case by requesting State a generally recognised principle of international law—Constitution of Ireland 1937, Article 29 3—Extradition Act 1965, Parts II and III. **Shannon v Attorney General** [1985] 449, HC, SC.

Treaty

Anglo-Irish Agreement—Locus Standi—Provisions of Constitution concerning re-integration of national territory—Whether claim of legal right—Whether agreement constitutes abandonment of claim to re-integration of national territory—Agreement recognises de facto situation in Northern Ireland—Whether estoppel created in international law—Whether agreement fettered power of Government to conduct external relations—Whether agreement constituted disregard of interests of majority community in Northern Ireland—Constitution of Ireland 1937, Articles 2, 3, 28, 29, 40 1, 40 3 1—Anglo-Irish Agreement 1985, Articles 1, 2, 4, 5. **McGimpsey v Ireland** [1989], HC; [1990] 440, SC.

Extradition—Treaty involving expense—Treaty not specifically approved by Dáil Éireann—Whether State bound by treaty—Extradition Act 1965, s. 5. **State (McCaud) v Governor of Mountjoy Prison** [1986] 129, HC.

Extradition—Treaty laid before both Houses of the Oireachtas—No resolution passed by Dáil Éireann approving of the terms—Whether Treaty involved a charge on public funds—Treaty formed subject matter of a statutory instrument—Whether such order invalid—Constitution of Ireland 1937, Articles 27.4.1, 29.5—Extradition Act 1965 (Part II) (No 20) Order 1984. **State (Gilliland) v Governor of Mountjoy Prison** [1986] 381, HC; [1987] 278, SC.

Ratification—Single European Act—Government intending to ratify treaty—Obligations to engage in foreign policy co-operation—Whether limiting ability to engage in independent foreign policy making—Whether in conflict with sovereignty of Irish State and People—Whether consistent with Constitution—Constitution of Ireland 1937, Articles 1, 5, 6, 28, 29 4 1, 29 4 3—Single European Act [Treaty] Title III, Article 30. **Crotty v An Taoiseach** [1987] 400, HC, SC.

Interpretation
Principles applicable

Provisions in apparent conflict—Literal interpretation giving way to more fundamental rule—General constitutional scheme. **Tormey v Attorney General** [1985] 375, SC.

Purposive or literal approach

Whether court precluded from considering the principles of social policy—Onus of proof—Constitution of Ireland 1937, Articles 38, 40 3 1 and 2, 45 3 1—Post Office Act 1908. **Attorney General v Paperlink Ltd** [1984] 373, HC.

Right to procreate of married couple within prison

Whether right protected and recognised under provisions of Constitution relating to

CONSTITUTION
Interpretation
Right to procreate of married couple within prison continued
family or relating to personal (unenumerated) rights—Constitution of Ireland 1937, Arts 40 3, 41. **Murray v Attorney General** [1985] 542, HC.

Inviolability of dwelling of citizen. *See* Personal rights—Inviolability of dwelling (*below*).

Irish language. *See* National language (*below*).

Irish nationality and citizenship
Discrimination
Sexes—Statute—Validity—Male alien marrying Irish citizen—Application for certificate of naturalisation—Different provisions for female aliens marrying Irish citizens—Whether diversity of arrangements amounts to discrimination—Whether plaintiff capable of asserting constitutional rights—Locus standi—Natural justice—Jurisdiction of court to indicate appropriate form of enactment—Irish Nationality and Citizenship Act 1956, ss. 8, 15, 17. **Somjee v Minister for Justice** [1981] 324, HC.

Liberty of the individual. *See* Personal rights—Liberty (*below*).

Life of unborn. *See* Personal rights—Right to life of unborn (*below*).

Locus standi
Apprehension of breach of rights
Whether sufficient locus standi. **Curtis v Attorney General** [1986] 428, HC.

Challenge to validity of legislation
Freedom of expression—Broadcasting—Election broadcast—Ministerial order preventing access by Provisional Sinn Fein candidates to radio and television—Prosecutor one of candidates—Whether sufficient locus standi to maintain proceedings—Constitution of Ireland 1937, Article 40.6.1—Broadcasting Authority Act 1960, s. 31(1)—Broadcasting Authority (Amendment) Act 1976, s. 16. **State (Lynch) v Cooney** [1982] 190; [1983] 89, SC.

Fisheries—Foreign fishing vessel arrested and detained—Whether open to the master of the vessel to argue that the legislation affected the constitutional rights of the vessel's owner—Locus standi—Whether detention of the vessel amounted to a deprivation of the right to earn a livelihood—Whether physical presence of plaintiff necessary—Constitution of Ireland 1937, Article 40 3—Fisheries Consolidation Act 1959, ss. 221, 222 (A), 232, 232 (A), 234 (1), 235 (2)—Fisheries Amendment Act 1978, ss. 2(2), 12, 13, 14, **L'Henryenat v Ireland** [1984] 249, HC, SC.

Hypothetical arguments—Residential property tax- -Constitution of Ireland 1937, Articles 40 1, 40 3, 41, 43—Finance Act 1983. **Madigan v Attorney General** [1986] 136, HC, SC.

Whether action can be maintained where it cannot be shown that the right of any person will be thereby vindicated or protected. **Somjee v Minister for Justice** [1981] 324, HC.

Whether facts at issue established in evidence—Whether court should embark on moot trial—Appellate function of Supreme Court. **Brady and Others v Donegal Co Council** [1989] 282, SC.

Enforcement of personal right
Right to life of unborn. *See* Personal rights—Right to life of unborn—Enforcement—Locus standi (*below*).

International treaty
Anglo-Irish Agreement—Provisions of Constitution concerning re-integration of national territory—Locus standi of non-citizens. *See* International relations—Treaty—Anglo-Irish Agreement—Locus standi (*above*).

Legislation giving effect to international treaty—Application for injunction to prevent deposit of deeds of ratification—Whether plaintiff affected by legislation—Whether

CONSTITUTION
Locus standi
International treaty continued

injunction necessary to protect constitutional rights—Whether exceptional circumstances established. **Crotty v An Taoiseach** [1987] 400, HC, SC.

Non-citizens

Citizens of Northern Ireland—Challenge to constitutionality of international treaty—Anglo-Irish Agreement—Provisions of Constitution concerning re-integration of national territory. *See* International relations—Treaty—Anglo-Irish Agreement—Locus standi (*above*).

Public right

Assertion of public right by private citizen—Common law limitation—Whether limitations carried over by the Constitution—Whether private citizen has locus standi to assert breach of public right without showing particular loss or damage. **Irish Permanent Building Society v Caldwell** [1979] 273, HC; [1981] 242, HC.

Relator proceedings

Role of Attorney General—Whether necessary to consider issue of standing of relator—Whether relator had locus standi prior to conversion of proceedings to relator action. **Attorney General (ex rel SPUC) v Open Door Counselling Ltd** [1987] 477, HC; [1989] 19, SC.

Right to life of unborn

Enforcement of Article 40 3 3—Whether Attorney General had exclusive right to enforce Article 40 3 3—Whether plaintiff could maintain action without the relation of the Attorney General— Constitution of Ireland 1937, Article 40 3 3. **Society for the Protection of Unborn Children (Ireland) Ltd v Coogan** [1989] 526, HC; [1990] 70, SC.

Marriage
Divorce

Recognition—Whether concept of dependent domicile survived enactment of Constitution—Constitution of Ireland 1937, Articles 40 1, 40 3, 41. **C M v T M** [1988] 456, HC.

Married couple

Income tax—Statute with retrospective effect—Enacted in consequence of decision that portion of income tax legislation unconstitutional—Whether lawful for the State to collect arrears of tax due under the unconstitutional provisions—Finance Act 1980, s. 21—Constitution of Ireland 1937, Articles 40.1, 40.3, 41. **Muckley v Attorney General** [1986] 64, HC, SC.

Procreation rights—Husband and wife each serving sentence of imprisonment for life—Whether absence of facilities to procreate within prison a denial of rights of married couple. *See* Personal rights—Procreation—Married couple (*below*).

Social Welfare—Implementation of EC Council Directive—Equal treatment for men and women in matters of social security—Implementation effected in such a way that certain married couples adversely treated—Whether failure on the part of state to vindicate the institution of marriage—Constitution of Ireland 1937, Article 41 3 1—Council Directive 79/7—Social Welfare (No 2) Act 1985, s. 12(4). **Hyland v Minister for Social Welfare** [1989] 196, HC; [1990] 213, SC.

Matrimonial property

Wife seeking a declaration of interest in husband's house—Wife contributing no money towards acquisition—Full time wife and mother—Whether entitled to an interest in light of the provisions of the Constitution—Constitution of Ireland 1937, Article 41—Married Women's Status Act 1957, s. 12. **B L v M L** [1989] 528, HC.

Procreation rights

Married couple—Prisoners—Husband and wife each serving sentence of imprisonment

CONSTITUTION
Marriage
Procreation rights continued

for life—Whether absence of facilities to procreate within prison a denial of rights of married couple. *See* Personal rights—Procreation—Married couple (*below*).

Protection

Administrative scheme—Validity—Implementation of EC Council directive. *See* Administrative scheme—Validity (*above*).

Minor offence
Whether minor offence triable summarily. See Trial of offences—Minor offence (*below*).

National language
Promotion

Requirement of knowledge of Irish language for appointment to full-time teaching post—Knowledge not required for performance of teaching duties—Compatibility with European Community law—EEC Treaty, Articles 48(3), 177—Council Regulation 1612/68, Article 3—Constitution of Ireland 1937, Article 8—Vocational Education Act 1930, s. 23. **Groener v Minister for Education** [1990] 335, ECJ.

Use of Irish in court

Whether Justice obliged to hear case in Irish without assistance of interpreter—Natural justice—Courts of Justice Act 1924, s. 71—Constitution of Ireland 1937, Article 8. **Ó Monacháin v An Taoiseach** [1986] 660, SC.

Non-citizens
Constitutional rights. See ALIEN (Constitutional rights).

Locus standi

Challenge to constitutionality of legislation—Citizens of Northern Ireland—Challenge to constitutionality of Anglo-Irish Agreement—Provisions of Constitution concerning re-integration of national territory. *See* International relations—Treaty—Anglo-Irish Agreement—Locus standi (*above*).

Personal rights
Access to courts

Inspection—Action for trespass—Application for an order allowing plaintiffs to carry out an inspection of defendant's mining activities—Attempt to ascertain whether such trespass has taken place—Whether necessary for plaintiffs to establish prima facie case—Constitutional right of access to the courts—RSC O 50, r 4. **Bula Ltd v Tara Mines Ltd** [1988] 149, HC.

Legal aid—Custody and maintenance proceedings—Application for civil legal aid refused—Whether infringement of right of access to the courts—Scheme for Legal Aid and Advice 1979, paras 4, 7. **E v E** [1982] 497, HC.

Scope of right—Whether includes right to compel suit or prosecution—Irish citizen in custody in Northern Ireland—Extra-territorial offence—Prosecutor wishing to opt for trial in the Republic—Director of Public Prosecutions indicating that proceedings would not be instituted in this jurisdiction—Whether prosecutor deprived of his constitutional right of access to the courts of this jurisdiction. **State (McCormack) v Curran** [1987] 225, HC, SC.

Scope of right—Whether includes right to trial by jury—Claim in tort—Action for damages for personal injuries—Proceedings commenced in the High Court—Motion to remit case to District or Circuit Court—Damages likely to be within District Court jurisdiction—Whether plaintiff right to a jury trial—Courts of Justice Act 1924, s. 94—Courts Act 1971, s. 6. **McDonald v Galvin** [1976–7] 41, HC.

CONSTITUTION
Personal rights *continued*
Access to solicitor

Right of access to solicitor while in detention—Denial of access by Gardai—Whether right of reasonable access to solicitor was a constitutional right—Constitution of Ireland 1937, Article 40 3. **People (DPP) v Conroy** [1988] 4, CCA, SC.

Right of access to solicitor while in detention—Whether delay by Gardai in permitting access by solicitor to client constituted a denial of right of access—Whether right of reasonable access to solicitor was a constitutional right—Constitution of Ireland 1937, Article 40 3. **DPP v Healy** [1990] 313, SC.

Aliens

Whether aliens entitled to the protection of the Constitution. *See* ALIEN (Constitutional rights).

Bodily integrity

Statute—Validity—Planning permission—Asbestos waste—Whether injurious to health—Whether relevant to constitutionality of planning legislation—Constitution of Ireland 1937, Articles 40 1, 40 3—Local Government (Planning and Development) Act 1976. **Finnegan v An Bord Pleanála** [1979] 134, HC, SC.

Breach

Apprehension of breach—Criminal law—Extradition—Probability of being subjected to torture and degrading treatment. *See* EXTRADITION—Constitutional rights—Probability of being subjected to assault, torture and degrading treatment.

Invasion—Deliberate violation—Invasion by persons on behalf of the Executive—Jurisdiction of courts—Constitution of Ireland 1937, Articles 40.3.1, 40.4.2—Extradition Act 1965 Part II. **Trimbole v Governor of Mountjoy Prison** [1985] 465, HC, SC.

Unconstitutionally obtained evidence—Statements by accused while in unlawful detention—Admissibility—Constitution of Ireland 1937, Article 34 4 3—Courts (Establishment and Constitution) Act 1961, s. 3—Courts (Supplementary Provisions) Act 1961, s. 12—Courts of Justice Act 1924, ss. 29, 31. **DPP v Lynch** [1981] 389, SC.

Unconstitutionally obtained evidence—Criminal proceedings—Whether evidence obtained in breach of constitutional rights is inadmissible—Circumstances where such evidence may be admitted—Rationale for exclusionary rule. **People (DPP) v Kenny** [1990] 569, SC.

Communication

Right to communicate—Right to earn livelihood—Statutory monopoly in respect of the conveying of 'letters'—Whether violative of personal and property rights—Interpretation—Purposive of literal approach—Whether court precluded from considering the principles of social policy—Onus of proof—Constitution of Ireland 1937, Articles 38, 40 3 1 and 2, 45 3 1—Post Office Act 1908. **Attorney General v Paperlink Ltd** [1984] 373, HC.

Right to communicate—Convicted prisoner—Interference with right to communicate—Written communication to prisoner intercepted—Whether prisoner entitled to damages—Constitution of Ireland 1937, Articles 40.3, 40.6.1. **Kearney v Minister for Justice** [1987] 52, HC.

Right to communicate—Convicted prisoner—Effect of imprisonment on rights of family—Inquiry into lawfulness of detention—Constitution of Ireland 1937, Article 40.4.2. **State (Gallagher) v Governor of Portlaoise Prison** [1987] 45, HC.

Enforcement

Locus standi—Right to life of unborn. *See* Personal rights—Right to life of unborn—Enforcement—Locus standi—Whether Attorney General had exclusive right to enforce Article 40.3.3.

CONSTITUTION

Personal rights *continued*

Equality before the law. See Equality (*above*).

Extradition cases. See EXTRADITION (Constitutional rights).

Fair procedures. See Fair procedures (*above*).

Freedom of association

Garda Síochána—Rights of members of Garda Representative Association and Association of Garda Sergeants and Inspectors—Limitation of ranks within the Garda Síochána—Rights of freedom of association for members of Garda Síochána—Limitation on extent to which members of the force may organize—Garda Síochána Act 1977, s. 1—Constitution of Ireland 1937, Article 40 6 1(iii). **Aughey v Attorney General** [1986] 206, HC; [1989] 87, SC.

Plaintiff offered position as principal of a primary school—Plaintiff not being a member of trade union—Pressure exerted on manager to cancel appointment—Whether defendants engaged in actionable conspiracy to cause plaintiff to abandon his constitutional right to disassociate. **Cotter v Ahern** [1976–7] 248, HC.

Freedom of expression

Book written by deceased member of British intelligence service—Application to restrain publication in Ireland—Confidentiality—Whether different criteria applied to government information—Constitution of Ireland 1937, Article 40 6 1. **Attorney General for England and Wales v Brandon Book Publishers Ltd** [1987] 135, HC.

Election broadcast—Political party—Ministerial order preventing access by Provisional Sinn Fein candidates to radio and television to promote their electoral campaign—Whether Minister's opinion that the broadcasting would be likely to promote, or incite to crime, reviewable by the courts—Statute—Validity—Locus standi of prosecutor—Constitution of Ireland 1937, Article 40 6 1—Broadcasting Authority Act 1960, s. 31(1)—Broadcasting Authority (Amendment) Act 1976, s. 16. **State (Lynch) v Cooney** [1982] 190, HC; [1983] 89, SC.

Freedom of the press—Right to communicate—Criminal law—Conviction—Pending appeal—Publication of a magazine article based on material supplied by sole witness for the prosecution—Application to restrain publication—Whether article likely to prejudice the appeal—Constitution of Ireland 1937, Article 40 6. **Cullen v Toibin** [1984] 577, HC.

Infringement

Infringement by private person—Whether injunction may issue to prevent infringement—Constitution of Ireland 1937, Articles 40 3, 45. **Parsons v Kavanagh** [1990] 560, HC.

Inviolability of dwelling

Criminal law—Arrest—Legality—Gardai entering dwelling—Whether arrest lawful—Road Traffic Act 1961, s. 107—Constitution of Ireland 1937, Article 40 5. **DPP v Gaffney** [1986] 657, HC; [1988] 39, SC.

Criminal law—Evidence—Admissibility—Evidence obtained after forcible entry of accused's house—Invalid search warrant—Circumstances where such evidence may be admitted—Rationale for exclusionary rule. **People (DPP) v Kenny** [1990] 569, SC.

Liberty

Appellant detained in pursuance of extradition order—Evidence that appellant likely to be ill-treated if delivered out of the jurisdiction—Whether extradition should be refused in such circumstances. **Clarke v McMahon** [1990] 648, HC, SC.

Appellant detained in pursuance of extradition order—Evidence that appellant likely to be ill-treated if delivered out of the jurisdiction—Whether extradition should be refused in such circumstances—Constitution of Ireland 1937, Article 40 3 4. **Finucane v McMahon** [1990] 505, SC.

CONSTITUTION
Personal rights
Liberty continued
Inquiry into legality of detention under Article 40—Habeas corpus. *See* HABEAS CORPUS.

Prisoner
Married couple—Right to procreate. *See* Personal rights—Procreation (*below*).

Subsisting constitutional rights—Whether rights subsist subsequent to conviction—Extent to which rights circumscribed by requirements of security and good order in prison—Complaint by prisoner that conditions of confinement conflict with health and privacy rights—Whether State in breach of duties under Constitution and prison rules—Requirements of security and good order in prison—Remedies available—Access to courts—Constitution of Ireland 1937, Article 40 3—Rules for the Government of Prisons 1947, rules 34, 46, 108, 172. **State (Richardson) v Governor of Mountjoy Prison** [1980] 82, HC.

Privacy
Telephone tapping—Whether right to privacy one of the citizen's fundamental personal rights—Whether plaintiffs entitled to punitive or aggravated damages—Constitution of Ireland 1937, Article 40.3—Civil Liability Act 1961, ss. 7(2), 14(4). **Kennedy & Arnold v Ireland** [1988] 472, HC.

Procreation
Married couple—Prisoners—Whether absence of facilities to procreate within prison a denial of rights of married couple—Basis for restriction on prisoners' rights by State—Whether husband and wife constitute family—Constitution of Ireland 1937, Articles 40.3, 41. **Murray v Attorney General** [1985] 542, HC.

Protection
Extradition—Probability of being subjected to assault, torture or inhuman treatment. *See* EXTRADITION (Constitutional rights—Probability of being subjected to assault, torture or inhuman treatment).

Right to earn livelihood
Civil service—Suspension—Natural justice—Whether injunction be granted—Civil Service Regulation Act 1956, s. 13. **Yeates v Minister for Posts and Telegraphs** [1978] 22, HC.

Fisheries—Arrest of foreign fishing vessel—Detention order made—Vessel released upon provision of security—Challenge to the constitutionality of the relevant legislation—Whether open to the master of the vessel to argue that the legislation affected the constitutional rights of the vessel's owner—Locus standi—Whether detention of the vessel amounted to a deprivation of the right to earn a livelihood—Whether physical presence of plaintiff necessary—Constitution of Ireland 1937, Article 40.3—Fisheries Consolidation Act 1959, ss. 221, 222 (A), 232, 232 (A), 234 (1), 235 (2)—Fisheries Amendment Act 1978, ss. 2(2), 12, 13, 14, **L'Henryenat v Ireland** [1984] 249, HC, SC.

Gaming—Restrictions imposed on use of slot machines—Whether impact of inflation constituted unjust attack on exercise of right to earn livelihood—Statute—Validity—Gaming and Lotteries Act 1956, s. 14—Gaming and Lotteries Act 1979, s. 1—Constitution of Ireland 1937, Article 40 3. **Cafolla v Attorney General** [1986] 177, HC.

Infringement by private person—Whether injunction may issue to prevent infringement—Constitution of Ireland 1937, Articles 40 3, 45. **Parsons v Kavanagh** [1990] 560, HC.

Right to life of unborn
Enforcement—Locus standi—Whether Attorney General had exclusive right to enforce Article 40.3.3—Whether plaintiff could maintain action without the relation of the Attorney General—Constitution of Ireland 1937, Article 40.3.3. **Society for the Protection of Unborn Children (Ireland) Ltd v Coogan** [1989] 526, HC; [1990] 70, SC.

CONSTITUTION
Personal rights
Right to life of unborn continued
Information on abortion—Clinic—Non-directive counselling with regard to abortion in England—Whether in breach of right to life of unborn—Scope of relief—Right of communication—Conflict with right to life of unborn—Jurisdiction of courts to defend and vindicate a constitutionally guaranteed right—Locus standi—Relator proceedings—Role of Attorney General—Constitution of Ireland 1937, Articles 6.1, 15.2, 40.3.3—Offences against the Person Act 1861, ss. 58, 59—Health (Family Planning) Act 1979, s. 10. **Attorney General (ex rel SPUC (Ireland) Ltd) v Open Door Counselling Ltd** [1987] 477, HC; [1989] 19, SC.

Information on abortion—Students' groups—Publication of information about identity, location and means of communicating with abortion clinics outside the State—Whether right to give or receive such information under European Community law—Constitution of Ireland 1937, Article 40 3 3. **Society for the Protection of Unborn Children (Ireland) Ltd v Grogan** [1990] 350, SC.

Non-directive counselling with regard to abortion in England—Whether such activity unlawful having regard to the Constitution—Whether such activity amounts to a conspiracy to corrupt public morals. **Attorney General (SPUC) v Open Door Counselling** [1987] 477, HC.

Right to travel
Injunction application—Irish rugby football tour of South Africa—Whether tour in breach of plaintiff's constitutional rights—Whether injunction be granted—Constitutional rights to travel and play rugby abroad. **Lennon v Ganly** [1981] 84, HC.

Right to work
Trade union—Meeting—Resolution for the introduction of a compulsory retirement scheme—Resolution passed—Plaintiff not present when vote taken—Whether resolution valid—Whether natural justice infringed—Whether infringement of plaintiff's right to work—Constitution of Ireland 1937, Articles 40 3 1, 45. **Rodgers v ITGWU** [1978] 51, HC.

Waiver
Habeas corpus inquiry—Right of detainer to certify in writing the grounds of detention—Appearance before Special Criminal Court for purpose of charging prisoner—Application made to presiding judge to sit on his own as a judge of the High Court to hear habeas corpus application—Absolute order made—Whether judge jurisdiction to make such order—Whether opportunity of justifying detention a dispensable preliminary—Waiver—Constitution of Ireland 1937, Article 40 4 2—RSC O 84, rr 2, 9. **State (Rogers) v Galvin** [1983] 149, SC.

Privacy. *See* Personal rights—Privacy (*above*).

Procreate, right to. *See* Personal rights—Procreation (*above*).

Property rights
Agriculture
Regulations giving effect to EC milk levy—Such regulations having retrospective effect—Whether unjust—Whether unjustified attack on property rights—Whether any such infringement necessitated by membership of the European Community—Council Regulations 804/84, 856/84, 857/84—Commission Regulation 1271/84—European Communities (Milk Levy) Regulations 1985, reg 4, 12—Constitution of Ireland 1937, Articles 29.4.3, 40.3.2, 43. **Lawlor v Minister for Agriculture** [1988] 400, HC.

Compulsory imposition of structures on land
Compensation—Erection of electricity pylons on land—Power to cut or lop trees—Absence of independent means of assessing compensation—Whether justifiable interference with property rights—Whether unjust attack on property rights—Electricity

CONSTITUTION
Property rights
Compulsory imposition of structures on land continued
(Supply) Act 1927, ss. 53, 98—Electricity (Supply) (Amendment) Act 1941, s. 5—
Electricity (Supply) (Amendment) Act 1945, s. 46—Constitution of Ireland 1937, Arts
40 3, 43. **Electricity Supply Board v Gormley** [1985] 494, SC.

Compulsory purchase
Bord na Móna—Power to compulsorily acquire bogland—Whether power of judicial
nature—Absence of right of appeal—Whether statutory provisions invalid—Whether
procedures adopted in breach of natural justice—Distinction between procedures in
relation to the decision to acquire and procedures in relation to the assessment of fair
compensation—Constitution of Ireland 1937, Articles 40.3, 43—Turf Development
Act 1946, ss. 17, 28, 30–36. **O'Brien v Bord na Mona** [1983] 314, SC.

Land Commission—Price fixed at sum payable in Land Bonds equal in nominal value
to the sum fixed—Whether statutory provisions enabling the price to be paid in such
a way instead of cash ceased to be part of the law on the coming into force of the
Constitution—Whether provision inconsistent with Articles 40 or 43—Constitution of
Ireland 1937, Articles 40 3, 43, 50—Land Act 1923, ss. 3, 25—Land Bond Act 1934,
ss. 2, 4(3)—Land Act 1950, ss. 5(1), 27. **Dreher v Irish Land Commission** [1984] 94, SC.

Confiscation of property
Offences Against the State legislation—Minister empowered to freeze moneys in a
bank account and cause them to be paid into the High Court—Whether such power
amounts to confiscation of property—Whether such powers permissible delimitation
of property rights—Whether open to plaintiff to raise questions as to the constitutionality of the 1939 legislation—Constitution of Ireland 1937, Articles 40 3 2, 43—
Offences Against the State Act 1939, ss. 18, 19, 20, 22—Offences Against the State
(Amendment) Act 1985, ss. 2, 3, 4, 5. **Clancy v Ireland** [1989] 670, HC.

Costs
Statutory prohibition—Criminal trial—District Court Rules prohibiting award of costs
against member of Garda Síochána acting in discharge of his duties as police officer—
Whether unconstitutional discrimination—Whether justified on grounds of social
function—Whether unjust attack on property rights—Constitution of Ireland 1937,
Articles 40.1, 40.3—Prosecution of Offences Act 1974, s. 3—District Court Rules
1948, r 67. **Dillane v Attorney General and Ireland** [1980] 167, SC.

Intoxicating liquor licence
Forfeiture—Licensing offences—Whether forfeiture provisions an unjust attack on
property rights—Whether offences minor offences—Constitution of Ireland 1937,
Articles 38.2, 40.3—Intoxicating Liquor Act 1927, ss. 28, 30(1). **State (Pheasantry Ltd)
v Donnelly** [1982] 512, HC.

Landlord and Tenant
Bill—Validity—Bill affecting rent and security of tenure—Landlords receiving an
amount of rent substantially less than the market rent—Whether unjust attack on
their property rights—Constitution of Ireland 1937, Articles 26, 40.3.2—In re Housing
(Private Rented Dwellings) Bill 1981 [1983] 246, SC.

Rent Restrictions Acts—Arbitrary definition of controlled dwellings—Failure to
provide for review—Permanent alienation of right of possession—Statute—Validity—
Whether unjust attack on property rights of landlords—Social effect of Court's
decision—Jurisdiction in future claims for possession—Constitution of Ireland 1937,
Articles 40, 43—Rent Restrictions Act 1960 and 1967—Landlord and Tenant
(Amendment) Act 1971. **Blake and Madigan v Attorney General** [1981] 34, SC.

National monument
Preservation order—Statute—Validity—Whether unjust attack on property rights—

CONSTITUTION
Property rights
National monument continued
Whether order made in conformity with principles of natural justice—Constitution of
Ireland 1937, Articles 40, 43—National Monuments Act 1930, ss. 8, 14—National
Monuments (Amendment) Act 1954, s. 3. **O'Callaghan v Commissioners of Public Works**
[1983] 391, HC; [1985] 364, SC.

Planning
Purchase of land with benefit of planning permission—Such permission granted by
Minister of State—Supreme Court subsequently ruling such permission *ultra vires*—
Whether State had failed to vindicate the property rights of the plaintiff—Constitution
of Ireland 1937, Articles 40 3 1, 40 3 2. **Pine Valley Developments Ltd v Minister for
the Environment** [1987] 747, HC, SC.

Shareholder
Industrial and provident society—Registered provident society engaged in the business
of banking—Legislation enacted prohibiting such societies from accepting or holding
deposits—Whether legislation invalid—Whether unjust attack on property rights of
shareholders—Whether shareholder has property rights capable of being invoked—
Whether prohibition infringed shareholders' right of association—Constitution of
Ireland 1937, Articles 40 3, 40 6 1(iii)—Industrial and Provident Societies (Amendment)
Act 1978, s. 5(2). **PMPS Ltd v Attorney General** [1984] 88, SC.

Succession
Illegitimate child—Intestate succession—Deceased's illegitimate daughter claiming
share of the estate—Whether illegitimate child 'issue' of the deceased—Whether
statutory discrimination between child born inside and outside marriage invalid—
Constitution of Ireland 1937, Articles 40.1 and 3, 43 1.2—Succession Act 1965, ss.
67, 69, 110. **In re Walker: O'Brien v s.** [1982] 327, HC; [1985] 86, SC.

Taxation
Residential property tax levied on properties over certain value—Whether unjust
attack on property and family rights—Whether constituting invidious discrimination—
Presumption of constitutionality in taxation matters—Locus standi—Constitution of
Ireland 1937, Articles 40 1, 40 3, 41, 43—Finance Act 1983. **Madigan v Attorney
General** [1986] 136, HC, SC.

Valuation
Agricultural land—Valuation carried out between 1852 and 1866—No revaluation
ever taking place. *See* Statute—Validity—Valuation—Agricultural land (*below*).

Religion
Seminary
Dismissal of teacher—Teacher also a priest—Seminary obtaining funds from State—
Funds applied for lay purposes as recognised college of university—Whether primarily
seminary or university—Rights of religious denomination to manage its own affairs—
Domestic tribunal—Natural justice—Bias—Constitution of Ireland, Articles 44 3 3, 44
2 5—Maynooth College Establishment Act 1795, s. 3—Irish Universities Act 1908, s.
2(4)—Higher Education Authority Act 1971, s. 1(4). **McGrath and O Ruairc v
Maynooth College** [1979] 166, SC.

Right to earn livelihood. *See* Personal rights—Right to earn livelihood (*above*).

Right to life of unborn. *See* Personal rights—Right to life of unborn (*above*).

Right to travel. *See* Personal rights—Right to travel (*above*).

Right to work. *See* Personal rights—Right to work (*above*).

CONSTITUTION *continued*
Separation of powers
Judicial power
Administration of justice. *See* Administration of justice (*above*).

Whether court jurisdiction to entertain a claim for damages for alleged breach of constitutional duty by State—Housing—Travelling community—Whether State under a constitutional duty to provide serviced halting sites. **O'Reilly v Limerick Corporation** [1989] 181, HC.

Legislative power
Delegation—Whether unconstitutional delegation of legislative power vested in the Oireachtas—Imposition of duties—Powers of Government—Whether order could be validated by confirmation in the Oireachtas—Constitution of Ireland 1937, Article 15 2 1—Imposition of Duties Act 1957, s. 1—Finance Act 1976, s. 46—Imposition of Duties (Excise Duties) Order 1975. **McDaid v Sheehy** [1989] 342, HC.

Whether statute authorised the carrying out of legislative function by Minister—Constitution of Ireland 1937, Article 15 2—Social Welfare Act 1952, s. 75—Social Welfare (Overlapping Benefits) (Amendment) Regulations 1979, rule 4. **Harvey v Minister for Social Welfare** [1990] 185, SC.

State
Sovereignty
Prerogative—Treasure trove—Royal Prerogative—Whether such prerogative carried over into Irish law—Whether necessary ingredient of sovereignty—Constitution of Ireland 1937, Articles 5, 10. **Webb v Ireland** [1988] 565, HC, SC.

Subversion
Unlawful organisation—Objective of reintegration of national territory by force of arms—Whether objectives of organisation to subvert the Constitutional organs of the State—Extradition—Political offence—Whether political offence exception available—Constitution of Ireland 1937, Article 6—Extradition Act 1965, s. 50. **Russell v Fanning** [1986] 401, HC; [1988] 333, SC.

Unlawful organisation—Objective of reintegration of national territory by force of arms—Extradition—Political offence—Whether persons pursuing policy of reunification of country by violence qualify for political exemption—Constitution of Ireland 1937, Article 6—Extradition Act 1965, s. 50. **Finucane v McMahon** [1990] 505, SC.

Statute
Interpretation. See Statutory interpretation (*below*).

Validity
Administration of justice—Collector General of the Revenue Commissioners—Estimation of tax liability—Default provisions—Whether administration of justice. *See* Administration of justice—Revenue Commissioners (*above*).

Administration of justice—Admittance of persons to bail—Whether conferral of such power on peace commissioner invalid—Constitution of Ireland 1937, Article 34 1—Criminal Justice Act 1951, s. 15—Criminal Justice Act 1984, s. 26. **O'Mahony v Melia** [1990] 14, HC.

Administration of justice—Criminal law—District Justice discharging accused—DPP directing that accused be sent forward for trial in Circuit Court in respect of the same charges—Whether provisions under which DPP purported to act constitutionally valid. *See* DIRECTOR OF PUBLIC PROSECUTIONS (Powers—Validity—Power to send person forward for trial).

Administration of justice—Interference with judicial process—Betting—Register of bookmaking offices—Application to Garda Superintendent for certificate of suitability—Objection—Appeal—Statute providing that objector not entitled to be heard

CONSTITUTION
Statute
Validity continued

nor to adduce evidence in opposition. *See* Administration of justice—Judicial process—Interference—Betting (*above*).

Administration of justice—Judicial power—Interference—Street and house to house collections—Opinion that proceeds of collection would benefit an unlawful organisation—Appeal—Review of opinion excluded—Whether appeal procedure constitutionally invalid—Whether unwarranted invasion of the judicial power. *See* Administration of justice—Judicial power—Interference—Street and house-to-house collection (*above*).

Administration of justice—Trial on indictment—Preliminary examination—Accused sent forward for trial by District Justice—Substitution by DPP of new counts—Whether invasion of judicial domain. *See* DIRECTOR OF PUBLIC PROSECUTIONS (Powers—Validity—Trial on indictment—Preliminary examination—DPP substituting new counts).

Administration of justice—Trial on indictment—Preliminary examination—DPP inserting additional counts—Whether invasion of judicial domain. *See* DIRECTOR OF PUBLIC PROSECUTIONS (Powers—Validity—Trial on indictment—Preliminary examination—DPP inserting additional counts).

Adoption—Statutory provision excluding widower from obtaining adoption order—Whether arbitrary discrimination. *See* Equality—Adoption—Exclusion—Widower (*above*).

Aliens—Deportation order—Whether deportation order would infringe plaintiff's constitutional rights—Effect of marriage—Validity of Aliens Act 1935 and statutory orders thereunder—Constitution of Ireland 1937, Articles 9, 40, 41, 42—Aliens Act 1935, ss. 4, 5, 12—Irish Nationality and Citizenship Act 1956, ss. 8, 16—Aliens Order 1935, reg 13—Aliens Amendment Order 1975. **Osheku v Ireland** [1987] 330, HC.

Broadcasting—Unlicensed possession and use of apparatus for wireless telegraphy—Apparatus seized—Fair procedures. *See* BROADCASTING (Radio station—Unlicensed possession and use of apparatus for wireless telegraphy).

Broadcasting—Election broadcast—Ministerial order preventing access by members of Provisional Sinn Fein—Freedom of expression. *See* Personal rights—Freedom of expression—Election broadcast—Political party (*above*).

Children– Industrial school—District Court order that child be sent to industrial school—Father consenting to said order—Father subsequently seeking return of child—Minister refusing to order child's release—Whether statutory provisions unconstitutional. *See* Education—Industrial school. (*above*).

Compulsory imposition of structures on land—Erection of electricity pylons on land—Absence of independent means of assessing compensation. *See* Property rights—Compulsory imposition of structures on land—Compensation (*above*).

Compulsory purchase powers—Bord na Mona—Power to compulsorily acquire bogland—Whether power of judicial nature—Absence of right of appeal—Whether statutory provisions invalid. *See* Property rights—Compulsory purchase powers—Bord na Mona (*above*).

Compulsory purchase powers—Land Commission—Price fixed at sum payable in Land Bonds equal in nominal value to the sum fixed. *See* Property rights—Compulsory purchase—Land Commission (*above*).

Courts—Jurisdiction—Criminal Law—Trial—Accused sent forward for trial to Dublin Circuit Court—Accused seeking trial in High Court (Central Criminal Court)—Prohibition on transfer—Whether statutory provisions prohibiting transfer repugnant to Constitution. *See* Courts—Jurisdiction—Criminal Law—Trial—Accused sent forward for trial to Dublin Circuit Court (*above*).

CONSTITUTION
Statute
Validity continued

Courts—Jurisdiction—Statute providing for the transfer of the trial of a person from the Circuit Court before which he is triable to the Dublin Circuit Court—Whether Dublin Circuit Court jurisdiction to try the case. *See* Courts—Jurisdiction—Circuit Court—Criminal jurisdiction—Transfer of trial (*above*).

Delegated legislation—Agriculture—Regulations giving effect to EC milk levy—Regulations having retrospective effect—Whether unjust—Whether unjustified attack on property rights—Whether any such infringement necessitated by membership of the European Community. *See* Property rights—Agriculture—Regulations giving effect to EC milk levy (*above*).

Delegated legislation—Broadcasting—Ministerial order preventing access by Provisional Sinn Fein candidates to radio and television to promote their electoral campaign. *See* Personal rights—Freedom of expression—Broadcasting (*above*).

Delegated legislation—District Court Rules—Criminal trial—District Court—Costs—Statutory rules of procedure prohibiting award of costs against member of Garda Siochána acting in discharge of duties as police officer—Whether unconstitutional discrimination—Equality guarantee—Whether justified on grounds of social function—Whether unjust attack on property rights—Harmonious interpretation of Constitution—Constitution of Ireland 1937, Articles 40.1 and 3—Prosecution of Offences Act 1974 s. 3—District Court Rules 1948, r 67. **Dillane v Attorney General** [1980] 167, SC.

Delegated legislation—Health services—Ministerial regulations rendering victims of road traffic accidents ineligible for free medical services—Whether exclusive law making authority of the National Parliament eroded by such delegation of power—Whether Minister acted *ultra vires*—Whether regulations unconstitutional as being discriminatory— Whether Minister acted in accordance with the principles of natural justice—Constitution of Ireland 1937, Articles 15, 40.3—Health Act 1970, ss. 45, 46, 51(1), 52(1), 53, 56, 72—Health Services Regulations 1971, Article 6(3)—Health Services (Limited Eligibility) Regulations 1979. **Cooke v Walsh** [1983] 429, HC; [1984] 208, SC.

Delegated legislation—Order—Whether such order a "law" within the meaning of Article 40 4 3 so as to allow the High Court to state a case to the Supreme Court—Whether 'one judgment' rule applied—Extradition—Order extending Part II of the 1965 Act to the USA—Detention—Challenge to the legality of the detention—Constitution of Ireland 1937, Articles 15 2 1, 29 5 2, 34 4 5, 40 4 3—Extradition Act 1965, ss. 4, 8(1)—Extradition Act 1965 (Part II) Order 1984. **State (Gilliland) v Governor of Mountjoy Prison** [1987] 278, SC.

Elections—Ballot papers—Challenge to the alphabetical listing of election candidates required by statute. *See* Dáil Éireann—Elections—Ballot papers—Alphabetical listing of candidates (*above*).

Elections—Dáil Éireann—Right to vote—Physically incapacitated citizens—Absence of facilities for postal voting. *See* Dáil Éireann—Elections—Right to vote—Physically incapacitated citizens (*above*).

Extradition—Procedure—Whether extradition arrangements safeguard personal rights of citizen—Presumption of constitutionality. *See* Personal rights—Extradition—Procedure—Statute—Validity (*above*).

Fisheries—Arrest of foreign fishing vessel—Detention order made—Vessel released upon provision of security—Whether requirement to give security amounted to a requirement to give bail—If so, whether such bail oppressive—Whether contrary to fair procedures—Major or minor offence—Constitution of Ireland 1937, Articles 38 1, 40 3—Fisheries Consolidation Act 1959, ss. 221, 222(A), 232, 235(2)(a) and (b)—Fisheries Amendment Act 1978, ss. 2(2), 5, 7, 14. **L'Henryenat v Ireland** [1984] 249, HC, SC.

CONSTITUTION
Statute
Validity continued

Gaming—Restrictions on use of slot machines—Impact of inflation—Whether constituted unjust attack on exercise of right to earn livelihood. *See* Personal Rights—Right to earn livelihood—Gaming (*above*).

Industrial and provident societies—Property rights—Shareholder—Provident society engaged in the business of banking—Legislation prohibiting such societies from accepting or holding deposits—Whether unjust attack on property rights of shareholders. *See* Property rights—Shareholder—Industrial and provident society (*above*).

Irish nationality and citizenship—Discrimination—Sexes—Male alien marrying Irish citizen—Different provisions for female aliens marrying Irish citizens—Whether discrimination. *See* Irish Nationality and citizenship—Discrimination—Sexes (*above*).

Landlord and tenant—Rent Restrictions Acts—Arbitrary definition of controlled dwellings—Failure to provide for review—Permanent alienation of right of possession—Whether unjust attack on property rights of landlords. *See* Property rights—Landlord and tenant—Rent Restrictions Acts (*above*).

Locus standi. *See* Locus standi—Challenge to validity of legislation (*above*).

National monument—Preservation order—Whether unjust attack on property rights. *See* Property Rights—National monument—Preservation order—Statute—Validity (*above*).

Offences Against the State legislation—Property rights—Minister empowered to freeze moneys in a bank account and cause them to be paid into the High Court—Whether such power amounts to confiscation of property—Whether open to plaintiff to raise questions as to the constitutionality of the 1939 legislation. *See* Property Rights—Confiscation of property—Offences Against the State legislation (*above*).

Planning and development—Appeal—Requirement of lodgment of deposit—Whether arbitrary discrimination. *See* Equality—Planning appeal—Requirement of lodgment of deposit—Whether arbitrary discrimination (*above*).

Planning and development—Planning permission—Asbestos waste—Whether injurious to health—Whether relevant to constitutionality of planning legislation—Right to bodily integrity—Constitution of Ireland 1937, Articles 40 1, 40 3—Local Government (Planning and Development) Act 1976. **Finnegan v An Bord Pleanála** [1979] 134, HC, SC.

Planning and Development—Time limits—Decision of planning authority—Two month time limit within which to challenge validity—Whether constitutional—Constitution of Ireland 1937, Article 40 3 2—Local Government (Planning and Development) Act 1963, s. 82(3A). **Brady v Donegal County Council** [1989] 282, SC.

Presumption of constitutionality. **Shannon v Attorney General** [1985] 449, HC, SC.

Presumption of constitutionality. **State (Boyle) v Governor of the Curragh Military Detention Barracks** [1980] 242, HC.

Presumption of constitutionality—Interpretation of statute. *See* Statutory interpretation—Presumption of constitutionality (*below*).

Presumption of constitutionality—Re-enactment of pre-Constitutional legislation—Whether re-enacted legislative entitled to presumption of constitutionality. **Electricity Supply Board v Gormley** [1985] 494, SC.

Presumption of constitutionality—Taxing statute. **Madigan v Attorney General** [1986] 136, HC, SC.

CONSTITUTION
Statute
Validity continued

Presumption of constitutionality—Whether legislation, by virtue of its purported amendment in 1961, entitled to the benefit of the presumption of constitutionality. **Brennan v Attorney General** [1983] 449, HC; [1984] 355, SC.

Procedure—Case stated—Whether permissible to raise constitutional issue by way of case stated from District Court—Constitution of Ireland 1937, Article 34 3 2. **Minister for Labour v Costello** [1989] 485, HC.

Procedure—Certiorari—Whether certiorari an appropriate procedure for challenging the validity of legislation—Constitution of Ireland 1937, Article 40.6.1—Broadcasting Authority Act 1960, s. 31(1)—Broadcasting Authority (Amendment) Act 1976, s. 16. **State (Lynch) v Cooney** [1982] 190, HC; [1983] 89, SC.

Procedure—Certiorari proceedings—Whether open to prosecutor, on an application for certiorari, to challenge the constitutionality of legislation—Constitution of Ireland 1937, Article 34—Street and House-to-House Collections Act 1962, s. 13(4). **State (McEldowney) v Kelleher and Attorney General** [1982] 568, HC; [1985] 10, SC.

Revenue—Administration of justice—Estimation of tax liability—Default provisions—Whether administration of justice—Whether Collector General exercising judicial function. *See* Administration of justice—Revenue Commissioners—Enforcement procedure (*above*).

Revenue—Income tax—Husband and wife—Statute with retrospective effect—Enacted in consequence of decision that portion of income tax legislation unconstitutional—Whether lawful for the State to collect arrears of tax due under the unconstitutional provisions—Finance Act 1980, s. 21—Constitution of Ireland 1937, Articles 40.1, 40.3, 41. **Muckley v Attorney General** [1986] 364, HC, SC.

Revenue—Residential property tax levied on properties over certain value—Whether unjust attack on property and family rights—Whether constituting invidious discrimination—Presumption of constitutionality in taxation matters—Locus standi—Constitution of Ireland 1937, Articles 40 1, 40 3, 41, 43—Finance Act 1983. **Madigan v Attorney General** [1986] 136, HC, SC.

Succession—Intestacy—Illegitimate child—Whether illegitimate child 'issue' of the deceased. *See* Equality—Succession rights—Illegitimate child. (*above*).

Trial of offences—Issue of facts in dispute—Court precluded from determining issue. *See* Trial of offences—Interference with judicial determination (*below*).

Trial of offences—Minor offence—Whether minor offence triable summarily—Fisheries—Unlawful possession of salmon—Summary conviction—Fine and confiscation of catch—Whether minor offence—Whether need to review the criteria laid down in the decided cases—Petty Sessions (Ireland) Act 1851, s. 22—Fisheries (Consolidation) Act 1959, ss. 182(2)(a), 182(4). **O'Sullivan v Hartnett** [1983] 79, SC.

Valuation—Agricultural land—Valuation carried out between 1852 and 1866—No revaluation ever taking place—Whether an unjust attack on property rights—Whether arbitrary and unjust discrimination— Whether legislation, by virtue of its purported amendment in 1961, entitled to the benefit of the presumption of constitutionality—Constitution of Ireland 1937, Articles 40 1, 40 3, 43—Valuation (Ireland) Act 1852, ss. 5, 11, 32, 33, 34—Local Government Act 1946, ss. 11, 12. **Brennan v Attorney General** [1983] 449, HC; [1984] 355, SC.

Statutory discretion
Minister

Transfer of prisoner from civilian to military custody—Whether imposition of punishment—Whether exercise of judicial power—Whether regime different from that pertaining

CONSTITUTION
Statutory discretion
Minister continued

in civilian prisons—Whether administration of Act affects its constitutionality—Presumption of constitutionality—Prisons Act 1972 s. 2(3), (4), (9), (10). **State (Boyle) v The Governor of the Curragh Military Detention Barracks** [1980] 242, HC.

Power

Exercise—Whether to be exercised in judicial manner—Principles of natural and constitutional justice—Registered land—Inhibition—Whether notice to affected parties required—Registration of Title Act 1964, s. 121. **State (Philpott) v Registrar of Titles** [1986] 499, HC.

Statutory interpretation
Presumption of constitutionality

Extradition—Offence committed to further overthrow by violence of the Constitution and the organs of State—Whether political offence—Whether courts could interpret legislation to further objectives of organisation aimed at overthrow of State—Extradition Act 1965, s. 50(2). **Quinn v Wren** [1985] 411, SC.

Infant—Adoption and guardianhsip—Permanent interests of infant—Infant legitimised as member of family—Constitution of Ireland 1937, Article 42 5—Guardianship of Infants Act 1964, ss. 2, 3. **In re J H (otherwise R), an Infant** [1985] 302, HC.

Retrospectivity—Legislation enacted rendering conveyance of the family home void without prior notice to the wife—Whether legislation only designed to prevent dispositions in future—Constitution of Ireland 1937, Articles 40 3 2, 43—Interpretation Act 1937, s. 21 (1)—Family Home Protection Act 1976, ss. 2, 3, 4. **Dunne v Hamilton; Hamilton v Hamilton** [1982] 290, HC.

Statutory power
Exercise

Fisheries—Application for injunction—Whether an interlocutory injunction may be granted to restrain the exercise of a statutory power presumed to be in accordance with the Constitution—Fisheries (Consolidation) Act 1959, s. 222(b)—Fisheries (Amendment) Act 1983, s. 2. **Pesca Valentia Ltd v Minister for the Environment** [1986] 68, SC.

Treaty. *See* International relations—Treaty (*above*).

Trial of offences
Fair procedures

Delay—Trial abandoned—Proposed re-trial—Whether prejudice arising—Whether interlocutory injunction to restrain said trial be granted—Constitution of Ireland 1937, Articles 38 1, 40 3. **O'Connor v DPP** [1987] 723, HC.

Interference with judicial determination

Statute—Validity—Excise offences—Issue of facts in dispute—Court precluded from determining issue—Whether interference unconstitutional—Constitution of Ireland 1937, Articles 34 3 4, 38 1, 38 2, 38 5—Finance Act 1963, ss. 34(4)(d)(i), 34(4)(d)(iii). **Curtis v Attorney General** [1986] 428, HC.

Minor offence

Bookmaker—Failure to forward returns to Collector of Customs and Excise in respect of bets—Whether obligation to make returns within a specified time—Whether failure to do so gives rise to a separate offence in respect of each individual bet—Whether offence of a criminal nature—Whether minor offence—Criteria for distinguishing a minor offence—Object of penalty—Value of penalty—Constitution of Ireland 1937, Article 38(2) and (5)—Finance Act 1926, ss. 25(2), 42, 43—Betting Act 1931, ss. 6, 15—Betting Duty (Certified Returns) Regulations 1934, regs 27, 29. **State (Rollinson) v Kelly** [1982] 249, HC; [1984] 625, SC.

CONSTITUTION
Trial of offences
Minor offence continued
Bookmaker—Infringement of betting duty regulations—Whether minor offence—
Matters to which the court is to have regard—Constitution of Ireland 1937, Article 38
2—Finance Act 1926, ss. 24, 25—Betting Duty (Certified Returns) Regulations 1934,
regs 8, 18, 23, 29. **Charlton v Ireland** [1984] 39, HC.

District Court prosecution—Claim that offence not a minor offence—Submission that
statutory pension invalid—Whether open to the defendant to rely on this plea—Whether
permissible to raise the constitutional issue by way of case stated—Constitution of
Ireland 1937, Article 34 3 2. **Minister for Labour v Costello** [1989] 485, HC.

Fisheries—Summary conviction—Fine and forfeiture of equipment—Whether offence
minor offence—Severity of punishment—Whether forfeiture primary punishment—
Constitution of Ireland 1937, Art 38—Fisheries (Consolidation) Act 1959, s. 221.
Kostan v Ireland [1978] 12, HC.

Fisheries—Unlawful possession of salmon—Summary conviction—Fine and confiscation
of catch—Whether minor offence triable summarily—Whether need to review the
criteria laid down in the decided cases—Petty Sessions (Ireland) Act 1851, s. 22—
Fisheries (Consolidation) Act 1959, ss. 182(2)(a), 182(4). **O'Sullivan v Hartnett** [1981]
469, HC; [1983] 79, SC.

Indictable offence—Consent to District Court proceedings—Application for copies of
statements of evidence of the intended witnesses refused—Injunction sought to prevent
prosecution—Whether the offence a minor offence fit to be tried summarily—Inability
of High Court to anticipate District Justice's conclusion—Offences Against the Person
Act 1861, s. 47—Criminal Justice Act 1951, s. 2—Criminal Procedure Act 1967. **Clune
v DPP** [1981] 17, HC.

Licensing offences—Licence thereupon becoming forfeit—Whether forfeiture provisions an unjust attack on property rights—Whether punishment by reason of its
severity took the offences out of the category of minor offences triable summarily—
Constitution of Ireland 1937, Articles 38.2, 40.3—Intoxicating Liquor Act 1927, ss. 28,
30(1). **State (Pheasantry Ltd) v Donnelly** [1982] 512, HC.

Location of offences—Multiplicity of offences—Whether relevant to consideration of
nature of offences—District Court Rules 1948, rr 25, 44—Social Welfare (Consolidation)
Act 1981, s. 115. **State (Wilson) v Neilan** [1987] 118, HC.

Severity of penalty—Forfeiture of gaming instrument—Whether consequence too
remote in character—Distinction between primary and secondary punishment—
Constitution of Ireland 1937, Article 38 2—Gaming and Lotteries Act 1956, ss.
4(1)(c), 47. **Cartmill v Ireland** [1988] 430, HC.

Right to trial in due course of law
Interpretation—Whether includes right to compel Director of Public Prosecutions to
bring him to trial in the Republic—Extra-territorial offence—Irish citizen in custody
in Northern Ireland—Prosecutor seeking to be delivered in the custody of the
Gardai—Director of Public Prosecutions indicating that proceedings ould not be
instituted. **State (McCormack) v Curran** [1987] 225, HC, SC.

Right to trial with reasonable expedition
Delay—Whether such as to prejudice accused's right to fair trial—Constitution of
Ireland 1937, Article 38 1. **State (O'Connell) v Fawsitt** [1986] 639, HC, SC.

Special Criminal Court
Members appointed and removable at will by Government—Whether court independent.
See Courts—Judicial independence—Criminal law—Trial—Special Criminal Court
(*above*).

CONSTITUTIONAL JUSTICE. *See* NATURAL AND CONSTITUTIONAL JUSTICE.

CONSTITUTIONAL RIGHTS
Breach
Damages. See DAMAGES (Constitutional right—Breach)

Generally. See CONSTITUTION (Personal rights—Breach).

Extradition cases. *See* EXTRADITION (Constitutional rights).

Interference
Damages. See DAMAGES (Constitutional rights—Interference).

CONSTITUTIONAL TORT
Breach of constitutional obligations of the State
Invalid inquiry
Garda Síochána disciplinary investigation—Whether plaintiff entitled to costs and
expenses of his representation and attendance at the inquiry—Appropriate defendant—
Constitution of Ireland 1937—Garda Síochána (Discipline) Regulations 1971, reg 8.
McHugh v Commissioner of An Garda Síochána [1987] 181, SC.

CONSTRUCTION
Building contract. *See* BUILDING CONTRACT (Interpretation).

Constitution. *See* CONSTITUTION (Interpretation).

Contract. *See* CONTRACT (Construction).

Employment contract. *See* EMPLOYMENT (Contract—Construction).

Statute. *See* STATUTORY INTERPRETATION.

Will. *See* WILL (Construction).

CONSTRUCTIVE DISMISSAL
Unfair dismissal. *See* EMPLOYMENT (Unfair dismissal—Constructive dismissal).

CONSTRUCTIVE TRUST. *See* TRUST (Constructive trust).

CONSULTATIVE CASE STATED
Circuit Court
Jurisdiction
Consultative case stated from Circuit Court to Supreme Court—Evidence not
completed in Circuit Court—Whether case stated lies in those circumstances. **Doyle v
Hearne** [1988] 318, SC.

CONSUMER PROTECTION
Advertising
Building societies
Meaning of 'annual percentage rate of charge'—Whether cost of house insurance and
mortgage protection insurance included—Consumer Information Act 1978, ss. 11,
12—Consumer Information (Consumer Credit) Order 1987, Art 3. **Director of
Consumer Affairs v Irish Permanent Building Society** [1990] 743, HC.

Defective premises
Liability in tort. See NEGLIGENCE (Defective premises).

Defective products
Dealing as consumer. See SALE OF GOODS (Dealing as consumer).

Liability in tort. See NEGLIGENCE (Defective products).

CONSUMER PROTECTION *continued*
Investigative procedure
Powers conferred on 'authorised officers'
Authorisation required to indicate the matters in respect of which the officer may act—Whether provision satisfied by a recital in the authorisation of the powers which he is authorised to exercise—Consumer Information Act 1978, s. 16. **Director of Consumer Affairs v Joe Walsh Tours Ltd** [1985] 273, SC.

Offence
False statements
False statements as to the provision of services, accommodation or facilities—Whether defendant knew statements to be false—Whether defendant reckless—Penalty—Whether court should provide for the payment of compensation—Consumer Information Act 1978, ss. 6, 17(3)(a), 22(2). **Director of Consumer Affairs v Sunshine Holidays Ltd** [1984] 551, DC.

CONSUMER SUBSIDIES
Bread
Agreement to provide subsidy on retail price of bread
Whether retailer in breach of terms—Whether subsidy may be recouped. **Kylemore Bakery Ltd v Minister for Trade, Commerce and Tourism** [1986] 529, HC.

CONTEMPT OF COURT
Civil contempt
Committal
Jurisdiction of court—Deliberate disobedience of court order—Occupation of employer's premises—High Court order restraining defendants—Deliberate disobedience—No serious effort to purge contempt—Nature of Court's jurisdiction—Whether defendants be committed to prison—Prohibition of Forcible Entry and Occupation Act, 1971. **Ross Co Ltd v Swan** [1981] 416, HC.

Criminal contempt
Criminal contempt in the face of the court
Whether triable summarily—Necessity to protect proper administration of justice—Whether contempt trial necessary where alleged contempt involved witness in civil action who proceeded to testify in the action. **In re Kelly and Deighan** [1984] 424, HC, SC.

Ex parte application by accused
Inadvertent comment—Immediate steps taken to avoid any possible prejudice—Taoiseach receiving letter from accused—Taoiseach authorising publication in the national press—Publication of photograph of accused—Whether contempt of court. **In re MacArthur** [1983] 355, HC.

Newspaper publication
Article stating that DPP intended to bring charges against a local authority councillor—Political party to which councillor belonged referred to—Name of councillor not given—Whether publication could tend to prejudice the trial of proceedings that were pending. **State (DPP) v Independent Newspapers Ltd** [1985] 183, HC.

CONTINUOUS EMPLOYMENT *See* EMPLOYMENT (Continuity of employment).

CONTRACEPTIVES
Unlawful sale
Authority of Gardai to enter premises. See CRIMINAL LAW (Health offences—Family planning).

CONTRACT
Agency
Auctioneer

Fees—Auction cancelled—Vendor subsequently selling premises by private treaty—
Whether auctioneer entitled to fees. **Daniel Morrissey and Sons Ltd v Nalty** [1976–7]
269, HC.

Breach
Consumer subsidy agreement

Agreement to provide subsidy on retail price of bread—Whether retailer in breach of
terms—Whether subsidy may be recouped. **Kylemore Bakery v Minister for Trade,
Commerce & Tourism** [1986] 529, HC.

Building contract. See BUILDING CONTRACT (Breach).

Damages

Assessment. *See* DAMAGES (Breach of contract).

Damages in lieu of specific performance—Assessment. *See* DAMAGES (Breach of
contract—Sale of land—Damages in lieu of specific performance).

Employment contract. See EMPLOYMENT (Contract—Breach).

Inducement. See TORT (Inducement of breach of contract).

Quasi-contract

Damages—Assessment. *See* QUASI-CONTRACT.

Sale of goods

Claim for damages. *See* SALE OF GOODS (Contract—Breach).

Sale of land. See SALE OF GOODS (Contract—Breach).

Standard form agreement

Supply of electricity—Contract of adhesion—Disconnection of supply to customer—
Whether customer in breach of agreement—Whether supply may be disconnected
without notice—Whether court order required to disconnect supply. Electricity (Supply)
Act 1927, s 99. **McCord v Electricity Supply board** [1980] 153, SC.

Statutory duty

Damages—Measure. *See* Statutory duty (*below*).

Building contract. *See* BUILDING CONTRACT.

Collateral contract
Inducement of breach

Whether contract in existence—Whether injunction lies—Balance of convenience—
Relevance of foreign arbitration clause. **Mitchelstown Co-operative Society Ltd v
Societè des Produits Nestle SA** [1989] 582, SC.

Condition
Sale of land. See SALE OF LAND (Contract—Condition).

Waiver

Condition inserted exclusively for benefit of one party—Whether capable of waiver by
that party. **Sepia Ltd v M & P Hanlon Ltd** [1979] 11, HC.

Specified time for compliance with condition—Unilateral waiver of condition after
time for compliance expired—Whether waiver effective—Whether term to be implied
for discharge of contract—Whether mutual benefit of parties—Whether capable of
unilateral waiver—Contract for sale of land. **Maloney v Elf Investments** [1979] 253,
HC.

Conflict of laws. *See* Proper law (*below*).

CONTRACT *continued*
Construction
Building contract. See BUILDING CONTRACT (Interpretation).

Employer's liability insurance
Use of word "or"—Whether conjunctive or disjunctive—Whether obervance of claims procedure a condition precedent to the liability of the underwriters. **Gaelcrann Teo v Payne** [1985] 109, HC.

Employment contract. See EMPLOYMENT (Contract—Construction).

Insurance contract. See INSURANCE (Contract—Interpretation).

Letting of land for grazing
Public auction—Letting made on the eleven months system—Letting commenced on 23rd March 1979—Price agreed—No written or oral term as to date of termination. **Collins v O'Brien** [1981] 328, HC.

Damages for breach. See DAMAGES (Breach of contract).

Debt
Discharge
Cheque—Cheque drawn by creditor in favour of debtor and endorsed back to creditor—Cheque referred to drawer—Whether payment by cheque conditional or unconditional discharge of existing debt—Intention of parties. **Private Motorists Provident Society Ltd v Moore** [1988] 526, HC.

Deposit
Sale of land. See SALE OF LAND (Deposit).

Employment. See EMPLOYMENT (Contract).

Enforcement
Certainty of terms
Agreement for the supply of milk—Sale of supplier's creameries—Undertaking on contract of sale as to no diminution on the supply—Dispute over requirements and prices—Whether relevant clause legally enforceable—Whether void for uncertainty—Whether trust of contractual rights created. **Cadbury Ireland Ltd v Kerry Cooperative Creameries Ltd** [1982] 77, HC.

Husband and wife
Separation agreement—Term providing that parties would obtain divorce a vinculo—Parties domiciled in Ireland—Application to have agreement made a rule of court—Whether contrary to public policy—Family Law (Maintenance of Spouses and Children) Act 1976, ss 8, 9. **Dalton v Dalton** [1982] 418, HC.

Sale of liquor licence
Failure to complete—Whether licence unattached to premises is alienable—Whether specific performance of such agreement can be ordered—Whether agreement in reality payment for consent to the extinguishing of the licence. **Macklin v Greacen & Co** [1981] 315, HC; [1982] 182, SC.

Specific performance. See Specific performance (*below*).

Exclusive supply contract
Breach
Purchaser subsequently entering into similar contract with another supplier—Whether inducement of breach of contract—Position of person who innocently enters into contract without knowledge of prior inconsistent contract—Whether under duty to cease supplies. **Flogas Ltd v Ergas Ltd** [1985] 221, HC.

CONTRACT *continued*
Exemption clause
Building contract
Further clause that purchaser not deprived of his common law rights—Claim for damages for remedying defects and for diminution in value—Whether caught by exclusion clause. **Johnson v Longleat Properties (Dublin) Ltd** [1976–7] 93, HC.

Conditions of trade
Cold storage facilities—Failure to produce goods on demand—Whether reasonable notice given of the conditions of trade—Whether parties competent to include exemption clause—Quantification of damages. **Western Meats Ltd v National Ice and Cold Storage Co Ltd** [1982] 99, HC.

Sale of goods
Distributorship agreement—Claim for damages for breach of agreement—Negotiations between Department of Industry and Commerce, UK manufacturers and Irish Car Assemblers—Document drawn up—Character of such document—Whether new agreement reached arising out of these tripartite negotiations—Whether unfairness of original agreement a matter with which the court is concerned—Whether claim defeated by exclusion clause. **British Leyland Exports Ltd v Brittain Group Sales Ltd** [1982] 359, HC.

Existence
Whether concluded enforceable agreement in existence
Subject to contract—Distinction between conditions precedent and subsequent. **Dorene Ltd v Suedes Ireland Ltd** [1982] 126, HC.

Formation
Consent
Settlement of action—Landlord and tenant—Consent order—Settlement not in writing—Consent not drawn up—Denial by plaintiffs that action settled—Validity of order—Authority of legal advisers to settle. **Barrett v W J Lenehan & Co Ltd** [1981] 206, HC.

Intention to establish legal relations. See Intention to establish legal relations (*below*).

Mistake
Settlement of action—Plaintiff entering into settlement agreement with second defendant without adverting to the question of the first defendant's costs—Whether unilateral mistake rendering agreement a nullity. **Reen v Bank of Ireland Finance Ltd** [1983] 507, HC.

Sale of land. See SALE OF LAND (Contract—Formation).

Settlement of action
Whether agreement to settle proceedings reached. **Tattan v Cadogan** [1979] 61, HC.

"Subject to contract"
Meaning. *See* SALE OF LAND (Contract—Formation—"Subject to contract").

Frustration
Employment
Appointment terminable for stated or other reasons—Whether circumstances required to terminate appointment had arisen—Whether contract frustrated. **Browne v Mulligan: In re Shiel** [1976–7] 327, SC.

Licence agreement
Whether performance rendered impossible—Whether contract discharged in accordance with the provisions thereof—Whether fraudulent misrepresentation. **Neville and Sons Ltd v Guardian Builders Ltd** [1990] 601, HC.

Hire-purchase agreement
Vendor in breach of contract
Action for damages against vendor and finance company—No privity of contract

CONTRACT

Hire-purchase agreement

Vendor in breach of contract continued

between plaintiff and finance company—Whether action against finance company be dismissed. **Halpin v Rothwell** [1984] 613.

Illegality

Contract of employment tainted with illegality

Whether illegal aspect severable—Consequence of illegality—Whether contract void or unenforceable—Unfair Dismissals Act 1977, ss 1, 6. **Lewis v Squash Ireland Ltd** [1983] 363, EAT.

Sale of goods

Whether contract void for illegality—Onus of proof—Sale of Goods Act 1893, s 51. **Whitecross Potatoes (International) Ltd v Coyle** [1978] 31, HC.

Sale of land

Auction—Agent for vendor bidding—Whether contract rendered illegal—Sale of Land by Auction Act 1867, s 3. **Airlie v Fallon** [1976–7] 1, HC.

Implied term

Agency

Sole selling agent—Whether term to be implied—Intention of parties. **G F Galvin (Estates) Ltd v Hedigan** [1985] 295, HC.

Necessity

Sale of goods—Price—Letters of credit—Time within which credits to be opened—Whether parties ad idem—Whether statutory requirements complied with—Whether implied term necessary to give business efficacy to agreement—Sale of Goods Act 1893, s 4. **Tradax (Ireland) Ltd v Irish Grain Board Ltd** [1984] 471, SC.

Impossibility of performance. *See* Frustration (*above*).

Inducement of breach. *See* TORT (Inducement of breach of contract).

Insurance. *See* INSURANCE (Contract).

Intention to establish legal relations

Collective agreement

Employees dismissed for redundancy—Employees seeking declaration that the company gave them a guarantee that they would not be made redundant before a certain date—Company denying that such guarantee contemplated legal relations—Onus of proof. **O'Rourke v Talbot** (Ireland) Ltd [1984] 587, HC.

Interpretation. *See* Construction (*above*).

Licence or tenancy

Solus agreement. See Solus agreement (*below*).

Mistake

Sale of land

Deposit paid—Purchaser seeking to withdraw—Whether vendor entitled to forfeit deposit—Whether deposit paid under mistake of fact. **Siebel and Seum v Kent** [1976–7] 127, HC.

Settlement of action

Mutual mistake—Document authenticated by signatures of counsel—Lack of Consensus ad idem—Whether compromise enforceable—Whether agreement a nullity. **Mespil Ltd v Capaldi** [1986] 373, SC.

Plaintiff entering into settlement agreement with second defendant without adverting to the question of the first defendant's costs—Whether unilateral mistake rendering agreement a nullity. **Reen v Bank of Ireland Finance Ltd** [1983] 507, HC.

CONTRACT
Mistake
Settlement of action continued

Supply of seed potatoes
Both parties contracting on assumption which proved false—Crop failure—Whether contract rendered void—Whether implied obligations remaining. **Western Potato Co-Operative Ltd v Durnan** [1985] 5, CC.

Nature of contract
Whether contract of service or partnership
Fishermen—Captain of vessel engaging crew at commencement of each separate voyage—Remuneration based on custom and agreement—Whether arrangement in reality partnership—Revenue—Income tax—Employer. **DPP v McLoughlin** [1986] 493, HC.

Privity
Agency
Renewal—Option to renew agreement—Agent claiming privity with party to separate agreement—Whether separate agreements to be considered as single arrangement—Whether agency terminated on reasonable notice. **Henley Forklift (Ireland) Ltd v Lansing Bagnall & Co Ltd** [1979] 257, SC.

Hire-purchase agreement
Vendor in breach of contract—Action for damages against vendor and finance company—No privity of contract between plaintiff and finance company—Whether action against finance company be dismissed. **Halpin v Rothwell** [1984] 613, HC.

Proper law
Loan agreement
Terms of contract stating that disputes be settled in accordance with Irish law—Contract having no connection with Ireland—Whether service out of jurisdiction permissible—RSC 1986, O 11, r 1(e)(iii), O 12 r 26. **Kutchera v Buckingham International Holdings Ltd** [1988] 1, HC; [1988] 501, SC.

Mortgage of land
Judgment—Enforcement—Currency—Disparity arising between value of money in Northern Ireland and the value of money in Ireland—Whether amount should be payable in Irish pounds or in sterling. **Northern Bank Ltd v Edwards** [1986] 167, SC.

Quantum meruit. *see* QUASI-CONTRACT (Restitution).

Quasi-contract
Damages
Assessment. *See* QUASI-CONTRACT (Damages—Assessment).

Restitution
Quantum meruit. *see* QUASI-CONTRACT (Restitution).

Repudiation
Sale of land. See SALE OF LAND (Contract—Repudiation).

Rescission
Illegality
Sale of land—Auction—Licensed premises—Whether representation as to turnover—Agent for vendor bidding—Whether contract rendered illegal—Sale of Land by Auction Act 1867, s 3. **Airlie v Fallon** [1976–71] 1, HC.

Sale of land. See SALE OF LAND (Contract—Rescission).

Restitution
Quantum meruit
Quasi-contract. *See* QUASI-CONTRACT (Restitution).

Restraint of trade. *See* Restraint of Trade.

CONTRACT *continued*
Retention of title clause
Sale of goods. *See* SALE OF LAND (Retention of title clause).

Sale of goods. *See* SALE OF GOODS (Contract).

Sale of land. *See* SALE OF LAND (Contract).

Service. *See* EMPLOYMENT (Contract).

Severance
Whether general character of contract would be altered
Intention of the parties. **Taylor v Smyth** [1990] 377, HC.

Solus agreement
Licence or lease
Agreement to allow occupation and user of premises—Termination of agreement—Agreement held to constitute tenancy—Continued occupation and user—Whether constituted licence or tenancy—Intention of parties. **Irish Shell & BP Ltd v John Costello Ltd** [1985] 554, SC.

Specific performance
Building contract
Whether specific performance lies. *See* BUILDING CONTRACT (Specific performance).

Damages in lieu
Assessment. *See* DAMAGES (Breach of contract—Sale of land—Damages in lieu of specific performance).

Interest
Contract to build and sell a house—Completion—Interest—Dispute as to whether contract completed on certain dates—Basis on which interest to be awarded—Contract price placed on deposit—Interest gained on deposit. **Treacy v Dwyer Nolan Developments Ltd** [1979] 163, HC.

Sale of land. See SALE OF LAND (Specific performance).

Sale of licensed premises
Memorandum containing no express terms as to licence—Whether enforceable agreement that existing licence was to pass with premises—Whether vendor lacked capacity to enter into such agreement—Laches—Whether decree of specific performance be granted—Statute of Frauds 1695. **White v McCooey** [1976–7] 72, HC.

Sale of liquor licence
Whether contract enforceable—Whether licence unattached to premises is alienable—Whether agreement in reality payment for consent to the extinguishing of the licence. **Macklin v Greacen & Co** [1981] 315, HC; [1982] 182, SC.

Standard form agreement
Contract of adhesion
Supply of electricity—Disconnection of supply to customer—Whether customer in breach of agreement. *See* Breach—Standard form agreement (*above*).

Statutory duty
Substitution by agreement of parties for statutory obligations
Estoppel—Party to agreement estopped for insisting on enforcement of statutory obligations—Statute providing for ferry service—Party providing facilities—Facilities not used—Breach of contract—Measure of damages. **Waterford Harbour Commrs v British Railways** [1979] 296, HC, SC.

Termination
Employment
Dismissal. *See* EMPLOYMENT (Dismissal).

CONTRACT *continued*
Terms
Ambiguity
Arbitration—Foreign award—Agreement to arbitrate—Intention of parties. **Cremer GmbH & Co v Co-operative Molasses Traders Ltd** [1985] 564, HC, SC.

Bank
Guarantee—Company debts guaranteed by majority shareholder and managing director—Change of ownership and management and variation of the company's banking arrangements. Whether guarantor discharged from his obligations—Terms of guarantee—Whether rules in Clayton's case applicable—Whether bank negligent. **MacEnroe v Allied Irish Banks Ltd** [1980] 171, SC.

Enforcement. See Enforcement (*above*).

Negative term
Breach—Shareholders agreement—Plaintiff seeking compliance with negative term—Application for injunction to restrain the granting of a service agreement. **TMG Group Ltd v Al Babtain Holding and Construction Co Ltd** [1982] 349, HC.

Validity
Landlord and tenant—Rent review clause restricting application of statutory provisions. *See* LANDLORD AND TENANT (Rent review clause—Validity).

Waiver. See Condition—Waiver (*above*).

Sale of land. *See* SALE OF LAND (Contract—Terms—Waiver).

Trust of contractual rights
Agreement for the supply of milk
Sale of supplier's creameries—Undertaking on contract of sale as to no diminution on the supply—No collateral agreement between purchaser and new owner—Whether new owner under any obligation to supply a specified quantity of milk—Whether relevant clause legally enforceable—Whether trust of contractual rights created. **Cadbury Ireland Ltd v Kerry Cooperative Creameries Ltd** [1982] 77, HC.

Uberrima fides
Disclosure of material facts. See INSURANCE (Contract—Uberrima fides).

Waiver of terms
Condition. See Condition—Waiver (*above*).

Sale of land. See SALE OF LAND (Contract—Terms—Waiver).

CONTRIBUTORY NEGLIGENCE. *See* NEGLIGENCE (Contribution).
Damages. *See* DAMAGES (Contributory negligence).

CONTROLLED DRUG
Possession. *See* CRIMINAL LAW (Misuse of drugs).

CONTROLLED DWELLING
Rent Restrictions Acts. *See* LANDLORD AND TENANT (Rent Restrictions Acts—Controlled dwelling).

CONVERSION
Damages. *See* COPYRIGHT (Infringement—Damages—Measure of damages—Whether plaintiffs entitled to damages for conversion in addition to damages for infringement).

CONVEYANCE
Negligence
Solicitor. See SOLICITOR (Negligence—Sale of land).

CONVEYANCE *continued*
Family home. *See* SALE OF LAND (Family home).

Purchasers protection clause
Advisability. See SALE OF LAND (Contract—Purchasers protection clause).

Requisitions on title
Planning permission
No special condition relating to planning permission—Standard form warranty—Purchaser put an enquiry as to unauthorised use—Whether purchaser entitled to raise the matter by way of requisition—Whether certificate of discharge of capital acquisitions tax required to be furnished. **Meagher v Blount** [1984] 671, CC.

"Subject to contract". *See* SALE OF LAND (Contract—Formation—"Subject to contract").

Waiver
Terms. See SALE OF LAND (Contract—Terms—Waiver).

CONVICTED PRISONER *See* PRISONS (Prisoner).

CONVICTION See CRIMINAL LAW (Conviction).
Appeal. *See* CRIMINAL LAW (Appeal—Conviction).

Application to quash. *See* CERTIORARI (Conviction).

CO-OPERATIVES
Farming co-operatives
Application of EC competition rules. See AGRICULTURE (Co-operatives—Competition).

COPYRIGHT
Infringement
Compilation
Reliance on copyright owner's compilation—Unfair benefit—Compensation—Whether for breach of copyright or unjust enrichment. **Allied Discount Card Ltd v Bord Fáilte Éireann** [1990] 811, HC.

Damages
Assessment—Measure of damages—Whether plaintiffs entitled to damages for conversion in addition to damages for infringement—Whether award of exemplary damages permitted—Measure of damages for conversion—Claim for interest—Copyright Act 1963, ss 22, 24. **Allibert s. A v O'Connor** [1982] 40, HC.

Diffusion service
Transmission of foreign TV broadcasts containing musical works of foreign authors—Whether infringement of copyright—Whether broadcasts to be treated as being first made within the State—Copyright Act 1963, ss 7, 8, 10, 19, 21, 43, 52—Copyright (Foreign Countries) Order 1978, Articles 2, 3—Copyright (Foreign Countries) (No 2) Order 1978, Articles 2, 3. **Performing Rights Society Ltd v Marlin Communal Aerials Ltd** [1982] 269, SC.

Registered design
Sportswear—Similar designs—Whether obvious imitation of registered design—Application for interlocutory relief—Proposed counterclaim for rectification of register on grounds of prior publication—Whether prior publication was in circumstances making it contrary to good faith to republish—Balance of convenience—Industrial and Commercial Property (Protection) Act 1927, ss 72, 75. **Three Stripe International v Charles O'Neill & Co Ltd** [1989] 124, HC.

TV and radio programme schedules
Whether a compilation and a literary work in which copyright subsisted—Copyright Act 1963, ss 2(1), 8(1). **Radio Telefís Éireann v Magill TV Guide Ltd** [1990] 534, HC.

COPYRIGHT *continued*
Musical works. *See* Infringement—Diffusion service (*above*).

Passing off. *See* PASSING OFF.

CORONER
Inquest
Verdict
Suicide—Whether permissible. *See* INQUEST (Verdict).

Jurisdiction
Inquest
Adjournment. *See* INQUEST (Adjournment).

CORPORATION TAX *See* REVENUE (Corporation tax).

CORRESPONDING OFFENCE *See* EXTRADITION (Corresponding offence).

COSTS
Criminal case
Legal aid. See CRIMINAL LAW (Legal aid).

Statutory prohibition
District Court—Rules of procedure prohibiting award of costs against member of Garda Síochána acting in discharge of his duties as police officer—Whether unconstitutional discrimination. *See* CRIMINAL LAW (Costs—District Court proceedings).

Interest
Award of costs
Dispute as to the period in relation to which the interest thereon should be calculated—Whether interest payable from date of High Court order or from when costs were taxed—Application for directions—Regularity of procedure—Whether application could be initiated by a motion on notice. **Lambert v Lambert** [1987] 390, HC.

Constitutional issue
Defendant being unsuccessful in High Court but succeeding in Supreme Court on appeal—Supreme Court awarding costs against Attorney General—Whether interest should run only from date of taxation of costs—Debtors (Ireland) Act 1840, s. 27—RSC O 42 r 15. **Cooke v Walsh** [1989] 322, SC.

Indemnity
No legal liability to pay interest on sums due—Whether entitled to claim indemnity. **Attorney General (ex rel McGarry) v Sligo Co Council** (No 2) [1989] 785, SC.

Judicial review
Circuit Court order made in excess of jurisdiction
Order to extend time for appeal against decision of Employment Appeals Tribunal—Whether order for costs as against Circuit Court judge valid—Whether Attorney General liable to indemnity in respect of costs. **McIlwraith v Fawsitt** [1990] 1, SC.

Legal aid. *See* LEGAL AID.

Lien. *See* SOLICITOR (Lien).

Relator action
Locus standi of relator
Whether relator had standing as artificial person—Obligation to uphold constitutional rights. **Attorney General (ex rel SPUC) v Open Door Counselling** [1987] 477, HC.

Security for costs
Application
Claim for damages for personal injuries—Plaintiff residing outside the jurisdiction—Plaintiff unable to comply with order for security—Factors to be taken into consideration in exercising discretion. **Collins v Doyle** [1982] 495, HC.

COSTS
Security for costs *continued*
Company
Limited company—Corporate plaintiff's action dismissed with costs—Appeal to Supreme Court—Plaintiff insolvent—Defendant seeking security for costs—Whether order discretionary—Constitution of Ireland 1937, Article 34.4.3—Companies Act 1963, s. 390. s. **E E Co Ltd v Public Lighting Services Ltd** [1987] 255, SC.

Limited company instituting proceedings—If unsuccessful company unable to meet defendant's costs—Whether order of security be made—Companies Act 1963, s. 390. **Jack O'Toole Ltd v MacEoin Kelly Associates** [1987] 269, SC.

Liquidation—Limited liability company—Payment made by insolvent company— Action by liquidator—Fraudulent preference alleged—Application for security for costs—Principles to be applied—Companies Act 1963, ss 281, 285, 286, 290. **Comhlucht Paipear Riomhaireachta Teo v Udaras na Gaeltachta** [1990] 266, SC.

Liquidation—Liquidator instituting proceedings—Defendant seeking security for costs—Liquidator consenting to an order—Liquidator subsequently seeking to have consent order set aside—Whether consent order be set aside. **Irish Commercial Society Ltd v Plunkett** [1986] 624, HC; [1987] 504, SC.

Liquidation—Liquidator seeking to aggregate the assets of various companies—One company applying for security for costs—Conduct of person in actual control— Whether to be taken into account—Whether prima facie evidence of fraudulent preference—Companies Act 1963, s. 390. **Irish Commercial Society Ltd (In liquidation) v Plunkett** [1989] 461, HC.

Solicitor's lien. *See* SOLICITOR (Lien).

Statutory prohibition
District Court proceedings
Criminal trial—Rules of procedure prohibiting award of costs against member of Garda Síochána acting in discharge of his duties as police officer—Whether unconstitutional discrimination. *See* CRIMINAL LAW (Costs—District Court proceedings).

Taxation
Counsel's fees
Appeal—Several actions—Whether regard should be had to the fact that same solicitor acting in all cases—Scale fee allowed in one case and nominal fees in the others— Whether taxing master erred in principle—RSC, O 99, r 37. **Ormond (An infant) v Ireland** [1988] 490, HC.

Review. *See* Taxation—Review—Counsel's fees (*below*).

Legal costs accountant
Company—Winding up—Costs properly incurred in winding up—Whether fees of legal costs accountant constitute same—Companies Act 1963, s. 281. **In re Castle Brand Ltd** [1990] 97, HC.

Whether legal costs accountant right of audience before taxing master. **Magauran v Dargan** [1983] 7, HC.

Review
Counsel's fees—Brief fees marked by counsel and agreed to by instructing solicitor— Disbursement disallowed—Whether taxing master erred in principle. **State (Gallagher Shatter & Co) v de Valera** [1987] 555, HC.

Counsel's fees—Solicitors' disbursements for counsel's fees—Principles to be applied— Discretion of taxing master—RSC 1962, O 31 rr 12, 24, O 32 r 12, O 52 r 17(5), O 99 rr 11(2), 37(10), 38. **Irish Trust Bank Ltd v Central Bank of Ireland** [1976–7] 50, HC.

COSTS
Taxation
Review continued

Counsel's fees—Standard applicable by taxing master—Whether solicitor acted reasonably and prudently in agreeing to the fees marked—RSC 1962, O 99, r. 38. **Kelly v Breen** [1978] 63, HC.

Counsel's fees—Whether taxing master entitled to substitute his own view as to the adequacy of fees—Principles to be applied—RSC 1986, O 99 r 38. **Crotty v An Taoiseach** [1990] 617, HC.

Town agent's charges—Whether taxing master entitled to disallow claim—Whether special item—Whether claimant precluded from raising on appeal point not made before taxing master—RSC 1962, O 99 rr 13(2), 38(3). **O'Sullivan v Hughes** [1986] 555, HC.

Witnesses' expenses—Appeal from decision of taxing master to disallow or reduce fees or expenses of professional witnesses—Principles to be observed by taxing master—RSC 1962, O 61 r 12, O 99 r 37 (8). **Crown Chemicals Co (Ireland) Ltd v Cork Co Council** [1984] 555, HC.

Solicitor and client bill paid by client

Application to taxing master to tax under RSC O 99 r 15(e)—Appeal—Jurisdiction to tax in absence of a court order—Attorneys and Solicitors (Ireland) Act 1849, ss 2, 6—RSC 1962, O 99 r 15(e). **State (Gallagher Shatter & Co) v de Valera** [1986] 3, SC.

Solicitor's instruction fee

Family law action—Solicitor choosing not to instruct counsel—Whether appropriate to increase fee. **H P v W P** [1985] 527, HC.

Taxing master

Whether legal costs accountant right of audience before taxing master—Whether taxing master exercising a judicial function—Nature of documents—Whether duplication of charge—Solicitors Act 1954, s. 58. **Magauran v Dargan** [1983] 7, HC.

Town agent's charges

Review. *See* Taxation—Review—Town agent's charges (*above*).

Witnesses' expenses

Review. *See* Taxation—Review—Witnesses' expenses (*above*).

Winding up
Costs properly incurred in winding up

Whether fees of legal costs accountant constitute same—Companies Act 1963, s. 281. **In re Castle Brand Ltd** [1990] 97, HC.

COUNSEL
Fees
Taxation of costs. See COSTS (Taxation—Counsel's fees).

Generally. *See* BARRISTER.

COURIER SERVICE
Conveying of letters
Injunction to restrain

Whether defendant's trading in breach of post office monopoly. *See* POST OFFICE (Monopoly).

COURT OF CRIMINAL APPEAL
Jurisdiction
Appeal against conviction

Whether Court of Criminal Appeal has jurisdiction to substitute its own subjective

COURT OF CRIMINAL APPEAL
Jurisdiction
Appeal against conviction continued
view of evidence for the verdict of a jury—Courts of Justice Act 1924, ss 30, 34—Courts (Supplemental Provisions) Act 1961, s. 12. **People (DPP) v Egan** [1990] 780, SC.

Extension of time
Leave to appeal—Application for enlargement of time within which leave to appeal against conviction could be brought—Criteria to be considered—Whether documents served out of time irregular or void—RSC O 86, rr 5, 8, 40. **People (DPP) v Kelly** [1982] 1, SC.

COURTS
Abuse of process. *See* ABUSE OF PROCESS.

Access to court, right of. *See* CONSTITUTION (Personal rights—Access to court).

Administration of justice
Constitution. See CONSTITUTION (Courts—Administration of justice).

Justice to be administered in public
Circumstances which justify hearing other than in public—Statutory provision and denial of justice—Whether circumstances existed on a s. 205 application. **In re R Ltd** [1989] 757.

Central Criminal Court. *See* CENTRAL CRIMINAL COURT.

Circuit Court. *See* CIRCUIT COURT.

Contempt. *See* CONTEMPT OF COURT.

Court of Criminal Appeal. *See* COURT OF CRIMINAL APPEAL.

District Court. *See* DISTRICT COURT.

High Court. *See* HIGH COURT.

Irish language
Use in court. See CONSTITUTION (National language—Use in court).

Judge. *See* JUDGE.

Judgment. *See* JUDGMENT.

Judicial independence. *See* CONSTITUTION (Courts—Judicial independence).

Judicial review. *See* JUDICIAL REVIEW.

Jurisdiction
Constitution. See CONSTITUTION (Courts—Jurisdiction).

Generally. See under individual courts.

Labour Court. *See* LABOUR COURT.

Special Criminal Court. *See* SPECIAL CRIMINAL COURT.

Supreme Court. *See* SUPREME COURT.

Wardship jurisdiction. *See* WARD OF COURT.

COVENANT
Exclusive trading covenant. *See* RESTRAINT OF TRADE (Contract—Lease—Exclusive trading covenant).

Lease. *See* LANDLORD AND TENANT (Covenant).

Breach. See LANDLORD AND TENANT (Breach of covenant).

COVENANT *continued*
Restrictive covenant
  Contract. See RESTRAINT OF TRADE (Contract—Sale of business—Restrictive covenant).

  Lease. See LANDLORD AND TENANT (Covenant—Restriction as to user).

CREDIT UNION
Amendment to rules
  Function and jurisdiction of Registrar of Friendly Societies
    Registrar refusing to register amendment. *See* INDUSTRIAL AND PROVIDENT SOCIETY
    (Credit union—Amendment to rules).

CRIME PREVENTION
Preventative detention
  Habitual criminals
    Lengthy sentence imposed—Whether amounting to preventative detention—Whether
    attempt to reform by prevention appropriate basis for sentence—Prevention of Crime
    Act 1908, s. 10. **People (DPP) v Carmody** [1988] 370, CCA.

CRIMINAL INJURIES *See* Malicious Injuries.

CRIMINAL INVESTIGATION
Forcible entry of accused's home
  Constitutional right to inviolability of dwelling.
    Search warrant—Invalidity—Evidence—Admissibility. **People (DPP) v Kenny** [1990]
    569, SC.

  Search warrant. *See* CRIMINAL LAW (Search warrant).

Surveillance
  Overt surveillance
    Manner and purpose—Whether amounts to continuing detention—Whether amounts
    to unlawful harassment—Constitution of Ireland 1937, Article 40 4—Conspiracy and
    Protection of Property Act 1875—Offences Against the State Act 1939, s. 30. **Kane v
    Governor of Mountjoy Prison** [1988] 724, HC, SC.

CRIMINAL LAW
Accused
  Generally. See ACCUSED.

  Admission of responsibility
    Admissibility in evidence. *See* Evidence—Admission (*below*).

  Arrest and detention
    Legality. *See* ARREST (Legality).

  Right of access to solicitor
    Whether arises as a constitutional right—Constitution of Ireland 1937, Article 40 3—
    Criminal Justice Act 1984, s. 4. **People (DPP) v Conroy** [1988] 4, CCA, SC.

    Whether delay by Gardai in permitting access by solicitor to client constituted a denial
    of right of access—Whether right of reasonable access to solicitor was a constitutional
    right—Constitution of Ireland 1937, Article 40.3. **DPP v Healy** [1990] 313, SC.

  Statement
    Admissibility in evidence. *See* Evidence—Statement by accused (*below*).

Acquittal
  Appeal
    Acquittal by direction of trial judge—Appeal to Supreme Court—Appeal dismissed—
    Reasons. **People (DPP) v O'Shea (No 2)** [1983] 592, SC.

CRIMINAL LAW
Acquittal
Appeal continued

Case stated—Whether DPP had validly invoked the jurisdiction of the High Court—Necessary steps—Whether complied with—Whether possible to state case against acquittal—Summary Jurisdiction Act 1857, s. 2—Courts of Justice Act 1924, ss. 36, 91—Courts (Supplemental Provisions) Act 1961, s. 51—RSC O 62 r 5—District Court Rules 1948, r 201. **DPP v Nangle** [1984] 171, HC.

Central Criminal Court—Appeal to Supreme Court—Appeal allowed—Whether Supreme Court empowered to order re-trial—Whether consistent with principle of autrefois acquit—Whether re-trial would result in arbitrary discrimination—Whether legislative will thereby be set aside—Constitution of Ireland 1937, Articles 34 4, 40 1—Criminal Procedure Act 1967, s. 34(1)—RSC 1986, O 87. **People (DPP) v Quilligan** (No 2) [1989] 245, SC.

Jurisdiction of Supreme Court—Charge on indictment before Central Criminal Court—Jury, at the direction of the judge, recording verdict of not guilty—Whether open to DPP to bring an appeal against such verdict—Extent of Supreme Court's appellate jurisdiction—Plea of autrefois acquit explained—Constitution of Ireland 1937, Arts 34 3 1, 34 4 3, 38 1, 38 5, 38 6—Courts of Justice Act 1924, ss. 31, 63—Courts (Supplemental Provisions) Act 1961, ss. 11(1), 48—Criminal Procedure Act 1967, s. 34(1). **People (DPP) v O'Shea** (No 1) [1983] 549, SC.

Autrefois acquit. See Autrefois acquit *(below).*

Adjournment. *See* Trial—Adjournment *(below).*

Aiding and abetting
Licensing offence

Manager holding license as nominee of company—Liability of manager for aiding and abetting—Intoxicating Liquor Act 1960, s. 28. **McMahon v Murtagh Properties Ltd** [1982] 342, HC.

Appeal
Acquittal

Jurisdiction of Supreme Court. *See* Acquittal—Appeal *(above).*

Circuit Court

Jurisdiction—Whether defendant entitled to raise point not made in District Court on appeal to Circuit Court—Nature of appeal—Petty Sessions Act 1851, s. 10. **DPP (Nagle) v Flynn** [1989] 65, SC.

Conviction

Circuit Court—Jurisdiction—Circuit Court affirming conviction and increasing sentence. *See* Sentence—Increase—Circuit Court—Jurisdiction *(below).*

Court of Criminal Appeal—Jurisdiction—Whether Court of Criminal Appeal has jurisdiction to substitute its own subjective view of evidence for the verdict of a jury—Courts of Justice Act 1924, ss. 30, 34—Courts (Supplemental Provisions) Act 1961, s. 12. **People (DPP) v Egan** [1990] 780, SC.

Court of Criminal Appeal

Whether point of law of exceptional public importance—Whether desirable in public interest that appeal be carried to Supreme Court—Courts of Justice Act 1924, s. 29. **DPP v Littlejohn** [1978] 147, CCA.

Defect in trial

Proviso—Whether miscarriage of justice actually occurred—Whether shown that trial court disregarded inadmissible evidence. **People (DPP) v Prunty** [1986] 716, CCA.

CRIMINAL LAW
Appeal *continued*
Prejudice
Publication—Injunction to restrain—Conviction—Pending appeal to Court of Criminal Appeal—Publication of magazine article based on material supplied by sole witness for the prosecution—Whether article likely to prejudice the appeal—Freedom of the press—Constitution of Ireland 1937, Article 40 6. **Cullen v Toibin** [1984] 577, HC, SC.

Reinstatement of dismissed appeal
Jurisdiction—Circuit Judge indicating that if compensation were to be paid within a prescribed time custodial sentence would not be imposed—Whether judge had jurisdiction to reinstate appeals which had been dismissed—Certiorari. **State (Dunne) v Martin** [1982] 18, SC.

Sentence. See Sentence (*below*).

Time limit
Extension—Application for enlargement of time within which application for leave to appeal against conviction could be brought—Criteria to be considered—Whether documents served out of time irregular or void—RSC O 86, rr 5, 8, 40. **People (DPP) v Kelly** [1982] 1, SC.

Arrest. *See* ARREST.

Arrest warrant
Absence. See ARREST (Legality—Arrest without warrant).

Delay in execution of warrant
Judicial review—Certiorari—Conduct of applicant contributing to delay—Sentence—Commencement. **O'Driscoll v Governor of Cork Prison** [1989] 239, HC.

Warrant issued on foot of conviction
Warrant going out of date—Warrant issued by District Justice—Whether summons duly issued by an authorised person—Whether District Justice jurisdiction to re-issue a warrant. **Connors v Delap** [1989] 93, HC.

Autrefois acquit
Accused's conviction quashed
Whether matter should be remitted to the District Court—Distinction between conviction void ab initio and conviction where accused was entitled to be acquitted—Industrial Relations Act 1969, s. 10(3). **Singh v Ruane** [1990] 62.

Quashing of order
Whether the quashing of an order amounts to an acquittal—Grounds for granting an order of certiorari—Distinction between a proceeding commenced without jurisdiction and one validly commenced during which jurisdiction is exceeded. **State (Keeney) v O'Malley** [1986] 31, HC.

Bail *See also* BAIL
Extradition
Test—Likelihood of prisoners being available for extradition—Test to be applied on bail application—Whether different from that pertaining in domestic criminal matters. **People (AG) v Gilliland** [1986] 357, SC.

Objection
DPP opposing granting of bail—Grounds of objection—Whether likelihood of commission of future offences by applicant a valid ground of objection—Whether judicial discretion to refuse bail to prevent apprehended commission of crime—Constitution of Ireland 1937, Article 40 3 1—Malicious Damage Act 1861, s. 51—Prevention of Crime Act 1908—Larceny Act 1916, s. 23(A)—Criminal Procedure Act 1967, ss. 22, 28(3)—Criminal Justice Act 1984, s. 11. **DPP v Ryan** [1989] 333, SC.

CRIMINAL LAW *continued*
> *Powers of Peace Commission. See* BAIL (Admittance of Persons to bail)

> *Station bail*
>> Procedure—Recognisance returnable for four days later, being the next day the arresting officer was rostered for duty—Intervening sitting of the District Court—Validity of procedure—Whether 'appropriate time'—Whether attendance of accused on the stated date and the entering there on the charge constitute a valid complaint and conferred jurisdiction on the District Court—Criminal Procedure Act 1967, s. 31—District Court (Criminal Procedure Act 1967) Rules 1985. **State (Lynch) v Ballagh** [1987] 65, SC.

Bigamy
> *Husband obtaining church annulment and remarrying before obtaining civil annulment*
>> First marriage voidable—Offences against the Person Act 1861, s. 57—Constitution of Ireland 1937, Article 41 3. **F M L v Registrar General of Marriages** [1984] 667, HC.

Burglary
> *Whether crime against property*
>> Malicious injury claim—Test applicable. *See* Larceny—Burglary *(below)*.

Charge
> *Delay in prosecuting*
>> Whether such delay excessive—Whether defendant deprived of his right to a fair trial. **Maguire v DPP and Kirby** [1988] 166, HC.

> *Emergency powers legislation*
>> Accused charged in garda station—Whether lawful to charge accused otherwise than in District Court or Special Court—Emergency Powers Act 1976, s. 2. State (Brennan) v Mahon [1978] 17, HC.

> *Striking out of charge. See* Procedure—Striking out of charge—District Court *(below)*.

Complaint
> *Time limit*
>> Whether made within statutory period—Whether evidence before courts as to valid issue of summons. *See* Summons—Validity—Issue—Whether complaint made within statutory period *(below)*.

> *Validity*
>> Whether matter of defence—Whether defendant entitled to raise point not made in District Court on appeal to Circuit Court—Nature of appeal—Petty Sessions Act 1851, s. 10. **DPP (Nagle) v Flynn** [1989] 65, SC.

> *Withdrawal*
>> Powers of DPP—Complaint by garda as common informer—DPP directing that charge be withdrawn—District Justice entertaining the case—Conviction—Application to quash—Whether DPP had power to intervene—Constitution of Ireland 1937, Art 30 3—Minister and Secretaries Act 1924, s. 6(1)—Criminal Justice Administration Act 1924—Prosecution of Offences Act 1974, s. 3. **State (Collins) v Ruane** [1984] 443, HC; [1985] 349, SC.

Confession of accused
> *Admissibility. See* Evidence—Admission *(below)*.

Conspiracy to corrupt public morals
> *Offence*
>> Whether established—Danger of usurping function of jury—Whether court should issue declaration—Non-directive counselling regarding abortion. **Attorney General (SPUC) v Open Door Counselling** [1987] 477, HC.

Constitutional rights
> *Extradition cases. See* EXTRADITION (Constitutional rights).

CRIMINAL LAW

Constitutional rights *continued*

Unconstitutionally obtained evidence

Admissibility. *See* Evidence—Admissibility—Unconstitutionally obtained evidence (*below*).

Consumer information

False statements as to the provision of services, accommodation or facilities

Whether defendant knew statement to be false—Whether defendant reckless—Penalty—Whether court should provide for the payment of compensation—Consumer Information Act 1978, ss. 6, 17 (3) (a), 22 (2). **Director of Consumer Affairs v Sunshine Holidays Ltd** [1984] 551, DC.

Contempt of Court. *See* CONTEMPT OF COURT (Criminal contempt).

Conviction

Appeal. See Appeal—Conviction (*above*).

Certiorari to quash. See CERTIORARI (Conviction).

Fair procedures. See CERTIORARI (Conviction—Fair procedures).

Judicial review

Certiorari. *See* CERTIORARI (Conviction).

Whether solicitor representing accused allowed proper opportunity to present case—Whether conviction made within jurisdiction—Whether judicial review appropriate remedy. **Gill v Connellan** [1988] 448, HC.

Validity

Scheduled offence—Road traffic—Driving without insurance—Validity of conviction before ten day period to produce certificate has elapsed—Criminal Justice Act 1951, s. 2, as amended. **State (McDonagh) v Sheerin** [1981] 149, HC.

Scheduled offence—Summary trial only with consent of accused—Prosecutor tried summarily and convicted on two charges—Failure to inform prosecutor of his right to trial by jury. *See* CERTIORARI (Conviction—Validity—Scheduled offence—Summary trial only with consent of accused).

Corresponding offence. *See* EXTRADITION (Correspondence of offence).

Costs

District Court proceedings

Statutory prohibition—District Court Rules prohibiting award of costs against member of Garda Síochána acting in discharge of his duties as police officer—Whether unconstitutional discrimination—Constitution of Ireland 1937, Articles 40 1 and 3—Prosecution of Offences Act 1974, s. 3—District Court Rules 1948, r 67. **Dillane v Attorney General** [1980] 167, SC.

Legal aid. See Legal aid (*below*).

Criminal investigation. *See* CRIMINAL INVESTIGATION.

Damage to property. *See* MALICIOUS INJURIES.

Defence

Insanity or diminished responsibility

Murder—Whether jury to consider defence of diminished responsibility an alternative verdict of manslaughter—Whether concept of diminished responsibility recognised in Irish law. **People (DPP) v O'Mahony** [1986] 244, SC.

Detention

Generally. See DETENTION.

Legality. See ARREST (Detention—Legality).

CRIMINAL LAW
Detention
Legality continued
Inquiry under Constitution. *See* HABEAS CORPUS.

Drugs
Misuse. See Misuse of drugs (*below*).

Escape from custody
Extradition application. See EXTRADITION (Escape from custody).

Evidence
Accused. See Evidence—Statement by accused (*below*).

Admissibility
Entry on premises—Gardai entering premises and obtaining evidence—Absence of search warrant—Licensed premises—Offences under gaming and lotteries legislation detected by plain clothes gardai—Whether evidence admissible—Relevance of power to enter under intoxicating liquor code—Spirits (Ireland) Act 1854, s. 12—Beer Houses (Ireland) Act 1864, s. 11—Licensing Act (Ireland) 1874, s. 23—Intoxicating Liquor Act 1927, s. 22—Gaming and Lotteries Act 1956, ss. 9, 38, 39. **DPP v McMahon** [1987] 87, SC.

Entry on premises—No order authorising entry—Whether evidence admissible—Family planning—Unlawful sale of contraceptives—Discretion to exclude evidence—Health Act 1947, s. 96(1)—Health (Family Planning) Act 1979, s. 4(4). **DPP v McCutcheon** [1986] 433, HC.

Hearsay evidence. *See* Evidence—Hearsay (*below*).

Illegally obtained evidence. *See* Evidence—Admissibility—Entry on premises (*above*).

Inadmissible statement erroneously given to jury—Jury discharged—Case re-entered—Whether prosecution could tender in evidence statements ruled inadmissible. **Ryan v DPP** [1989] 466, HC.

Statement by accused. *See* Evidence—Statement by accused (*below*).

Unconstitutionally obtained evidence—Statement made while in Garda custody—Access to solicitor denied. **People (DPP) v Conroy** [1988] 4, CCA, SC.

Unconstitutionally obtained evidence—Statement made while in Garda custody—Delay in permitting access to solicitor—Whether denial of accused's right of access to solicitor—Whether such right a constitutional right—Constitution of Ireland 1937, Article 40.3. **DPP v Healy** [1990] 313, SC.

Unconstitutionally obtained evidence—Whether evidence obtained in breach of constitutional rights is inadmissible—Circumstances where such evidence may be admitted—Rationale for exclusionary rule. **People (DPP) v Kenny** [1990] 569, SC.

Voir dire—Effect on subsequent trial—Accused alleging detention in Garda custody unlawful—Whether issue to be tried by judge on voir dire or by jury. *See* Evidence—Statement by accused—Admissibility—Statements made while in police custody—Accused alleging detention in Garda custody unlawful (*below*).

Admission
Statement by accused (*generally*). *See* Evidence—Statement by accused (*below*).

Statement by accused admitting responsibility—Whether admission induced by gardai—Whether inducement improper—Appropriate test. **People (DPP) v Hoey** [1988] 666, SC.

Character
Unruly character—Young person—Whether evidence of unruly character must be tested by cross-examination—Natural justice—Children's Act 1908, s. 102(3). **State (O'Donoghue) v Kennedy** [1979] 109, HC.

CRIMINAL LAW
  Evidence *continued*
    Circumstantial
      Murder—Statement of accused—Whether sufficient to convict—Absence of body of victim. **People (DPP) v Towson** [1978] 122, CCA.

    Corresponding offence. See EXTRADITION (Correspondence of offence).

    Discretion to exclude
      Confession—Breach of Judge's Rules—Whether discretion should be exercised to introduce—Purpose of particular rule—Judges' Rules, rule 9. **People (DPP) v Towson** [1978] 122, CCA.

    Documents
      Admissibility—Reconstructed records from damaged originals—Unavailability of person compiling records—Whether documents admissible. **People (DPP) v Marley** [1985] 17, CCA.

      Certificate of Medical Bureau of Road Safety. *See* ROAD TRAFFIC OFFENCES (Drunken driving—Evidence).

      Medical certificate—Drunken driving. *See* ROAD TRAFFIC OFFENCES (Drunken driving—Evidence—Medical certificate).

      Medical certificate—Whether form signed by designated medical practitioner duly completed in the statutory manner—Whether legibility the hallmark of an effective signature. **DPP v Collins** [1981] 447, SC.

    Drunken driving. See ROAD TRAFFIC OFFENCES (Drunken driving—Evidence).

    Exclusion
      Statement by accused—Breach of Judge's Rules—Discretion to exclude—Whether discretion should be exercised to introduce—Purpose of particular rule—Judges' Rules, rule 9. **People (DPP) v Towson** [1978] 122, CCA.

      Statement by accused—Whether certain statements, made in circumstances in which there was not an exact compliance with the Judge's Rules, should be excluded. **DPP v Kelly** [1983] 271, SC.

      Unconstitutionally obtained evidence—Circumstances in which such evidence admissible—Rationale for exclusionary rule. **People (DPP) v Kenny** [1990] 569, SC.

    Exhibits
      Whether accused person entitled to inspect exhibits to be produced at trial—Theft of exhibits—Whether accused deprived of right to inspect. **State (Pletzer) v Magee** [1986] 441, HC.

    Hearsay
      Admissibility—Telephone calls—Tracing of calls—Whether evidence as to voice on telephone established by hearsay—Whether admissible—Whether retrial should be ordered—Proviso. **People (DPP) v Prunty** [1986] 716, CCA.

    Illegally obtained evidence
      Admissibility—Gardai entering premises and obtaining evidence—Absence of search warrant. *See* Evidence—Admissibility—Entry on premises (*above*).

      Admissibility—Gardai entering premises and obtaining evidence—No order authorising entry. *See* Evidence—Admissibility—Entry on premises—No order authorising entry (*above*).

    Identification
      Identification parade—Objection by accused to participation—Requirement as to jury direction. **People (DPP) v Marley** [1985] 17, CCA.

CRIMINAL LAW
Evidence
Identification continued

Misdescription of accused—Medical Bureau Certificate—Whether sufficient evidence—Whether accused the person named on the certificate—Road Traffic Act 1961, s. 49—Road Traffic Amendment Act 1978, s. 10. **DPP v McPartland** [1983] 411, HC.

Murder

Lengthy detention in police custody—Statement made—Conviction—Appeal to Supreme Court—Whether provisions relating to jurisdiction of Court of Criminal Appeal limit the appellate jurisdiction of Supreme Court—Admissibility of statements—Whether voluntary—Whether detention unlawful—Whether conscious and deliberate violation of constitutional rights—Role of Jury—burden of proof—Constitution of Ireland 1937, Arts. 29,34—Courts of Justice Act 1924, ss. 29,31—Courts (Establishment and Constitution) Act 1961, s. 3—Courts (Supplemental Provisions) Act 1961, s. 12. **People (DPP) v Lynch** [1981] 389, SC.

Prejudicial

Procedure—Conviction in Special Criminal Court—Whether inadmissible prejudicial evidence given during the trial—Whether trial held in accordance with statute—Forensic evidence—Whether findings based on inferences capable of more than one interpretation—Offences against the State Act 1939, s. 41 (4). **People (DPP) v McMahon** [1984] 461, CCA.

Preservation

Duty of Gardai to preserve evidence material to guilt or innocence—Charges related to stolen car—Judicial review—Garda disposal of vehicle—Whether prejudice arising—Whether injunction to restrain prosecution of said charges be granted—Constitution—Fair procedures. **Murphy v DPP** [1989] 71, HC.

Regulations

Road traffic offence—Drunken driving—Proof of regulations—Whether necessary for prosecution to give prima facie evidence of the regulations—Documentary Evidence Act 1925, s. 4(1). **DPP v Collins** [1981] 447, SC.

Statement by accused

Admissibility—Breach of Judge's Rules—Discretion to exclude—Whether discretion should be exercised to introduce—Purpose of particular rule—Judges' Rules, rule 9. **People (DPP) v Towson** [1978] 122, CCA.

Admissibility—Arrest and detention under s. 30 of Offences Against the State Act—Statements made in police custody—Finding by court of trial that such statements voluntary—Appeal—Approach of appeal court to such finding—Whether certain statements, made in circumstances in which there was not an exact compliance with the Judge's Rules, should be excluded—Courts of Justice Act 1924, s. 29—Interpretation Act 1937, s. 11(c)—Offences against the State Act 1939, ss. 30(3), 30(4), 52. **DPP v Kelly** [1983] 271, SC.

Admissibility—Detention—Legality—Extension—Garda Superintendent authorising detention now dead—Whether Superintendent's suspicion that accused had committed a scheduled offence need be expressly proved—Offences Against the State Act 1939, s. 30. **People (DPP) v Byrne** [1989] 613, SC.

Admissibility—Statement admitting responsibility—Whether admission induced by gardai—Whether inducement improper—Appropriate test. **People (DPP) v Hoey** [1988] 666, SC.

Admissibility—Statements made while in detention—Conviction—Legality of arrest and detention—Arrest in respect of scheduled offence—Questioning in respect of non-scheduled offence—Non-scheduled offence more serious—Whether arrest lawful—Offences Against the State Act 1939, ss. 30, 36. **People (DPP) v Quilligan** [1987] 606, CCC, SC.

CRIMINAL LAW
Evidence
Statement by accused continued
> Admissibility—Statements made while in police custody—Accused alleging detention in Garda custody unlawful—Onus of proof—Whether issue to be tried by judge on voir dire or by jury—Whether jury likely to be prejudiced by determining issue of lawfulness of detention or admissibility of evidence—Constitution of Ireland 1937, Articles 38 1, 38 5—Criminal Justice Act 1984, s. 25. **People (DPP) v Conroy** [1988] 4, CCA, SC.

> Admissibility—Statement made while in Garda custody—Access to solicitor denied—Whether right of access to solicitor a constitutional right—Constitution of Ireland 1937, Article 40 3—Criminal Justice Act 1984, s. 4. **People (DPP) v Conroy** [1988] 4, CCA, SC.

> Admissibility—Statement made while in Garda custody—Delay by Gardai in permitting access to solicitor—Whether constituted a denial of accused's right of access to solicitor—Whether such right a constitutional right—Constitution of Ireland 1937, Article 40 3. **DPP v Healy** [1990] 313, SC.

> Admissibility—Unlawful detention—Conviction of murder in Central Criminal Court—Appeal direct to Supreme Court—Whether statements freely and voluntarily made—Constitution of Ireland 1937, Article 34 4 3—Courts (Establishment and Constitution) Act 1961, s. 3—Courts (Supplementary Provisions) Act 1961, s. 12—Courts of Justice Act 1924, ss. 29 and 41. **DPP v Lynch** [1981] 389, SC.

> Admissibility—Young person—Statements made in Garda custody—Whether obligation to have parent or guardian present during questioning—Whether fear of obstruction of course of justice justified refusal to have parent present—Whether trial judge has discretion to admit evidence. **Travers v Ryan** [1985] 343, HC.

Sufficiency
> Procedure—Offences contrary to European Community regulations—Authorised Officers of the Minister for Agriculture—Whether certificate that officer had been appointed sufficient evidence of the fact of appointment—Whether oral evidence sufficient—Evidence Act 1845—Ministers and Secretaries Act 1924, ss. 15(4), 17(c)—Documentary Evidence Act 1925, s. 7(2)—European Communities (Marketing of Fertiliser) Regulations 1978, regs 2, 4, 6, 7(4). **Minister for Agriculture v Cleary** [1988] 294, HC.

Tape recordings
> Admissibility—Telephone calls—Whether defect in quality affects admissibility—Factors affecting weight to be given to evidence—Whether recording of telephone call made to person not then on trial admissible if part of transaction as a whole. **People (DPP) v Prunty** [1986] 716, CCA.

Unconstitutionally obtained evidence
> Admissibility. *See* Evidence—Admissibility—Unconstitutionally obtained evidence (*above*).

Undertaking of DPP. See DIRECTOR OF PUBLIC PROSECUTIONS (Undertaking—
> Preliminary examination—Undertaking that evidence given would not be used for the purpose of criminal proceedings against witness).

Extra-territorial offence
Trial
> Jurisdiction. *See* Trial—Jurisdiction—Extra-territorial offence (*below*).

Extradition. *See* EXTRADITION.

Fair procedures. *See* CONSTITUTION (Fair procedures).

CRIMINAL LAW
Firearms *continued*
Possession
Accused being constable in RUC—Whether possession for a lawful purpose—Accused believing that their lives would be in danger—Whether such belief honest and reasonable—Firearms Act 1964, s. 27A—Criminal Law Jurisdiction Act 1976, s. 8. **DPP v Kelso** [1984] 329, SPC.

Whether political offence—Test to be applied. *See* EXTRADITION (Political offence—Test to be applied—Appellant driver of car in which firearms discovered in possession of passenger).

Fisheries offences. *See* FISHERIES (Offence).

Gaming offences. *See* GAMING AND LOTTERIES (Offences).

Health offences
Family planning
Unlawful sale of contraceptives—Authority to enter premises—Whether in force—Whether evidence obtained without warrant admissible—Whether judge must exercise discretion to admit evidence—Nature and substance of evidence—Health Act 1947, s. 96(1)—Health (Family Planning) Act 1979, s. 4(4). **DPP v McCutcheon** [1986] 433, HC.

Indictment
Misuse of drugs
Whether possession for personal use or some other purpose—Whether indictment must distinguish between purposes for which drug is possessed. *See* Misuse of drugs—Controlled drugs (*below*).

Trial
Powers of DPP. *See* DIRECTOR OF PUBLIC PROSECUTIONS (Powers—Validity—Trial on indictment).

Insanity
Defence
Murder—Diminished responsibility. *See* Murder—Defence—Insanity—Diminished responsibility (*below*).

Jurisdiction
Circuit Court
Complaint—Validity—Whether matter of defence—Whether defendant entitled to raise point not made in District Court on appeal to Circuit Court—Nature of appeal—Petty Sessions Act 1851, s. 10. **DPP (Nagle) v Flynn** [1989] 65, SC.

Court of Criminal Appeal. See Appeal—Conviction—Court of Criminal Appeal (*above*).

District Court
Accused detained pursuant to statutory power—Whether remand order made by district justice valid—Whether District Court can embark on constitutional inquiry as to validity of detention—Whether unwarrantable and unlawful usurpation of the constitutional role of the High Court—Constitution of Ireland 1937, Article 40 4 2—Criminal Justice Act 1984, s. 4. **Keating v Governor of Mountjoy Prison** [1990] 850, SC.

Accused electing for summary trial—Whether District Justice subsequently entitled to decline jurisdiction—Offences against the Person Act 1861, s. 62—Penal Servitude Act 1891, s. 1—Criminal Justice Act 1951, ss. 2 (2)(a), 4(1). **State (O'Hagan) v Delap** [1983] 241, HC.

Indictable offence—Subsequent charge of summary offence—Applicant charged with obstructing police officers in the course of their duty—Applicant electing for trial by judge and jury—Subsequent charges of assault contrary to common law—DPP electing to have latter charges disposed of summarily—District Justice refusing to deal

CRIMINAL LAW
Jurisdiction
District Court continued

with charges summarily—Withdrawal of indictable charges—Whether District Justice entitled to assume jurisdiction over charges of common assault—Offences Against the Person Act 1861, ss. 38, 46—Criminal Justice Act 1951, s. 6. **O'Neill v DPP and Hussey** [1989] 881, HC.

Scheduled offence—Summary trial only with consent of accused—Prosecutor tried summarily and convicted on two charges—Certiorari—Failure to inform prosecutor of his right to trial by Jury—No objection to being tried summarily—Whether District Justice acted without jurisdiction—Malicious Damage Act 1861, s. 51—Road Traffic Act, 1961, s. 56 (1)—Criminal Justice Act 1961, s. 2—Offences Against the State Act 1939, s. 45 (2)—Offences against the State (Scheduled Offences) Order 1972. **State (McDonagh) v Sheerin** [1981] 149, HC.

Summary criminal offences—Issue of summons—Time limits—Whether parallel procedures—Whether 1986 Act duly authorises the issue of summons for the trial of offences in the District Court—Petty Sessions (Ireland) Act 1851, s. 10(4)—Courts Act 1986, ss. 1, 2. **DPP v Roche and Kelly; DPP v Nolan** [1989] 39, SC.

Whether District Justice had jurisdiction to reopen case and hear additional evidence for prosecution in absence of applicant's counsel—Applicant's counsel specifically excused from attending—Whether District Justice acted contrary to natural justice—Whether case should be remitted to District Court for further consideration—RSC 1986, O 84 r 27(4), (6). **Dawson v Hamill** [1990] 257, HC.

Special Criminal Court
Accused before the court on a warrant for a scheduled offence charged with a non-scheduled offence—Whether separate warrant or summons required in respect of each offence charged—Offences Against the State Acts 1939-1972 (Special Criminal Court) Rules 1975—Offences Against the State Act 1939, ss. 43 and 47. **McElhinney v Special Criminal Court and DPP** [1989] 411, SC.

Supreme Court
Re-trial—Appeal against acquittal—Appeal allowed—Whether Supreme Court empowered to order re-trial—Whether consistent with principle of autrefois acquit—Whether re-trial would result in arbitrary discrimination—Whether legislative will thereby be set aside—Constitution of Ireland 1937, Articles 34 4, 40 1—Criminal Procedure Act 1967 (No. 12), s. 34(1)—Rules of the Superior Courts 1986, O 87. **People (DPP) v Quilligan** (No 2) [1989] 245, SC.

Larceny
Burglary
Whether crime against property—Malicious injury claim—Requirement to show that damage was caused in the course of commission of a crime against property—Test applicable—Malicious Injuries Act 1981, ss. 5(1), (2)(d)—Larceny Act 1916, s. 23—Criminal Law (Jurisdiction) Act 1976, s. 6. **Shennick Lodge v Monaghan Co Council** [1986] 273, SC.

Offence
Department store—Accused arrested before leaving store—Whether offence of larceny complete. **DPP v Keating** [1989] 561, HC.

Entering premises as trespasser and stealing therein—Evidence of owner of premises—Whether offence established—Whether accused entered as trespasser—Distinction between breaking and entering—Larceny Act 1916, s. 23—Criminal Law (Jurisdiction) Act 1976, s. 6. **Travers v Ryan** [1985] 343, HC.

Receiving stolen goods—Extradition—Correspondence of offence—Charge of dishonestly receiving articles 'knowing or believing same to have been stolen'—Whether

CRIMINAL LAW
Larceny
Offence continued

less stringent degree of mens rea than 'knowing same to have been stolen'. *See* EXTRA-DITION (Political offence—Corresponding offence—Charge of receiving stolen goods).

Supermarket—Defendant leaving supermarket without paying for goods—Relationship of customer to goods between selection and completion of purchase—Whether bailment, licence or custody—Whether defendant guilty of larceny—Larceny Act 1916, ss. 1, 2. **DPP v Morrissey** [1982] 487, HC.

Simple larceny

Whether accused could be convicted on such charge notwithstanding that he might be charged with an offence under another section—Larceny Act 1916, ss. 2, 17. **DPP v Cassidy** [1990] 310, HC.

Legal aid
Choice of solicitor

Applicant requesting a particular solicitor from legal aid panel—District Justice following usual practice of nominating a solicitor from the panel in alphabetical order—Prosecutor refusing to accept solicitor appointed in this way—Whether order of prohibition be granted—Criminal Justice (Legal Aid) Act 1962, s. 2(1)—Criminal Justice (Legal Aid) Regulations 1965, reg 7(1). **State (Freeman) v Connellan** [1987] 470, HC.

Right of poor person charged with serious offence to free legal aid—Right of accused to nominate solicitor from panel—Whether court obliged to assign solicitor nominated by accused—Criminal Justice (Legal Aid) Act 1962. **Mulhall v O'Donnell and DPP** [1989] 367, HC.

Exceptional circumstances

Whether onus on defendant to establish existence of exceptional circumstances. Whether defendant to be informed by District Justice of right to legal aid—Criminal Justice (Legal Aid) Act 1962, s. 2. **O'Neill v Butler** [1979] 243.

Licensing offences. *See* LICENSING ACTS (Offences).

Conviction

License becoming forfeit—Whether offences minor offences—Whether forfeiture provisions an unjust attack on property rights—Constitution of Ireland 1937, Articles 38 2, 40 3—Intoxicating Liquor Act 1927, ss. 28, 30(1). **State (Pheasantry Ltd) v Donnelly** [1982] 512, HC.

Location of offences
Multiplicity of offences

Whether relevant to consideration of nature of offences—Whether major or minor offences—District Court Rules 1948, rr 25, 44—Social Welfare (Consolidation) Act 1981, s. 115. **State (Wilson) v Neilan** [1987] 118, HC.

Malicious damage to property. *See* MALICIOUS INJURIES (Crime against property damaged).

Manslaughter
Sentence

Severity. *See* Sentence—Manslaughter—Plea of guilty (*below*).

Maximum Prices Order
Intoxicating liquor

Breach. *See* LICENSING (Offence—Prices—Maximum Prices Order).

Mens rea
Shooting with intent to commit murder

Whether necessary to establish intention to commit murder. *See* Murder—Shooting with intent to commit murder (*below*).

CRIMINAL LAW *continued*
Minor offence
Whether minor offence triable summarily. See CONSTITUTION (Trial of offences—Minor offence).

Misuse of drugs
Controlled drugs
Cannabis resin—Whether possession for personal use or some other purpose—Whether indictment must distinguish between purposes for which drug is possessed—Whether triable summarily or on indictment—Misuse of Drugs Act 1977, ss. 3, 15, 27. **State (Bloomfield) v Neylon** [1985] 602, HC.

Search warrant
Nature of information required for issue of warrant—Nature of determination to issue warrant—Misuse of Drugs Act 1977, s. 26(1). **People (DPP) v Kenny** [1990] 569, SC.

Sentence
Purpose—Punishment or rehabilitation—Change of circumstances of offender—Removal from contact with proscribed drugs by parents—Probation officer reports making no reference to change of circumstances—Whether judge obliged to take account of change in devising regime of rehabilitation rather than punishment—Misuse of Drugs Act 1977, s. 28(2). **State (Slattery) v Roe** [1986] 511, HC.

Murder
Conviction
Appeal—Arrest—Legality—Motive—Arrest in respect of scheduled offence—Questioning in relation to non-scheduled offence—Whether arrest effected for spurious purpose unconnected with offence authorised by statutory power—Emergency Powers Act 1976, s. 2. **People (DPP) v Towson** [1978] 122, CCA.

Appeal—Arrest—Legality—Motive—Arrest in respect of scheduled offence—Questioning in relation to non-scheduled offence—Whether arrest merely colourable device—Purpose of statute—Whether applicable to subversive and non-subversive crime—Offences Against the State Act 1939, ss. 30, 45. **People (DPP) v Walsh** [1984] 84, CCC, CCA, SC.

Corresponding offence
Extradition—Whether offence of murder in law of New York corresponds to Irish law—Possible defences. **State (McCaud) v Governor of Mountjoy Prison** [1986] 129, HC.

Defence
Insanity—Diminished responsibility—Whether jury to consider defence of diminished responsibility an alternative verdict of manslaughter—Whether concept of diminished responsibility recognised in Irish law. **People (DPP) v O'Mahony** [1986] 244, SC.

Extradition
Political offence—Whether political nature of offence established—Extradition Act 1965, s. 50(2). **Shannon v Fanning** [1985] 385, HC, SC.

Intent
Shooting with intent to commit murder. *See* Murder—Shooting with intent to commit murder (*below*).

Shooting with intent to commit murder
Mens rea—Whether necessary to establish intention to commit murder—Whether reckless disregard of risk to killing as a likely outcome sufficient to constitution required intent—Offences Against the Person Act 1861, s. 14. **People (DPP) v Douglas** [1985] 25, CCA.

Nature of offence
Whether minor offence triable summarily. See CONSTITUTION (Trial of offences—Minor offence).

CRIMINAL LAW *continued*

Nolle prosequi

Plea of guilty in District Court

Case sent forward to Circuit Court for sentence—Change of plea to not guilty—DPP entering a nolle prosequi—Prosecutor discharged and rearrested—Sent forward to Special Criminal Court—Whether Special Criminal Court jurisdiction—Whether possible to institute a fresh prosecution following the entrance of a valid nolle prosequi— Delay between rearrest and application for conditional order of prohibition—Whether relevant—Criminal Justice Administration Act, 1924, s. 12—Offences against the State Act 1939, ss. 46(2), 48—Criminal Procedure Act 1967, s. 13(2), (4) (b). **State (Coveney) v Special Criminal Court** [1982] 284, HC.

Not guilty verdict

Appeal. See Acquittal—Appeal (*above*).

Obstruction of government. *See* Offence—Obstruction of government (*below*).

Offence

Aiding and abetting. See Aiding and abetting (*above*).

Alternative or separate and distinct offences

Onus of proof—Licensing offences. **McCarthy v Murphy** [1981] 213, HC.

Conspiracy to corrupt public morals

Whether established—Danger of usurping function of jury—Whether court should issue declaration—Non-directive counselling regarding abortion. **Attorney General (SPUC) v Open Door Counselling** [1987] 477, HC.

Entering premises as trespasser and stealing therein

Evidence of owner of premises—Whether offence established Whether accused entered as trespasser—Distinction between breaking and entering—Larceny Act 1916, s. 23— Criminal Law (Jurisdiction) Act 1976, s. 6. **Travers v Ryan** [1985] 343, HC.

Larceny. See Larceny (*above*).

Nature

Whether minor offence triable summarily. *See* CONSTITUTION (Trial of offences— Minor offence).

Obstruction of government

Constituent ingredients of such offence—Offences against the State Act 1939, s. 7(1)— Criminal Law Act 1976, s. 2—Diplomatic Relations and Immunities Act 1967, Schedule Art 22. **DPP v Kehoe** [1983] 237, CCA.

Public mischief

Offence of effecting a public mischief contrary to common law—Whether charge known to common law of Ireland—Whether creation of a new offence—Criminal Law Act 1976, s. 12. **DPP (Vizzard) v Carew** [1981] 91, HC.

Revenue. See Revenue offence (*below*).

Shooting with intent to commit murder

Whether necessary to establish intention to commit murder—Whether reckless disregard of risk to killing as a likely outcome sufficient to constitution required intent—Offences Against the Person Act 1861, s. 14. **People (DPP) v Douglas** [1985] 25, CCA.

Single or separate offences

Licensing—Maximum Prices Order—Breach—Whether evidence necessary of actual state of beverage—Price list displaying excess price on three drinks on two separate occasions—Interpretation of Order—Whether single offence—Prices Act 1958, s. 22— Maximum Retail Price (Beverages in Licensed Premises) Display Order 1979—Maximum Price (Intoxicating Liquor) (No 3) Order 1979. **Minister for Industry, Commerce and Tourism v Farrelly** [1981] 302, HC.

CRIMINAL LAW *continued*

Offences Against the State Acts

Arrest

Legality. *See* ARREST (Legality—Statutory power—Offences Against the State Acts).

Obstruction of government. See Offence—Obstruction of government (*above*).

Penalty

Mitigation

Jurisdiction of court—Excise offences—Whether court has discretion with regard to penalty incurred—Interpretation of statute—Excise Management Act 1827, s. 578—Finance Act 1926, s. 25(2)—Criminal Justice Act 1951, s. 8—Finance Act 1982, ss. 69(1)(b), 70. **DPP v Gray** [1987] 4, SC.

Plea

Autrefois acquit. See Autrefois acquit (*above*).

Guilty. see Trial—Plea of guilty (*below*).

Political offence. *See* EXTRADITION (Political offence).

Preliminary examination. *See* Procedure—Preliminary examination (*below*).

Prevention of crime. *See* CRIME PREVENTION.

Procedure

Appeal. See Appeal (*above*).

Autrefois acquit. See Autrefois acquit (*above*).

Case stated

Appeal against acquittal—Whether DPP had validly invoked the jurisdiction of the High Court—Necessary steps—Whether complied with—Whether possible to state case against acquittal—Summary Jurisdiction Act 1857, s. 2—Courts of Justice Act 1924, ss. 36, 91—Courts (Supplemental Provisions) Act 1961, s. 51—RSC O 65—District Court Rules 1948, r 201. **DPP v Nangle** [1984] 171, HC.

Charge. See Charge (*above*).

Complaint. See Complaint (*above*).

Conviction in District Court on various charges

Appeal to Circuit Court—Circuit Court judge allowing two appeals but dismissing the others and confirming the convictions and sentences—Certificates of conviction not correctly recording the orders spoken by the judges—Application for certiorari—Courts of Justice (District Court) Act 1946, s. 23. **State (O'Dare) v Sheehy** [1984] 99, HC.

Delay in prosecuting charges

Whether such delay excessive—Whether defendant deprived of his right to a fair trial. **Maguire v DPP and Kirby** [1988] 166, HC.

District Court prosecution

Plea of guilty—Legal aid denied—Charges not stated to accused in open court—Application for certiorari to quash conviction—Whether District Court orders good on their face—Whether orders made without or in excess of jurisdiction—Malicious Damage Act 1861, s. 52—Larceny Act 1916, s. 23(a)—Criminal Justice Act 1951, ss. 2, 8—Criminal Procedure Act 1967, s. 13(2)—Criminal Law (Jurisdiction) Act 1976, s. 6—District Court Rules 1972, rr 84, 85. **State (McDonagh) v Barry** [1983] 525, HC.

District Court Rules

Rules Committee of District Court making rules regulating the procedure to be adopted by members of the Gardai in relation to station bail—Extension of time for the appearance in court of the accused—Whether such rules ultra vires. **State (Lynch) v Ballagh** [1987] 65.

CRIMINAL LAW
Procedure *continued*
Emergency powers legislation
Charge—Accused charged in garda station—Whether lawful to charge accused otherwise than in District Court or Special Court—Emergency Powers Act 1976, s. 2. **State (Brennan) v Mahon** [1978] 17, HC.

Extradition cases. See EXTRADITION (Practice and procedure).

Indictable offence
Consent to District Court proceedings—Application for copies of statements of evidence of the intended witnesses refused—Injunction sought to prevent prosecution—Whether the offence a minor offence fit to be tried summarily—Inability of High Court to anticipate District Justice's conclusion—Prerogative writs—Powers and functions of High Court—Offences Against the Person Act 1861, s. 47—Criminal Justice Act 1951, s. 2—Criminal Procedure Act 1967. **Clune v DPP** [1981] 17, HC.

Initiation of criminal proceedings
District Court Rules—Validity—District Court Rules conferring on District Court Clerk the entitlement to receive a complaint and issue a summons—Whether clerk acting in a judicial capacity—Whether rules went beyond the adaptation and modification of legislation for practice and procedure purposes—Whether invalid rules severable—Petty Sessions (Ireland) Act 1851, s. 10—Courts of Justice Act 1924, s. 91—District Court Rules 1948, rr 29, 30—Constitution of Ireland 1937, Articles 34, 37. **Rainey v Delap** [1988] 620, HC.

Jurisdiction of trial. See Trial—Jurisdiction *(below)*.

Nolle prosequi. See Nolle prosequi *(above)*.

Preliminary examination
Depositions—Use of statements from Book of Evidence—Identification of accused—Additional witnesses—Refusal of adjournment—Extent of review on certiorari—Criminal Procedure Act 1967, ss. 6, 7. **State (Daly) v Ruane** [1988] 117, HC.

Exhibits—Whether accused person entitled to inspect exhibits to be produced at trial—Theft of exhibits—Whether accused deprived of right to inspect—Criminal Procedure Act 1967, s. 6(1). **State (Pletzer) v Magee** [1986] 441, HC.

Fair procedures
District Justice not permitting cross-examination of witness—Prosecutor sent forward for trial—Whether denial of fair procedures—Criminal Procedure Act 1967, ss. 5, 6, 7, 8 12, 14, 15. **State (Sherry) v Wine** [1985] 196, SC.

Statement of charge not setting out the time or place of the alleged offence—Failure to serve Book of Evidence—Application for an order of prohibition—Effect of non-compliance with statutory requirements—Whether objection to District Justice's jurisdiction be postponed—Criminal Procedure Act 1967, ss. 5,6,8. **State (Williams) v DPP** [1983] 285, HC; [1983] 537, SC.

Trial on indictment—DPP inserting additional counts—Whether invasion of judicial domain—Whether DPP exercising judicial function. *See* DIRECTOR OF PUBLIC PROSECUTIONS (Powers—Validity—Trial on indictment—Preliminary examination—DPP inserting additional counts).

Trial on indictment—Substitution by DPP of new counts—Whether DPP exercising judicial function—Whether procedure unfair or discriminatory. *See* DIRECTOR OF PUBLIC PROSECUTIONS (Powers—Validity—Trial on indictment—Preliminary examination—DPP substituting new counts).

Prosecution of offences. See Prosecution of offences *(below)*.

Remand in custody. See Remand in custody *(below)*.

CRIMINAL LAW
  Procedure continued
  Return for trial. See Return for trial (*below*).

  Station bail
    Validity of procedure. *See* Bail—Station bail (*above*).

  Striking out of charge
    District Court—Indictable offence—District Court order striking out charge—Accused rearrested and charged with same offences—Prohibition—Whether District Court order amounted to an acquittal—Offences Against the State Act 1939, s. 30—Criminal Justice Act 1967, ss. 6, 7, 8. **State (Hogan) v Carroll** [1981] 25, SC.

    District Court order striking out a charge—Whether appropriate order when court may not have jurisdiction—Whether DPP entitled to proceed with new charge—Whether DPP acted unfairly—Criminal Procedure Act 1967, s. 8. **Carpenter v Kirby** [1990] 764, HC.

  Summons. See Summons (*below*).

  Trial. See Trial (*below*).

Prosecution of offences
  Delay
    Whether such delay excessive—Whether defendant deprived of his right to a fair trial. **Maguire v DPP and Kirby** [1988] 166, HC.

    Whether such delay excessive—Summary offence—Delay in issuing and serving summonses—Whether such as to prejudice accused's right to fair trial—Whether delay caused by actions of defendants—Whether delay by State culpable—Natural justice— Petty Sessions Act 1851, s. 10(4)—Road Traffic Act 1961, s. 49. **State (Cuddy) v Mangan** [1988] 720, HC.

    Whether delay prejudiced right to fair trial—Judicial review—Arrest—Delay of 18 months between initial arrest and bringing of charges—Offences Against the State Act 1939, s. 30. **Hannigan v Clifford; O'Flynn v Clifford** [1990] 65, SC.

  Delegation of power
    Indictable offence—DPP delegating carriage of prosecution to solicitor being whole-time employee of company making criminal complaint against defendant—Whether delegation of power ultra vires the director—Whether risk of unfairness inherent in delegation—Prosecution of Offences Act 1974, ss. 4, 7. **Flynn v DPP** [1986] 290.

  District Justice discharging accused
    DPP directing that accused be sent forward for trial in Circuit Court in respect of the same charges—Whether provisions under which DPP purported to act constitutionally valid—Whether invasion of the judicial domain. *See* DIRECTOR OF PUBLIC PROSECUTIONS (Powers—Validity—Power to send person forward for trial).

  Extra-territorial offence
    Irish citizen in custody in Northern Ireland—Application to Garda Superintendent to seek a warrant—Prosecutor seeking to be delivered into the custody of the Garda Síochána—DPP indicating that proceedings would not be instituted in this jurisdiction— Garda Superintendent declining to seek a warrant—Application for orders of certiorari and mandamus—Whether decision of Garda Superintendent reviewable—Role of DPP—Whether DPP's decision reviewable—Whether prima facie case of mala fides made out—Whether prosecutor deprived of his constitutional rights of access to the courts of this jurisdiction. **State (McCormack) v Curran** [1987] 225, HC, SC.

  Failure to prosecute
    Trial and conviction for one offence—While serving that sentence applicant was charged with and convicted of another offence—Applicant could have been charged

CRIMINAL LAW
Prosecution of offences
Failure to prosecute continued
with this offence at the same time as the first offence—Whether unfair procedure—Whether sentence imposed by Special Criminal Court illegal. **State (McGlinchey) v Governor of Portlaoise Prison** [1982] 187, HC.

Fisheries
Whether District Justice required to furnish applicant with note of evidence taken at trial—Whether officer of Regional Fisheries Board authorised to act outside area of the board—Petty Sessions (Ireland) Act 1851, s. 20—Fisheries (Consolidation) Act 1959, ss. 92, 182(2), (4), 293(2)(a), 301, 308—Courts Act 1971, s. 14—District Court Rules 1948 to 1972, rules 4, 64(5). **Friel v McMenamin** [1990] 761, HC.

Nolle prosequi. See Nolle prosequi (*above*).

Powers of DPP
Validity. *See* DIRECTOR OF PUBLIC PROSECUTIONS (Powers—Validity).

Private prosecution
Common informer—District Court—Prosecution brought by garda as common informer—DPP directing that charge be withdrawn—District Justice entertaining the case—Conviction—Application to quash—Whether DPP had power to intervene—Whether District Justice acted without jurisdiction in hearing complaint when accused was without legal representation—Right of common informer to prosecute—Distinction between official and unofficial common informers—Constitution of Ireland 1937, Art 30 3—Minister and Secretaries Act 1924, s. 6(1)—Criminal Justice Administration Act 1924— Prosecution of Offences Act 1974, s. 3. **State (Collins) v Ruane** [1984] 443, HC; [1985] 349, SC.

Public mischief
Offence of effecting a public mischief contrary to common law
Whether charge known to common law of Ireland—Whether creation of a new offence—Criminal Law Act 1976, s. 12. **DPP (Vizzard) v Carew** [1981] 91, HC.

Public morals
Conspiracy to corrupt public morals
Offence—Whether established—Non-directive counselling regarding abortion. **Attorney General (SPUC) v Open Door Counselling** [1987] 477, HC.

Rape
Conviction by Jury
Uncorroborated evidence—Jurisdiction of CCA to intervene. **People (DPP) v Egan** [1990] 780, SC.

Sentence
Plea of guilty—Sentence of 21 years penal servitude—Appeal—Whether sentence appropriate—Whether court should lay down guidelines. **DPP v Tiernan** [1989] 149, SC.

Receiving stolen goods. *See* Larceny—Offence—Receiving stolen goods (*above*).

Remand in custody
Validity
Application for judicial review—Conviction in District Court—Appeal to Circuit Court—Applicant remanded in custody in accordance with Circuit Court procedure—Whether valid remand—Criminal Procedure Act 1967, s. 24. **Maguire v O'Hanrahan** [1988] 243, HC.

Young person
Certification of unruly character—Evidence—Whether evidence of unruly character must be tested by cross-examination—Natural justice—Children's Act 1908, s. 102(3). **State (O'Donoghue) v Kennedy** [1979] 109, HC.

CRIMINAL LAW *continued*
Re-trial
Supreme Court
Jurisdiction—Appeal against acquittal allowed—Whether Supreme Court empowered
to order re-trial—Whether consistent with principle of autrefois acquit—Whether re-
trial would result in arbitrary discrimination—Constitution of Ireland 1937, Articles
34 4, 40 1—Criminal Procedure Act 1967, s. 34(1)—Rules of the Superior Courts
1986, O 87. **People (DPP) v Quilligan** (No 2) [1989] 245, SC.

Return for trial
Error
Delay—Return to wrong Circuit Court—Circuit Court having no jurisdiction—Error
due to fault of the DPP—No contention that the accused was hindered in the conduct
of his defence—RSC 1986, O 84—Courts (Supplemental Provisions) Act 1961, s. 25.
DPP v Johnson [1988] 747, HC.

Special Criminal Court
DPP—Return for trial on non-scheduled offences to Special Criminal Court—Opinion
of DPP that ordinary courts not adequate—Whether reviewable by the court—
Constitution of Ireland 1937, Article 38 3 1—Offences Against the State Act 1939, ss.
35, 45, 46(2)—Prosecution of Offences Act 1974, s. 3. **Savage v DPP** [1982] 385, HC.

DPP directing trial in Special Criminal Court—Whether power unconstitutional—
Opinion of DPP that ordinary courts inadequate—Whether reviewable by the courts—
Offences Against the State Act 1939, ss. 47, 48—Prosecution of Offences Act 1974, s.
3. **Judge v DPP; O'Reilly v DPP** [1984] 224, HC.

Revenue offence
Whether criminal offence
Payment of penalties in default of income tax returns—Whether penalties imposition
of punishment—Whether criminal matter—Whether offence clearly established—
Constitution of Ireland 1937, Article 34—Income Tax Act 1967, s. 500. **McLoughlin v
Tuite** [1986] 304, HC.

Recovery of penalty—Whether criminal proceeding—Purpose of section imposing
penalty—Employer—Failure to make returns—Income Tax Act 1967, s. 128. **Downes
v DPP** [1987] 665, HC.

Road traffic offences. *See* ROAD TRAFFIC OFFENCES.

Search warrant
Absence
Authority to enter premises—Whether in force—Whether evidence obtained without
warrant admissible—Whether judge must exercise discretion to admit evidence. **DPP v
McCutcheon** [1986] 433, HC.

Entry on premises—Gardai entering premises and obtaining evidence—Whether
evidence admissible—Relevance of power to enter under intoxicating liquor code.
DPP v McMahon [1987] 87, SC.

Invalidity
Forcible entry of accused's home—Evidence—Admissibility—Constitutional right to
inviolability of dwelling. **People (DPP) v Kenny** [1990] 569, SC.

Issue
Nature of information required for issue of warrant—Nature of determination to issue
warrant—Misuse of Drugs Act 1977, s. 26(1). **People (DPP) v Kenny** [1990] 569, SC.

Sentence
Appeal
Circuit Judge indicating that if compensation were to be paid within a prescribed time
custodial sentence would not be imposed—Accused failing to appear at adjourned

CRIMINAL LAW
Sentence
Appeal continued

appeals—Custodial sentences affirmed—Whether judge had jurisdiction to reinstate appeals which had been dismissed—Certiorari—Whether Circuit Court order affirming District Court order be quashed. **State (Dunne) v Martin** [1982] 18, SC.

Commencement

Not to occur before specified date—Arrest warrant—Delay in execution of warrant—Judicial review—Certiorari—Conduct of applicant contributing to delay—Judical discretion. **O'Driscoll v Governor of Cork Prison** [1989] 239, HC.

Consecutive sentence

Accused already serving sentence of imprisonment—Sentence to run from legal expiration at present being served—Whether void for uncertainty—Power to impose consecutive sentences. **State (Gleeson) v Martin** [1985] 577, HC.

Jurisdiction of court—Felony—Statute apparently giving power to impose consecutive sentences repealed by Statute Law Revision Act—Effect of repeal—Whether power existed independently of statute—Criminal Law (Ireland) Act 1828, s. 20—Statute Law Revision Act 1983, s. 2. **State (Dixon) v Martin** [1985] 240, HC.

Jurisdiction of court—Young offender—Detention in St Patrick's Institution—Whether a young offender may be sentenced in the District Court to consecutive periods of such detention exceeding twelve months—Nature of distinction between imprisonment and detention—Criminal Justice Act 1951, s. 5—Criminal Justice Act 1960, s. 13(1). **State (Clinch) v Connellan** [1986] 455, SC.

Increase

Circuit Court—Jurisdiction—Conviction in District Court—Sentence of imprisonment—Appeal against conviction—Sentence increased by Circuit Court—Whether increase made within jurisdiction—Procedure adopted in challenging Circuit Court order—Constitution of Ireland 1937, Article 40 4 2—Petty Sessions Act 1851, s. 24—Courts of Justice Act 1924, ss. 51, 85, 91—Courts of Justice Act 1928, s. 18—Courts (Establishment and Constitution) Act 1961, s. 5—Courts (Supplemental Provisions) Act 1961, ss. 22(3), 22(5)(a), 48, 50. **State (Aherne) v Governor of Limerick Prison** [1981] 169, HC; [1983] 17, SC.

Circuit Court—Jurisdiction—District Court Appeals—Whether absence of fairness in the procedure. **State (O'Rourke) v Martin; State (O'Flaherty) v Martin** [1984] 333, HC.

Manslaughter

Plea of guilty—Co-accused each sentenced to nine years penal servitude—Appellant receiving penal servitude for life—Appeal against severity of sentence—Whether sentence appropriate. **People (DPP) v Conroy** [1989] 139, SC.

Misuse of drugs

Purpose—Punishment or rehabilitation—Change of circumstances of offender—Removal from contact with proscribed drugs by parents—Probation officer reports making no reference to change of circumstances—Whether judge obliged to take account of change in devising regime of rehabilitation rather than punishment—Misuse of Drugs Act 1977, s. 28(2). **State (Slattery) v Roe** [1986] 511, HC.

Penal servitude

Manslaughter—Plea of guilty—Co-accused each sentenced to nine years penal servitude—Appellant receiving penal servitude for life—Appeal against severity of sentence. **People (DPP) v Conroy** [1989] 139, SC.

Rape—Plea of guilty—Sentence of 21 years penal servitude—Whether sentence appropriate. **DPP v Tiernan** [1989] 149, SC.

CRIMINAL LAW
Sentence
Penal servitudecontinued

Military custody—Whether sentence imposed laid down by law—Prisons Act 1972, ss. 2, 4. **State (Flannery) v Governor of Military Detention Barracks** [1976–7] 13, SC.

Preventative detention

Habitual criminals—Lengthy sentence imposed—Whether amounting to preventative detention—Whether attempt to reform by prevention appropriate basis for sentence—Prevention of Crime Act 1908, s. 10. **People (DPP) v Carmody** [1988] 370, CCA.

Rape

Plea of guilty—Sentence of 21 years penal servitude—Appeal—Whether sentence appropriate—Whether court should lay down guidelines. **DPP v Tiernan** [1989] 149, SC.

Remission

Detention sentence of ten years—Final four years to be suspended—Regulations providing for remission of sentence—Whether remission earned related to six years custodial sentence—Whether prisoner entitled to be released—Prisons Act 1972, s. 2(9)—Prisons Act 1972 (Military Custody) Regulations 1972, reg 35(1). **State (Beirnes) v Governor of Curragh Military Detention Barracks** [1982] 491, HC.

Road traffic

Conviction for drunken driving—Maximum permissible sentence six months—Sentence imposed of three months imprisonment and fine of £250, with six months imprisonment in default of payment—Prosecutor therefore liable to imprisonment for nine months—Whether order made in excess of jurisdiction—Petty Sessions (Ireland) Act 1851, s. 22—Criminal Justice Administration Act 1914, ss. 3, 16—Criminal Justice Act 1951, s. 5—Road Traffic Act 1961, ss. 49(2), 49(4)(a)—Road Traffic (Amendment) Act 1978, s. 10(4)(a)—District Court Rules 1948, r 65. State (Delaney) v Magee [1983] 45, HC.

Successive sentences

District Court—Jurisdiction—Aggregate sentences exceeding twelve months—Whether District Justice acting in excess of jurisdiction—Criminal Justice Act 1951, ss. 5, 41. **State (Payne) v Clifford** [1985] 70, HC.

Uncertainty

Commencement date—Ordered to begin at the expiration of the last of any sentence currently being served—Whether ambiguous—Whether void for uncertainty. **State (Dixon) v Martin** [1985] 240, HC.

Young Person

Plea of guilty—Circuit Court Judge certifying that defendant not a fit person to be detained in a place of detention for young persons—Whether court then entitled to impose such punishment as the law provides and the Court thinks proper—Children Act 1908, ss. 101(3), 102(3), 106, 131—Children Act 1941, s. 29. **State (Laffey) v Esmonde** [1983] 291, SC.

Validity

Habeas corpus application—Trial and conviction for one offence—While serving that sentence applicant was charged with and convicted of another offence—Applicant could have been charged with this offence at the same time as the first offence—Whether unfair procedure—Whether sentence imposed by Special Criminal Court illegal. **State (McGlinchey) v Governor of Portlaoise Prison** [1982] 187, HC.

Shoplifting
Conviction

Plea of guilty—Whether voluntary—Certiorari. *See* Trial—Plea of guilty—Whether voluntary—Shoplifting—Certiorari *(below)*.

CRIMINAL LAW *continued*
Social welfare offence
False statements
Unemployment benefit—Minor offence—Number of similar offences charged in the one summons—District Court—Jurisdiction. **The State (Wilson) v Neilan** [1987] 118, HC.

Special Criminal Court
Jurisdiction. See SPECIAL CRIMINAL COURT (Jurisdiction).

Street trading offences. *See* ROAD TRAFFIC OFFENCES (Street trading—Breaches of bye-laws).

Summons
Delay in issuing
Whether such delay excessive—Summary offence—Whether delay such as to prejudice accused's right to fair trial—Whether delay caused by actions of defendants—Whether delay by State culpable—Natural justice—Petty Sessions Act 1851, s. 10(4)—Road Traffic Act 1961, s. 49. **State (Cuddy) v Mangan** [1988] 720, HC.

Sufficiency
Conviction—Application to make absolute a conditional order of certiorari—District Court Clerk affixing signature to the summons by use of a rubber stamp—Whether open to prosecutor to challenge sufficiency of summons—Prosecutor acquiesing in adjournments of his case—Validity of concept of 'representation without prejudice' questioned. **State (O'Leary) v Neilan** [1984] 35, HC.

Validity
Delay in serving summons—Date of issue altered—Whether summons invalid—Road Traffic (Amendment) Act 1978, ss. 12(2), 13(3). **DPP v Clein** [1983] 76, SC.

Issue—Whether complaint made within statutory period—Whether summons invalidly issued—Date from which time runs in relation to complaint. **State (Clarke) v Roche** [1986] 565, HC; [1987] 309, SC.

Issue—Whether complaint made within statutory period—Whether evidence before courts as to valid issue of summons—Nature of summons—Petty Sessions (Ireland) Act 1851, s. 10(4). **DPP v Sheeran** [1986] 579, HC.

Issue—Whether complaint made within statutory period—Whether evidence before court as to valid issue of summons—Nature of summons—Petty Sessions (Ireland) Act 1851, s. 10(4). **State (Gartlan) v O'Donnell** [1986] 588, HC.

Non-compliance with form prescribed by District Court rules—Reversal of onus of proof—Whether summons saved—Whether applicant appeared and submitted to the jurisdiction of the District Court—Petty Sessions (Ireland) Act 1851, ss. 36 and 39. **McGirl v McArdle** [1989] 495, HC.

Peace Commissioner signing summons—Whether invalid as being an exercise of judicial power—Whether appearance in court cures defect in securing attendance—Constitution of Ireland 1937, Article 34 4 3. **Joyce v Circuit Court Judge for Western Circuit** [1987] 316, HC.

Road traffic offence—Summons originally issued in July for court hearing in September—Date of hearing altered to November—Service of summons not effected prior to original date of court hearing—Whether summons continued to be valid and effective. **DPP v Clein** [1981] 465, HC.

Summons issued from office of District Court clerks by means of computer printout—Summons not considered by clerk—Whether summons invalidly issued—Date from which time runs in relation to complaint—Petty Sessions (Ireland) Act 1851, ss. 10, 11—Courts of Justice Act 1924—Courts Officers' Act 1926, s. 48—Courts Officers'

CRIMINAL LAW
Summons
Validity continued
Act 1951—Criminal Justice Act 1951, s. 15—District Court Rules 1948, r 30. **State (Clarke) v Roche** [1986] 565, HC; [1987] 309, SC.

Summons issued by District Court Clerk—Conviction—Warrant issued on foot of conviction—Warrant going out of date—Warrant issued by District Justice—Whether summons duly issued by an authorised person—Whether District Justice jurisdiction to re-issue a warrant. **Connors v Delap** [1989] 93, HC.

Time limit—Indictable offence triable summarily—Application for issue of summons made more than six months after date of alleged offence—Whether time limit applicable—Petty Sessions (Ireland) Act 1881, s. 10—Criminal Justice Act 1951, s. 7—Courts (No 3) Act 1986, s. 1. **McGrail v Ruane** [1989] 498, HC.

Whether issue of summons an act of a judicial nature—Summons issued—Complaints not considered personally by District Court Clerk—Whether summons should be dismissed—Petty Sessions (Ireland) Act 1851, ss. 10, 11. **State (Clarke) v Roche** [1986] 565, HC; [1987] 309, SC.

Whether issue of summons a judicial act—District Court Rules conferring on District Court Clerk the entitlement to receive a complaint and issue a summons—Whether clerk acting in a judicial capacity—Validity—Whether ultra vires—Petty Sessions (Ireland) Act 1851, s. 10—Courts of Justice Act 1924, s. 91—District Court Rules 1948, rr 29, 30—Constitution of Ireland 1937, Articles 34, 37. **Rainey v Delap** [1988] 620, HC.

Trial
Abandonment
Proposed retrial—Whether prejudice arising—Constitution of Ireland 1937, Articles 38.1, 40.3. **O'Connor v DPP** [1987] 723, HC.

Adjournment. See also ADJOURNMENT.

Refusal—Defendant requesting adjournment to obtain legal representation and a witness—Whether refusal to grant adjournment breach of natural justice. **Flynn v Ruane** [1989] 690, HC.

Constitution. See CONSTITUTION (Trial of offences).

Delay
Fair procedures—Trial abandoned—Proposed re-trial—Whether prejudice arising—Whether interlocutory injunction to restrain said trial be granted—Constitution of Ireland 1937, Articles 38 1, 40 3. **O'Connor v DPP** [1987] 723, HC.

Whether such as to prejudice accused's right to fair trial—Whether delay caused by actions of defendants—Whether delay by State culpable—Constitution of Ireland 1937, Article 38 1. **State (O'Connell) v Fawsitt** [1986] 639, HC, SC.

Whether such as to prejudice accused's right to fair trial—Whether delay caused by actions of defendants—Whether delay by the State culpable—Constitution of Ireland 1937, Article 38 1. **State (O'Keeffe) v McMenamin** [1986] 653, HC.

Whether such as to prejudice accused's right to fair trial—Judicial review—Delay of 18 months between initial arrest and bringing of charges—Offences Against the State Act 1939, s. 30. Hannigan v Clifford: **O'Flynn v Clifford** [1990] 65, SC.

Evidence. See Evidence (*above*).

Indictable offence
Consent to District Court proceedings—Application for copies of statements of evidence of the intended witnesses refused—Injunction sought to prevent prosecution—

CRIMINAL LAW
Trial

Indictable offence continued

Procedure to be adopted by the Court—Whether to proceed without copies of the evidence being tendered contrary to natural and constitutional justice—Prerogative writs—Powers and functions of High Court—Offences Against the Person Act 1861, s. 47—Criminal Justice Act 1951, s. 2—Criminal Procedure Act 1967. **Clune v DPP** [1981] 17, HC.

Interference with judicial determination

Statute—Validity. *See* CONSTITUTION (Trial of offences—Interference with judicial determination—Statute—Validity—Excise offences).

Judge

Interventions by judge during conduct of defence—Whether excessive—Whether injustice resulted. **People (DPP) v Marley** [1985] 17, CCA.

Jurisdiction

Extra-territorial offence—Irish citizen in custody in Northern Ireland seeking to be delivered into the custody of the Garda Síochána—DPP indicating that proceedings would not be instituted in this jurisdiction—Whether decision of Garda Superintendent reviewable—Whether DPP's decision reviewable—Whether prosecutor deprived of his constitutional rights of access to the courts of this jurisdiction—Statutory right of individual to select the jurisdiction for his trial—When right arises—Criminal Law (Jurisdiction) Act 1976. **State (McCormack) v Curran** [1987] 225, HC, SC.

Jury See also JURY

Absence of some members during direction by judge—Whether trial unsatisfactory. **People (DPP) v Marley** [1985] 17, CCA.

Mode of trial

Nature of offence—Whether minor offence triable summarily. *See* CONSTITUTION (Trial of offences—Minor offence).

Plea of autrefois acquit. See Autrefois acquit (*above*).

Plea of guilty

Change to not guilty plea—DPP entering nolle prosequi. *See* Nolle prosequi (*above*).

Manslaughter—Sentence. *See* Sentence—Manslaughter—Plea of guilty (*above*).

Rape—Sentence. *See* Rape—Sentence (*above*).

Whether voluntary—Shoplifting—Conviction—Certiorari—Natural justice—Appeal to Circuit Court—Whether reason for refusing order of certiorari—Factors guiding Court in the exercise of its discretion. **State (Glover and Mulligan) v McCarthy** [1981] 47, HC.

Young person—Sentence. *See* Sentence—Young person—Plea of guilty (*above*).

Special Criminal Court

DPP directing trial in Special Criminal Court—Return for trial on non-scheduled offences to Special Criminal Court—Opinion of DPP that ordinary courts not adequate—Whether reviewable by the court—Constitution of Ireland 1937, Article 38 3 1—Offences Against the State Act 1939, ss. 35, 45, 46(2)—Prosecution of Offences Act 1974, s. 3. **Savage v DPP** [1982] 385, HC.

DPP directing trial in Special Criminal Court—Whether power unconstitutional—Opinion of DPP that ordinary courts inadequate—Whether reviewable by the courts—Offences Against the State Act 1939, ss. 47, 48—Prosecution of Offences Act 1974, s. 3. **Judge v DPP; O'Reilly v DPP** [1984] 224, HC.

Summary jurisdiction

Accused electing for summary trial—Whether District Justice subsequently entitled to

CRIMINAL LAW
Trial
Summary jurisdiction continued

decline jurisdiction—Offences against the Person Act 1861, s. 62—Penal Servitude Act 1891, s. 1—Criminal Justice Act 1951, ss. 2 (2)(a), 4(1). **State (O'Hagan) v Delap** [1983] 241, HC.

Transfer

Constitution—Accused sent forward for trial to Dublin Circuit Court—Accused seeking trial in High Court (Central Criminal Court)—Prohibition on transfer—Whether statutory provisions prohibiting transfer repugnant to the Constitution—Whether withdrawing jurisdiction from the High Court expressly conferred by the Constitution— Constitution of Ireland 1937, Articles 34 2, 34 3, 36 iii—Courts (Establishment and Constitution) Act 1961, s. 4—Courts (Supplemental Provisions) Act 1961, ss. 11, 25— Courts Act 1964, s. 4—Courts Act 1981, s. 32(1). **Tormey v Attorney General** [1984] 657, HC; [1985] 375, SC.

Trial on indictment

DPP inserting additional counts—Whether invasion of judicial domain—Whether DPP exercising judicial function. *See* DIRECTOR OF PUBLIC PROSECUTIONS (Powers—Vaidity— Trial on indictment—Preliminary examination—DPP inserting additional counts).

Substitution by DPP of new counts—Whether DPP exercising judicial function— Whether procedure unfair or discriminatory. *See* DIRECTOR OF PUBLIC PROSECUTIONS (Powers—Validity—Trial on indictment—Preliminary examination—DPP substituting new counts).

Venue

Indictable offence—Circuit Court—Return for trial—Courthouse destroyed by fire— Transfer of trial—Powers of President of Circuit Court—Whether infringement of accused's rights—Whether right to be tried by jury drawn from any particular locality— Courts of Justice Act 1947, s. 10—Courts (Supplemental Provisions) Act 1961, ss. 25, 26—Criminal Procedure Act 1967, s. 8—Juries Act 1967—District Court (Criminal Procedure Act 1967) Rules. **State (Hughes) v Neylon** [1982] 108, HC.

Verdict

Jurisdiction of CCA to substitute its own subjective view of evidence for the verdict of a jury. **People (DPP) v Egan** [1990] 780, SC.

Voir dire

Evidence—Admissibility—Statement by accused—Accused alleging detention in Garda custody unlawful—Onus of proof—Whether issue to be tried by judge on voir dire or by jury—Whether jury likely to be prejudiced by determining issue of lawfulness of detention or admissibility of evidence. **People (DPP) v Conroy** [1988] 4, CCA, SC.

Whether defendant lawfully before court

Whether defendant in unlawful custody at time of being charged in court—Whether relevant to jurisdiction of court to try case. **People (DPP) v Kehoe** [1986] 690, CCA.

Warrant
Arrest warrant. See Arrest warrant *(above)*.

Extradition. See EXTRADITION (Warrant).

Search warrant. See Search warrant *(above)*.

Young offender
Evidence

Admissibility—Statement by accused in Garda custody—Whether obligation to have parent or guardian present during questioning—Whether fear of obstruction of course of justice justifies refusal to have parent present. **Travers v Ryan** [1985] 343, HC.

CRIMINAL LAW
Young offender *continued*
Remand in custody
> Certification of unruly character—Evidence—Whether evidence of unruly character must be tested by cross-examination—Natural justice—Children's Act 1908, s. 102(3). **State (O'Donoghue) v Kennedy** [1979] 109, HC.

Sentence
> Plea of guilty—Circuit Court Judge certifying that defendant not a fit person to be detained in a place of detention for young persons—Whether court then entitled to impose such punishment as the law provides and the Court thinks proper—Children Act 1908, ss. 101(3), 102(3), 106, 131—Children Act 1941, s. 29. **State (Laffey) v Esmonde** [1983] 291, SC.

> Successive sentences—Detention in St Patrick's Institution—Whether a young offender may be sentenced in the District Court to consecutive periods of such detention exceeding twelve months—Criminal Justice Act 1951, s. 5—Criminal Justice Act 1960, s. 13(1). **State (Clinch) v Connellan** [1986] 455, SC.

CRIMINAL LEGAL AID. *See* CRIMINAL LAW (Legal aid).

CROWN PREROGATIVE
Treasure trove
Whether carried over into Irish law
> Constitution of Ireland 1937, Articles 5, 10. **Webb v Ireland** [1988] 565, HC, SC.

CRUELTY
Marriage
> *Divorce a mensa et thoro See* MARRIAGE (Divorce a mensa et thoro).

CURRENCY
Judgment. *See* JUDGMENT (Currency).

CUSTODY
Child
> *Adoption. See* ADOPTION.

> *Generally. See* CHILD (Custody).

> *Guardianship. See* CHILD (Guardianship and custody).

Escape from custody
> *Extradition proceedings. See* EXTRADITION (Escape from custody).

Garda Siochána
> *Statement made by accused while in custody*
> Admissibility in evidence. *See* CRIMINAL LAW (Evidence—Statement by accused).

> *Whether detention lawful. See* ARREST (Detention—Legality).

Military custody
> *Generally. See* PRISONS (Military custody).

> *Sentence. See* CRIMINAL LAW (Sentence—Penal servitude in military custody).

Remand in custody. *See* CRIMINAL LAW (Remand in custody).

CUSTOMER
Bank
> *Duty of care. See* BANK (Duty of care).

CRIMINAL LAW *continued*
Supermarket
Nature of relationship
Whether bailment, licence or custody—Defendant leaving supermarket without paying
for goods—Whether defendant guilty of larceny—Larceny Act 1916, ss. 1, 2. **DPP v
Morrissey** [1982] 487, HC.

CUSTOMS AND EXCISE
Betting duty
Offences. See Offence—Betting duty *(below).*

Excise duty
Agriculture
Levy on livestock—European Community—Common organisation of the markets—
Whether measure having effect equivalent to a customs duty—Whether duty *ultra vires*
as unreasonable—Whether decision on European law required—Imposition of Duties
(No 239) Agricultural Produce (Cattle and Milk) Order 1979—Agricultural Produce
(Cattle and Milk) Regulations 1979. **Doyle v An Taoiseach** [1986] 693, HC, SC.

Deed of bond
Principal and surety—Priority—Excise Collection and Management Act 1841, s. 24.
Attorney General v Sun Alliance and London Insurances Ltd [1985] 522, SC.

Practice
Company importing goods for processing and exporting them for sale—Exemption from
duty—Appointment of receiver—Receiver selling goods on the home market—Whether
full duty now payable—Whether duty payable in priority to the other creditors—
Customs Consolidation Act 1876, s. 177—Finance Act 1932, ss. 38, 45—European
Communities (Customs) Regulation 1972, reg 11. **Spain v Revenue Commissioners**
[1980] 21, HC.

Excise offence. *See* Offence *(below).*

Offence
Betting duty
Whether single or multiple offences—Whether minor offences triable summarily—
Finance Act 1926, s. 25(2)—Betting Duty (Certified Returns) Regulations 1934—Con-
stitution of Ireland 1937, Articles 38.2, 38.5. **State (Rollinson) v Kelly** [1984] 625, SC.

Whether minor offence triable summarily—Matters to which the court is to have
regard—Constitution of Ireland 1937, Article 38.2—Finance Act 1926, ss. 24, 25—
Betting Duty (Certified Returns) Regulations 1934, regs 8, 18, 23, 29. **Charlton v Ireland**
[1984] 39, HC.

Issue of facts in dispute
Determination of value of goods—Statute providing for final and unappealable
determination to be made by District Justice—Offence triable with jury—Jury precluded from determining issue—Whether statute inconsistent with Constitution—
Constitution of Ireland 1937, Articles 34.3.4, 38.1, 38.2, 38.5—Finance Act 1963, ss.
34(4)(d)(i), 34(4)(d)(iii). **Curtis v Attorney General** [1986] 428, HC.

Penalty
Mandatory penalty on conviction—Whether court has jurisdiction to mitigate
penalty—Whether court has discretion with regard to penalty incurred—Interpretation
of statute—Excise Management Act 1827, s. 78—Finance Act 1926, s. 25(2)—Criminal
Justice Act 1951, s. 8—Finance Act 1982, ss. 69(1)(b), 70. **DPP v Gray** [1987] 4, SC.

Statute
Interpretation
Table water duties—Ice pops—Whether 'table waters'—Whether product something
intended to be drunk—Finance (New Duties) Act 1916, ss. 4(1)(2), 6(3)—Table Waters

CRIMINAL LAW
Statute
Interpretation continued
Duties Regulations 1916, reg 6. **Attorney General v Palmer Products Ltd; Attorney General v Leaf Ltd** [1982] 441, HC.

CY-PRÈS DOCTRINE
Charitable gifts. *See* CHARITY (Cy-près).

DÁIL ÉIREANN
Dissolution
Injunction
Whether courts can prevent the Taoiseach from advising the President to dissolve Dáil Éireann—Duty of Oireachtas to revise Dáil constituencies—Ratio not complying with requirements of Constitution—Constitution of Ireland 1937, Articles 13.2.1, 13.2.2, 13.8.1, 16.3.1, 16.2. **O'Malley v An Taoiseach** [1990] 461, HC.

Elections. *See* ELECTORAL LAW.

Extradition treaty
Approval
Whether treaty a charge on the public funds. *See* CONSTITUTION (International relations—Treaty—Extradition treaty—Treaty involving expense).

Revision of constituencies
Duty of Oireachtas
Ratio not complying with requirements of Constitution—Constitution of Ireland 1937, Article 16.2.3. **O'Malley v An Taoiseach** [1990] 461, HC.

Statement by Minister in the Dáil
Reliance. See MINISTER (Statement in Dáil Éireann—Reliance).

DAIRY CO-OPERATIVES
Competition
Application of European Community rules. See AGRICULTURE (Co-operatives—Competition)

DAIRY FARMING
Milk quotas. *See* AGRICULTURE (Milk quotas).

Milk levy. *See* AGRICULTURE (Milk levy).

DAMAGES
Aggravated damages
Constitutional right
Breach—Right to privacy—Telephone tapping—Whether plaintiff entitled to punitive or aggravated damages—Constitution of Ireland 1937, Article 40.3—Civil Liability Act 1961, ss. 7(2), 14(4), HC.

Defamation
Libel—Appeal against quantum—Measure of damages—Whether damages adequate to compensate plaintiff—Conduct of proceedings—Whether relevant. **Kennedy v Hearne** [1988] 52, 531, SC.

Lease
Covenant—Quiet enjoyment—Interference by landlord—Intimidation—Whether aggravated damages be awarded—Whether damages recoverable for breach of covenant to repair—Landlord and Tenant (Ireland) Act 1860, ss. 17, 41—Landlord and Tenant Act 1931, s. 5. **Whelan v Madigan** [1978] 136, HC.

DAMAGES *continued*
Appeal
Award
> Personal injuries—Appeal to Supreme Court—Whether events subsequent to High
> Court order constitute grounds of appeal—Admissibility of new evidence—Relevance—
> Rules of the Superior Courts 1986, O 58, rr 3(4), 8. **Dalton v Minister for Finance**
> [1989] 519, SC.

> Supreme Court—Jurisdiction—Whether Supreme Court may substitute award of High
> Court—Constitution of Ireland 1937, Article 34 4 3—Courts of Justice Act 1924, s.
> 96. **Holohan v Donohue** [1986] 250, SC.

> Whether excessive—Defamation—Purpose of award compensatory. **Barrett v
> Independent Newspapers Ltd** [1986] 601, SC.

> Whether excessive—Personal injuries. *See* Personal injuries—Award—Whether excessive
> (*below*).

Apportionment
Concurrent wrongdoers
> Whether appropriate to apportion damage between defendants—Civil Liability Act
> 1961, s. 11. **Riordan's Travel Ltd v Acres** [1979] 3, HC.

Assessment
Appeal court. See Appeal (*above*).

Personal injuries. See Personal injuries (*below*).

Supreme Court
> Jurisdiction—Whether Supreme Court may substitute award of High Court—
> Constitution of Ireland 1937, Article 34 4 3—Courts of Justice Act 1924, s. 96.
> **Holohan v Donohue** [1986] 250, SC.

> Supreme Court assessing and awarding damages in first instance. **Bahkt v Medical
> Council** [1990] 840, SC.

Award
Appeal. See Appeal (*above*).

Contributory negligence
> Whether just and equitable to reduce award to nil Behaviour of plaintiff—Civil
> Liability Act 1961, s. 34(1). **McCord v Electricity Supply Board** [1980] 153, SC.

Deductions
> Personal injuries—Social welfare benefits. *See* Personal injuries—Deduction from
> award (*below*).

Whether excessive
> Defamation—Purpose of award compensatory. **Barrett v Independent Newspapers Ltd**
> [1986] 601, SC.

Whether excessive
> Personal injuries. *See under* Personal injuries (*below*).

Breach of contract
Building contract
> Defects—Alleged defects in workmanship and materials—Repairs deferred while
> liability disputed—Rescission in accordance with commercial good sense—Date by
> reference to which damages should be assessed—Plaintiff's financial stringency. **Corrigan
> v Crofton** [1985] 189, HC.

> Defects—Assessment—Whether purchaser entitled to loss in letting value or loss of
> interest on capital. **Fitzpatrick v Frank McGivern Ltd.** [1976–7] 239, HC.

DAMAGES
Breach of contract *continued*
Employment contract
Termination of appointment—Whether circumstances required to terminate appointment had arisen—Whether contract frustrated. In re Shiel: **Browne v Mulligan** [1976–7] 327, SC.

Wrongful dismissal—Office holder—Failure to pay salary on due dates—Loss of availability of salary—Whether dismissal resulted in injury to health—Whether due to unlawful nature of dismissal—Exemplary damages—Loss arising from arbitrary nature of dismissal. **Garvey v Ireland** [1979] 266, HC.

Loss of income
Assessment—Whether claim sustainable for loss in provision of unused capital asset—Whether claim amounts to double compensation—Whether loss of income reasonably in contemplation of parties. **Waterford Harbour Commrs v British Railways** [1979] 296, HC, SC.

Loss of profits
Assessment of damages—Principles to be applied—Whether inflationary decrease in purchasing power relevant in assessing damages—Whether award taxable in hands of claimant—Whether award to be reduced to take account of liability to tax. **Hickey & Co Ltd v Roches Stores** (Dublin) Ltd [1980] 107, HC.

Sale of land
Damages for failure to complete—Vendor's delay—Vendor obtaining income from property while contract completed—Whether purchaser entitled to damages in addition to decree for specific performance. **O'Brien v White-Spunner** [1979] 240, HC.

Damages in lieu of specific performance—Whether damages appropriate remedy. **White v McCooey** [1976–7] 72, HC.

Damages in lieu of specific performance—Whether to be assessed by reference to the value of the premises at date of judgment—Evidence as to market value—Whether damages to include loss of profits—Rule in *Hadley v Baxendale*. **In re Fuller & Co Ltd: O'Connor v McCarthy** [1982] 201, HC.

Damages in lieu of specific performance—Interest—Whether a capital sum within the meaning of the Act—Incidence of capital gains tax in regard to damages—Capital Gains Tax Act 1976, ss. 3, 8, 11, 25—Capital Gains Tax (Amendment) Act 1978, ss. 2, 4. **Vandeleur v Dargan** [1981] 75, HC.

Building contract
Breach. See Breach of contract—Building contract (*above*).

Exclusion clauses
Defects. *See* Defective premises—Building contract—Exclusion clause—Further clause that purchaser not deprived of his common law rights (*below*).

Constitutional obligation
Breach
Resulting harm to plaintiff—Whether damages recoverable. **Hosford v John Murphy and Sons Ltd** [1988] 300, HC.

Constitutional right
Breach
Communication—Convicted prisoner—Whether tort—Whether damages may be granted—Whether loss suffered—Whether nominal damages appropriate—Constitution of Ireland 1937, Articles 40 3, 40 6 1(i). **Kearney v Minister for Justice** [1987] 52, HC.

Right to privacy—Telephone tapping—Whether plaintiffs entitled to punitive or aggravated damages—Constitution of Ireland 1937, Article 40.3—Civil Liability Act 1961, ss. 7(2), 14(4). **Kennedy & Arnold v Ireland** [1988] 472, HC.

DAMAGES

Constitutional right *continued*

Infringement

Family. *See* Family—Constitutional rights—Non-pecuniary benefits deriving from parent-child relationship (*below*).

Interference

Guardianship of infants—Removal of children from jurisdiction by wife—Passports obtained despite husband's objections—Entitlement to damages. *See* Statutory rights—Infringement—Guardianship of infants—Husband and wife—Removal of children from jurisdiction by wife (*below*).

Right to free primary education—Trade dispute—Union directing members not to enrol pupils from affected schools—Claim for damages—Whether such claim a claim in tort—Constitution of Ireland 1937, Article 42 2—Trade Disputes Act 1906, s. 4. **Hayes v Ireland** [1987] 651, HC.

Contributory negligence

Award

Whether just and equitable to reduce award to nil—Behaviour of plaintiff—Civil Liability Act 1961, s. 34(1). **McCord v Electricity Supply Board** [1980] 153, SC.

Personal injuries. See Personal injuries—Contributory negligence (*below*).

Conversion

Copyright See Copyright (*below*)

Copyright

Infringement

Measure of damages—Whether plaintiffs entitled to damages for conversion in addition to damages for infringement—Whether award of exemplary damages permitted—Measure of damages for conversion—Claim for interest—Copyright Act 1963, ss. 22, 24. **Allibert S.A. v O'Connor and Others** [1982] 40, HC.

Deduction from award

Social welfare benefits. See Personal injuries—Deduction from award (*below*).

Defamation

Libel

Award—Aggravated damages—Appeal against quantum—Measure of damages—Whether damages adequate to compensate plaintiff—Conduct of proceedings—Whether relevant. **Kennedy v Hearne** [1988] 52, 531, SC.

Award—Whether excessive—Purpose of award compensatory—Whether jury awarded sum not reasonable in circumstances. **Barrett v Independent Newspapers Ltd** [1986] 601, SC.

Defective premises

Building contract

Breach. *See* Breach of contract—Building contract—Defects (*above*).

Exclusion clause—Further clause that purchaser not deprived of his common law rights—Claim for damages for remedying defects and for diminution in value—Whether caught by exclusion clause—Whether purchaser entitled to damages for inconvenience and loss of engagement. **Johnson v Longleat Properties** (Dublin) Ltd. [1976–7] 93, HC.

Damages recoverable

Whether damages recoverable for defective workmanship and for inconvenience as well as for dangerous faults—Apportionment of loss—Concurrent wrongdoers—Contribution or indemnity—Housing Act 1966, s. 39—Housing Authorities (Loans for Acquisition or Construction of Houses) Regulations 1972—Civil Liability Act 1961, s. 21(2). **Ward v McMaster** [1986] 43, HC.

DAMAGES
Defective premises *continued*
Measure of damages
Agreement to build house—Dispute as to alleged defects in workmanship and materials—Repairs deferred while liability disputed—Decision in accordance with commercial good sense—Date by reference to which damages should be assessed—Plaintiff's financial stringency—Whether relevant. **Corrigan v Crofton** [1985] 189, HC.

Exemplary damages
Copyright
Infringement—Measure of damages—Whether award of exemplary damages permitted—Claim for interest—Copyright Act 1963, ss. 22, 24. **Allibert s. A v O'Connor and Others** [1982] 40, HC.

Wrongful dismissal
Office holder——Loss arising from arbitrary nature of dismissal. **Garvey v Ireland** [1979] 266, HC.

False imprisonment
Arrest
Personal injuries—Garda in scuffle with young person—Whether acting in the course of his duty—Whether reasonable force used. **Dowman v Ireland** [1986] 111, HC.

Family
Constitutional rights
Non-pecuniary benefits deriving from parent-child relationship—Whether recoverable at common law—Industrial accident—Victim suffering brain damage—Whether employer owed duty of care to victim's children—Whether defendant's carelessness infringed the plaintiffs' constitutional rights—Constitution of Ireland 1937, Articles 41, 42, HC.

Foreseeability
Loss of premises
Interest on loan for premises—Whether recoverable—Whether reasonably foreseeable—Civil Liability Act 1961, s. 11. **Riordan's Travel Ltd v Acres** [1979] 3, HC.

Remoteness. See Remoteness—Foreseeability (*below*).

Future loss of earnings
Personal injuries. See under Personal injuries—loss of earnings (*below*).

Future loss of profits
Destruction of brochures used in mail order business
Foreseeability—Remoteness—Failure to mitigate loss. **William Egan & Sons Ltd v John Sisk & Sons Ltd** [1986] 283, SC.

General damages
Personal injuries. See Personal injuries (*below*).

Inflation
Relevance
Claim in quasi-contract—Whether inflation to be taken into account. *See* Quasi-contract (*below*).

Whether inflationary decrease in purchasing power relevant in assessing damages. *See* Breach of contract—Loss of profits (*above*).

Interest
Injury to property
Road traffic accident—Damage to vehicle—Money borrowed to pay for the repairs—Whether defendant liable for interest charged on borrowed money—Whether necessity to borrow too remote a consequence. **Murphy v McGrath** [1981] 364, HC.

DAMAGES
Interest *continued*
Negligence
Solicitor—Sale of land—Booking deposit—Date from which interest to run. **Desmond v Brophy** [1986] 547, HC.

Landlord and tenant
Covenant
Quiet enjoyment—Interference by landlord—Intimidation—Whether aggravated damages be awarded—Whether damages recoverable for breach of covenant to repair—Landlord and Tenant (Ireland) Act 1860, ss. 17, 41—Landlord and Tenant Act 1931, s. 5. **Whelan v Madigan** [1978] 136, HC.

Loss of earnings
Personal injuries. See Personal injuries (*below*).

Loss of income
Breach of contract
Whether claim sustainable for loss in provision of unused capital asset—Whether claim amounts to double compensation—Whether loss of income reasonably in contemplation of parties. **Waterford Harbour Commrs v British Railways** [1979] 296, HC, SC.

Loss of premises
Interest on loan for premises
Whether recoverable—Whether reasonably foreseeable—Mitigation of loss—Award—Apportionment—Concurrent wrongdoers—Civil Liability Act 1961, s. 11. **Riordan's Travel Ltd v Acres** [1979] 3, HC.

Loss of profits
Future loss
Destruction of brochures used in mail order business—Foreseeability of loss—Remoteness—Failure to mitigate loss. **William Egan & Sons Ltd v John Sisk & Sons Ltd** [1986] 283, SC.

Principles to be applied
Whether inflationary decrease in purchasing power relevant in assessing damages. *See* Breach of contract—Loss of profits (*above*).

Malicious injuries. *See* MALICIOUS INJURIES (Compensation).

Measure
Copyright
Infringement. *See* Copyright—Infringement (*above*).

Defamation
Appeal—Whether damages adequate to compensate plaintiff—Conduct of proceedings—Whether relevant. **Kennedy v Hearne** [1988] 52, 531, SC.

Pain and suffering. *See* Personal injuries—Pain and suffering (*below*).

Personal injuries
Award
Appeal to Supreme Court on quantum—Whether events subsequent to High Court order constitute grounds of appeal. **Dalton v Minister for Finance** [1989], SC.

Whether excessive—Burning—Scarring. **Rooney v Connolly** [1987] 768, SC.

Whether excessive—Future loss of earnings—General damages—Appeal to Supreme Court. **Reddy v Bates** [1984] 197, SC.

Whether excessive—Future pain and suffering—Appeal to Supreme Court. **Brennan v Savage Smyth & Co Ltd** [1982] 223, SC.

DAMAGES
Personal injuries
Award continued

Whether excessive—General damages—Appeal to Supreme Court—Principles to be applied where damages assessed under several heads. **Griffiths v Van Raaj** [1985] 582, SC.

Whether excessive—Negligence—Occupier's liability—Injury to infant licensee. **Rooney v Connolly** [1987] 768, SC.

Whether excessive—Pain and suffering—Appeal to Supreme Court—Jurisdiction— Whether Supreme Court may substitute award of High Court. **Holohan v Donohue** [1986] 250, SC.

Whether excessive—Whether defendants negligent—Whether plaintiff contributorily negligent—Garda Síochána—Injury to person while in detention. **McKevitt v Ireland** [1987] 541, SC.

Brain damage

Infant—Future economic loss—Risk of unemployment or redundancy—Appropriate multiplier—Rate of interest—Cost of future care—General damages—Whether account to be taken of plaintiff's lack of awareness or appreciation of his condition. **Cooke v Walsh** [1984] 208, SC (*reversing* [1983] 429*]*.

Infant—Medical negligence—Matters to be considered in assessing general damages. **Dunne (an Infant) v National Maternity Hospital and Jackson** [1989] 735, SC.

Jury award of damages—Appeal to Supreme Court—Whether damages excessive— Future loss of earnings—Actuarial evidence—Risk of unemployment or redundancy— General damages—Principles applicable. **Reddy v Bates** [1984] 197, SC.

Burning

Scarring—Infant—Award—Whether excessive. **Rooney v Connolly** [1987] 768, SC.

Civil liability

Plaintiff obtaining judgment—Defendant company in liquidation—Plaintiff claiming against defendant's insurance company—Whether onus on plaintiff to prove no right to rescind or repudiate the policy had arisen. **Dunne v P J White Construction Co Ltd** [1989] 803, SC.

Contributory negligence

Compensation for pain, suffering and disablement—Future loss. **Clancy v Commissioners of Public Works** [1988] 268, HC.

Road traffic accident—Failure to wear seat belt—Proportion of fault appropriate— General damages—Factors to be considered in compensating victim—Civil Liability Act 1961, s. 21—Road Traffic Act 1961, s. 118. **Sinnott v Quinnsworth Ltd** [1984] 523, SC.

Deduction from award

Social welfare disability benefit—Pay related benefit—Whether possible future social welfare payments deductible from damages—Social Welfare Act 1984, s. 12. **O'Loughlin v Teeling** [1988] 620, HC.

Future economic loss

Brain damage—Actuarial evidence—Notional investment of capital sum—Rate of interest—Trustee (Authorised Investments) Act 1958, ss. 1, 2 (1), 3(1)—Trustee (Authorised Investments) Order 1977—Trustee (Authorised Investments) (No 2) Order 1972. **Cooke v Walsh** [1983] 429, HC (*reversed in* [1984] 208, SC).

Brain damage—Risk of unemployment or redundancy—Appropriate multiplier—Rate of interest—Cost of future care—General damages—Whether account to be taken of plaintiff's lack of awareness or appreciation of his condition. **Cooke v Walsh** [1984] 208, SC (*reversing* [1983] 429).

DAMAGES

Personal injuries *continued*

Garda Siochána

Liability—Plaintiff taken to garda station—Plaintiff alleging that he was left with matches—Plaintiff setting fire to cell and suffering extensive burns—Whether defendants negligent—Whether plaintiff contributorily negligent and, if so, to what extent—Whether damages awarded excessive. McKevitt v Ireland [1987] 541, SC.

General damages

Assessment—Matters to be considered. **Dunne (An infant) v National Maternity Hospital and Jackson** [1989] 735, SC.

Contributory negligence—Factors to be considered in compensating victim—Civil Liability Act 1961, s. 21—Road Traffic Act 1961, s. 118. **Sinnott v Quinnsworth Ltd** [1984] 523, SC.

Infant—Brain damage—Whether account to be taken of plaintiff's lack of awareness or appreciation of his condition. **Cooke v Walsh** [1984] 208, SC.

Principles applicable. **Reddy v Bates** [1984] 197, SC.

Principles to be applied where damages assessed under several heads. **Griffiths v Van Raaj** [1985] 582, SC.

Loss of earnings

Future loss—Actuarial evidence—Risk of unemployment or redundancy—General damages—Principles applicable. **Reddy v Bates** [1984] 197, SC.

Pain and suffering. **Murphy v McCarthy** [1989] 678, HC.

Pain and suffering

Award—Whether excessive—Appeal to Supreme Court. **Holohan v Donohue** [1986] 250, SC.

Future pain and suffering—Whether damages awarded excessive—Appeal to Supreme Court. **Brennan v Savage Smyth & Co Ltd** [1982] 223, SC.

Loss of earnings. **Murphy v McCarthy** [1989] 678, HC.

Planning decision

Delay—Failure to give notice of decision within statutory time limit—Local Government (Planning and Development) Act 1963, s. 26(4), (5). **O'Neill v Clare Co Council** [1983] 141, HC.

Quantum

Appeal against award

Whether events subsequent to High Court order constitute grounds of appeal—Admissibility of new evidence. **Dalton v Minister for Finance** [1989] 519, SC.

Quasi-contract

Assessment

Discussion concerning publication—Publishing company expending money on project—Claim for indemnity against money expended and damages for breach of contract—Claim in quasi contract—Whether interest on sum payable allowed—Whether inflation to be taken into account. **Folens & Co Ltd v Minister for Education** [1984] 265, HC.

Remoteness

Foreseeability

Injury to property—Destruction of brochures used in mail order business—Future loss of profits—Test—Failure to mitigate loss. **William Egan & Sons Ltd v John Sisk & Sons Ltd** [1986] 283, SC.

Injury to property—Interest—Road traffic accident—Damage to vehicle—Money borrowed to pay for the repairs—Whether defendant liable for interest charged on

DAMAGES
Remoteness
Foreseeability continued

borrowed money—Whether necessity to borrow too remote a consequence. **Murphy v McGrath** [1981] 364, HC.

Loss of premises—Demolition work—Interest on loan for alternative premises—Whether recoverable—Whether reasonably foreseeable. **Riordan's Travel Ltd v Acres** [1979] 3, HC.

Sale of land
Breach of contract

Damages for failure to complete. *See* Breach of contract—Sale of land—Damages for failure to complete (*above*).

Damages in lieu of specific performance. *See* Breach of contract—Sale of land—Damages in lieu of specific performance (*above*).

Negligence
Solicitor *See* Solicitor (*below*)

Solicitor
Negligence

Sale of land—Booking deposit—Interest—Date from which interest to run. **Desmond v Brophy** [1986] 547, HC.

Statutory rights
Infringement

Guardianship of infants—Husband and wife—Removal of children from jurisdiction by wife—Passports having been issued despite husband's objection—Entitlement to damages—Extent of relief husband entitled to obtain—Ministers and Secretaries Act 1924, s. 1—Adoption Act 1952, s. 40—Guardianship of Infants Act 1964, ss. 6, 10, 11—Constitution of Ireland 1937, Articles 40, 41, 42. **Cosgrove v Ireland** [1982] 48, HC.

Undertaking
Relator action

Injunction—Undertaking as to damages—Fiat of Attorney General not extending to undertaking. **Attorney General (ex rel Martin) v Dublin Corporation** [1983] 254, SC.

Wrongful dismissal
Office holder

Failure to pay salary on due dates—Loss of availability of salary—Whether dismissal resulted in injury to health—Whether due to unlawful nature of dismissal—Exemplary damages—Loss arising from arbitrary nature of dismissal. **Garvey v Ireland** [1979] 266, HC.

DANCE HALL
Licensing
Special exemption order

Application—Public dance hall—Whether a "special occasion". *See* LICENSING (Exemption orders—Special exemption order—Dance hall).

DEATH
Fatal injury compensation

Garda Síochána. See GARDA SÍOCHÁNA. (Compensation—Assessment—Fatal injury).

Joint tenant

Next-of-kin of deceased owner remaining in possession. See ADVERSE POSSESSION (Joint tenants).

DEATH *continued*
Suicide
Inquest
Whether verdict of suicide available. *See* INQUEST (Verdict—Suicide).

Succession. *See* SUCCESSION.

Survival of cause of action
Unfair dismissal claim
Death of employer—Whether claim should proceed against personal representatives—
Civil Liability Act 1961, s. 8(1)—Succession Act 1965, s. 8—Unfair Dismissals Act
1977, ss. 1, 15. **Hutton v Philippi** [1982] 578, EAT.

DEBENTURE. *See* COMPANY (Charge).

DEBT
Common agricultural policy
Monetary compensation amounts
Claim for interest. *See* AGRICULTURE (Common agricultural policy—Export of
cereals—Carousel fraud).

Company
Charge. *See* COMPANY (Charge).

Discharge
Cheque
Whether conditional or unconditional discharge of debt—Cheque drawn by creditor in
favour of debtor and endorsed back to creditor—Cheque referred to drawer—Whether
cheque accepted as unconditional payment of defendant's indebtedness. **Private
Motorists Provident Society Ltd v Moore** [1988] 526, HC.

Recovery
Currency
Whether a judgment for a sterling debt obtained at a time when the currencies of the
State and of the United Kingdom were of equal value—Whether amount payable in
Irish pounds or in sterling. **Northern Bank Ltd v Edwards** [1986] 167, SC.

Limitation of actions
Claim in respect of deductions made by Pigs and Bacon Commission. *See* LIMITATION
OF ACTIONS (Debt—Recovery).

Surety. *See* SURETY.

DECISION
Minister
Judicial review. See MINISTER (Decision).

Planning. *See* PLANNING (Decision).

Social welfare appeals officer
Judicial review. See SOCIAL WELFARE (Decision—Appeals officer).

DECLARATION
Dismissal
Office-holder
Delegation of power to dismiss. **Heneghan v Western Regional Fisheries Board** [1986]
225, HC.

Farm tax office
Discontinuance of farm tax
Termination of appointment of farm tax inspectors—Validity— Whether inspectors
having legitimate expectation of permanent appointment—Locus standi. *See* JUDICIAL
REVIEW (Farm tax office—Discontinuance of farm tax).

DECLARATION *continued*
General Medical Services Scheme
Complaints of abuse of scheme
Referral of matter to Minister—Establishment of Committee of Inquiry—Failure to inform fully of nature of complaint—Whether invalidates decision to refer to Minister— Health Act 1970, s. 58. **O'Flynn v Mid-Western Health Board** [1990] 149, HC.

Locus standi
Whether aggrieved persons
Whether sufficient interest—Building society—Plaintiffs seeking to restrain society carrying on business. Irish Permanent **Building Society v Cauldwell** (Registrar of Building Societies) [1981] 242, HC.

Revenue
Advance rulings
Whether inspector of taxes bound by opinion given to taxpayer by Revenue Commissioners. **Pandion Haliaetus Ltd v Revenue Commissioners** [1988] 419, HC.

Scope of action in Irish law. Irish Permanent Building Society v Cauldwell (Registrar of Building Societies) [1981] 242, HC.

DEDUCTION
Compensation award
Criminal injuries
Deduction of social welfare benefits. *See* MALICIOUS INJURIES (Compensation— Deduction).

Damages award
Social welfare benefits. See DAMAGES (Personal injuries—Deduction from award).

Income tax. *See* REVENUE (Income tax—Deductions).

DEED
Execution
Validity
Company—Mortgage—Whether valid directors' meeting to approve contents of mortgage—Whether mortgagee entitled to believe meeting properly constituted. **Ulster Investment Bank Ltd v Euro Estates Ltd** [1982] 57, HC.

Title deeds
Deposit with bank
Whether bank entitled to claim lien over deeds—Deeds taken as security for loan. In re Farm Fresh Frozen Foods Ltd [1980] 131, HC.

Transfer of land
Reservation of right of residence, care and support
Whether undue influence—Whether deed improvident. **Leonard v Leonard** [1988] 245, HC.

DEFAMATION
Libel
Damages
Aggravated damages—Appeal against quantum—Measure of damages—Whether damages adequate to compensate plaintiff—Conduct of proceedings—Whether relevant. **Kennedy v Hearne** [1988] 52, 531, SC.

Whether excessive—Purpose of award compensatory—Whether jury awarded sum not reasonable in circumstances. **Barrett v Independent Newspapers Ltd** [1986] 601, SC.

Defence
Particulars—Rolled up plea—Plaintiff seeking further and better particulars—Whether

DEFAMATION
Libel
Defence continued
defendant obliged to specify which words complained of were true and to specify facts relied on to support factual statements made—RSC 1962, O 19 r 6(1). **Cooney v Browne** [1985] 673, HC.

Particulars—Rolled up plea—Further and better particulars—Compliance with court order—Whether sufficient compliance. **Cooney v Browne** (No 2) [1986] 444, HC.

Function of judge
Judge determining words were defamatory—Whether usurping role of jury—Damages—Whether excessive—Purpose of award. **Barrett v Independent Newspapers Ltd** [1986] 601, SC.

Qualified privilege
Whether evidence of malice—Interpretation of letter written by plaintiff's solicitor—Allegations of blackmail—Whether reckless exaggeration. **Hartery v Welltrade** (Middle East) Ltd [1978] 38, HC.

Whether an occasion of qualified privilege could arise out of an honest belief that the recipient had a duty or interest in the matters referred to—Whether such an occasion could arise if the recipient had an honest and reasonable belief—Malice—Constitution of Ireland 1937, Articles 40.3.1, 40.3.2, 40.6.1. **Hynes-O'Sullivan v O'Driscoll** [1989] 349, SC.

Revenue
Enforcement notice—Default in making PAYE returns—Enforcement procedure activated—Computer-based programme—Payment due received before enforcement notice issued—Whether publication of enforcement notice a libel—Finance Act 1968, s. 7. **Kennedy v Hearne** [1988] 52, HC.

DEFECTIVE PREMISES
Building contract
Breach
Action for damages. *See* BUILDING CONTRACT (Breach—Defects in premises).

Damages
Assessment. See DAMAGES (Defective premises).

Limitation of actions
Accrual of cause of action
Whether date of damage or date of discoverability—House built on unsuitable foundations developing structural fault—Statute of Limitations 1957, ss. 11(1), 11(2)(a), 71(1). **Morgan v Park Developments Ltd** [1983] 156, HC.

Negligence actions. *See* NEGLIGENCE (Defective premises).

DEFECTIVE PRODUCTS
Drink dispensing machine
Defects manifesting themselves
Whether purchaser entitled to refund of monies paid and damages for loss of profit—Whether purchaser 'dealing as a consumer'—Sale of Goods and Supply of Services Act 1980, s. 3(1). **O'Callaghan v Hamilton Leasing** (Ireland) Ltd [1984] 146, HC.

Liability of supplier
Onus of proof. **Cole v Webb Caravan Services Ltd** [1985] 1, HC.

Negligence
Concurrent wrongdoers
Whether vendor entitled to claim contribution or indemnity against manufacturer—

DEFECTIVE PRODUCTS
Negligence
Concurrent wrongdoers continued
Civil Liability Act 1961, s. 21—RSC, O 16 rr 7, 11. **Cole v Webb Caravan Services Ltd** [1985] 1, HC.

Practice
Service out of jurisdiction—Choice of law—Defective heart valve—Plaintiff resident in Ireland—Valve manufactured in United States—RSC 1962, O 11 r 1(f). **Grehan v Medical Incorporated and Valley Pines Associates** [1986] 627, SC.

DEFENCE
Laches. *See* EQUITY (Laches).

Libel
Particulars
Rolled up plea. *See* DEFAMATION (Libel—Defence).

Murder
Diminished responsibility. *See* CRIMINAL LAW (Defence—Insanity or diminished responsibility)

DEFENCE FORCES
Dismissal
Fair procedures
Natural justice—Certiorari—Delay—Lack of candour—Whether disentitling to relief. **State (Furey) v Minister for Justice** [1988] 89, SC.

Navy
Officer—Natural justice—Audi alteram partem—Notification of decision given but postponed to allow representations—No representations made—Whether sufficient compliance with rules of natural justice. **State (Duffy) v Minister for Defence** [1979] 65, SC.

Negligence
Duty of care
UN service—Injury to soldier—Whether soldier owed duty of care by superior officers—Whether State enjoys common law immunity from suit during armed conflict or hostilities—Whether sufficient case for jury—Constitution of Ireland 1937, Articles 28, 40.3.1 and 40.3.2—Defence Act 1954, s. 111—Defence (Amendment) Act 1960, s. 4. **Ryan v Ireland** [1989] 544, SC.

Pensions
Army Pensions Board
Application for widow's allowance rejected—Denial of oral hearing—Refusal to furnish evidence on which decision based—Whether breach of natural justice—Nature of Board—Whether judicial or administrative—Whether Board's power to grant allowance enabling or mandatory—Army Pensions Act 1962, Second Schedule—Army Pensions Act 1968, s. 11(1)(c)—Army Pensions (Investigations of Applications) Regulations 1927, reg 8,10. **State (Williams) v Army Pensions Board** [1981] 379, HC; [1983] 331, SC.

DELAY *See also* LIMITATION OF ACTIONS; TIME LIMIT.
Access to solicitor
Detained person
Statement made while in Garda custody—Delay in permitting access to solicitor—Whether denial of accused's right of access to solicitor—Whether such right a constitutional right—Constitution of Ireland 1937, Article 40.3. **DPP v Healy** [1990] 313, SC.

DELAY *continued*

Action

Dismissal for want of prosecution. See PRACTICE (Dismissal for want of prosecution).

Infant plaintiff
Proceedings instituted sixteen years after cause of action accrued—Whether unreasonable delay—Whether abuse of process—Statute of Limitations 1957, s. 49. **O'Domhnaill v Merrick** [1985] 40, SC.

Certiorari application. *See* CERTIORARI (Delay).

Contract
Completion
Sale of land—Whether delay explained—Whether specific performance should be refused. **Horgan v Deasy** [1979] 71, HC.

Sale of land—Whether delay entitled parties to treat agreement as repudiated. **Taylor v Smith** [1990] 377, HC.

Extradition
Arrest
Warrants relating to offences committed seven years previously—Whether excessive delay—Whether unfair discrimination. **Harte v Fanning** (No 1) [1988] 70, HC.

Special summons
Inordinate delay between hearing of summons and delivery of judgment—Whether delay a ground for refusing extradition. **Hanlon v Fleming** [1982] 69, SC.

Injunction application
Interlocutory relief
Delay in bringing proceedings—No explanation given—Whether application should succeed. **Lennon v Ganly** [1981] 84, HC.

Judicial review application
Return for trial
Error—Error due to fault of DPP—Charges hanging over accused for longer period—Whether delay in seeking relief such as to deprive applicant of relief sought. **DPP v Johnson** [1988] 747, HC.

Nullity proceedings
Whether delay excessive
Whether approbation. **A M N v J P C** [1988] 170, HC.

Planning decision
Planning authority required to make and give notice of decision within 5 weeks from date of final determination
Registered letter containing notice of refusal received after expiry of period—Whether notice given within period—Last day of five-week period falling on a Sunday. **Freeney v Bray UDC** [1982] 29, HC.

Prohibition application
Whether relevant
Whether disentitling prosecutor to relief—No explanation given. **State (Coveney) v Special Criminal Court** [1982] 284, HC.

Prosecution of offences. *See* CRIMINAL LAW (Prosecution of offences—Delay).

Reference of dispute to Labour Court
Whether caught by statutory time-bar
Employment Equality Act 1977, ss. 2(b), 3, 19, 20, 27(2), 34. **State (Aer Lingus Teo) v Labour Court** [1987] 373, HC, SC.

DELAY *continued*
Return for trial
Error. See CRIMINAL LAW (Return for trial—Error—Delay).

Summons
Issue. See CRIMINAL LAW (Summons—Delay in issuing).

Service
Validity—Date of issue altered—Whether summons invalid. **DPP v Clein** [1983] 76, SC.

Trial
Abandonment of trial
Proposed re-trial—Fair procedures—Whether prejudice arising. **O'Connor v DPP** [1987] 723, HC.

Whether such as to prejudice accused's right to fair trial. See CRIMINAL LAW (Trial—Delay—Whether such as to prejudice accused's right to fair trial).

Warrant
Execution
Arrest warrant—Conduct of applicant contributing to delay—Sentence—Commencement. **O'Driscoll v Governor of Cork Prison** [1989] 239, HC.

DELEGATED LEGISLATION
District Court Rules
Validity
Whether ultra vires. *See* DISTRICT COURT RULES (Validity).

Government order
Validity
Whether order a "law" within meaning of Articles 34.4.5 and 40.4.3 of the Constitution—Extradition Act 1965 (Part II) (No 20) Order 1984. **State (Gilliland) v Governor of Mountjoy Prison** [1986] 381, HC; [1987] 278, SC.

Retrospectivity
Agriculture
Levy on livestock—Presumption against retrospectivity—Imposition of Duties (No 239) Agricultural Produce (Cattle and Milk) Order 1979—Agricultural Produce (Cattle and Milk) Regulations 1979. **Doyle v An Taoiseach** [1986] 693, HC.

Regulations giving effect to EC milk levy—Whether unjustified attack on property rights—European Communities (Milk Levy) Regulations 1985, regs 4, 12—Constitution of Ireland 1937, Articles 29.4.3, 40.3.2, 43. **Lawlor v Minister for Agriculture** [1988] 400, HC.

Status
Constitution
Whether statutory instrument a "law"—Government order extending Part II of 1965 Act to the USA. *See* Government order (*above*).

Validity
See also CONSTITUTION (Statute—Validity—Delegated legislation).

Aliens
Deportation order—Whether deportation order would infringe plaintiff's constitutional rights—Constitution of Ireland 1937, Articles 9, 40, 41, 42—Aliens Act 1935, ss. 4, 5, 12—Aliens Order 1935, reg 13—Aliens Amendment Order 1975. **Osheku v Ireland** [1987] 330, HC.

Casual trading
Bye-laws—Proposal to designate land as casual trading area subject to conditions—Whether decision perverse—Whether draft bye-laws *ultra vires* Casual Trading Act 1980. **Comerford v O'Malley** [1987] 595, HC.

DELEGATED LEGISLATION
Validity *continued*
Health services
Exclusion of certain road traffic accident victims from class of persons entitled to hospital services free of charge—Whether ultra vires—Intention of legislature—Presumption of constitutionality—Health Act 1970, s. 72. Health Services Regulations 1971, reg 6. **Cooke v Walsh** [1983] 429, HC; [1984] 208, SC.

Prison regulations
Access to legal advisers—Certain solicitors excluded—Rules of the Government of Prisons 1976. **Incorporated Law Society v Minister for Justice** [1978] 112, HC.

Road traffic
New regulations providing for breathalyser—Authorising legislation enacted but not yet operative—Whether regulations "necessary or expedient" for implementation of legislation when operative—Road Traffic Act Regulations 1978—Interpretation Act 1937, s. 10(1)(b). **State (McColgan) v DPP** [1980] 75, SC.

Rules of Court
District Court rules. *See* DISTRICT COURT RULES (Validity).

Rules of the Superior Courts—Whether *ultra vires*—Discovery of documents—Non-party discovery. *See* DISCOVERY (Non-party discovery—Rules of court).

Social welfare
Regulations—Appellant prevented from receiving both blind pension and widow's pension—Whether provisions in direct breach of statute—Social Welfare Act 1979, s. 7—Social Welfare (Overlapping Benefits) Regulations 1953, art 38—Social Welfare (Overlapping Benefits) (Amendment) Regulations 1979. **Harvey v Minister for Social Welfare** [1990] 185, SC.

Supplementary welfare allowance—Regulations providing for payment of allowance on means test—Departmental circular excluding from scheme persons on short-term social welfare—Whether circular *ultra vires* the Minister—Social Welfare (Supplementary Welfare Allowances) Act 1975, s. 11—Social Welfare (Supplementary Welfare Allowances) Regulations 1977, art 6. **State (Kershaw) v Eastern Health Board** [1985] 235, HC.

Whether arbitrary or unreasonable
Whether confirmed by subsequent enactment—Presumption against retrospection. *See* Retrospectivity—Agriculture—Levy on livestock (*above*).

DELEGATION OF POWERS
Director of Public Prosecutions. *See* DIRECTOR OF PUBLIC PROSECUTIONS (Powers—Delegation).

DEMOLITION WORK
Damage to adjoining premises
Independent contractor carrying out work
Whether negligence—Whether defendant vicariously liable. **Boylan v Northern Bank Ltd** [1976–7] 287, HC.

DEPENDANT
Family provision
Moral duty of testator. See SUCCESSION (Family provision).

Maintenance. *See* Family Law (Maintenance)

DEPORTATION ORDER. *See* ALIEN (Deportation order).

DEPOSIT
Fraudulent misappropriation. *See* BANK (Deposit—Fraudulent misappropriation).

Interest
Liability to tax
Company liquidation. *See* COMPANY (Winding up—Deposit interest—Liability to tax).

Planning appeal. *See* PLANNING (Appeal—Deposit).

Sale of land. *See* SALE OF LAND (Deposit).

Title deeds
Equitable mortgage. See BANK (Deposit of title deeds).

DESIGN
Copyright
Infringement. See COPYRIGHT (Infringement—Registered design).

Passing off. *See* PASSING OFF (Design).

DESIGNATED AREA
Capital allowances. *See* REVENUE (Income tax—Capital allowances—Plant—Plant and machinery used in designated area).

DETENTION
Continuing detention. *See* CRIMINAL INVESTIGATION (Surveillance—Overt surveillance—Manner and purpose—Whether amounts to continuing detention).

Legality. *See* ARREST (Detention).

Inquiry under Constitution. See HABEAS CORPUS.

Preventative detention
Habitual criminals. See CRIME PREVENTION (Preventative detention).

Right of access to solicitor while in detention. *See* CRIMINAL LAW (Access to solicitor)

Sentence. *See* CRIMINAL LAW (Sentence).

Remission. See CRIMINAL LAW (Sentence—Remission).

Statement made while in detention
Admissibility. See CRIMINAL LAW (Evidence—Statement by accused).

Young person
Sentence
Consecutive periods of detention in St Patrick's Institution. *See* CRIMINAL LAW (Young offender—Sentence—Consecutive sentences—Detention in St Patrick's Institution).

Judge certifying that defendant not a fit person to be detained in a place of detention for young persons. *See* CRIMINAL LAW (Young offender—Sentence—Plea of guilty).

DETINUE
Proceedings for recovery of goods
Find of ancient hoard
Hoard deposited with museum—Title to goods—Bailee denying bailor's title—Treasure trove. **Webb v Ireland** [1988] 565, HC, SC.

DEVELOPMENT
Planning control. *See* PLANNING.

DEVELOPMENT PLAN
Material contravention. *See* PLANNING (Development plan—Contravention).

DIMINISHED RESPONSIBILITY
Defence
Murder
Whether jury to consider defence of diminished responsibility an alternative verdict of manslaughter—Whether concept of diminished responsibility recognised in Irish law. **People (DPP) v O'Mahony** [1986] 244, SC.

DIRECTIVE
European Community. *See* EUROPEAN COMMUNITY (Directive).

DIRECTOR
Company. *See* COMPANY (Director).

DIRECTOR OF PUBLIC PROSECUTIONS
Appeal against acquittal
Case stated
Whether DPP had validly invoked the jurisdiction of the High Court—Necessary steps—Whether complied with. *See* CRIMINAL LAW (Acquittal—Appeal—Case stated).

Charge on indictment before Central Criminal Court
Jury recording verdict of not guilty at direction of trial judge—Whether open to DPP to bring an appeal against such verdict—Extent of Supreme Court's appellate jurisdiction. *See* CRIMINAL LAW (Acquittal—Appeal—Jurisdiction of Supremen Court).

Decision
Whether reviewable by the courts
Extra-territorial offence—Irish citizen in custody in Northern Ireland *see*king to be delivered into the custody of the Garda Síochána—DPP indicating that proceedings would not be instituted in this jurisdiction—Certiorari—Mandamus—Role of DPP—Whether DPP's decision reviewable—Whether prima facie case of mala fides made out—Whether prosecutor deprived of his constitutional rights of access to the courts. **State (McCormack) v Curran** [1987] 225, HC, SC.

Function
Local elections
Election petition—Prosecution of Offences Act 1974, s. 3(1). **Boyle v Allen** [1979] 281, CC.

Nolle prosequi
Whether possible to institute a fresh prosecution following the entrance of a valid nolle prosequi. See CRIMINAL LAW (Nolle prosequi).

Opinion
Whether reviewable by the courts
Power to direct trial in Special Criminal Court—Opinion of DPP that ordinary courts inadequate—Offences Against the State Act 1939, ss. 47, 48—Prosecution of Offences Act 1974, s. 3. **O'Reilly and Judge v DPP** [1984] 224, HC.

Return for trial on non-scheduled offences to Special Criminal Court—Offences Against the State Act 1939, ss. 35, 45, 46—Prosecution of Offences Act 1974, s. 3. **Savage v DPP** [1982] 385, HC.

Powers
Delegation
Prosecution of indictable offence—Delegation of carriage of prosecution to solicitor—Solicitor being employee of company making criminal complaint against defendant—Whether delegation *ultra vires*—Prosecution of Offences Act 1974, ss. 4, 7. **Flynn v DPP** [1986] 290, SC.

Exercise
Injunction to restrain—Indictable offence dealt with summarily—Application for

DIRECTOR OF PUBLIC PROSECUTIONS
Powers
Exercise continued

injunction restraining DPP from proceeding in the District Court—Presumption that DPP will conform with principles of natural justice—Criminal Justice Act 1951—Criminal Procedure Act 1967. **Clune v DPP** [1981] 17, HC.

Existence

Power to end private prosecutions—Prosecution brought by garda as common informer—DPP directing that charge be withdrawn—District Justice entertaining the case—Whether DPP had power to intervene—Right of common informer to prosecute—Distinction between official and unofficial common informers—Constitution of Ireland 1937, Art 30 3—Minister and Secretaries Act 1924, s. 6(1)—Criminal Justice Administration Act 1924—Prosecution of Offences Act 1974, s. 3. **State (Collins) v Ruane** [1984] 443, HC; [1985] 349, SC.

Validity

Power to send person forward for trial—Whether power unconstitutional—Whether DPP exercising judicial function—Preliminary investigation in District Court—Discharge of accused—DPP directing that accused be sent forward for trial in Circuit Court in respect of the same charges—Whether provisions under which DPP purported to act constitutionally valid—Whether invasion into the judicial domain—Constitution of Ireland 1937, Articles 6, 34—Courts of Justice Act 1936, s. 62(1)—Courts (Supplemental Provisions) Act 1961, s. 48 (3)—Criminal Procedure Act 1967, ss. 5(1), 6, 7, 8—Prosecution of Offences Act 1974, ss. 2(4), 3. **Costello v DPP** [1983] 489, HC; [1984] 413, SC.

Power to direct trial in Special Criminal Court—Whether power unconstitutional—Opinion of DPP that ordinary courts inadequate—Whether reviewable by the courts—Offences Against the State Act 1939, ss. 47, 48—Prosecution of Offences Act 1974, s. 3. **O'Reilly and Judge v DPP** [1984] 224, HC.

Trial on indictment—Preliminary examination—DPP substituting new counts—Whether invasion of judicial domain—Whether DPP exercising judicial function—Constitution of Ireland 1937, Articles 6, 30.3, 34—Criminal Justice (Administration) Act 1924, s. 6—Criminal Procedure Act 1967, ss. 5, 6, 7, 8, 18. **O'Shea v DPP** [1989] 309, HC, SC.

Trial on indictment—Preliminary examination—DPP inserting additional counts—Whether invasion of judicial domain—Whether Director exercising judicial function—Whether counsel obliged to sign indictment—Criminal Procedure Act 1967, ss. 8, 18. **Walsh v President of the Circuit Court** [1989] 325 HC, SC.

Undertaking
Preliminary examination

Undertaking that evidence given would not be used for the purpose of criminal proceedings against witness—Effect of such undertaking. **State (Williams) v DPP** [1983] 285, HC.

DISABLED PERSON
Personal injuries
Damages

Award—Deduction—Whether possible future social welfare disability payments deductible from award. **O'Loughlin v Teeling** [1988] 617, HC.

Voting in elections
Inability to attend at polling station

Whether absence of postal facilities frustrating the right to vote—Statute—Validity. *See* ELECTORAL LAW (Dáil Éireann elections—Polling—Inability to attend at polling station).

DISADVANTAGED AREAS
Farming
Compensatory payments. See AGRICULTURE (Disadvantaged areas—Compensatory payments).

DISCIPLINE
Athlete
Suspension. See NATURAL AND CONSTITUTIONAL JUSTICE (Athletic body).

Employment
Dismissal. See EMPLOYMENT (Dismissal).

Suspension. See EMPLOYMENT (Suspension).

Garda Síochána. *See* GARDA SÍOCHÁNA (Discipline).

School
Natural justice
> Certiorari—Suspension and expulsion—Whether failure to interview pupil expelled rendered expulsion invalid—Whether legal representation required at hearing—Whether draft article of management of school consistent with requirements of natural justice. **State (Smullen) v Duffy** [1980] 46, HC.

Trade union
Powers of ICTU. See TRADE UNION (Discipline).

University disciplinary committee. *See* UNIVERSITY (Disciplinary committee—Charge of plagiarism).

DISCLAIMER
Onerous lease. *See* LANDLORD AND TENANT (Disclaimer of onerous lease).

Onerous property
Company liquidation. See COMPANY (Winding up—Disclaimer of onerous property—Application to disclaim a lease).

DISCLOSURE OF INFORMATION
Bank. *See* BANK (Disclosure of information).

Central Bank
Statutory privilege claim
> Subpoena *duces tecum* issued requiring officer of Central Bank to produce documents—Oath of secrecy—Whether summons be set aside—Central Bank Act 1942, ss. 6(1), 31. **Cully v Northern Bank Finance Corporation** [1984] 683, HC.

Guarantee
Disclosure of information to guarantor
> Company in receivership—Guarantor and sundry creditors seeking information concerning the proposed purchase price of the assets. *See* GUARANTEE (Disclosure of information to guarantor).

Government information
Publication
> Injunction to restrain. *See* INJUNCTION (Interlocutory—Breach of confidence—Publication—Book written by deceased member of British intelligence service—Application to restrain publication in Ireland).

Insurance contract
Material facts
> Uberrima Fides. *See* INSURANCE (Contract—*Uberrima fides*).

DISCLOSURE OF INFORMATION *continued*
Motor insurance policy
Duty of insurers
Obligation to keep records and to give information to members of Garda Síochána—Request for information—Refusal to supply—Validity of regulations. *See* MOTOR INSURANCE (Information—Duty of insurers).

Privilege
Discovery of documents. See DISCOVERY (Privilege).

Revenue matters. *See* REVENUE (Disclosure of information).

DISCOUNT
Bill of exchange
Bank
Duty of care. *See* BANK (Duty of care—Discount of foreign bills).

DISCOVERY
Affidavit
Format
Identification of documents—Whether individual listing required—Further discovery—Privilege—Whether deponent final say on what is relevant. **Bula Ltd v Crowley** [1990] 756, SC.

Inspection
Bank account
Jurisdiction of High Court to make an order for inspection with extra territorial effect—Bankers' Books Evidence Act 1879, s. 7—Bankers' Books Evidence (Amendment) Act 1959, s. 2. **Chemical Bank v McCormack** [1983] 350, HC.

Non-party discovery
Order against non-party to proceedings
Whether court satisfied of likelihood that relevant documents are in possession of non-party—Parties to be served with notice—RSC 1986, O 31 r 29. **Holloway v Belenos Publications** [1987] 790, HC.

Rules of court
Whether rule *ultra vires* rulemaking committee—Whether committee has power to impose obligation to make discovery or allow inspection of documents in possession, custody or power of notice party—Courts of Justice Act 1924, s. 36—RSC 1986, O 31 r 29. **Holloway v Benelos Publications Ltd** (No 2) [1988] 685, HC.

Whether rule *ultra vires* rulemaking committee—Privilege—Public interest—Objection to production by statutory body—Judicial discretion to order production—Whether rule related to practice and procedure—RSC 1986, O 31 r 29. **Fitzpatrick v Independent Newspapers** [1988] 707, HC.

Privilege
Adoption
Prospective parents applying for an order dispensing with consent of mother—Prospective parents seeking discovery of certain documents—Whether in best interests of child to disclose documents—Adoption Act 1976, s. 8. s. **M v G M** [1985] 186, HC.

Executive privilege
Garda Síochána—Communication between members of the Gardai—Whether such communications inadmissible in evidence because, as a class, their admission would be against the public interest—Whether claim for privilege should be rejected. **DPP (Hanley) v Holly** [1984] 149, HC.

Legal professional privilege
Contemplation of litigation—Whether purpose of documents' existence was preparation

DISCOVERY
Privilege
Legal professional privilege continued
for apprehended litigation—Whether disclosure contrary to the public interest. **Silver Hill Duckling Ltd & Ors v Minister for Agriculture** [1987] 516, HC.

Correspondence with legal advisers—Documents procured to obtain legal advice—Whether privilege attaches—Importance of principle of legal professional privilege—Internal documents—Whether relevant to issues raised by pleadings—Purpose for which documents prepared—Precedent—Conflict between English authorities—Long-established principle—Approach of Irish courts—RSC 1986, Order 31. **Tromso Sparebank v Beirne** (No 2) [1989] 257, HC.

Correspondence between client and solicitor—Whether distinction between legal advice and legal assistance—Companies Act 1963, s. 17. **Smurfit Paribas Bank Ltd v AAB Export Finance Ltd** [1990] 588, SC.

Marriage counsellor
Priest acting as marriage counsellor—Communications—Privilege that of the spouses—Constitution of Ireland 1937, Article 41. **R v R** [1981] 125, HC.

Public interest
Objection to production by statutory body—Judicial discretion to order production. **Fitzpatrick v Independent Newspapers** [1988] 707, HC.

Order for discovery of documents in possession of Minister—Privilege—Confidentiality versus administration of justice. **Folens & Co Ltd v Minister for Education** [1981] 21, HC.

State privilege
Factors to be taken into consideration—Injustice to applicant or potential damge to public service. **Incorporated Law Society of Ireland v Minister for Justice** [1987] 42, HC.

Statutory privilege
Subpoena duces tecum issued requiring officer of the Central Bank to produce documents—Oath of secrecy—Statutory privilege—Whether summons be set aside—Central Bank Act 1942, ss. 6 (1), 31. **Cully v Northern Bank Finance Corp Ltd** [1984] 676, HC.

DISCRIMINATION
Employment
Sex or marital status. See EMPLOYMENT (Equality of treatment).

Equality before the law. *See* CONSTITUTION (Equality).

Health services
Regulations rendering victims of traffic accidents ineligible for free medical services
Whether unconstitutional discrimination. *See* HEALTH SERVICES (Regulations—Validity).

Irish nationality and citizenship
Differentiation between alien men and women
Whether breach of guarantee of equality—Interests of the common good—Irish Nationality and Citizenship Act 1956, ss. 8, 15, 16. **Somjee v Minister for Justice** [1981] 324, HC.

Marital status
Employment. See EMPLOYMENT (Equality of treatment—Marital status).

Religious. *See* RELIGIOUS DISCRIMINATION.

DISEASE
Animals
Eradication scheme. See AGRICULTURE (Diseases of animals).

DISEASE *continued*
Occupational
    Employer's liability. See NEGLIGENCE (Employer—Occupational disease).

DISHONESTY
    Solicitor. *See* SOLICITOR (Misconduct—Dishonesty).

DISMISSAL
Action
    Abuse of process. See ABUSE OF PROCESS.

    Delay. See PRACTICE (Dismissal for want of prosecution).

    Employee. *See* EMPLOYMENT (Dismissal).

    Unfair dismissal. See EMPLOYMENT (Unfair dismissal).

DISPUTE
    Trade dispute. *See* TRADE DISPUTE.

DISSOLUTION
    Marriage. *See* MARRIAGE (Divorce).

DISTRICT COURT
Conviction
    Validity
        Certiorari. *See* CERTIORARI (Conviction—District Court).

Costs
    Criminal trial
        District Court Rules prohibiting award of costs against member of Garda Síochána acting in discharge of duties as police officer. *See* DISTRICT COURT RULES (Validity—Costs).

Discretion
    Exercise
        Discretion to adjourn or to refuse to adjourn—Whether properly exercised—Appeal pending to Circuit Court—Whether certiorari available. **State (Pheasantry Ltd) v Donnelly** [1982] 512, HC.

Judicial independence
    Constitution
        Sole and exclusive authority to control and supervise conduct of proceedings within limits of jurisdiction. **Clune v DPP** [1981] 17, HC.

Jurisdiction
    Criminal law
        Detention—Validity—Detention pursuant to statutory power—Whether District Court can embark on constitutional inquiry as to validity of detention—Whether unwarrantable and unlawful usurpation of the constitutional role of the High Court—Constitution of Ireland 1937, Article 40.4.2—Criminal Justice Act 1984, s. 4. **Keating v Governor of Mountjoy Prison** [1990] 850, SC.

        Generally. See CRIMINAL LAW (Jurisdiction—District Court).

        Indictable offence—Subsequent charge of summary offence—DPP electing to have latter charges disposed of summarily—District Justice refusing to deal with charges summarily—Withdrawal of indictable charges. *See* CRIMINAL LAW (Jurisdiction—District Court—Indictable offence—Subsequent charge of summary offence).

DISTRICT COURT
Jurisdiction
Criminal law continued

Minor offences—Location of offences—Multiplicity of offences—Whether relevant to consideration of nature of offences—Certiorari—Discretion of court—Alternative remedy—District Court Rules 1948, rr 25, 44—Social Welfare (Consolidation) Act 1981, s. 115. **State (Wilson) v Neilan** [1987] 118, HC.

Scheduled offence—Summary trial only with consent of accused—Failure to inform accused of right to be tried by jury—Criminal Justice Act 1951, s. 2. **State (McDonagh) v Sheerin** [1981] 149, HC.

Sole and exclusive authority within limits of jurisdiction—Indictable offence dealt with summarily—Conditional order of prohibition granted prohibiting hearing of prosecutions without copies of the statements of evidence being furnished—Application for absolute order—Jurisdiction of High Court—Presumption that District Justice will act in accordance with principles of natural justice and fairness—Criminal Justice Act 1951, s. 2—Criminal Procedure Act 1967. **Clune v DPP** [1981] 17, HC.

Order
Validity

Error—Licensing Acts—Order renewing publican's licence made in error—Whether order made within jurisdiction—Whether certiorari available. In re Riordan [1981] 2, HC.

Procedure
Case stated

Interpretation of statutory provisions—Whether reference must be on basis of particular circumstances arising. **O'Neill v Butler** [1979] 243, HC.

Election for summary trial

Whether District Justice subsequently entitled to decline jurisdiction—Offences against the Person Act 1861, s. 62—Penal Servitude Act 1891, s. 1—Criminal Justice Act 1951, ss. 2 (2)(a), 4(1). **State (O'Hagan) v Delap** [1983] 241, HC.

Irregularities

Criminal case—Plea of guilty—Legal aid denied—Charges not stated to accused in open court—Prosecutor having no clear idea of the charges to which the sentences related—Certiorari—Whether orders made without or in excess of jurisdiction—Criminal Justice Act 1951, ss. 2, 8—Criminal Procedure Act 1967, s. 13(2)(b)—District Court Rules 1972, rr 84, 85. **State (McDonagh) v Barry** [1983] 525, HC.

Legal aid certificate

Exceptional circumstances—Factors to be considered by District Justice. **O'Neill v Butler** [1979] 243, HC.

Natural justice

Audi alteram partem—Landlord and tenant hearing—Tenant not represented at hearing—Tenant not invited to give evidence—Whether hearing in breach of natural justice—Housing Act 1966, s. 62. **State (Crothers) v Kelly** [1978] 167, HC.

Remand in custody—Young offender—Certificate of unruly character—Evidence on which decision made—Whether evidence must be tested by cross-examination—Children's Act 1908, s. 102(3). **State (O'Donoghue) v Kennedy** [1979] 109, HC.

Reopening of case sought by DPP—District Justice admitting additional evidence for prosecution in absence of applicant's counsel—Applicant's counsel specifically excused from attending—Jurisdiction of court—Whether case should be remitted to District Court for further consideration—RSC 1986, O 84 r 27(4), (6). **Dawson v Hamill** [1990] 257, HC.

Preliminary examination

Generally. *See* CRIMINAL LAW (Procedure—Preliminary examination).

DISTRICT COURT
Procedure
Preliminary examination continued
Book of evidence—Failure to serve—Non-compliance with statutory requirements—Prohibition—Whether objection to District Justice's jurisdiction be postponed—Criminal Procedure Act 1967, ss. 5, 6, 8. **State (Williams) v DPP and Kelliher** [1983] 285, HC; [1983] 537, SC.

Striking out of charge. See CRIMINAL LAW (Procedure—Striking out of charge—District Court).

Rules
Validity
Whether ultra vires. *See* DISTRICT COURT RULES (Validity).

Summons
Issue
Validity. *See* CRIMINAL LAW (Summons—Validity).

DISTRICT COURT RULES
Validity
Costs
Rules prohibiting award of costs against member of Garda Síochána acting in discharge of duties as police officer—Whether discrimination—Whether justified on grounds of social function—Constitution of Ireland 1937, Articles 40.1, 40.3—Prosecution of Offences Act 1974, s. 3—District Court Rules 1948, r 67. **Dillane v Attorney General** [1980] 167, SC.

Initiation of criminal proceedings
District Court Rules conferring on District Court Clerk the entitlement to receive a complaint and issue a summons—Whether clerk acting in a judicial capacity—Whether rules went beyond the adaptation and modification of legislation for practice and procedure purposes—Whether invalid rules severable—Petty Sessions (Ireland) Act 1851, s. 10—Courts of Justice Act 1924, s. 91—District Court Rules 1948, rr 29, 30—Constitution of Ireland 1937, Articles 34, 37. **Rainey v Delap** [1988] 620, HC.

Station bail
Whether rules ultra vires rule-making committee—Rules regulating the procedure to be adopted by members of the Gardai in relation to station bail—Extension of time for the appearance in court of the accused—Criminal Procedure Act 1967, s. 31(1)—Criminal Justice Act 1984, s. 26—District Court (Criminal Procedure Act 1967) Rules 1985. **State (Lynch) v Ballagh** [1987] 65, SC.

DISTRIBUTIONS
Corporation tax. *See* REVENUE (Corporation tax—distributions).

DISTURBANCE
Compensation. *See* LANDLORD AND TENANT (Compensation for disturbance).

DIVIDENDS
Taxation. *See* REVENUE (Corporation tax—Dividends).

DIVORCE. *See* MARRIAGE (Divorce).

DOCKS. *See* HARBOURS.

DOCTOR *See* MEDICAL PRACTITIONER.

DOCUMENTS
Deed. *See* DEED.

DOCUMENTS *continued*
Discovery. *See* DISCOVERY.

Evidence
Generally. *See* CRIMINAL LAW (Evidence—Documents).

Medical certificate
Driving while drunk—Validity of form signed by doctor—Illegible signature—Capacity of person not stated—Road Traffic Act 1961, s. 49(2)—Road Traffic (Amendment) Act 1978. **DPP v Collins** [1981] 447, SC.

DOG
Guard dog
Injury to plaintiffs
Liabilty of owner—Whether owner strictly liable—Whether defence to show that its escape was caused by the wrongful act of a third party. **Kavanagh v Centreline Ltd** [1987] 306, HC.

DOMICILE
Generally. *See* PRIVATE INTERNATIONAL LAW.

Husband and wife
Dependent domicile
Legislation abolishing dependent domicile—Whether retrospective in effect—Whether dependent domicile concept existed up to enactment of legislation—Whether concept of dependent domicile survived enactment of Constitution—Constitution of Ireland 1937, Articles 40.1, 40.3, 41—Domicile and Recognition of Foreign Divorces Act 1986, s. 5. **C M v T M** [1988] 262, HC; [1988] 456, HC.

Divorce
Recognition of foreign decree. *See* MARRIAGE (Divorce—Recognition of foreign decree—Domicile).

Separation
Husband seeking custody of children—Whether husband abandoned Irish domicile of origin—Guardianship of Infants Act 1964. **J W v M W** [1978] 119, HC.

DOUBLE TAXATION AGREEMENT. *See* REVENUE (Corporation tax—Double taxation agreement).

DRAINAGE SCHEME *See* ARTERIAL DRAINAGE.

DRIVER
Duty of care. *See* NEGLIGENCE (Road accident—Driver of motor vehicle—Duty of care).

Offences. *See* ROAD TRAFFICE OFFENCES.

DRUGS
Misuse. *See* CRIMINAL LAW (Misuse of drugs).

DRUNKEN DRIVING. *See* ROAD TRAFFICE OFFENCES (Drunken driving).

DURESS *See also* UNDUE INFLUENCE.
Marriage
Nullity proceedings. *See* MARRIAGE (Nullity—Duress).

Statement of accused
Admission of responsibility
Admissibility—Whether voluntary statement—Whether admission induced by gardai—Whether inducement improper—Appropriate test. **People (DPP) v Hoey** [1988] 666, SC.

DUTY
Statutory. *See* STATUTORY DUTY.

DUTY OF CARE. *See* NEGLIGENCE (Duty of care).

DWELLING *See also* HOUSING.
Burial ground proposed within 100 yards of dwelling-house
Approval of Minister
Whether consent of owner of dwellinghouse required—Public Health (Ireland) Act 1878, ss. 160, 174—Local Government (Sanitary Services) Act 1948, s. 44. **McCarthy v Johnson** [1989] 706, SC.

Defects in construction. *See* DEFECTIVE PREMISES.

Family home. *See* FAMILY LAW (Property—Family home).

Inviolability
Constitutional right. See CONSTITUTION (Personal rights—Inviolability of dwelling).

Service charges
Local authority. See LOCAL GOVERNMENT (Service charges).

Taxation
Residential property tax
Whether unjust attack on property rights—Constitution of Ireland 1937, Articles 40 1, 40 3, 41, 43—Finance Act 1983, Part VI. **Madigan v Attorney General** [1986] 136, HC, SC.

Temporary. *See* TEMPORARY DWELLINGS.

EARNINGS
Loss. *See* DAMAGES (Personal injuries—Loss of earnings).

EASEMENT
Right of way
Entitlement
Absence of defined path—Evidence of user—Lack of defined *terminus a quo* and *terminus ad quem*—Whether use of the way over the land sufficient in extent and regularity— Whether knowledge of such user to be imputed to the owner of the land. **Flanagan v Mulhall** [1985] 134, HC.

Estoppel by conduct—Whether evidence of any detrimental act done with the knowledge or encouragement of the defendant. **Dunne v Molloy** [1976–7] 266, HC.

Overgrown and little used path—Whether intention to abandon right—Whether mere evidence of non-user sufficient to bring about the extinguishment of a private right of way. **Carroll v Sheridan** [1984] 451, HC.

Public right of way
Action to establish—Fiat of Attorney General—Whether action maintainable. **Dunne v Rattigan** [1981] 365, CC.

ECCLESIASTICAL COURTS
Annulment of marriage. *See* CHURCH ANNULMENT.

ECONOMIC INTERESTS
Unlawful interference. *See* TORT (Unlawful interference with economic interests).

ECONOMIC LOSS. *See* DAMAGES (Personal injuries—Future economic loss).

EDUCATION
Constitutional right
Right to free primary education
Interference—Trade dispute—Teachers' union directing members not to enrol pupils from affected schools—Claim for damages—Whether such claim a claim in tort—Constitution of Ireland 1937, Article 42.2—Trade Disputes Act 1906, s. 4. **Hayes v Ireland** [1987] 651, HC.

Industrial school *See* INDUSTRIAL SCHOOL

Professions
Law school
System of entry. *See* SOLICITOR (Entry to profession).

School
Admission of students
School Board of Management—Decision—Whether subject to judicial review—Whether arbitrary—Criteria applied. **O hUallachain v Burke** [1988] 693, HC.

Discipline
Natural justice—Suspension and expulsion of pupil—Suspension after investigation by school principal affirmed by expulsion by board of management—Whether failure to interview pupil expelled rendered expulsion invalid—Whether legal representation required at hearing to expel student—Whether draft articles of management of school consistent with requirements of natural justice. **State (Smullen) v Duffy** [1980] 46, HC.

Teacher
Appointment
Legitimate expectation—Whether Minister estopped from exercising discretion to refuse to appoint applicant as teacher—Whether applicant had legitimate expectation that she would be appointed—Whether Minister could exercise discretion to appoint applicant to a position other than that applied for—Vocational Education Act 1930, ss. 23, 30. **Devitt v Minister for Education** [1989] 639, HC.

Requirement of linguistic knowledge—Knowledge not required for the performance of teaching duties—Compatibility of such requirement with European Community law—Free movement of workers—Treaty of Rome, Articles 48(3), 177—Council Regulation 1612/68, article 3—Constitution of Ireland 1937, Article 8—Vocational Education Act 1930, s. 23. **Groener v Minister for Education** [1990] 335, ECJ.

Validity—Scheme for establishment of posts of responsibility—Appointment as vice principal—Appeal Board ruling appointee ineligible—Whether appointment valid. **Ahern v de Hora** [1980] 203, HC.

Cancellation of appointment
Breach of contract—Pressure exerted on manager of primary school to cancel appointment of plaintiff as principal—Plaintiff not being member of trade union—Whether manager in breach of contract—Whether defendants induced or procured such breach. **Cotter v Ahern** [1976–7] 248, HC.

Dismissal
Natural justice—Seminary—Teacher also priest—Seminary receiving funds from State but applied for lay purposes as recognised college of university—Whether dismissal in breach of natural justice. **McGrath and O Ruairc v Maynooth College** [1979] 166, SC.

Pregnancy—Unmarried woman teacher in convent secondary school—Whether teacher dismissed by reason of her pregnancy—Whether substantial grounds justifying dismissal—Unfair Dismissals Act 1977, ss. 6(1), 6(2)(f). **Flynn v Power** [1985] 336, HC.

University. *See* UNIVERSITY.

EJECTMENT
Action for possession
Trespass. See TRESPASS (Ejectment).

Action for recovery of land. *See* LAND (Recovery of possession).

Limitation of actions
Action by personal representative. See LIMITATION OF ACTIONS (Ejectment).

Tenant. *See* LANDLORD AND TENANT (Ejectment).

EJUSDEM GENERIS RULE *See* STATUTORY INTERPRETATION (*Ejusdem generis rule*).

ELECTORAL LAW
Dáil Éireann elections
Ballot papers
Listing of candidates' names—Statute pending for alphabetical listing of candidates—
Alleged distortion in voting patterns in favour of candidates at head of ballot paper—
Challenge to the validity of the legislation. *See* CONSTITUTION (Dáil Éireann—Elections—
Ballot papers).

Election broadcast
Political party—Ministerial order prohibiting access to radio or TV by Provisional Sinn
Fein candidates to promote their electoral campaign—Constitution—Validity—Freedom
of expression—Whether order reviewable by the courts. *See* BROADCASTING (Election
broadcast—Ministerial order—Judicial review).

Franchise
Extension—Bill conferring rights to vote on British citizens—Whether repugnant to
the Constitution—Constitution of Ireland 1937, Articles 6, 12, 16, 47. **In re Electoral
(Amendment) Bill 1983** [1984] 539, SC.

Polling
Inability to attend at polling station—Physically incapacitated citizen—Dáil Éireann
elections—Absence of provision for postal voting—Whether absence of postal facilities
frustrating the right to vote—Whether provision of postal voting for certain classes of
voters arbitrary—Whether extension of postal voting would lead to increased risk of
abuse—Statute—Validity—Constitution of Ireland 1937, Articles 16 1 2, 16 7, 40 1, 40
3—Electoral Act 1963, ss. 5, 22, 26. **Draper v Attorney General** [1984] 643, HC, SC.

Local elections
Petition
Irregularity—Final count—Returning officer declaring result of election immediately
after declaring final count—No opportunity given to unsuccessful candidate or his agent
to request a recount—Whether action of returning officer amounted to an irregularity
'likely to have affected' the result of the election—Onus of proof—Returning officer
failing to exercise discretion—Whether recount should be ordered—Local Elections
(Petitions and Disqualifications) Act 1974, ss. 1, 2(1), 5, 7, 8—Prosecution of Offences
Act 1974, ss. 3(1), 4(b)—Local Elections Regulations 1965, Arts 11, 71. **Boyle v Allen**
[1979] 281, CC.

Service—Functions of DPP—Prosecution of Offences Act 1974, s. 3(1). **Boyle v Allen**
[1979] 281, CC.

Vacancy
County council—Death of member—Standing orders providing for co-option of a
person from the same electoral area—Whether *ultra vires*. *See* LOCAL GOVERNMENT
(Authority—Membership—Vacancy).

Postal voting
Physically incapacitated persons. See Dáil Éireann elections—Polling—Inability to attend
at polling station (*above*).

ELECTRICITY SUPPLY BOARD
Statutory power
Exercise
Compulsory imposition of structures on land—Erection of electricity pylons—Absence of independent means of assessing compensation—Whether justifiable interference with property rights—Constitution—Statute—Validity—Whether constitutes unjust attack on property rights—Electricity (Supply) Act 1927, ss. 52, 98—Electricity ((Supply) (Amendment) Act 1941, s. 5—Electricity (Supply) (Amendment) Act 1945, s. 46—Constitution of Ireland 1937, Articles 40.3, 43. **Electricity Supply Board v Gormley** [1985] 494, SC.

Reasonableness—Disconnection of supply to customer—Standard form contract—Whether customer in breach of agreement—Whether supply may be disconnected without notice—Whether court order required—Electricity (Supply) Act 1927, s. 99. **McCord v Electricity Supply Board** [1980] 153, SC.

EMERGENCY POWERS ACT 1976
Arrest
Legality. See ARREST (Legality—Motive—Arrest under statutory power—Emergency Powers Act).

Procedure
Charge
Whether lawful to charge accused otherwise than in District Court or Special Court. *See* CRIMINAL LAW (Charge—Emergency Powers Legislation).

EMPLOYER'S LIABILITY
Injury to employee. *See* NEGLIGENCE (Employer).

Insurance
Contract
Interpretation. *See* INSURANCE (Contract—Interpretation—Employer's liability insurance).

Vicarious liability. *See* NEGLIGENCE (Employer—Vicarious liability).

EMPLOYMENT
Access to post
Age limit for entry
Upper age limit—Discrimination—Sex or marital status. *See* Equality of treatment—Access to employment (*below*).

Qualification for appointment
Requirement of linguistic knowledge—Teacher—Knowledge of Irish langauge—Knowledge not required for the performance of teaching duties—Compatibility of such requirement with European Community law—Free movement of workers. *See* EDUCATION (Teacher—Appointment—Requirement of linguistic knowledge).

Accident to employee
Employer
Duty of care. *See* NEGLIGENCE (Employer).

Appeal
Employment Appeals Tribunal determination
Appeal to Circuit Court—Whether further right of appeal lay to High Court. *See* HIGH COURT (Jurisdiction—Appeal—Circuit Court decision—Appeal from Employment Appeals Tribunal determination).

Labour Court determination. See LABOUR COURT

Tribunal. See EMPLOYMENT APPEALS TRIBUNAL.

EMPLOYMENT *continued*

Appointment

Cancellation

Teacher—Pressure exerted on manager of primary school to cancel appointment of plaintiff as principal. *See* EDUCATION (Teacher— Cancellation of appointment).

Legitimate expectation

Teacher—Whether Minister estopped from exercising discretion to refuse to appoint applicant as teacher—Whether applicant had legitimate expectation that she would be appointed. *See* EDUCATION (Teacher—Appointment—Legitimate expectation).

Teacher. See EDUCATION (Teacher—Appointment).

Validity

Teacher—Scheme for establishments of posts of responsibility—Appointment as vice principal—Appeal Board ruling appointee ineligible—Whether appointment valid. **Ahern v de Hora** [1980] 203, HC.

Civil service. *See* CIVIL SERVICE.

Collective agreement

Equal pay. See Equal pay—Collective agreement (*below*).

Whether intention to establish legal relations

Employees dismissed for redundancy—Employees seeking declaration that the company gave them a guarantee that they would not be made redundant before a certain date—Company denying that such guarantee contemplated legal relations—Whether intention to enter into legal relations—Onus of proof. **O'Rourke v Talbot (Ireland) Ltd** [1984] 587, HC.

Continuity of employment

Redundancy

Compensation—Requirement of continuous employment—Meaning of "week"—Whether "week" means calendar week—Redundancy Payments Act 1967, s. 2(1)—Interpretation Act 1937, Schedule, rule 34. **Gormley v McCartin Brothers (Engineering) Ltd** [1982] 215, EAT.

Contract

Breach

Cancellation of appointment—Pressure exerted on manager of primary school to cancel appointment of plaintiff as principal. *See* EDUCATION (Teacher—Cancellation of appointment).

Damages. *See* DAMAGES (Breach of contract—Employment contract).

Employee on holiday—Serious situation developing requiring employee's attention—Whether lawful and reasonable of employer to require employee to interrupt his holiday—Employee failing to return —Employment terminated—Whether cancellation and rearrangement of holiday constituted a breach of contract. **Hartery v Welltrade (Middle East) Ltd** [1978] 38, HC.

Collective agreement

Whether intention to establish legal relations. *See* Collective agreement (*above*).

Construction

Probationary period—Whether duty of certifying satisfactory service could be delegated—Whether certification should take place within probationary period—Whether bias. **O'Neill v Beaumont Hospital Board** [1990] 419, HC.

Contract of service or for services

Dispute over termination of contract—Picketing—Whether entitled to statutory protection—Whether picketer an "employee"—Whether plaintiff the employer—Trade Disputes Act 1906, ss. 2, 5(3)—Constitution of Ireland 1937, Article 40. **Lamb Brothers Dublin Ltd v Davidson** [1978] 226, HC.

EMPLOYMENT

Contract *continued*

Contract of service or partnership

Fishermen—Captain engaging crew at commencement of each separate voyage—
Remuneration of crew based on custom and agreement—Whether element of control
by captain outweighed by other factors—Whether arrangement in reality partnership—
Revenue—Returns—Employer—Income Tax (Employments) Regulation 1960—Social
Welfare (Collection of Employment Contributions by the Collector General) Regulations
1979. **DPP v McLoughlin** [1986] 493, HC.

Existence

Trade dispute—Sub-contractor—Whether protection of trade disputes legislation
available—Trade Disputes Act 1906, s. 3. **J Bradbury Ltd v Duffy** [1979] 51, HC.

Frustration

Appointment terminated for stated or other reasons—Whether circumstances required
to terminate appointment had arisen—Whether contract frustrated. **Browne v Mulligan:
In re Shiel** [1976–7] 327, SC.

Restraint of trade clause

Whether restraint reasonable—Valid interest to be protected—Injunction—Balance of
convenience. **European Chemical Industries Ltd v Bell** [1981] 345, HC.

Termination

Dismissal. *See* Dismissal (*below*).

Unfair dismissal. *See* Unfair dismissal (*below*).

Terms. See Terms (*below*).

Discipline

Inquiry

Garda Siochána. *See* GARDA SIOCHÁNA (Discipline).

Discrimination

Sex or marital status. See Equality of treatment (*below*).

Dismissal

Constructive dismissal. See Unfair dismissal—Constructive dismissal (*below*).

Defence forces

Constitution—Fair procedures—Certiorari—Delay—Whether disentitling prosecutor
to relief. **State (Furey) v Minister for Defence** [1988] 89, SC.

Naval officer—Inefficiency—Whether sufficient compliance with rules of natural
justice. **State (Duffy) v Minister for Defence** [1979] 65, SC.

Fair procedures

Defence forces—Certiorari—Delay—Whether disentitling prosecutor to relief. **State
(Furey) v Minister for Defence** [1988] 89, SC.

Garda Siochána. See GARDA SIOCHÁNA (Dismissal).

Natural justice

Defence forces—Naval officer—Inefficiency—Notification of decision given but
postponed to allow representation—No representations made—Whether sufficient compliance with rules of natural justice. **State (Duffy) v Minister for Defence** [1979] 65, SC.

Delegation of power to dismiss. *See* Dismissal—Office-holder—Delegation of power
to dismiss (*below*).

Garda Siochána—Summary dismissal by Commissioners—Absence of formal inquiry—
Limitation of rules of natural justice in context of certain State services. *See* GARDA
SIOCHÁNA (Dismissal—Natural justice).

EMPLOYMENT
Dismissal
Natural justice continued
Probationer. *See* Dismissal—Office holder—Probationer (*below*).

Office holder
Delegation of power to dismiss—Whether *ultra vires* or whether dismissal in breach of principles of natural justice. **Heneghan v Western Regional Fisheries Board** [1986] 225, HC.

Probationer—Garda Síochána—Whether dismissal *ultra vires*. *See* GARDA SÍOCHÁNA (Dismissal—Natural justice—Probationer).

Probationer—Natural justice—Whether reasons required—Whether reasons be disclosed—Civil Service Regulation Act 1956, ss. 5, 7—Civil Service Regulation (Amendment) Act 1958, s. 3. **State (Daly) v Minister for Agriculture** [1988] 173, HC.

Teacher. *See* EDUCATION (Teacher—Dismissal).

Unfair dismissal claim—Whether entitlement to claim unfair dismissal. *See* Unfair dismissal—Exclusion—Officer—Health board (*below*).

Wrongful dismissal—Damages—Failure to pay salary on due dates—Loss of availability of salary—Exemplary damages—Loss arising from arbitrary nature of dismissal. **Garvey v Ireland** [1979] 266, HC.

Unfair dismissals. See Unfair dismissal (*below*).

Wrongful dismissal. See Wrongful dismissal (*below*).

Employer's insolvency
Arrears of weekly remuneration
Application for payment out of Redundancy and Employers' Insolvency Fund—Trade union dues deducted from remuneration—Dues not paid to trade union—Whether deduction notice operated as an assignment—Protection of Employees (Employers' Insolvency) Act 1984, s. 6(1), (2). **In re Solus Teo: Minister for Labour v O'Toole** [1990] 180, HC.

Employer's liability. *See* NEGLIGENCE (Employer).

Employer's liability insurance. *See* INSURANCE (Contract Interpretation—Employer's liability insurance).

Equal pay
Collective agreement providing for the implementation of unisex salary structure
Agreement proposed and accepted as 'in full and final settlement of claims'—Whether employees estopped from claiming arrears of equal pay—Appeal from Labour Court determination—Whether Labour Court erred in law—Anti-Discrimination (Pay) Act 1974, ss. 2(1), 4, 5, 7. **PMPA Insurance Co Ltd v Keenan** [1982] 367, LC; [1985] 173, HC, SC.

Labour Court determination
Appeal—Grounds other than sex—Like work—Whether difference in pay amounts to discrimination—Anti-Discrimination (Pay) Act 1974, ss. 2(1), (3), 3, 7(3). **An Chomhairle Oiliuna Talmhaiochta v Doyle** [1990] 21, HC.

Appeal—Whether Labour Court acted without jurisdiction—Comparator used not named in union's original submission—Anti-Discrimination (Pay) Act 1974, s. 7. **State (Polymark (Ireland) Ltd) v Labour Court** [1987] 357, HC.

Appeal—Whether Labour Court erred in law—Retrospection of equal pay. **PMPA Insurance Co Ltd v Keenan** [1985] 173, HC, SC.

NOT TO BE REMOVED
FROM LIBRARY

EMPLOYMENT

Equal pay *continued*

"*Like work*"

Work higher in value—Female employees engaged in work of greater value than male comparator—Male comparator being paid more—Legislation providing equal pay for like work—Determination that employees' work of higher value—Legislation not allowing for equal pay determination in such circumstances—Intention of legislature—Anti-Discrimination (Pay) Act 1974, ss. 2, 3. **Murphy v Bord Telecom Eireann** [1986] 483, HC.

Work higher in value—Female employees engaged in work of greater value than male comparator—Male comparator being paid more—Whether female employees entitled to equal pay—National legislation providing for an entitlement to equal pay where employees engaged in work of equal value—Whether national legislation compatible with European Community law—Extent of Community law principle—Treaty of Rome, Article 119—Council Directive 75/117—Anti-Discrimination (Pay) Act 1974, ss. 2, 3. **Murphy v Bord Telecom Eireann** [1989] 53, ECJ, HC.

Equality of treatment

Access to employment

Age limit for entry to post—Whether discriminatory against married women—Whether essential requirement—Proportion of married women able to comply—Entitlement to compensation—Employment Equality Act 1977, ss. 2(c), 3(1), 22. **North Western Health Board v Martyn** [1982] 584, LC.

Age limit for entry to post—Discrimination—Sex or marital status—Labour Court determination—Appeal to High Court—Labour Court finding that discrimination occurred being based on uncontested assumptions of fact—Whether open to High Court to require these facts to be proved—Employment Equality Act 1977, ss. 2(c), 3 (1), 22. **North Western Health Board v Martyn** [1985] 226, HC; [1988] 519, SC.

Labour Court

Jurisdiction—Appeal from equality officer—Whether jurisdiction to deal with the issue of discrimination outside six month period—Judicial review—Appellate nature of Labour Court—Function in disputes as to whether discrimination has occurred—Employment Equality Act 1977, s. 19. **Aer Rianta v Labour Court** [1990] 193, HC.

Marital staus

Access to employment—Age limit for entry to post—Whether discriminatory against married women. *See* Equality of treatment—Access to employment (*above*).

Complainants dismissed on marriage prior to enactment of equality legislation—Complainants rehired subsequently—Whether failure to take premarriage service into account constituted discrimination—Whether referral out of time—Employment Equality Act 1977, ss. 2, 3, 10, 19(5)—Council Directive 76/207/EEC, Article 6. **Aer Lingus Teo v Labour Court** [1990] 485, HC.

Procedure

Labour Court—determination—Appeal on a point of law—Whether appeal out of time—Health Act 1970, s. 18—Employment Equality Act 1977, ss. 2(c), 3, 12(3), 20, 21(4), 22, 24(2). **North Western Health Board v Martyn** [1985] 226, HC.

Statutory time-bar for reference of disputes—Alleged general practice of discrimination—Reference to Labour Court by Employment Equality Agency—Whether reference caught by statutory time-bar. **State (Aer Lingus) v Labour Court** [1987] 373, HC, SC.

European Community

Free movement of workers. See EUROPEAN COMMUNITY (Free movement of workers).

Garda Siochána. *See* GARDA SIOCHÁNA.

EMPLOYMENT *continued*

Health and safety

Injury to employee

Employer's duty of care. *See* NEGLIGENCE (Employer).

Occupational disease

Folliculitis—Employer's liability—Whether employee's contraction of the disease was reasonably foreseeable. **Brady v Beckman Instruments** [1986] 361, SC.

Liability

Employer

Duty of care—Injury to employee. *See* NEGLIGENCE (Employer).

Vicarious liability. *See* NEGLIGENCE (Employer—Vicarious liability).

Maternity protection

Entitlement to return to work

Employee not notifying employer in writing of intention to return to work—Whether mandatory condition—Whether failure to allow an employee who had not complied with the condition to return a dismissal—If dismissed, whether unfair—Maternity Protection of Employees Act 1981, ss. 16, 22, 26, 27. **Ivory v Ski-Line Ltd** [1989] 433, HC.

Minimum notice

Lay off

Claim for compensation—Notice of intention to claim redundancy payment—Effect on contract of employment—Whether employment ceased due to termination of employer—Whether waiver of right to notice—Whether employees estopped—Redundancy Payments Act 1967, ss. 11, 12, 13—Redundancy Payments Act 1971, s. 11—Minimum Notice and Terms of Employment Act 1973, ss. 4, 5, 7, 1st Schedule—Unfair Dismissals Act 1977, s. 20. **Industrial Yarns Ltd v Greene** [1984] 15, HC.

Termination of employment

Constructive dismissal—Whether question of minimum notice entitlement arises—Minimum Notice and Terms of Employment Act 1973. **Halal Meat Packers (Ballyhaunis) Ltd v Employment Appeals Tribunal** [1990] 293, HC, SC.

Notice—Continuance of business—Purported extension of notice—Whether permissible—Whether employees received their statutory entitlement—Minimum Notice and Terms of Employment Act 1973, ss. 7(1), 11(2). **Bolands Ltd v Ward** [1988] 382, HC, SC.

Minimum wage. *See* Pay—Minimum wage (*below*).

Office holder

Dismissal. See Dismissal—Office holder (*above*).

Suspension

Civil servants—Application for injunction restoring plaintiffs to their position. *See* CIVIL SERVICE (Suspension).

Garda Síochána. *See* GARDA SÍOCHÁNA (Discipline—Suspension).

Pay

Equal pay. See Equal pay (*above*).

Minimum wage

Statutory minimum wage levels—Offence—Employer prosecuted for failure to observe statutory wage levels—District Court—Jurisdiction—Whether jurisdiction to order employer to pay amount of underpayment for period prior to date of alleged offence—Courts (Supplemental Provisions) Act 1961, s. 52—Industrial Relations Act 1946, ss. 45 and 49—Employment Regulation Order (Catering Joint Labour Committee) 1986. **Minister for Labour v Costello** [1989] 485, HC.

EMPLOYMENT *continued*
Promotion
Garda Siochána
Proposed change in system of promotion. *See* GARDA SIOCHÁNA (Promotion).

Remuneration. See Terms *(below)*.
Qualification for appointment
Requirement of knowledge of Irish language
Teacher. *See* EDUCATION (Teacher—Appointment—Requirement of linguistic knowledge).

Redundancy
Compensation
Exclusions and qualifications—Requirement of continuous employment—Meaning of "week"—Whether "week" means calendar week—Redundancy Payments Act 1967, s. 2(1)—Interpretation Act 1937, Schedule, rule 34. **Gormley v McCartin Brothers (Engineering) Ltd** [1982] 215, EAT.

Road traffic accident
Vehicle used in course of employment
Indemnity—Employer seeking indemnity from employee using vehicle in course of employment—Employee guilty of negligence—Civil Liability Act 1961, s. 21—Road Traffic Act 1961, s. 118. **Sinnott v Quinnsworth Ltd** [1984] 523, SC.

Staff association
Civil service
New staff association seeking recognition from Minister for the Public Service. *See* CIVIL SERVICE (Staff association).

Suspension
Civil servants
Application for injunction restoring plaintiffs to their position. *See* CIVIL SERVICE (Suspension).

Office holder
Garda Siochána—Disciplinary investigation and inquiry—Natural justice—Whether member entitled to make representation on suspension. *See* GARDA SIOCHÁNA (Discipline—Suspension).

Terms
Office
Teacher—Teacher accepting post on basis of adhering to college statutes—Certain statutes in disuse—Whether affecting validity of dismissal under other provisions of statutes—Whether statutes inimical of academic freedom—College also pontifical university—Whether rules of pontifical university part of canon law—Whether recognisable in court of law. **McGrath v Maynooth College** [1979] 166, SC.

Promotion
Remuneration—Health Board officer—Calculation of commencing salary requiring approval of Minister—Increased salary granted pending approval—Refusal resulting in reduced salary—Whether Minister acting intra vires—Whether officer entitled to receive payments in accordance with original determination—Health Act 1970, s. 14. **Murphy v Eastern Health Board** [1979] 100, HC.

Trade dispute. *See* TRADE DISPUTE.

Transfer of undertaking
Unfair dismissal. See Unfair dismissal—Transfer of undertaking *(below)*.

Unfair Dismissal
Compensation
Assessment—Termination of employment on grounds of redundancy—Proceedings for redress—Jurisdiction of the High Court—Whether dismissal wholly or mainly due

EMPLOYMENT
Unfair Dismissal
Compensation continued

to redundancy—Onus of proof—Extent to which the financial loss was attributable to applicant's own conduct—Whether confined to conduct after dismissal—Whether failure to mitigate loss—Whether deduction of financial loss attributable to applicant to be made from maximum permitted amount or from full amount of the financial loss—Assessment of compensation—Redundancy Payments Act 1967, s. 7—Redundancy Payments Act 1971, s. 4—Unfair Dismissals Act 1977, ss. 1, 6. **McCabe v Lisney & Son** [1981] 289, HC.

Constructive dismissal

Whether question of minimum notice entitlement arises—Minimum Notice and Terms of Employment Act 1973. **Halal Meat Packers (Ballyhaunis) Ltd v Employment Appeals Tribunal** [1990] 293, HC, SC.

Exclusion

Contract of employment tainted with illegality—Whether illegal aspect severable—Consequence of illegality—Whether contract void or unenforceable—Unfair Dismissals Act 1977. **Lewis v Squash Ireland** [1983] 363, EAT.

Contract of service—Claimant consultant surgeon—Whether an employee—Unfair Dismissals Act 1977, s. 1. **O'Friel v St Michael's Hospital** [1982] 260, EAT.

Officer—Health board—Statutory registered psychiatric nurse—Termination of employment—Determination of EAT—Appeal to Circuit Court—Whether further appeal lay to High Court—Whether action 'a civil action or manner'—Whether claimant employed under a contract of service—Whether claimant an officer and thereby excluded from provisions of Act—Courts of Justice Act 1936, ss. 31, 38—Health Act 1970, ss. 14, 15—Unfair Dismissals Act 1977, ss. 2(1) (j), (2), 10(4)—Mental Hospitals (Officers and Servants) Order 1966, Arts 3(3), 4. **Western Health Board v Quigley** [1982] 390, HC.

Maternity protection

Entitlement to return to work—Employee not notifying employer in writing of intention to return to work—Whether mandatory condition—Whether failure to allow an employee who had not complied with the condition to return a dismissal—If dismissed, whether unfair—Maternity Protection of Employees Act 1981, ss. 16, 22, 26, 27. **Ivory v Ski-Line Ltd** [1989] 433, HC.

Natural justice

Gradual deterioration of working relationship—Termination of employment—Whether compliance with requirements of natural justice—Relevance of fair procedures—Assessment of compensation—Contribution by claimant—Unfair Dismissals Act 1977, s. 7. **Bunyan v UDT (Ireland) Ltd** [1982] 404, EAT.

Procedure

Initiation of claim—Death of employer—Whether claim should proceed against the personal representatives of the employer—Nature of proceedings before Employment Appeals Tribunal—Whether employee dismissed—Remedy—Civil Liability Act 1961, s. 8(1)—Succession Act 1965, s. 8—Unfair Dismissals Act 1977, ss. 1, 15. **Hutton v Philippi** [1982] 578, EAT.

Initiation of claim—Time limit—Whether mandatory requirement on employee to notify employer—Unfair Dismissals Act, 1977, s. 8. **IBM Ireland Ltd v Feeney** [1983] 50, CC.

Initiation of claim—Time limit—Whether mandatory requirement on employee to notify employer—Unfair Dismissals Act 1977, s. 8. **State (IBM Ireland Ltd) v Employment Appeals Tribunal** [1984] 31, HC.

EMPLOYMENT
Unfair Dismissal *continued*
Reason for dismissal
> Whether substantial grounds justifying dismissal—Female teacher in convent school—
> Whether teacher dismissed by reason of her pregnancy—Unfair Dismissals Act 1977,
> ss. 6(1), 6(2)(f). **Flynn v Power** [1985] 336.

Remedy
> Compensation. *See* Unfair dismissal—Compensation (*above*).

> Re-engagement—Tribunal determining dismissal unfair—Appropriate remedy—
> Claimant indicating preferred remedy compensation—Tribunal directing claimant be
> re-engaged—Whether Tribunal acted *ultra vires*. *See* EMPLOYMENT APPEALS TRIBUNAL
> (Natural justice—Unfair dismissals appeal—Re-engagement ordered).

Transfer of undertaking
> Employee dismissed for redundancy prior to transfer—Whether Employment Appeals
> Tribunal jurisdiction to hear claim of unfair dismissal against transferee—Whether
> regulations apply where transferor insolvent—Council Directive 77187, Articles 1, 3(1),
> 4(1)—European Communities (Safeguarding of Employees' Rights on Transfer of
> Undertakings) Regulations 1980, regs 3, 5, 6—Unfair Dismissals Act 1977, ss. 13, 19.
> **Mythen v Employment Appeals Tribunal** [1989] 844, HC.

Tribunal
> Natural justice—Failure by employer to deliver notice of appearance—Tribunal refusing
> to hear employer—Judicial review—Whether violation of natural and constitutional
> justice—Whether error within jurisdiction. *See* EMPLOYMENT APPEALS TRIBUNAL
> (Natural justice—Unfair dismissals appeal—Failure by employer to deliver notice of
> appearance).

> Natural justice—Fair procedures—Appropriate remedy—Claimant indicating preferred
> remedy compensation—Tribunal directing claimant be re-engaged—Whether Tribunal
> acted *ultra vires*. *See* EMPLOYMENT APPEALS TRIBUNAL (Natural justice—Unfair
> dismissals—Re-engagement ordered).

Wrongful dismissal
Damages
> Office holder—Failure to pay salary on due dates—Loss of availability of salary—
> Whether dismissal resulted in injury to health—Whether due to unlawful nature of
> dismissal—Exemplary damages—Loss arising from arbitrary nature of dismissal. **Garvey
> v Ireland** [1979] 266, HC.

EMPLOYMENT APPEALS TRIBUNAL
Appeal from determination
Appeal to Circuit Court
> Whether further right of appeal lay to High Court. *See* HIGH COURT (Jurisdiction—
> Appeal—Circuit Court decision—Appeal from Employment Appeals Tribunal
> determination).

Natural justice
Unfair dismissals appeal
> Failure by employer to deliver notice of appearance—Tribunal refusing to hear
> employer—Judicial review—Whether violation of natural and constitutional justice—
> Whether error within jurisdiction Constructive dismissal—Whether entitlement to
> minimum notice—Redundancy Appeals Tribunal Regulations 1968, reg 23—Unfair
> Dismissals (Claims and Appeals) Regulations 1977, regs 5, 9, 10—Maternity Pro-
> tection (Disputes and Appeals) Regulations 1981, reg 15—Unfair Dismissals Act 1977,
> ss. 8, 9, 10. **Halal Meat Packers (Ballyhaunis) Ltd v Employment Appeals Tribunal**
> [1990] 293, HC, SC.

EMPLOYMENT APPEALS TRIBUNAL
Natural justice
Unfair dismissals appeal continued
Re-engagement ordered—Remedy not argued by parties to hearing—Failure to give employer notice of its intention to consider such remedy—No opportunity given to meet the case—Whether in breach of fair procedures. **State (Irish Pharmaceutical Union) v Employment Appeals Tribunal** [1987] 36, SC.

EMPLOYMENT CONTRIBUTIONS. *see* SOCIAL WELFARE (Employment contributions).

EMPLOYMENT EQUALITY. *See* EMPLOYMENT (Equality of treatment).

EMPLOYMENT INSURANCE
Social welfare. *See* SOCIAL WELFARE (Employment contributions).

ENFORCEMENT
Judgment. *See* JUDGMENT (Enforcement).

Planning control. *See* PLANNING (Enforcement).

Revenue. *See* REVENUE (Income tax—Default procedure).

ENTERTAINMENT
Dance hall licence. *See* LICENSING (Exemption orders—Special exemption order—Dance hall).

Gaming
Slot machines. See GAMING AND LOTTERIES.

ENTRY ON PREMISES
Forcible entry
Employees
Occupation of employer's premises—Civil contempt—Committal—Jurisdiction of court—Deliberate disobedience of court order. *See* CONTEMPT OF COURT (Civil contempt—Committal).

Garda Síochána
Admissibility of evidence obtained. See CRIMINAL LAW (Evidence—Admissibility—Entry on premises).

Arrest
Legality—Whether gardai empowered to enter a private dwelling without permission of occupant. *See* ARREST (Legality—Place of arrest—Dwelling of citizen).

Criminal investigation
Forcible entry of accused's home. *See* CRIMINAL INVESTIGATION (Forcible entry of accused's home).

ENVIRONMENT
Development control. *See* PLANNING.

Local government. *See* LOCAL GOVERNMENT.

Nuisance. *See* NUISANCE.

Public health. *See* LOCAL GOVERNMENT (Public health).

Pollution. *See* POLLUTION.

ENVIRONMENTAL IMPACT ASSESSMENT
EC directive. *See* PLANNING (Environmental impact assessment directive).

EQUAL PAY. *See* EMPLOYMENT (Equal pay).

EQUALITY BEFORE THE LAW. *See* CONSTITUTION (Equality).

EQUALITY OF TREATMENT
Employment
Sex or marital status. See EMPLOYMENT (Equality of treatment).

Social welfare
European Community directive
Failure to fully implement directive. *See* SOCIAL WELFARE (Equal treatment—European Community directive—Failure to fully implement directive).

EQUITY
Action for possession
Plaintiff's lands built on by defendants
Court's exercise of equitable jurisdiction to refuse order for possession—Rule in *Ramsden v Dyson.* **McMahon v Kerry Co Council** [1981] 419, HC.

Landlord
Relief against forfeiture—Leaseholder assigning interest without consent of owner—Change of use—Whether evidence entitling leaseholder to relief from forfeiture—Discretion of court to order lease to vest in under-lessee—Whether equitable to force owner into privity of contract with under-lessee—Conveyancing Act 1892, s. 4—Conveyancing and Law of Property Act 1881. **O'Connor v J G Mooney & Co Ltd** [1982] 373, HC.

Beneficial interest
Matrimonial property
Wife seeking declaration of interest. *See* FAMILY LAW (Property—Beneficial interest).

Unmarried couple
Purchase of house—Whether resulting trust to be inferred. *See* TRUST (Resulting trust—Unmarried couple).

Breach of confidence. *See* CONFIDENTIALITY (Breach).

Clean hands doctrine
Trust
Enforcement—Husband purchasing property in name of wife—Husband procuring wife to make false declaration in conveyance—Husband subsequently invoking court's aid to enforce trust—Whether husband entitled to relief in equity. *See* TRUST (Enforcement—Clean hands doctrine).

Constructive trust. *See* TRUST (Constructive trust).

Conversion. *See* CONVERSION.

Duress. *See* DURESS.

Equitable mortgage
Deposit of title deeds
Banker's lien. *See* BANK (Deposit of title deeds).

Family home. *See* Family Law (Property—Family home—Equitable mortgage).

Estoppel. *See* ESTOPPEL.

Fraudulent concealment
Defective premises
Accrual of right of action—Statute of Limitations—Whether statements made by defendant's agent can be considered as fraudulent concealment—Statute of Limitations 1957, ss. 11(1), 11(2)(a), 71(1). **Morgan v Park Developments Ltd** [1983] 156, HC.

Injunction. *See* INJUNCTION.

EQUITY *continued*

Joint tenancy. *See* JOINT TENANCY.

Laches

Contract for the sale of licensed premises

Action for specific performance—Whether plaintiff barred from relief by delay in bringing the proceedings. **White v McCooey** [1976–7] 72, HC.

Contract for the sale of a site

Oral agreement—Action for specific performance—Whether defence of laches available—Defendant allowed to incur expense in putting in roads and drainage on the site—Defendant aware of plaintiff's intention to institute proceedings—Delay not significant. **Guardian Builders Ltd v Kelly** [1981] 127, HC.

Mistake. *See* MISTAKE.

Partnership

Dissolution

Purchase of shares by remaining partners—Disagreement—General equitable principles—Whether excluded. **Williams v Harris** [1980] 237, SC.

Relief against forfeiture. *See* LANDLORD AND TENANT (Forfeiture—Recovery of possession).

Resulting trust. *See* TRUST (Resulting trust).

Retention of title clause

Sale of goods

Whether equitable charge only created—Whether sufficient to retain property in the goods. **Frigoscandia (Contracting) Ltd v Continental Irish Meat Ltd** [1982] 396, HC.

Specific performance

Contract

Building contract. *See* BUILDING CONTRACT (Specific performance).

Generally. *See* CONTRACT (Specific performance).

Sale of land. *See* SALE OF LAND (Specific performance).

Tracing

Money paid in error

Claim for repayment—Whether tracing available—Mixed fund—Whether money held in trust—Whether subject to set off—Constructive trust—Purpose of such trust—Estoppel—Whether person claiming set off acting to its detriment. **In re Irish Shipping Ltd (In liquidation)** [1986] 518, HC.

Trust. *See* TRUST.

Trust of contractual rights. *See* TRUST (Contractual rights).

Undue influence. *See* UNDUE INFLUENCE.

Unjust enrichment. *See* UNJUST ENRICHMENT.

ERROR *See* MISTAKE.

ERROR OF LAW *See* CERTIORARI.

ESCAPE FROM CUSTODY

Extradition application. *See* EXTRADITION (Escape from custody).

ESTATE AGENT. *See* AUCTIONEER.

ESTOPPEL
Bailment
Title
Bailee denying bailor's title—Whether exceptions to well-established principle applicable—Whether bailee entitled to claim rights of third party. **Webb v Ireland** [1988] 565, HC, SC.

Conduct
Acceptance
Landlord and tenant—Decontrolled premises—Death of statutory tenant—Whether dependants entitled to tenancy—Whether acceptance by landlord of dependant as tenant precluded landlord from denying contractual tenancy. **Byrne v O'Neill** [1979] 47, SC.

Acquiescence
Breach of covenant—Landlord and tenant—Restrictive covenant as to user—Subletting—Different use—No consent in writing—Tacit acquiescence over previous years—Proceedings to restrain breach—Whether plaintiff estopped from enforcing covenant. **Green Property Co Ltd v Shalaine Modes Ltd** [1978] 222, HC.

Assent to sale of premises
Licence attached—Premises mortgaged—No reference to licence—Whether licence caught by mortgage—Whether assentor precluded from substituting hypothetical basis for sale. **In re Sherry-Brennan** [1979] 113, HC, SC.

Collective agreement
Equal pay—Collective agreement providing for the implementation of unisex salary structure—Whether individual employees estopped from claiming arrears of equal pay—Whether agreement not to pursue equal pay claim void as being contrary to public policy. **PMPA v Keenan** [1982] 367, LC; [1985] 173, HC, SC.

Contractual arrangement
Contract providing for variation of statutory obligations—Whether parties to agreement estopped from reverting to prior position—Statute providing for ferry service on certain basis—Parties agreeing alternative service—Whether plaintiffs estopped from insisting on compliance with statutory obligation. **Waterford Harbour Commissioners v British Railways Board** [1979] 296, HC, SC.

Encouragement to act to detriment
Claim to right of way—Evidence failing to establish acquisition of right—Plea of estoppel by conduct—Whether evidence of any detrimental act done with the knowledge or encouragement of the defendant. **Dunne v Molloy** [1976–7] 266, HC.

Estoppel in pais
Representation—Reliance. *See* Representation (*below*).

Equitable estoppel
Claim—Whether statute-barred—Limitation period having expired—Whether acknowledgment—Whether defendants estopped from pleading the statute—Correspondence—Whether calculated to lead plaintiff to believe that defendants would not rely on their strict legal rights—Whether constituted encouragement to plaintiff to act on that belief. **Smith v Ireland** [1983] 300, HC.

Expenditure allowed
Plaintiff's lands built on by defendant—Bona fide mistake—Plaintiff never securing site nor keeping surveyance of it—Principles of equity—Conduct of both parties to be considered—No intrinsic value in land—Whether order for possession should be refused. **McMahon v Kerry Co Council** [1981] 419, HC.

Inconsistency with subsequent claim
Planning authority—S. 27 application—Unauthorised change of use—Whether authority estopped by causing the premises to be rated as used for office purposes—Whether

ESTOPPEL
Conduct
Inconsistency with subsequent claim continued
inconsistency between exercise of powers as rating authority and planning authority—Local Government (Planning and Development) Act 1976, s. 27. **Dublin Corporation v Garland** [1982] 104, HC.

Mistake
Money paid in error—Claim for repayment—Mixed fund—Whether money held in trust—Whether subjet to set-off—Constructive trust—Purpose of such trust—Estoppel—Whether person claiming set-off acting to his detriment—Whether estoppel arising. **In re Irish Shipping Ltd** [1986] 518, HC.

Estoppel in pais
Representation
Reliance. *See* Representation (*below*).

Injunction
Planning injunction
Non-compliance with enforcement notice. *See* Planning authority—Enforcement of planning control—S. 27 application (*below*).

Issue estoppel
Interlocutory application
Additional ground argued—Application to dismiss for want of prosecution—Application unsuccessful—Further delay—Second application—Whether applicant estopped from raising grounds of prejudice other than those relied on on first application. **Sweeney v Horan's Hotel (Tralee) Ltd** [1987] 240, SC.

Res judicata
Civil proceedings following criminal proceedings—Civil action for damages for assault—Criminal proceedings involving same issue finding no assault took place—Whether plaintiff estopped from bringing civil proceedings—Whether defendants estopped from denying plaintiff's ability to bring civil proceedings—Defendants not party to criminal prosecution—Additional evidence—Whether sufficient to overcome plea of estoppel. **Kelly v Ireland** [1986] 318, HC.

Civil proceedings following criminal proceedings—Dismissal of complaint in District Court—Not guilty finding—Whether such dismissal a bar to civil proceedings being brought in respect of the same matter. **Meath Co Council v Daly** [1988] 274, HC.

Nullity proceedings—Whether point arising in second action was put in issue and determined in earlier proceedings—Distinction between issue estoppel and cause of action estoppel. **D v C** [1984] 173, HC.

Personal injury action—Whether defendant in second action estopped from alleging negligence or contributory negligence on part of plaintiff—Whether issue considered and finally determined in earlier proceedings. **Gilroy v McLoughlin** [1989] 133, HC.

Landlord and tenant
Entitlement to tenancy
Dependants of statutory tenant—Whether acceptance by landlord of dependent as tenant precluded landlord from denying contractual tenancy. **Byrne v O'Neill** [1979] 47.

Local authority. *See* Planning authority (*below*).

Matrimonial proceedings
Barring order application
Whether res judicata—Different circumstances prevailing. *See* Res judicata—Different circumstances prevailing—Barring order application (*below*).

ESTOPPEL
Matrimonial proceedings *continued*
Nullity
Plea of res judicata—Whether plea available—Whether validity of marriage an issue determined in earlier proceedings. **D v C** [1984] 173, HC.

Parties
Adding party as defendant
Personal injury action—Claim made against driver of vehicle—Driver dying from injuries received—Liberty sought to join insurers as defendants—Whether insurers estopped from opposing such an order. **Boyce v McBride** [1987] 95, SC.

Planning authority
Enforcement of planning control
S. 27 application—Unauthorised change of use—Whether authority estopped by causing the premises to be rated as used for office purposes—Local Government (Planning and Development) Act 1976, s. 27. **Dublin Corporation v Garland** [1982] 104, HC.

S. 27 application—Whether *res judicata*—Dismissal of complaint in District Court—Whether such dismissal a bar to civil proceedings being brought in respect of the same matter. **Meath Co Council v Daly** [1988] 274, HC.

Exempted development
Agent of authority representing that development exempt—Whether authority estopped from denying that development exempt—Local Government (Planning and Development) Act 1963, ss. 5, 26. **Dublin Corporation v McGrath** [1978] 208, HC.

Promissory estoppel
Agreement
Equal pay—Collective agreement providing for the implementation of unisex salary structure—Whether individual employees estopped from claiming retrospection of equal pay—Whether agreement not to pursue equal pay claim void as being contrary to public policy—Whether unjust to allow claimants to insist on their strict legal rights. **PMPA v Keenan** [1982] 367, LC; [1985] 173, HC, SC.

Legitimate expectation. See LEGITIMATE EXPECTATION.

Reliance on representation
Legitimate expectation—Garda Siochána—Conciliation and Arbitration scheme—Changes proposed—Plaintiffs claiming legitimate expectation that they would be consulted before changes implemented—Ministerial statement made in Dáil Éireann—Whether such statement may be relied on by plaintiff—Whether evidence to show that plaintiffs relied on Minster's statement so as to invoke support for promissory estoppel. **Garda Representative Association v Ireland** [1989] 1, HC.

Personal injury action—Road traffic accident—Driver dying from injuries received—Liberty sought to join insurers of deceased driver as defendants—Whether insurers estopped from opposing such an order—Whether evidence that insurers impliedly promised that they would not rely on the invalidity of the proceedings—Whether case for estoppel made out. **Boyce v McBride** [1987] 95, SC.

Whether doctrine applicable
Agreement to provide subsidy on retail price of bread—Dispute over compliance—Refusal to pay. **Kylemore Bakery Ltd v Minister for Trade, Commerce and Tourism** [1986] 529, HC.

Proprietary estoppel
Action for possession of land
Plaintiff's lands built on by defendant county council—Mistake—Whether excusable—Court's exercise of equitable jurisdiction to refuse order of possession—Matters to be considered—Conduct and consequences. **McMahon v Kerry Co Council** [1981] 419, HC.

ESTOPPEL
Proprietary estoppel *continued*
Assent to sale of premises
Licence attached—Premises mortgaged—Whether assentor precluded from substituting hypothetical basis for sale. *See* Conduct—Assent to sale of premises (*above*).

Reasonable expectation. *See* Promissory estoppel (*above*); *see also* LEGITIMATE EXPECTATION.

Representation
Agent
Planning authority—Agent of planning authority representing that development exempt—Whether authority estopped from denying that development exempt—Local Government (Planning and Development) Act 1963, ss. 5, 26. **Dublin Corporation v McGrath** [1978] 208, HC.

Defective premises
Accrual of right of action—Whether statements made by defendant's agent precluded defendant from pleading the Statute of Limitations—Statements of opinion—Whether reasonable inference drawn—Plaintiff acting unreasonably and with undue delay in failing to take proper remedial action—Statute of Limitations 1957, ss. 11(1), 11(2)(a), 71(1). **Morgan v Park Developments Ltd** [1983] 156, HC.

Existence of contractual relationship
Agreement for supply of milk—Sale of supplier's creameries—Undertaking as to no diminution of supply—No collateral agreement between purchaser and new owner of creameries—Dispute—Whether new owner under any obligation to supply a specified quantity of milk—Whether a trust of contractual rights created—Whether plea of estoppel fails. **Cadbury Ireland Ltd v Kerry Co-operative Creameries Ltd** [1982] 77, HC.

Reliance
Estoppel *in pais*—Company—Winding up—Issue and allocation of shares—Technical irregularity—Whether petitioner acquiesced in the arrangement—Whether petitioner estopped from asserting transaction was irregular. **In re Greenore Trading Co Ltd** [1980] 94, HC.

Estoppel *in pais*—Company—Guarantee and mortgage—Transaction *ultra vires*—Company sending memorandum and articles of association to lender—Whether amounting to representation that company had power to question—Whether lender relied on such act—Whether lender acted to their detriment—Whether company estopped from relying on *ultra vires* nature of transaction. **Northern Bank Finance v Quinn** [1979] 221, HC.

Expenditure—Defendant milk suppliers making complaints about efficiency of purchaser's plant—Plaintiff expending money on capital improvements to plant—Whether expenditure done on assumption that future supplies would be secure. **Cadbury Ireland Ltd v Kerry Co-operative Creameries** [1982] 77, HC.

Promissory estoppel. *See* Promissory estoppel (*above*).

Res judicata
Cause of action estoppel
Nullity proceedings—Whether validity of marriage a cause of action in earlier proceedings—Whether estoppel arose—Distinction between cause of action estoppel and issue estoppel explained. **D v C** [1984] 173, HC.

Civil proceedings following criminal proceedings
Whether plaintiff estopped from bringing civil proceedings—Whether defendants estopped from denying plaintiff's ability to bring civil proceedings. *See* Issue estoppel—Res judicata—Civil proceedings following criminal proceedings (*above*).

Different circumstances prevailing
Barring order application—Jurisdiction of High Court—Previous Circuit Court order

ESTOPPEL
  Res judicata
  Different circumstances prevailing continued
    refusing order—Whether different circumstances prevailing—Resumption of residence
    by defendant. **O'B v O'B** [1984] 1, SC.

  Issue estoppel. See Issue estoppel (*above*).

EUROPEAN COMMUNITY
  Agriculture
  Claim for levies
    Whether claim maintainable in light of Community law—Levies financed export bonus
    scheme—Whether scheme contrary to Community law—Reference to European Court
    of Justice—Whether Court condemned part of the scheme only—Whether these activities
    distinguishable and separable from the other activities—Pigs and Bacon Acts (Amend-
    ment) Act 1939, ss. 34, 38. **Pigs and Bacon Commission v McCarren and Co** [1981] 237,
    SC.

  Common agricultural policy
    Company liquidation—Monetary compensation levies—Intervention agent claiming
    right of set off. *See* AGRICULTURE (Common agricultural policy—Intervention scheme—
    Company liquidation).

    Export of cereals to other member states—Monetary compensation amounts—To whom
    payable—Frauds and irregularities. *See* AGRICULTURE (Common agricultural policy—
    Export of cereals—Carousel fraud).

    Monetary compensation amounts—Description of goods on import-export docu-
    mentation between EEC states. *See* AGRICULTURE (Common agricultural policy—
    Intervention scheme—Monetary compensation amounts).

  Competition
    Application of competition rules to the activities of farmers' co-operatives. *See* AGRI-
    CULTURE (Co-operatives—Competition—European Community competition rules).

  Compensatory payments
    Disadvantaged areas—Implementation by administrative scheme—Constitution—
    Validity. *See* AGRICULTURE (Disadvantaged areas—Compensatory payments to persons
    farming in disadvantaged areas).

  Excise duty on livestock
    Whether measure having effect equivalent to a customs duty—Whether duty *ultra
    vires. See* AGRICULTURE (Export levy on livestock).

  Milk levy
    Regulations giving effect to EC milk levy—Regulations having retrospective effect—
    Whether unjustified attack on property rights. *See* AGRICULTURE (Milk levy—Regu-
    lations giving effect to EC milk levy).

  Milk quotas
    'Mulder Regulations'—Interpretation. *See* AGRICULTURE (Milk quotas).

  Competition
  Abuse of dominant position
    Whether Co Kerry a substantial part of the Common Market—Treaty of Rome, Article
    86. **Cadbury Ltd v Kerry Cooperative Creameries Ltd** [1982] 77, HC.

  Agricultural co-operatives
    Application of competition rules to the activities of farmers' co-operatives—Whether
    exemption available—Jurisdiction of Irish courts to apply such Council Regulation.
    See AGRICULTURE (Co-operatives—Competition).

EUROPEAN COMMUNITY
Competition *continued*
Breach of competition rules alleged
Shareholder allegedly suffering damage by reason of reduction in share value—Whether such claim subject to national limitations—Rule in *Foss v Harbottle*—Treaty of Rome, Articles 85, 86. **O'Neill v Ryan** [1990] 140, HC.

Policy
Whether trade between Member States affected—Whether possibility of distortion of competition—Whether concerted practice—Whether abuse of a dominant position—Treaty of Rome, Articles 85, 86. **Radio Telefis Eireann v Magill TV Guide Ltd** [1990] 534, HC.

Directive
Direct effect
Equal treatment in matters of social security—Failure to fully implement directive—Whether directive has direct effect—Whether directive sufficiently unconditional and precise—Whether in the absence of implementing measures, women entitled to the benefits under the same condition as men—Council Directive 79/7EEC, Article 4(1)—Social Welfare (No. 2) Act 1985, ss. 2, 6(c). **McDermott and Cotter v Minister for Social Welfare** [1987] 324, ECJ.

Implementation
Administrative scheme—Validity—Constitution. *See* CONSTITUTION (Administrative scheme—Validity).

Planning and Development—Directive requiring certain information to be included in application—Whether directive implemented—Administrative circular letter—Council Directive 85/337/EEC. **Browne v An Bord Pleanála** [1989] 865, HC.

Social welfare—Implementation effected in such a way that certain married couples adversely treated—Constitutional obligation—Marriage—Whether failure on the part of the State to vindicate the institution of marriage—Constitution of Ireland 1937, Article 41.3.1—Social Welfare (No. 2) Act 1985, s. 12(4). **Hyland v Minister for Social Welfare** [1990] 213, SC.

Enforcement of Judgments
Brussels Convention See JUDGMENT (Enforcement—Brussels Convention).

Environmental impact assessment directive. *See* PLANNING (Environmental impact assessment).

Equal pay
Directly enforceable Community right
Whether such rights only capable of protection in High Court—Treaty of Rome, Articles 117, 119—Constitution of Ireland 1937, Articles 15, 29. 4.3—European Communities Act 1972, s. 2—Anti-Discrimination (Pay) Act 1974, ss. 2(1), 3. **Murphy v Bord Telecom Eireann** [1989] 53, ECJ, HC.

Like work
Work higher in value—Legislation lacuna allowing employee to be paid lower wages in respect of male employee whose work was of less value—Whether consistent with Treaty of Rome, Article 119. **Murphy v Bord Telecom Éireann** [1986] 483, HC; [1989] 53, ECJ, HC.

Free movement of workers
Teacher
Appointment to full-time teaching post—Requirement of linguistic knowledge—Irish language—Knowledge not required for the performance of teaching duties—Policy of maintaining and promoting the use of Irish—Compatibility of such requirement with European Community law—Treaty of Rome, Articles 48(3), 177—Council Regulation 1612/68, article 3—Constitution of Ireland 1937, Article 8—Vocational Education Act 1930, s. 23. **Groener v Minister for Education** [1990] 335, ECJ.

EUROPEAN COMMUNITY *continued*
Freedom to provide services
Whether includes right to give or receive information
Abortion—Public policy—Whether issue of community law arising—Reference to Court of Justice—Whether reference necessary—Treaty of Rome 1957, Article 177. **Society for the Protection of Unborn Children (Ireland) Ltd v Grogan** [1990] 350, SC.

Fuel
Supply and distribution
Government powers to regulate acquisition, supply, distribution and marketing—Whether incompatible with Community obligations—Whether mandatory regime a quantitive restriction or measure having equivalent effect—Application for interlocutory injunction—Whether injunction be granted—Treaty of Rome, Articles 30, 31, 36, 85, 86, 90—Fuels (Controls of Supplies) Act 1971, ss. 2, 3—Fuels (Controls of Supplies) Act 1982, s. 3 (1)—Fuels (Control of Supplies) Order 1982. **Campus Oil Ltd v Minister for Industry and Energy** [1983] 258, HC; [1984] 45, HC, SC.

Law
Application
Limitation of actions—Prohibition against defeat by government agency of legitimate expectation of agricultural producers—Prohibition against discrimination by government agency—Whether applies to right of government agency to rely upon a statutory time limit—Statute of Limitations 1957, ss. 3, 11, 56—European Communities Act 1972, s. 2. **Smith v Ireland** [1983] 300, HC.

Procedure
Reference to European Court of Justice
Supreme Court—Issue arising for first time. Consideration of mandatory reference—Treaty of Rome 1957, Art 177. **Macken v O'Reilly** [1979] 79, HC, SC.

Whether necessary—Supreme Court—Whether issue of community law arising—Treaty of Rome 1957, Articles 59, 60, 177. **Attorney General (ex rel Society for the Protection of Unborn Children (Ireland) Ltd) v Open Door Counselling Ltd** [1989] 19, SC.

Regulations
National regulations giving effect to EC regulations
Milk levy—Regulations having retrospective effect—Whether unjust—Whether unjustified attack on property rights—Whether any such infringement necessitated by membership of the European Community—Council Regulations 804/84, 856/84, 857/84—Commission Regulation 1271/84—European Communities (Milk Levy) Regulations 1985, reg 4, 12—Constitution of Ireland 1937, Articles 29.4.3, 40.3.2, 43. **Lawlor v Minister for Agriculture** [1988] 400, HC.

Treaty
Amendment
Constitution authorising membership of Communities—Whether amendments effect change in nature of Communities—Whether outside scope of constitutional provision—Change in voting procedure by Council of Ministers—Additional functions for Council—Enabling provision for new court structure—Constitution of Ireland 1937, Article 29.4.3—European Communities (Amendment) Act 1986. **Crotty v An Taoiseach** [1987] 400, HC, SC.

Challenge to validity
Single European Act—Government intending to ratify treaty—Obligations to engage in foreign policy co-operation—Whether limiting ability to engage in independent foreign policy making—Whether in conflict with sovereignty of Irish State and People—Whether consistent with Constitution—Constitution of Ireland 1937, Articles 1, 5, 6, 28, 29.4.1, 29.4.3—Single European Act [Treaty] Title III, Article 30. **Crotty v An Taoiseach** [1987] 400, HC, SC.

EUROPEAN CONVENTION ON HUMAN RIGHTS
Application
Succession Rights
Illegitimate child. **In re Walker: O'Brien v S.** [1982] 327, HC.

Whether State bound by Convention
Legal aid—Matrimonial proceedings—Convention on Human Rights and Fundamental Freedoms 1953 Art 6, 8—Scheme for Civil Legal Aid and Advice 1979, paras 4, 7. **E v E** [1982] 497, HC.

EVIDENCE *See also* CRIMINAL LAW (Evidence).
Admissibility
Affidavit
Objection to introduction of evidence at trial without prior notice—Case involving constitutional rights of citizen—Whether principles of ordinary litigation ought to be waived—RSC 1962, O 39 r 1. **Shannon v Attorney General** [1985] 449, HC, SC.

Challenge to constitutionality of legislation
Legislation conferring statutory monopoly on Post Office—Evidence as to alleged inefficiency in the administration of the postal service—Whether admissible—Whether relevant. **Attorney General v Paperlink Ltd** [1984] 373, HC.

Extrinsic evidence
Contract terms—Written agreement—Contract for sale of ordinary publican's licence—Whether extrinsic evidence admissible to vary the terms of the document. **Macklin v Greacen** [1981] 315, HC; [1982] 182, SC.

Will—Construction—Admissibility of extrinsic evidence to show testator's intention. **In re Clinton: O'Sullivan v Dunne** [1988] 80, HC.

Marriage settlement
Original deed destroyed by fire—Whether secondary evidence of contents of deed admissible. **Savage v Nolan** [1978] 151, HC.

New evidence
Appeal—Damages award—Whether events subsequent to High Court order consitute grounds of appeal—RSC 1986, O 58 rr 3(4), 8. **Dalton v Minister for Finance** [1989] 519, SC.

Paternity of child
Evidence of wife that child not the child of the marriage—Whether admissible. *See* CHILD (Paternity).

Privilege. See Privilege (*below*).

Discovery. *See* DISCOVERY (Privilege).

Statement of accused. See CRIMINAL LAW (Evidence—Statement by accused).

Tape recordings
Telephone calls—Whether defect in quality affects admissibility—Whether recording of telephone call made to person not then on trial admissible if part of transaction as a whole. **People (DPP) v Prunty** [1986] 716, CCA.

Telephone calls
Criminal law—Tape recording—Tracing of calls—Whether evidence as to voice on telephone established by hearsay—Whether admissible—Whether retrial should be ordered. **People (DPP) v Prunty** [1986] 716, CCA.

Unconstitutionally obtained evidence. See CRIMINAL LAW (Evidence—Admissibility—Unconstitutionally obtained evidence).

EVIDENCE *continued*
Appointment
Certificate of appointment
Sufficiency—Authorised officers of Minister for Agriculture—Whether certificate that officer had been appointed sufficient evidence of the fact of appointment—European Communities (Marketing of Fertiliser) Regulations 1978, reg 7(4). **Minister for Agriculture v Cleary** [1988] 294, HC.

Certificate
Sufficiency
Certificate of appointment. *See* Appointment—Certificate of appointment—Sufficiency (*above*).

Criminal law. *See* CRIMINAL LAW (Evidence).

Documents
Admissibility
Affidavit. *See* Admissibility—Affidavit (*above*).

Claim of privilege. *See* DISCOVERY.

Reconstructed records from damaged originals—Unavailability of person compiling records—Whether documents admissible. **People (DPP) v Marley** [1985] 17, CCA.

Discovery. See DISCOVERY.

Sufficiency
Certificate of appointment. *See* Sufficiency—Documentary evidence—Certificate of appointment (*below*).

Estoppel. *See* ESTOPPEL.

Extrinsic evidence
Admissibility. See Admissibility—Extrinsic evidence (*above*).

Findings of fact
Appellate review
Primary and secondary findings of fact—Finding as to state of mind of person at a particular point in time—Whether such finding a primary or second finding of fact. **J M and G M v An Bord Uchtala** [1988] 203, SC.

Hearsay
Tape recordings
Admissibility. *See* Admissibility—Tape recordings—Telephone calls (*above*).

Telephone calls
Admissibility. *See* Admissibility—Telephone calls (*above*).

Identification of accused. *See* CRIMINAL LAW (Evidence—Identification).

Illegally obtained evidence
Admissibility. See CRIMINAL LAW (Evidence—Admissibility—Entry on premises).

Issue estoppel. *See* ESTOPPEL (Issue estoppel).

Marriage
Non-consummation
Proof—Evidence indicating that marriage was not consummated—Trial judge inferring collusion between parties—Whether inference open to judge—Whether in accordance with natural justice—Whether decree of nullity should be granted on the basis of evidence presented only—Whether rehearing of issues required. **M v M** [1979] 160, SC.

Marriage settlement
Original deed destroyed by fire
Whether secondary evidence of contents of deed admissible. **Savage v Nolan** [1978] 151, HC.

EVIDENCE *continued*
  Onus of proof
    Security for costs
      Limited company instituting proceedings—If unsuccessful company unable to meet
      defendant's costs—Application for security to be given—Onus of proof on company
      seeking to avoid order for security—Prima facie special circumstance—Whether making
      of mere bald statement a sufficient discharge of the onus of proof—Companies Act
      1963, s. 390. **Jack O'Toole Ltd v MacEoin Kelly Associates** [1987] 269, SC.

  Paternity of child
    Evidence of wife that child not the child of the marriage
      Whether admissible. *See* CHILD (Paternity).

  Preservation
    Duty of Gardai. See CRIMINAL LAW (Evidence—Preservation—Duty of Gardai to preserve
      evidence material to guilt or innocence).
  Privilege
    Discovery of documents. See DISCOVERY (Privilege).

    Legal professional privilege. See DISCOVERY (Privilege—Legal professional privilege).

    Marriage counsellor
      Priest acting as marriage counsellor—Communications—Privilege that of the spouses—
      Constitution of Ireland 1937, Article 41. **R v R** [1981] 125, HC.

    Statutory privilege
      Central Bank officer—Subpoena duces tecum issued requiring officer to produce certain
      documents—Claim of statutory privilege—Whether summons be set aside—Central
      Bank Act 1942, ss. 6(1), 31. **Cully v Northern Bank Finance Corporation** [1984] 683, HC.

  Professional witness
    Costs
      Taxation. *See* COSTS (Taxation—Review—Witnesses' expenses).

  Regulation. *See* CRIMINAL LAW (Evidence—Regulations—Road traffic offence).

  Res judicata
    Estoppel. See ESTOPPEL (Res judicata).

  Statement of accused
    Admissibility. See CRIMINAL LAW (Evidence—Statement by accused).

  Sufficiency
    Documentary evidence
      Certificate of appointment. *See* Appointment—Certificate of appointment—Sufficiency
      (*above*).

    Medical negligence
      Findings of fact—Whether evidence before the jury to support certain of its findings—
      Whether findings should be set aside—Brain damage suffered by infant while in
      mother's womb—Expert medical evidence—Whether capable of supporting challenged
      findings. **Dunne (an infant) v National Maternity Hospital** [1989] 735, SC.

  Tape recordings
    Admissibility. See Admissibility—Tape recordings (*above*).

  Telephone calls
    Tape recording
      Admissibility. *See* Admissibility—Telephone calls (*above*).

  Will
    Construction
      Admissibility of extrinsic evidence to show testator's intention. **In re Clinton: O'Sullivan
      v Dunne** [1988] 80, HC.

EVIDENCE *continued*
Witness
Professional witness
Costs—Taxation. *See* COSTS (Taxation—Review—Witnesses' expenses).

EXCISE DUTY *See* CUSTOMS AND EXCISE.

EXCISE OFFENCES *See* CUSTOMS AND EXCISE (Offence).

EXCLUSIVE SUPPLY CONTRACT
Breach
Whether inducement
Purchaser subsequently entering into similar contract with another supplier—Position
of person who innocently enters into contract without knowledge of prior inconsistent
contract—Whether under duty to cease supplies on being informed of prior contract.
Flogas Ltd v Ergas Ltd [1985] 221, HC.

EXECUTIVE PRIVILEGE
Documents
Admissibility in evidence
Communications between members of the Gardai—Public interest—Whether executive
privilege can be claimed in respect of a class of documents. **DPP (Hanley) v Holly**
[1984] 149, HC.

EXEMPLARY DAMAGES *See* DAMAGES (Exemplary).

EXEMPTED DEVELOPMENT *See* PLANNING (Exempted development).

EXEMPTION CLAUSE
Contract. *See* CONTRACT (Exemption clause).

EXPLORATION WORK
Minerals. *See* MINES (Mineral exploration).

EXPORT LEVIES
Livestock. *See* AGRICULTURE (Export levy on livestock).

EXPORT SALES RELIEF *see* REVENUE (Corporation tax—Export sales relief).

EXPRESSION, FREEDOM OF *See* FREEDOM OF EXPRESSION.

EXTENSION OF TIME *See* TIME LIMIT (Extension).

EXTRA-TERRITORIAL OFFENCE
Jurisdiction of trial
Statutory right of individual to select jurisdiction
When right arises. *See* CRIMINAL LAW (Trial—Jurisdiction—Extra-territorial offence).

EXTRADITION
Bail
Test applicable
Likelihood of prisoner's being available for extradition—Test to be applied on bail
application—Whether different from that pertaining in domestic criminal matters.
People (Attorney General) v Gilliland [1986] 357, SC.

Constitutional rights
Fair procedures
Statutory scheme for production of documents—Whether entitlement to production of
sworn informations on which warrant based—Whether such production a requirement
of the right to fair procedures—Constitution of Ireland 1937, Articles 4, 29.4.1—
Extradition Act 1965, ss. 54(1), 55. **Ellis v O'Dea** [1990] 87, SC.

EXTRADITION
Constitutional rights *continued*
Liberty
Arrest—Validity—Overt surveillance—Garda Siochána anticipating request for extradition warrant—Whether surveillance operation justified—Whether garda authority in executing extradition warrant more restricted than authority to detect crime—Constitution of Ireland 1937, Article 40.4—Conspiracy and Protection of Property Act 1875—Offences against the State Act 1939, s. 30. **Kane v Governor of Mountjoy Prison** [1988] 724, HC, SC.

Probability of being subjected to assault, torture or inhuman treatment
Escape from custody—Extradition sought to serve remainder of sentence—Whether real danger that appellant would be ill-treated if delivered out of the jurisdiction. Constitution of Ireland 1937, Article 40.3.4. **Clarke v McMahon** [1990] 648, HC, SC.

Onus of proof—Escape from custody—Whether evidence of ill-treatment in prison from which escape took place established—Extradition Act 1965, s. 50—Criminal Law (Jurisdiction) act 1976, Constitution of Ireland 1937, Article 38.1. **Russell v Fanning** [1986] 401, HC; [1988] 333, SC.

Appellant detained in pursuance of extradition order—Evidence that appellant likely to be ill-treated if delivered out of the jurisdiction—Whether extradition should be refused in such circumstances—Constitution of Ireland 1937, Article 40.3.4. **Finucane v McMahon** [1990] 505, SC.

Conflict of evidence—Appellant in detention pursuant to warrant for his extradition—jurisdiction—Whether extradition should be refused in the circumstances—Constitution of Ireland 1937, Article 40. **Carron v McMahon** [1990] 802, SC.

Violation
Arrest—Illegality—Abuse of process—Whether illegality taints subsequent proceedings—Extradition Act 1965, s. 47—Constitution of Ireland 1937, Articles 40.3.1, 40.4.2. **Trimbole v Governor of Mountjoy Prison** [1985] 465, HC, SC.

Whether extradition arrangements safeguard personal rights of citizens
Whether procedures in courts of Northern Ireland meet minimum standards applicable in this State—Constitution of Ireland 1937, Article 34.1—Extradition Act 1965, Part III. **Shannon v Attorney General and Ireland** [1985] 449, HC, SC.

Correspondence of offence
Abuse of process
Illegality of arrest—Whether illegality taints subsequent proceedings—Extradition Act 1965, s. 47. **Trimbole v Governor of Mountjoy Prison** [1985] 465, HC, SC.

Charge of receiving stolen goods
Extradition order—Special summons—Whether delay a ground for refusing extradition—Whether offence political—Whether required correspondence with an offence under Irish Law—Charge of dishonestly receiving articles 'knowing or believing same to have been stolen'—Whether less stringent degree of *mens rea* than 'knowing same to have been stolen'—Larceny Act 1916, s. 33(1). **Hanlon v Fleming** [1982] 69, SC.

Extradition treaty
USA—Narcotics offences prior to date of treaty—Whether acts criminal within law of Ireland—Dangerous Drugs Act 1934—Murder—Whether offence of murder in law of New York corresponds with Irish law—Possible defences—Dangerous Drugs Act 1934, s. 17—Extradition Act 1965, s. 5—Extradition Act 1965 (Part II) Order 1984, Arts XVI, XVII—Constitution of Ireland 1937, Article 29.5.2. **State (McCaud) v Governor of Mountjoy Prison** [1986] 129, HC.

Order
Whether an extradition order must specify the offence in Irish law corresponding to

EXTRADITION
Correspondence of offence
Order continued

those for which the extradition has been sought—Extradition Act 1965, Part II. **State (Gilliland) v Governor of Mountjoy Prison** [1986] 381, HC.

Warrant

Uncertainty—Whether warrant void for uncertainty—Whether sufficient correspondence of offences—Whether necessary to establish total identity—Offences against the Person Act 1861, s. 62—Criminal Law (Amendment) Act 1935, s. 14—Extradition Act 1965, s. 50. **Harris v Wren** [1984] 120, HC.

Delay
Arrest on foot of warrants relating to offences committed seven years previously

Whether excessive delay—Whether unfair discrimination. **Harte v Fanning** [1988] 70, HC.

Escape from custody
Extradition sought to serve remainder of sentence

Whether real danger that appellant would be ill-treated if delivered out of the jurisdiction. **Clarke v McMahon** [1990] 648, HC, SC.

Whether political offence

Custody based on commission of robbery and unlawful possession of firearms—Furtherance of liberation of Northern Ireland from British rule. *See* Political offence—Escape from lawful custody—Custody based on commission of robbery and unlawful possession of firearms (*below*).

Whether evidence of ill-treatment in prison from which escape took place established. *See* Political offence—Escape from lawful custody—Offences connected with escape committed for purpose of promoting objectives of illegal paramilitary organisation (*below*).

Fair procedures
Re-arrest

Arrest on foot of foreign warrant—Order of habeas corpus granted because of matters which happened after arrest—Re-arrest on foot of same warrant—Whether lawful—Habeas Corpus (Ireland) Act 1781, s. 5. **State (McFadden) v Governor of Mountjoy Prison** (No 2) [1981] 120, HC.

Jurisdiction of court
Appellant escaped from lawful custody

Extradition sought to serve remainder of sentence—Appellant's conviction based on self-incriminating statement—Appellant alleging statement untrue and obtained by means of ill-treatment—Whether court can enquire into validity of conviction recorded in State requesting extradition—Constitution of Ireland 1937, Article 40.3—Extradition Act 1965. **Clarke v McMahon** [1990] 648, HC, SC.

Political offence
Corresponding offence

Charge of receiving stolen goods—Whether required correspondence with an offence under Irish Law—Charge of dishonestly receiving articles 'knowing or believing same to have been stolen'—Whether less stringent degree of mens rea than 'knowing same to have been stolen'—Larceny Act 1916, s. 33(1). **Hanlon v Fleming** [1982] 69, SC.

Criminal law

Robbery—Motive—No evidence upon which trial judge could have held robbery instigated on behalf of IRA or motivated by desire to assist IRA—Burden of proof—Extradition Act 1965, s. 50. **Maguire v Keane** [1986] 235, SC.

Definition

Warrant for arrest issued by foreign judicial authority on a complaint of murder—

EXTRADITION
  Political offence
   Definition continued
     Extradition order made—Application to High Court—Affidavit swearing the offence
     referred to was a political offence or an offence connected with a political offence—
     Definition of political offence—Consideration of whether murder could ever be a
     political offence—Extradition Act 1965, s. 50(2). **McGlinchey v Wren** [1983] 169, SC.

   Escape from lawful custody
     Custody based on commission of robbery and unlawful possession of firearms—
     Furtherance of liberation of Northern Ireland from British rule—Membership of para-
     military organisation—Whether political nature of offence established—Constitution
     of Ireland 1937, Articles 15.4.1, 40.1—Extradition Act 1965, s. 50(2). **McMahon v
     Leahy** [1985] 432, HC, SC.

     Offences connected with escape committed for purpose of promoting objectives of illegal
     paramilitary organisation—Whether political offences or offences connected with political
     offences—Whether trial in courts of Northern Ireland likely to prejudice accused's
     trial rights—Whether evidence of lack of impartiality of Northern Ireland judiciary
     established—Whether evidence of ill-treatment in prison from which escape took place
     established—Extradition Act 1965, s. 50—Criminal Law (Jurisdiction) act 1976, Con-
     stitution of Ireland 1937, Article 38.1. **Russell v Fanning** [1986] 401, HC; [1988] 401, SC.

   Member of unlawful organisation
     Whether objectives of this organisation to subvert the Constitution—Whether political
     offence exception available—Requirement that warrant be signed by a judicial
     authority—Whether justice of the peace a judicial authority—Constitution of Ireland
     1937, Articles 2, 6—Extradition Act 1965, s. 50. **Russell v Fanning** [1988] 333, SC.

   Offence connected with political offence
     Uttering of documents with intent to defraud—Offence committed on instructions of
     organisations aimed at overthrow of State—Whether offence exempted from extra-
     dition arrangements on ground of political motivation—Whether courts could interpret
     legislation to further objectives of organisation aimed at overthrow of State—
     Extradition Act 1965, s. 50(2). **Quinn v Wren** [1985] 411, HC, SC.

   Onus of proof
     Damage to property—Possession of firearms—Whether political offence—Onus of
     proof. **Harte v Fanning** [1988] 75, HC.

     Robbery—Motive—Whether evidence upon which trial judge could have held robbery
     instigated on behalf of IRA—Burden of proof—Extradition Act 1965, s. 50. **Maguire
     v Keane** [1986] 235, SC.

   Principles to be applied
     Murder—Whether political nature of offence established—Whether substantial
     grounds for believing that person would be prosecuted for some other offence—
     Extradition Act 1965, s. 50(2). **Shannon v Fanning** [1985] 385, HC, SC.

   Qualification for exemption
     Whether persons pursuing policy of reunification of country by violence qualify for
     political exemption—Whether such policy equivalent to subversion of Constitution—
     Constitution of Ireland 1937, Article 6—Extradition Act 1965, s. 50. **Finucane v
     McMahon** [1990] 505, SC.

   Test to be applied
     Appellant driver of car in which firearms discovered in possession of passenger—
     Appellant and passenger charged with firearms offences—Appellant denying knowledge
     of presence of firearms in car—Appellant disavowing objective of reuniting Ireland by
     force of arms—Whether appellant entitled in the circumstances to claim that offences

EXTRADITION
Political offence
Test to be applied continued

were political—Whether appellant's alleged offences were connected with political offences—Test to be adopted in deciding whether an offence is connected with a political offence—Extradition Act 1965, s. 50. **Carron v McMahon** [1990] 802, SC.

Practice and procedure
Abuse of process

Arrest—Legality—Whether illegality taints subsequent proceedings—Whether applicant be released—Extradition Act 1965, s. 47. **Trimbole v Governor of Mountjoy Prison** [1985] 465, HC, SC.

Constitutional rights

Whether extradition arrangements safeguard rights of citizen. *See* Constitutional rights—Whether extradition arrangements safeguard personal rights of citizen (*above*).

Delay

Charge of receiving stolen goods—Extradition order—Special summons—Inordinate delay between hearing of summons and delivery of judgment—Whether delay a ground for refusing extradition. **Hanlon v Fleming** [1982] 69, SC.

Hearing before District Court

Statutory scheme for production of documents—Whether entitlement to production of sworn informations on which warrant based—Whether such production a requirement of the right to fair procedures—Constitutionally correct name of the State—Constitution of Ireland 1937, Articles 4, 29.4.1—Extradition Act 1965, ss. 54(1), 55. **Ellis v O'Dea** [1990] 87, SC.

Order extending application of Act to Australia

Whether order *ultra vires*—Meaning of reciprocal—Whether requirement that the procedures be completely identical—Power of minister under Part II—Constitution of Ireland 1937, Art 29.5.2—Extradition Act 1965, ss. 8(1), 10(1), 10(3), 10(4), 25, 26(3), 26(4), 27, 29—Extradition Act 1965 (Part II), Order 1984. **Trimbole v Governor of Mountjoy Prison** [1985] 465, HC, SC.

Procedures prior to and at extradition hearings

Alien brought before District Court on foot of English warrant—Order for delivery at point of departure—Whether valid—Procedure antedating the making of the order—Whether unfair—No legal representation—Whether sufficient for Garda Officer executing the warrant to provide and read the warrant—Whether Garda Officer should hand over a copy of the warrant—Entitlement of prosecutor to fairness of procedures—Constitution of Ireland 1937, Art 40—Extradition Act 1965 ss. 43,45,47,50. **State (McFadden) v Governor of Mountjoy Prison** (No 1) [1981] 113, HC.

Specialty rule

Whether rule infringed by trying defendant in Special Criminal Court—Extradition Act 1965, s.39. **Director of Public Prosecutions v Littlejohn** [1978] 147, CCA.

Treaty
Validity

Whether binding—Treaty involving charge on public funds—Treaty not specifically approved by Dáil Éireann—Constitutional requirement that terms of international agreements involving a charge upon public funds be approved by Dáil Éireann—Whether State bound by treaty. *See* CONSTITUTION (International relations—Treaty—Extradition).

Warrant
Requirement that warrant be signed by a judicial authority

Whether justice of the peace a judicial authority—Extradition Act 1965, s. 50. **Russell v Fanning** [1988] 333, SC.

EXTRADITION
Warrant *continued*
Statutory assumption that warrants duly issued
Whether good reason for rejecting such assumption—Extradition Act 1965, s. 55(1). **McMahon v McClafferty** [1990] 32, HC.

Uncertainty
Whether warrant void for uncertainty—Whether sufficient correspondence of offences—Offences against the Person Act 1861, s. 62—Criminal Law (Amendment) Act 1935, s. 14—Extradition Act 1965, s. 50. **Harris v Wren** [1984] 120, HC.

Whether sufficient evidence that respondent a person named or described in the warrant. **Crowley v McVeigh** [1990] 220, HC.

EXTRINSIC EVIDENCE
Admissibility. *See* EVIDENCE (Admissibility—Extrinsic evidence).

FACTORY
Emissions
Injuries and damage. See NUISANCE (Emissions from factory).

FAIR PROCEDURES
Compulsory purchase. *See* COMPULSORY PURCHASE (Fair procedures).

Constitutional guarantee. *See* CONSTITUTION (Fair procedures).

Extradition. *See* EXTRADITION (Fair procedures).

Natural justice. *See* NATURAL AND CONSTITUTIONAL JUSTICE.

Tribunal. See TRIBUNAL (Fair procedures).

FAIR TRADING *See* RESTRICTIVE PRACTICES; *See also* EUROPEAN COMMUNITY (Competition).

FAIRS AND MARKETS *See* MARKETS AND FAIRS.

FALSE IMPRISONMENT
Arrest
Reasonable use of force
Garda in scuffle with young person—Whether acting in the course of duty—Whether reasonable force used. **Dowman v Ireland** [1986] 111, HC.

Person of unsound mind
Detention
Subsequent discharge—Plaintiff seeking to institute proceedings for assault, battery and false imprisonment—Requirement that plaintiff shows substantial grounds for contending that the Board, through its officers, acted in bad faith or without reasonable care—Whether claim made out—Meaning of 'substantial'—Mental Treatment Act 1945, s. 260. **O'Dowd v North Western Health Board** [1983] 186, SC.

FALSE STATEMENT
Social welfare benefit. *See* SOCIAL WELFARE (Offence—False statements).

FAMILY HOME. *See* FAMILY LAW (Property—Family home).

FAMILY LAW
Barring order
Breakdown of marriage
Application for barring order—Whether husband's conduct seriously affected wife's and child's welfare—Entitlement to a decree of judicial separation on grounds of

FAMILY LAW
Barring order
Breakdown of marriage continued
cruelty—Whether proof of physical violence required—Whether intention to injure required—Matrimonial Causes and Marriage Law (Ireland) Act 1870, s. 13—Family Law (Maintenance of Spouses and Children) Act 1981. **McA v McA** [1981] 361, HC.

Maintenance application
Husband's failure to pay mortgage instalments—Whether conduct as may lead to loss of interest in family home—Whether order on transfer of family home should be granted—Guardianship of Infants Act 1964—Family Law (Maintenance of Spouses and Children) Act 1976, s. 22—Family Home Protection Act 1976, s. 5. **D C v A C** [1981] 357, HC.

Whether the evidence of the facts constituted proper grounds for making such order
Meaning of 'safety' and 'welfare'—Whether positive action by respondent spouse required before order made—Family Law (Maintenance of Spouses and Children) Act 1976, ss. 11, 22—Family Law (Maintenance of Spouses and Children) Act 1981, ss. 2, 5, 6, 7, 17. **O'B v O'B** [1984] 1, SC.

Child
Adoption. See ADOPTION.

Affiliation order. See AFFILIATION ORDER.

Care
Fit person order—Child committed to care of Health Board as 'fit person'. *See* CHILD (Care—Health board—Fit person order).

Place of safety order—Constitution—Inquiry into legality of detention—Whether fair procedures observed. *See* CHILD (Care—Health board—Place of safety order).

Custody. See CHILD (Custody).

Paternity
Evidence admissible to prove paternity—Evidence of wife that child not the child of the marriage—Whether admissible. *See* CHILD (Paternity).

Wardship. See CHILD (Ward of court).

Constitutional rights of family
Aliens
Family consisting of alien parents and children who are Irish citizens—Whether right to reside in the State. *See* CONSTITUTION (Family—Rights—Aliens—Whether a family consisting of alien parents and children who are Irish citizens has the right to reside in the State).

Whether aliens entitled to the protection of the Constitution—Child—Custody—Wrongful removal of infant from foreign jurisdiction. *See* CHILD (Custody—Removal from jurisdiction—Child born of lawfully married parents who were citizens of and domiciled abroad—Wrongful removal of infant from foreign jurisdiction).

Extent
Whether any right to protection from a negligent act of a private person which interferes with its constitution or authority—Industrial accident—Father of family suffering brain damage—Whether employer owed duty of care to victim's children. *See* CONSTITUTION (Family—Rights—Extent of guarantee).

Father of family a convicted prisoner
Effect of imprisonment on rights of family. *See* CONSTITUTION (Family—Rights—Father convicted prisoner).

FAMILY LAW
Constitutional rights of family *continued*
Husband and wife

Procreation—Convicted prisoners—Husband and wife each serving sentence of imprisonment for life—Whether absence of facilities to procreate within prison a denial of rights of married couple. *See* CONSTITUTION (Personal rights—Procreation—Married couple—Prisoners).

Infringement

Damages—Non-pecuniary benefits deriving from parent-child relationship—Whether recoverable. *See* CONSTITUTION (Family—Rights—Infringement—Damages).

Revenue

Income tax—Statute with retrospective effect—Enacted in consequence of decision that portion of income tax legislation unconstitutional. *See* CONSTITUTION (Marriage—Married couple—Income tax—Statute with retrospective effect).

Costs
Matrimonial proceedings

Legal aid—Custody and maintenance proceedings coming before the High Court on a number of occasions—Defendant unable to continue paying costs of legal representation—Application for civil legal aid refused—Whether defendant's right of access to the courts infringed—Locus standi—European Convention on Human Rights—Whether state bound by Convention—Convention on Human Rights and Fundamental Freedoms 1953 Art 6, 8—Scheme for Civil Legal Aid and Advice 1979, paras 4, 7. **E v E** [1982] 497, HC.

Nullity—Discretion of court—Whether general rule that wife be given her costs irrespective of whether she had been successful—Matrimonial Causes and Marriage Law (Ireland) Amendment Act 1870, s. 27—RSC 1986, O 70 r 75. **F v L** [1990] 886, HC.

Damages
Statutory rights

Infringement—Damages—Guardianship of infants—Removal of children from jurisdiction by wife—Passports having been issued despite husband's objection—Entitlement to damages—Extent of relief husband entitled to obtain—Ministers and Secretaries Act 1924, s. 1—Adoption Act 1952, s. 40—Guardianship of Infants Act 1964, ss. 6, 10, 11—Constitution of Ireland 1937, Articles 40, 41, 42. **Cosgrove v Ireland** [1982] 48, HC.

Desertion
Maintenance. See Maintenance—Desertion (*below*).

Divorce
Recognition of foreign decree. See MARRIAGE (Divorce).

Legal aid. *See* Costs—Legal aid (*above*).

Maintenance
Agreement

Variation—Index-linked payments—Absence of a provision allowing for the future variation of the terms of the agreement—Agreement made a rule of court—Whether the court has jurisdiction to vary the terms—Family Law (Maintenance of Spouses and Children) Act 1976, ss. 6 and 8. **JD v BD** [1985] 688, HC.

Alimony

Divorce *a mensa et thoro*—Cruelty—Adultery—Whether subsequent misconduct revives adultery and cruelty previously condoned—Principles to be applied in awarding alimony. **BL v ML** [1989] 528, HC.

Motion for order reducing alimony—Claim for judicial separation and alimony having been settled on agreement terms—Court order merely recording parties' agreement—

FAMILY LAW
Maintenance
Alimony continued

Whether an 'allotment of alimony'—Whether review procedure applicable to proceedings settled without a hearing. Family Law (Maintenance of Spouses and Children) Act 1976, ss. 6, 8, 30—RSC O 70 rr 54, 55. **MC v JC** [1982] 562, HC.

Barring order. See Barring order (*above*).

Desertion

Application by wife for maintenance—Whether wife's action in leaving family home amounted to desertion. **NAD v TD** [1985] 153, HC.

Divorce

Foreign domicile—Wife obtaining a divorce—Order requiring husband to pay a lump sum in lieu of maintenance—Husband avoiding being made amenable to pay—Monies lodged in an Irish bank—Whether contrary to public policy for the court to grant aid in the execution of this payment. **Sachs v Standard Chartered Bank (Ireland) Ltd** [1987] 297, SC.

Parties divorced in the United Kingdom—Whether applicant husband domiciled in Britain—Parties resident for time in Ireland—Parties both British citizens—Whether domicile of origin displaced—Onus of proof—Whether legislation abolishing dependent domicile retrospective in effect—Whether dependent domicile concept existed up to enactment of legislation—Motion to stay proceedings—Whether motion should be granted before decree made absolute. **CM v TM** [1988] 456, HC.

Principles to be applied

Enquiries required by court—Income potential of spouse and minimum reasonable requirements of children—True take-home pay and minimum standard of living requirements of spouse making maintenance payments—Family Law (Maintenance of Spouses and Children) Act 1976, s. 5. **RH v NH** [1986] 352, SC.

Marriage. *See* MARRIAGE.

Nullity of marriage. *See* MARRIAGE (Nullity).

Property
Beneficial interest

Wife's application for declaration of interest—Family home—Husband purchasing house in own name—Wife's contributions to household expenses—Whether wife entitled to beneficial share of ownership by virtue of contributions. **R v R** [1979] 1, HC.

Wife's application for declaration of interest—Family home built directly under supervision of husband—Husband paying for site and obtaining loan—Wife contributing some money towards construction costs—Whether wife entitled to an interest in the family home—Whether trust to be imposed in wife's favour. **NAD v TD** [1985] 153, HC.

Wife's application for declaration of interest—Farm registered in name of husband—Application of joint and separate savings to stock, equipment and improvements—Whether wife entitled to beneficial interest—Extent of interest. **W v W** [1981] 202, HC.

Wife's application for declaration of her interest—House purchased in sole name of husband—Contribution by wife to family finances—Mortgage repayment not met directly out of family finances—Whether wife contributed to the acquisition of the equity of redemption—Computation of beneficial share. **FG v PG** [1982] 155, HC.

Wife's application for declaration of interest—Husband purchasing house—Wife contributing to purchase of furniture. **McC v McC** [1986] 1, SC.

Wife's application for declaration of interest—House purchased by husband—Wife contributing no money towards acquisition—Whether wife entitled to an interest in

FAMILY LAW
Property
Beneficial interest continued

light of the provisions of the Constitution—Constitution of Ireland 1937, Article 41. **B L v M L** [1989] 528, HC.

Family home

Beneficial interest—Wife seeking declaration of interest. *See* Property—Beneficial interest—Wife's application for declaration of interest—Family home (*above*).

Conveyance. *See* SALE OF LAND (Family home).

Equitable mortgage—Advances made on foot of deposit of title deeds—Deposit made prior to Act coming into effect—Further advances—Whether consent of spouse required—Family Home Protection Act 1976, ss. 2, 3(1). **Bank of Ireland v Purcell** [1988] 480, HC; [1990] 106, SC.

Joint tenancy—Order for sale in lieu of partition—Whether jurisdiction to make order—Repeal of statutory power by statute law revision legislation—Whether power existed prior to statutory power—Act for Joint Tenants 1542—Statute Law Revision (Pre-Union Irish Statutes) Act 1962, s. 2(1). **FF v CF** [1987] 1, HC.

Judgment mortgage—No prior consent of wife—Whether a purported conveyance of husband's interest—Nature of judgment mortgage—Whether it comes into existence by operation of statute—Nature of wife's veto—Judgment Mortgage Act 1850, s. 6—Registration of Title Act 1964, ss. 52, 71(4)—Family Home Protection Act 1976, s. 3. **Murray v Diamond** [1982] 113, HC.

Sale—Consent of spouse—Generally. *See* SALE OF LAND (Family home).

Sale—Validity—Agreement to sell prior to enactment of legislation rendering conveyance of the family home void if executed without prior notice to the wife—Failure to complete—Statute—Interpretation—Presumption against retroaction—Pre-existing contractual rights—Purchaser entitled to specific performance—Constitution of Ireland 1937, Articles 40.3.2, 43—Interpretation Act 1937, s. 21(1)—Family Home Protection Act 1976, ss. 2, 3, 4. **Dunne v Hamilton; Hamilton v Hamilton** [1982] 290, SC.

Transfer of ownership—Claim by wife—Husband's failure to pay mortgage instalments—Whether conduct as may lead to loss of interest in family home—Whether order on transfer of family home should be granted—Maintenance—Barring order—Guardianship of Infants Act 1964—Family Law (Maintenance of Spouses and Children) Act 1976, s. 22—Family Home Protection Act 1976, s. 5. **DC v AC** [1981] 357, HC.

Transfer of ownership—Claim by wife—Husband substantially in debt—Deposit of title deeds by way of equitable mortgage—Whether husband engaged in such conduct as might lead to the loss of the family home—Whether husband any intention of depriving the wife of residence—Meaning of intention—Claim for maintenance—Family Home Protection Act 1976,s 5(1). **CP v DP** [1983] 380, HC.

Transfer of ownership—Claim by wife—Husband acting improvidently and incurring substantial debts—Whether husband any intention of depriving wife of residence—Meaning of intention—Family Home Protection Act 1976, s. 5(1). **S. v S.** [1983] 387, HC.

Validity of marriage. *See* MARRIAGE (Validity).

FAMILY PLANNING
Contraceptives
Unlawful sale

Criminal offence—Authority of gardai to enter premises—Admissibility of evidence obtained without warrant. *See* CRIMINAL LAW (Health offences—Family planning).

FAMILY PROVISION
Testator
Moral duty. See SUCCESSION (Family provision).

FARM TAX OFFICE
Discontinuance of farm tax
Termination of appointment of farm tax inspectors
Judicial review—Whether inspectors having legitimate expectation of permanent appointment. *See* JUDICIAL REVIEW (Farm tax office—Discontinuance of farm tax).

FARMING *See* AGRICULTURE.

FATAL INJURY
Compensation
Criminal injuries
Tribunal rejecting claim. *See* MALICIOUS INJURIES (Fatal injury)

Garda Siochána. See GARDA SIOCHÁNA (Compensation—Fatal injury).

FEE
Administrator of company. *See* COMPANY (Administration—Remuneration of administrator).

Auctioneer. *See* AUCTIONEER (Contract—Fees).

Counsel
Taxation of costs. See COSTS (Taxation—Counsel's fees).

Liquidator. *See* COMPANY (Winding up—Liquidator—Remuneration).

FERRY SERVICE
Suspension
Suspension of service by decision of English government
Whether decision having extra-territorial effect—Whether statutory obligations suspended by Oireachtas—Adaptation of enactments. *See* CONSTITUTION (Continuance of laws—Adaptation of enactments).

FINANCE
Local government. *See* LOCAL GOVERNMENT (Service charges).

Rating. *See* RATING AND VALUATION.

Taxation. *See* REVENUE.

FINANCE COMPANY
Hire-purchase agreement
Breach by vendor
Action for damages against vendor and finance company. *See* HIRE-PURCHASE AGREEMENT (Contract—Breach by vendor).

FIRE
Insurance
Contract
Interpretation. *See* CONTRACT (Interpretation—Fire insurance).

Uberrima fides—Repudiation of liability—Non-disclosure of previous fire. *See* INSURANCE (Contract—*Uberrima fides*—Disclosure of material facts—Fire).

Malicious injury claims. *See* MALICIOUS INJURIES (Fire).

Possession
Offence. See CRIMINAL LAW (Firearms).

FISCAL NULLITY
Tax avoidance scheme
Statutory interpretaton
    Capital Gains Tax Act 1975, ss. 5(1), 33(5)—Corporation Tax Act 1976, s. 102. **McGrath v McDermott** [1988] 181, HC; 647, SC.

FISHERIES
Aquaculture
Designated area
    Ministerial order—Objections—Inquiry—Appeal—Whether order be set aside—Subsequent scientific survey yielding evidence that proposed activities would cause serious pollution—Fisheries Act 1980, s. 54(7)—Aquaculture (Smerwick Harbour) Order 1987. **Courtney v Minister for the Marine** [1989] 605, HC.

Fishing rights. *See* FISHING RIGHTS.

Licence
Offshore fishing
    Conditions of nationality attached to licence—Arrest of foreign fishing vessel for fishing in breach of conditions—Plaintiffs seeking injunction restraining enforcement of terms of licence—Fisheries (Consolidation) Act 1959, s. 222(b)—Fisheries (Amendment) Act 1983, s. 2. **Pesca Valentia Ltd v Minister for Fisheries** [1986] 68, SC.

    Conditions of nationality attached to licence—Vessel arrested for fishing in breach of condition—Plaintiff seeking order restraining enforcement of condition. **Ardent Fisheries Ltd v Minister for Tourism, Fisheries and Forestry** [1987] 528, HC.

    Conditions of nationality attached to licence—Licence requiring 75% of crew be EEC nationals—Challenge to validity of statutory provision under which licence granted—Reference to European Court of Justice—Whether plaintiffs entitled to injunction restraining enforcement of licence—Fisheries (Amendment) Act 1983, s. 2. **Beara Fisheries and Shipping Ltd v Minister for the Marine** [1988] 221, HC.

Offence
Detention order
    Fishery trawler—Whether detention order bad on its face—Absolute orders of certiorari and habeas corpus—Natural justice—Whether certiorari lies in relation to the making of a detention order—Whether success of appeal having no practical effect a bar to proceedings—Whether habeas corpus still available under the 1782 Act—Conflict with Constitution—Constitution of Ireland 1937, Article 40 4 2—Habeas Corpus (Ireland) Act 1782, s. 12—RSC O 84 rr 2 and 9—Fisheries (Consolidation) Act 1959. **In re Zwann** [1981] 333, SC.

Failure to keep log book
    Accused fined and ordered to forfeit catch and fishing gear—Catch and gear previously released pursuant to an order of a District Justice subject to the provision of security—Whether value of catch and gear together with total of fine and costs be deducted from security—Whether statutory provision for the deduction of a sum of money in lieu of forfeiture—Whether judge power to decline to release any part of the security—Fisheries (Consolidation) Act 1959, ss. 235(2)(a), 317—Fisheries (Amendment) Act 1968, ss. 2(5), 14—Sea Fisheries (Control of Catches) Order 1985. **Attorney General v Sheehy** [1989] 303, HC.

Powers of sea fisheries protection officer
    Detention of boat and all persons on board—Power to extend detention conferred on District Justice or Peace Commissioner—Whether application made as soon as may be—Fisheries (Consolidation) Act 1959, ss. 233(1), 233(A), 234. **Rederij Kennemerland BV v The Attorney General** [1989] 821, HC, SC.

FISHERIES
Offence *continued*
  Prosecution
    Whether District Justice required to furnish applicant with note of evidence taken at trial—Whether officer of Regional Fisheries Board authorised to act outside area of the board—Petty Sessions (Ireland) Act 1851, s. 20—Fisheries (Consolidation) Act 1959, ss. 92, 182(2), (4), 293(2)(a), 301, 308—Courts Act 1971, s. 14—District Court Rules 1948 to 1972, rules 4, 64(5). **Friel v McMenamin** [1990] 761, HC.

  Trial
    Whether minor offence triable summarily—Arrest of foreign fishing vessel—Detention order—Vessel released upon provision of security—Whether requirement to give security amounted to a requirement to give bail—If so, whether such bail oppressive—Major or minor offence—Constitution of Ireland 1937, Articles 38 1, 40 3—Fisheries (Consolidation) Act 1959. ss. 221, 222(A), 232, 235(2)(a) and (b)—Fisheries Amendment Act 1978, ss. 2(2), 5, 7, 14. **L'Henryenat v Attorney General and Ireland** [1984] 249, HC, SC.

    Whether minor offence triable summarily—Foreign fishing vessel—Summary conviction—Fine and forfeiture of equipment—Whether offence minor offence—Severity of punishment—Whether forfeiture primary punishment—Constitution of Ireland 1937, Article 38—Fisheries (Consolidation) Act 1959, s. 221. **Kostan v Ireland** [1978] 12, HC.

    Whether minor offence triable summarily—Unlawful possession of salmon—Summary conviction—Severity of penalty—Fine and confiscation of catch—Whether need to review the criteria laid down in the decided cases—Petty Sessions (Ireland) Act 1851, s. 22—Fisheries (Consolidation) Act 1959, s. 182—Constitution of Ireland 1937, Article 38. **O'Sullivan v Hartnett** [1983] 79, SC.

  Unlawful possession of salmon
    Summary conviction—Severity of penalty—Fine and confiscation of catch. **O'Sullivan v Hartnett** [1983] 79, SC.

Revenue
  Income tax
    Returns—Employer—Whether contract of service or partnership existed—Fishermen—Captain of vessel engaging crew at commencement of each voyage—Remuneration based on custom and agreement—Whether in reality partnership. **DPP v McLoughlin** [1986] 493, HC.

FISHING RIGHTS
Interference
  Lakes and rivers
    Outdoor education centre—Canoeing—Interference with fishing—Ownership of bed and soil of lake and river—Whether plaintiff entitled only to *profit a prendre*—Form of injunction. **Tennent v Clancy** [1988] 214, HC.

FIT PERSON ORDER *See* CHILD (Care—Health board—Fit person order).

FIXTURES
Value added tax
  Whether television aerials "fixtures". See REVENUE (Value added tax).

FORCE
Arrest
  Reasonable use of force. See FALSE IMPROVEMENT (Arrest—Reasonable use of force—Garda).

FORCIBLE ENTRY
Employees
Occupation of employer's premises
Civil contempt—Committal—Jurisdiction of court—Deliberate disobedience of court order. *See* CONTEMPT OF COURT (Civil contempt—Committal).

Garda Siochána
Criminal investigation
Forcible entry of accused's home. *See* CRIMINAL INVESTIGATION (Forcible entry of accused's home).

FOREIGN CURRENCY
Judgment. *See* JUDGMENT (Currency).

FOREIGN DIVORCE
Recognition. *See* MARRIAGE (Divorce—Recognition of foreign decree).

FOREIGN DOCTOR
Registration. *See* MEDICAL PRACTITIONER (Registration).

FOREIGN DOMICILE
Divorce
Recognition. *See* MARRIAGE (Divorce—Recognition of foreign divorce—Domicile).

FOREIGN FISHING VESSEL
Arrest
Offence
Trial. *See* FISHERIES (Offence—Trial—Whether minor offence triable summarily).

FOREIGN GOVERNMENT
Confidential information
Breach
Whether different criteria applied to government information. *See* CONFIDENTIALITY (Breach—Publication—Book written by deceased member of British intelligence service—Application to restrain publication in Ireland).

FOREIGN JUDGMENT
Enforcement. *See* JUDGMENT (Enforcement—Foreign judgment).

FOREIGN LAW
Conflict of laws. *See* PRIVATE INTERNATIONAL LAW.

FOREIGN MARRIAGE
Validity
Moslem marriage ceremony in South Africa. See MARRIAGE (Validity—Moslem marriage).

FOREIGN RELATIONS *See* CONSTITUTION (International relations).

FOREIGN WARRANT. *See* EXTRADITION (Warrant).

FOREIGN WILL
Construction. *See* WILL (Construction—Foreign will).

FOREIGNER
Immigration. *See* ALIEN.

FORESEEABILITY
Damages. *See* DAMAGES (Foreseeability).

FORESEEABILITY *continued*
Negligence. *See* NEGLIGENCE (Foreseeability).

FORFEITURE
Deposit
Sale of land. See SALE OF LAND (Deposit—Forfeiture).

Fishing catch and gear
Offence. See FISHERIES (Offence—Failure to keep log book—Accused fined and ordered to forfeit catch and fishing gear).

> *Whether minor offence. See* FISHERIES (Offence—Trial—Whether minor offence triable summarily).

Gaming instrument
Gaming offence. **Cartmill v Ireland** [1988] 430, HC.

Intoxicating liquor licence. *See* LICENSING ACTS (Forfeiture of licence).

Lease. *See* LANDLORD AND TENANT (Lease—Forfeiture).

FORGERY
Passport
Entry of child's name on wife's passport
> Husband's consent forged—Whether Minister obliged to cancel entry of child. **P I v Ireland** [1989] 810, SC.

FORMATION OF CONTRACT
Sale of land. *See* SALE OF LAND (Contract—Formation).

FOSTERAGE *See* CHILD (Custody—Foster parents).

FRANCHISE
Dáil Éireann elections. *See* ELECTORAL LAW (Dáil Éireann Elections—Franchise).

Fairs and markets. *See* FAIRS AND MARKETS.

FRAUD
Fraudulent misappropriation
Bank deposit
> Foreign company—Money lodged in bank account—Claim that this money consisted of funds fraudulently misappropriated—Whether sufficient inference of fraud—Obligations of receiving bank—Whether required to repay the funds actually advanced. **Banco Ambrosiano v Ansbacher & Co** [1987] 669, HC, SC.

Fraudulent preference
Company
> Charge—Winding up—Charge registered one month before winding up—Whether charge void as being fraudulent preference—Companies Act 1963, s. 286. **Corran v Bank of Ireland Finance Ltd** [1976–7] 175, HC.

Fraudulent trading
Company
> Winding up. *See* COMPANY (Winding up—Fraudulent trading).

Medical practitioner
General medical scheme
> Allegations of fraudulent payments—Referral of matter to Minister—Whether referral *ultra vires*. *See* HEALTH SERVICES (General medical services scheme—Complaints of abuse of scheme).

FRAUD *continued*
Passport
Entry of child's name on wife's passport
Forged consent of husband—Removal of child from jurisdiction—Whether Minister obliged to cancel entry of child—Ministers and Secretaries Act 1924. **P I v Ireland** [1989] 810, SC.

Payment
Employer's liability insurance. See MISTAKE (Payment—Recovery—Payment induced by fraud).

FREE MOVEMENT OF WORKERS. *See* EUROPEAN COMMUNITY (Free movement of workers).

FREEDOM OF ASSOCIATION. *See* CONSTITUTION (Personal rights—Freedom of association).

FREEDOM OF EXPRESSION. *See* CONSTITUTION (Personal rights—Freedom of expression).

FREEDOM OF THE PRESS. *See* PRESS (Freedom).

FREEDOM TO PROVIDE SERVICES. *See* EUROPEAN COMMUNITY (Freedom to provide services).

FRIENDLY SOCIETIES
Registrar
Powers of investigation and control
Building society—Advertising control. *See* BUILDING SOCIETY (Advertising—Control by Registrar).

Industrial and provident society—Winding up—Duty of care—Minister—Whether sufficient relationship of proximity between Registrar of Friendly Societies and plaintiff. *See* INDUSTRIAL AND PROVIDENT SOCIETY (Winding up—Duty of care—Minister).

Registration of building society. See BUILDING SOCIETY (Registration).

FRUSTRATION OF CONTRACT *See* CONTRACT (Frustration).

FUEL
Control of supplies. *See* EUROPEAN COMMUNITY (Fuel—Supply and distribution).

FUEL ALLOWANCE *See* SOCIAL WELFARE (Supplementary welfare allowance—Fuel allowance).

FUNDAMENTAL RIGHTS *See* CONSTITUTION (Personal rights).

FUTURE ECONOMIC LOSS
Damages. *See* DAMAGES (Personal injuries—Future economic loss).

FUTURE LOSS OF EARNINGS
Damages. *See* DAMAGES (Personal injuries—Loss of earnings—Future loss).

GAMING AND LOTTERIES
Betting
Bookmaker. See BOOKMAKER.

Gaming licence
Application
Amusement hall—Local authority—Resolution permitting gaming halls in authority's area—Applicant seeking licence—Application refused by District Court—Local authority giving notice of intention to rescind resolution allowing gaming—Local

GAMING AND LOTTERIES
Gaming licence
Application continued

authority resricting gaming—Whether applicant carried out business—Whether decision of local authority *ultra vires* by reason of bad faith—Gaming and Lotteries Act 1956, Part III. **State (Divito) v Arklow UDC** [1986] 123, SC.

Expiry

Application to renew refused—Appeal—Local authority rescinding resolution adopting the relevant part of the statute—Whether rescinding resolution operated to prevent the grant of certificate of appeal—Whether invasion of judicial process—Gaming and Lotteries Act 1956, ss. 4, 12, 13, 15, 18(1), (3). **Camillo v O'Reilly** [1988] 738, SC.

Gaming machine
Slot machine

Statutory restrictions—Limits on stake to be wagered—Whether impact of inflation constituted unjust attack on exercise—Constitution—Statute—Validity—Right to earn a livelihood—Gaming and Lotteries Act 1956, s. 14—Gaming and Lotteries Act 1979, s. 1—Constitution of Ireland 1937, Article 40 3. **Cafolla v Attorney General** [1986] 177, HC.

Whether player engaged in gaming—Whether gaming unlawful—Whether human banker a necessary participant in gaming as defined—Gaming and Lotteries Act 1956, ss. 2, 4, 10, 44—Gaming and Lotteries Act 1970, s. 1—Gaming and Lotteries Act 1979, ss. 1 2(2). **DPP (McGrath) v Murphy** [1982] 143, HC.

Lottery
Application for licence

Branch of political party—Proceeds of lottery to enable party members attend seminars and conventions—Whether purpose philanthropic—Gaming and Lotteries Act 1956, s. 28(2). **Gurhy v Goff** [1980] 103, SC.

Game promoted through newspapers

Game effectively in two parts—Whether first part depended wholly on chance—Whether lottery requires purchase of tickets—Gaming and Lotteries Act 1956, ss. 2, 21. **Flynn v Denieffe** [1990] 391, HC.

Offences
Evidence

Admissibility—Licensed premises—Offences detected by plain clothes gardai—No search warrant—Whether evidence admissible—Relevance of power to enter under intoxicating liquor code—Spirits (Ireland) Act 1854, s. 12—Beer Houses (Ireland) Act 1864, s. 11—Licensing Act (Ireland) 1874, s. 23—Intoxicating Liquor Act 1927, s. 22—Gaming and Lotteries Act 1956, ss. 9, 38, 39. **DPP v McMahon** [1987] 87, SC.

Gaming machines

Gaming machines in which both the stake to be hazarded and amount to be won exceeded statutory limits—Owners of machines holding gaming and gaming machine licences—Effect of subsequent legislation—Whether operation of machine a criminal offence. **DPP v Olympic Amusements** (Bundoran) Ltd [1987] 320, SC.

Licensed premises

Offences under gaming and lotteries legislation detected by plain clothes gardai—No search warrant. *See* Offences—Evidence—Admissibility (*above*).

Nature

Whether minor offences triable summarily—Penalty—Severity—Forfeiture of gaming instrument—Whether consequence too remote in character—Distinction between primary and secondary punishment—Constitution of Ireland 1937, Article 38 2—Gaming and Lotteries Act 1956, ss. 4(1)(c), 47. **Cartmill v Ireland** [1988] 430, HC.

GAMING AND LOTTERIES *continued*
Statute
Validity
Right to earn livelihood—Restrictions imposed on use of slot machines. *See* Gaming machine—Slot machine—Statutory restrictions (*above*).

GARDA SÍOCHÁNA
Arrest
Legality. See ARREST (Legality).

Reasonable use of force
Garda in scuffle with young person—Whether acting in the course of duty—Whether reasonable force used. **Dowman v Ireland** [1986] 111, HC.

Associations
Garda Representative Association
Association of Garda Sergeants and Inspectors—Rights of members—Limitations of ranks within the Garda Síochána—Right of freedom of association for members of Garda Síochána—Limitations on extent to which members of the Force may organise. *See* CONSTITUTION (Personal rights—Freedom of association—Garda Siochána).

Compensation
Fatal injury
Assessment of compensation—Special pension—Whether compensation should be reduced to take into account the value of special pensions and allowances payable on death or injury—Statute—Interpretation—Apparent incongruity of provisions—Amending legislation—Garda Siochána (Compensation) Act 1941, s. 9. **McLoughlin v Minister for the Public Service** [1986] 28, HC.

Conciliation and Arbitration scheme
Chairman's decision
Grounds of review—Whether decision irrational or unreasonable—Legitimate expectation—Promissory estoppel—Whether ministerial statement made in Dáil Éireann may be relied on by plaintiff—Constitution of Ireland 1937, Article 15 1—Garda Siochána Act 1924, s. 13—Garda Síochána Act 1977, s. 1—Police Forces Amalgamation Act 1925, ss. 8(1), 12, 14. **Garda Representative Association v Ireland** [1989] 1, HC.

Costs
Criminal trial
Statutory rules of procedure prohibiting award of costs against member of Garda Síochána acting in discharge of duties as police officer—Whether unconstitutional discrimination—Whether justified on grounds of social function—Whether unjust attack on property rights—Constitution of Ireland 1937, Articles 40 1, 40 3—Prosecution of Offences Act 1974, s. 3—District Court Rules 1948, r 67. **Dillane v Attorney General and Ireland** [1980] 167, SC.

Criminal investigation
Absence of search warrant. See CRIMINAL LAW (Search warrant).

Forcible entry of accused's home
Search warrant—Invalidity—Evidence—Admissibility. **People (DPP) v Kenny** [1990] 569, SC.

Overt surveillance
Garda Siochána anticipating request for extradition warrant—Whether surveillance operation justified. **Kane v Governor of Mountjoy Prison** [1988] 724, HC, SC.

Detention in custody
Accused making statement while in custody
Admissibility in evidence. *See* CRIMINAL LAW (Evidence—Statement by accused).

GARDA SÍOCHÁNA

Detention in custody *continued*

Denial of access to solicitor

Statement—Admissibility. *See* CRIMINAL LAW (Evidence—Statement by accused—Admissibility—Statement made while in Garda custody—Access to solicitor denied).

Delay in permitting access to solicitor

Statement—Admissibility. *See* CRIMINAL LAW (Evidence—Statement by accused—Admissibility—Statement made while in Garda custody—Delay by Gardai in permitting access to solicitor).

Legality. See ARREST (Detention—Legality).

Discipline

Inquiry

Allegation that conflict of evidence required investigation into separate breaches of discipline—Whether principles of natural justice observed—Invalid inquiry—Whether plaintiff entitled to costs and expenses of his representation and attendance at the inquiry—Appropriate defendant—Constitution of Ireland 1937—Garda Síochána (Discipline) Regulations 1971, reg 8. **McHugh v Commissioner of the Garda Síochána** [1987] 181, SC.

Appeals board—Judicial review—Certiorari—Declaration—Whether applicant guilty of conduct prejudicial to the interests of An Garda Síochána—Whether conduct justified dismissal—Whether decision of appeal board reasonable. **Stroker v Doherty** [1989] 428, HC.

Details of alleged breach of discipline not disclosed—Whether violation of fair procedures—Whether regulations unconstitutional—Constitution of Ireland 1937, Article 40—Garda Siochána Act 1924, ss. 4(2), 5—Police Forces Amalgamation Act 1925, s. 14(1)—Garda Síochána (Discipline) Regulations 1971, regs 6, 8(2), 9, 11, 12, 13, 14, 15, 31, 34. **Hogan v Minister for Justice** [1976–7] 184, HC.

Discontinuance—Garda Commissioner directing that a new inquiry be held into same allegations—Judicial review—Certiorari—Whether appointment of new board of inquiry be quashed—Garda Siochána (Discipline) Regulations 1971. **McGowan v Wren** [1988] 744, HC.

Garda acquitted of criminal charges—Disciplinary inquiry—Whether inquiry could subsequently investigate charges arising out of identical allegations of corruption—Whether estoppel—Whether unfair and oppressive procedure—Garda Siochána (Discipline) Regulations 1971, reg 6. **McGrath v Commissioner of the Garda Síochána** [1990] 5, HC; [1990] 817, SC.

Two stage procedure—Matter being referred to Appeal Board—Board deciding that it had no jurisdiction to hear appeal—Whether jurisdictional error—Whether invalidated finding at initial stage—Garda Síochána (Discipline) Regulations 1971, regs 16, 20. **State (Sheehan) v McMahon** [1976–7] 305, HC, SC.

Suspension

Disciplinary investigation and inquiry—Natural justice—Whether member entitled to make representation on suspension—Nature of decision on suspension—Distinction between investigation and inquiry—Conflict of evidence—Whether inquiry into conflict required—Delay in instituting disciplinary proceedings—Constitution of Ireland 1937, Art 40 1—Garda Síochána (Discipline) Regulations 1971, regs 8, 9, 31(1). **McHugh v Commissioner of the Garda Síochána** [1985] 606, HC; [1987] 181, SC.

Dismissal

Natural justice

Probationer—Dismissal for not being likely to become efficient and well-conducted guard—Previous breaches of discipline as basis for dismissal—Pending enquiry into

GARDA SÍOCHÁNA
Dismissal
Natural justice continued
breach of discipline discontinued—Whether dismissal ultra vires—Garda Síochána (Appointment) Regulations 1945, arts 8, 9. **State (Burke) v Garvey** [1979] 232, SC.

Summary dismissal—Absence of formal inquiry—Limitation of rules of natural justice in context of certain State services—Acquittal of dismissed garda at trial on charge of assault on suspect—Counsel for dismissed garda seeking admission that witness at trial committed the assault—Absence of such allegation in statement of dismissed garda—Dismissal by Commissioner on ground that statement considered falsehood or prevarication—Opportunity given to advance reasons against dismissal—Garda Síochána (Discipline) Regulations 1971, Regs 6, 34. **State (Jordan) v Commissioner of the Garda Síochána** [1987] 107, HC.

Wrongful dismissal
Commissioner—Damages—Assessment. **Garvey v Ireland** [1979] 266, HC.

Entry on premises. *See* ENTRY ON PREMISES (Garda Síochána).

Evidence
Preservation
Duty to preserve evidence material to guilt or innocence. *See* CRIMINAL LAW (Evidence—Preservation).

Liability
Injuries to detainee
Plaintiff arrested and detained in Garda station—Plaintiff alleging that he was left with matches—Plaintiff setting fire to cell and suffering extensive burns—Whether defendants negligent—Whether defendant contributorily negligent—Damages—Whether excessive. **McKevitt v Ireland** [1987] 541, SC.

Privilege
Communication between members
Claim of privilege—Whether such communication inadmissible in evidence because, as a class, their admission would be against the public interest—Whether claim for privilege should be rejected. **DPP (Hanley) v Holly** [1984] 149, HC.

Promotion
Proposed change in system of promotion
"Vertical' and "horizontal' promotions—Powers of Garda Commissioner—Powers of Minister for Justice—Rights of members of Garda Representative Association and Association of Garda Sergeants and Inspectors—Limitations of ranks within the Garda Síochána. *See* CONSTITUTION (Personal rights—Freedom of association—Garda Síochána).

Station bail
District Court rules. *See* CRIMINAL LAW (Bail—Station bail).

GARNISHEE
Judgment creditor
Equitable assignments
Whether order be made absolute—Precedence of competing claims. **Fitzpatrick v DAF Sales Ltd and Allied Irish Finance Company Ltd** [1989] 777, HC.

GIFT
Bequest
Condition. See WILL (Construction—Condition).

Charitable gift
Cy-pres. See CHARITY (Cy-pres).

GIFT TAX *See* REVENUE (Capital acquisitions tax).

GOOD ESTATE MANAGEMENT
Refusal of new tenancy. *See* LANDLORD AND TENANT (New tenancy—Refusal—Good estate management).

Restrictive covenant. *See* LANDLORD AND TENANT (Covenant—Restrictive covenant as to user).

GOVERNMENT
Civil service. *See* CIVIL SERVICE.

Confidential information
Breach
Publication—Foreign government—Book written by deceased member of British intelligence service—Application to restrain publication in Ireland. *See* CONFIDENTIALITY (Breach—Publication).

International relations
Treaty
Single European Act—Intention to ratify treaty—Obligations to engage in foreign policy co-operation—Whether limiting ability to engage in independent foreign policy making—Whether in conflict with sovereignty of Irish State and People. *See* CONSTITUTION (International relations—Treaty—Ratification).

Local government. *See* LOCAL GOVERNMENT.

Minister. *See* MINISTER.

Obstruction
Offence
Constituent ingredients of such offence. *See* CRIMINAL LAW (Offence—Obstruction of government).

Order
Whether a "law" within meaning of Articles 34.4.5 and 40.4.3 of the Constitution
Extradition order. **State (Gilliland) v Governor of Mountjoy Prison** [1986] 381, HC; [1987] 278, SC.

GRAVEYARD *See* BURIAL GROUND.

GRAZING *See* AGRICULTURE (Grazing of land).

GROUND RENT *See* LANDLORD AND TENANT (Ground rent).

GUARANTEE
Bank
Charge to bank to secure loan to company
Associated company acting as surety—Directors also guaranteeing loan and charging property—Default in repayments—Proceedings against corporate surety—Decree for possession of property—Appeal to Supreme Court pending—Proceedings also instituted against directors—Whether bank entitled to exercise its rights to possession of director's property until they have exercised their rights against the principal debtor and co-surety—Whether doctrine of marshalling applicable. **Lombard and Ulster Banking Ltd v Murray** [1987] 522, HC.

Company
Receivership
Information sought by guarantor. *See* Disclosure of information (*below*).

Ultra vires
Notice—Guarantee and mortgage by company of third party debt—Transaction *ultra vires*—Creditor reading company's memorandum and articles before guarantee

GUARANTEE
Company
Ultra vires continued
> executed—Creditor failing to understand effect of memorandum and articles—Whether creditor had actual notice of guarantee being *ultra vires* company—Subsequent resolution empowering company to execute guarantee—Whether resolution having retrospective effect—Whether company estopped from relying on *ultra vires* nature of guarantee—Companies Act 1963, ss. 7, 8(1), 10(1). **Northern Bank Finance Corporation Ltd v Quinn** [1979] 221, HC.

Disclosure of information to guarantor
Receiver
> Guarantor and sundry creditors seeking information concerning the proposed purchase price of the assets—Whether guarantor entitled to the information—Whether sale be restrained—Negligence—Duty of care—Company in receivership—Whether receiver owes duty of care to guarantor. **McGowan v Gannon** [1983] 516, HC.

Rule in Clayton's case
Company debts guaranteed by majority shareholder and managing director
> Change of ownership and management and variation of the company's banking arrangements—Whether guarantor discharged from his obligations—Terms of guarantee—Whether rule in Clayton's Case applicable—Whether bank negligent. **MacEnroe v Allied Irish Banks Ltd** [1980] 171, SC.

GUARD DOG *See* ANIMALS (Negligence—Liability of owner—Personal injuries caused by animal—Guard dog).

GUARDIANSHIP OF CHILDREN
Adoption proceedings. *See* ADOPTION.

Generally. *See* CHILD (Guardianship and custody).

Wardship. *See* CHILD (Ward of court).

GUILTY PLEA *See* CRIMINAL LAW (Trial—Plea of guilty).

GUNS *See* CRIMINAL LAW (Firearms—Possession).

HABEAS CORPUS
Absolute order made in first instance
Validity
> Natural justice. *See* Procedure—Absolute order made in first instance (*below*).

Adjournment
Validity
> Inquiry under Constitution—Convicted prisoner—Arrest and detention under emergency powers legislation—Allegation that prosecutor had not been charged with the offences of which he was convicted—Principal authority on which prosecutor relied in the course of being reviewed by the Supreme Court—Matter adjourned by consent to the next list and prosecutor admitted to bail—Whether such procedure unconstitutional—Whether an adjournment upon a return date warranted under the provisions of Article 40—Constitution of Ireland 1937, Article 40 4. **State (Whelan) v Governor of Mountjoy Prison** [1983] 52, HC.

Appropriate form of relief
Prisoner
> Conditions of confinement—Whether habeas corpus or Article 40.4 inquiry appropriate form of relief. *See* Prisoner—Conditions of confinement (*below*).

HABEAS CORPUS *continued*
Arrest
Legality
Extradition request—No extradition treaty—Order extending application of Extradition Act—Arrest under s. 30 of Offences against the State Act 1939—Arrest made to ensure applicant be available for detention under Part II—Whether misuse of arrest powers amounts to conscious and deliberate violation of constitutional rights—Duty of courts to protect against invasion of constitutional rights—Constitution of Ireland 1937, Articles 40.3.1, 40.4.2—Extradition Act 1965, Part II. **Trimbole v Governor of Mountjoy Prison** [1985] 465, HC, SC.

Re-arrest—Extradition request—English warrant—Re-arrest on same warrant after absolute order granted—Validity of re-arrest—Habeas Corpus (Ireland) Act 1781, s. 5—Constitution of Ireland 1937, Article 40. **State (McFadden) v Governor of Mountjoy Prison** (No 2) [1981] 120, HC.

Surveillance—Overt surveillance—Garda Síochána anticipating request for extradition warrant—Whether surveillance operation justified—Constitution of Ireland 1937, Article 40.4. **Kane v Governor of Mountjoy Prison** [1988] 724, HC, SC.

Child
Detention
English Court ordering that infant be placed in the custody of a county council—Father removing child from jurisdiction of English courts—Council seeking an order of habeas corpus—Whether appropriate to make the order sought—Principle of comity between courts—Constitution of Ireland 1937, Articles 40, 41, 42. **Kent Co Council v S.** [1984] 292, HC.

Fit person order
Child committed to care of Health Board as 'fit person'—Nature of District Court order—Whether fair procedures—Whether child should be returned to custody of parents—Children Act 1908. **State (D & D) v G and Others** [1990] 10, SC.

Place of safety order
Children taken from custody of parent—Inquiry into legality of detention—Whether fair procedures observed—Whether failure to bring case before District Court within a reasonable time—Whether failure to give parent adequate information about detention of children within a reasonable time—Children Act 1908, ss. 20, 24—Summary Jurisdiction Rules 1909, rules 6, 12. **State (F) v Superintendent, B Garda Station** [1990] 243, HC.

Extradition
Legality of detention
Appellant in detention pursuant to warrant for his extradition—Appellant claiming possibility of assault and torture if removed from the jurisdiction—Conflict of oral evidence—Whether extradition should be refused in the circumstances—Constitution of Ireland 1937, Article 40. **Carron v McMahon** [1990] 802, SC.

Corresponding offences—USA—Conspiracy charges—Narcotics offences—Murder—Dangerous Drugs Act 1934, s. 17—Extradition Act 1965, s. 5—Extradition Act 1965 (Part II) (No 20) Order 1984, Arts XVI, XVII—Constitution of Ireland 1937, Article 29 5 2. **State (McCaud) v Governor Mountjoy Prison** [1986] 129, HC.

Procedures
Procedures prior to and at extradition hearings—Entitlement of prosecutor to fair procedures. **State (McFadden) v Governor of Mountjoy Prison** (No 1) [1981] 113, HC.

Fair procedures
Imprisonment
Applicant sentenced to four years penal servitude—While serving that sentence applicant was charged with and convicted of another offence—Applicant could have been

HABEAS CORPUS
Fair procedures
Imprisonment continued

charged with this offence at the same time as the first offence—Whether unfair procedure—Constitution of Ireland 1937, Article 40. **State (McGlinchey) v Governor of Portlaoise Prison** [1982] 187, HC.

Re-arrest

Arrest on foot of foreign warrant—Extradition order—Order of habeas corpus granted because of matters which happened after arrest—Re-arrest on foot of same warrant—Whether lawful—Habeas Corpus (Ireland) Act 1782, s. 5. **State (McFadden) v Governor of Mountjoy Prison** (No 2) [1981] 120, HC.

Immigration
Alien

Landing permission—Refusal. *See* ALIENS (Landing permission—Refusal—Habeas corpus).

Inquiry under Constitution
Procedure. See Procedure—Inquiry under Constitution (*below*).

Jurisdiction
District Court

Whether District Court can embark on constitutional inquiry as to validity of detention—Whether unwarrantable and unlawful usurpation of the constitutional role of the High Court—Constitution of Ireland 1937, Article 40 4 2—Criminal Justice Act 1984, s. 4. **Keating v Governor of Mountjoy Prison** [1990] 850, SC.

High Court

Absolute order made in first instance. *See* Procedure—Absolute order made in first instance (*below*).

Locus standi
Aliens

Whether non-citizens can seek relief by way of habeas corpus—Constitution of Ireland 1937, Article 40 4 2. **State (Kugan) v Station Sergeant, Fitzgibbon St Garda Station** [1986] 95, HC.

Inquiry under Constitution

Whether necessary for prosecutor to establish procedural defect in the detention before relief could be sought. **State (Kugan) v Station Sergeant, Fitzgibbon St Garda Station** [1986] 95, HC.

Prisoner
Conditions of confinement

Breaches of prison regulations—Allegations of ill-treatment—Whether breaches of regulations rendered detention unlawful—Whether appropriate to be dealt with in enquiry into legality of detention—Whether alternative relief may be sought—Constitution of Ireland 1937, Article 40 4 2. **Cahill v Governor of Military Detention Barracks** [1980] 191, HC.

Whether habeas corpus or Article 40 4 inquiry appropriate form of relief—Constitution of Ireland 1937, Articles 40 3, 40 4. **State (Richardson) v Governor of Mountjoy Prison** [1980] 82, HC.

Health

Effect of imprisonment—Effect not normally contemplated by court in imposing sentence—Prisoner suffering from reactive depression—Whether detention rendered illegal—Whether habeas corpus should issue. **State (Smith) v Governor of Curragh Military Detention Barracks** [1980] 208, HC.

HABEAS CORPUS *continued*
Procedure
Absolute order made in first instance
Validity—Natural justice—Jurisdiction—No opportunity given to detaining person to justify detention—Whether habeas corpus still available under Habeas Corpus (Ireland) Act—Constitution of Ireland 1937, Article 40—RSC O 84, rules 2 and 9—Fisheries (Consolidation) Acts 1959 to 1978. **In re Zwann** [1981] 333, SC.

Validity—Natural justice—Jurisdiction—No opportunity given to detaining person to certify in writing the grounds of detention—No opportunity given to have legal advice or representation—Special Criminal Court sitting for purpose of charging prisoner—Application to presiding judge to sit on his own to hear habeas corpus application—Absolute order made—Whether jurisdiction to make such order—Whether opportunity of justifying detention a dispensible preliminary—Whether waiver of respondent's rights—Constitution of Ireland 1937, Art 40 4 2—RSC O 84, rr 2, 9. **State (Rogers) v Galvin** [1983] 149, SC.

Inquiry under Constitution
Post-conviction application—Whether within the competence of any rule making authority to make rules regulating the procedure—Whether the method of a conditional order followed by an order absolute an appropriate procedure—Distinction between judge of the High Court and the High Court itself—Whether release by habeas corpus open to applicant—Constitution of Ireland 1937, Article 40 4 1 and 2. **State (Aherne) v Governor of Limerick Prison** [1983] 17, SC.

Requirement of immediate inquiry—Detention in police custody—Effect of order for release—Constitution of Ireland 1937, Article 40.4.2. **State (Bowes) v Fitzpatrick** [1978] 195, HC.

Re-arrest
Validity
English warrant—Re-arrest on same warrant after absolute order granted—Validity of re-arrest—Habeas Corpus (Ireland) Act 1781, s. 5—Constitution of Ireland 1937, Article 40. **State (McFadden) v Governor of Mountjoy Prison** (No 2) [1981] 120, HC.

Remand order
Jurisdiction of District Court
Accused detained pursuant to statutory power—Whether remand order made by district justice valid—Whether District Court can embark on constitutional inquiry as to validity of detention. *See* Jurisdiction—District Court (*above*).

Remand prisoner
Legality of detention
Removal to punishment section for security and administrative reasons—Whether in accordance with regulations—Whether irregularity such as to make detention unlawful—Constitution of Ireland 1937, Art 40—Prisons (Ireland) Act 1877, ss. 12, 13—Rules for the Government of Prisons 1947, rr 66, 192. **State (Comerford) v Governor of Mountjoy Prison** [1981] 86, HC.

HABITUAL CRIMINALS
Preventative detention. *See* CRIME PREVENTION (Preventative detention—Habitual criminals).

HARBOURS AND PIERS
Canal
Lack of maintenance
Flooding—Nuisance—Whether harbour commissioners' duty to maintain canal. *See* CANAL (Lack of maintenance).

HARBOURS AND PIERS *continued*
Harbour authority
Tug operating licence
Refusal—Judicial review of decision—Natural and consitutional justice—Whether licence necessary for the operation of tugs in the Shannon Estuary—Whether applicant entitled to damages—Whether applicant entitled to be told of criteria employed in and the reasons for the decision. **C W Shipping Company Ltd v Limerick Harbour Commissioners** [1989] 416, HC.

HEALTH AND SAFETY
Employer's liability insurance
Contract
Interpretation. *See* INSURANCE (Contract—Intepretation—Employer's liability insurance).

Family planning
Offence
Unlawful sale of contraceptives—Authority to enter premises—Whether evidence obtained without warrant admissible—Nature and substance of evidence—Health Act 1947, s. 96(1)—Health (Family Planning) Act 1979, s. 4(4). **DPP v McCutcheon** [1986] 433, HC.

Occupational disease
Employer's liability. *See* Negligence (Employer—Occupational disease).

Prisoner. *See* PRISONS (Prisoner—Health and safety).

Workplace
Injury to employee
Employer's duty of care. *See* Negligence (Employer).

HEALTH BOARD
Care of child
Fit person order. *See* CHILD (Custody—Fit person order).

Place of safety order. *See* CHILD (Custody—Place of safety order).

Duty of care
Detention of person as being of unsound mind
Subsequent discharge—Requirement that person show substantial grounds for contending that the board, through its officers, acted in bad faith or without reasonable care—Whether claim made out—Whether evidence of want of reasonable care—Mental Treatment Act 1945, s. 260. **O'Dowd v North Western Health Board** [1983] 186, SC.

Employment
Age limit for entry to post
Whether discriminatory. *See* EMPLOYMENT (Equality of treatment—Access to employment—Age limit).

Injury to employee
Home help employed in the community—Defective condition of patient's home—Responsibility of health board. **Mulcare v Southern Health Board** [1988] 689, HC.

Officer
Dismissal—Entitlement to claim unfair dismissal. *See* EMPLOYMENT (Unfair dismissal—Exclusion—Officer—Health board).

Remuneration—Promotion—Calculation of commencing salary requiring approval of Minister—Increased salary granted pending approval—Refusal resulting in reduced salary—Whether officer entitled to receive payments in accordance with original determination. **Murphy v Eastern Health Board** [1979] 100, HC.

HEALTH EDUCATION BUREAU
Duty of care
Campaign to help members of the public give up smoking
Whether duty of care owed to conduct the campaign so as not to damage the property rights of those engaged in the tobacco trade. **Gallaher Ltd v Health Education Bureau** [1982] 240, HC.

HEALTH SERVICES
Chargeabilty
Hospital care
Ward of court—Geriatric patient—County home or similar institution—Whether maintenance to be construed as "institutional assistance" under 1953 Act or "inpatient services" under 1970 Act—Whether inmates receiving more than shelter and main-tenance—Mental Treatment Act 1945, s. 158—Health Act 1947, s. 2—Health Act 1953, ss. 6, 54—Health Act 1970, ss. 3, 51. **In re Maud McInerney** [1976–7] 229, HC, SC.

General medical services scheme
Investigation procedure
Complaints of abuse of scheme—Allegation of fraudulent payments for pharmaceutical products—Health board referring matter to Minister—Establishment of committee of inquiry—Failure to inform fully of nature of complaint—Whether invalidates decision to refer to Minister—Whether referral ultra vires—Certiorari—Declaration—Health Act 1970, s. 58. **O'Flynn v Mid-Western Health Board** [1990] 149, HC.

Payments—Doctor—Procedure for investigation of claims indicating excessive rate of attendance—Decision of appeal committee—Whether in accordance with natural justice—Conduct of proceedings—No cross-examination of witnesses—Whether proper exercise of discretion by appeal committee. **State (Boyle) v General Medical Services (Payments) Board** [1981] 14, HC.

Hospital
Chargeability for services. See Chargeability (*above*).

Closure
Private hospital. *See* HOSPITAL (Closure).

Discontinuance of services. See HOSPITAL (Discontinuance of services).

Negligence
Duty of care. *See* NEGLIGENCE (Hospital).

Medical practitioner. *See* MEDICAL PRACTITIONER.

Regulations
Validity
Whether *ultra vires*—Legislation empowering Minister to make regulations—Regu-lations rendering victims of road traffic accidents ineligible for free medical services—Whether unconstitutional delegation of legislative power—Whether Minister acted *ultra vires*—Validity—Constitution—Natural justice—Health Act 1970, s. 72—Health Services Regulations 1971, art 6(3). **Cooke v Walsh** [1983] 429, HC; [1984] 208, SC.

HEARSAY EVIDENCE
Admissibility
Telephone calls
Tape recording—Whether evidence as to voice on telephone established by hearsay. **People (DPP) v Prunty** [1986] 716, CCA.

HEREDITAMENT
Valuation. *See* RATING AND VALUATION.

HIGH COURT
Decision
Interlocutory injunction proceedings
High Court judge deciding to refer certain questions to the European Court of Justice—Whether decision by the High Court declining to grant an injunction constitutes a decision appealable to the Supreme Court. **SPUC Ireland Ltd v Grogan** [1990] 350, SC.

Judge
Meaning of phrase 'judge of the High Court'
Statute—Interpretation—Whether statute should be construed so as to include Registrar or Master within meaning of the phrase—Courts Act 1981, ss. 19(1), 22(1). **Mellowhide Products Ltd v Barry Agencies Ltd.** [1983] 152, HC.

Jurisdiction
Affiliation order
Whether mother may institute proceedings in High Court—Legislation conferring jurisdiction on High Court but contemplating the making of rules as to relevant procedures to be followed—No such rules of Court made—Whether High Court inherent jurisdiction—Courts Act 1971, s. 19—Illegitimate Children (Affiliation Orders) Act 1930, s. 2(1). **O'B v W** [1982] 234, SC.

Appeal
Circuit Court decision—Appeal from decision of the Employment Appeals Tribunal—Whether further right of appeal lay to High Court—Unfair Dismissals Act 1977, ss. 1, 6, 7—Redundancy Payments Acts. **McCabe v Lisney and Son** [1981] 289, HC.

Circuit Court decision—Appeal from decision of the Employment Appeals Tribunal—Whether further right of appeal lay to High Court—Whether action a "civil action or matter"—Courts of Justice Act 1936, s. 38—Unfair Dismissals Act 1977, s. 10(4). **Western Health Board v Quigley** [1982] 390, HC.

Labour Court determination—Employment equality—Labour Court finding that discrimination occurred being based on uncontested assumptions of fact—Whether open to High Court to require these facts to be proved—Employment Equality Act 1977, s. 2(c). **North Western Health Board v Martyn** [1988] 519, SC.

Registrar of Building Societies—Decision—Nature of appeal from decision—Whether confined to a point of law—Building Societies Act 1976, s. 19(7). **Ireland Benefit Building Society v Registrar of Building Societies** [1981] 73, HC.

Case stated
Arbitration—Lease—Terms—Construction—Rent review clause. **Hynes Ltd v O'Malley Property Ltd** [1989] 619, SC.

Findings of fact—Revenue—Extent of judicial review of finding of fact by Appeal Commissioner. **Mara v Hummingbird Ltd** [1982] 421, HC, SC.

Malicious injuries—Jurisdiction to state case to Supreme Court—Malicious Injuries Act 1981, s. 18. **W J Prendergast & Son Ltd v Carlow Co Council** [1990] 749, SC.

Constitution
Original jurisdiction in "all matters and questions"—Exclusion—Validity—Criminal trial—Transfer—Circuit Court—Accused seeking trial in High Court—Statutory prohibition on transfer—Whether provision prohibiting transfer repugnant to the Constitution—Whether withdrawing jurisdiction from High Court expressly conferred by Constitution—Constitution of Ireland 1937, Articles 34 2, 34 3, 36 iii—Courts Act 1964, s. 4—Courts Act 1981, s. 32(1). **Tormey v Attorney General and Ireland** [1984] 657, HC; [1985] 375, SC.

Contempt of court
Criminal contempt in the face of the court—Whether power to try summarily and

HIGH COURT
Jurisdiction

Contempt of court continued

immediately—Necessity to protect administration of justice—Alleged subornation of witness—Whether necessity to try the contempt where witness proceeded to give his evidence. **In re Kelly and Deighan** [1984] 424, HC.

District Court procedure

Prohibition—*Quia timet* injunction—Criminal case—Indictable offence dealt with summarily—Statements of evidence requested by defendant—Application for order restraining District Justice from hearing the case—Presumption that District Justice will act in accordance with principles of justice and fairness—Criminal Justice Act 1951, s. 2. **Clune v DPP** [1981] 17, HC.

Habeas corpus

Absolute order made in first instance. *See* HABEAS CORPUS (Procedure—Absolute order made in first instance).

Inspection

Bank account—Jurisdiction to make an order for inspection with extra-territorial effect—Bankers' Books Evidence Act 1879, ss. 7, 9—Bankers' Books Evidence (Amendment) Act 1959, s. 2. **Chemical Bank v McCormack** [1983] 350, HC.

Judicial review

Domestic tribunal—Decision—Function of court—Nature of jurisdiction. **McGrath v Maynooth College** [1979] 166, SC.

Minister—Decision-making power affecting personal rights—Precondition to exercise—Opinion—Whether High Court jurisdiction to give ruling as to whether precondition validly complied with—Constitution of Ireland 1937, Article 40 6 1—Broadcasting Authority Act 1960, s. 31(1). **State (Lynch) v Cooney** [1983] 89, SC.

Mareva injunction

Whether jurisdiction confined to cases where defendant is resident outside the State—Supreme Court of Judicature (Ireland) Act 1877, s. 28(8). **Fleming v Ranks (Ireland) Ltd** [1983] 541, HC.

Planning injunction

Extent of jurisdiction—Planning authority refusing permission for change of use—Whether Court may review decision of the planning authority regarding the granting or witholding of permission—Local Government (Planning and Development) Act 1976, s. 27. **Dublin Corporation v Garland** [1982] 104, HC.

Extent of jurisdiction—Unauthorised building work—Development carried out without complying with conditions—Whether High Court has jurisdiction to order demolition of part of building—Local Government (Planning and Development) Act 1976, s. 27(2). **Morris v Garvey** [1982] 177, SC.

Interpretation of statute—Whether High Court jurisdiction to make mandatory order—Local Government (Planning and Development) Act 1976, s. 27. **Dublin Co Council v Kirby** [1985] 325, HC.

Wardship proceedings

Lunacy matters—Mentally retarded girl—Application for inquiry as to her soundness of mind—Whether condition precedent for the jurisdiction to bring persons of unsound mind into the wardship of the court that they be entitled to property which requires management or protection—Constitution of Ireland 1937, Articles 40 3 2, 40 4 2—Lunacy Regulations (Ireland) Act 1871—Mental Treatment Act 1945—Courts (Supplemental Provisions) Act 1961, s. 9. **In re Midland Health Board** [1988] 251, SC.

HIGH COURT *continued*
Precedent
Whether High Court bound to follow pre-Treaty English decisions
Constitution of Ireland 1937, Article 50—**Irish Shell Ltd v Elm Motors Ltd** [1984] 595, SC.

Procedure
Personal injuries action
One party commencing proceedings in the Circuit Court claiming damages for his car—Other party issuing proceedings in High Court claiming damages for personal injuries—Whether Circuit Court action to be stayed—Courts of Justice Act 1924, s. 94—Civil Liability Act 1961, ss. 34(1), 37(1)—Courts Act 1971, s. 6—Circuit Court Rules, 1950, 0 30, r 11. **Murphy v Hennessy** [1985] 100, HC.

HIGHWAY
Animal on highway
Cattle straying—Liability of owner or keeper for damage caused. *See* ANIMALS (Negligence—Straying onto main road).

Bridge over highway
Vertical clearance
Whether local authority's roadworks in reducing clearance *below* statutory minimum wanting in due course. *See* Highway authority—Negligence—Breach of statutory duty (*below*).

Danger adjacent to highway. *See* Tree adjacent to highway (*below*).

Highway authority
Maintenance of road. See Maintenance (*below*).

Negligence
Breach of statutory duty—Apportionment of fault—Railway bridge—Minimum clearance required—Whether local authority's roadworks in reducing clearance below statutory minimum wanting in due care—Whether advance warning system agreed between railway company and local authority—Railway Clauses Consolidation Act 1845, s. 49. **CIE v Carroll** [1983] 173, HC; [1986] 312, SC.

Injury to pedestrian—Difference in road levels—Lay-by provided by developers—Layout agreed with defendants as planning authority—Jury finding of negligence—Whether defendant authority liable for contractor's negligence. **Weir v Dun Laoghaire Corporation** [1984] 113, SC.

Maintenance
Civil liability
Non-feasance—Statutory provision amending law to come into operation by governmental order—No such order made—Mandamus application—Whether government's discretion to bring section into operation—Civil Liability Act 1961, s. 60. **State (Sheehan) v Ireland** [1988] 437, HC, SC.

Road works
Negligence—Breach of statutory duty. *See* Highway authority—Negligence—Breach of statutory duty (*above*).

Non-feasance
Civil liability. See Maintenance—Civil liability—Non-feasance (*above*).

Street trading offence. *See* ROAD TRAFFIC OFFENCES (Street trading).

Tree adjacent to highway
Liability of landowner
Tree falling to ground and damaging passing car—Whether landowner in breach of a duty of care—Whether tree a danger to persons using the highway. **Lynch v Hetherton** [1990] 857, HC.

HIRE-PURCHASE AGREEMENT
Privity of contract
Vendor in breach of contract
Action for damages against vendor and finance company—No privity of contract between plaintiff and finance company—Whether action against finance company be dismissed. **Halpin v Rothwell** [1984] 613, HC.

HISTORIC BUILDING
Preservation
Effectiveness of planning legislation. See PLANNING (Enforcement—Section 27 application—Breach of conditions—Building of historic interest).

HISTORIC MONUMENT *See* NATIONAL MONUMENT.

HOMICIDE
Manslaughter
Sentence. See CRIMINAL LAW (Sentence—Manslaughter).

Murder. *See* CRIMINAL LAW (Murder).

HORSE
Showjumping
Prohibition on use of non-Irish horses by Irish showjumpers in international competitions
Whether unreasonable restraint of trade. *See* RESTRAINT OF TRADE (Reasonableness—Public policy—Equestrian rule-making body).

HOSPITAL
Chargeability for services. *See* HEALTH SERVICES (Chargeabiltiy fo services).

Closure
Private hospital
Whether repeal of legislation required—Withdrawal of public funds—Whether requirement of public subvention established—Barrington's Hospital Act 1830. **Governors of Barrington's Hospital v Minister for Health** [1989] 77, HC.

Discontinuance of services
Validity of direction
Minister discontinuing certain in-patient services in particular hospital—Whether decision *ultra vires*—Whether discontinuance of service amounted to direction relating to the arrangements for providing services in hospital—Health Act 1970, s. 38. **McMeel v Minister for Health** [1985] 616, SC.

Negligence. *See* NEGLIGENCE (Hospital).

HOTEL
Development
Increase in trade
Ground floor reconstructed to incorporate a lounge bar—Whether material change of use constituting development. *See* PLANNING (Development—Material change of use—Hotel premises).

Intoxicating liquor licence
Application. See Licensing Acts (Licence—Application—Hotel licence).

Renewal
Objection. *See* LICENSING ACTS (Licence—Renewal—Hotel licence).

Rateable valuation
Reduction
Basis upon which rateable valuation of premises may be reduced—Rateable Valuation (Ireland) Act 1852, s. 11. **Rosses Point Hotel v Commissioner of Valuation** [1987] 512, HC.

HOUSE TO HOUSE COLLECTION *See* STREET AND HOUSE TO HOUSE COLLECTIONS.

HOUSING

Accommodation

Travelling community
Provision of serviced sites. *See* Travelling community (*below*).

Ejectment

Local authority tenant
Notice to quit. *See* Local authority—Notice to quit (*below*).

House

Contract to build and sell
Specific performance—Completion—Interest—Dispute as to whether contract was completed on certain date—Basis on which interest to be awarded. **Treacy v Dwyer Nolan Developments Ltd** [1979] 163, SC.

Defects. See DEFECTIVE PREMISES.

Dwelling of citizen
Constitutional inviolability. *See* CONSTITUTION (Personal rights—Inviolability of dwelling).

Family home. See FAMILY LAW (Property—Family home).

Loan for acquisition
Defects manifesting themselves—Liability of Housing authority. *See* Local authority—Duty of Care—Defective premises—Whether duty of care owed to purchaser by a housing authority granting a loan under statutory powers (*below*).

Sale
Family home. *See* SALE OF LAND (Family home).

Local authority

Allocation of houses
Whether *ultra vires*—Allocation of houses to person residing outside housing authority's functional area—Whether authority acting *ultra vires*—Housing Act 1966, ss. 53, 60, 109. **McNamee v Buncrana UDC** [1984] 77, SC.

Compulsory purchase powers. See COMPULSORY PURCHASE (Local authority).

Decision
Validity—Application for permission to use premises other than for human habitation refused—Whether such decision invalid—Default procedure—Whether operative—Local Government (Planning and Development) Act 1963, ss. 2, 26—Housing Act 1969, ss. 4, 10. **Creedon v Dublin Corporation** [1983] 339, SC.

Duty of Care
Defective premises—Whether duty of care owed to purchaser by a housing authority granting a loan under statutory powers—Consequential loss to purchaser—Housing Act 1966, s. 39—Housing Authorities (Loans for Acquisition or Construction of Houses) Regulations 1972—Civil Liability Act 1961, s. 21(2). **Ward v McMaster** [1986] 43, HC; [1989] 400, SC.

Notice to quit
Demand for possession—Corporation flat—District Court hearing—Natural justice—Tenant not represented—Tenant not invited to give evidence—Housing Act 1966, s. 62. **State (Crothers) v Kelly** [1978] 167, HC.

Demand for possession—No explanation given nor complaint brought to tenant's attention—District Court order for possession—Appeal—Certiorari—Whether corporation obliged to give evidence of motive or justification—Whether form of notice to quit and demand for possession correct—Landlord and Tenant Law (Amendment) Act 1860, ss. 86, 87, 88—Housing Act 1966, ss. 62, 118. **State (Litzouw) v Johnson** [1981] 273, HC.

HOUSING
Local authority *continued*
Service charges. See LOCAL GOVERNMENT (Service charges).

Statutory duty
> Breach—Loan to purchaser—Duty of care—Defective premises—Whether duty of care owed to purchaser by a housing authority granting a loan under statutory powers. *See* Local authority—Duty of care—Defective premises (*above*).

> Travelling community—Provision of serviced halting sites—Whether housing authority under a statutory duty to provide serviced sites for plaintiffs. *See* Travelling community (*below*).

Redemption of annuity
Overpayment
> Mistake of law—Whether recoverable—Housing Act 1966, s. 99. **Rogers v Louth Co Council** [1981] 144, SC.

Rent. *See* LANDLORD AND TENANT (Rent).

Service charges
Domestic dwelling. See LOCAL GOVERNMENT (Service charges).

Taxation
Residential property tax
> Constitutional validity—Property rights—Family rights—Tax levied on properties over certain value—Whether constituting invidious discrimination—Constitution of Ireland 1937, Articles 40 1, 40 3, 41, 43—Finance Act 1983, Part VI. **Madigan v Attorney General** [1986] 136, HC, SC.

Temporary dwellings
Unlicensed caravan site. See TEMPORARY DWELLINGS.

Travelling community
Serviced halting sites
> Whether housing authority under statutory duty to provide serviced sites—Whether State under a constitutional duty to provide such sites—Duty of corporation to review its building programme so as to include proposals for provision of serviced sites—Constitution of Ireland—Housing Act 1966, ss. 53, 54, 56, 58, 60, 111. **O'Reilly and Others v Limerick Corporation** [1989] 181, HC.

HUMAN RIGHTS *See* EUROPEAN CONVENTION ON HUMAN RIGHTS

HUSBAND AND WIFE
Barring order. *See* FAMILY LAW (Barring order).

Bigamy. *See* CRIMINAL LAW (Bigamy).

Custody of children. *See* CHILD (Custody).

Divorce. *See* MARRIAGE (Divorce).

Family home. *See* FAMILY LAW (Property—Family home).

Income tax
Statute with retrospective effect
> Validity. *See* CONSTITUTION (Marriage—Married couple—Income tax).

Joint tenancy
Order for sale in lieu of partition. See JOINT TENANCY (Partition).

Maintenance. *See* FAMILY LAW (Maintenance).

Marriage. *See* MARRIAGE.

HUSBAND AND WIFE *continued*
Marriage settlement. *See* MARRIAGE SETTLEMENT.

Nullity of marriage. *See* MARRIAGE (Nullity).

Property. *See* FAMILY LAW (Property).

Separation. *See* MARRIAGE (Separation).

Social welfare allowances
Implementation of EC Council Directive
Implementation effected in such a way that certain married couples adversely treated.
See CONSTITUTION (Marriage—Married couple—Social welfare).

Validity of marriage. *See* MARRIAGE (Validity).

IDENTIFICATION OF ACCUSED *See* CRIMINAL LAW (Evidence—Identification).

ILLEGAL CONTRACT *See* CONTRACT (Illegality).

ILLEGAL ORGANISATION
Collection
Street and house to house collection
Opinion of Garda superintendent that proceeds of collection would benefit an unlawful organisation. *See* STREET AND HOUSE TO HOUSE COLLECTIONS.

Member
Offence
Extradition application—Whether political offence exception available. *See* EXTRADITION (Political offence).

Objectives
Objective of reintegration of national territory by force of arms
Whether objectives of organisation to subvert the Constitutional organs of the State—Extradition proceedings—Whether political offence exception available. *See* CONSTITUTION (State—Subversion—Unlawful organisation—Objective of reintegration of national territory by force of arms).

ILLEGALLY OBTAINED EVIDENCE
Admissibility. *See* CRIMINAL LAW (Evidence—Admissibility—Entry on premises).

ILLEGITIMATE CHILD
Adoption. *See* ADOPTION.

Affiliation order
Whether mother may institute proceedings in High Court. See AFFILIATION ORDER.

Guardianship and custody
Natural father's application. See CHILD (Guardianship and custody—Natural father's application).

Registration of birth
Paternity
Evidence admissible to prove paternity—Evidence of wife that child not the child of the marriage—Rule in *Russell v Russell*—Whether part of the common law of Ireland. *See* CHILD (Paternity).

Succession rights
Intestacy
Whether "issue" of deceased—Right of illegitimate child to intestate succession to father's estate. *See* SUCCESSION (Intestacy—Illegitimate child).

IMMIGRATION *See* ALIEN.

IMMUNITY FROM SUIT
State. *See* STATE (Immunity from suit).

IMPLIED TERMS
Contract. *See* CONTRACT (Implied terms).

IMPOTENCE *See* MARRIAGE (Nullity—Impotence).

IMPRISONMENT
Damages action
False imprisonment. See FALSE IMPRISONMENT.

Detention
Legality. See ARREST (Detention—Legality).

Generally. *See* PRISONS.

Inquiry into legality of detention. *See* HABEAS CORPUS.

Sentence. *See* CRIMINAL LAW (Sentence).

IMPROVEMENTS
Lessee
Rent review
Whether improvements lawfully made by the lessee to be taken into account in fixing rent. **Hynes Ltd v O'Malley Property Ltd** [1989] 619, SC.

INCAPACITY
Marriage. *See* MARRIAGE (Nullity—Capacity).

Testator. *See* WILL (Validity—Capacity of testator).

INCOME TAX *See* REVENUE (Income tax).

INCORPORATED LAW SOCIETY
Compensation fund
Solicitor dishonestly obtaining a loan
Creditor suffering loss—Whether creditor entitled to claim compensation. *See* SOLICITOR (Misconduct—Dishonesty—Law Society Compensation Fund).

Law school
System of entry
Examination. *See* SOLICITOR (Entry to profession—Examination—Law Society—Student unsuccessful—Whether student reached standard required to pass examination).

Whether limit on numbers imposed—Examination—Compensation rules—Whether Education Committee acted arbitrarily. *See* SOLICITOR (Entry to profession—System of entry).

INCUMBRANCE ON LAND. *See* REAL PROPERTY (Incumbrance).
Mortgage. *See* MORTGAGE.

INDEMNITY
Insurance
Professional indemnity policy
Interpretation of contract. *See* INSURANCE (Contract—Interpretation—Intention of parties—Professional indemnity and public liability policies).

INDEMNITY *continued*
Road traffic accident
Employer seeking indemnity from employee using vehicle in course of employment
Employee guilty of negligence—Civil Liability Act 1961, s. 21—Road Traffic Act 1961, s. 118. **Sinnott v Quinnsworth Ltd** [1984] 523, SC.

INDICTMENT *See* CRIMINAL LAW (Indictment).

INDUCEMENT OF BREACH OF CONTRACT. *See* TORT (Inducement of breach of contract).

INDUSTRIAL AND PROVIDENT SOCIETY
Credit union
Amendment to rules
Registrar of Friendly Societies refusing to register such amendment—Whether Registrar so entitled—Function and jurisdiction of Registrar—Industrial and Provident Societies Act 1893, s. 10(3)—Credit Union Act 1966, ss. 1, 2(3), 3, 6, 13, 17, 27, 33, 35—Industrial and Provident Societies (Amendment) Act 1978. **Prison Service Credit Union Ltd v Registrar of Friendly Societies** [1987] 367, HC.

Members
Powers
Power to manage affairs—Power to alter capital—Power to amend rules—Industrial and Provident Societies Act 1893,ss 10, 21, 22. **Kerry Co-Operative Creameries v An Bord Bainne** [1990] 664, HC.

Rules
Amendment
Registration—Function and jurisdiction of Registrar. *See* Credit union—Amendment to rules (*above*).

Registration
Function of Registrar of Friendly Societies—Industrial and Provident Societies Act 1893, s. 10(3). **Kerry Co-Operative Creameries v An Bord Bainne** [1990] 664, HC.

Shareholder
Property rights
Registered provident society engaged in the business of banking—Legislation enacted prohibiting such societies from accepting or holding deposits—Whether legislation invalid—Whether unjust attack on property rights of shareholders—Whether shareholder has property rights capable of being invoked—Whether prohibition infringed shareholders' right of association—Constitution of Ireland 1937, Articles 40 3, 40 6 1(iii)—Industrial and Provident Societies (Amendment) Act 1978, s. 5(2). **PMPS Ltd v Attorney General** [1984] 88, SC.

Rights of shareholders in or over assets of society—Industrial and Provident Societies Act 1893. **Kerry Co-Operative Creameries v An Bord Bainne** [1990] 664, HC.

Winding up
Duty of care
Minister—Depositor lodging money with industrial and provident society—Society subsequently going into liquidation—Depositor receiving a dividend of only part of sum lodged—Whether Minister owed duty of care—Registrar of Friendly Societies—Powers of investigation and control—Whether sufficient relationship of proximity between Registrar of Friendly Societies and plaintiff—Central Bank Act 1971, s. 7(1)(4)—Industrial and Provident Societies (Amendment) Act 1978, s. 5(2)—Insurance (No 2) Act 1983. **McMahon v Ireland** [1988] 610, HC.

INDUSTRIAL PROPERTY PROTECTION *See* COPYRIGHT; PASSING OFF; PATENTS; TRADE MARK.

INDUSTRIAL RELATIONS
Generally. *See* EMPLOYMENT.

Trade dispute. *See* TRADE DISPUTE.

Trade union. *See* TRADE UNION.

INDUSTRIAL SCHOOL
District Court order that child be sent to industrial school
Father consenting to said order
> Father subsequently seeking return of child—Minister refusing to order child's release—Whether provisions unconstitutional. **In re Doyle (An infant): State (Doyle) v Minister for Education** [1989] 277, SC.

INDUSTRIAL TRAINING GRANTS
Corporation tax
Assessment
> Whether training grants capital or revenue receipts—Industrial Development Act 1969, s. 239. **Jacob International Ltd Inc v O Cleirigh (Inspector of Taxes)** [1985] 651, SC.

INDUSTRIAL TRIBUNAL. *See* EMPLOYMENT APPEALS TRIBUNAL; LABOUR COURT

INFANT
Adoption. *See* ADOPTION.

Custody. *See* CHILD (Custody).

Generally. *See* CHILD.

Illegitimate child. *See* ILLEGITIMATE CHILD.

Passport. *See* PASSPORT (Child).

Paternity. *See* CHILD (Paternity).

Personal injuries
Brain damage
> Damages—Assessment. *See* DAMAGES (Personal injuries—Brain damage—Infant).

Limitation of actions. See Limitation of Actions (Personal injuries—Infant).

Occupier's liability
> Infant licensee—Church—Damages—Whether excessive. **Rooney v Connolly** [1987] 768, SC.

Removal from jurisdiction. *See* CHILD (Custody—Removal from jurisdiction).

Wardship. *See* CHILD (Wardship).

Young offender. *See* CRIMINAL LAW (Young offender).

INFLATION
Damages
Claim in quasi-contract
> Whether inflation to be taken into account. *See* DAMAGES (Quasi-contract).

Loss of profits
> Whether inflationary decrease in purchasing power relevant in assessing damages. *See* DAMAGES (Breach of contract—Loss of profits).

INFORMATION
Abortion. *See* ABORTION (Information).

Consumer information. *See* CONSUMER PROTECTION.

INFORMATION *continued*
Disclosure. *See* DISCLOSURE OF INFORMATION.

Negligence. *See* NEGLIGENCE (Advice or information).

INFORMER *See* COMMON INFORMER.

INHERITANCE RIGHTS. *See* SUCCESSION.

INJUNCTION
Barring order
Exclusion from matrimonial home. See FAMILY LAW (Barring order).

Breach
Contempt of court
Deliberate disobedience of High Court order—Trade union members—Power to commit to prison—Alternative remedy. **Ross Co Ltd (In receivership) v Swan** [1981] 416, HC.

Estoppel
Planning injunction
Unauthorised change of use—Enforcement notice—Proceedings for non-compliance— Whether Corporation estopped by causing the premises to be rated as used for office purposes—Discretion of court to refuse injunction on grounds of hardship—Local Government (Planning and Development) Act 1976, s. 27. **Dublin Corporation v Garland** [1982] 104, HC.

Interlocutory
Balance of convenience
Building contract—Action for specific performance—Whether prejudice likely to result—Sub-contractor—Nomination of alternative sub-contractor. **Lift Manufacturers v Irish Life Assurance Co** [1979] 277, HC.

Company—Shareholders' agreement—Sole distribution and assembly of Datsun motor vehicles —Negative term—Restricted transaction—Prohibition of grant of contract of service—Termination of chief executive's appointment—Appointment of other executives—Proposal to grant fork lift truck franchise—Injunction to restrain— Principles to be applied on an application for an interlocutory injunction—Balance of convenience. **TMG Group Ltd v Al Babtain Trading & Contracting Co** [1982] 349, HC.

Fair question to be tried—Validity of law—Fisheries—Offshore fishing licence—Penal statute—Crew nationality conditions—Challenge to validity of statutory provision under which licence granted—Reference to European Court of Justice—Whether plaintiffs entitled to injunction restraining enforcement of licence—Fisheries (Amendment) Act 1983, s. 2. **Beara Fisheries & Shipping Ltd v Minister for the Marine** [1988] 221, HC.

Landlord and tenant—Lease—Forfeiture by landlord—Claim by 'underlesee' for relief—Person 'claiming as under-lessee' having unenforceable agreement with tenant for a sub-lease—Whether claim maintainable—Conveyancing Act 1892, ss. 4, 5— Landlord and Tenant (Amendment) Act 1980, s. 78. **Enock v Lambert Jones Estates Ltd** [1983] 532, HC.

Nuisance—Operation of quarry—Noise—Damage to property. **Stafford v Roadstone Ltd** [1980] 1, HC.

Restraint of trade—Valid interest to be protected. **European Chemical Industries ltd v Bell** [1981] 345, HC.

Breach of confidence
Publication—Book written by deceased member of British intelligence service— Application to restrain publication in Ireland—Duty of confidentiality—Whether different criteria applied to government information—Constitution of Ireland 1937,

INJUNCTION
Interlocutory
Breach of confidence continued

Article 40 6 1. **Attorney General for England and Wales v Brandon Book Publishers Ltd** [1987] 135, HC.

Broadcasting

Unlicensed possession and use of apparatus for wireless telegraphy—Seizure of apparatus. *See* Interlocutory—Mandatory injunction—Broadcasting (*below*).

Constitutional action

Presumption of constitutionality—Fair question to be tried—Balance of convenience—Whether abuse of process of court—Forum shopping—Domestic legislation to ratify international treaty—Injunction sought to prevent deposit of deeds of ratification—Effect of potential embarrassment for government if injunction granted—European Communities (Amendment) Act 1986. **Crotty v An Taoiseach** [1987] 400, HC, SC.

Constitutional right

Protection—Balance of convenience—Competing constitutional right. **Society for the Protection of Unborn Children (Ireland) Ltd v Grogan** [1990] 350, SC.

Contract

Terms—Enforcement—Restraint of trade—Solus agreement—Principles to be applied. **Irish Shell Ltd v Elm Motors Ltd** [1982] 519, HC; [1984] 595, SC.

Decision of court

Deferral or postponement—Reference to European Court—Whether reference to Court of Justice necessary to determine interlocutory issues. **Society for the Protection of Unborn Children (Ireland) Ltd v Grogan** [1990] 350, SC.

Employment

Civil service—Suspension—Application for injunction restoring plaintiffs to their position—Whether suspension in breach of natural justice—Whether breach of right to earn livelihood—Whether injunction be granted—Whether case established—Whether damages adequate remedy—Civil Service Regulation Act 1956, s. 13. **Yeates v Minister for Posts and Telegraphs** [1978] 22, HC.

Fair prima facie case to be tried

Inducement of breach of contract—Whether damages adequate remedy—Balance of convenience. **Reno Engrais et Produits Chemiques S.A. v Irish Agricultural Wholesale Society Ltd** [1976–7] 179, HC.

Fiat of Attorney General secured

Injunction granted on undertaking to abide by any order as to damages—Fiat not extended to this understanding—Error in High Court record—Whether plaintiffs able to rely on this—Whether Attorney General liable in respect of plaintiff's loss. **Attorney General (ex rel Martin) v Dublin Corporation** [1983] 254, SC.

Fisheries

Offshore fishing licence—Conditions as to nationality—Challenge to validity of statutory provision—Whether plaintiffs entitled to injunction restraining enforcement of licence—Fisheries (Amendment) Act 1983, s. 2. **Beara Fisheries & Shipping Ltd v Minister for the Marine** [1988] 221, HC.

Offshore fishing licence—Conditions as to nationality—Vessel arrested for fishing in breach of condition—Plaintiff seeking order restraining enforcement of condition. **Ardent Fisheries Ltd v Minister for Tourism, Fisheries and Forestry** [1987] 528, HC.

Fishing rights

Interference—Outdoor education centre—Canoeing—Ownership of bed and soil of lake and river—Form of injunction—Whether plaintiffs entitled to injunction to restrain interference. **Tennent v Clancy** [1988] 214, HC.

INJUNCTION
Interlocutory *continued*
Health services
Hospital—Closure—Ministerial decision—Whether repeal of legislation required—
Withdrawal of public funds—Whether requirement of public subvention established.
Governors of Barrington's Hospital v Minister for Health [1989] 77, HC.

Inducement of breach of contract
Collateral contract—Whether contract in existence—Whether injunction lies—Balance
of convenience—Relevance of foreign arbitration clause. **Mitchelstown Co-Operative
Society Ltd v Societè des produits Nestlè S.A.** [1989] 582, SC.

Trade dispute—Picketing. *See* Interlocutory—Trade dispute—Picketing (*below*).

Mandatory injunction
Breach of contract—Solus agreement—Lessor granted mandatory injunction at
interlocutory stage. **Irish Shell Ltd v Elm Motors Ltd** [1982] 519, HC; [1984] 595, SC.

Broadcasting—Unlicensed possession and use of apparatus for wireless telegraphy—
Apparatus seized—Constitutional challenge to the seizure procedure—Application for
an injunction restraining interference with the broadcasting—Application for a
mandatory injunction requiring return of apparatus—Whether injunctions be
granted—Wireless Telegraphy Act 1926, ss. 3, 5, 8, 12. **Nova Media Services Ltd v
Minister for Posts and Telegraphs** [1984] 161, HC.

Broadcasting—Unlicensed possession and use of apparatus for wireless telegraphy—
Apparatus seized—Constitutional challenge to the seizure procedure—Application for
a mandatory injunction requiring return of apparatus. **Sunshine Radio Productions
Ltd v Attorney General** [1984] 170, HC.

Principles on which such injunctions granted—Whether different at interlocutory
stage—Need for certainty. **Bula Ltd v Tara Mines Ltd** [1988] 157, HC.

Mareva injunction
Jurisdiction to grant—Whether confined to cases where defendant is resident outside
the State—Whether real risk of removal or disposal of defendant's assets—Balance of
convenience—Judicature (Ireland) Act 1877, s. 28 (8). **Fleming v Ranks (Ireland) Ltd**
[1983] 541, HC.

Jurisdiction to grant—Whether confined to cases where defendant is resident outside
the State—Whether real risk of removal or disposal of defendant's assets. **Powerscourt
Estates v Gallagher** [1984] 123, HC.

Whether injunction should issue—Plaintiffs and defendants having no connection with
jurisdiction—Defendants' assets consisting of aeroplane within jurisdiction—Mareva
injunction sought on endorsement of claim—Whether service out of jurisdiction permissible—Distinction between interlocutory and substantive relief—Whether policy
considerations relevant—RSC 1962, O 4 r 2, O 11 r 1(g). **Serge Caudron v Air Zaire**
[1986] 10, HC, SC.

Nuisance
Mineral exploration work—Noise and vibration—Rural locality—Physical damage—
Whether caused by defendant's activities—Whether appropriate to grant an
injunction. **Halpin v Tara Mines Ltd** [1976-7] 28, HC.

Operation of quarry—Noise—Damage to property. **Stafford v Roadstone Ltd** [1980] 1,
HC.

Principles to be applied
Balance of convenience—Date for determination of balance of convenience—Negative
covenant—Restraint of trade—Solus agreement. **Irish Shell Ltd v Elm Motors Ltd**
[1982] 519, HC; [1984] 595, SC.

INJUNCTION
Interlocutory
Principles to be applied continued

"Come into court with clean hands"—Offshore fishing licence—Conditions as to nationality attaching—Vessel arrested for fishing in breach of condition—Plaintiff seeking order restraining enforcement of condition—Whether plaintiff came to court with clean hands—Balance of convenience—Whether order be refused. **Ardent Fisheries Ltd v Minister for Tourism, Fisheries and Forestry** [1987] 528, HC.

Disputed facts—Serious questions of law demanding detailed argument—Balance of convenience—Whether injunction be granted. **Campus Oil Ltd v Minister for Industry and Energy** [1983] 258, HC; [1984] 45, HC, SC.

Publication

Freedom of expression—Confidentiality—Book written by deceased member of British intelligence service—Application to restrain publication in Ireland. *See* Interlocutory—Breach of confidence—Publication (*above*).

Freedom of the press—Criminal conviction—Pending appeal to Court of Criminal Appeal—Publication of a magazine article on material supplied by sole witness for the prosecution—Application to restrain publication—Whether article likely to prejudice the appeal—Constitution of Ireland 1937, Article 40 6. **Cullen v Toibin** [1984] 577, HC, SC.

Reference to European Court

Effect—-Whether postponement of decision—Whether reference to Court of Justice necessary to determine interlocutory issues. **Society for the Protection of Unborn Children (Ireland) Ltd v Grogan** [1990] 350, SC.

Restraint of trade

Balance of convenience—Valid interest to be protected. **European Chemical Industries Ltd v Bell** [1981] 345, HC.

Contract for the sale of a business—Enforceability of restraint clauses—Whether restraint reasonable. **John Orr Ltd v Orr** [1987] 702, HC.

Solus agreement—Principles to be applied. **Irish Shell Ltd v Elm Motors Ltd** [1982] 519, HC; [1984] 595, SC.

Sporting activity

Irish Rugby Football tour of South Africa—Interlocutory injunction to restrain identification with Ireland—Use of word "Irish" or association with Ireland—Legal principles applicable—Whether substantial question to be tried—Right to travel—Breach of international law—Particular damage—Machinery to enforce order—Delay. **Lennon v Ganly** [1981] 84, HC.

Statutory power

Exercise—Fisheries—Whether an interlocutory injunction may be granted to restrain the exercise of a statutory power presumed to be in accordance with the Constitution—Fisheries (Consolidation) Act 1959, s. 222(b)—Fisheries (Amendment) Act 1983, s. 2. **Pesca Valentia v Minister for Fisheries** [1986] 68, SC.

Exercise—Fisheries—Offshore fishing licence—Vessel arrested for fishing in breach of condition—Plaintiff seeking order restraining enforcement of condition—Whether order be refused. **Ardent Fisheries Ltd v Minister for Tourism, Fisheries and Forestry** [1987] 528, HC.

Trade dispute

Picketing—Inducement of breach of contract—Contract terminated—Whether appropriate to grant injunction in respect of continuing picketing. **J. Bradbury Ltd v Duffy** [1979] 51, HC.

INJUNCTION

Interlocutory

Trade dispute continued

Picketing—Inducement of breach of contract—Dispute over termination of contract—Whether picketing entitled to statutory protection—Whether picketer the "employee" of the plaintiff—Trade Disputes Act 1906, ss. 2, 5(3)—Constitution of Ireland 1937, Article 40. **Lamb Brothers Dublin Ltd v Davidson** [1978] 226, HC.

Labour injunction

Picketing. See Interlocutory—Trade dispute—Picketing (*above*).

Mandatory injunction

Breach of contract

Solus agreement—Lessor granted mandatory injunction at interlocutory stage. **Irish Shell Ltd v Elm Motors Ltd** [1982] 519, HC; [1984] 595, SC.

Principles on which such injunctions granted

Whether different at interlocutory stage—Need for certainty. **Bula Ltd v Tara Mines Ltd** [1988] 157, HC.

Slaughter-house licence

County council refusing licence—Plaintiff instituting proceedings to order council to grant licence—Public Health—Town Improvement Clauses Act 1847, ss. 125-131—Slaughter of Animals Act 1935. **Doupe v Limerick County Council** [1981] 456, HC.

Mareva injunction. *See* Interlocutory—Mareva injunction (*above*).

Planning

Enforcement of planning control. See PLANNING (Enforcement—Section 27 application).

Quia timet

Quiet and peaceable enjoyment

Landlord—Interference—Probability of further interference. **Whelan v Madigan** [1978] 136, HC.

Remedy

Breach of statute

Restrictive practices—Retail prices regulation—Advertising goods at cost less than net invoice price—Whether injunction appropriate remedy—Restrictive Practices Act 1972, s. 19—Restrictive Practices (Groceries) (Amendment) (No 2) Order 1978, Art 5. **Irish Assoc of Distributive Trades Ltd v Three Guys Ltd** [1979] 269, HC.

Restrictive practices

Breach of statute. See Remedy—Breach of statute—Restrictive practices (*above*).

Statute

Breach

Whether injunction appropriate remedy. *See* Remedy—Breach of statute (*above*).

Enforcement

Private individual seeking injunction to enforce statutory provisions—Whether statute passed for benefit of small class of persons—Constitution—Right to earn livelihood—Whether breach of right requires enforcement through injunction. **Parsons v Kavanagh** [1990] 560, HC.

Trespass

Action for ejectment

Family home—Conveyance without consent of wife—Purchaser taking up residence—Supreme Court declaring conveyance void—Application by wife for possession—Family Home Protection Act 1976, ss. 3(1), 4(1), 5. **Weir v Somers** [1983] 343, SC.

INJUNCTION *continued*
Vexatious or frivolous action
Planning
Application for injunction restraining continuing development and declaration that planning permission was invalid—Whether claim frivolous or vexatious—RSC, O 19 r 28. **McCabe v Harding Investments Ltd** [1984] 105, SC.

INJURY
Criminal injuries. *See* MALICIOUS INJURIES.

Damages. *See* DAMAGES (Personal injuries).

Employer's liability. *See* NEGLIGENCE (Employer).

Fatal. *See* FATAL INJURY.

Occupier's liability. *See* NEGLIGENCE (Occupier).

INQUEST
Adjournment
Jurisdiction of coroner
Whether coroner has jurisdiction to adjourn sine die or whether it must be for a definite period—Certiorari—Natural justice—Coroners Act 1962,ss 5, 17, 25(1), 25(2), 30. **State (Costello) v Bofin** [1980] 233, SC

Verdict
Suicide
Whether permissible—Whether finding of criminal or civil liability—Presumption against suicide—Evidence—Natural justice—Notice to next-of-kin—Coroners Act 1962, s. 20. **State (McKeown) v Scully** [1986] 133, HC.

INQUIRY
Disciplinary inquiry
Garda Síochána. See GARDA SÍOCHÁNA (Discipline—Inquiry).

INSANITY
Defence
Murder
Diminished responsibility—Whether jury to consider defence of diminished responsibility an alternative verdict of manslaughter—Whether concept of diminished responsibility recognised in Irish law. **People (DPP) v O'Mahony** [1986] 244, SC.

Treatment. *See* MENTAL TREATMENT.

INSOLVENCY
Bankruptcy. *See* BANKRUPTCY.

Company. *See* COMPANY (Winding up).

Industrial and provident society. *See* INDUSTRIAL AND PROVIDENT SOCIETY (Winding up).

INSPECTION
Bank account
Jurisdiction of High Court. See PRACTICE (Inspection—Documents—Bank account).

Discovery. *See* DISCOVERY.

Property
Action for trespass. See PRACTICE (Inspection—Property).

INSPECTOR
Taxes. *See* REVENUE (Tax inspectors).

INSURANCE
Broker
Duty of care
Advice—Contract of insurance—Proposal—Non-disclosure of material facts—Fire—Insurance company repudiating liability—Liability of brokers to plaintiff in contract and tort—Marine Insurance Act 1906, s. 18. **Chariot Inns Ltd v Assicurazioni Generali SPA** [1981] 173, SC.

Contract
Disclosure of material facts
Uberrima fides. *See* Contract—Uberrima fides (*below*).

Dispute
Arbitration clause—Reinsurance contracts—Disputes to be referred to arbitration as condition precedent to any right of action—Whether clause operative when serious and complex issues of law involving allegations of fraud raised—Allegation of fraud made by party opposing stay of action—Application to revoke authority of arbitrator. **Adminstratia Asigurarilor de Stat v Insurance Corporation of Ireland plc** [1990] 159, HC.

Interpretation
Employer's liability insurance—Dispute referred to arbitration—Questions of intepretation arising—Use of word "or"—Whether conjunctive or disjunctive—Whether obervance of claims procedure a condition precedent to the liability of the underwriters. **Gaelcrann Teo v Payne** [1985] 109, HC.

Fire insurance—Destruction of premises by fire—Whether contract of insurance contained a re-instatement clause—Assessment of loss. **St Alban's Investment Co v Sun Alliance and London Insurance Co Ltd** [1984] 501, HC, SC.

Intention of parties—Professional indemnity and public liability policies—Claim of indemnity—Whether claim covered under either policy. **Rohan Construction Ltd v Insurance Corporation of Ireland plc** [1986] 419, HC; [1988] 373, SC.

Life insurance policy—Whether warranty by proposer as to state of health—Whether required to disclose facts of which unaware—Principles of construction of life insurance contracts. **Keating v New Ireland Assurance Company plc** [1990] 110, SC.

Mortgage protection policy—Advertisement—Meaning of 'annual percentage rate of charge'. *See* Mortgage protection policy—Intepretation (*below*).

Warranties—Marine insurance—Cruiser damaged by explosion while laid up—Whether caused by want of due diligence—Warranty that during lay-up period vessel would only be fitted out for customary overhauling—Use of vessel for cooking for friend of insured person—Whether customary—Whether terms relevant to ocean-going vessels suitable to pleasure craft—Marine Insurance Act 1906, ss. 18, 33. **Brady v Irish National Insurance Co** [1986] 669, HC, SC.

Repudiation
Life insurance policy—Material fact that proposer suffering from angina—Whether non-disclosure of material fact—Construction of policy—Whether warranty by proposer as to state of health—Whether required to disclose facts of which unaware—Principles of construction of life insurance contracts. **Keating v New Ireland Assurance Company plc** [1990] 110, SC.

Uberrima fides
Disclosure of material facts—Fire—Repudiation of liability on grounds of failure to disclose material facts—Non-disclosure of previous fire—Duty of uberrima fides—Origin of duty—Onus of proof—Standard of materiality—Whether test in Marine

INSURANCE
Contract
Uberrima fides continued

Insurance Act 1906 applicable to non Marine insurance—Insurance practice—credibility of witness—Extent of review of trial judge's findings—Whether liability for negligence. Marine Insurance Act 1906, s. 18(2). **Chariot Inns Ltd v Assicurazioni Generali SpA** [1981] 173, SC.

Motor insurance policy—Obligation on insurers to keep records and to give information to members of Garda Síochána—Whether regulations valid—Whether natural rights of insured invaded—Road Traffic Act 1961, s. 75—Road Traffic (Compulsory Insurance) Regulations 1962, arts 7, 9. **Murphy v PMPA Insurance Co** [1978] 25, HC.

Employer's liability insurance
Interpretation of contract. See Contract—Interpretation—Employer's liability insurance (*above*).

Information
Disclosure of material facts. See Contract—*Uberrima fides* (*above*).

Duty of insurers

Motor insurance—Obligation on insurers to keep records and to give information to members of Garda Síochána—Validity of regulations. *See* MOTOR INSURANCE (Information—Duty of insurers).

Liability of insurer
Motor insurance

Accident occurring in grounds of country house—Personal injuries—Judgment entered against defendant—Plaintiff failing to recover—Plaintiff seeking liberty to execute judgment against defendant's motor insurance company—Whether liability for which an approved policy of insurance required—Whether accident in a 'public place'—Road Traffic Act 1961, ss. 3, 56, 76. **Stanbridge v Healy** [1985] 290, HC.

Motor Insurers' Bureau of Ireland

Agreement—Interpretation—Ex gratia payments—Whether Bureau sole arbiter of conditions which might lead to making of such payment. **Bowes v Motor Insurers' Bureau of Ireland** [1990] 59, SC.

Repudiation

Fraud—Employer's liability insurance—Infant plaintiff sustaining serious injury in the course of employment—Lodgement of money into court—Mistaken assumption of liability induced by fraud—Policy repudiated—Whether plaintiff any title to the lodged money. RSC O 22 rr 4, 10, 13. **Carey v Ryan Ltd** [1982] 121, SC.

Life insurance policy
Interpretation. See Contract—Interpretation—Life insurance policy (*above*).

Repudiation of liabilities. See Contract—Repudiation—Life insurance policy (*above*).

Mortgage protection policy
Interpretation

Building society—Advertisement—Meaning of 'annual percentage rate of charge'—Whether cost of house insurance and mortgage protection insurance included—Consumer Information Act 1978, ss. 11, 12—Consumer Information (Consumer Credit) Order 1987, Art. 3. **Director of Consumer Affairs v Irish Permanent Building Society** [1990] 743, HC.

Motor vehicle
Generally. See MOTOR INSURANCE.

Offences. See ROAD TRAFFIC OFFENCES (Insurance).

INSURANCE *continued*
Policy
Benefits
Company—Benefits stated to be payable to company—Whether intention to pay benefits to employees—Whether company holding benefits in trust for employees. **McCann v Irish Board Mills** [1980] 216, HC.

Social welfare. *See* SOCIAL WELFARE (Employment contributions).

Treaty of reinsurance
Interpretation
Provision for inspection of books—Whether includes right to take photocopies— Dispute over selection of persons to inspect—Costs. **Winterthur Swiss Insurance Co v The Insurance Corporation of Ireland PLC** (Under Administration) [1989] 13, HC.

Uberrima fides. *See* Contract—*Uberrima fides (above)*.

INSURANCE COMPANY
Administration
Expenses
Administrator appointed receiver and manager of the property and assets of a body connected with the insurance company—Administrator's appointment ceasing upon appointment of liquidator—Administrator retaining certain funds to defray expenses— Whether certain items of expenditure be paid out by the retained funds. **In re PMPA Insurance Co** [1986] 524, HC; [1988] 109, SC.

INTEREST
Beneficial *See* BENEFICIAL INTEREST

Claim in quasi contract for money expended
Whether interest on sum payable. See QUASI-CONTRACT (Damages—Assessment).

Contract
Contract to build and sell a house
Completion—Interest—Dispute as to whether contract completed on certain dates— Basis on which interest to be awarded—Contract price placed on deposit—Interest gained on deposit. **Treacy v Dwyer Nolan Developments Ltd** [1979] 163, HC.

Specific performance
Contract for sale of land—Dispute as to whether contract completed on certain date—Basis on which interest to be awarded. **Treacy v Dwyer Nolan Developments Ltd** [1979] 163, HC.

Costs. *See* COSTS (Interest).

Damages award. *See* DAMAGES (Interest).

Judgment
Jurisdiction of Master of the High Court
Whether within the jurisdiction of the Master of the High Court to make an order as to interest. *See* PRACTICE (Judgment—Interest).

Partnership shares
Retirement of partner
Purchase of shares—Disagreement—Arbitration award—Whether interest payable on plaintiff's share of partnership assets. *See* PARTNERSHIP (Retirement of partner— Purchase of shares).

INTERLOCUTORY INJUNCTION. *See* INJUNCTION (Interlocutory).

INTERNATIONAL LAW
Conflict of laws. *See* PRIVATE INTERNATIONAL LAW.

INTERNATIONAL LAW *continued*
European Community law. *See* EUROPEAN COMMUNITY.

European Convention on Human Rights
  Application See EUROPEAN CONVENTION ON HUMAN RIGHTS

Extradition proceedings. *See* EXTRADITION.

Removal of child from jurisdiction. *See* CHILD (Custody—Removal from jurisdiction).

INTERNATIONAL RELATIONS
See CONSTITUTION (International relations).

INTERNATIONAL TREATY *See* CONSTITUTION (International relations—Treaty).

INTERPRETATION
Building contract. *See* BUILDING CONTRACT (Interpretation).

Constitution. *See* CONSTITUTION (Interpretation).

Contract. *See* CONTRACT (Construction).

Employment contract. *See* EMPLOYMENT (Contract—Construction).

Insurance contract. *See* INSURANCE (Contract—Interpretation).

Statute. *See* STATUTORY INTERPRETATION.

Will. *See* WILL (Construction).

INTERVENTION BY JUDGE
Trial. *See* JUDGE (Trial—Intervention).

INTERVENTION SCHEME
Common agricultural policy. *See* AGRICULTURE (Common agricultural policy—Intervention scheme).

INTESTACY *See* SUCCESSION (Intestacy).

INTIMIDATION
Landlord
  Damages
    Whether aggravated damages be awarded. **Whelan v Madigan** [1978] 136, HC.

INTOXICATING LIQUOR LICENSING *See* LICENSING ACTS.

INVALIDITY
Statute. *See* CONSTITUTION (Statute—Validity).

Ultra vires. *See* ULTRA VIRES.

INVENTION *See* PATENT.

IRELAND State. *See* STATE.

IRISH CONGRESS OF TRADE UNIONS
Disciplinary powers. *See* TRADE UNION (Discipline).

IRISH LAND COMMISSION *See* LAND COMMISSION.

IRISH LANGUAGE
Knowledge
  Appointment to post
    Requirement of knowledge of Irish language for appointment to full-time teaching post—Knowledge not required for performance of teaching duties—Compatibility

IRISH LANGUAGE
Knowledge
Appointment to post continued
with European Community law—EEC Treaty, Articles 48(3), 177—Council Regulation 1612/68, Article 3—Constitution of Ireland 1937, Article 8—Vocational Education Act 1930, s. 23. **Groener v Minister for Education** [1990] 335, ECJ.

Use in court
Whether Justice obliged to hear case in Irish without assistance of interpreter
Natural justice—Courts of Justice Act 1924, s. 71—Constitution of Ireland 1937, Article 8. **Ó Monacháin v An Taoiseach** [1986] 660, SC.

IRISH NATIONALITY AND CITIZENSHIP. *See* CITIZENSHIP.

ISSUE
Estoppel. *See* ESTOPPEL (Issue estoppel).

Meaning
Succession Act
Whether "issue" includes illegitimate child of deceased. *See* SUCCESSION (Intestacy—Illegitimate child).

JOINT TENANCY
Adverse possession
Next-of-kin of deceased owner remaining in possession
Whether interest of other next-of-kin defeated by adverse possession—Whether shares of those excluded from possession acquired as joint tenants or as tenants in common—Administration of Estates Act 1959, ss 13, 22—Succession Act 1965, s. 125(1). **Maher v Maher** [1987] 582, HC.

Partition
Order for sale in lieu of partition
Whether jurisdiction to make order extant—Repeal of statutory power by statute law revision legislation—Whether power existed prior to statutory power—Act for Joint Tenants 1542—Statute Law Revision (Pre-Union Irish Statutes) Act 1962, s. 2(1). **F F v C F** [1987] 1, HC.

JUDGE
Charge to jury
Medical negligence
General and approved practice—Failure of judge to draw jury's attention to legal principles applicable in cases of medical negligence—New trial ordered. **Dunne (an infant) v National Maternity Hospital** [1989] 735, SC.

Discretion
Exercise
Discretion to adjourn or to refuse to adjourn. **State (Pheasantry) Ltd v Donnelly** [1982] 512, HC.

Judicial function
Administration of justice. See CONSTITUTION (Courts—Administration of justice).

Judicial independence
Constitution. See CONSTITUTION (Courts—Judicial independence).

Jurisdiction
Reinstatement of dismissed appeal
Appeal against sentence—Judge indicating that if compensation were to be found

JUDGE
Jurisdiction
Reinstatement of dismissed appeal continued
within a prescribed time custodial sentence would not be imposed—Failure of accused to appear at adjourned appeals—Custodial sentences affirmed. **State (Dunne) v Martin** [1982] 18, SC.

Trial
Intervention
Interventions during conduct of defence—Whether excessive—Whether injustice resulted. **People (DPP) v Marley** [1985] 17, CCA.

Whether solicitor representing accused allowed proper opportunity to present case—Whether conviction made within jurisdiction—Whether judicial review appropriate remedy. **Gill v Connellan** [1988] 448, HC.

JUDGE'S RULES
Breach
Evidence
Admission of statement of accused—Discretion to exclude—Whether discretion should be exercised to introduce—Purpose of particular rule—Judge's Rules, Rule 9. **People (DPP) v Towson** [1978] 122, CCA.

JUDGMENT
Currency
Contract for the sale of goods
Money of account being Dutch guilders—Whether judgement could be given in foreign currency—Conversion rate. **Damen v O'Shea** [1976–7] 275, HC.

Proper law of contract
Whether a judgment for a sterling debt obtained at a time when the currencies of the State and of the United Kingdom were of equal value—Whether amount should be payable in Irish pounds or in sterling. **Northern Bank Ltd v Edwards** [1986] 167, SC.

Enforcement
Brussels Convention
Procedural requirements—Address for service within the jurisdiction—Judgment of a court of a contracting State—Evidence that judgments were ones to which the 1968 Convention applied—Appeal against enforcement order—RSC 1986, O 34—Jurisdiction of Courts and Enforcement of Judgments (European Communities) Act 1988, ss 3, 5—Convention on the Enforcement and Recognition of Judgments in Civil and Commercial Matters (1968), Articles 31, 32, 33, 34(1), 35, 36. **Rhatigan v Textiles y Confecciones Europeas SA** [1989] 659, HC; [1990] 825, SC.

Protective measures—Master of the High Court—Order for enforcement granted but protective measures refused—Whether Master entitled to refuse protective measures—Ex parte appeal to High Court—Whether judicial review for mandamus more appropriate—Jurisdiction of Courts and Enforcement of Judgments (European Communities) Act 1988, ss 5, 11(3), Schedules—Convention on the Enforcement and Recognition of Judgments in Civil and Commercial Matters (1968), Articles 24, 31, 39. **Elwyn (Cottons) Ltd v Pearle Designs Ltd** [1989] 162, HC.

Foreign judgment
Foreign divorce—Order requiring husband to pay lump sum in lieu of maintenance—Husband avoiding being made amenable to pay—Monies lodged in an Irish bank—Whether contrary to public policy for the court to grant aid in the execution of this payment. **Sachs v Standard Chartered Bank (Ireland) Ltd** [1987] 297, SC.

JUDGMENT *continued*
Evidence
Nullity
Non-consummation—Evidence indicating marriage was not consummated—Trial judge inferring collusion between parties—Whether inference open to judge—Natural justice—Whether rehearing required. **M v M** [1979] 160, SC.

Interest
Jurisdiction of Master of High Court
Monies due and owing for goods supplied and delivered—Matter coming before Master of the High Court—Order that plaintiff be at liberty to enter final judgment for amount claimed together with interest—Order made in default of appearance—Whether within the jurisdiction of the Master to make an order in respect of interest— Meaning of phrase 'judge of the High Court'—Matter coming before High Court for leave to enter judgment—Whether order for interest should be made—Summons not including a claim for interest—Whether relevant—Debtors (Ireland) Act 1840, s. 26—Courts Act 1981, ss 19(1), 22(1). **Mellowhide Products Ltd v Barry Agencies Ltd** [1983] 152, HC.

Precedent. *See* PRECEDENT.

JUDGMENT MORTGAGE
Family home
Registered judgment mortgage
No prior consent of wife—Whether a purported conveyance of husband's interest— Nature of judgment mortgage—Whether it comes into existence by operation of statute—Nature of wife's veto—Judgment Mortgage Act 1850, s. 6—Registration of Title Act 1964, ss 52, 71(4)—Family Home Protection Act 1976, s. 3. **Murray v Diamond** [1982] 113, HC.

Nature
Whether comes into existence by operation of statute
Judgment Mortgage Act 1850, s. 6. **Murray v Diamond** [1982] 113, HC.

JUDICIAL FUNCTION
Administration of justice. *See* CONSTITUTION (Administration of justice).

JUDICIAL INDEPENDENCE *See* CONSTITUTION (Courts—Judicial independence).

JUDICIAL NOTICE
Regulations
Road traffic offence
Evidence—Whether necessary for prosecution to give prima facie evidence of the regulations—Judge entitled to take notice of regulations—Documentary Evidence Act 1925, s. 4(1). **DPP v Collins** [1981] 447, SC.

JUDICIAL REVIEW
Administrative action
Test of irrationality
Whether decision fundamentally at variance with reason and common sense. **State (Keegan) v Stardust Victims Compensation Tribunal** [1987] 202, HC, SC.

Administrative authority
Discretionary powers
Exercise—Resolution by county council directing county manager to grant planning permission—Manager refusing to comply with resolution——Whether reasonable— Certiorari—Mandamus. **P & F Sharpe Ltd v Dublin City and County Manager** [1989] 565, HC, SC.

JUDICIAL REVIEW *continued*

Alternative remedy available

Appeal

Employment Appeals Tribunal determination—Whether bad on its face—Whether certiorari be granted—Whether more appropriate to appeal to Circuit Court—Unfair Dismissals Act 1977, s. 10(4). **Mythen v Employment Appeals Tribunal** [1989] 844, HC.

Appeal by way of case stated

District Court conviction—Whether certiorari appropriate remedy. **Gill v Connellan** [1988] 448, HC.

Whether restrictive on certiorari proceedings

Planning. **State (Abenglen Properties Ltd) v Dublin Corporation** [1981] 54, HC; [1982] 590, SC.

Availability of relief

District Court conviction

Alternative remedy of appeal by way of case stated—Whether certiorari appropriate remedy. **Gill v Connellan** [1988] 448, HC.

Tribunal

Decision—Whether subject to judicial review—Natural justice—Criminal Injuries Compensation Scheme. **State (Hayes) v Criminal Injuries Compensation Tribunal** [1982] 210, HC.

Ultra vires decision

Decision plainly and unambiguously at variance with fundamental reason and common sense—Implied constitutional limitation of jurisdiction. **State (Keegan) v Stardust Victims Compensation Tribunal** [1987] 202, HC, SC.

Certiorari. *See* CERTIORARI.

Constitutionality of legislation

Whether certiorari an appropriate procedure for challenging validity of legislation. See CERTIORARI (Constitutionality of legislation).

Costs

Availabilty

Order to extend time for appeal against decision of Employment Appeals Tribunal—Order made in excess of jurisdiction—Whether order for costs as against Circuit Court judge valid—Whether Attorney General liable to indemnity in respect of costs. **McIlwraith v Fawsitt** [1990] 1, SC.

Criminal law

Procedure

Conviction in District Court—Appeal to Circuit Court—Applicant remanded in custody in accordance with Circuit Court procedure—Whether valid remand—Whether judicial review available—Criminal Procedure Act 1967, s. 24. **Maguire v O'Hanrahan** [1988] 243, HC.

Declaratory relief. *See* DECLARATION.

Delay in applying. *See* CERTIORARI (Delay).

Director of Public Prosecutions

Opinion

Return for trial on non-scheduled offences to Special Criminal Court—Whether opinion of DPP reviewable by the court—Constitution of Ireland 1937, Article 38.3.1—Offences Against the State Act 1939, ss 35, 45, 46(2)—Prosecution of Offences Act 1974, s. 3. **Savage v DPP** [1982] 385, HC.

Discretion of court

Factors guiding court in exercise of its discretion. **State (Litzouw) v Johnson** [1981] 273, HC.

JUDICIAL REVIEW *continued*
Extradition
Jurisdiction of District Court
Extradition Act 1965, Part III. **Carron v McMahon** [1990] 802, SC.

Farm tax office
Discontinuance of farm tax
Termination of appointment of farm tax inspectors—Whether *ultra vires*—Appointment made in acting capacity—Whether inspectors having legitimate expectation of permanent appointment—Whether inspectors locus standi to challenge decision to cease to charge any levy farm tax—Civil Service Commissioner Act 1956, s. 20—Farm Tax Act 1985, ss 4, 9, 14—Constitution of Ireland 1937, Articles 15.2.1, 28.2. **Duggan v An Taoiseach** [1989] 710, HC.

Function of court
Administrative action
Proper purpose of remedy—Court having no function to substitute its opinion for that of lawfully constituted authority. **State (Keegan) v Stardust Victims Compensation Tribunal** [1987] 202, HC, SC.

Domestic tribunal
Exercise of discretion—Validity—Whether court entitled to review exercise of discretion where tribunal acted honestly and reasonably—Whether discretion exercised *ultra vires*. **McGrath v Maynooth College** [1979] 166, SC.

Harbour authority
Licence
Refusal—Tug operating licence—Whether licence necessary for the operation of tugs in the Shannon Estuary—Whether applicant entitled to damages—Whether applicant entitled to be told of criteria employed in and the reasons for the decision. **C W Shipping Company Ltd v Limerick Harbour Commissioners** [1989] 416, HC.

Incorporated Law Society
System of entry into Law School
Whether limit on numbers imposed—Examination—Compensation rules—Whether Education Committee acted arbitrarily—Solicitors Act 1954 (Apprenticeship and Education) (Amendment No 1) Regulations 1974—Solicitors Acts 1954 and 1960 (Apprenticeship and Education) Regulations 1975. **MacGabhann v Incorporated Law Society of Ireland** [1989] 854, HC.

Jurisdiction
Tribunal
Decision—Whether subject to judicial review—Natural justice—Criminal Injuries Compensation Scheme. **State (Hayes) v Criminal Injuries Compensation Tribunal** [1982] 210, HC.

Labour Court determination. *See* LABOUR COURT

Locus standi
Challenge to act of executive
Farm tax office—Discontinuance of farm tax—Termination of appointment of farm tax inspectors. *See* Farm tax office—Discontinuance of farm tax *(above)*.

Local authority
Estimates meeting—Whether resolution adopting estimates null and void—Whether meeting conducted in accordance with natural justice—Whether councillor having locus standi to seek judicial review of meeting—Appropriate relief—RSC 1986, O 84 r 26(4)—City and County Management (Amendment) Act 1955, s. 10(1), (4). **Ahern v Kerry Co Council** [1988] 392, HC.

Mandamus. *See* MANDAMUS.

JUDICIAL REVIEW *continued*
Ministerial decision
Nature of decision
Whether administrative or judicial—Public Service—Staff associations—New Staff association seeking negotiation from Minister for the Public Service—Refusal of recognition— Whether refusal of recognition supported by evidence before Minister. **Inspector of Taxes' Association v Minister for Public Service** [1986] 296, SC.

Prohibition. *See* PROHIBITION.

Remand in custody
Circuit Court procedure
Whether valid remand—Whether judicial review available—Criminal Procedure Act 1967, s. 24. **Maguire v O'Hanrahan** [1988] 243, HC.

Restraint of trade
Regulation
Equestrian Federation—Prohibition of use of non-Irish horses by Irish showjumpers in international competitions—Fair and equal position to be given in competitive arena—Whether prohibition *ultra vires.* **Macken v O'Reilly** [1979] 79, HC, SC.

Revenue
Decision of Collector-General
Tax clearance certificates—Circumstances in which mandamus will lie. **State (Melbarian Enterprises Ltd) v Revenue Commissioners** [1986] 476, HC.

Disclosure of information
Notice served by Revenue Commissioners requiring information—Whether notice ultra vires —Whether notice unduly burdensome and oppressive—Finance Act 1974, s. 59. **Warnock v Revenue Commissioners** [1986] 37, HC.

Income tax
Appeal Commissioner's findings—Extent of judicial review of findings of fact by Appeal Commissioner—Nature of case stated—Income Tax Act 1967, s. 1, Schedule D—Finance (Miscellaneous Provisions) Act 1968, s. 17. **Mara v Hummingbird Ltd** [1982] 421, HC, SC.

School
Admission of students
Criteria applied—Whether subject to judicial review. **Ó hUallachain v Burke** [1988] 693, HC.

Statute
Operation of section
Section to come into operation on day fixed by governmental order—Application for an order of mandamus requiring government to make such order. *See* MANDAMUS (Statute—Operation of section).

Validity
Constitution—Whether certiorari an appropriate procedure for challenging validity of legislation. *See* CERTIORARI (Constitutionality of legislation).

Tribunal
Generally. See TRIBUNAL.

Ultra vires
Administrative body
Regulation in restraint of trade—Prohibition of use of non-Irish horses by Irish showjumpers in international competitions. **Macken v O'Reilly** [1979] 79, HC, SC.

University
Committee of discipline
Charge of plagiarism—Natural justice—Whether fair procedures followed—Whether committee required to act judicially. **Flanagan v University College Dublin** [1989] 469, HC.

JURISDICTION
Courts
Constitution. See CONSTITUTION (Courts—Jurisdiction).

Specific courts. See under individual courts.

Removal of child from jurisdiction. See CHILD (Custody—Removal from jurisdiction).

Service out of jurisdiction. See PRACTICE (Service out of jurisdiction).

JURISDICTIONAL ERROR See CERTIORARI.

JURY
Coroner's court
Verdict. See INQUEST (Verdict).

Direction
Admissibility of evidence
Identification parade—Objection by accused to participation—Requirement as to direction of jury. **People (DPP) v Marley** [1985] 17, CCA.

Medical negligence
Conflicting medical evidence—Duty of judge in civil cases—Whether jury appropriately directed—Failure of judge to draw jury's attention to legal principles applicable in cases of medical negligence. **Dunne (an infant) v National Maternity Hospital** [1989] 735, SC.

Findings of fact
Appeal
Supreme Court—Jurisdiction to set aside finding. **Dunne (An infant) v National Maternity Hospital** [1989] 735, SC.

Evidence
Sufficiency—Whether evidence before the jury to support certain of its findings—Whether findings should be set aside—Conflicting medical evidence—Duty of judge in civil cases—Whether jury appropriately directed. **Dunne (an infant) v National Maternity Hospital** [1989] 735, SC.

Statutory exclusion of issue of fact from jury
Statute authorising District Justice to decide issue of fact—Decision of District Justice to be final and unappealable—Constitution—Validity—Constitution of Ireland 1937, Articles 34.3.4, 38.1, 38.2, 38.5. **Curtis v Attorney General** [1986] 428, HC.

Function
Defamation trial
Judge determining words were defamatory—Whether usurping role of jury. **Barrett v Independent Newspapers Ltd** [1986] 601, SC.

Right to trial by jury
Criminal law
Nature of offence—Whether minor offence triable summarily. See CONSTITUTION (Trial of offences—Minor offence).

Requirement to inform accused as to right—Failure to inform accused—Prosecutor tried summarily and convicted on two charges—Validity. See CERTIORARI (Conviction—Validity—Scheduled offence—Summary trial only with consent of accused).

Scheduled offence—Summary trial only with consent of accused—Statutory requirement first to inform the accused of his right to be tried with a jury before proceeding in a summary manner. **State (McDonagh) v Sheerin** [1981] 149, HC.

Personal injuries action
Proceedings commenced in High Court—Motion to remit case to District or Circuit

JURY
Right to trial by jury
Personal injuries action continued
Court—Damages likely to be within District Court jurisdiction—Whether plaintiff right to a jury trial—Courts of Justice Act 1924, s. 94—Courts Act 1971, s. 6. **McDonald v Galvin** [1976–7] 41, HC.

Trial
Absence of some members of jury during direction by judge
Whether trial unsatisfactory. **People (DPP) v Marley** [1985] 17, CCA.

Change of venue
Criminal trial—Courthouse destroyed by fire—Whether right to be tried by jury from any particular locality. **State (Hughes) v Neylon** [1982] 108, HC.

Verdict
Inquest. See INQUEST (Verdict).

Jurisdiction of Court of Criminal Appeal
Whether Court of Criminal Appeal has jurisdiction to substitute its own subjective view of evidence for the verdict of a jury. **People (DPP) v Egan** [1990] 780, SC.

Not guilty verdict
Whether open to DPP to bring appeal against such verdict. *See* CRIMINAL LAW (Acquittal—Appeal).

JUVENILE OFFENDER. *See* CRIMINAL LAW (Young offender).

LABOUR COURT
Determination
Appeal to High Court
Jurisdiction—Employment equality—Labour Court finding that discrimination occurred being based on uncontested assumptions of fact—Whether open to High Court to require these facts to be proved—Employment Equality Act 1977, s. 2(c). **North Western Health Board v Martyn** [1988] 519, SC.

Judicial review
Application to quash—Employment equality—Whether error of law as to jurisdiction—Employment Equality Act 1977, ss. 19, 20. **State (Aer Lingus Teo) v Labour Court** [1987] 373, HC, SC.

Application to quash—Whether Labour Court acted without jurisdiction—Equal pay determination—Comparator used not named in union's original submission—Whether Labour Court acted in breach of principles of natural justice in taking legal advice on its jurisdiction in the absence of the parties—Certiorari—Extent of court's discretion to refuse to grant order—Anti-Discrimination (Pay) Act 1974,s 7. **State (Polymark (Irl) Ltd) v Labour Court** [1987] 357, HC.

Jurisdiction
Appeal from equality officer
Labour Court refusing to entertain appeal—Whether correct—ssues raised by some of the grounds of appeal governed by earlier decision of court—Judicial review—Employment Equality Act 1977, s. 19. **Aer Rianta v Labour Court** [1990] 193, HC.

Procedure
Employment equality
Jurisdiction—Appeal from equality officer—Whether jurisdiction to deal with the issue of discrimination outside six month period—Judicial review—Appellate nature of Labour Court—Function in disputes as to whether discrimination has occurred—Employment Equality Act 1977, s. 19. **Aer Rianta v Labour Court** [1990] 193, HC.

LABOUR COURT
Procedure
Employment equality continued
Jurisdiction—Complaint of discrimination—Referral to Equality Officer—Objection to jurisdiction—Whether Labour Court erred in law—Whether Labour Court has a discretion as to whether to hold a preliminary hearing as to receivability—Employment Equality Act 1977, s. 19(5). **Aer Lingus Teo v Labour Court** [1990] 485, HC, SC.

LABOUR INJUNCTION
Trade dispute
Picketing
Application to restrain. *See* INJUNCTION (Interlocutory—Trade dispute—Picketing).

LABOUR LAW *See* EMPLOYMENT; TRADE DISPUTE; TRADE UNION

LACHES *See* EQUITY (Laches).

LAKES AND RIVERS
Fishing rights
Outdoor education centre
Canoeing—Interference with fishing—Ownership of bed and soil of lake and river—Whether plaintiff entitled only to a *profit-a-prendre*—Form of injunction. **Tennent v Clancy** [1988] 214, HC.

LAND
Action for possession
Local authority building on land belonging to another
Owner only becoming aware of situation when houses virtually complete—Whether owner estopped—Conduct of both parties—Failure to fence off land—Circumstances of acquisition of property—Land possessing no intrinsic value—Compensation—Right of local authority to be registered as owner—**McMahon v Kerry County Council** [1981] 419, HC.

Administrator
Limitation of actions. *See* SUCCESSION (Administration—Administrator seeking to recover possession of land).

Adverse possession. *See* ADVERSE POSSESSION.

Agricultural land
Valuation
Valuation unrelated to present-day circumstances—Whether unjust attack on property rights. *See* AGRICULTURAL LAND (Valuation).

Annuity
Redemption
Incorrect assessment of redemption value—Mistake—Overpayment—Whether recoverable—Housing Act 1966, s. 99. **Rogers v Louth Co Council** [1981] 144, SC.

Compulsory acquisition. *See* COMPULSORY PURCHASE.

Charge on land. *See* REAL PROPERTY (Incumbrance—Charge).

Charge on land
Mortgage. See MORTGAGE.

Compulsory acquisition. *See* COMPULSORY PURCHASE.

Conveyance. *See* SALE OF LAND (Conveyance)

Development
Planning control. See PLANNING.

LAND *continued*
Easement
Right of way. See EASEMENT (Right of way).

Grazing letting
Letting on eleven-month system
No memorandum or note in writing—Dispute over date of termination—Plaintiff required to leave before end of eleven months—Whether eleven month system adopted. **Collins v O'Brien** [1981] 328, HC.

Incumbrance
Lis pendens. See REAL PROPERTY (Incumbrance—Lis pendens).

Occupation
Licence
Expiry—Adverse possession. *See* LICENCE (Occupation of lands—Expiry).

Partition
Order for sale in lieu of partition
Joint tenancy—Whether jurisdiction to make order extant. *See* JOINT TENANCY (Partition).

Preservation order
National monument on land
Effect of order—Prohibition on ploughing or disturbing the ground within or near the monument—Constitution—Validity—Whether unjust attack on property rights. *See* NATIONAL MONUMENT (Preservation order).

Reclaimed land
Valuation
Whether such land may be valued by Commissioner of Valuation. *See* RATING AND VALUATION (Reclaimed land).

Recovery of possession. *See* Action for possession (*above*).

Registered land
Inhibition. See REGISTRATION OF TITLE (Inhibition).

Registration. *See* REGISTRATION OF TITLE.

Transfer
Deed
Reservation of right of residence, care and support—Application to cancel transfer— Whether undue influence. **Leonard v Leonard** [1988] 245, HC.

Valuation. *See* RATING AND VALUATION.

LAND ACTS
Compulsory purchase. *See* COMPULSORY PURCHASE (Land Acts).

LAND COMMISSION
Acquisition of lands
Generally. See COMPULSORY PURCHASE (Land Acts).

Procedure
Natural justice—Objectors' application for sight of certain documents refused— Whether procedure adopted fair and in accordance with principles of natural justice— Land Act 1965, ss. 12, 45. **State (Hussey) v Irish Land Commission** [1983] 407, HC.

Sale of land
Condition of sale that contract dependent on Land Commission approval
Whether prospective purchaser has standing to object to compulsory acquisition of the land—Land Act 1923, s. 40(6). **State (Callaghan) v Irish Land Commission** [1978] 201, SC.

LAND COMMISSION *continued*

Vesting

Building ground excepted from scheme of general vesting

Application by tenant to have Land Commission acquire landlord's interest—Whether acquisition in the interest of the country—Land Act 1923, s. 24—Land Act 1939, s. 40(1). **In re Estate of Soden** [1985] 685, SC.

LANDLORD AND TENANT

Action

Settlement

Authority of legal adviser—Consent order—Settlement not in writing—Denial by plaintiffs that action settled—Validity of order—Authority of legal advisers to negotiate and settle. **Barrett v W J Lenehan & Co Ltd** [1981] 206, HC.

Action for possession. *See* Ejectment (*below*).

Arbitration

Dispute as to construction of rent review clause

Whether improvements lawfully made by the lessee to be taken into account in fixing rent. **Hynes Ltd v O'Malley Property Ltd** [1989] 619, SC.

Assignment of lease

Refusal of consent

Premises in shopping centre—Proposed assignee a financial institution—Landlord withholding consent—Avoidance of dead frontages—Whether reason based on valid estate management ground. **O H S. Ltd v Green Property Co** [1986] 451, HC.

Breach of covenant

Forfeiture. See Forfeiture (*below*).

Quiet enjoyment

Interference by landlord—Trespass—Intimidation—Application for damages and injunction—Whether aggravated damages be awarded—Whether damages recoverable for breach of covenant to repair—Landlord and Tenant (Ireland) Act 1860, ss. 17, 41—Landlord and Tenant Act 1930, s. 55. **Whelan v Madigan** [1978] 136, HC.

Premises being authorised structure—Failure to obtain planning permission—Whether breach of covenant for quiet enjoyment—Landlord and Tenant Law Amendment (Ireland) Act 1860, s. 41. **Fitzpatrick v Frank McGivern Ltd** [1976–7] 239, HC.

Repair

Whether damages recoverable for breach of covenant to repair—Landlord and Tenant (Ireland) Act 1860, ss. 17, 41—Landlord and Tenant Act 1930, s. 55. **Whelan v Madigan** [1978] 136, HC.

Case stated

Compensation

Appeal against award. *See* Compensation for disturbance—Assessment—Case stated (*below*).

Compensation for disturbance

Assessment

Case stated—Application for new tenancy refused—Appeal against award of compensation—Landlord subsequently offering to grant 21 year lease—Whether court when fixing compensation entitled to treat subsequent offer of new lease as relevant consideration—Landlord and Tenant Act 1931, ss. 22, 23—Courts of Justice Act 1936, s. 38. **Aherne v Southern Metropole Hotel Co Ltd** [1989] 693, SC.

Covenant

Breach. See Breach of covenant (*above*).

LANDLORD AND TENANT

Covenant *continued*

Enforcement

Restraint of trade—Solus agreement—Injunction—Principles to be applied—Negative covenants. **Irish Shell Ltd v Elm Motors Ltd** [1984] 595, SC.

Restriction as to user

Premises in shopping centre—Change of use—Consent—Refusal—Landlord withholding consent—Avoidance of dead frontages—Whether reason based on valid estate management grounds. **O H S. Ltd v Green Property Co** [1986] 451, HC.

Retail units in shopping centre—Subletting—Different use—No consent in writing—Proceedings to restrain breach of covenant—Whether plaintiff estopped from enforcing covenant. **Green Property Co Ltd v Shalaine Modes Ltd** [1978] 222, HC.

Tenant seeking permission for change of user—Landlord refusing consent—Whether refusal unreasonable—Objections from other tenants—Whether landlord likely to suffer loss. **White v Carlisle Trust Ltd** [1976–7] 311, HC.

Disclaimer of onerous lease

Company in liquidation

Application to disclaim lease—Whether lease "onerous"—Position of guarantors—Whether the disclaimer would end the liability of the guarantors—Companies Act 1963, s. 290. **Tempany v Royal Liver Trustees Ltd** [1984] 273, HC.

Ejectment

New tenancy application. See New tenancy—Ejectment proceedings—Order of possession stayed pending appeal (*below*).

Notice to Quit

Local authority tenant—Corporation flat—District Court hearing—Tenant not represented—Tenant not invited to give evidence—Possession awarded to Corporation—Whether hearing in breach of natural justice—Housing Act 1966, s. 62. **State (Crothers) v Kelly** [1978] 167, HC.

Local authority tenant—No explanation given nor complaint brought to tenant's attention—Requests for explanation unanswered—District Court order for possession—Appeal to Circuit Court—Application to High Court to make absolute a conditional order of certiorari—Whether Corporation obliged to give evidence of motive or justification—Whether form of notice to quit and demand for possession correct—Landlord and Tenant Law (Amendment) Act 1860, ss. 86, 87, 88—Housing Act 1966, ss. 62, 118. **State (Litzouw) v Johnson** [1981] 273, HC.

Forfeiture

Breach of covenant

Re-entry by landlord—Whether peaceable—Conveyancing and Law of Property Act 1881, s. 14. **F G Sweeney Ltd v Powerscourt Shopping Centre Ltd** [1985] 442, HC.

Claim by 'underlessee' for relief

Person 'claiming as underlessee' having unenforceable agreement with tenant for a sub-lease—Whether claim maintainable—Application for interlocutory injunction—Conveyancing Act 1892, ss. 4, 5—Landlord and Tenant (Amendment) Act 1980, s. 78. **Enock v Lambert Jones Estates Ltd** [1983] 532, HC.

Recovery of possession of premises

Lease-holder assigning interest without consent of owner—Change of use—Whether evidence entitling leaseholder to relief from forfeiture—Discretion of court to order lease to vest in under-lessee—Whether equitable to force owner into privity of contract with under-lessee—Conveyancing Act 1892, s. 4—Conveyancing and Law of Property Act 1881. **O'Connor v J G Mooney & Co Ltd** [1982] 373, HC.

LANDLORD AND TENANT
Forfeiture *continued*
Relief against forfeiture

Liquidation of company—Sale of interest in lease—Whether proceeds belong to company or lessor—Whether s. 2 applicable to limited companies—Conveyancing Act 1882, ss. 2, 3, 14. **MCB Galway Ltd v Industrial Development Authority** [1981] 58, SC.

Ground rent
Purchase of fee simple

Fixing of price in absence of agreement—Whether provisions regarding purchase workable—Impossibility of determining rent—Landlord and Tenant (Reversionary Leases) Act 1958 s. 18—Landlord and Tenant (Ground Rents) Act 1967 s. 18—Landlord and Tenant (Ground Rents) (No 2) Act 1978, s. 17. **Gilsenan v Foundary House Investments Ltd** [1980] 273, SC.

Lease
Assignment. See Assignment (*above*).

Disclaimer. See Disclaimer of onerous lease (*above*).

Forfeiture. See Forfeiture (*above*).

Option to purchase fee simple

Price calculation as if rent were a ground rent—Whether option enforceable—Whether refusal of county registrar to deal with matter subject to arbitration—Arbitration Act 1954, s. 18—Landlord and Tenant (Ground Rents) Act 1967, ss. 17, 22. **Carr v Phelan** [1976–7] 149, HC.

Rent review clause. See Rent—Rent review clause (*below*).

Licence or lease
Agreement

Letting of site and equipment of garage—Occupation of premises under successive yearly agreements—Nature of agreements—Whether licence or lease—Landlord and Tenant (Ireland) Act 1860, s. 3. **Irish Shell & BP Ltd v John Costello Ltd** [1981] 66, SC.

Termination—Agreement to allow occupation and user of premises—Agreement held to constitute tenancy—Continued occupation and user—Whether constitute licence to occupy or tenancy—Whether tenancy at will or tenancy from month to month for a time uncertain—Intention of the parties. **Irish Shell & BP Ltd v John Costello Ltd** [1985] 554, SC.

New tenancy
Ejectment proceedings

Order of possession stayed pending appeal—Application for new tenancy under new legislation—Whether deliberate omission from the benefits of the new legislation of a tenant who had a decree of ejectment against him—Interpretation of words "or otherwise"—Interpretation Act 1931, s. 21—Landlord and Tenant (Amendment) Act 1980, ss. 11, 29. **Kenny v Quinn** [1981] 385, CC.

Entitlement

Periodic letting—Tenancy not yet determined—Tenant fearful of a possible sale and determination—Application for a declaration of entitlement to a new tenancy—Landlord and Tenant (Amendment) Act 1980, ss. 13, 17, 20, 21. **Mealiffe v G N Walsh Ltd** [1987] 301, HC.

Existing statutory right

Tenancy granted by Circuit Court—Appeal pending when new legislation introduced—Whether existing rights affected—Whether new legislation operated with retroactive effect—Landlord and Tenant (Amendment) Act 1980, ss. 23(5), 29. **Caulfield v D H Bourke and Son Ltd** [1980] 223, HC.

LANDLORD AND TENANT
New tenancy *continued*
Notice of intention to claim relief
Lessor having no reversion in tenement—Notice served on superior landlord—Whether lessor served a copy of such notice on superior landlord—Amount of new rent—Landlord and Tenant (Ireland) Act 1860, s. 5—Landlord and Tenant Act 1931,ss 2, 24, 25, 31, 33. **Eamonn Andrews Productions Ltd v Gaiety Theatre** (Dublin) Ltd [1976–7] 119, HC.

Time for service—Notice not served within statutory period—Whether time should be extended—Landlord and Tenant Act 1931, ss. 24, 31. **The Grey Door Hotel Company Ltd v Pembroke Trust Ltd** [1976–7] 14, HC.

Time for service—Periodic letting—Tenancy not yet determined—Tenant fearful of a possible sale and determination—Application for a declaration of entitlement to a new tenancy—Whether tenant can serve notice of intention to claim relief prior to service of notice to quit—Whether tenant entitled to apply to have tenancy determined when no notice to quit has been served—Landlord and Tenant (Amendment) Act 1980, ss. 13, 17, 20, 21. **Mealiffe v G N Walsh Ltd** [1987] 301, HC.

Refusal
Good estate management—Compensation—Appeal against award of compensation—Landlord subsequently offering to grant 21 year lease—Case stated—Whether court when fixing compensation entitled to treat subsequent offer of new lease as relevant consideration—Landlord and Tenant Act 1931, ss. 22, 23—Courts of Justice Act 1936, s. 38. **Aherne v Southern Metropole Hotel Co Ltd** [1989] 693, SC.

Rent
Calculation—Commercial premises—Theatre—Fixing of new rent—Appeal—Comparison with other premises—Rent based on covenants in former lease concerning repairs and insurance—Responsibility for repair and insurance—Landlord and Tenant Act 1931, s. 29(f)—Landlord and Tenant Acts 1931 to 1978. **Olympia Productions Ltd v Olympia Theatres Ltd** [1981] 424, HC.

Calculation—Inability of valuers to fix rent—Uncertain economic climate—Jurisdiction of Circuit Court to fix an inflationary rent—Whether contrary to public policy—Case stated—Landlord and Tenant Act 1931, ss. 27, 29. **McGovern v Governors and Guardians of Jervis Street Hospital** [1981] 197, SC.

Rent
Fixing of rent
Landlord' repairing obligation not complied with—Whether rent should be fixed on the basis that the premises are in good repair—Whether allowance be made for future inflation—Housing (Private Rented Dwellings) Act 1982, ss. 12 (2), 13. **Dowd v Pierce** [1984] 653, CC.

New tenancy application. *See* New tenancy—Rent—Calculation (*above*).

Rent review clause—Interpretation—Arbitration—Whether improvements lawfully made by the lessee to be taken into account in fixing rent. **Hynes Ltd v O'Malley Property Ltd** [1989] 619, SC.

Rent tribunal—Application to fix gross rent—Dispute over landlord's income—Tribunal refusing tenant's request for more information as to landlord's means—Whether tribunal erred in law—Housing (Private Rented Dwellings) Act 1982, s. 13. **Quirke v Folio Homes Ltd** [1988] 496, SC.

Rent review clause
Dispute going to arbitration—Arbitrator required to determine the rent a willing lessee not in occupation would give—Whether lessor should be excluded as a prospective lessee. **Macey Ltd v Tylers Ltd** [1978] 82, HC.

LANDLORD AND TENANT
Rent
Rent review clause continued

Interpretation—Arbitration—Dispute as to construction of rent review clause—Whether improvements lawfully made by the lessee to be taken into account in fixing rent. **Hynes Ltd v O'Malley Property Ltd** [1989] 619, SC.

Validity—Enforcement—Estoppel—Multiplier clause—Rent far in excess of current commercial rent—Whether clause designed to put tenant under compelling pressure to surrender—Surrender excluding tenant from right to claim new tenancy—Whether lessor estopped from enforcing clause—Landlord and Tenant (Amendment) Act 1980, ss. 17(1)(a)(iii), 23, 24, 85. **Bank of Ireland v Fitzmaurice** [1989] 452, HC.

Validity—Multiplier clause—Rent following recalculation in accordance with multiplier clause far in excess of current commercial rent—Whether clause designed to put tenant under compelling pressure to surrender—Whether clause invalidated—Whether lessor estopped from enforcing clause—Landlord and Tenant (Amendment) Act 1980, ss. 17(1)(a)(iii), 23, 24, 85. **Bank of Ireland v Fitzmaurice** [1989] 452, HC.

Rent Restrictions Acts
Bill

Validity—Constitution—Bill affecting rent and security of tenure—Landlords receiving an amount of rent substantially less than the market rent—Whether unjust attack on their property rights—Constitution of Ireland 1937, Articles 26, 40 3 2—**In re Housing (Private Rented Dwellings) Bill 1981** [1983] 246, SC.

Controlled dwelling

Arbitrary definition of controlled dwellings—Failure to provide for review—Permanent alienation of right of possession—Statute—Validity—Constitution—Whether unjust attack on property rights of landlords—Social effect of Court's decision—Jurisdiction in future claims for possession—Constitution of Ireland 1937, Articles 40, 43—Rent Restrictions Act 1960 and 1967—Landlord and Tenant (Amendment) Act 1971. **Blake and Madigan v Attorney General** [1981] 34, SC.

Landlords claiming letting was "furnished letting"—Residential flat—Monthly tenancy—Purported termination—Whether controlled dwelling—Rent included payment for the use of furniture—Apportionment of rent as between flat and furnishings—Rent Restrictions Act 1960, s. 3(2)(d). **Fridberg v Doyle** [1981] 370, CC.

Statutory tenancy
Decontrolled premises

Death of tenant intestate—Whether acceptance of widow as tenant precluded landlord from denying that the contractual tenancy had passed to her—Whether dependant entitled to statutory tenancy on death of contractual tenant—Landlord and Tenant Act 1931, Part III—Rent Restrictions Act 1950, ss. 2(1), 31(3)—Rent Restrictions (Amendment) Act 1967, ss. 2(4), 13(2) (3). **Byrne v O'Neill** [1979] 47, SC.

Termination of tenancy
Natural justice

Corporation flat—Notice to quit and demand for possession—District Court hearing—Tenant not represented—Tenant not invited to give evidence—Possession awarded to Corporation—Whether hearing in breach of natural justice—Housing Act 1966, s. 62. **State (Crothers) v Kelly & Ors** [1978] 167, HC.

Notice to quit. See Ejectment—Notice to quit (*above*).

Overholding

Agreement to allow occupation and user of premises—Agreement held to constitute tenancy—Continued occupation and user—Whether constitute licence to occupy or tenancy—Intention of the parties. **Irish Shell & BP Ltd v John Costello Ltd** [1985] 554, SC.

LANDOWNER
Duty of care
Tree adjacent to highway
Tree falling to ground and damaging passing car—Whether landowner in breach of a duty of care—Whether tree a danger to persons using the highway. **Lynch v Hetherton** [1990] 857, HC.

LANGUAGE *See* IRISH LANGUAGE.

LARCENY *See* CRIMINAL LAW (Larceny).

LAW SOCIETY *See* INCORPORATED LAW SOCIETY.

LAWYER *See* BARRISTER; SOLICITOR. *See also* LEGAL PROFESSION.

LEASE *See* LANDLORD AND TENANT (Lease).

LEGAL ADVICE
Privilege
Discovery of documents
Correspondence between client and solicitor—Whether distinction between legal advice and legal assistance. **Smurfit Paribas Bank Ltd v AAB Export Finance Ltd** [1990] 588, SC.

LEGAL ADVISER *See* SOLICITOR.

LEGAL AID
Civil legal aid
Family law
Custody and maintenance proceedings—Matter coming before the High Court on a number of occasions—Defendant unable to continue paying costs of legal representation—Application for civil legal aid refused—Whether defendant's right of access to the courts infringed—European Convention on Human Rights—Whether State bound by Convention—Scheme for Civil Legal Aid and Advice 1979 paras 4, 7. **E v E** [1982] 497, HC.

Criminal legal aid. See CRIMINAL LAW (Legal aid).

LEGAL COSTS *See* COSTS.

LEGAL PROFESSION
Barrister. *See* BARRISTER

Education
Solicitors
System of entry to law school. *See* SOLICITOR (Entry to profession).

Privilege
Discovery of documents. See DISCOVERY (Privilege—Legal professional privilege).

Solicitor. *See* SOLICITOR.

LEGAL RIGHT
Spouse. *See* SUCCESSION (Legal right).

LEGISLATION *See* STATUTE.
Validity
Constitution. See CONSTITUTION (Statute—Validity).

LEGITIMACY *See* ILLEGITIMATE CHILD.

LEGITIMATE EXPECTATION
Agricultural producer
Claim for payment of debt
Claim in respect of deductions made by Pigs and Bacon Commission—Whether claim statute-barred—Whether legitimate expectation that plaintiff's claim would be satisfactorily discharged in due course—European Community law—Prohibition against defeat by government agency of legitimate expectation of agricultural producers—Whether government agency estopped from pleading statute—Statute of Limitations 1957, ss. 3, 11, 56—European Communities Act 1972, s. 2. **Smith v Ireland** [1983] 300, HC.

Education
Admission of students to school
Whether parents had any legitimate expectation as to criteria to be applied. **O hUallachain v Burke** [1988] 693, HC.

Employment
Farm tax office
Discontinuance of farm tax—Termination of appointment of farm tax inspectors—Judicial review—Whether inspectors having legitimate expectation of permanent appointment. *See* JUDICIAL REVIEW (Farm tax office—Discontinuance of farm tax).

Teacher *See* Ministerial decision—Estoppel (*below*).

Local authority
Estimates meeting
Whether resolution adopting estimates null and void—Whether meeting conducted in accordance with natural justice—Whether councillor having legitimate expectation that meeting would consider each estimate separately—Judicial review—Form of relief—RSC 1986, O 84 r 26(4)—City and County Management (Amendment) Act 1955, ss. 10(1), 10(4). **Ahern v Kerry Co Council** [1988] 392, HC.

Ministerial decision
Estoppel
Exercise of statutory discretion—Appointment of teacher—Whether Minister estopped from exercising discretion to refuse to appoint applicant as teacher—Whether applicant had legitimate expectation that she would be appointed—Vocational Education Act 1930, ss. 23, 30. **Devitt v Minister for Education** [1989] 639, HC.

Promissory estoppel
Garda Síochána
Conciliation and Arbitration scheme—Changes proposed—Plaintiffs claiming legitimate expectation that they would be consulted before changes implemented—Ministerial statement made in Dáil Éireann—Whether such statement may be relied on by plaintiff—Whether evidence to show that plaintiffs relied on Minister's statement so as to invoke support for promissory estoppel. **Garda Representative Association v Ireland** [1989] 1, HC.

Treasure trove
Finder of ancient hoard depositing same with museum—Promise that finder would be honourably treated—Whether finder has legitimate expectation of reasonable reward. **Webb v Ireland** [1988] 565, HC.

Social welfare
Widow's contributory pension
Disqualification on ground of cohabitation—Whether dependants had legitimate expectation that the benefit would continue to be paid. **Foley v Moulton** [1989] 169, HC.

LETTERS
Conveying of letters
Post office monopoly
Private courier service—Whether in breach of the monopoly. *See* POST OFFICE
(Monopoly).

LETTERS OF CREDIT
Sale of goods
Time within which credits to be opened. See SALE OF GOODS (Contract—Implied terms—
Letters of credit).

LEVY
Livestock. *See* AGRICULTURE (Export levy on livestock).

Milk. *See* AGRICULTURE (Milk levy).

Monetary compensation
European Community. See AGRICULTURE (Common agricultural policy).

Orders
Severance
Bonus scheme financed from levies. *See* AGRICULTURE (Levy orders).

LIBEL *See* DEFAMATION.

LIBERTY, RIGHT TO. *See* CONSTITUTION (Personal rights—Liberty).
Habeas corpus applications
Procedure specified by Constitution. See HABEAS CORPUS.

LIBERTY OF EXPRESSION. *See* CONSTITUTION (Personal rights—Freedom of expression).

LIBERTY OF THE PRESS. *See* PRESS (Freedom).

LICENCE
Abattoir
Refusal of application
Natural justice—Mandamus proceedings—Towns Improvement Clauses Act 1847, ss.
125–131—Slaughter of Animals Act 1935. **Doupe v Limerick Co Council** [1981] 456, HC.

Amusement halls
Gaming machines. See GAMING AND LOTTERIES (Gaming licence)

Licence or lease. *See* LANDLORD AND TENANT (Licence or lease).

Occupation of lands
Expiry
Occupation continuing—Nature of occupation—Whether as a result of a tenancy at
will—Adverse possession—Whether owner's title extinguished—Statute of Limitations
1957, ss. 13(2), 17(1), 18, 24, 51 (1). **Bellew v Bellew** [1983] 128, SC.

Sea fishing. *See* FISHERIES (Licence—Offshore fishing).

Tour operator
Breach of condition
Decision to revoke—Appeal to High Court—Whether applicant fit and proper to
carry on business. *See* TOUR OPERATOR (Licence).

LICENSED PREMISES
Mortgage
No reference to licence
Whether licence caught by mortgage—Whether licence capable of separation from
licensed premises. **In re Sherry-Brennan** [1979] 113, HC, SC.

LICENSING ACTS
Club licence
Renewal. See Licence—Renewal—Club licence (*below*).

Exemption orders
Special exemption order
Dance—Public dance hall—Hotel ballroom—Whether dance a "special occasion"—Prohibition on granting exemption orders for any time on a Sunday—Whether District Justice can grant exemption order in respect of only part of a special occasion—Extent of discretion—Substantial meal—Whether persons attending must eat the meal—Price—Mode of service—Intoxicating Liquor Act 1927, ss. 1, 5—Public Dance halls Act 1935—Intoxicating Liquor Act 1943, s. 6—Intoxicating Liquor Act 1960, s. 11—Intoxicating Liquor Act 1962, ss. 9, 12. **Murray v O Colmain** [1981] 137, SC.

Forfeiture of licence
Offences
Whether forfeiture provisions an unjust attack on property rights—Constitution of Ireland 1937, Articles 38.2, 40.3—Intoxicating Liquor Act 1927, ss. 28, 30(1). **State (Pheasantry Ltd) v Donnelly** [1982] 512, HC.

Hotel licence
Application. See Licence—Application—Hotel licence (*below*).

Renewal
Objection. *See* Licence—Renewal—Hotel licence (*below*).

Licence
Alienation
Whether licence unattached to premises is alienable—Contract for the sale of ordinary publican's licence—Failure to complete—Whether specific performance of such agreement can be ordered—Whether agreement in reality payment for consent to the extinguishing of the licence—Whether such agreement enforceable. **Macklin v Greacen & Co Ltd** [1981] 315, HC; [1982] 182, SC.

Whether existing separately from licensed premises—Whether capable of being sold separately—Mortgage of premises—No reference to licence—Whether licence caught by mortgage. In re **Sherry-Brennan** [1979] 113, HC, SC.

Application
Hotel licence—Objection to grant of licence—Character and misconduct of applicant—Whether unreasonable detriment to other licensed premises in the area—Fitness and convenience of premises to be licensed—Intensification of use—Licensing (Ireland) Act 1902, s. 2(2)—Intoxicating Liquor Act 1960, s. 21(1). **In re Fox Court Developments Ltd** [1989] 806, HC.

New premises—Substitution for demolished licensed premises—Objections—Locus standi of objectors—Whether objectors required to be inhabitants of parish where the premises located—Licensing (Ireland) Act 1833, s. 4—Intoxicating Liquor Act 1960, s. 14. **Jaggers Restaurant Ltd v Ahearne** [1988] 553, SC.

New premises—Substitution for demolished licensed premises—Publican's seven day ordinary on-licence—Whether new premises in 'the immediate vicinity' of demolished premises—Whether grant of licence might have a materially adverse effect on licensed premises in neighbourhood. **In re Thank God It's Friday Ltd** [1990] 228.

Off-licence—Case stated—Beer and spirit retailer's off-licence—Consent to extinguishing two publican's seven day on-licences—Whether off-licence should be granted—Whether licences of same character—Intoxicating Liquor Act 1960, s. 13. **O'Rourke v Grittar** [1990] 877, HC.

On-licence—Restaurant certificate—Whether premises required to be in use as a restaurant at time of application—Whether licence could be granted when public bar

LICENSING ACTS
Licence
Application continued

was on the premises—Intoxicating Liquor Act 1927, s. 12A. **Whelan v Tobin** [1976–7] 199, HC.

On-licence—Whether premises "fit and convenient"—Supermarket—Procedure for obtaining off-licence not available—Statutory provisions only applicable to County Boroughs—Carlow not a County Borough—Application for an on-licence—Anomalies in licensing legislation—Licensing (Ireland) Act 1902, ss. 2, 4—Intoxicating Liquor Act 1927, ss. 61, 62—Intoxicating Liquor Act 1960, s. 15—Intoxicating Liquor Act 1962, s. 28. **In re Powers Supermarkets Ltd** [1981] 270, HC.

Forfeiture. See Forfeiture (*above*).

Holder

Company—Public house—Breaches of Licensing Acts—Complaint against company—Manager, as nominee of company, holding licence—Summons dismissed—Case stated—Right of limited liability company to hold an intoxicating liquor licence—Whether company liable as 'real' licensee—Liability of manager for aiding and abetting—Intoxicating Liquor Act 1960, s. 28. **McMahon v Murtagh Properties Ltd** [1982] 342, HC.

Renewal

Club licence—Club being a limited company—Whether supply of exciseable liquor under the control of the members—Registration of Clubs (Ireland) Act 1904, s. 4. **In re Parnell GAA Club Ltd** [1984] 246, HC.

Hotel licence—Objection—No evidence that hotel registered with Bord Failte—Whether too late to go behind the orders previously made in respect of the premises—Whether material that the premises to which the licence relates were licensed before the 1960 Act came into operation—Licensing (Ireland) Act 1902, s. 2 (ii)—Intoxicating Liquor Act 1960, ss. 13, 15 (1), 17, 20, 23. **In re Bannerton** [1984] 662, HC; [1986] 471, SC.

Publican's licence—Objection—Validity of licence—Convictions under Licensing Acts—Convictions not endorsed on the licence—Licence should have been forfeited—Licence renewed on five occasions—Death of holder—Application by widow for an ad-interim licence—Order renewing licence made in error—Whether error made by District Justice an error within his jurisdiction—Validity of issue of licence by Customs and Excise in the name of the deceased—Intoxicating Liquor Act 1927, ss. 25, 28(1), 30 (1), 31, 32—Intoxicating Liquor Act 1943, s. 14—Intoxicating Liquor Act 1960, s. 37—Courts Act 1971, s. 13. **In re Riordan** [1981] 2, HC.

Refusal—Appeal—Premises burnt down—Application for renewal of licence refused because no business had been carried on in the premises during the preceding licensing year—Appeal—Whether Circuit Court jurisdiction—Whether intention to rebuild—Spirits (Ireland) Act 1854, ss. 11 **Breen v Keane** [1981] 279, CC.

Transfer

Application for certificate of transfer—Applicant company having only two share-holders—Such shareholders being sole directors of the company—Such persons having previously been convicted for licensing offences—Whether such conviction be recorded on the licence applied for—Intoxicating Liquor Act 1927, s. 30—Interpretation Act 1937, s. 11 (c). **In re Hesketh Investments Ltd** [1984] 134, HC.

Offence
Aiding and abetting

Manager holding licence as nominee of company—Liability of manager for aiding and abetting—Intoxicating Liquor Act 1960, s. 28. **McMahon v Murtagh Properties Ltd** [1982] 342, HC.

LICENSING ACTS
Offence *continued*
Liability
Holder of licence—Company—Manager holding licence as nominee of company—
Whether company liable as "real" licensee—Liability of manager for aiding and
abetting—Intoxicating Liquor Act 1960, s. 28. **McMahon v Murtagh Properties Ltd**
[1982] 342, HC.

Major or minor offence
Wine retailer's on licence—Holder convicted of various licensing offences—Licence
thereupon becoming forfeit—Whether minor offences triable summarily—Whether
forfeiture provisions an unjust attack on property rights—Constitution of Ireland
1937, Articles 38 2, 40 3—Intoxicating Liquor Act 1927, ss. 28, 30 (1). **State (Pheasantry
Ltd) v Donnelly** [1982] 512, HC.

Prices
Maximum Prices Order—Breach—Whether evidence necessary of actual state of bev-
erage—Price list displaying excess price on three drinks on two separate occasions—
Interpretation of Order—Whether single offence—Whether restrictions on maximum
price at which drinks 'may be sold' refers to maximum price proposed by publican for
the sale of the drinks—Prices Act 1958, s. 22—Maximum Retail Price (Beverages in
Licensed Premises) Display Order 1979—Maximum Price (Intoxicating Liquor) (No 3)
Order 1979. **Minister for Industry, Commerce and Tourism v Farrelly** [1981] 302, HC.

Prohibited hours
Conviction—Appeal—Case stated—Substantial meal supplied and eaten with the
drinks remaining not fully consumed—Interpretation of exemption—Whether liquor
'being consumed' at the same time—Intoxicating Liquor Act 1927, s. 13—Intoxicating
Liquor Act 1960, s. 5—Intoxicating Liquor Act 1962, s. 4. **DPP v O'Toole** [1983] 41,
HC.

Permitting persons to be on the premises at a prohibited time—Case stated—Whether
separate and distinct offences—Nature of offences—Onus of proof—Whether evidence
of the address of the premises is sufficient evidence that the premises are within the
County Borough of Dublin—Licensing Act 1872, s. 51 (4)—County Officers and
Courts (Ireland) Act 1877, s. 78—Intoxicating Liquor Act 1927 ss. 2, 17—Intoxicating
Liquor Act 1962, ss. 2, 29, 36. **McCarthy v Murphy** [1981] 213, HC.

Off-licence application. *See* Licence—Application—Off-licence (*above*).

Prohibited hours. *See* Offence—Prohibited hours (*above*).

Restaurant certificate
On-licence application
Whether premises required to be in use as a restaurant at time of application—
Whether licence could be granted when public bar was on the premises—Intoxicating
Liquor Act 1927, s. 12A. **Whelan v Tobin** [1976–7] 199, HC.

Special occasion
Whether dance a "special occasion". *See* Exemption orders—Special exemption order—
Dance (*above*).

LICENSOR AND LICENSEE
Church
Negligence
Infant licensee—Infant plaintiff suffering extensive burns after her sleeve caught fire
whilst lighting a candle on a candelabra—Whether concealed danger—Whether defen-
dant negligent. **Rooney v Connolly** [1987] 768, SC.

LIEN
Banker's lien
Deposit of title goods
Whether bank entitled to claim lien over title deeds taken as security for loan. *See* BANK (Deposit of title deeds).

Purchaser's lien
Sale of land. See SALE OF LAND (Lien).

Solicitor's lien. *See* SOLICITOR (Lien).

LIFE INSURANCE *See* INSURANCE (Life insurance policy).

LIFE OF UNBORN *See* CONSTITUTION (Personal rights—Right to life of unborn).

LIMITATION OF ACTIONS
Accrual of cause of action
Defective premises. See Defective premises (*below*).

Malicious injuries claim. See Malicious injuries claim (*below*).

Personal injuries
Medical negligence. *See* Personal injuries—Medical negligence (*below*).

Adverse possession. *See* Land—Adverse possession (*below*).

Defective premises
Accrual of cause of action
House built on unsuitable foundations developing structural fault—Date when cause of action accrued—Whether date of damage or date of discoverability of damage—Whether date of accrual further extended on the grounds of equitable estoppel or fraudulent concealment—Statute of Limitations 1957, ss. 11(1), 11(2)(a), 71 (1). **Morgan v Park Developments Ltd** [1983] 156, HC

Debt
Recovery
Pigs and Bacon Commission—Claim in respect of deductions made by Commission—Whether claim statute barred—Limitation period having expired—Whether acknowledgement—Whether defendants estopped from pleading the statute—Whether European Community Law prohibits defendants from pleading the statute—Statute of Limitations 1957, ss. 3(1), 56(1)—European Communities Act 1972, s. 2. **Smith v Ireland** [1983] 300, HC.

Ejectment
Personal representative
Whether statute barred—Statute of Limitations as amended by Succession Act 1965, s. 126—Whether applicable to the estates of persons dying before commencement of the Act—Statute of Limitations 1957, s. 45—Succession Act 1965 s. 126. **Drohan v Drohan** [1981] 473, HC.

Family provision
Proceedings by widow and children
Late application—Succession Act 1965, ss. 117, 121, 127. **D v D** [1981] 179, HC.

Land
Adverse possession
Occupation of lands with approval and consent of owner—Occupation continuing beyond what was originally contemplated to the exclusion of the owner—Nature of occupation—Whether as a result of a tenancy at will—Whether owner's title extinguished—Statute of Limitations 1957, ss. 13(2), 17(1), 18, 24, 51 (1). **Bellew v Bellew** [1983] 128, SC.

LIMITATION OF ACTIONS
Land
Adverse possession continued

Recovery of possession—Personal representative—Claim by personal representative to recover assets of the deceased from a person holding adversely to the estate—Whether statute barred—Amending legislation—Whether applicable to the estates of persons dying before commencement of the Act—Relevant period of limitation—Statute of Limitations 1957, s. 45—Succession Act 1965 s. 126. **Drohan v Drohan** [1981] 473, HC.

Malicious injuries claim
Accrual of cause of action

Time limits—Proceedings commenced outside statutory period—Whether court power to extend time—Statute—Interpretation—Malicious Injuries Act 1981, ss. 8, 14, 23. **Dublin Corporation v Murdon Ltd** [1988] 86, HC.

Negligence
Defective premises. See Defective premises (*above*).

Personal injuries. See Personal injuries (*below*).

Personal injuries
Infant

Accident occurring four years before attaining majority—Writ issued two years after attaining majority—Whether claim statute barred—Statute of Limitations s. 49(2) (a)(ii). **Campbell v Ward** [1981] 160, HC.

Delay—Proceedings instituted on behalf of infant sixteen years after cause of action accrued—Whether delay unreasonable—Whether an abuse of the process of the courts—Statute of Limitations 1957, s. 49—Convention for the Protection of Human Rights and Fundamental Freedoms (1950), Art 6(1). **O'Domhnaill v Merrick** [1985] 40, SC.

Medical negligence

Accrual of cause of action—Surgical operation—Plaintiff discovering subsequently that operation not successful—Institution of proceedings—Whether statute-barred—Accrual of cause of action—Whether date of damage or date of discoverability. **Hegarty v O'Loughran** [1987] 603, HC; [1990] 403, SC.

LIQUIDATION
Company. *See* COMPANY (Winding up).

LIQUOR LICENSING *See* LICENSING ACTS.

LIS PENDENS. *See* REAL PROPERTY (Incumbrance—Lis pendens).

LIVELIHOOD, RIGHT TO EARN. *See* CONSTITUTION (Personal rights—Right to earn livelihood).

LOAN
Security
Deposit of title deeds

Whether bank entitled to claim lien over deeds. **In re Farm Fresh Frozen Foods Ltd** [1980] 131, HC.

LOCAL ELECTIONS
Generally. *See* ELECTORAL LAW (Local elections).

Vacancy
County council

Death of member. *See* LOCAL GOVERNMENT (Authority—Membership—Vacancy).

LOCAL GOVERNMENT
Authority
Decision

Validity—Housing authority—Application for permission to use premises other than for human habitation refused—Whether such decision invalid—Local Government (Planning and Development) Act 1963, ss. 2, 26—Housing Act 1969, ss. 4, 10. **Creedon v Dublin Corporation** [1983] 339, SC.

Compulsory purchase. See COMPULSORY PURCHASE (Local authority).

Duty of care. See NEGLIGENCE (Local authority).

Highway authority. See HIGHWAY.

Housing authority. See HOUSING (Local authority).

Meeting

Estimates meeting. *See* Meeting (*below*).

Membership

Vacancy—Replacement—County council—Death of member—Standing orders providing that such vacancies be filled by co-option—Standing orders further providing that co-option be of a person from the same electoral area—Council meetings—Whether vacancy remained unfilled—Whether standing order ultra vires—Electoral Act 1863, s. 82—Local Government Act 1955, s. 62—Local Government (Application of Enactments) Order 1898, art 14—Local Elections Regulations 1965, reg 87. **McNelis v Donegal Co Council** [1978] 230, HC.

Negligence. See NEGLIGENCE (Local authority).

Non-feasance

Civil liability—Road authority—Statutory provision amending law to come into operation by governmental order—No such order made—Mandamus application—Whether government's discretion to bring section into operation—Civil Liability Act 1961, s. 60. **State (Sheehan) v Ireland** [1988] 437, HC, SC.

Order

Validity—Natural justice—Sanitary services—Temporary dwellings—Unlicensed caravan site—County Council prohibiting the erection or retention of any temporary dwellings on the site—Whether order void—Whether sufficient compliance with principles of natural justice—Local Government (Sanitary Services) Act 1948, ss. 31, 34—Local Government Act 1955, s. 66. **Gammell v Dublin Co Council** [1983] 413, HC.

Planning authority. See PLANNING.

Statutory duty

Breach—Negligence. *See* NEGLIGENCE (Local authority).

Burial grounds—Cattle poisoned by eating yew leaves—Wall damaged—Whether authority negligent. *See* Public health—Burial ground (*below*).

Ultra vires

Housing authority—Allocation of houses—Whether authority acting *ultra vires*—Housing Act 1966, ss. 53, 60, 109. **McNamee v Buncrana UDC** [1984] 77, SC.

Resolution—Gaming licence—Local authority giving notice of intention to rescind resolution allowing gaming—Whether decision of local authority ultra vires by reason of bad faith—Gaming and Lotteries Act 1956, Part III. **State (Divito) v Arklow UDC** [1986] 123, SC.

Service charges—Imposition—Sanitary authority—Sewer—Connection. *See* Public health—Sewer—Connection—Charges (*below*).

Vacancy. See Authority—Membership—Vacancy (*above*).

LOCAL GOVERNMENT *continued*
Compulsory acquisition. *See* COMPULSORY PURCHASE.

Finance
Rating. See RATING AND VALUATION.

Service charges. See Service charges (*below*).

Highway authority. *See* HIGHWAY (Highway authority).

Housing. *See* HOUSING (Local authority).

Licence
Abattoir
Refusal of application—Natural justice—Mandamus proceedings—Towns Improvement Clauses Act 1847, ss. 125–131—Slaughter of Animals Act 1935. **Doupe v Limerick Co Council** [1981] 456, HC.

Amusement halls
Gaming machines. *See* GAMING AND LOTTERIES (Gaming licence).

Markets and fairs
Casual trading licence. *See* CASUAL TRADING.

Meeting
Estimates meeting
Whether resolution adopting estimates null and void—Whether each estimate must be considered separately—Whether composite adoption sufficient—Whether motion adopting estimates and motion striking rate to be separate—Whether meeting conducted in accordance with natural justice—Whether councillor having legitimate expectation that meeting would consider each estimate separately—Whether councillor having locus standi to seek judicial review of meeting—Judicial review—Form of relief—Remittal to local authority—RSC 1986, O 84 r 26(4)—City and County Management (Amendment) Act 1955, ss. 10(1), 10(4). **Ahern v Kerry Co Council** [1988] 392, HC.

Member of authority
Death
Vacancy. *See* Authority—Membership—Vacancy (*above*).

Municipal rate
Relief
Statute—Interpretation. *See* RATING AND VALUATION (Relief—Municipal rate).

Non-feasance
Civil liability. See Authority—Non-feasance (*above*).

Planning. *See* PLANNING.

Public health
Burial ground
Minister's consent—Whether burial ground can be located within 100 yards of a dwelling-house without owner's consent—Public Health (Ireland) Act 1878, ss. 160, 174—Local Government (Sanitary Services) Act 1948, s. 44. **McCarthy v Johnson** [1989] 706, SC.

Statutory duty—Breach—Cattle poisoned by eating yew leaves—Wall damaged—Whether local authority negligent or in breach of statutory duty in not having wall repaired—Public Health (Ireland) Act 1878, ss. 181, 185, 193, 234. **Walsh v Kilkenny Co Council** [1978] 1, HC.

Refuse dump
Sanitary authority proposing to establish refuse dump on site of national monument—Whether dump constitutes material contravention of development plan—Whether constitutes breach of national monuments legislation. *See* PLANNING (Development plan—Contravention—National monument on lands—Refuse dump).

LOCAL GOVERNMENT
Public health *continued*

Sewer

Connection—Application for permission to connect a sewer—No formal dispute to the claim for connection—Property arbitrator appointed—Whether developers precipitate—Whether excessive delay—Public Health (Ireland) Act 1878, ss. 24, 216, 217. **Kildare Co Council v McKone Estates Ltd** [1984] 313, HC.

Connection—Charges—Trade effluent—Licence granted conditional on payment of certain charges purported to be levied pursuant to statute—Whether relevant statutory provisions applied to a sanitary authority—Whether authority acted ultra vires in imposing such charges. Public Health (Ireland) Act 1878, s. 23—Local Government (Water Pollution) Act 1977, ss. 1, 16—Local Government (Financial Provisions) (No 2) Act 1983, s. 2. **Ballybay Meat Exports Ltd v Monaghan Co Council** [1990] 864, HC.

Rating. *See* RATING AND VALUATION.

Sanitary services

Burial ground. See Public health—Burial ground *(above).*

Charges

Sewer—Connection. *See* Public health—Sewer—Connection—Charges *(above).*

Connection. See Public health—Sewer—Connection *(above).*

Temporary dwellings

Unlicensed caravan site—Prohibition of erection or retention of any temporary dwellings on the site—Whether order void—Whether sufficient compliance with principles of natural justice—Local Government (Sanitary Services) Act 1948, ss. 31, 34—Local Government Act 1955, s. 66. **Gammell v Dublin County Council** [1983] 413, HC.

Service charges

Sewer

Connection—Discharge of trade effluent—Licence conditional on payment of certain charges—Whether authority acted ultra vires in imposing such charges. *See* Public health—Sewer—Connection—Charges *(above).*

Water supply

Statutory authority—Whether authority exists for aggregating charges for services provided by local authority—Whether water service provided by "enactment'—Whether order for water charges may be deemed lawful by court supplying evidence overcoming deficiency—Public Health (Ireland) Act 1878, s. 65A—Local Government (Sanitary Services) Act 1962, s. 7—Local Government (Financial Provisions) (No 2) Act 1983, ss. 1(3), 2(1), 8. **Athlone UDC v Gavin** [1986] 277, SC.

Temporary dwellings

Halting site for members of travelling community

Whether housing authority under statutory duty to provide serviced halting sites. *See* HOUSING (Travelling community).

Unlicensed caravan site. See Sanitary services—Temporary dwellings *(above).*

LOCAL TAXATION *See* RATING AND VALUATION.

LOCUS STANDI
Constitutional action. *See* CONSTITUTION (Locus standi).

Declaratory relief

Administrative decision

Building society—Registration—Issue of certificate of registration—Whether null and void—Injunction sought to restrain society carrying on business—Locus standi of plaintiffs to seek relief—Whether aggrieved persons—Whether sufficient interest—

LOCUS STANDI
Declaratory relief
Administrative decision continued
Building Societies Acts 1874 and 1876—RSC 1962, O 19 r 28. **Irish Permanent Building Society v Registrar of Building Societies** [1981] 242, HC.

Habeas corpus application. *See* HABEAS CORPUS (Locus standi).

Judicial review. *See* JUDICIAL REVIEW (Locus standi).

Mandamus
Enforcement of statutory duty
Test to be applied—Failure of government to make order bringing section of statute into operation—Whether applicant has necessary locus standi to apply for order of mandamus requiring government to make such order. **State (Sheehan) v Ireland** [1988] 437, SC.

Objector
Intoxicating liquor licence
Whether objectors required to be inhabitants of parish where the premises located—Licensing (Ireland) Act 1833, s. 4—Intoxicating Liquor Act 1960, s. 14. **Jaggers Restaurant Ltd v Ahearne** [1988] 553, SC.

Planning decision. See PLANNING (Decision—Objection—Locus standi).

Personal right
Enforcement. See CONSTITUTION (Personal rights—Right to life of unborn—Enforcement).

Public right
Assertion by private citizen
Common law limitation—Whether limitations carried over by the Constitution—Whether private citizen has locus standi to assert breach of public right without showing particular loss or damage—Whether aggrieved persons—Whether sufficient interest—RSC 1962, O 19 r 28. **Irish Permanent Building Society v Caldwell (Registrar of Building Societies)** [1979] 273, HC; [1981] 242, HC.

Relator proceedings
Role of Attorney General
Whether necessary to consider issue of standing of relator—Whether relator had locus standi prior to conversion of proceedings to relator action. **Attorney General (ex rel SPUC) v Open Door Counselling Ltd** [1987] 477, HC; [1989] 19, SC.

LOTTERY. *See* GAMING AND LOTTERIES (Lottery).

MACHINE
Gaming. *See* GAMING AND LOTTERIES (Gaming machine).

MACHINERY
Valuation
Exclusion
Brewery—Tanks and vessels—Whether rateable—Whether "machinery"—Annual Revision of Rateable Property (Ireland) Act 1860, s. 7. **Beamish & Crawford Ltd v Commissioner of Valuation** [1980] 149, SC.

Wear and tear
Capital allowances. See REVENUE (Income tax—Capital allowances).

MAIL
Conveyance of letters
Statutory monopoly
Post office. *See* POST OFFICE.

MAINTENANCE
Affiliation order. *See* AFFILIATION ORDER.

Canal
Lack of maintenance
Flooding. *See* CANAL.

Family provision
Testator
Moral duty. *See* SUCCESSION (Family provision).

Road. *See* HIGHWAY (Maintenance).

Spouse and children. *See* FAMILY LAW (Maintenance).

MALICE
Claim for damages
Whether such action lay in respect of instituting a civil action
Meaning of malice—Proof of damage—Cause of loss. **Dorene Ltd v Suedes (Ireland) Ltd** [1982] 126, HC.

MALICIOUS ABUSE OF PROCESS. *See* ABUSE OF PROCESS (Tort—Malicious abuse).

MALICIOUS INJURIES
Appeal
Supreme Court
Jurisdiction of Application dismissed on appeal in High Court—Whether substantive appeal lies to Supreme Court—Whether case stated lies from High Court to Supreme Court under statutory scheme—Courts of Justice Act 1936, ss. 38, 39—Malicious Injuries Act 1981, ss. 17, 18—Constitution of Ireland 1937, Article 34 4 3. **W J Prendergast & Son Ltd v Carlow Co Council** [1990] 749, SC.

Case stated
High Court
Jurisdiction of High Court to state case to Supreme Court—Malicious Injuries Act 1981, s. 18. **W J Prendergast & Son Ltd v Carlow Co Council** [1990] 749, SC.

Compensation
Deduction
Social welfare benefits—Criminal Injuries Compensation Tribunal—Whether decision subject to judicial review—Natural justice—Criminal Injuries Compensation Scheme 1974, paras 1, 2, 3, 4, 6, 15, 16, 25, 26. **State (Hayes) v Criminal Injuries Compensation Tribunal** [1982] 210, HC.

Crime against property damaged
Test applicable
Burglary—Entering premises with intent to steal therein—Destruction of portion of premises in course of burglary—Goods stolen—Whether offences offences against property damaged—Malicious Injuries Act 1981, ss. 5(1), 5(2)(d)—Larceny Act 1916, s. 23—Criminal Law (Jurisdiction) Act 1976, s. 6. **Shennick Lodge v Monaghan Co. Council** [1986] 273, SC.

Unauthorised taking and user of motor vehicle
Damage to vehicle—Whether caused in the course of committing a crime against the property damaged—Extended meaning of "maliciously"—Road Traffic Act 1961, s. 112(1)—Malicious Injuries Act 1981, s. 5(2)(d)—Road Traffic Act 1968, s. 65. **Fitzgerald v Limerick Corporation** [1985] 445, SC.

MALICIOUS INJURIES *continued*
Fatal injury
Whether sustained in course of attempting to save human life
Tribunal rejecting claim—Certiorari—Whether decision at variance with reason and common sense—Scheme of Compensation for Personal Injuries Criminally Inflicted 1974, rule 4(d). **State (Creedon) v Criminal Injuries Compensation Tribunal** [1989] 104, SC.

Fire
Malice
Evidence—Chromatogram tests—Malicious Injury (Ireland) Act 1853. **Taylor v Monaghan Co Council** [1981] 383, HC.

Proof—Inference from facts—Factory damaged by fire—Whether onus of proof discharged—Local Government (Ireland) Act 1898. **Sean Dillon Ltd v Dublin Corporation** [1989] 46, HC.

Proof—Fire started carelessly by employee—No intention to injure—Whether act malicious—Meaning of "caused"—Malicious Injuries Act 1981, s. 5(2). **Lally v Meath Co Council** [1985] 269, HC.

Proof—Fire caused by employee—Whether fire caused deliberately or by an act of wanton recklessness—Whether employee knew what he did was likely to cause damage. **Agra Trading Ltd v Waterford Co Council** [1985] 249, HC.

Malice
Proof
Fire. See Fire—Malice—Proof (*above*).

Inference from facts—Factory damaged by fire—Whether onus of proof discharged—Local Government (Ireland) Act 1898. **Sean Dillon Ltd v Dublin Corporation** [1989] 46, HC.

Time limit for claim
Accrual of cause of action
Proceedings commenced outside limitation period—Whether court power to extend time—Statute—Interpretation—Malicious Injuries Act 1981, ss. 8, 14, 23. **Dublin Corporation v Murdon Ltd** [1988] 86, HC.

Tribunal
Decision
Reasonableness—Whether at variance with reason and common sense—Whether inference from facts open to tribunal—Whether tribunal obliged to give reasons for decision—Scheme of Compensation for Personal Injuries Criminally Inflicted 1974, rule 4(d). **State (Creedon) v Criminal Injuries Compensation Tribunal** [1989] 104, SC.

Reviewability—Natural justice—Fatal injury directly attributable to a crime of violence—Whether tribunal entitled to reduce the gross loss suffered by the value of social welfare benefits payable—Criminal Injuries Compensation Scheme 1974, paras 1, 2, 3, 4, 6, 15, 16, 25, 26. **State (Hayes) v Criminal Injuries Compensation Tribunal** [1982] 210, HC.

MANDAMUS
Alternative remedy
Planning permission
Refusal—Appeal—Application for mandamus—Whether lodgment of appeal precludes application for mandamus—Whether mandamus more appropriate remedy where merits of case not in issue. **State (NCE) Ltd v Dublin Co Council** [1979] 249, HC.

Availability
Existence of adequate alternative remedy. **State (McInerney & Co Ltd) v Dublin County Council** [1985] 513, HC.

MANDAMUS *continued*
District Court
Penalty

Plea of guilty to various summonses—District Justice finding accused guilty on one count only and taking the others into consideration in imposing the penalty—DPP applying for judicial review—Such application not made promptly—Whether time limit be extended. **DPP v Macklin** [1989] 113, HC.

Effectiveness of order
Husband and wife

Entry of child's name on wife's passport—Forged consent of husband—Removal of child from jurisdiction by wife—Whether Minister obliged to cancel entry of child— Ministers and Secretaries Act 1924. **P I v Ireland** [1989] 810, SC.

Locus standi
Statutory duty

Enforcement—Test to be applied—Failure of government to make order bringing section of statute into operation—Whether applicant has necessary locus standi to apply for order of mandamus requiring government to make such order. **State (Sheehan) v Ireland** [1988] 437, SC.

Medical Council
Failure to register doctor with foreign qualifications

Failure to make rules specifying qualifications necessary for registration—Application for mandamus to direct Council to register applicant and to make and issue rules. **Bakht v Medical Council** [1990] 840, SC.

Planning decision
Purchase notice

Local authority refusing to purchase—Whether refusal made within statutory time limit—Alternative remedies—Whether exhausted—Whether default procedure implicit in statutory provisions. **State (McInerney & Co Ltd) v Dublin Co Council** [1985] 513, HC.

Time limit

Statute—Interpretation—Time limit for challenging decisions—Whether appropriate to seek relief by way of mandamus. **Freeney v Bray UDC** [1982] 29, HC.

Prison
Breaches of prison regulations

Whether mandamus appropriate remedy—Remand prisoner—Unlawful detention— Whether appropriate to make absolute order of mandamus. **State (Comerford) v Governor of Mountjoy Prison** [1981] 86, HC.

Whether mandamus appropriate remedy—Habeas corpus application—Enquiry under Constitution—Informal nature of procedure—Whether appropriate to use enquiry as method of obtaining alternative relief—Whether mandamus may be granted as alternative relief—Constitution of Ireland 1937, Article 40 4 2. **Cahill v Governor of Military Detention Barracks** [1980] 191, HC.

Revenue Commissioners
Tax clearance certificate

Rrequirement of tax clearance certificate with tenders for Government contracts— Refusal to issue by Collector General—Whether Revenue Commissioners can have regard to tax default of previous "connected' company—Whether Collector General's decision amenable to judicial review—Duty to act judicially—Requirement not based on statutory provisions. **State (Melbarian Enterprises) v Revenue Commissioners** [1986] 476, HC.

Sanitary authority
Service charges

Sewer—Licence granted by respondent permitting applicant to discharge trade effluent

MANDAMUS
Sanitary authority
Service charges continued

into respondent's sewer—Application granted by letter conditionally upon payment of certain charges purporting to be levied pursuant to statute—Whether relevant statutory provisions applied to a sanitary authority—Whether respondent acted *ultra vires* in imposing said charges. **Ballybay Meat Exports Ltd v Monaghan Co Council** [1990] 864, HC.

Statutory duty
Enforcement

Statute—Section to come into operation on day fixed by governmental order—No such order made—Application for order of mandamus requiring government to make such order—Whether government's discretion to bring section into operation—Civil Liability Act 1961, s. 60. **State (Sheehan) v Government of Ireland** [1988] 437, HC, SC.

Time limit
Extension

DPP applying for judicial review of decision of District Justice—Such application not made promptly—Whether time limit be extended. **DPP v Macklin** [1989] 113, HC.

Tribunal
Failure to furnish reasons for decision

Whether supervisory jurisdiction of court may be invoked to require Tribunal to give reasons—Natural justice—Duty to act judicially—Trade marks Application to remove trade mark from register—Application refused—Applicant wishing to appeal. **Anheuser Busch Inc v Controller of Patents** [1988] 247, HC.

MANDATORY INJUNCTION *See* INJUNCTION (Mandatory injunction).

MANDATORY PROVISION
Statute. *See* STATUTORY INTERPRETATION (Mandatory or directory).

MANSLAUGHTER
Sentence
Severity. See CRIMINAL LAW (Sentence—Manslaughter—Plea of guilty).

MANUFACTURE OF GOODS
Export sales relief
Goods manufactured within the State. See REVENUE (Corporation tax—Export sales relief).

Meaning
Statute

Interpretation. *See* WORDS AND PHRASES (Manufacture of goods).

MAREVA INJUNCTION *See* INJUNCTION (Interlocutory—Mareva injunction).

MARINE INSURANCE
Contract
Interpretation

Warranties—Whether terms relevant to ocean-going vessels suitable to pleasure craft—Cruiser damaged by explosion while laid up—Whether caused by "want of due diligence"—Warranty that during lay-up period vessel would only be fitted out for customary overhauling—Use of cooking facilities while vessel laid up—Marine Insurance Act 1906, ss. 18, 23. **Brady v Irish National Insurance Co Ltd** [1986] 669, HC, SC.

MARITAL STATUS
Discrimination
Employment. See EMPLOYMENT (Equality of treatment—Marital status).

MARK
Trade mark. *See* TRADE MARK.

MARKETS AND FAIRS
Casual trading. *See* Casual TRADING.

Legality of market
Authorisation
Presumption of immemorial usage from which a lost grant presumed—Street traders—Convictions for breach of bye-laws made for the control of traffic—Whether vehicle being used in connection with the sale of goods in a lawful market—Road Traffic Act 1961, ss. 89(1), (7), 90(1), 92—Constitution of Ireland 1937, Article 40. **DPP (Long) v McDonald** [1983] 223, SC.

Market right
Franchise to carry on market and fair
Failure to hold market or fair—Legislation regulating carrying on of markets and fairs by licence—Whether franchise survived legislation even though not in use—Whether non-user by grantee of market would result in extinguishment of market—Whether individual trader could constitute a concourse of traders—Casual Trading Act 1980, ss. 1, 2(2)(h), 3, 5, 9. **Skibbereen UDC v Quill** [1986] 170, HC.

Street trading. *See* STREET TRADING.

MARRIAGE
Barring order. *See* FAMILY LAW (Barring order).

Bigamy. *See* CRIMINAL LAW (Bigamy).

Breakdown
Divorce. See Divorce *(below).*

Separation. See Separation *(below).*

Capacity
Nullity proceedings. See Nullity—Capacity *(below).*

Constitutional protection
Administrative scheme
Validity—Agriculture—Scheme implementing EC directive—Compensatory payments to persons farming in disadvantaged areas—Payment limited to applicants whose income together with that of their spouses did not exceed a specific figure—Whether breach of constitutional pledge to guard the institution of marriage—Whether condition necessitated by membership of European Community—Council Directive 75/268/EEC—Constitution of Ireland 1937, Articles 29 4 3, 41. **Greene v Minister for Agriculture** [1990] 364. HC.

Constitutional rights
Income tax
Statute with retrospective effect—Enacted in consequence of decision that portion of income tax legislation unconstitutional—Aggregation of earned incomes of married couples—Whether lawful for the State to collect arrears of tax due under the unconstitutional provisions—Finance Act 1980, s. 21—Constitution of Ireland 1937, Arts 40.1, 40.3, 41. **Muckley v Ireland** [1986] 364, HC, SC.

Matrimonial property
Wife seeking a declaration of interest in husband's house—Wife contributing no money towards acquisition—Full time wife and mother—Whether entitled to an interest in light of the provisions of the Constitution—Constitution of Ireland 1937, Article 41—Married Women's Status Act 1957, s. 12. **B L v M L** [1989] 528, HC.

MARRIAGE
Constitutional rights *continued*
Procreation
Husband and wife each serving sentence of imprisonment for life—Whether absence of facilities to procreate within prison a denial of rights of married couple. *See* CONSTITUTION (Personal rights—Procreation—Married couple).

Social welfare
European directive—Implementation—Certain married couples adversely treated—Whether failure on the part of the State to vindicate the institution of marriage. **Hyland v Minister for Social Welfare** [1989] 196, HC; [1990] 213, SC.

Discrimination
Constitutional protection. See Constitutional rights (*above*).

Employment. See EMPLOYMENT (Equality of treatment—Marital status).

Divorce
Recognition of foreign decree
Decree obtained by collusion—Whether decree invalid—Whether parties domiciled in State where decree obtained—Whether court should recognise decree—Whether dwelling shared by parties to be regarded as a family home—Whether wife entitled to maintenance from husband—Family Home Protection Act 1976 s. 2. **L B v H B** [1980] 257, HC.

Domicile—Husband—Burden of proof—Procedure adopted by High Court in case stated—Power of High Court to refer matters back to District Justice—Summary Jurisdiction Act 1857, s. 2—Courts (Supplemental Provisions) Act 1961, s. 51. **M T T v N T** [1982] 217, SC.

Domicile—Whether decree consistent with law of husband's domicile—Appropriate test—Rejection of test of real and substantial connection with country of court granting decree. **K E D (Otherwise K C) v M C** [1987] 189, SC.

Domicile—Parties divorced in the UK—Whether husband domiciled in Britain—Parties resident for time in Ireland—Parties both British citizens—Whether domicile of origin displaced—Whether legislation abolishing dependent domicile retrospective in effect—Wife's application for maintenance—Motion to stay proceedings—Domicile and Recognition of Foreign Divorces Act 1986, s. 5—Family Law (Maintenance of Spouses and Children) Act 1976, s. 5—Guardianship of Infants Act 1964, s. 11. **C M v T M** [1988] 456, HC.

Divorce a mensa et thoro
Cruelty
Adultery—Whether subsequent misconduct revives adultery and cruelty previously condoned—Principles to be applied in awarding alimony. **B L v M L** [1989] 528, HC.

Cruelty without physical violence—Entitlement to a decree of judicial separation on grounds of cruelty—Whether proof of physical violence required—Whether intention to injure required—Matrimonial Causes and Marriage Law (Ireland) Act 1870, s. 13—Family Law (Maintenance of Spouses and Children) Act 1981. **McA v McA** [1981] 361, HC.

Foreign divorce
Recognition. See Divorce—Recognition of foreign decree (*above*).

Foreign marriage
Validity
Moslem marriage ceremony in South Africa. *See* Validity—Moslem marriage (*below*).

Invalidity. *See* Validity (*below*).

Judicial separation. *See* Divorce a mensa et thoro (*above*).

MARRIAGE *continued*
Matrimonial property
Family home. See FAMILY LAW (Property—Family home).

Wife seeking a declaration of interest. See FAMILY LAW (Property—Beneficial interest).

Nullity
Capacity
Impotence. *See* Nullity—Impotence (*below*).

Non-consummation. *See* Nullity—Non-consummation (*below*).

Psychiatric illness. *See* Nullity—Psychiatric illness (*below*).

Consent
Duress. *See* Nullity—Duress (*below*).

Delay
Approbation—Whether delay excessive—Whether party approbated—Party subsequently obtaining church annulment and marrying another party in church—Party having children and then separating from second partner—Party denying marriage—Whether approbation of first marriage—Whether public policy requires legalisation of second marriage to establish legitimacy of children—Non-consummation of first marriage—Whether impotence of one party established. **A M N v J P C** [1988] 170, HC.

Duress
Capacity—Husband's petition for nullity of marriage—Whether petitioner induced to be a party to the marriage through pressure, fear, duress or undue influence—History of psychiatric illness—Whether petitioner suffering from such a disease of the mind that he was unable to maintain and sustain a normal marital relationship—Petitioner at all material times understanding the nature, purposes and consequences of the ceremony—Onus of proof—Matrimonial Causes and Marriage (Ireland) Amendment Act 1870, s. 13. **R S. J v J D J** [1982] 263, HC.

Pregnancy—Petitioner becoming pregnant—Parents taking view that marriage only possible solution—Petitioner and father of her child acquiescing in parents' wishes—Petitioner and father of child entering into contract of marriage—Whether consent to marriage real or apparent—Whether free will of petitioner vitiated by influence of parents—Whether marriage a nullity—Whether application for church annulment relevant to judicial determination of validity of marriage—Need for law reform regarding nullity—Matrimonial Causes and Marriage Law (Ireland) Amendment Act 1870, s. 13. **N (otherwise K) v K** [1986] 75, HC, SC.

Pregnancy—Petitioner becoming pregnant—Parental pressure to marry respondent—Whether marriage to be avoided on grounds of duress—Nature of duress—Whether restricted to violence or threats thereof—Matrimonial Causes and Marriage Law (Ireland) Amendment Act 1870, s. 13. **M K (McC) v McC** [1982] 277, HC.

Pregnancy—Marriage in consequence of pregnancy and wife's threat to procure an abortion—Whether marriage contracted under duress—Refusal of wife to cohabit in normal relationship with husband—Whether indicative of disease of mind—Absence of wife from trial after previous correspondence about intended proceedings—Whether evidence of collusion. **E P v M C** (otherwise P) [1985] 34, HC.

Impotence
Failure to inseminate—Whether ground for granting nullity—Whether ground recognised by ecclesiastical courts—Matrimonial Causes and Marriage Law (Ireland) Amendment Act 1870, s. 13. **M M (otherwise G) v P M** [1986] 515, HC.

Non-consummation—Impotence of one partner to another—Whether ground for declaring marriage a nullity—Whether impotence of both parties required to be shown. **L C v B C** [1986] 618, HC.

MARRIAGE
Nullity
Impotence continued
Respondent refusing to have intercourse—Respondent not impotent generally—Whether marriage null and void—Matrimonial Causes and Marriage Law (Ireland) Amendment Act 1870, s. 13. **S. v S.** [1976–7] 156, SC.

Non-Consummation
Proof—Evidence indicating that marriage was not consummated—Trial judge inferring collusion between parties—Whether inference open to judge—Whether in accordance with natural justice—Whether decree of nullity should be granted on the basis of evidence presented only—Whether rehearing of issues required. **M v M** [1979] 160, SC.

Whether failure due to incapacity on part of respondent—Whether petitioner approbated the marriage—Delay. **N F v M T** [1982] 545, HC.

Whether incapable—Presumption—Refusal to consummate—Whether incapacity to be presumed. **O'H (otherwise F) v P F** [1986] 489, HC.

Psychiatric illness
Petitioner suffering from schizophrenia—Inability to form and sustain normal marriage relationship—Respondent obtained nullity decree from ecclesiastical court—Whether relevant to the determination of civil court. **DC (Otherwise DW) v DW** [1987] 58, HC.

Whether petitioner entitled to decree of nullity on basis of respondent's inability to enter into and sustain normal marriage relationship due to psychiatric illness—Whether marriage void or voidable—Whether petitioner approbated marriage—Whether petitioner estopped by earlier matrimonial proceedings against respondent—Matrimonial Causes and Marriage Law (Ireland) Amendment Act 1870. **D v C** [1984] 173, HC.

Polygamous
Potentially polygamous. See Validity—Moslem marriage (*below*).

Property of marriage. *See* FAMILY LAW (Property).

Separation agreement
Application to have separation agreement made a rule of court
Clause providing that the parties agree to obtain a decree of divorce a vinculo—Parties domiciled in Ireland—Whether contrary to public policy—Family Law (Maintenance of Spouses and Children) Act 1976, ss. 8, 9. **Dalton v Dalton** [1982] 418, HC.

Validity
Case stated
Moslem marriage potentially polygamous—Correct inference of law raised by trial judge—No valid marriage at common law. **Conlon v Mohamed** [1989] 523, SC.

Moslem marriage
Ceremony in South Africa joining persons of different race—Marriage without formal validity in South Africa—Moslem marriage potentially polygamous—Subsequent exchange of marriage vows—Whether the parties thereby intended a monogamous union—Whether such an exchange may be recognised as a valid marriage at common law. **Conlon v Mohamed** [1987] 172, HC; [1989] 523, SC.

Non-compliance with statutory formalities
Marriages (Ireland) Act 1844, s. 49. **I E v W E** [1985] 691, HC.

Second marriage
Church annulment of first marriage—Husband marrying again before obtaining civil annulment of first marriage—First marriage voidable—Whether second marriage valid—Constitution of Ireland 1937, Article 41 3—Offences Against the Person Act 1861, s. 57. **F M L v Registrar General of Marriages** [1984] 667, HC.

MARRIAGE *continued*
Will
Revocation. See WILL (Revocation—Marriage).

MARRIAGE COUNSELLING
Privilege attached to communications
Parish priest acting as marriage counsellor
Whether entitled to claim privilege—Confidentiality—Possible injury to relationship—Privilege that of the spouses—Constitution of Ireland 1937, Article 41. **E R v J R** [1981] 125, HC.

MARRIAGE SETTLEMENT
Construction
Lost deed
Original deed destroyed by fire—Whether secondary evidence of the contents of the deed admissible—Construction of admitted document. **Savage v Nolan** [1978] 151, HC.

MARRIED WOMAN
Discrimination
Employment. See EMPLOYMENT (Equality of treatment—Marital status).

MASTER AND SERVANT *See* EMPLOYMENT.

MASTER OF THE HIGH COURT
Jurisdiction
Judgment
Monies due and owing for goods supplied and delivered—Matter coming before Master of the High Court—Order plaintiff be at liberty to enter final judgment for amount together with interest—Whether within jurisdiction to make an order as to interest—Meaning of phrase "judge of the High Court"—Courts Act 1981, ss. 19(1), 22(1). **Mellowhide Products Ltd v Barry** [1983] 152, HC.

MATERIAL CHANGE OF USE *See* PLANNING (Development—Material change of use).

MATERIAL CONTRAVENTION OF DEVELOPMENT PLAN. *See* PLANNING
(Development plan—Contravention).

MATERIAL FACT
Disclosure
Insurance policy. See INSURANCE (Contract—*Uberrima fides*).

MATERNITY PROTECTION LEGISLATION *See* EMPLOYMENT (Maternity protection).

MATRIMONIAL HOME *See* FAMILY LAW (Property—Family home).

MATRIMONIAL PROCEEDINGS
Costs
Discretion of court
Whether general rule that wife be given her costs irrespective of whether she had been successful—Matrimonial Causes and Marriage Law (Ireland) Amendment Act 1870, s. 27—RSC 1986, O 70 r 75. **F v L** [1990] 886, HC.

Maintenance. *See* FAMILY LAW (Maintenance).

Nullity. *See* MARRIAGE (Nullity).

MATRIMONIAL PROPERTY *See* FAMILY LAW (Property).

MAYNOOTH COLLEGE
Status
Whether primarily seminary or university
Dismissal—Teacher—Teacher also a priest—Whether decision in breach of rules of

MAYNOOTH COLLEGE
Status
Whether primarily seminary or university continued
> natural justice—Maynooth College Establishment Act 1795, s. 3—Irish Universities Act 1908, s. 2(4)—Higher Education Authority Act 1971, s. 1(c). **McGrath v Maynooth College** [1979] 166, SC.

MEASURE OF DAMAGES *See* DAMAGES (Measure).

MEDIA *See* BROADCASTING; PRESS

MEDICAL BUREAU OF ROAD SAFETY
Certificate *See* ROAD TRAFFIC OFFENCES (Drunken driving).

MEDICAL CERTIFICATE
Drunken driving. *See* ROAD TRAFFIC OFFENCES (Drunken driving—Evidence—Medical certificate).

MEDICAL COUNCIL
Registration
Foreign doctors
> Statutory obligation to make rules specifying qualifications necessary for registration of foreign doctors—Mandamus application—Whether Council should be compelled to register applicant and make rules required—Whether compensation payable for loss suffered by applicant.*See* MEDICAL PRACTITIONER (Registration).

MEDICAL PRACTITIONER
Dismissal. *See* Surgeon—Dismissal (*below*).

General medical scheme
Complaints of abuse of scheme
> Allegation of fraudulent payments—Referral of matter to Minister—Whether referral *ultra vires*. *See* HEALTH SERVICES (General medical services scheme—Complaints of abuse of scheme).

Investigation
> Procedure—Remuneration—Investigation of claims indicating excessive rate of attendance—Decision of appeal committee—Natural justice—Conduct of proceedings— No cross-examination of witnesses—Whether proper exercise of discretion by appeal committee. **State (Boyle) v General Medical Services (Payments) Board** [1981] 14, HC.

Negligence
General and approved practice
> Jury trial—Whether evidence before the jury to support certain of its findings—Whether jury appropriately directed—Assessment of damages. **Dunne (an Infant) v National Maternity Hospital and Jackson** [1989] 735, SC.

Health board officers
> Psychiatrists—Detention of person as being of unsound mind—Subsequent discharge— Requirement that person show substantial grounds for contending that the board, through its officers, acted in bad faith or without reasonable care—Whether claim made out—Whether evidence of want of reasonable care—Mental Treatment Act 1945, s. 260. **O'Dowd v North Western Health Board** [1983] 186, SC.

Limitation of actions. See Negligence—Surgical operation (*below*).

Psychiatrist. See Negligence—Health board officers—Psychiatrists (*above*).

Surgical operation
> Limitation of actions—Plaintiff discovering subsequently that operation not successful— Institution of proceedings—Whether statute-barred—Accrual of cause of action—

MEDICAL PRACTITIONER
Negligence
Surgical operation continued
Whether date of damage or date of discoverability. **Hegarty v O'Loughran** [1987] 603, HC; [1990] 403, SC.

Registration
Medical Council failing to register applicant
Applicant qualified as doctor outside jurisdiction—Council under obligation to make rules specifying courses of training and exams necessary for qualification for registration—Failure to make rules—Whether Council should be compelled to register applicant—Whether Council could be compelled to make and issue rules—Damages—Assessment—Loss of livelihood—Medical Practitioners Act 1955, ss. 3 and 6—Medical Practitioners Act 1978, ss. 6, 26, 27, 28, 29. **Bahkt v Medical Council** [1990] 840, SC.

Surgeon
Dismissal from employment
Hospital—Consultant surgeon—Whether entitlement to claim unfair dismissal—Whether an employee. **O'Friel v St Michael's Hospital** [1982] 260, EAT.

Negligence. See Negligence—Surgical operation (*above*).

MEDICAL SERVICES *See* HEALTH SERVICES.

MEETING
Local authority. *See* LOCAL GOVERNMENT (Meeting).

MEMORANDUM
Contract for sale of land
Whether sufficient note or memorandum. See SALE OF LAND (Contract—Formation).

MEMORANDUM OF ASSOCIATION
Company
Transaction ultra vires
Guarantee of third party debt—Creditor failing to understand effect of memorandum and articles. *See* COMPANY (Powers—Exercise—*Ultra vires*).

MEN AND WOMEN
Employment equality. *See* EMPLOYMENT (Equality of treatment).

Equal pay. *See* EMPLOYMENT (Equal pay).

MENS REA
Shooting with intent to commit murder
Whether necessary to establish intention
Whether reckless disregard of risk of killing as a likely outcome sufficient to constitute required intent—Offences Against the Person Act 1861, s. 14. **People (DPP) v Douglas** [1985] 25, CCA.

MENTAL CAPACITY
Marriage. *See* MARRIAGE (Nullity—Psychiatric illness).

Will
Execution. See WILL (Validity—Capacity of testator).

MENTAL HANDICAP
Wardship proceedings
High Court
Jurisdiction—Mentally retarded girl—Application for inquiry as to her soundness of mind. *See* HIGH COURT (Jurisdiction—Wardship proceedings—Lunacy matters).

MENTAL HOSPITAL *See also* MENTAL TREATMENT
Employment
Psychiatric nurse
Dismissal—Whether entitlement to claim unfair dismissal. *See* EMPLOYMENT (Unfair dismissal—Exclusion—Officer—Health board).

MENTAL ILLNESS *See also* PSYCHIATRIC ILLNESS
Criminal law
Defence of insanity. See INSANITY.

MENTAL INJURY
Brain damage. *See* DAMAGES (Personal injuries—Brain damage).

MENTAL TREATMENT
Chargeability of services
Ward of court
Senile patient—Transfer to nursing home—Whether inmates receiving more than shelter and maintenance. *See* HEALTH SERVICES (Chargeability).

Detention of person as being of unsound mind
Health board
Subsequent discharge—Person seeking to institute proceedings arising out of his detention—Requirement that person show substantial grounds for contending that the board, through its officers, acted in bad faith or without reasonable care—Whether claim made out—Whether evidence of want of reasonable care—Mental Treatment Act 1945, s. 260. **O'Dowd v North Western Health Board** [1983] 186, SC.

Wardship proceedings
Jurisdiction of High Court
Mentally retarded girl—Whether condition precedent for the jurisdiction to bring persons of unsound mind into the wardship of the court that they be entitled to property which requires management or protection. *See* HIGH COURT (Jurisdiction—Wardship proceedings—Lunacy matters).

MILITARY CUSTODY *See* PRISONS (Military custody).

MILK
Levy
European Community. See AGRICULTURE (Milk levy).

Quotas
Mulder Regulations
Interpretation. *See* AGRICULTURE (Milk quotas).

GARDA SIOCHANA COLLEGE
2 2 DEC 1992
LIBRARY
TEMPLEMORE. Co. TIPPERARY.

MINES
Mineral exploration
Noise and vibration
Nuisance—Action for damages—Rural locality—Physical damage—Whether caused by defendant's activities—Whether appropriate to grant an injunction. **Halpin v Tara Mines Ltd** [1976–7] 28, HC.

Mining profits
Taxation
Relief—Termination—Calculation of tax liability—Avoidance of retrospective imposition of tax—Income Tax Act 1967, s. 386—Finance (Taxation of Profits of Certain Mines) Act 1974, ss. 15, 16. **Mogul of Ireland Ltd v O Riain** [1979] 75, HC.

MINIMUM NOTICE *See* EMPLOYMENT (Minimum notice).

MINISTER
Administrative scheme
Validity

Constitution—Agriculture—Implementation of EC Council directive—Compensatory payments to persons farming in disadvantaged areas—Whether breach of constitutional pledge to guard the institution of marriage. *See* CONSTITUTION (Administrative scheme—Validity—Agriculture).

Authorised officers
Appointment

Evidence—Sufficiency—Certificate—Whether certificate that officer had been appointed sufficient evidence of the fact of appointment—European Communities (Marketing of Fertilisers) Regulations 1978, regs 2, 4, 6, 7(4)—Ministers and Secretaries Act 1924, ss. 15(4), 17(c). **Minister for Agriculture v Cleary** [1988] 294, HC.

Decision
Nature

Whether administrative or judicial—Civil service—New staff association seeking recognition from Minister for the Public Service—Refusal—Whether refusal supported by evidence before Minister—Judicial review—Administrative act—Civil Service Regulations Act 1956, s. 17. **Inspector of Taxes Association v Minister for the Public Service** [1986] 296, SC.

Whether administrative or judicial—Prisoner—Transfer to military custody—Whether Minister under obligation to give reasons for his decision—**State (Boyle) v Governor of Curragh Military Detention Barracks** [1980] 242, HC, SC.

Review

Order—Aquaculture—Designated area—Objections—Inquiry—Appeal to High Court—Whether order be set aside—Whether Minister fully informed at time of making of decision—Fisheries Act 1980, s. 54(7)—Aquaculture (Smerwick Harbour) Order 1987. **Courtney v Minister for the Marine** [1989] 605, HC.

Ultra vires. See Ultra vires—Decision (*below*).

Validity

Excess of jurisdiction—Planning appeal—Minister granting outline planning permission in material contravention of development plan—Failure to consider objections of planning authority and those entitled to get notice of such contravention—Local Government (Planning and Development) Act 1963, ss. 26 (3), 26(4), 82(3A). **State (Pine Valley Developments Ltd) v Dublin Co Council** [1982] 169, SC.

Hospital—Closure—Whether repeal of legislation required. *See* HEALTH SERVICES (Hospital—Closure).

Hospital—Discontinuance of services—Whether decision *ultra vires*. *See* HEALTH SERVICES (Hospital—Discontinuance of services).

Order. *See* Order (*below*).

Discretion
Exercise

Validity—Transfer of prisoner from civilian to military custody—Opinion that transfer to military custody required on grounds of insufficiency of ordinary prison accommodation—Whether Minister exercising administrative discretion—Whether under an obligation to furnish reasons for his decision—Whether statutory power had lapsed—Prisons Act 1972, ss. 2(3), 2(4)—Prisons Act 1974, s. 1. **State (Boyle) v Governor of Curragh Military Detention Barracks** [1980] 242, HC, SC.

Validity—Transfer of prisoner from civilian to military custody—Opinion that transfer to military custody required on grounds of insufficiency of ordinary prison accommodation—Whether reviewable—Security context of exercise of discretion—Prisons

MINISTER
Discretion
Exercise continued

Act 1972, s. 2(3). **State (Smith) v Governor of Curragh Military Detention Barracks** [1980] 208, HC.

Duty of care
Industrial and provident society

Winding up—Loss to depositor—Whether Minister owed duty of care to depositor—Central Bank Act 1971, s. 7(1)(4)—Industrial and Provident Societies (Amendment) Act 1978—Insurance (No 2) Act 1983. **McMahon v Ireland** [1988] 610, HC.

Function
Planning appeal

Persona designata—Minister not exercising executive functions—Minister having no function outside those either expressly or by necessary implication conferred upon him by statute—Local Government (Planning and Development) Act 1963, ss. 26 (3), 26(4), 82(3A)—Local Government (Planning and Development) Act 1976, s. 42. **State (Pine Valley Developments Ltd) v Dublin Co Council** [1982] 169, SC.

Negligence
Exercise of statutory discretion

Minister granting planning permission—Legal advice that he had power so to do—Supreme court subsequently ruling that such permission *ultra vires*—Whether Minister negligent. **Pine Valley Developments Ltd v Minister for the Environment** [1987] 747, HC, SC.

Opinion
Review. See Discretion—Exercise—Validity (*above*).

Order
Validity

Whether reviewable by courts—Whether certiorari available to quash the decision—Broadcasting—Ministerial order preventing access by Provisional Sinn Fein candidates to radio and television to promote their electoral campaign—Whether Minister's opinion that the broadcasting would be likely to promote, or incite to crime, reviewable by the courts—Decision-making power affecting personal rights—Presumption that power would be exercised in conformity with the Constitution—Broadcasting Authority Act 1960, s. 31(1)—Broadcasting Authority (Amendment) Act 1976, s. 16. **State (Lynch) v Cooney** [1982] 190, HC; [1983] 89, SC.

Passport
Fraud

Whether court should direct Minister for Foreign Affairs to cancel passport—Entry of child's name on wife's passport—Forged consent of husband—Removal of child from jurisdiction by wife—Mandamus—Effectiveness of order—Whether Minister obliged to cancel entry of child—Ministers and Secretaries Act 1924. **P I v Ireland** [1989] 810, SC.

Powers
Exercise

Injunction to restrain—Challenge to validity of statutory power—Fisheries—Penal statute—Licensing requirements—Challenge to validity of statutory provision under which licence granted—Reference to European Court of Justice—Whether plaintiffs entitled to injunction restraining enforcement of licence—Balance of convenience—Fisheries (Amendment) Act 1983, s. 2. **Beara Fisheries and Shipping Ltd v Minister for the Marine** [1988] 221, HC.

Injunction to restrain—Challenge to validity of statutory power—Whether an interlocutory injunction may be granted to restrain the exercise of a statutory power

MINISTER
Powers
Exercise continued
presumed to be in accordance with the Constitution—Whether presumption of constitutionality relevant where allegation that statute in conflict with European Community
law—Fisheries (Consolidation) Act 1959, s. 222(b)—Fisheries (Amendment) Act 1983, s.
2. **Pesca Valentia Ltd v Minister for Fisheries** [1986] 68, SC.

Validity—Decision. *See* Decision—Validity (*above*).

Validity—Impermissible intervention in legislative function—Whether statute authorised
the carrying out of legislative function by Minister—Constitution—Separation of
powers—Constitution of Ireland 1937, Article 15.2—Social Welfare Act 1952, s. 75—
Social Welfare (Overlapping Benefits) (Amendment) Regulations 1979, rule 4. **Harvey
v Minister for Social Welfare** [1990] 185, SC.

Validity—Whether *ultra vires*. *See Ultra vires*—Exercise of powers (*below*).

Validity
Offences Against the State Acts— Minister empowered to freeze moneys in a bank
account and cause them to be paid into the High Court—Whether such power amounts
to confiscation of property—Whether such powers permissible delimitation of
property rights. **Clancy v Ireland** [1989] 670, HC.

Privilege
Discovery
Public interest—Documents in possession of Minister—Confidentiality versus adminis-
tration of justice. **Folens & Co Ltd v Minister for Education** [1981] 21, HC.

Statement in Dáil Éireann
Reliance
Whether Ministerial statement may be relied on by plaintiff—Whether evidence to
show that plaintiffs relied on Minister's statement so as to invoke support for plea of
promissory estoppel. **Garda Representative Association v Ireland** [1989] 1, HC.

Ultra vires
Decision
Whether *ultra vires*—Dismissal—Civil service probationer—No prior warning—
Whether reasons required—Whether reasons be disclosed—Whether notice must be
given—Natural justice—Exercise of powers in conformity with Constitution—Duty
of court—Civil Service Regulation Act 1956, ss. 5, 7—Civil Service Regulation
(Amendment) Act 1958, s. 3. **State (Daly) v Minister for Agriculture** [1988] 173, HC.

Grant of planning permission—Supreme Court subsequently ruling such permission
ultra vires—Whether an action in damages for breach of statutory duty or negligence
lay against the Minister. **Pine Valley Developments Ltd v Minister for the Environment**
[1987] 747.

Deportation order
Whether *ultra vires* authority conferred by Aliens Act 1935. **Osheku v Ireland** [1987]
330, HC.

Exercise of powers
Natural justice—Legislation empowering Minister to make regulations in respect of
medical services—Minister making regulations rendering victims of road traffic
accidents ineligible for free medical services—Exclusion not authorised or
contemplated by the Act—Whether *ultra vires*—Intention of legislature—Presumption
of constitutionality—Health Act 1970, s. 72(1)—Health Services Regulations 1971, art
6(iii). **Cooke v Walsh** [1983] 429, HC; [1984] 208, SC.

Social welfare—Supplementary welfare allowance—Regulations providing for payment
of allowance on means test—Departmental circular excluding from scheme persons

MINISTER
Ultra vires
Exercise of powers continued

on short term social welfare—Whether circular *ultra vires* the Minister—Whether decisions based on guidelines in circular valid—Social Welfare (Consolidation) Act 1981, ss. 209, 312—Social Welfare (Supplementary Welfare Allowances) Act 1975, s. 11—Social Welfare (Supplementary Welfare Allowances) Regulations 1977, art 6. **State (Kershaw) v Eastern Health Board** [1985] 235, HC.

MINISTER OF RELIGION *See* PRIEST.

MINOR *See* CHILD.

MINOR OFFENCE
Whether minor offence triable summarily. *See* CONSTITUTION (Trial of offences—Minor offence).

MINORITY SHAREHOLDER
Oppression. *See* COMPANY (Oppression of minority).

MISCONDUCT
Arbitrator. *See* ARBITRATION (Misconduct).

Company
Winding up petition

Whether petitioner guilty of misconduct disentitling relief—Company with two directors—Companies Act 1963, s. 213(f). **In re Vehicle Buildings and Insulations Ltd** [1986] 239, HC.

Solicitor. *See* SOLICITOR (Misconduct).

MISDESCRIPTION
Sale of land
Compensation. See SALE OF LAND (Misdescription).

MISREPRESENTATION
Fraudulent misrepresentation
Payment induced by fraud

Insurance—Mistaken assumption of liability induced by fraud—Whether payment recoverable. *See* MISTAKE (Payment—Recovery—Payment induced by fraud—Employer liability insurance).

Negligent misrepresentation
Auctioneers

Sale of land—Pre-contractual representation—Purchaser relying on representation— Claim for damages for loss suffered. **Stafford v Mahony** [1980] 53, HC.

MISTAKE
Agreement
Settlement of action

Action commenced against two defendants—Plaintiff entering into settlement agreement with second defendant without adverting to the question of the first defendant's costs—Whether unilateral mistake rendering agreement a nullity. **Reen v Bank of Ireland Finance Ltd** [1983] 507, HC.

Mutual mistake—Document authenticated by signatures of counsel—Lack of Consensus ad idem—Whether compromise enforceable—Whether agreement a nullity. **Mespil Ltd v Capaldi** [1986] 373, SC.

MISTAKE *continued*
  Contract
    Sale of land
      Deposit paid—Purchaser seeking to withdraw—Whether vendor entitled to forfeit deposit—Whether deposit paid under mistake of fact. **Siebel and Seum v Kent** [1976–7] 127, HC.

    Supply of seed potatoes
      Both parties contracting on assumption which proved false—Crop failure—Whether contract rendered void—Whether implied obligations remaining. **Western Potato Co-Operative Ltd v Durnan** [1985] 5, CC.

  Payment
    Recovery
      Company in liquidation—Money paid by mistake to company prior to liquidation—Whether constituting assets of company subsequent to liquidation—Whether subject to right of set-off—Whether company holding money as trustee—Purpose of constructive trust—Estoppel—Whether arising. **In re Irish Shipping Ltd** [1986] 518, HC.

      Mistake of law—Money paid voluntarily—Whether recoverable—Case stated—Statute—Interpretation—Housing Act 1966, s. 99. **Rogers v Louth Co Council** [1981] 144, SC.

      Mixed fund—Whether tracing available. **In re Irish Shipping Ltd** [1986] 518, HC.

      Payment induced by fraud—Employer liability insurance—Infant plaintiff sustaining serious injury in the course of employment—Lodgment of money into court—Mistaken assumption of liability induced by fraud—Policy repudiated—Whether plaintiff any title to the lodged money—RSC O 22, rr 4, 10, 13. **Carey v W H Ryan Ltd** [1982] 121, SC.

  Payment into court
    Fraud. See Payment—Recovery—Payment induced by fraud (*above*).

  Registrar of Building Societies
    Registration of new society
      Whether mistake of law necessarily meant that Registrar acted outside his jurisdiction—Building Societies Act 1976—RSC O 19, r 28. **Irish Permanent Building Society v Registrar of Building Societies** [1981] 242, HC.

  Settlement of action. *See* Agreement—Settlement of action (*above*).

  Statute
    Draftsman's error
      Defective clause in penal provision—Whether provision inoperable. *See* STATUTE (Mistake—Draftsman's error).

MISUSE OF DRUGS *See* CRIMINAL LAW (Misuse of drugs).

MONEY
  Currency of judgment. *See* JUDGMENT (Currency).

  Payment
    Mistake. See MISTAKE (Payment).

MONOPOLY
  Postal service
    Statutory monopoly in respect of the conveying of "letters"
      Private courier service—Minister seeking an injunction. *See* POST OFFICE (Monopoly).

MONUMENT *See* NATIONAL MONUMENT.

MORTGAGE
Charge on land
Deed of charge
Extent of property mortgaged—Receiver—Whether entitled to appropriate all income from land—Whether receiver entitled to portion of proceeds of land—Conveyancing and Law of Property Act 1881, s. 24. **Donohoe v ACC** [1987] 26, HC.

Equitable mortgage
Deposit of title deeds
Banker's lien. *See* BANK (Deposit of title deeds).

Family home. *See* FAMILY LAW (Property—Family home—Equitable mortgage).

Judgment mortgage. *See* JUDGMENT MORTGAGE.

Licensed premises
No reference to licence
Sale of licensed premises—Whether licence caught by mortgage—Whether licence capable of separation from licensed premises. In re Sherry-Brennan [1979] 113, HC, SC.

Prior mortgage
Liquidation
Debenture granted subject to rights of a prior mortgagee—Particulars registered—Failure to register particulars of mortgagee—Mortgagee obtaining order extending time for registration—Sale of property—Whether debenture holder priority over mortgagee—Companies Act 1963, ss. 99, 106, 316. In re Clarets Ltd: **Spain v McCann** [1978] 215, HC.

Premises subject to a charge to secure apportioned rent—Whether such charge a "prior mortgage"—Whether building society precluded from lending money on such premises. **Rafferty v Crowley** [1984] 350, HC.

Registered land
Possession
Entitlement—Whether owner of charge entitled to possession without order of court—Deed conferring power of possession—Whether contractual licence to enter lands only created. **Gale v First National Building Society** [1987] 30, HC.

Validity
Company
Whether valid directors' meeting to approve contents of mortgage—Whether mortgagee entitled to believe meeting properly constituted. **Ulster Investment Bank Ltd v Euro Estates Ltd** [1982] 57, HC.

Lis pendens
Registration—Mortgage executed subsequent to registration of lis pendens—Whether equitable interest entitled to priority over mortgagee's interest—Whether mortgage valid. In re Kelly's Carpetdrome Ltd: **Byrne v UDT Bank Ltd** [1984] 418, HC.

Registration
Certificate of Registrar—Conclusiveness—Mortgage not registered within twelve days of creation—Mortgage subsequently registered—Whether certificate of registration conclusive evidence that requirements complied with—Companies Act 1963, ss. 99, 104. **Lombard & Ulster Banking (Ir) Ltd v Amurec Ltd** [1976-7] 222, HC.

MORTGAGE PROTECTION POLICY
Interpretation. *See* INSURANCE (Mortgage protection).

MOSLEM MARRIAGE
Validity. *See* MARRIAGE (Validity—Moslem marriage).

MOTOR INSURANCE
Compulsory insurance scheme
Road Traffic Acts
Whether court's duty to safeguard position of third parties—Regulations—Limitation of cover permitted—Jurisdiction of Circuit Court to rule on whether the regulations were *ultra vires*. *See* ROAD TRAFFIC OFFENCES (Insurance—Driving without insurance—Approved policy of insurance in force in respect of vehicle—Defendant not covered by policy).

Information
Duty of insurers
Insurers obliged to keep records and to give information to members of Garda Síochána—Request for information—Refusal to supply—Whether regulations valid—Whether natural rights of insured invaded—*Uberrimae fides*—Road Traffic Act 1961, s. 75—Road Traffic (Compulsory Insurance) Regulations 1962, arts 7, 9. **Murphy v PMPA Insurance Co** [1978] 25, HC.

Liability of insurer
Whether accident in a "public place"
Accident occurring in grounds of country house—Personal injuries—Judgment entered against defendant—Plaintiff seeking liberty to execute judgment against defendant's motor insurance company—Whether liability for which an approved policy of insurance required—Whether accident in a 'public place'—Road Traffic Act 1961, ss. 3, 56, 76. **Stanbridge v Healy** [1985] 290, HC.

Motor Insurers' Bureau of Ireland
Liability
Untraced driver—Agreement—Interpretation—Ex gratia payments—Whether Bureau sole arbiter of conditions which might lead to making of such payment. **Bowes v Motor Insurers' Bureau of Ireland** [1990] 59, SC.

Offences. *See* ROAD TRAFFIC OFFENCES (Insurance).

MOTOR VEHICLE
Insurance. *See* MOTOR INSURANCE.

Malicious damage
Compensation claim
Unauthorised taking and user of motor vehicle—Damage to vehicle—Whether caused in the course of committing a crime against the property damaged—Road Traffic Act 1961, s. 112(1)—Malicious Injuries Act 1981,s 5(2)(d)—Road Traffic Act 1968, s. 65. **Fitzgerald v Limerick Corporation** [1985] 445, SC.

Parking offences. *See* ROAD TRAFFIC OFFENCES (Parking).

Seat belt
Failure to wear
Road traffic accident—Damages—Assessment—Apportionment of fault. **Sinnott v Quinnsworth Ltd** [1984] 523, SC.

MOTORING ACCIDENTS. *See* ROAD TRAFFIC ACCIDENTS.

MOTORING OFFENCES. *See* ROAD TRAFFIC OFFENCES.

MUNICIPAL RATE
Relief
Whether reduction relates only to premises occupied at date of passing of statute. See RATING AND VALUATION (Relief—Municipal rate).

MURDER
Defence
Insanity

Diminished responsibility—Whether jury to consider defence of diminished responsibility an alternative verdict of manslaughter—Whether concept of diminished responsibility recognised in Irish law. **People (DPP) v O'Mahony** [1986] 244, SC.

Generally. *See* CRIMINAL LAW (Murder).

MUSICAL WORKS
Copyright
Infringement

Diffusion service—Transmission of foreign TV broadcasts containing musical works of foreign authors. *See* COPYRIGHT (Infringement—Diffusion service).

NATIONAL LANGUAGE. *See* IRISH LANGUAGE.

NATIONAL MONUMENT
Development on site
Injunction application

Fiat of Attorney General secured—Injunction granted on undertaking to abide by any order as to damages. *See* INJUNCTION (Interlocutory—Fiat of Attorney General secured).

Planning Permission

Material contravention of development plan— Whether planning authority had power to grant permission by default. *See* PLANNING (Development plan—Contravention—National monument on lands—Default procedure—Whether available).

Sanitary authority proposing to establish refuse dump on site of national monument—Whether material contravention of development plan. *See* PLANNING (Development plan—Contravention—National monument on lands—Refuse dump proposal).

Discovery of ancient hoard
Finder trespassing

Rights of ownership and possession as between landowner and finder—Treasure trove—Whether royal prerogative of treasure trove carried over into Irish law—Whether necessary ingredient of sovereignty—Delivery of hoard into custody of National Museum—Whether finder entitled to reward—Reasonable reward—National Monuments Act 1930, ss. 8, 14(1), 26. **Webb v Ireland** [1988] 565, HC, SC.

Occupier's liability. *See* NEGLIGENCE (Occupier—Ancient castle—Injury to visitor).

Preservation order
Validity

Whether unjust attack on property rights—Whether order made in conformity with principles of natural justice—Constitution of Ireland 1937, Articles 40, 43—National Monuments Act 1930, ss. 8, 14—National Monuments (Amendment) Act 1954, s. 3. **O'Callaghan v Commissioners of Public Works** [1983] 391, HC; [1985] 364, SC.

NATIONAL PARLIAMENT *See* DÁIL ÉIREANN; OIREACHTAS.

NATIONALITY *See also* ALIEN
Conditions attached to fishing licence. *See* FISHERIES (Licence—Offshore fishing—Conditions of nationality).

NATURAL AND CONSTITUTIONAL JUSTICE
Appeal committee
Decision

Conduct of proceedings—Refusal to allow cross-examination—Whether requirements

NATURAL AND CONSTITUTIONAL JUSTICE
Appeal committee
Decision continued
of natural and constitutional justice disregarded. **State (Boyle) v General Medical Services (Payment) Board** [1981] 14, HC.

Athletic body
Suspension of athlete
Dope testing procedure—Failure of athlete to undergo test—Whether suspension contrary to principles of natural justice. **Quirke v Bord Luthchleas na hEireann** [1989] 129, HC.

Bord na Móna
Power to compulsorily acquire bogland
Whether power of judicial nature—Absence of right of appeal—Requirements of fair procedures and compliance with rules of natural and constitutional justice—Giving of notice and hearing of objections—*Audi alteram partem*—Constitution of Ireland 1937, Articles 40.3, 43—Turf Development Act 1946, ss. 17, 28, 30–36. **O'Brien v Bord na Móna** [1983] 314, SC.

Criminal Injuries Compensation Tribunal
Compensation
Deduction of social welfare benefits payable—Whether Tribunal acted contrary to natural justice in assessing the value of the benefits without giving prosecutrix an opportunity of making submissions with regard to same. **State (Hayes) v Criminal Injuries Compensation Tribunal** [1982] 210, HC.

Defence Forces
Widow
Application for allowance—Army Pensions Board—Denial of oral hearing—Refusal to furnish the evidence on which decision based—Whether breach of natural justice—Whether rules of natural justice applicable to administrative decisions. **State (Williams) v Army Pensions Board** [1981] 379, HC; [1983] 331, SC.

Deportation order
Alien
Whether order in conflict with rights of family—Whether order must comply with requirements of natural justice. **Pok Sun Shum v Ireland** [1986] 593, HC.

District Court
Conviction
Plea of guilty—Voluntary nature of plea—Certiorari—Natural justice—Criminal procedure—Conditional order discharged. **State (Glover) v McCarthy** [1981] 47, HC.

Procedure
Criminal case—Indictable offence dealt with summarily—Whether absolute order of prohibition should issue prohibiting District Justice from hearing the prosecutions for indictable offences without copies of the statements of evidence being furnished—Presumption that District Justice will act in accordance with principles of natural justice and fairness—Criminal Justice Act 1951—Criminal Procedure Act 1967. **Clune v Director of Public Prosecutions** [1981] 17, HC.

Criminal case—Preliminary examination—Refusal of cross-examination of witnesses—Criminal Procedure Act 1967, ss. 5, 6, 7, 8, 12, 14, 15. **State (Sherry) v Wine** [1985] 196, SC.

Employment
Dismissal
Bias—Domestic tribunal—Predisposition of tribunal to dismiss—Whether such affects validity of dismissal—Seminary—Dismissal of teacher—Teacher also priest. **McGrath and O'Ruairc v Maynooth College** [1979] 166, SC.

NATURAL AND CONSTITUTIONAL JUSTICE
Employment
Dismissal continued

Garda probationer—Dismissal for not being likely to become efficient and well-conducted guard—Previous breaches of discipline as basis for dismissal—Pending inquiry into breach of discipline discontinued—Garda Síochána (Disciplinary) Regulations 1945, arts 8, 9. **State (Burke) v Garvey** [1979] 232, SC.

Garda Síochána—Summary dismissal—Absence of formal inquiry—Limitations of rules of natural justice in context of certain State services. **State (Jordan) v Commissioner of the Garda Síochána** [1987] 107, HC.

Office holder—Delegation of power to dismiss—Whether *ultra vires* or in breach of principles of natural justice—Party to dispute acting as prosecutor and judge. **Heneghan v Western Regional Fisheries Board** [1986] 225, HC.

Office holder—Civil servant—Probationer—Whether reasons required—Whether reasons be disclosed. **State (Daly) v Minister for Agriculture** [1988] 173, HC.

Officer—Naval service—Dismissal notified but postponed to allow representations—No representations made—Whether sufficient compliance with *audi alteram partem* rules. **State (Duffy) v Minister for Defence** [1979] 65, SC.

Unfair dismissal—Gradual deterioration of working relationship—Termination of employment—Whether compliance with requirements of natural justice—Relevance of fair procedures. **Bunyan v UDT (Ireland) Ltd** [1982] 404, EAT.

Probationary period

Certification of satisfactory service—Delegation of duty of certification—Challenge to certificate—Board proceeding to institute inquiry as to whether plaintiff's service was satisfactory—Whether likelihood of bias—Pre-judgment—Test to be applied. **O'Neill v Beaumont Hospital Board** [1990] 419, HC, SC.

Suspension

Civil servants—Suspension without hearing—Plaintiffs knowing reason for suspension. **Yeates v Minister for Posts and Telegraphs** [1978] 22, HC.

Office holder—Garda Síochána—Disciplinary investigation and inquiry—Whether member entitled to make representations on suspension—Nature of decision on suspension—Garda Síochána (Discipline) Regulations 1971, reg 31. **McHugh v Commissioner of the Garda Síochána** [1985] 606, HC; [1987] 181, SC.

Employment Appeals Tribunal
Unfair dismissal claim

Failure by employer to deliver notice of appearance—Tribunal refusing to hear employer—Whether violation of natural and constitutional justice—Whether error within jurisdiction. *See* CERTIORARI (Employment Appeals Tribunal).

Evidence
Nullity proceedings

Non-consummation—Trial judge inferring collusion between parties—Whether inference open to judge—Whether in accordance with natural justice. **M v M** [1979] 160, SC.

Fair procedures
Criminal law

District Court—Whether District Justice had jurisdiction to reopen case and hear additional evidence for prosecution in absence of applicant's counsel—Applicant's counsel specifically excused from attending—Whether District Justice acted contrary to natural justice—RSC 1986, O 84 r 27(4), (6). **Dawson v Hamill** [1990] 257, HC.

NATURAL AND CONSTITUTIONAL JUSTICE *continued*

Habeas corpus
Certiorari

Absolute orders made at first instance—Whether denial of natural justice. **In re Zwann** [1981] 333, SC.

Harbour authority
Tug operating licence

Refusal—Whether applicant entitled to be told of criteria employed in and the reasons for the decision. **C W Shipping Company Ltd v Limerick Harbour Commissioners** [1989] 416, HC.

Inquest
Verdict

Suicide—Whether verdict available—Notice of inquest not served on next-of-kin— Failure to give opportunity to be heard. **State (McKeown) v Scully** [1986] 133, HC.

Labour Court
Legal advice

Challenge to Labour Court's jurisdiction—Labour court taking legal advice and pro- ceeding with the appeal—Employer not made aware of advice and given no opportunity of commenting on it—Whether breach of natural justice—Whether, if so, employer entitled as of right to have the determination quashed. **State (Polymark (Irl) Ltd) v Labour Court** [1987] 357, HC.

Land Commission
Acquisition of lands

Objectors' application for sight of certain documents refused—Whether procedure adopted fair and in accordance with principles of natural justice—Land Act 1965, ss. 12, 45. **State (Hussey) v Irish Land Commission** [1983] 407, HC.

Landlord and tenant
Termination of tenancy

Notice to quit—District Court hearing—**Audi alteram partem**—Tenant not represented— Tenant not invited to give evidence—Possession awarded to Corporation—Whether hearing in breach of natural justice—Housing Act 1966, s. 62. **State (Crothers) v Kelly** [1978] 167, HC.

Licensing authority
Refusal of licence

Slaughterhouse licence—Duties of licensing authority to act in accordance with natural justice—Extent of duty—*Audi alteram partem*—Fair procedures—Towns Improvement Clauses Act 1847—Slaughter of Animals Act 1935. **Doupe v Limerick County Council** [1981] 456, HC.

Local authority
Estimates meeting

Whether conducted in accordance with natural justice—Whether each estimate to be considered separately. **Ahern v Kerry Co Council** [1988] 392, HC.

Gaming and lotteries

Licence—Application—Local authority rescinding resolution allowing gaming— Whether decision of local authority *ultra vires*—Whether resolution made as a result of bias or interest—Whether made in disregard of the essentials of justice. **State (Divito) v Arklow UDC** [1986] 123, SC.

Sanitary authoirty. See sanitary authority (*below*).

Medical Bureau of Road Safety
Certificate of analysis of blood specimen

Accused not receiving copy of certificate until just before the trial. **State (O'Regan) v Plunkett** [1984] 347, HC.

NATURAL AND CONSTITUTIONAL JUSTICE *continued*
Minister
Party political broadcast
Ministerial order preventing access by Provisional Sinn Fein candidates to radio and television to promote their electoral campaign—No advance notice given nor representations invited—Relevance of time factor. **State (Lynch) v Cooney** [1982] 190, HC; [1983] 89, SC.

National monument
Preservation order
Whether order made in conformity with principles of natural justice. *See* NATIONAL MONUMENT (Preservation order).

Nemo iudex in causa sua
Compulsory purchase powers
Bord na Móna—Absence of right of appeal. **O'Brien v Bord na Mona** [1983] 314, SC.

Planning appeal
Refusal of permission
Whether objector entitled to be heard on appeal. **State (Haverty) v An Bord Pleanála** [1988] 545, HC.

Prison
Temporary release
Revocation—Whether fair procedures required to be observed—Whether fact that releasee had been charged with an offence a sufficient reason for revocation—No investigation of offence carried out by prison governor—Criminal Justice Act 1960, ss. 2, 4, 6, 7—Prisoners (Temporary Release) Rules 1960, rr 3(2), 5, 6, 7. **State (Murphy) v Governor of St Patrick's Institution** [1982] 475, HC; [1985] 141, SC.

Racing Board
Licensed bookmaker
Revocation of course betting permit—Appeal—Fair procedures—Whether hearing contrary to natural justice—Hearing of appeal by same body which heard the original complaint. **McCann v Attorney General** [1983] 67, HC.

Sanitary authority
Unlicensed caravan site
Order prohibiting erection or retention of temporary dwellings on the site—Order having no effect until person aggrieved has been given an opportunity of stating reasons as to why it should not come into operation—Whether sufficient compliance with principles of natural justice—*Audi alteram partem*—Local Government (Sanitary Services) Act 1948, ss. 31, 34—Local Government Act 1955, s. 66. **Gammell v Dublin Co Council** [1983] 413, HC.

Schools
Discipline
Suspension and expulsion—Suspension after investigation by school principal affirmed by expulsion by board of management—Whether failure to interview pupil expelled rendered expulsion valid—Whether legal representation required at hearing to expel student—Whether draft articles of management of school consistent with requirements of natural justice. **State (Smullen) v Duffy** [1980] 46, HC.

Trade union
Disciplinary powers
ICTU—Whether principles of natural justice must be observed. **IDATU v Carroll** [1988] 713, HC.

Meeting
Resolution—Validity—Plaintiff not present when vote taken. **Rodgers v ITGWU** [1978] 51, HC.

NATURAL AND CONSTITUTIONAL JUSTICE *continued*
Trial
Adjournment
Refusal—Defendant requesting adjournment to obtain legal representation and a witness—Whether refusal to grant adjournment breach of natural justice. **Flynn v Ruane** [1989] 690, HC.

District Court
Conduct of trial—Whether solicitor representing accused allowed proper opportunity to present case—Interventions by judge during cross-examination. **Gill v Connellan** [1988] 448, HC.

Tribunal
Bias
Employment—Certification of satisfactory service—Board proceeding to institute inquiry as to whether plaintiff's service was satisfactory—Whether likelihood of bias—Test to be applied. **O'Neill v Beaumont Hospital Board** [1990] 419, HC, SC.

Evidence
Determination of remedy by tribunal not argued by parties to hearing—Whether in breach of natural justice—Whether in breach of fair procedures. **State (Irish Pharmaceutical Union) v Employment Appeals Tribunal** [1987] 36, SC.

NATURAL FATHER
Guardianship proceedings. *See* CHILD (Guardianship and custody—Natural father's application).

NAVAL SERVICE
Officer
Dismissal. See DEFENCE FORCES (Dismissal—Navy).

NEGLIGENCE
Accountant
Duty of care
Duty of care owed to third party—Preparation of accounts—Third party investing in company for whom accountant acted as auditor—Whether auditor owing duty of care to third party—Whether auditor in breach of duty—Whether accounting standards as to audits complied with—Whether negligent—Whether accounts prepared by auditor resulted in misleading impression in third party. **Kelly v Boland** [1989] 373, HC.

Accrual of cause of action
Defective premises. See Defective premises—Accrual of cause of action (*below*).

Personal injuries. See LIMITATION OF ACTIONS (Personal injuries).

Advice or information
Auctioneer
Building society agent—Defective premises—Negligent advice—Liability of building society in respect of agent acting as an auctioneer. **Irish Permanent Building Society v O'Sullivan and Collins** [1990] 598, HC.

Pre-contractual representation—Representation made to plaintiff's brother—Plaintiff relying on representation—Premises found unsuitable for use as residence—Whether duty of care owed to plaintiff by auctioneer—Whether negligent misrepresentation. **Stafford v Mahony and Others** [1980] 53, HC.

Banker. See BANK (Duty of care—Advice or information).

Broker
Contract of insurance—Proposal—Non-disclosure of material facts—Fire—Insurance company repudiating liability—Liability of brokers to plaintiff in contract and tort—Marine Insurance Act 1906, s. 18. **Chariot Inns Ltd v Assicurazioni Generali SPA** [1981] 173, SC.

NEGLIGENCE *continued*
Animals
Liability of owner for injuries caused by animal. See ANIMALS (Negligence—Liability of owner).

Poisoning
Cattle wandering into cemetery—Cattle poisoned by eating yew leaves—Liability of local authority. *See* ANIMALS (Cattle—Poisoning).

Straying onto main road
Liability of owner or keeper for damage caused. *See* ANIMALS (Negligence—Straying onto main road).

Architect
Building defects
Contribution—Engineer's certificate as to structural stability—Architect's certificate based on such certificate—Whether builder or architect negligent—Contribution as between defendants—Damages. **Quinn v Quality Homes Ltd** [1976–7] 314, HC.

Foreseeability
Contribution—Accident—Plaintiff falling from roof—Institution of proceedings against occupier—Occupier joining architects as third party—Trial judge finding occupier liable but holding that architect pay 30% contribution in respect of the damages payable—Appeal against the findings in respect of contribution—Whether architects concurrent wrongdoers—Whether architects could reasonably have foreseen this accident—Civil Liability Act 1961, ss. 22, 29. **Crowley v Allied Irish Banks** [1988] 225, SC.

Auctioneer
Advice or information
Defects subsequently discovered. *See* Advice or information—Auctioneer (*above*).

Inspection of property
Duty of care—Whether duty of care owed to the purchaser by an auctioneer inspecting the dwelling on behalf of the housing authority—Failure to discover serious defects—Standard of care. **Ward v McMaster** [1986] 43, HC.

Auditor
Duty of care to third party. See Accountant—Duty of care—Duty of care owed to third party (*above*).

Bank
Duty of care. See BANK (Duty of care).

Broker
Duty of care
Advice—Contract of insurance—Non-disclosure of material facts—Company repudiating liability. *See* Advice or information—Broker (*above*).

Builder
Defective premises. See Defective premises (*below*).

Duty of care
Defective premises—Contribution—Architect. *See* Defective premises—Contribution—Architect—Builder (*below*).

Defective premises—Whether duty of care extends to defects in quality or confined to defects constituting damage to health or safety—Second purchaser suing builder. *See* Defective premises—Duty of care—Builder—Dwelling house—Second purchaser suing builder for financial loss incurred in making good the defects (*below*).

Building society
Agency
Negligent advice—Building society agent acting as auctioneer—Liability of building

NEGLIGENCE
Building society
Agency continued

society in respect of agent acting as an auctioneer. **Irish Permanent Building Society v O'Sullivan and Collins** [1990] 598, HC.

Concurrent wrongdoers
Damages

Award—Apportionment—Each defendant responsible for event causing loss to plaintiff. **Riordan's Travel Ltd v Acres & Co Ltd** [1979] 3, HC.

Defective product

Jury finding defendants negligent and apportioning fault—Whether vendor entitled to claim contribution or indemnity against manufacturer—Civil Liability Act 1961, s. 21—RSC, O 16, rr 7, 11. **Cole v Webb Caravan Services Ltd** [1985] 1, HC.

Occupier

Architects—Plaintiff falling from roof—Proceedings against occupier—Occupier joining architects as third party— Whether architects concurrent wrongdoers—Civil Liability Act 1961, ss. 22, 29. **Crowley v Allied Irish Banks** [1988] 225, SC.

Indemnity

Road traffic accident—Employer seeking indemnity from employee using vehicle in course of employment—Employee guilty of negligence—Civil Liability Act 1961, s. 21—Road Traffic Act 1961, s. 118. **Sinnott v Quinnsworth Ltd** [1984] 523, SC.

Contribution
Canal

Lack of maintenance—Flooding. *See* Statutory duty—Canal (*below*).

Concurrent wrongdoers. See Concurrent wrongdoers (*above*).

Defective premises. See Defective premises (*below*).

Garda Síochána

Plaintiff arrested and detained in Garda station—Injury. *See* Garda Síochána—Duty of care (*below*).

Occupier

Architects—Plaintiff falling from roof—Proceedings against occupier—Occupier joining architects as third party— Whether architects concurrent wrongdoers—Civil Liability Act 1961, ss. 22, 29. **Crowley v Allied Irish Banks** [1988] 225, SC.

Visitor—Ancient castle—Plaintiff falling down hole—Injuries—Contribution—Whether plaintiff contributorily negligent. **Clancy v Commissioners of Public Works** [1988] 268, HC.

Damages. *See* DAMAGES.

Defective premises
Accrual of cause of action

Statute of Limitations—House built on unsuitable foundations developing structural fault—Date when cause of action accrued—Whether date of damage or date of discoverability of damage—Whether date of accrual further extended on the grounds of equitable estoppel or fraudulent concealment—Statute of Limitations 1957, ss. 11(1), 11(2)(a), 71(1). **Morgan v Park Developments Ltd** [1983] 156, HC.

Contribution

Architect—Builder—Engineer's certificate as to structural stability—Architect's certificate based on such certificate—Whether builder or architect negligent— Contribution as between defendants—Damages. **Quinn v Quality Homes Ltd** [1976–7] 314, HC.

Duty of care

Auctioneer—Dwelling built on land owned by builder—Whether duty of care owed to

NEGLIGENCE
Defective premises
Duty of care continued

the purchaser by an auctioneer inspecting the dwelling on behalf of the housing authority—Housing Act 1966, s. 39—Housing Authorities (Loans for Acquisition or Construction of Houses) Regulations 1972—Civil Liability Act 1961, s. 21(2). **Ward v McMaster** [1986] 43, HC.

Builder—Dwelling built on land owned by builder—Whether duty of care owed by builder to the purchaser—Whether duty of care owed to such purchaser by a housing authority granting a loan to him under statutory powers—Whether duty of care owed to the purchaser by an auctioneer inspecting the dwelling on behalf of the housing authority—Extent of liability—Whether consequential loss—Financial loss recoverable—Housing Act 1966, s. 39—Housing Authorities (Loans for Acquisition or Construction of Houses) Regulations 1972—Civil Liability Act 1961, s. 21(2). **Ward v McMaster** [1986] 43, HC.

Builder—Dwelling house—Second purchaser suing builder for financial loss incurred in making good the defects—Whether duty extends to defects in quality or confined to defects constituting damage to health or safety—Whether liability excluded by the fact that defects could have been discovered if plaintiff had had house surveyed before purchase—Civil liability Act 1961, s. 34(2)(f). **Colgan v Connolly Construction Co (Ireland) Ltd** [1980] 33, SC.

Building society—Building society agent acting as auctioneer—Negligent advice—Liability of building society in respect of agent acting as an auctioneer. **Irish Permanent Building Society v O'Sullivan and Collins** [1990] 598, HC.

Housing authority—Whether duty of care owed to purchaser by a housing authority granting a loan under statutory powers—Consequential loss to purchaser—Housing Act 1966, s. 39—Housing Authorities (Loans for Acquisition or Construction of Houses) Regulations 1972—Civil Liability Act 1961, s. 21(2). **Ward v McMaster** [1986] 43, HC; [1989] 400, SC.

Planning authority—Grant of planning permission—Whether authority in granting planning permission owed a duty of care to occupiers to avoid damage due to defective siting and construction—Local Government (Planning and Development) Act 1963, ss. 26, 28. **Sunderland v Louth Co Council** [1990] 658, SC.

Defective products
Concurrent wrongdoers

Jury finding defendants negligent and apportioning fault—Whether vendor entitled to claim contribution or indemnity against manufacturer—Civil Liability Act 1961, s. 21—RSC, O 16, rr 7, 11. **Cole v Webb Caravan Services Ltd** [1985] 1, HC.

Floodlighting masts

Strong wind—Mast collapsing—Whether defendant negligent—Method of installation—Relevant standard—Whether mast inherently defective. s. **E E Co Ltd v Public Lighting Services** [1988] 677, SC.

Liability of supplier

Onus of proof. **Cole v Webb Caravans Ltd** [1983] 595, HC.

Practice

Service out of jurisdiction—Choice of law—Defective heart valve—Fitting of heart valve in Ireland—Plaintiff resident in Ireland—Valve manufactured in United States—RSC 1962, O 11, r 1(f). **Grehan v Medical Incorporated and Valley Pines Associates** [1986] 627, SC.

NEGLIGENCE *continued*
Defence forces
UN service
Injury to soldier—Whether soldier owed duty of care by superior officers—Whether State enjoys common law immunity from suit during armed conflict or hostilities— Whether sufficient case for jury. **Ryan v Ireland** [1989] 544, SC.

Demolition work
Adjoining premises
Demolition work causing damage to plaintiff's premises—Whether work carried out negligently—Work being carried out by independent contractor—Whether defendant vicariously liable. Boylan v Northern Bank Ltd [1976–7] 287, HC.

Loss of premises
Damages—Assessment—Foreseeability. *See* DAMAGES (Loss of premises).

Doctor. *See* MEDICAL PRACTITIONER (Negligence).

Duty of care
Accountant
Auditor—Duty of care to third party. *See* Accountant (*above*).

Auctioneer. See Auctioneer (*above*).

Bank. See Bank (Duty of care).

Builder. See Builder (*above*).

Building society. See Building society (*above*).

Defence forces
Injury to soldier. *See* Defence forces (*above*).

Driver of motor vehicle. See Road accident
Driver of motor vehicle—Duty of care. (*below*).

Employer. See Employer (*below*).

Garda Síochána
Duty owed to person detained in Garda station. *See* Garda Síochána (*above*).

Hospital. See Hospital (*below*).

Housing authority
Loan to purchaser—Whether duty of care owed by housing authority granting a loan under statutory powers. See Defective premises—Duty of care—Housing authority (*above*).

Insurance broker
Advice or information. *See* Advice or information—Broker (*above*).

Landowner
Tree falling on highway. *See* Highway—Tree adjacent to highway (Landowner (*below*).

Local authority. See Local authority (*below*).

Minister. See Minister (*below*).

Planning authority
Defective premises. *See* Defective premises—Duty of care—Planning authority (*above*).

Prison authorities. See Prison authorities (*below*).

Receiver. See Receiver (*below*).

Solicitor. See SOLICITOR (Negligence).

Statutory authority. See Statutory duty (*below*).

NEGLIGENCE *continued*
Employer
Accident at work
Plaintiff employed by first defendant, an independent contractor working under contract with second defendant—Employee of second defendant directing plaintiff in accordance with specifications on contract—Plaintiff injured while carrying out such directions—Whether second defendants liable. **O'Donnell v Begley and Bord Telecom Eireann** [1987] 105, HC.

Victim suffering brain damage—Permanent hospitalisation—Whether defendant owed duty of care to victim's children not to deprive them of the non-pecuniary benefits derived from parent-child relationships—Whether defendants' carelessness infringed the plaintiffs' constitutional rights—Constitution of Ireland 1937, Articles 41, 42. **Hosford v John Murphy & Sons Ltd** [1988] 300, HC.

Whether employer negligent—Risk becoming manifest—Simple method of overcoming it. **Fortune v P E Jacob and Co Ltd** [1976–7] 277, SC.

Concurrent wrongdoers
Indemnity—Road traffic accident—Employer seeking indemnity from employee using vehicle in course of employment—Employee guilty of negligence—Civil Liability Act 1961, s. 21—Road Traffic Act 1961, s. 118. **Sinnott v Quinnsworth Ltd** [1984] 523, SC.

Duty of care
Notice given that employee fit for work only—Employer taking no further action—Whether employer in breach of duty of care—Whether *prima facie* case of negligence established. **Rafferty v C A Parsons of Ireland Ltd** [1987] 98, SC.

Occupational disease
Folliculitis—Whether employee's contraction of the disease was reasonably foreseeable. **Brady v Beckman Instruments** [1986] 361, SC.

Safe place of work
Health board—Home help employed in the community—Personal injuries—Defective condition of patient's home—Responsibility of Health Board. **Mulcare v Southern Health Board** [1988] 689, HC.

Personal injuries—Absence of provision of protective clothing—Whether duty upon employer to provide employee with protective clothing—Whether scope of duty limited by foreseeability of type of injury—Evidence—Degree of evidence necessary to allow case to go to jury—Test applicable to determination of employer's liability. **Kennedy v Hughes Dairy Ltd** [1989] 117, SC.

Vicarious liability
Employee engaged in criminal activity—Whether employer liable—Goods stolen from factory guarded by employer—Whether employer liable to factory owner for cost price or retail price of goods. **Johnson & Johnson v C P Security Ltd** [1986] 559, HC.

Independent contractor—Demolition work—Damage to adjoining premises—Whether work carried out negligently—Whether defendant vicariously liable. **Boylan v Northern Bank Ltd** [1976–7] 287, HC.

Foreseeability
Architects
Plaintiff falling from roof—Institution of proceedings against occupier—Occupier joining architects as third party— Whether architects concurrent wrongdoers. *See* Occupier—Contribution—Architect—Foreseeability (*below*).

Employer
Injury to employee—Evidence necessary to allow case to go to jury. *See* Foreseeability—Evidence (*below*).

NEGLIGENCE
Foreseeability
Employer continued

Occupational disease—Folliculitis—Whether employee's contraction of the disease was reasonably foreseeable. **Brady v Beckman Instruments** [1986] 361, SC.

Evidence

Degree of evidence necessary to allow case to got to jury—Employer—Dairy—Employee injured by broken glass—Absence of provision of protective clothing—Whether duty to supply protective clothing—Whether scope of duty limited by foreseeability of type of injury—Test applicable to determination of employer's liability. **Kennedy v Hughes Dairy Ltd** [1989] 117, SC.

Garda Síochána
Duty of care to detainee in Garda station

Personal injuries—Plaintiff arrested and detained in Garda station—Plaintiff drunk and incapable—Plaintiff alleging that he was left with matches—Plaintiff setting fire to cell and suffering extensive burns—Whether defendants negligent—Whether defendant contributorily negligent—Damages—Whether excessive. **McKevitt v Ireland** [1987] 541, SC.

Health board
Mental treatment

Detention of person as being of unsound mind—Subsequent discharge—Requirement that person show substantial grounds for contending that the Board, through its officers, acted in bad faith or without reasonable care—Whether claim made out—Whether evidence of want of reasonable care—Mental Treatment Act 1945, s. 260. **O'Dowd v North Western Health Board** [1983] 186, SC.

Health Education Bureau
Duty of care

Campaign to help members of the public give up smoking—Whether duty of care owed to conduct the campaign so as not to damage the property rights of those engaged in the tobacco trade. **Gallaher Ltd v Health Education Bureau** [1982] 240, HC.

Highway
Highway authority

Injury to pedestrian—Condition of planning permission that lay by be provided by developers—Layout agreed with defendants as planning authority—Difference in road levels—Pedestrian injured—Jury finding of negligence—Whether defendant authority liable for contractor's negligence. **Weir v Dun Laoghaire Corporation** [1984] 113, SC.

Tree adjacent to highway

Tree falling to ground and damaging passing car—Landowner—Duty of care—Whether landowner in breach of a duty of care—Whether tree a danger to persons using the highway. **Lynch v Hetherton** [1990] 857, HC.

Hospital
Duty of care

Patient known to suffer from epileptic fits and connected psychotic behaviour—Patient taken off medication—Patient falling from first floor window—Whether reasonable for hospital authorities to allow patient to be alone without supervision—Whether hospital authorities negligent—Trial judge's directions to jury—Whether mistrial—Whether damages awarded excessive—RSC, O 58 r 72. **Kelly v Board of Governors of St Laurence's Hospital** [1989] 437, SC.

General and approved practice

Jury trial—Whether evidence before the jury to support certain of its findings—Whether jury appropriately directed—Assessment of damages. **Dunne (an Infant) v National Maternity Hospital and Jackson** [1989] 735, SC.

NEGLIGENCE *continued*
Housing authority
Loan to purchaser
Defective premises. *See* Defective premises—Duty of care—Housing authority (*above*).

Immunity from suit
State
Injury to soldier on UN service—Whether State enjoys common law immunity from suit during armed conflict or hostilities—Whether sufficient case for jury—Constitution of Ireland 1937, Articles 28, 40 3 1 and 40 3 2—Defence Act 1954, s. 111—Defence (Amendment) Act 1960, s. 4. **Ryan v Ireland** [1989] 544, SC.

Jurisdiction of courts
Conflict of laws
Explosion on French registered ship in Irish waters—Fatal damages claim—Victims French nationals employed under French contracts of service—RSC 1962, O 12, r 26. **O'Daly v Gulf Oil Terminals Ltd** [1983] 163, HC.

Landowner
Tree adjacent to highway
Tree falling to ground and damaging passing car—Duty of care. *See* Highway—Tree adjacent to highway (*above*).

Limitation of actions
Personal injuries. See LIMITATION OF ACTIONS (Personal injuries).

Local authority
Cemetery
Cattle poisoned by eating yew leaves—Wall between pastureland and cemetery damaged—Whether local authority negligent or in breach of statutory duty in not having wall repaired. *See* ANIMALS (Cattle—Poisoning).

Duty of care
Road works—Overhead railway bridge—Minimum clearance required by statute of railway company—Whether local authority's roadworks in reducing clearance *below* statutory minimum wanting in due course—Whether advanced warning system agreed between railway company and local authority—Railway Clauses Consolidation Act 1845, s. 49. **Coras Iompair Eireann v Carroll** [1983] 173, HC; [1986] 312, SC.

Highway authority. See Highway authority (*above*).

Housing authority
Loan to purchaser—Defective premises. *See* Defective premises—Duty of care—Housing authority (*above*).

Planning authority
Grant of permission—Defective premises. *See* Defective premises—Duty of care—Planning authority (*above*).

Manufacturer's liability
Defective products
Concurrent wrongdoers—Whether vendor entitled to claim contribution or indemnity against manufacturer. **Cole v Webb Caravan Services Ltd** [1985] 1, HC.

Medical practitioner. *See* MEDICAL PRACTITIONER (Negligence).

Minister
Duty of care
Depositor lodging money with industrial and provident society—Society subsequently going into liquidation—Depositor received a dividend of only part of sum lodged—Whether Minister owed duty of care—Whether sufficient relationship of proximity between Registrar of Friendly Societies and plaintiff. **McMahon v Ireland** [1988] 610, HC.

NEGLIGENCE
Minister *continued*

Exercise of statutory discretion

Minister granting planning permission—Legal advice that he had power so to do— Supreme court subsequently ruling that such permission ultra vires—Whether Minister negligent. **Pine Valley Developments Ltd v Minister for the Environment** [1987] 747, HC, SC.

Occupier
Ancient castle

Injury to visitor— Plaintiff falling down hole—Contribution—Whether plaintiff contributorily negligent—Assessment of damages. **Clancy v Commissioners of Public Works** [1988] 268, HC.

Contribution

Architect—Foreseeability—Plaintiff falling from roof—Institution of proceedings against occupier—Occupier joining architects as third party—Trial judge finding occupier liable but holding that architect pay 30% contribution in respect of the damages payable—Appeal against the findings in respect of contribution—Whether architects concurrent wrongdoers—Whether architects could reasonably have foreseen this accident—Civil Liability Act 1961, ss. 22, 29. **Crowley v Allied Irish Banks** [1988] 225, SC.

Licensee

Church—Infant licensee—Personal injuries—Infant plaintiff suffering extensive burns after her sleeve caught fire whilst lighting a candle on a candelabra—Whether concealed danger—Whether defendant negligent—Whether damages awarded excessive. **Rooney v Connolly** [1987] 768, SC.

Trespasser

Contribution—Architect. *See* Occupier—Contribution—Architect—Foreseeability (*above*).

Visitor. See Occupier—Ancient castle—Injury to visitor (*above*).

Personal injuries
Damages. See DAMAGES (Personal injuries).

Practice
Summons

Service out of jurisdiction—Defective product. *See* Defective products—Practice— Service out of jurisdiction (*above*).

Prison authorities
Duty of care

Whether duty of care owed to prisoner—Prisoner injured by another prisoner during recreation—Whether supervision of prisoners adequate—Whether prison authorities required to conduct searches of prisoners before recreation. **Muldoon v Ireland** [1988] 367, HC.

Professional
Accountant. See Accountant (*above*).

Advice or information. See Advice or information (*above*).

Architect. See ARCHITECT (*above*).

Broker

Advice—Contract of insurance. *See* Advice or information—Broker (*above*).

Medical practitioner. See MEDICAL PRACTITIONER (Negligence).

Solicitor. See SOLICITOR (Negligence).

NEGLIGENCE *continued*
Railway authority
Destruction of overhead bridge
Derailment of train—Clearance between road surface and underside of the bridge less than the prescribed statutory dimension—Diminution in clearance due to road works carried out by second defendant—Whether negligence or breach of statutory duty on part of plaintiffs—Railway Clauses Consolidation Act 1845, ss. 46, 49, 52–57—Local Government Act 1925, Part III. **Coras Iompair Eireann v Carroll** [1983] 173, HC.

Receiver
Duty of care
Duty of care owed to guarantor—Company in receivership—Guarantor and sundry creditors seeking information concerning purchase price of the assets—Whether guarantor entitled to the information—Whether sale be restrained—Whether receiver owes duty of care to guarantor. **McGowan v Gannon** [1983] 516, HC.

Road traffic accident
Apportionment of fault
Failure to wear seat belt—Damages. **Sinnott v Quinnsworth Ltd** [1984] 523, SC.

Driver of motor vehicle
Duty to take care—Infant plaintiff—Whether finding of negligence justifiable—Apportionment of fault—Assessment of damages for future pain and suffering. **Brennan v Savage Smith & Co Ltd** [1982] 223, SC.

Personal injuries
Claim made against driver of vehicle—Driver dying from injuries received—Liberty sought to join insurers as defendants in place of deceased—Whether insurers estopped from opposing such an order. **Boyce v McBride** [1987] 95, SC.

Damages. *See* DAMAGES—Personal injuries.

Ship
Explosion
Explosion on French registered ship in Irish waters—Fatal damages claim—Victims French nationals employed under French contracts of service—Jurisdiction of Irish courts. **O'Daly v Gulf Terminals Ltd** [1983] 163, HC.

Solicitor. *See* SOLICITOR (Negligence).

Statutory duty
Canal
Lack of maintenance—Flooding—Nuisance—Whether commissioners' duty to maintain canal—Whether commissioners negligent—Whether plaintiff contributorily negligent—Damages—Wexford Harbour Embankment Act 1852, ss. 25, 26, 45. **Stelzer v Wexford North Slob Commissioners** [1988] 279, HC.

Local authority
Cemetery—Cattle poisoned by eating yew leaves—Wall between pastureland and cemetery damaged—Whether local authority negligent or in breach of statutory duty in not having wall repaired. *See* ANIMALS (Cattle—Poisoning).

Prison authorities. See Prison authorities (*above*).

Planning authority
Grant of planning permission—Defective premises—Whether authority in granting planning permission owed a duty of care to occupiers to avoid damage due to defective siting and construction. *See* Defective premises—Duty of care—Planning authority (*above*).

Surgeon. *See* MEDICAL PRACTITIONER (Negligence—Surgical operation).

NEGLIGENCE *continued*
Vicarious liability
Employer. See Employer—Vicarious liability (*above*).

Highway authority
Injury to pedestrian—Lay by provided by developers—Difference in road levels—Pedestrian injured—Jury finding of negligence—Whether defendant authority liable for contractor's negligence. **Weir v Dun Laoghaire Corporation** [1984] 113, SC.

Principal and agent
Third party given use of motor vehicle by employee of owner—Third party involved in motor accident—Third party negligent—Whether agency in existence—Whether owner liable. **Kett v Shannon** [1987] 364, SC.

NEGOTIABLE INSTRUMENTS
Bill of exchange
Discounting of foreign bills
Duty of care—Bank. *See* BANK (Duty of care—Discounting of foreign bills).

Cheque
Conditional or unconditional payment. See CHEQUE (Conditional or unconditional payment).

Duty of care of paying banker. See BANK (Duty of care—Contractual duty to exercise care and skill).

NEGOTIATION LICENCE *See* TRADE UNION (Negotiation licence).

NEWSPAPER
Advertisment
Planning application. See PLANNING (Application—Advertisement).

Defamation. *See* DEFAMATION.

Lottery. *See* GAMING AND LOTTERIES (Lottery—Game promoted through newspapers).

Press freedom *See* PRESS (Freedom).

NOISE AND VIBRATION
Nuisance
Mineral exploration work. See NUISANCE (Mineral exploration work)

Operation of quarry See NUISANCE (Quarry)

NOLLE PROSEQUI *See* CRIMINAL LAW (Nolle prosequi).

NON-CITIZENS *See* ALIENS.

NON-PARTY DISCOVERY *See* DISCOVERY (Non-party discovery).

NORTHERN IRELAND
Anglo-Irish Agreement 1985
Challenge to constitutionality
Whether agreement constituted disregard of interests of majority community in Northern Ireland—Whether contrary to Articles 2 and 3 of Constitution of Ireland. *See* CONSTITUTION (International relations—Treaty—Anglo-Irish Agreement).

Courts
Procedure
Whether procedure in courts of Northern Ireland meet minimum standards applicable in this State—Extradition order—Challenge. **Shannon v Attorney General** [1985] 449, HC, SC.

Whether procedure in courts of Northern Ireland meet minimum standards applicable in this State—Extradition order—Challenge. **Shannon v Fanning** [1985] 385, HC, SC.

NOTARY PUBLIC
Appointment
Appointment of person other than a member of the solicitor's profession
    Whether exceptional circumstances justifying appointment. **In re McCarthy** [1990] 84, CCJ.

NOTICE
Acquisition notice. *See* PLANNING (Acquisition notice).

Commercial transation
Ultra vires
    Constructive notice inapplicable. **Northern Bank Finance v Quinn** [1979] 221, HC.

Enforcement notice
Planning control. See PLANNING (Enforcement—Enforcement notice).

Judicial notice. *See* JUDICIAL NOTICE.

Notice to quit. *See* LANDLORD AND TENANT (Ejectment—Notice to quit).

Planning application. *See* PLANNING (Application—Advertisement).

Purchase notice. *See* PLANNING (Purchase notice).

Service
Date
    Purchase notice—Postal delivery—Notice deemed to be received on date of delivery rather than on date on which planning department stated it had been received. **State (McInerney & Co Ltd) v Dublin Co Council** [1985] 513, HC.

Time limit
    Initiation of claim—Unfair dismissal—Whether mandatory requirement to notify employer—Unfair Dismissals Act 1977, s. 8. **IBM (Ireland) Ltd v Feeney** [1983] 50, CC.

    Planning authority decision—Letter received after expiry of period for giving notice of decision—Whether notice given within period. **Freeney v Brady UDC** [1982] 29, HC.

Termination of employment
Minimum notice. See EMPLOYMENT (Minimum notice).

NUISANCE
Canal
Lack of maintenance
    Flooding—Whether commissioners' duty to maintain canal—Whether commissioners negligent—Whether plaintiff contributorily negligent—Damages—Wexford Harbour Embankment Act 1852, ss. 25, 26, 45. **Stelzer v Wexford North Slob Commissioners** [1988] 279, HC.

Cattle straying onto main road
Road traffic accident
    Whether cattle constituted a public nuisance. **Gillick v O'Reilly** [1984] 402, HC.

Emissions from factory
Injuries and damage
    Whether emissions shown to be cause of injuries claimed to have been suffered—Onus of proof—Whether defendants under obligation to disprove plaintiffs' claim in nuisance—Whether plaintiffs' onus at common law amounts to failure to vindicate property rights—Whether proof of offensive smells may support claim in nuisance—Whether interference with property beyond what was reasonable—Whether on balance of probabilities medical evidence corraborated plaintiffs' claims—Injuries to animals—Whether caused by factory emissions—Damage to plant life—Whether caused by factory emissions. **Hanrahan & Ors v Merck Sharp & Dohme** [1988] 629, SC.

NUISANCE *continued*
Highway
Tree adjacent to highway
Tree falling to ground and damaging passing car—Whether landowner in breach of duty of care—Whether tree a danger to persons using the highway. **Lynch v Hetherton** [1990] 857, HC.

Intended blasting operations
Building project delayed
Interference with cash flow—Plaintiff unable to take up all his site options—Plaintiff losing credit and discount facilities—Assessment of damages—Whether plaintiff's impecuniosity relevant. **Rabbette v Mayo Co Council** [1984] 156, HC.

Mineral exploration work
Noise and vibration
Rural locality—Physical damage—Whether caused by defendant's activities—Whether appropriate to grant an injunction. **Halpin v Tara Mines Ltd** [1976–7] 28, HC.

Quarry
Blasting operations
Heavy traffic—Dust and noise—Standard of comfort—Whether landlord liable for nuisance caused by the tenant's act—Whether plaintiffs entitled to damages and injunction—Contributions as between defendants—Civil Liability Act 1961, ss. 21, 34. **Patterson v Murphy** [1978] 85, HC.

Noise
Damage to property—Application for interlocutory injunction—Balance of convenience. **Stafford v Roadstone Ltd** [1980] 1, HC.

Tree. *See* Highway—Tree adjacent to highway (*above*).

NULLITY
Marriage. *See* MARRIAGE (Nullity).

NURSE
Dismissal
Psychiatric nurse
Whether entitlement to claim unfair dismissal. *See* EMPLOYMENT (Unfair dismissal—Exclusion—Officer—Health board).

OBSTRUCTION OF GOVERNMENT
Offence. *See* CRIMINAL LAW (Offence—Obstruction of government).

OCCUPATIONAL DISEASE
Employer's liability. *See* NEGLIGENCE (Employer—Occupational disease).

OCCUPATIONAL INJURIES
Employer's liability. *See* NEGLIGENCE (Employer).

OCCUPIER'S LIABILITY. *See* NEGLIGENCE (Occupier).

OFFENCE
Excise offence. *See* CUSTOMS AND EXCISE (Offence).

Fisheries. *See* FISHERIES (Offence).

Gaming and lotteries. *See* GAMING AND LOTTERIES (Offence).

Generally. *See* CRIMINAL LAW (Offence).

OFFENCE *continued*
Licensing. *See* LICENSING ACTS (Offence).

Nature
Whether minor offence triable summarily. See CONSTITUTION (Trial of offences—Minor offence).

Political. *See* EXTRADITION (Political offence).

OFFENCES AGAINST THE STATE ACTS
Arrest
Legality
Generally. *See* ARREST (Legality—Statutory power—Offences Against the State Acts).

Motive of arrest. *See* ARREST (Legality—Motive—Arrest under statutory power—Offences Against the State Acts).

Freezing of money in bank account
Powers of Minister
Minister empowered to freeze moneys in a bank account and cause them to be paid into the High Court—Whether such power amounts to confiscation of property—Whether such powers permissible delimitation of property rights. *See* CONSTITUTION (Property rights—Confiscation of property).

Trial
Court
Non-scheduled offences—Return for trial to Special Criminal Court—Opinion of DPP that ordinary courts inadequate—Whether opinion reviewable—Offences Against the State Act 1939, ss, 35, 45, 46—Prosecution of Offences Act 1974, s. 3. **Savage v DPP** [1982] 385, HC.

OFFICE HOLDER
Dismissal. *See* EMPLOYMENT (Dismissal—Officeholder).

OFFICER
Authorised officer. *See* AUTHORISED OFFICERS.

OFF-LICENCE APPLICATIONS. *See* LICENSING ACTS (Licence—Application—Off-licence)

OIREACHTAS
Bill
Validity. See CONSTITUTION (Bill—Validity).

Legislation
Validity. See CONSTITUTION (Statute—Validity).

Legislative power
Delegation. See DELEGATED LEGISLATION.

Revision of Dáil Constituencies
Duty of Oireachtas
Ratio not complying with requirements of Constitution—Whether courts can prevent the Taoiseach from advising the President to dissolve Dáil Éireann. *See* DÁIL ÉIREANN (Dissolution—Injunction).

ONEROUS LEASE
Disclaimer. *See* LANDLORD AND TENANT (Disclaimer of onerous lease).

ONEROUS PROPERTY
Disclaimer. *See* COMPANY (Winding up—Disclaimer of onerous property).

OPEN SPACES
Acquisition notice. *See* PLANNING (Acquisition notice).

OPPRESSION
Minority shareholder. *See* COMPANY (Oppression of minority).

OPTION TO PURCHASE
Fee simple. *See* LANDLORD AND TENANT (Lease—Option to purchase fee simple).

ORAL CONTRACT
Sale of land. *See* SALE OF LAND (Contract—Formation—Oral contract).

ORAL HEARING
Planning appeal
See PLANNING (Appeal—Hearing—Whether oral hearing required).

ORDER
Absolute order
Certiorari. See CERTIORARI (Absolute order).

Habeas corpus. See HABEAS CORPUS (Practice and procedure—Absolute order made in first instance).

Affiliation. *See* AFFILIATION ORDER.

Amendment
Extra-territorial effect
Inspection of bank account—Jurisdiction of High Court to make order for inspection with extra-territorial effect—Bankers' Books Evidence Act 1879, ss. 7, 9—Bankers' Books Evidence (Amendment) Act 1959, s. 2. **Chemical Bank v McCormack** [1983] 350, HC.

Certiorari. *See* CERTIORARI.

Committal. *See* CONTEMPT OF COURT (Committal).

Compulsory purchase. *See* COMPULSORY PURCHASE.

Conviction
Certiorari. See CERTIORARI (Conviction).

Costs. *See* COSTS.

Deportation. *See* ALIEN (Deportation order).

Generally. *See* JUDGMENT.

Enforcement. *See* JUDGMENT (Enforcement).

Fit person order. *See* CHILD (Care—Fit person order).

Government order
Whether a "law". See DELEGATED LEGISLATION (Government order).

Injunction. *See* INJUNCTION

Judicial review. *See* JUDICIAL REVIEW

Maintenance. *See* FAMILY LAW (Maintenance).

Mandamus. *See* MANDAMUS.

Place of safety order. *See* CHILD (Care—Place of safety order).

Prohibition. *See* PROHIBITION.

Sale in lieu of partition. *See* JOINT TENANCY (Partition).

OUTLINE PLANNING PERMISSION. *See* PLANNING (Outline permission).

PAIN AND SUFFERING
Damages. *See* DAMAGES (Personal injuries—Pain and suffering).

PARTICULARS
Plea. *See* PRACTICE (Pleadings—Particulars).

PARTIES *See* PRACTICE (Parties).

PARTITION
Joint tenancy
Order for sale in lieu of partition
Whether jurisdiction to make order extant. *See* JOINT TENANCY (Partition).

PARTNERSHIP
Existence
Drug testing unit
Receipt of a share of the profits—Whether partnership existed—Terms of arrangement—Partnership Act 1890, s. 2(3). **O'Kelly v Darragh** [1988] 309, HC.

Fisheries
Contract of service or partnership—Revenue—Returns—Employer's annual obligation to provide information relating to employees—Captain of vessel engaging crew at commencement of each separate voyage—Remuneration based on custom and agreement—Whether employment or partnership in existence—Whether element of control by captain outweighed by other factors. **DPP v McLoughlin** [1986] 493, HC.

Limited partnership
Income tax—Claim by partners for initial allowances in respect of the purchase of plant—Close relationship between the partners and a hotel company to which the plant was leased—Whether partnership existed as a matter of law—Whether colourable transaction—Limited Partnerships Act 1907, ss. 4, 5, 8—Income Tax Act 1967, ss. 241(5), 252, 282, 296, 307. **MacCarthaigh v Daly** [1986] 116, HC.

Retirement of partner
Purchase of shares
Shares of outgoing partners to be purchased by remaining partners in shares proportionate to their shares in business—Disagreement over net value of shares—Arbitration award—Whether interest payable from date of retirement to date of award—Interpretation of partnership deed—Whether equitable principles excluded—Whether entitlement to an account of rent and profits—Supreme Court of Judicature (Ireland) Act 1877— Partnership Act 1870, ss. 42, 43. **Williams v Harris** [1980] 237, SC.

PASSING OFF
Design
Sportswear
Foreign company with international trading reputation marketing sportswear with distinctive design—Irish company using similar design—Neither design registered as a trademark—Whether plaintiffs could claim any exclusive property or reputation in respect of the design—Whether defendants passing off their goods as those of the plaintiffs—Whether mere copying of a design or taking advantage of a demand created by another's advertising sufficient to support an action for passing off. **Adidas Sportschuhfabriken v Charles O'Neill & Co Ltd** [1983] 122, SC.

Imitation of packaging
Damages
Whether product marketed in a manner calculated to deceive the public—Whether

PASSING OFF
Imitation of packaging
Damages continued
action might be maintained by a distributor or agent—Assessment of damages—
Whether account of profits be directed. **Grange Marketing Ltd v M & Q Plastic
Products Ltd** [1976–7] 144, HC.

PASSPORT
Child
Application by wife for passports for children
Passports issued despite husband's objections—Removal of children from jurisdiction
by wife—Extent of relief husband entitled to obtain. **Cosgrove v Ireland** [1982] 48, HC.

Entry of child's name on passport of mother
Forged consent of husband—Removal of child from jurisdiction by wife—Mandamus—
Effectiveness of order—Whether Minister obliged to cancel entry of child—Ministers
and Scretaries Act 1924. **P I v Ireland** [1989] 810, SC.

Endorsement
Alien's passport
Fair procedures. *See* ALIEN (Settlement permission—Refusal of leave to settle in the
State).

PATENT
Appeal
Decision of Controller
Registration application—Appeal to High Court—Whether further appeal lies to
Supreme Court—Statute—Interpretation—Patents Act 1964, s. 75. **Beecham Group v
Bristol Myers** [1983] 500, SC.

Expiry
Application for extension dismissed
Adequacy of remuneration—Research and development costs—Whether trial judge's
discretion erroneously exercised—Patents Act 1964, ss. 25, 26 (3), 27, 75, (7). **Fisons
Pharmaceutical Ltd's Petition** [1984] 393, HC, SC.

Income tax. *See* REVENUE (Income tax—Patent—Income from qualifying patent).

Patent office
Arrears of work
Controller promulgating policy of accelerated acceptance of patent specifications—
Examiners refusing to carry out this policy—Whether for them so to do would involve
a breach of their statutory obligations—Refusal of increment to those examiners
failing to implement this policy—Application for judicial review—Whether orders of
certiorari and mandamus be granted—Patents Act 1964, ss. 2, 8(6), 9, 11, 12, 13,
16(3), 77, 78(5), 79(1)—Patent Rules, rr 27, 117. **State (Rajan) v Minister for Industry &
Commerce** [1988] 231, HC.

PATERNITY OF CHILD
Evidence
Admissibility
Evidence of wife that child not the child of the marriage—Whether admissible—Rule
in *Russell v Russell*—Whether part of the common law of Ireland—Whether incompatible with provisions of the Constitution. *See* CHILD (Paternity).

PAY
Equal pay. *See* EMPLOYMENT (Equal pay).

Statutory minimum wage. *See* EMPLOYMENT (Pay—Minimum wage).

PAYMENT
Mistake
Recovery. See MISTAKE (Payment—Recovery).

PAYMENT INTO COURT
Mistake
Lodgment of money in court
Insurance company—Mistaken assumption of liability induced by fraud. *See* MISTAKE (Payment—Recovery—Payment induced by fraud).

PEACE COMMISSIONER
Jurisdiction
Bail
Admittance of persons to bail—Whether administration of justice—Whether conferral of such power on peace commissioner invalid—Constitution of Ireland 1937, Article 34 1—Criminal Justice Act 1951, s. 15—Criminal Justice Act 1984, s. 26. **O'Mahony v Melia** [1990] 14, HC.

Summons
Peace Commissioner signing summons—Whether invalid as being an exercise of judicial power. **Joyce v Circuit Court Judge for Western Circuit** [1987] 316, HC.

PENAL SERVITUDE. *See* CRIMINAL LAW (Sentence—Penal servitude).

PENALTY
Mitigation
Excise offences. See CRIMINAL LAW (Penalty—Mitigation).

Revenue offence. *See* REVENUE (Offence—Penalty).

PENSION
Army pensions. *See* DEFENCE FORCES (Pensions).

Social welfare. *See* SOCIAL WELFARE (Pensions).

PERSONAL INJURIES
Damages. *See* DAMAGES (Personal injuries).

Employer's liability. *See* NEGLIGENCE (Employer).

Fatal injury. *See* FATAL INJURY.

Industrial accident
Father of family suffering brain damage
Whether employer owed duty of care to victim's children not to deprive them of the non-pecuniary benefits derived from parent-child relationships. *See* CONSTITUTION (Family—Rights—Extent of guarantee).

Limitation of actions. *See* LIMITATION OF ACTIONS (Personal injuries).

Occupier's liability. *See* NEGLIGENCE (Occupier).

Road traffic accidents. *See* NEGLIGENCE (Road traffic accident).

PERSONAL REPRESENTATIVE
Expenses. *See* SUCCESSION (Administration—Expenses of personal representative).

Recovery of possession
Limitation period
Applicability to claim of a personal representative to recover assets of deceased. **Drohan v Drohan** [1981] 472, HC.

PERSONAL REPRESENTATIVE *continued*
Sale of land
Powers
Whether vendor, selling as personal representative, must satisfy the purchaser that he
has power to sell as such. *See* Succession (Administration—Sale of land by personal
representative).

PERSONAL RIGHTS *See* Constitution (Personal rights).

PETITION
Company
Winding up. See Company (Winding up).

Local election. *See* Electoral Law (Local elections).

Nullity. *See* Marriage (Nullity).

PICKETING
Injunction applications. *See* Trade Dispute (Picketing).

PLACE OF SAFETY ORDER *See* Child (Care—Health board).

PLANNING
Abattoir
Intensification of use. See Development—Intensification of use (*below*)

Abuse of process
Challenge to validity of decision
Residents' association challenging authority's decision to grant planning permission—
Developers seeking to have proceedings dismissed—Whether proceedings frivolous or
vexatious—Whether proceedings an abuse of the process of the courts. **Cavern
Systems Ltd v Clontarf Residents' Association** [1984] 24, HC.

Unauthorised change of use
Duplicitous use of mandamus procedure to obtain order compelling the Corporation
to grant planning permission—Whether affects s. 27 application. **Cork Corporation v
O'Connell** [1982] 505, SC.

Acquisition notice
Open spaces
Planning authority dissatisfied in manner in which plot of land was being maintained—
Notice served under s. 25—Non-compliance—Planning authority acquiring land—
Vesting order—Ejectment civil bill—Whether section operates prospectively only—
Local Government (Planning and Development) Act 1976, s. 25. **Dublin Co Council v
Grealey** [1990] 641, HC.

Appeal
Challenge to validity of decision. See Decision—Validity—Challenge (*below*).

Deposit
Requirement of lodgement of deposit—Whether arbitrary discrimination—Constitutional
validity of planning legislation—Constitution of Ireland, Articles 40.1, 40.3—Local
Government (Planning and Development) Act 1976, s. 15. **Finnegan v An Bord
Pleanála** [1979] 134, HC, SC.

Effectiveness of remedy
Mandamus application—Whether lodgement of appeal precludes application for
mandamus—Whether mandamus more effective remedy where merits of case are not
in issue. **State (N C E Ltd) v Dublin Co Council** [1979] 249, HC.

Grant of permission
Use of site for disposal of asbestos waste—Board granting permission subject to

PLANNING
Appeal
Grant of permission continued
conditions—Appeal against decision—Whether due consideration given to evidence as to danger of health arising from proposed user—Requirement of lodgment of deposit—Statute—Validity—Constitution—Whether permission given by Board *ultra vires* the statute—Constitution of Ireland 1937, Articles 40.1, 40.3—Local Government (Planning and Development) Act 1976, ss. 15, 16, 18. **Finnegan v An Bord Pleanála** [1979] 134, HC, SC.

Hearing
Whether oral hearing required—Power of Board to determine vexatious or dilatory appeals notwithstanding that no submission made—Fair procedures—Constitutional validity of planning legislation—Constitution, Articles 40.1, 40.3—Local Government (Planning and Development) Act 1976, ss. 16, 18. **Finnegan v An Bord Pleanála** [1979] 134, HC, SC.

Jurisdiction of Bord Pleanála
Retention application—Whether retention order made in excess of jurisdiction. *See* Retention permission—Jurisdiction of Bord Pleanála (*below*).

Notice
Failure to state grounds of appeal in written notice of appeal—Application for planning permission granted—Written appeal by local residents—Failure to state grounds—Whether mandatory requirements to state grounds—Local Government (Planning and Development) Act 1963, s. 26—Local Government (Planning and Development) Act 1976, ss. 17,24(2)—Local Government (Planning and Development) Regulations 1977, art 36. **State (Elm Developments Ltd) v An Bord Pleanála** [1981] 108, SC.

Failure to state grounds of appeal in written notice of appeal—Extension erected without planning permission—Permission to retain refused by planning authority—Appeal to An Bord Pleanála—Whether appeal valid—Natural justice—Local Government (Planning and Development) Act 1976, ss. 17, 18—Local Government (Planning and Development) Regulations 1977, art 35. **State (Genport Ltd) v An Bord Pleanála** [1983] 12, HC.

Objector's rights
Successful objection to planning authority for planning permission—Appeal to An Bord Pleanála—Whether objector entitled to be heard on appeal—Natural justice—Fair procedures. **State (Haverty) v An Bord Pleanála** [1988] 545, HC.

Refusal of permission
Function of Minister in hearing appeal against refusal—Minister granting outline permission for development in breach of development plan—Limited ouster of judicial intervention—Whether applies to decisions made before the exclusionary provisions came into operation—Local Government (Planning and Development) Act 1963, ss. 26 (3), (4), (5), (6), 82 (3A)—Local Government (Planning and Development) Act 1976, ss. 14(8), 46(3). **State (Pine Valley Developments) Ltd v Dublin Co Council** [1982] 169, SC.

Retention order
Whether retention order made without jurisdiction. *See* Retention permission (*below*).

Vexatious appeal
Power of Board to determine vexatious or dilatory appeals notwithstanding that no submission made—Fair procedures. **Finnegan v An Bord Pleanála** [1979] 134, HC, SC.

Application
Advertisement
Application for change of user—Whether validly made—Requirement that application comply with planning application regulations—Whether regulations mandatory or directory—Extent of failure to comply—Local Government (Planning and Development)

PLANNING
Application
Advertisement continued

Act 1963, s. 26(4)—Local Government (Planning and Development (Regulations 1977, Art 75. **Monaghan UDC v Alf-a-Bet Promotions Ltd** [1980] 64, SC.

Compliance with regulations—Description of location of property—Inadequate description—Permission invalid—Electricity supply cables—Permission invalid notwithstanding that complainant landowner purchased lands after publication of advertisement—Local Government (Planning and Development) Act 1963, s. 26—Local Government (Planning and Development) Regulations 1964, art 9, s. 4(a). **Electricity Supply Board v Gormley** [1985] 494, SC.

Compliance with regulations—Description of location of property—Whether sufficient—Whether in compliance with planning legislation—Local Government (Planning and Development) Regulations 1977, regs 15, 17 **State (N C E Ltd) v Dublin Co Council** [1979] 249, HC.

Compliance with regulations—Description of location of property—Whether adequate—Advertisement in national daily newspaper—Default permission—Whether applicable—Local Government (Planning and Development) Regulations 1977, arts 14, 15. **Crodaun Homes Ltd v Kildare Co Council** [1983] 1, SC.

Compliance with regulations

Extent of failure to comply—Whether *de minimis* principle applicable—Whether approach different to *inter partes* litigation—Local Government (Planning and Development) Regulations 1977, Arts 18, 20. **Dublin Co Council v Marren** [1985] 593, HC.

Decision of planning authority. See Decision (*below*).

Interest in land. See Application—Particulars required—Interest in land (*below*).

Particulars required

Change of use—Application for permission for change of use of one room of a dwellinghouse to office use—Default permission obtained—Housing authority requiring particulars as to whether premises were remaining primarily residential—Whether apppplicant obliged to furnish particulars—Local Government (Planning and Development) Act 1963, s. 26(4)—Housing Act 1969, ss. 1(1), 2(1),2(2),3,9(2), 10 (c). **State (Magauran) v Dublin Corporation** [1983] 145, SC.

Interest in land—Whether requirement of stating applicant's interest in the land satisfied by a general description of the interest—Local Government (Planning and Development) Regulations 1977, reg 17 (a). **McCabe v Harding Investments Ltd** [1984] 105, SC.

Status of applicant

Application on behalf of company—Company not incorporated on date of application—Whether permission granted to non-existent company a nullity—Local Government (Planning and Development) Acts 1963 to 1983. **Inver Resources Ltd v Limerick Corporation** [1988] 47, HC.

Asbestos waste disposal
Grant of permission for use of site for disposal of asbestos waste

Appeal against decision. *See* Appeal—Grant of permission—Use of site for disposal of asbestos waste (*above*).

Authority
Decision

Challenge to validity. *See* Decision—Validity (*below*).

Duty of care

Grant of planning permission—Defective premises—Whether authority in granting planning permission owed a duty of care to occupiers to avoid damage due to

PLANNING

Authority

Duty of care continued

defective siting and construction—Local Government (Planning and Development) Act 1963, ss. 26, 28. **Sunderland v Louth Co Council** [1990] 658, SC.

Building of historic interest

Preservation

Effectiveness of planning legislation to preserve buildings of historic interest. *See* Enforcement—Section 27 application—Breach of conditions—Building of historic interest (*below*).

Challenge to validity of decision. *See* Decision—Validity—Challenge (*below*).

Change of use

Whether material change of use constituting development. See Development—Material change of use (*below*).

Compensation

Compulsory acquisition

Subject land designated on the County Development Plan—Whether designation amounts to a reservation for a particular purpose—Whether, in the event of housing development taking place, sanitary authority would refuse a connection for sewerage—Whether claimant debarred from recovering compensation—Public Health (Ireland) Act 1878, s. 23—Acquisition of Land (Assessment of Compensation) Act 1919, s. 2—Local Government (Planning and Development) Act 1963, ss. 19, 55, 56(1) (b)(i), 69, Schedule 4 r 11. **Shortt v Dublin Co Council [1982] 117, HC; Dublin County Co v Shortt** [1983] 377, SC.

Exclusions. See Compensation—Refusal of planning permission—Exclusions (*below*).

Refusal of planning permission

Exclusions—Deficiency in public sewerage facilities—Compensation claim—Diminution in value of land—Whether compensation deniable by virtue of a deficiency in public sewerage facilities—Whether assessment of compensation be delayed pending exhausture of the procedure laid down in the 1878 Act—Public Health (Ireland) Act 1878, s. 24—Acquisition of Land (Assessment of Compensation) Act 1919—Local Government (Planning and Development) Act 1963, ss. 55, 56 (1) (b). **McKone Estates Ltd v Kildare Co Council** [1984] 313, HC.

Exclusions—Legal interest in land— Whether applicant required to have legal interest in land affected not only at time permission refused but also at time compensation assessed. **Dublin Corporation v Smithwick** [1976–7] 280, HC.

Exclusions—Legal interest in land—Whether claimant had sufficient interest in lands—Local Government (Planning and Development) Act 1963, ss. 55, 56, 57—Acquisition of Land (Assessment of Compensation) Act 1919—Property Values (Arbitrations and Appeals) Act 1960. **In re Grange Developments Ltd** [1987] 733, HC.

Exclusions—Refusal for certain specified reasons—Whether reasons given defeated claim for compensation—Planning documents—Construction—Local Government (Planning and Development) Act 1963, ss. 55, 56. **X J S. Investments Ltd v Dun Laoghaire Corporation.** [1987] 659, SC.

Exclusions—Undertaking to grant permission—Planning authority undertaking to grant permission for an alternative development—Whether authority has power to give such an undertaking—Whether such undertaking valid. **Byrne v Dublin Co Council** [1983] 213, HC.

Exclusions—Undertaking to grant permission—Undertaking by assistant city and county manager to grant permission subject to conditions—Whether such undertaking valid—Whether given in time—Whether void for want of detail and precision—

PLANNING
Compensation
Refusal of planning permission continued
Whether material contravention of development plan involved. **Grange Developments Ltd v Dublin Co Council** [1987] 245, SC.

Exclusions—Undertaking to grant permission—Planning authority undertaking to grant permission for a residential development—Such undertaking involving a departure from the area's development plan—Whether undertaking valid—Whether arbitrator should have regard to undertaking in determining reduction in value of land—Local Government (Planning and Development) Act 1963, ss. 55, 56, 57—Acquisition of Land (Assessment of Compensation) Act 1919—Property Values (Arbitrations and Appeals) Act 1960. **Grange Developments Ltd v Dublin Co Council** [1987] 733, HC; [1989] 145, SC.

Outline permission—Entitlement to compensation—Assessment of compensation—Whether claimant confined, in proving the probable reduction in value of his interest, to the development in respect of which permission was refused—Local Government (Planning and Development) Act 1963, ss. 55, 68. **Owenabue Ltd v Dublin Co Council** [1982] 150, HC.

Outline permission—Extent to which value of land reduced—Exclusions—Alternative potential development—Undertaking to grant permission for an alternative development—Whether such undertaking valid—Local Government (Planning and Development) Act 1963, ss. 55, 57. **Byrne v Dublin Co Council** [1983] 213, HC.

Compulsory purchase
Compensation
Generally. *See* Compensation—Compulsory acquisition (*above*).

Conditions
Breach
Section 27 applications. *See* Enforcement—Section 27 application—Breach of condition (*below*).

Invalidity
Severance—Planning permission granted subject to condition—Whether condition, if invalid, able to be severed from permission—Local Government (Planning and Development) Act 1963, ss. 19, 26(1), (2), (5). **State (F P H Properties SA) v An Bord Pleanála** [1989] 98, SC.

Non-compliance
Planning permission granted subject to conditions—Development carried out without complying with conditions—Section 27 application. *See* Enforcement—Section 27 application—Development not in conformity with conditions (*below*).

Outline permission
Decision to grant outline planning permission subject to conditions—Application to quash decision—Certiorari—Existence of adequate alternative remedy—Jurisdiction of planning authority. **State (Abenglen Properties Ltd) v Dublin Corporation** [1981] 54, HC; [1982] 590, SC.

Validity
Permission granted subject to condition—Reason for imposing condition—Whether adequate—Whether moot point—Local Government (Planning and Development) Act 1963, s. 26. **Killiney and Ballybrack Development Association v Minister for Local Government** [1978] 78, SC.

Constitutional validity of legislation
Grant of permission for use of site for disposal of asbestos waste
Whether injurious to health—Whether relevant to constitutionality of planning

PLANNING
Constitutional validity of legislation
Grant of permission for use of site for disposal of asbestos waste continued
legislation—Right to bodily integrity—Constitution of Ireland 1937, Articles 40 1, 40 3—Local Government (Planning and Development) Act 1976. **Finnegan v An Bord Pleanála** [1979] 134, HC, SC.

Decision
Invalidity
Grant of permission by Minister—Supreme court subsequently ruling such permission *ultra vires*—Constitutional rights—Whether State had failed to vindicate the property rights of the plaintiff—Whether action in damages for breach of statutory duty or negligence lay against the Minister—Constitution of Ireland 1937, Arts 40.3.1 and 2—Local Government (Planning and Development) Act 1963, s. 26—Local Government (Planning and Development) Act 1982, s. 6. **Pine Valley Developments Ltd v Minister for the Environment** [1987] 747, HC, SC.

Objection
Locus standi—Objector—Local member of public bringing application—Whether applicant having sufficient standing—Local Government (Planning and Development) Act 1976, s. 27. **Robinson v Chariot Inns Ltd** [1986] 621, HC.

Time for giving
Computation of period—Application for planning permission and permission to demolish—Planning authority required to make and give notice of their decision within five weeks of date of final determination—Registered letter containing notice of refusal accepted for posting—Letter received after expiry of period—Whether notice given without period—Time limit for bringing proceedings questioning the validity of the planning authority's decision—Whether appropriate to seek relief by way of mandamus—Whether continued user of premises unlawful—RSC O 108 rr 2, 3—Local Government (Planning and Development Act) 1976, s. 27—Housing Act 1966, s. 10—Housing Act 1969, ss. 3,4(6)(b), 10—Interpretation Act 1937, ss. 11(h), s. 18—Sunday Observance Act 1695—Statute Law Revision (Pre-Union Irish Statutes) Act 1962, s. 1. **Freeney v Bray UDC** [1982] 29, HC.

Delay—Damages—Failure to give notice of decision within statutory time limit—Local Government (Planning and Development) Act 1963, s. 26(4), (5). **O'Neill v Clare Co Council** [1983] 141, HC.

Purchase notice—Whether refusal made within statutory time limit. *See* Purchase notice—Decision—Time for giving (*below*).

Request for further information—Whether a valid request—Whether decision given within appropriate period. **State (N C E) v Dublin Co Council** [1979] 249, HC.

Whether planning authority failed to adjudicate on and give notice of decision within prescribed period—Effective date of application—Entitlement to damages—Assessment of damages—Local Government (Planning and Development) Act 1963, s. 26(4) (5). **O'Neill v Clare Co Council** [1983] 141, HC.

Whether planning authority failed to notify decision within two months—Whether plaintiffs should first have applied for planning permission to demolish habitable houses—Whether existence of alternative remedy of appeal to An Bord Pleanála grounds for refusing declaration—Failure to comply with 1977 planning regulations—*De minimis* rule—Whether permission should be regarded as having been granted—Local Government (Planning and Development) Act 1963, s. 26(4)—Local Government (Planning and Development) Regulations 1977, rregs 17, 18, 19, 20. **Molloy and Walsh v Dublin Co Council** [1990] 633, HC.

PLANNING

Decision *continued*

Validity

Application to quash—Certiorari—Existence of adequate alternative remedy—Whether error appearing on the face of the record—Discretion—Whether certiorari should issue *ex debito justitiae*. **State (Abenglen Properties Ltd) v Dublin Corporation** [1981] 54, HC; [1982] 590, SC.

Challenge—Abuse of process—Planning appeal to be conducted by way of oral hearing—Residents' association instituting High Court proceedings challenging authority's decision to grant planning permission—Residents' association not serving summons or disclosing its existence—Developers seeking to have proceedings dismissed—Whether proceedings frivolous or vexatious—Whether proceedings an abuse of the process of the courts—Local Government (Planning and Development) Act 1976, s. 42—RSC O 19, rr 27, 28, O84, r 10. **Cavern Systems Ltd v Clontarf Residents' Association** [1984] 24, HC.

Challenge—Grant of permission—Judicial review—Jurisdiction of An Bord Pleanála—Whether estoppel or waiver on the part of the applicants—EC Directive—Environmental impact assessment—Whether directive implemented—Whether environmental impact study submitted included information required by directive—Whether failure to include information in breach of mandatory provision of planning regulations—Local Government (Planning and Development) Act 1963, ss. 25, 26—Local Government (Planning and Development) Regulations 1977, reg 26—Council Directive 85/337/EEC, Article 6(2). **Browne v An Bord Pleanála** [1989] 865, HC.

Challenge—Locus standi— Whether permission granted may be challenged by person unaffected by grant—Whether authority granting permission must be party to proceedings—Local Government (Planning and Development) Regulations 1964, Art 9—Local Government (Planning and Development) Act 1963, s. 26(1). **Electricity Supply Board v Gormley** [1985] 494, SC.

Challenge—Expiry of period—Whether decision *ultra vires*—Whether decision subject to judicial review—Permission granted to non-existent company—Local Government (Planning and Development) Act 1963, ss. 8, 82(3A)—Whether a real application was before the planning authority. **Inver Resources Ltd v Limerick Corporation** [1988] 47, HC.

Challenge—Time limit—Two month time limit within which to challenge validity—Whether constitutional—Locaal Government (Planning and Development) Act 1963, s. 82(3A). **Brady and Ors v Donegal Co Council** [1989] 282, HC, SC.

Whether *ultra vires*—Permission granted subject to conditions—Application to quash—Default procedure—Whether a decision given in excess of jurisdiction a 'decision'—Certiorari—Whether available—Alternative remedy in existence. **State (Abenglen Properties Ltd) v Dublin Corporation** [1982] 590, SC.

Default procedure

Purchase notice

Whether default procedures implicit in statutory provisions where planning authority does not reply to purchase notice. **State (McInerney & Co Ltd) v Dublin Co Council** [1985] 513, HC.

Whether applicable. **Crodaun Homes Ltd v Kildare Co Council** [1983] 1, SC.

Proposed development in contravention of development plan—Whether default procedure operates to produce an effect equivalent to the granting of permission in a case where the application is for something prohibited by statute—Limited ouster of judicial intervention—Whether applies to decisions made before the exclusionary provisions came into operation. **State (Pine Valley Developments) Ltd v Dublin Co Council** [1982] 169, SC.

SUBJECT MATTER

SUBJECT MATTER 353

PLANNING
Default procedure
Whether applicable continued
Proposed development in contravention of development plan—Whether local authority had power to grant permission by default. **Dublin Co Council v Marren** [1985] 593, HC.

Development
Exempted development. See Exempted development (*below*).

Intensification of use
Whether material change of use constituting development—Abattoir—Slaughtering activity carried on since the 1940's for the purpose of providing animal food. **Monaghan Co Council v Brogan** [1987] 564, HC.

Whether material change of use constituting development—Land used for the purpose of manufacturing concrete blocks—Whether unauthorised use or exempted development—Discontinued user—Redemption of original user. **Dublin Co Council v Tallaght Block Co Ltd** [1982] 534, HC.

Whether material change of use constituting development—Quarry—Whether operation of quarry exempted development—Reference to Minister to determine whether development exempted—Local Government (Planning and Development) Act 1976, s. 27. **Stafford v Roadstone Ltd** [1980] 1, HC.

Whether material change of use constituting development—Section 27 applications *generally. See* Enforcement—Section 27 application—Unauthorised use—Intensification of use (*below*).

Whether material change of use constituting development—Use of agricultural land to store caravans and fuel oils—Whether intensification or abandonment of use—Whether exempted development. **Furlong v A F & G W McConnell Ltd** [1990] 48, HC.

Material change of use
Hotel premises—Hotel acquiring ordinary seven day licence—Ground floor reconstructed to incorporate a lounge bar—Increase in trade—Whether material change of use constituting development—Whether, if so, such development exempted development—Local Government (Planning and Development) Act 1963, s. 5—Housing Act 1969, s. 10. **Carrick Hall Holdings Ltd v Dublin Corporation** [1983] 268, HC.

Licensed premises with cabaret—Installation of snooker tables—Whether change of user. **Robinson v Chariot Inns Ltd** [1986] 621, HC.

Quarry used as sand and gravel pit—Extraction of rock by blasting—Planning permission not obtained—Whether material change of use constituting development. **Dublin Co Council v Sellwood Quarries Ltd** [1981] 23, HC.

Section 27 applications. *See* Enforcement—Section 27 application—Unauthorised use—Material change of use (*below*).

Non-compliance with conditions
Section 27 application. *See* Enforcement—Section 27 application—Development not in conformity with conditions (*below*).

Development plan
Contravention
Grant of permission—Outline permission granted, on appeal, by Minister for Environment—Whether Minister power to grant permission—Function of Minister in hearing appeal against refusal—Default procedure—Whether operates to produce an effect equivalent to the granting of permission in a case where the application is for something prohibited by statute—Local Government (Planning and Development) Act 1963, ss. 26 (3), (4), (5), (6), 82 (3A)—Local Government (Planning and Development)

PLANNING
Development plan
Contravention continued

Act 1976, ss. 14(8), 46(3). **State (Pine Valley Developments) Ltd v Dublin Co Council** [1982] 169, SC.

National monument on lands—Default procedure—Whether applicable—Difficulty of local authority in replying to application—Postal strike—Whether permission obtained by default—Permission amounting to material contravention of development plan—Whether local authority had power to grant permission by default—Local Government (Planning and Development) Act 1976, s. 39(d)—Local Government (Planning and Development) Act 1963, s. 26(3) **Dublin Co Council v Marren** [1985] 593, HC.

National monument on lands—Refuse dump proposal—Sanitary authority proposing to establish refuse dump on site of national monument—Whether dump constitutes material contravention of development plan—Whether constitutes breach of national monuments legislation—National Monuments Act 1930, s. 14—Local Government (Planning and Development) Act 1963, s. 19, 3rd Schedule. **Attorney General (ex rel McGarry) v Sligo Co Council** [1989] 768, SC.

Undertaking to grant permission—Such undertaking involving a departure from the area's development plan—Whether undertaking valid. **Grange Developments Ltd v Dublin Co Council** [1987] 733, HC; [1989] 145, SC.

Enforcement
Enforcement notice

Application to quash by way of certiorari—Claim that development exempted—No application made to An Bord Pleanála for ruling—Whether certiorari be granted—Local Government (Planning and Development) Act 1963, s. 31. **O'Connor v Kerry Co Council** [1988] 660, HC.

Open spaces. See Acquisition notice *(above)*.

Section 27 application

Breach of conditions—Building of historic interest—Grant of permission subject to special conditions ensuring preservation of historic building—Whether developers guilty of breaches of the conditions—Effectiveness of planning legislation to preserve buildings of historic interest—Interpretation of conditions—Local Government (Planning and Development) Act, 1963, ss. 19(1), 26—Local Government (Planning and Development) Act, 1976, s. 27. **Dun Laoghaire Corporation v Frescati Estates Ltd** [1982] 469, HC.

Breach of conditions—Company in voluntary liquidation—Whether order justified against the liquidator—Whether court able to make an order against the directors of the company—Whether appropriate—Local Government (Planning and Development) Act 1976, s. 27. **Dublin Co Council v Elton Homes Ltd** [1984] 297, HC.

Breach of conditions—Failure to complete—Application for order compelling compliance with planning conditions—Company—Directors—Whether order should issue against directors—Whether veil of incorporation should be lifted—Whether application under planning laws appropriate procedure for raising issues of malfeasance of directors—Whether plenary procedure more appropriate—Local Government (Planning and Development) Act 1976, s. 27. **Dublin Co Council v O'Riordan** [1986] 104, HC.

Change of user—Whether material change of use constituting development. *See* Enforcement—Section 27 application—Unauthorised use—Material change of use *(below)*.

Development not in conformity with permission conditions—Failure to complete—Failure to comply with conditions of permission—Development company insolvent—Whether directors of company personally liable for default of development company—

PLANNING
Enforcement
Section 27 application continued

Local Government (Planning and Development) Act 1976, s. 27—Companies Act 1963, ss. 131, 148. **Dun Laoghaire Corporation v Parkhill Developments Ltd** [1989] 235, HC.

Development not in conformity with permission conditions—Whether High Court has jurisdiction to order demolition. **Morris v Garvey** [1982] 177, SC.

Intensification of use—Whether material change of use constituting development. *See* Enforcement—Section 27 application—Unauthorised use—Intensification of use (*below*).

Jurisdiction of High Court—Whether High Court authority to make a mandatory order—Local Government (Planning and Development) Act 1976, s. 27. **Dublin Co Council v Kirby** [1985] 325, HC.

Jurisdiction of High Court—Development not in conformity with permission conditions—Whether High Court has jurisdiction to order demolition. **Morris v Garvey** [1982] 177, SC.

Locus standi—Local member of public bringing application—Whether applicant having sufficient standing. **Robinson v Chariot Inns Ltd** [1986] 621, HC.

Unauthorised development—Advertisement hoardings—Works representing considerable improvement to the appearance of the premises—Subsequent application for permission to retain refused—Appeal to An Bord Pleanála—Whether court power to direct removal—Whether pending appeal inhibits the granting of an injunction—Local Government (Planning and Development) Act 1976, s. 27. **Dublin Corporation v Maiden Poster Sites Ltd** [1983] 48, HC.

Unauthorised development—Building in course of construction—Whether in accordance with planning permission—Whether applicants for order preventing completion need have any interest in land—Whether damages need be shown—Nature of s. 27 order—Whether discretionary—Local Government (Planning and Development) Act 1976, s. 27. **Avenue Properties Ltd v Farrell Homes Ltd** [1982] 21, HC.

Unauthorised use—Convictions and fines—Enforcement notice—Injunction application—Power of Court to review planning authority's decision—Whether corporation estopped by causing the premises to be rated as used for office purposes—Discretion of court to refuse injunction on grounds of hardship—Local Government (Planning and Development) Act 1976, s. 27. **Dublin Corporation v Garland** [1982] 104, HC.

Unauthorised use—Intensification of use—Area zoned as agricultural land in development plan—Use of land to store caravans and fuel oils—Whether intensification or abandonment of use—Whether exempted development—Stay on prohibition of continuance of unauthorised use. **Furlong v A F & G W McConnell Ltd** [1990] 48, HC.

Unauthorised use—Intensification of use—Land used for the purpose of manufacturing concrete blocks—Whether unauthorised use or exempted development—Discontinued user—Redemption of original user—Local Government (Planning and Development) Act 1976, s. 27. **Dublin Co Council v Tallaght Block Co Ltd** [1982] 534, HC.

Unauthorised Use—Intensification of Use—Premises used as abattoir. **Monaghan Co Council v Brogan** [1987] 564, HC.

Unauthorised use—Intensification of use—Reference to Minister to determine whether development exempted—Whether s. 27 application be adjourned pending Minister's decision—Whether court under duty to issue injunction once unauthorised use established—Local Government (Planning and development) Act 1976, s. 27. **Stafford v Roadstone Ltd** [1980] 1, HC.

PLANNING
Enforcement
Section 27 application continued

Unauthorised use—Material change of use—Mobile ice cream van parking in driveway of residential property at night—Whether unauthorised development—Whether material change of use—Local Government (Planning and Development) Act 1976, s. 27—Local Government (Planning and Development) Regulations 1977, 3rd Schedule cl 16. **Dublin Corporation v Moore** [1984] 339, SC.

Unauthorised use—Material change of use—Quarry—Extraction of rock by blasting—Planning permission not obtained—Whether material change of use constituting development. **Dublin Co Council v Sellwood Quarries Ltd** [1981] 23, HC.

Unauthorised use—Substantial change of user—Planning permission not having been obtained—Attempt to stave off consequences of disregarding requirements—Whether injunction should be granted while appeal that the change was 'exempted development' pending—Abuse of process—Duplicitous use of mandamus procedure to obtain order compelling the Corporation to grant planning permission—Whether affects s. 27 application—Local Government (Planning and Development) Act 1963, ss. 3, 4, 5, 24, 26(4)—Local Government (Planning and Development) Act 1976, s. 27—Local Government (Planning and Development) Regulations 1977, Arts 9, 10, 12. **Cork Corporation v O'Connell** [1982] 505, SC.

Unauthorised use—User commenced prior to legislation coming into force—User interrupted by various unauthorised users—Whether user liable to authorisation as a result of abandonment—Whether matter *res judicata*—Local Government (Planning and Development) Act 1963, s. 24—Local Government (Planning and Development) Act 1976, s. 27. **Meath Co Council v Daly** [1988] 274, HC.

Environmental impact assessment
EC directive

Whether directive implemented—Whether environmental impact study submitted included information required by directive—Whether failure to include information in breach of mandatory provision of planning regulations—Local Government (Planning and Development) Act 1963, ss. 25, 26—Local Government (Planning and Development) Regulations 1977, reg 26—Council Directive 85/337/EEC, Article 6(2). **Browne v An Bord Pleanála** [1989] 865, HC.

Exempted development
Conversion works

Change of use from multiple bed-sitter type residence to two flats—Whether conversion works exempted development—Whether appearance considered inconsistent with neighbouring structures—External staircase and balcony erected at rear of terraced house—Whether planning permission required—Local Government (Planning and Development) Act 1963, ss. 2(1), 4(1)(g)—Local Government (Planning and Development) Act 1976, s. 27. **Cairnduff v O'Connell** [1986] 465, SC.

Estoppel

Agent of planning authority representing that development exempt—Whether authority estopped from denying the development exempt—Whether representation *ultra vires*—Local Government (Planning and Development Act 1963, ss. 5, 26. **Dublin Corporation v McGrath** [1978] 208, HC.

Fried fish shop

Conditions implied as to opening hours—Whether violated by selling fish and chips outside opening hours—Local Government (Planning and Development Act 1963 (Exempted Development) Regulations 1967, r 4. **Dublin Corporation v Raso** [1976-7] 139, HC.

SUBJECT MATTER

357

PLANNING

Exempted development *continued*
Land used for the purpose of manufacturing concrete blocks
Whether unauthorised use or exempted development. **Dublin Co Council v Tallaght Block Co Ltd** [1982] 534, HC.

Quarry
Whether operation of quarry exempted development—Reference to Minister to determine whether development exempted—Whether s. 27 application be adjourned pending Minister's decision. **Stafford v Roadstone Ltd** [1980] 1, HC.

Historic building
Preservation
Effectiveness of planning legislation to preserve buildings of historic interest. *See* Enforcement—Section 27 application—Breach of conditions—Building of historic interest *(above)*.

Intensification of use. *See* Development—Intensification of use *(above)*.

Section 27 applications. See Enforcement—Section 27 application—Unauthorised use—Intensification of use *(above)*.

Material change of use. *See* Development—Material change of use *(above)*.

Section 27 applications. See Enforcement—Section 27 application—Unauthorised use—Material change of use *(above)*.

National Monument on Lands. *See* Development plan—Construction—National monument on Lands *(above)*.

Objector
Locus standi
Local member of public bringing section 27 application. **Robinson v Chariot Inns Ltd** [1986] 621, HC.

Open spaces. *See* Acquisition notice *(above)*.

Outline permission
Decision to grant outline permission
Application to quash decision—Certiorari—Jurisdiction of planning authority. **State (Abenglen Properties Ltd) v Dublin Corporation** [1981] 54, HC; [1982] 590, SC.

Jurisdiction of Minister to grant
Appeal against refusal of permission—Function of Minister in hearing appeal against refusal—Minister granting outline permission—Whether power to grant permission. **State (Pine Valley Developments) Ltd v Dublin Co Council** [1982] 169, SC.

Refusal to grant
Compensation. *See* Compensation—Refusal of permission—Outline permission *(above)*.

Premature development—Whether valid ground for refusal—Adequacy of notification or refusal—Certiorari. **State (Sweeney) v Minister for Environment** [1979] 35, HC.

Permission
Conditions. See Conditions *(above)*.

Contract for sale of land
Agreement subject to obtaining planning permission. *See* SALE OF LAND (Contract—Condition—Planning permission).

Extension
Refusal—Whether ultra vires planning authority—Whether development carried out under existing permission—Whether completion possible within reasonable time—Whether irrelevant factors considered by planning authority—Local Government

PLANNING
Permission
Extension continued
(Planning and Development) Act 1982, s. 4(1). **State (McCoy) v Dun Laoghaire Corporation** [1985] 533, HC.

Grant
Appeal against decision. *See* Appeal—Grant of permission (*above*).

Contravention of development plan. *See* Development plan—Contravention—Grant of permission (*above*).

Invalidity—Minister granting permission—Supreme Court ruling permission *ultra vires*—Whether action in damages lay against the Minister. *See* Decision—Invalidity—Grant of permission by Minister (*above*).

Mistake—Permission granted to company seeking change of user from dwellinghouse to amusement centre—Mistake in name of company causing grant to non-existent company—Genuine mistake—Objection—Appellant owning amusement centre in adjoining premises—Whether objector under any misapprehension as to real identity of owner—Whether Corporation jurisdiction to make the order—Certiorari—Application to quash order granting permission—Delay—Whether extension of time available—Local Government (Planning and Development) Act 1976, ss. 8, 26—RSC O 81 r10. **State (Toft) v Galway Corporation** [1981] 439, SC.

Section 4 resolution—Resolution by County Council directing county manager to grant planning permission—Manager refusing to comply with resolution—Proper exercise of discretionary power by administrative authority—Whether reasonable—Certiorari—Mandamus—Application of s. 4 of the City and County Management (Amendment) Act 1955—Function of An Bord Pleanála confined to proper planning and development of the area—Local Government (Planning and Development) Act 1963. **P & F Sharpe Ltd v Dublin City and County Manager** [1989] 565, HC, SC.

Slaughter house—Whether County council obliged to grant slaughter house licence—Principles of natural justice—Town Improvement Clauses Act 1847, ss. 125, 126, 128—Slaughter of Animals Act 1935 s. 11—Local Government (Planning and Development) Act 1963. **Doupe v Limerick Co Council** [1981] 456, HC.

Waste disposal—Asbestos waste—Appeal against decision. *See* Appeal—Grant of permission—Use of land for disposal of asbestos waste (*above*).

Non-compliance with conditions
Section 27 application. *See* Enforcement—Section 27 application—Development not in conformity with conditions (*above*).

Outline permission. See Outline permission (*above*).

Refusal
Appeal. *See* Appeal—Refusal of permission (*above*).

Compensation. *See* Compensation—Refusal of permission (*above*).

Deficiency in public sewerage facilities—Exclusion of compensation. *See* Compensation—Refusal of permission—Exclusions—Deficiency in public sewerage facilities (*above*).

Premature development—Compulsory purchase order on lands—Whether valid ground for refusal—Whether order made in compliance with housing legislation—Adequacy of notification or refusal—Certiorari. **State (Sweeney) v Minister for Environment** [1979] 35, HC.

Purchase notice. *See* Purchase notice (*below*).

Retention of unauthorised development
Whether retention order made without jurisdiction. *See* Retention permission (*below*).

PLANNING
Permission *continued*
Undertaking to grant
Compensation—Exclusion. *See* Compensation—Refusal of planning permission—Exclusions—Undertaking to grant permission (*above*).

Premature development. *See* Permission—Refusal—Premature development (*above*).

Purchase notice
Decision
Time for giving—Local authority refusing to purchase—Whether refusal made within statutory time limit—Date from which time runs—Date of posting notice or date of receipt—Alternative remedies—Whether exhausted—Whether default procedures implicit in statutory provisions where planning authority does not reply to purchase notice—Local Government (Planning and Development) Act 1963, ss. 2, 29—Local Government (Planning and Development) Act 1976, s. 14(5). **State (McInerney & Co Ltd) v Dublin Co Council** [1985] 513, HC.

Price
Failure to agree on price—Matter referred to arbitration—Date at which land should be valued—Local Government (No 2) Act 1960, s. 10(1)—Local Government (Planning and Development) Act 1963, s. 29(3)—Local Government (No 2) Act 1960, s. 19(1)—Local Government (Planning and Development) Act 1963, s. 29(3)—Housing Act 1966, ss. 76, 79,80,81,84,86. **Portland Estates (Limerick) Ltd v Limerick Corporation** [1980] 77, SC.

Quarrying
Intensification of use
Whether material change of use constituting development—Quarry—Whether operation of quarry exempted development—Reference to Minister to determine whether development exempted. **Stafford v Roadstone Ltd** [1980] 1, HC.

Whether unauthorised use
Whether material change of use. **McGrath Limestone Works Ltd v Galway Co Council** [1989] 602, HC.

Whether material change of use—Extraction of rock by blasting—Planning permission not obtained. **Dublin Co Council v Sellwood Quarries Ltd** [1981] 23, HC.

Refusal of permission. *See* Permission—Refusal (*above*).

Refuse dump proposal
National monument on lands
Whether dump constitutes material contravention of development plan. *See* Development plan—Contravention—National monument on lands—Refuse dump proposal (*above*).

Retention permission
Jurisdiction of Bord Pleanála
Development not in accordance with planning permission—Section 27 application—Application for retention permission—Application granted on appeal—Whether retention order made without jurisdiction—Matters to be taken into account in considering application—Local Government (Planning and Development) Act 1976, s. 27. **State (Fitzgerald) v An Bord Pleanála** [1985] 117, HC, SC.

Section 4 resolutions
Grant of permission. See Permission—Grant—Section 4 resolution (*above*).

Section 27 applications. *See* Enforcement—Section 27 application (*above*).

Time limit
Challenge to validity of decision
Two month time limit within which to challenge validity—Whether constitutional—

PLANNING
Time limit
Challenge to validity of decision continued
Constitution of Ireland 1937, Article 40 3 2—Local Government (Planning and Development) Act 1963, s. 82(3A). **Brady v Donegal Co Council** [1989] 282, SC.

Decision of planning authority. See Decision—time for giving (*above*).

Unauthorised development
Injunction applications. See Enforcement—Section 27 application—Unauthorised development (*above*).

Retention permission. See Retention permission (*above*).

Unauthorised use
Definition
Quarrying—Whether unauthorised use—Whether material change of use—Whether planning permission for mushroom growing implemented—Construction of planning documents—Local Government (Planning and Development) Act 1963, s. 2. **McGrath Limestone Works Ltd v Galway Co Council** [1989] 602, HC.

Injunction applications. See Enforcement—Section 27 application—Unauthorised use (*above*).

Undertaking to grant permission
Exclusion of compensation. See Compensation—Refusal of planning permission—Exclusions—Undertaking to grant permission (*above*).

Waste disposal
Asbestos waste. See Appeal—Grant of permission—Use of site for disposal of asbestos waste (*above*).

Refuse dump
Sanitary authority proposing to establish refuse dump on site of national monument—Whether dump constitutes material contravention of development plan. *See* Development plan—Contravention—National monument on lands—Refuse dump proposal (*above*).

PLANT
Capital allowances. *See* REVENUE (Income tax—Capital allowances).

PLEA
Autrefois acquit. *See* CRIMINAL LAW (Autrefois acquit).

Guilty plea *See* CRIMINAL LAW (Trial—Plea of guilty).

PLEADINGS *See* PRACTICE (Pleadings).

POLICE *See* GARDA SÍOCHÁNA
Arrest
Legality. See ARREST.

POLICE INFORMER *See* COMMON INFORMER.

POLITICAL OFFENCE
Extradition. *See* EXTRADITION.

POLITICAL PARTY
Election broadcast
Ministerial prohibition
Ministerial order prohibiting access to radio or TV by Provisional Sinn Fein candidates to promote their electoral campaign—Constitution—Validity—Freedom of expression—

POLITICAL PARTY
Election broadcast
Ministerial prohibition continued
Whether order reviewable by the courts. *See* BROADCASTING (Election broadcast—Ministerial order—Judicial review).

Lottery
Application for licence
Branch of political party—Proceeds of lottery to enable party members attend seminars and conventions—Whether purpose philanthropic—Gaming and Lotteries Act 1956, s. 28(2). **Gurhy v Goff** [1980] 103, SC.

POLLUTION
Emissions from factory
Injuries and damage
Nuisance. *See* NUISANCE (Emissions from factory).

Waste disposal
Asbestos waste
Grant of permission for use of site for disposal of asbestos waste—Appeal against decision. *See* PLANNING (Appeal—Grant of permission—Use of site for disposal of asbestos waste).

Water pollution
Trade effluent
Charges for connection to sewer. *See* LOCAL GOVERNMENT (Public health—Sewer—Connection—Charges).

PONTIFICAL UNIVERSITY *See* University (Pontifical university).

PORTS *See* HARBOURS AND PIERS.

POST OFFICE
Employee
Criminal law
Prosecution—Indictable charge against employee of Post Office—Solicitor employed by Post Office having carriage of prosecution—Whether delegation of carriage of case by DPP *ultra vires*—Whether likely to create unfairness in procedure—Postal and Telecommunications Services Act 1983—Prosecution of Offences Act 1974, ss. 4, 7. **Flynn v DPP** [1986] 290, SC.

Monopoly
Statutory monopoly in respect of the conveying of 'letters'
Private courier service—Minister seeking an injunction—Whether defendants trading in breach of the monopoly—Meaning of 'letters'—Whether relevant provisions unconstitutional—Post Office Act 1908, s. 34. **Attorney General v Paperlink Ltd** [1984] 373, HC.

POSTAL VOTING
Absence of facilities
Physically incapacitated persons. See ELECTORAL LAW (Dáil Éireann elections—Polling—Inability to attend at polling station).

PRACTICE
Abuse of process. *See* ABUSE OF PROCESS.

Accrual of cause of action. *See* LIMITATION OF ACTIONS (Accrual of cause of action).

Action
Compromise. See ACTION (Compromise).

PRACTICE

Action *continued*
  Dismissal. See Dismissal (*below*).

  Generally. See ACTION.

  Stay of proceedings. See Stay of action (*below*).

Adjournment. *See* ADJOURNMENT.

Affiliation order. *See* AFFILIATION ORDER.

Appeal
  Extension of time
    Appeal from High Court to Supreme Court—Whether Supreme Court has same powers as High Court to extend time for appeal—RSC 1962, O 58 r 8, O 108 r 70, O 111, r 1. **Hughes v O'Rourke** [1986] 538, SC.

  Findings of fact
    Whether disturbable on appeal—Adoption—Consent of mother—Finding of fact by trial judge that consent not free and informed—Whether such finding could be disturbed on appeal. In re M; **J M and G M v An Bord Uchtala** [1988] 203, SC.

  Supreme Court
    Function of Court—Primary and secondary facts—Whether Supreme Court empowered to reach different conclusions to those of trial court in relation to inferences from primary facts. **Hanrahan & Ors v Merck Sharp & Dohme** [1988] 629, SC.

    Occupier's liability—Case tried in High Court on basis of duty owed to licensee— Whether appropriate for Supreme Court to decide case on basis of a different duty. **Rooney v Connolly** [1987] 768, SC.

  Time for taking
    Appeal from Labour Court determination—Whether appeal out of time—Health Act 1970, s. 18—Employment Equality Act 1977, ss. 2(c), 3, 12(3), 20, 21(4), 22, 24(2). **North Western Health Board v Martyn** [1985] 226, HC.

Appearance
  Barristers and solicitors
    Presumption that counsel and solicitor appear on express instruction of the client— **L'Henryenat v Ireland** [1984] 249, SC.

Attachment
  Contempt of court
    Civil contempt—Committal—Jurisdiction of court—Deliberate disobedience of court order—No serious effort to purge contempt—Nature of Court's jurisdiction—Whether defendants be committed to prison—Prohibition of Forcible Entry and Occupation Act, 1971. **Ross Co Ltd v Swan** [1981] 416, HC.

Attorney General. *See* ATTORNEY GENERAL; *see also* Relator proceedings (*below*).

Bank account
  Inspection. See Inspection—Documents—Bank account (*below*).

Benjamin order. *See* SUCCESSION (Administration of estates—Ascertainment of next-of-kin).

Case stated. *See* CASE STATED

Cause of action. *See* ACTION (Cause).

Compromise of action. *See* ACTION (Compromise).

Concurrent wrongdoers
  Apportionment of damage
    Whether appropriate to apportion damage between defendants—Civil Liability Act 1961, s. 11. **Riordan's Travel Ltd v Acres** [1979] 3, HC.

PRACTICE *continued*
Constitutional action
Certiorari
Whether appropriate form of action in constitutional matter. **State (McEldowney) v Kelleher** [1985] 10, SC.

Contempt of court. *See* CONTEMPT OF COURT.

Contribution or indemnity
Negligence
Vendor and manufacturer—Jury finding defendants negligent and apportioning fault—Whether vendor entitled to claim contribution or indemnity against manufacturer—Civil Liability Act 1961, s. 21—RSC 1962, O 16, rr 7, 11. **Cole v Webb Caravan Services Ltd** [1985] 1, HC.

Costs. *See* COSTS.

Criminal law. *See* CRIMINAL LAW (Procedure).

Date listed for hearing
Personal injuries claim
Damages awarded less than lodgment—Question as to costs—Whether action first listed for hearing only when it appeared in a list of cases to be heard on a specified date—RSC 1986, O 22 rr 1(2), 46. **Donohue v Dillon** [1988] 654, HC.

Defamation
Defence
Particulars—Rolled-up plea. *See* Pleadings—Particulars—Defamation (*below*).

Delay of action
Dismissal for want of prosecution. See Dismissal for want of prosecution (*below*).

Infant plaintiff
Proceedings instituted on behalf of infant sixteen years after cause of action accrued—Whether delay unreasonable—Inordinate delay—Whether an abuse of the process of the courts—Statute of Limitations 1957, s. 49—Convention for the Protection of Human Rights and Fundamental Freedoms (1950) Art 6(1). **O'Domhnaill v Merrick** [1985] 40, SC.

Discovery
Documents. See DISCOVERY.

Dismissal
Abuse of process. See ABUSE OF PROCESS.

Delay. See Dismissal for want of prosecution (*below*).

Dismissal for want of prosecution
Delay
Application to have action dismissed—Application unsuccessful—Further delay—Second application—Whether applicant estopped from raising grounds of prejudice other than those relied on on first application—Whether action to be dismissed for want of prosecution—Balance of justice. **Sweeney v Horans (Tralee) Ltd** [1987] 240, SC.

Request for particulars by defendant—Order to deliver same—Action to stand dismissed with costs unless particulars delivered within specified time—Inordinate and inexcusable delay—Jurisdiction to extend time where "unless" order not complied with—Discretion—Nature of action—Particulars within the knowledge of the defendant—Whether defendant unreasonably prejudiced—Balance of justice. **Brennan v Kelly** [1988] 306, HC.

Documents
Discovery. See DISCOVERY.

Inspection. See Inspection (*below*).

PRACTICE
Documents *continued*
Production
Privilege—Subpoena duces tecum issued requiring officer of the Central Bank to produce documents—Oath of secrecy—Statutory privilege—Whether summons be set aside—Central Bank Act 1942, ss. 6 (1), 31. **Cully v Northern Bank Finance Corp Ltd** [1984] 676, HC.

Enforcement of judgments. *See* JUDGMENT (Enforcement).

Estoppel
Issue estoppel. See ESTOPPEL (Issue estoppel).

Objection to being joined as defendants
Road traffic accident—Driver dying from injuries—Application to have insurers joined as defendants in place of deceased—Whether insurers estopped from opposing such an order. **Boyce v McBride** [1987] 95, SC.

Evidence
Admissibility
Affidavit—Objection to introduction of evidence at trial without prior notice—Case involving constitutional rights of citizen—Whether principles of ordinary litigation ought to be waived—Rules of the Superior Courts 1962, O 39 r 1. **Shannon v Attorney General** [1985] 449, HC.

Extension of time. *See* TIME LIMIT (Extension).

Frivolous or vexatious action
Motion to strike out
Application for an injunction restraining continued development and declaration that the planning application was invalid—Motion to strike out—Whether claim frivolous or vexatious—RSC O 19, r 28. **McCabe v Harding Investments Ltd** [1984] 105, SC.

Locus standi—Whether plaintiff has locus standi to maintain action—Claim of breach of statutory requirements—No damage or loss alleged by plaintiff—Whether court should strike out at preliminary stage—Whether action requires full consideration by the court—RSC 1962, O 19, r 28. **Irish Permanent Building Society v Caldwell** [1979] 273, HC.

Garnishee order
Judgment creditor
Equitable assignments—Whether order be made absolute—Precedence of competing claims. **Fitzpatrick v DAF Sales Ltd and Allied Irish Finance Company Ltd** [1989] 777, HC.

Immunity from suit. *See* STATE (Immunity from suit).

In camera hearing
Circumstances which justify hearing other than in public
Statutory provision and denial of justice—Whether circumstances existed on a s. 205 application—Courts (Supplemental Provisions) Act 1961, s. 45—Companies Act 1963, s. 205—Constitution of Ireland 1937, Article 34. **In re R Ltd** [1989] 757, SC.

Inspection
Documents
Bank account—Jurisdiction of High Court to make an order for inspection with extra territorial effect—Bankers' Books Evidence Act 1879, s. 7—Bankers' Books Evidence (Amendment) Act 1959, s. 2. **Chemical Bank v McCormack** [1983] 350, HC.

Property
Action for trespass—Application for an order allowing plaintiffs to carry out an inspection of defendant's mining activities—Attempt to ascertain whether such trespass

PRACTICE
Inspection
Property continued
has taken place—Whether necessary for plaintiffs to establish prima facie case—Constitutional right of access to the courts—RSC, O 50 r 4. **Bula Ltd v Tara** Mines [1988] 149, HC.

Interest. *See* INTEREST.

Issue estoppel. *See* ESTOPPEL (Issue estoppel).

Judgment
Currency. *See* JUDGMENT (Currency).

Enforcement. *See* JUDGMENT (Enforcement).

Interest. *See* JUDGMENT (Interest).

Judicial review. *See* JUDICIAL REVIEW.

Jurisdiction of courts
Circuit Court
Equity—Whether court having jurisdiction to issue injunction to enforce statutory provisions—Submission to jurisdiction—Right to transfer case to High Court. **Parsons v Kavanagh** [1990] 560, HC.

Conflict of laws
Explosion on French registered ship in Irish waters—Fatal damages claim—Victims French nationals employed under French contracts of service—Rules of the Superior Courts 1962, O 12, r 26. **O'Daly v Gulf Oil Terminals Ltd** [1983] 163, HC.

Legal professional privilege. *See* DISCOVERY (Privilege—Legal professional privilege).

Locus standi. *See* LOCUS STANDI.

Maintenance of action
Abuse of process
Malice—Claim for damages—Whether such action lay in respect of instituting a civil action. **Dorene Ltd v Suedes (Ireland) Ltd** [1982] 126, HC.

Mareva Injunction
Generally. *See* INJUNCTION (Interlocutory—Mareva injunction).

Service out of jurisdiction
Foreign plaintiffs and defendants having no connection with jurisdiction—Whether order for service out of the jurisdiction should issue. *See* Service out of jurisdiction—Mareva injunction (*below*).

Non-party discovery. *See* DISCOVERY (Non-party discovery).

Parties
Adding party as defendants
Road traffic accident—Driver dying from injuries—Application to have insurers joined as defendants in place of deceased—Whether insurers estopped from opposing such an order. **Boyce v McBride** [1987] 95, SC.

Locus standi. *See* LOCUS STANDI.

Service of notice
Election petition—Statutory requirement to serve notice on DPP 'as soon as may be'—DPP assuming functions of Attorney General—Petitioner unaware of requirement—Whether proceedings should be avoided by reason of lack of service—Whether any material damage caused to any of the parties by reason of lack of service. **Boyle v Allen** [1979] 281, CC.

NOT TO BE REMOVED
FROM LIBRARY

PRACTICE

Parties *continued*
> *Third party notice. See* Third party notice (*below*).

Payment into court
> *Mistake*
>> Fraud—Employer liability insurance—Infant plaintiff sustaining serious injury in the course of employment—Lodgment of money into court—Mistaken assumption of liability induced by fraud—Policy repudiated—Whether plaintiff any title to the lodged money—RSC O 22 rr 4, 10, 13. **Carey v W H Ryan Ltd** [1982] 121, SC.

Pleadings
> *Particulars*
>> Defamation—Libel—Defence—Rolled-up plea—Plaintiff seeking further and better particulars—Whether defendant obliged to specify which words complained of were true and to specify facts relied on to support factual statements made—RSC 1962, O 19, r 6(1). **Cooney v Browne (No 1)** [1985] 673, HC, SC.
>>
>> Defamation—Libel—Defence—Rolled-up plea—Further and better particulars—Compliance with court order—Whether sufficient compliance. **Cooney v Browne (No 2)** [1986] 444, HC.
>>
>> Undue influence claim—Probate application—Claim that the making of the will was procured by undue influence—Whether full particulars of undue influence required—RSC O 19 r 5, O 111. **In re Rutledge: Hanly v Finnerty** [1981] 198, HC.

Point of law
> *Revenue case*
>> Statutory provision requiring person to express dissatisfaction with the determination of a point of law ' immediately after the determination'—Whether 'immediately' to be interpreted strictly—Whether provision directory or mandatory—Income Tax Act 1967, ss. 428, 430. **State (Multiprint Label Systems Ltd) v Neylon** [1984] 545, HC.

Pre-trial relief
> *Injunction. See* INJUNCTION (Interlocutory).

Precedent. *See* PRECEDENT.

Privilege
> *Discovery of documents. See* DISCOVERY (Privilege).
>
> *Production of documents*
>> Statutory privilege—Subpoena duces tecum issued requiring officer of the Central Bank to produce documents—Oath of secrecy—Whether summons be set aside—Central Bank Act 1942, ss. 6 (1), 31. **Cully v Northern Bank Finance Corp Ltd** [1984] 676, HC.

Relator proceedings
> *Costs*
>> Locus standi of relator—Whether relator had standing as artificial person—Obligation to uphold constitutional rights. **Attorney General (SPUC) v Open Door Counselling** [1987] 477, HC.
>
> *Fiat*
>> Refusal—Action to establish public right of way—Whether decision of Attorney General subject to review by the courts—Whether action maintainable in absence of fiat of Attorney General. **Dunne v Rattigan** [1981] 365, CC.
>
> *Locus standi*
>> Role of Attorney General—Whether necessary to consider issue of standing of relator—Whether relator had locus standi prior to conversion of proceedings to relator action. **Attorney General (ex rel SPUC) v Open Door Counselling Ltd** [1987] 477, HC; [1989] 19, SC.

PRACTICE

Relator proceedings *continued*
Role of Attorney General
Whether Attorney General liable in respect of plaintiff's loss—Injunction granted on undertaking to abide by any order as to damages—Fiat of Attorney General not extending to this undertaking—Whether giving of Attorney General's consent indication of approval of proceedings. **Attorney General (ex rel Martin) v Dublin Corporation** [1983] 253, SC.

Revenue case
Point of law. See Point of law—Revenue case (*above*).

Security for costs. *See* COSTS (Security for costs).

Service
Case stated
Not possible to serve respondent with notice of appeal and copy of case stated—Whether service on solicitor, who acted in the District Court proceedings on behalf of the respondent, sufficient—Summary Jurisdiction Act 1857, s. 2. **Crowley v McVeigh** [1990] 220, HC.

Service out of jurisdiction
Choice of law
Whether significant connection with jurisdiction—Negligence proceedings—Fitting of heart valve in Ireland—Plaintiff resident in Ireland—Valve manufactured in United States—RSC 1962, O 11 r 1(f). **Grehan v Medical Incorporated and Valley Pines Associates.** [1986] 627, SC.

Mareva injunction
Foreign plaintiffs and defendants having no connection with jurisdiction—Application for interlocutory Mareva injunction as part of endorsement of claim—Whether appropriate to claim interlocutory relief on endorsement setting out substantive claim—Whether order for service out of the jurisdiction should issue—RSC 1962, O 4 r 2, O 11 r 1 (g). **Serge Caudron v Air Zaire** [1986] 10, HC, SC.

Whether permissible
Contract terms stating that disputes be settled in accordance with Irish law—Contract having no connection with Ireland—RSC 1986, O 11, r 1(e)(iii), O 12 r 26. **Kutchera v Buckingham International Holdings Ltd** [1988]1, HC; [1988] 501, SC.

Set off
Company
Assets—Liquidation—Money paid by mistake to company prior to liquidation—Whether constituting assets of company subsequent to liquidation—Whether subject to right of set-off—Whether company holding money as trustee—Purpose of constructive trust—Estoppel—Whether arising—Whether person acted to his detriment. **In re Irish Shipping Ltd** [1986] 518, HC.

European Communities
Common agricultural policy—Company in liquidation—Company owing a sum for monetary compensation levies—Company owed a sum for monetary compensation payments on farm levies—Intervention agent claiming a right of set off. **Continental Irish Meat Ltd v Minister for Agriculture** [1983] 503, HC.

Summary judgement
RIAI standard form building contract—Whether provisions of same inconsistent with right of set-off—Whether defendant entitled to set-off. **Sisk and Son Ltd v Lawter Products BV** [1976–7] 204, HC.

RIAI standard form building contract—Whether provisions of contract inconsistent with right of set off—Motion to stay proceedings—Stay dependent upon entitlement

PRACTICE
Set off
Summary judgement continued
   to set-off—Arbitration Act 1980, s. 5—RSC 1986, O 42 r 17. **Rohan Construction Ltd
   v Antigen Ltd** [1989] 783, HC.

Settlement of action. *See* ACTION (Compromise).

State
Immunity from suit. See STATE (Immunity from suit).

Stay of action
Allegation that action had been settled
   Whether evidence supported allegation—Contract—Formation—Whether agreement
   to settle proceedings reached. **Tattan v Cadogan** [1979] 61, HC.

Arbitration
   Discretion of court to refuse—Fraud alleged by party opposing stay—Contracts of
   reinsurance—Arbitration clause—Whether clause operative when serious and complex
   issues of law involving allegations of fraud raised—Application to revoke authority of
   arbitrator—Arbitration Act 1954, ss. 12, 39—Arbitration Act 1980, s. 5—Insurance
   (No 2) Act 1983. **Adminstratia Asigurarilor de Stat v Insurance Corporation of Ireland
   plc** [1990] 159, HC.

   Notice of motion served—Agreement to strike out motion and allow extended time
   for the filing of defence—Subject matter of claim being a matter agreed to be referred
   to arbitration—Application to stay proceedings—Whether seeking to consent for
   extension of time 'a step in the proceedings'—Arbitration Act 1980, s. 5. **O'Flynn v An
   Bord Gais Eireann** [1982] 324, HC.

   Power to stay proceedings—Whether any court before which an action has been
   commenced may stay proceedings or whether such power is exclusively vested in the
   High Court—Arbitration Act 1954, ss. 2, 12(1)—Arbitration Act 1980, s. 5 (1).
   Mitchell v Budget Travel Ltd [1990] 739, SC.

Concurrent proceedings
   Separate courts—Principles to be applied—Road traffic accident—One party commencing proceedings in the Circuit Court claiming damages for his car—Other party
   issuing proceedings in the High Court claiming damages for personal injuries—Circuit
   Court case coming on for hearing before High Court action was heard—Application
   to have Circuit Court proceedings stayed—Courts of Justice Act 1924, s. 94—Civil
   Liability Act 1961, ss. 34(1), 37(1)—Courts Act 1971, s. 6—Circuit Court Rules 1950,
   0 30, r 11. **Murphy v Hennessy** [1985] 100, HC.

Summary judgment
Set off. See Set off (*above*).

Summons
Criminal law. See CRIMINAL LAW (Summons).

Delay in serving
   Date of issue altered—Whether summons invalid—Road Traffic (Amendment) Act 1978,
   ss. 12(2), 13(3). **DPP v Clein** [1983] 76, SC.

Renewal
   Plenary summons issued but not served—Limitation period expiring—Application to
   renew—Whether defendant prejudiced by lapse of time—RSC 1962, 0 8, r 1. **Walshe v
   Coras Iompair Eireann** [1985] 180, HC.

Service out of jurisdiction. See Service out of jurisdiction (*above*).

Survival of cause of action
Death of respondent. See ACTION (Cause—Survival—Death of respondent).

PRACTICE *continued*
Taxation of costs. *See* COSTS (Taxation).

Third party notice
Personal injuries action
Third party notice not served until after conclusion of plaintiff's claim—Whether
served as soon as was reasonably possible—Whether service of a third party notice the
only method of claiming contribution from a person not already a party to the
action—Civil Liability Act 1961, ss. 21, 27(1), 31. **Kelly v St Laurence's Hospital** [1989]
877, SC.

Service out of jurisdiction
Order granting leave to serve notice out of jurisdiction—Application to set aside—
Whether third party a proper person—English proceedings relating to same cause of
action—Whether court obliged to decline jurisdiction because of English proceedings—
Convention on Jurisdiction and the Enforcement of Judgments in Civil and Commercial
Matters 1968, Articles 21, 54—Accession Convention 1978, Article 34(1). **International
Commercial Bank plc v Insurance Corporation of Ireland plc** [1989] 788, HC.

Time limit
Computation. See TIME LIMIT (Computation of time).

Extension. See TIME LIMIT (Extension).

Trial
Jury trial
Whether right to trial by jury deriving from Constitutional right of access to the
courts—Whether absolute right—Claim in tort—Action for damages for personal
injuries—Proceedings commenced in the High Court—Motion to remit case to District
or Circuit Court—Damages likely to be within District Court jurisdiction—Whether
plaintiff right to a jury trial—Courts of Justice Act 1924, s. 94—Courts Act 1971, s. 6.
McDonald v Galvin [1976–7] 41, HC.

Several causes of action
Damages for personal injuries—Two distinct and separate causes of action—Plaintiff
seeking to join unrelated defendants—Whether causes of action could be conveniently
tried or disposed of together—Civil Liability Act 1961, ss. 11(1), 12(2)—RSC O 12 rr
1, 8. **Byrne v Triumph Engineering Ltd** [1982] 317, SC.

Want of prosecution
Dismissal of action. See Dismissal for want of prosecution (*above*).

PRECEDENT
Decisions of European Court of Human Rights
Precedent value
Succession—Intestacy—Illegitimate child—Whether illegitimate child "issue" of the
deceased. **In re Walker: O'Brien v s.** [1985] 86, HC.

Decisions of United States Supreme Court
Precedent value
Succession—Intestacy—Illegitimate child—Whether illegitimate child "issue" of the
deceased. **In re Walker: O'Brien v s.** [1985] 86, HC.

Pre-Treaty English decisions
Whether High Court bound to follow pre-Treaty English decisions
Constitution of Ireland 1937, Article 50—**Irish Shell Ltd v Elm Motors Ltd** [1984] 595,
SC.

Stare decisis
High Court decision
Whether based on insufficient authority or incorrect submissions—Whether grounds

PRECEDENT
Stare decisis
High Court decision continued
for departure from judgment established. **Irish Trust Bank Ltd v Central Bank** [1976–7] 50, HC.

Previous decisions of Supreme Court on issue of when case stated lies—Interpretation of relevant statutory provision—Whether compelling reasons for departing from court's previous interpretation—Status of three-judge court decisions. **Doyle v Hearne & Ors** [1988] 318, SC.

Supreme Court decision
Earlier decision overruled where legal principle incorrectly applied. **Finucane v McMahon** [1990] 505, SC.

Ratio decidendi not followed. **Costello v DPP** [1983] 489, HC; [1984] 413, SC.

PREFERENTIAL PAYMENTS *See* COMPANY (Winding up—Preferential payments).

PREGNANCY
Marriage
Whether consent to marriage. See MARRIAGE (Nullity—Duress—Pregnancy).

Maternity protection. *See* EMPLOYMENT (Maternity protection).

Teacher
Dismissal on grounds of pregnancy. See EDUCATION (Teacher—Dismissal—Pregnancy).

Termination
Abortion. See ABORTION.

PREJUDICIAL EVIDENCE *See* CRIMINAL LAW (Evidence—Prejudicial).

PRELIMINARY EXAMINATION
Generally *See* CRIMINAL LAW (Procedure—Preliminary examination).

Powers of DPP. See DIRECTOR OF PUBLIC PROSECUTIONS (Powers—Validity—Trial on indictment—Preliminary examination—DPP substituting new counts).

Undertaking of DPP. See DIRECTOR OF PUBLIC PROSECUTIONS (Undertaking—Preliminary examination—Undertaking that evidence given would not be used for the purpose of criminal proceedings against witness).

PREMISES
Defective. *See* DEFECTIVE PREMISES.

Entry on. *See* ENTRY ON PREMISES.

PREROGATIVE
State
Immunity from suit. See STATE (Immunity from suit).

Treasure trove
Whether necessary ingredient of sovereignty—Whether former Royal prerogative of treasure trove carried over into Irish law—Constitution of Ireland 1937, Articles 5, 10. **Webb v Ireland** [1988] 565, HC, SC.

PRESERVATION
Evidence
Duty of Gardai to preserve evidence material to guilt or innocence. See CRIMINAL LAW (Evidence— Preservation).

PRESERVATION ORDER
National monument on land
Whether unjust attack on property rights
Whether order *ultra vires*. See NATIONAL MONUMENT (Preservation order).

PRESIDENT OF IRELAND
Dissolution of Dáil
Duty of Taoiseach to advise President
Whether courts can prevent the Taoiseach from advising the President to dissolve Dáil Éireann—Constitution of Ireland 1937, Article 13.2.1. **O'Malley v An Taoiseach** [1990] 461, HC.

Reference of Bill to Supreme Court. *See* CONSTITUTION (Bill—Validity).

PRESS
Defamation
Ordinary meaning of words
Judge determining words were defamatory—Whether usurping role of jury—Damages—Whether excessive—Purpose of award. **Barrett v Independent Newspapers Ltd** [1986] 601, SC.

Freedom
Contempt of court
Newspaper publication—Article stating that DPP intended to bring charges against a local authority councillor—Political party to which councillor belonged referred to—Name of councillor not given—Whether publication could tend to prejudice the trial of proceedings that were pending—Whether facts justified extension of law. **State (DPP) v Independent Newspapers Ltd** [1985] 183, HC.

Injunction application to restrain publication
Criminal conviction—Pending appeal to Court of Criminal Appeal—Publication of a magazine article on material supplied by sole witness for the prosecution—Whether article likely to prejudice the appeal—Constitution of Ireland 1937, Article 40 6. **Cullen v Toibin** [1984] 577, HC, SC.

PRESUMPTION
Constitutionality of legislation. *See* CONSTITUTION (Statute—Validity—Presumption of constitutionality).

Courts
Natural justice
Presumption that District Justice will act in accordance with principles of natural justice and fairness—Criminal Justice Act 1951—Criminal Procedure Act 1967. **Clune v DPP** [1981] 17, HC.

Statutory interpretation. *See* STATUTORY INTERPRETATION (Presumption).

PREVENTATIVE DETENTION
See CRIME PREVENTION (Preventative detention—Habitual criminals).

PRICES
Maximum Prices Order
Breach
Intoxicating liquor. *See* LICENSING ACTS (Offence—Prices—Maximum Prices Order).

PRIEST
Privilege
Priest acting as marriage counsellor
Communications—Privilege that of the spouses. **R v R** [1981] 125, HC.

PRIEST *continued*
Teacher in seminary
Dismissal
Whether religious discrimination. *See* RELIGIOUS DISCRIMINATION (Seminary—Employment—Dismissal of teacher).

PRINCIPAL AND AGENT *See* AGENCY.

PRINCIPAL AND SURETY *See* SURETY.

PRIOR MORTGAGE. *See* MORTGAGE (Prior mortgage).

PRIORITY OF CREDITORS
Receivership. *See* COMPANY (Receivership—Priority of creditors).

Winding up. *See* COMPANY (Winding up—Priority of creditors).

PRISONS
Access to legal adviser
Validity of regulations. See Prison regulations—Validity (*below*).

Conditions of confinement
Rights of convicted prisoner. See Prisoner—Health and safety—Conditions of confinement (*below*).

Lighting and ventilation
Whether in accordance with prison regulations. See Prisoner—Health and safety—Accommodation—Lighting and ventilation of cell (*below*).

Military custody
Legality of detention. See Prisoner—Legality of detention—Military custody (*below*).

Transfer of prisoner to military custody. See Prisoner—Transfer—Military custody (*below*).

Prison authority
Duty of care
Whether duty of care owed to prisoner—Prisoner injured by another prisoner during recreation—Whether supervision of prisoners adequate—Whether prison authorities required to conduct searches of prisoners before recreation. **Muldoon v Ireland** [1988] 367, HC.

Prison regulations
Validity
Prisoners' access to legal advisers and legal advice—Certain solicitors excluded—Whether regulations unconstitutional—Whether specific regulations *ultra vires*—General Prisons (Ireland) Act 1877, ss. 12, 13(2)—Rules for the Government of Prisons 1976. **Incorporated Law Society v Moore and Minister for Justice** [1978] 112, HC.

Prisoner
Excape from custody
Extradition proceedings. *See* EXTRADITION (Escape from custody).

Communication. See Prisoner—Personal rights—Communication (*below*).

Family of prisoner
Rights—Subsisting rights of convicted prisoner's family—Right to communicate—Rules for the Government of Prisons 1947, Rules 59, 60. **State (Gallagher) v Governor of Portlaoise Prison** [1987] 45, HC.

Health and safety
Accommodation—Lighting and ventilation of cell—Whether in accordance with prison regulations—Whether regulation relating to lighting and ventilation applied only to punishment cells used for separate and close confinement of prisoners—

PRISONS
Prisoner
Health and safety continued

Military custody—Whether administration of rules by soldiers affects legality of detention—Prison order and discipline—Prisons Act 1972 s. 2(9)—Prisons Act 1972 (Military Custody) Regulations 1972, Regs 6, 7, 66, 68. **State (Boyle) v Governor of the Curragh Military Detention Barracks** [1980] 242, HC.

Conditions of confinement—Subsisting rights of convicted prisoner—Complaint by prisoner that conditions of confinement conflict with health and privacy rights—Whether motive for complaint relevant—Whether state in breach of duties under Constitution and Prison Rules—Appropriate remedy—Whether habeas corpus or Article 40 4 inquiry appropriate form of relief—Constitution of Ireland, 1937, Article 40 3—Rules for the Government of Prisons 1947, rr 34,46,108,172. **State (Richardson) v Governor of Mountjoy Prison** [1980] 82, HC.

Effect of imprisonment—Prisoner suffering from reactive depression—Effect not normally contemplated by court in imposing sentence—Whether detention rendered illegal—Whether habeas corpus should issue—Whether to be considered in discretion of Minister for Justice to remit sentence or grant parole—Prisons Act 1972, s. 2(3). **State (Smith and Fox) v Governor of Military Detention Barracks** [1980] 208, HC.

Injury during recreation—Duty of care of prison authority—Supervision. *See* Prison authority—Duty of care *(above)*.

Legality of detention

Military custody—Breaches of prison regulations established—Allegations of ill-treatment—Whether detention of prisoner rendered unlawful—Whether mandamus should issue as alternative form of relief—Prisons Act 1972 (Military Custody) Regulations 1972, Regs 8, 16, 19, 34, 39, 40, 50, 51, 62, 134. **Cahill v Governor of Curragh Military Detention Barracks** [1980] 191, HC.

Military custody—Inquiry under Constitution—Whether administration of rules by soldiers affects legality of detention—Prison order and discipline. **State (Boyle) v Governor of the Curragh Military Detention Barracks** [1980] 242, HC.

Remand prisoner—Inquiry under Constitution—Transfer to wing containing convicted prisoners—Whether irregularity such as to make the detention unlawful—Rules for the Government of Prisons 1947—Constitution of Ireland 1937, Article 40. **State (Comerford) v Governor of Mountjoy Prison** [1981] 86, HC.

Personal rights

Communication—Interception of correspondence—Unauthorised interference—Whether censorship of correspondence in breach of right to communicate—Whether damages for breach of right should issue—Rules for the Government of Prisons 1947, Rule 63—Constitution of Ireland 1937, Articles 40 3, 40 6 1. **Kearney v Minister for Justice** [1987] 52, HC.

Communication—Subsisting rights of convicted prisoner's family—Right to communicate—Rules for the Government of Prisons 1947, Rules 59, 60. **State (Gallagher) v Governor of Portlaoise Prison** [1987] 45, HC.

Procreation—Husband and wife serving lengthy sentences of imprisonment—Whether absence of facilities within prison to procreate a denial of rights as married couple—Basis on which exercise of power to imprison may restrict exercise of prisoners' rights—Whether provision of facilities would impose undue burdens on prison administration—Constitution of Ireland 1937, Art 40 3, 40 4, 41. **Murray and Murray v Attorney General** [1985] 542, HC.

Sentence

Generally. *See* CRIMINAL LAW (Sentence).

PRISONS
Prisoner
Sentence continued

Remission—Detention sentence of ten years—Final four years to be suspended—
Regulations providing for remission of sentence—Whether remission earned related to
six years custodial sentence—Whether prisoner entitled to be released—Prisons Act
1972, s. 2(9)—Prisons Act 1972 (Military Custody) Regulations 1972, reg 35(1). **State
(Beirnes) v Governor of Curragh Military Detention Barracks** [1982] 491, HC.

Transfer

Military custody—Opinion that transfer to military custody required on grounds of
insufficiency of ordinary prison accommodation—Whether reviewable—Security context
of exercise of discretion—Prisons Act 1972, s. 2(3). **State (Smith and Fox) v Governor
of Military Detention Barracks** [1980] 208, HC.

Military custody—Transfer by Minister—Whether prisoner entitled to reasons for
transfer—Administrative discretion—Lawful custody—Prisons Act 1972, s. 2(3), (4)—
Prisons Act 1974, s. 1. **State (Boyle) v The Governor of the Curragh Military Detention
Barracks** [1980] 242, HC.

Temporary release scheme
Breach of condition

Order for re-arrest of released prisoner—Failure to make arrest until after the expiry
of the prisoner's sentence—Whether subsequent imprisonment lawful or fair—Criminal
Justice Act 1960, s. 2. **Cunningham v Governor of Mountjoy Prison** [1987] 33, HC.

Revocation of order

Whether contrary to rules of natural justice—Whether fair procedures required to be
observed—Whether fact that releasee had been charged with an offence a sufficient
reason for revocation—Prisoners (Temporary Release) Rules 1960, r 6—Criminal
Justice Act 1960, ss. 2, 4, 6, 7—Offences Against the State Act 1939, s. 30. **State
(Murphy) v Governor of St Patrick's Institution** [1982] 475, HC; [1985] 141, SC.

PRIVACY, RIGHT TO. *See* CONSTITUTION (Personal rights—Privacy).

PRIVATE CITIZEN
Assertion of public right. *See* CONSTITUTION (Locus standi—Public right).

PRIVATE DWELLING
Inviolability. *See* CONSTITUTION (Personal rights—Inviolability of dwelling).

PRIVATE INTERNATIONAL LAW
Choice of law
Whether significant connection with jurisdiction

Appropriate choice of law rule to proceedings in question—Negligence—Defective
products—Fitting of heart valve manufactured in United States. **Grehan v Medical
Incorporated & Valley Pines Associates** [1986] 627, SC.

Comity of courts
Recognition of validity of English court order

Children—Committal into care of local authority in England—Removal by parents to
Ireland—Inquiry into detention of children by health board—Health board action
taken at request of English authority. **Saunders v Mid-Western Health Board** [1989]
229, HC.

Domicile
Irish domicile of origin

Whether acquisition of a foreign domicile of choice—Whether such a domicile if
acquired, subsequently abandoned—Onus of proof. **Revenue Commissioners v Shaw**
[1982] 433, HC.

PRIVATE INTERNATIONAL LAW
Domicile
Irish domicile of origin
Whether acquisition of a foreign domicile of choice—Evidence—Relevance of statement by deceased that he was domiciled in Ireland. **Rowan v Rowan** [1988] 65, HC.

Marriage
Dissolution—Foreign decree—Validity—Whether decree consistent with law of husband's domicile—Appropriate test—Rejection of test of real and substantial connection with country of court granting decree—Constitution of Ireland 1937, Article 41 3 3. **K E D (Otherwise K C) v M C** [1987] 189, HC, SC.

Dissolution—Foreign decree—Recognition—Domicile of husband—Burden of proof. **M T v N T** [1982] 217, HC, SC.

Dissolution—Foreign decree—Recognition—Whether concept of dependent domicile survived enactment of Constitution—Constitution of Ireland 1937, Articles 40 1, 40 3, 41. **C M v T M** [1988] 456, HC.

Validity—Succession—Will made in 1971—Deceased going through ceremony of marriage in 1977—Whether will revoked by this marriage—Whether deceased free to marry in 1977—Previous marriage annulled in 1968—Whether such order would be recognised—Succession Act 1965, ss. 27(4), 85. **In re Fleming (deceased)** [1987] 638, HC.

Evidence
Evidence of expert on provisions of English statute
Whether court bound to accept evidence—Whether evidence contradicted. **Waterford Harbour Commrs v British Railways Board** [1979] 296, HC, SC.

Jurisdiction of courts
Explosion on French registered ship in Irish waters
Fatal damages claim—Victims French nationals employed under French contracts of service—RSC 1962, O 12, r 26. **O'Daly v Gulf Oil Terminals Ltd.** [1983] 163, HC.

Fatal damages claim
Victims being French nationals employed on French registered ship employed under French contracts of service—Motion to set aside order authorising the institution of proceedings—Explosion occurring on board the vessel but within Irish waters—Whether occurring on French national territory—Whether Irish courts should decline jurisdiction in favour of French courts—RSC O 12,r 26. **O'Daly v Gulf Oil Terminals** [1983] 163, HC.

Proper law
Contract
Judgment mortgage—Enforcement—Currency—Disparity arising between value of money in Northern Ireland and the value of money in Ireland—Whether amount should be payable in Irish pounds or in sterling. **Northern Bank Ltd v Edwards** [1986] 167, SC.

Loan agreement—Terms of contract stating that disputes be settled in accordance with Irish law—Contract having no connection with Ireland—Whether service out of jurisdiction permissible—RSC 1986, O 11, r 1(e)(iii), O 12 r 26. **Kutchera v Buckingham International Holdings Ltd** [1988] 1, HC; [1988] 501, SC.

Sale of goods—Retention of title clause—German law—Whether clause a term of the contract. **Fried Krupp Huttenwerke AG v Quitmann Products Ltd** [1982] 551, HC.

Will
Construction—Testator domiciled abroad—Disposition of immovables—Intention of testator—Identity of beneficiary. In re Bonnet: **Johnston v Langheld** [1983] 359, HC.

PRIVATE PROPERTY *See* CONSTITUTION (Property rights)

PRIVATE PROSECUTION
Power of Attorney General to end private prosecutions
Whether such power devolved on the Attorney General after 1922. See ATTORNEY
GENERAL (Jurisdiction—Power to end private prosecutions).

PRIVILEGE
Documents
Discovery. See DISCOVERY (Privilege).

Executive privilege
Garda Síochána
Communication between members of the Gardai—Whether such communications
inadmissible in evidence because, as a class, their admission would be against the
public interest—Whether executive privilege can be claimed in respect of a class of
documents. **DPP (Hanley) v Holly** [1984] 149, HC.

Legal professional privilege. *See* DISCOVERY (Privilege—Legal professional privilege).

Marriage counselleor
Priest
Parish priest acting as marriage counsellor—Whether entitled to claim privilege. **E R v
J R** [1981] 125, HC.

Public interest. *See* DISCOVERY (Privilege—Public interest).

Qualified privilege
Libel. See DEFAMATION (Libel—Qualified privilege).

State privilege
Factors to be taken into consideration
Injustice to applicant or potential damge to public service. **Incorporated Law Society
of Ireland v Minister for Justice** [1987] 42, HC.

Statutory privilege
Central Bank officer
Production of documents—Subpoena *duces tecum* issued—Oath of secrecy—Whether
summons be set aside—Central Bank Act 1942, ss. 6 (1), 31. **Cully v Northern Bank
Finance Corp Ltd** [1984] 676, HC.

PRIVITY OF CONTRACT *See* CONTRACT (Privity).

PROBATE
Two wills
Purported revocation of second will
Whether effective—Whether court to give effect to intention of testatrix—Whether
photocopy of second will should be admitted to probate. *See* WILL (Revocation—
Two wills).

Undue influence claim. *See* WILL (Validity—Undue influence).

PROBATIONER
Dismissal. *See* EMPLOYMENT (Dismissal—Office holder—Probationer).

PROCEDURE
Certiorari. *See* CERTIORARI (Practice and procedure).

Constitution
Challenge to validity of statute. See CONSTITUTION (Statute—Validity—Procedure).

Consumer protection
Investigative procedure. See CONSUMER PROTECTION (Investigative procedure).

PROCEDURE *continued*
Criminal law. *See* CRIMINAL LAW (Procedure).

District Court. *See* DISTRICT COURT (Procedure).

Employment equality reference. *See* EMPLOYMENT (Equality of treatment—Procedure).

Extradition
Validity. *See* CONSTITUTION (Extradition —Procedure).

Fair procedures. *See* CONSTITUTION (Fair procedures).

Generally. *See* PRACTICE.

Habeas corpus inquiry. *See* HABEAS CORPUS (Procedure).

High Court. *See* HIGH COURT (Procedure).

Labour Court. *See* LABOUR COURT (Procedure).

Land Commission acquisition. *See* LAND COMMISSION (Procedure).

Planning
Default procedure. *See* PLANNING (Default procedure).

Revenue. *See* REVENUE (Practice and procedure).

Special Criminal Court. *See* SPECIAL CRIMINAL COURT (Procedure).

Unfair dismissals claim. *See* EMPLOYMENT (Unfair dismissal—Procedure).

PRODUCT LIABILITY. *See* Negligence (Defective products).

PROFESSIONS
Accountant. *See* ACCOUNTANT

Architect. *See* ARCHITECT

Auctioneer. *See* AUCTIONEER

Doctor. *See* MEDICAL PRACTITIONER

Education
Solicitors
Law school—System of entry. *See* SOLICITOR (Entry to profession).

Legal profession. *See* Barrister; Solicitor

Negligence
Generally. *See* NEGLIGENCE (Professional).

Registration. *See* MEDICAL PRACTITIONER (Registration).

PROFIT Á PRENDRE *See* FISHING RIGHTS (Interference).

PROHIBITION
Criminal trial
Delay
Whether such as to prejudice accused's rights to fair trial—Whether delay by State culpable—Whether delay so excessive as to justify granting absolute order of prohibition. **State (O'Connell) v Fawsitt** [1986] 639, HC, SC.

Garda Síochána
Disciplinary investigation
Garda acquitted of criminal charges—Disciplinary inquiry—Whether inquiry could subsequently investigate charges arising out of identical allegations of corruption—Whether estoppel—Whether unfair and oppressive procedure—Garda Síochána (Discipline) Regulations 1971, reg 6. **McGrath v Commissioner of An Garda Síochána** [1990] 5, HC; [1990] 817, SC.

PROHIBITION *continued*
Grounds for issue
Compensation tribunal
Solicitor of applicants having difficulty preparing case—Difficulty in advising clients as to their legal rights—Order of prohibition sought prohibiting Tribunal from hearing claims of certain named applicants—Whether prohibition available—Whether Tribunal usurping its jurisdiction. **State (Keegan) v Stardust Victims' Compensation Tribunal** [1987] 202, HC, SC.

PROMISSORY ESTOPPEL
Generally. *See* ESTOPPEL (Promissory estoppel).

Legitimate expectation. *See* LEGITIMATE EXPECTATION.

PROPER LAW *See* PRIVATE INTERNATIONAL LAW (Proper law).

PROPERTY *See also* REAL PROPERTY
Confiscation
Freezing of money in bank account
Powers of Minister under Offences Agains the State legislation. *See* CONSTITUTION (Property rights—Confiscation of property).

Forfeiiture. See FORFEITURE

Inspection. *See* PRACTICE (Inspection of property).

Matrimonial. *See* FAMILY LAW (Property).

Residential property tax. *See* REVENUE (Residential property tax).

Sale of land. *See* SALE OF LAND.

PROPERTY RIGHTS
Constitution. *See* CONSTITUTION (Property rights).

Shareholder
Industrial and provident society
Property rights. *See* INDUSTRIAL AND PROVIDENT SOCIETY (Shareholder—Property rights).

PROPRIETARY ESTOPPEL *See* ESTOPPEL (Proprietary estoppel).

PROSECUTION OF OFFENCES
Generally. *See* CRIMINAL LAW (Prosecution of offences).

Powers of DPP
Validity. *See* DIRECTOR OF PUBLIC PROSECUTIONS (Powers—Validity).

PSYCHIATRIC ILLNESS
See also MENTAL ILLNESS

Marriage
Capacity. *See* MARRIAGE (Nullity—Psychiatric illness).

PSYCHIATRIC NURSE
Dismissal
Health board officer
Whether entitlement to claim unfair dismissal. *See* EMPLOYMENT (Unfair dismissal—Exclusion—Officer—Health board).

PSYCHIATRIST
Negligence
Health board officers
  Detention of person as being of unsound mind. *See* NEGLIGENCE (Medical practitioner—
  Health board officers—Psychiatrists).

PUBLIC AUTHORITY
Challenge to validity of decision. *See* JUDICIAL REVIEW.

Health board. *See* HEALTH BOARD.

Local authority. *See* LOCAL GOVERNMENT (Authority).

Minister. *See* MINISTER.

Natural justice. *See* NATURAL AND CONSTITUTIONAL JUSTICE.

Statutory duty. *See* STATUTORY DUTY.

Statutory powers. *See* STATUTORY POWER.

PUBLIC FINANCE
Rating. *See* RATING AND VALUATION.

Revenue. *See* REVENUE.

PUBLIC FUNDS
Charge upon public funds
Treaty. *See* CONSTITUTION (International relations—Treaty—Extradition).

PUBLIC HEALTH
Generally. *See* LOCAL GOVERNMENT (Public health).

Nuisance. *See* NUISANCE.

Service charges. *See* LOCAL GOVERNMENT (Service charges).

Sewerage
Connection to public sewer. *See* LOCAL GOVERNMENT (Public health—Sewer—
Connection).

Deficiency in public facilities
  Refusal of planning permission. *See* PLANNING (Compensation—Refusal of permission—
  Exclusions—Deficiency in public sewerage facilities).

Trade effluent
  Charges for connection to public sewer. *See* LOCAL GOVERNMENT (Public health—
  Sewer—Connection—Charges—Trade effluent).

Slaughterhouse. See ABATTOIR

Temporary dwellings. *See* TEMPORARY DWELLINGS.

Waste disposal
Asbestos waste
  Grant of permission—for use of site for disposal of asbestos waste—Appeal against
  decision—Whether due consideration given to evidence as to danger of health arising
  from proposed user. *See* PLANNING (Appeal—Grant of permission—Use of site for
  disposal of asbestos waste).

Refuse dump proposal
  Site of national monument. *See* PLANNING (Development plan—Contravention—
  National monument on lands—Refuse dump).

PUBLIC HOUSING *See* HOUSING (Local authority).

PUBLIC INTEREST
Discovery of documents
Privilege. See DISCOVERY (Privilege—Public interest).

Trade union negotiation licence. *See* TRADE UNION (Negotiation licence).

PUBLIC INTERNATIONAL LAW
Treaty. *See* CONSTITUTION (International relations—Treaty).

PUBLIC MISCHIEF
Offence
Offence of effecting a public mischief contrary to common law
Whether charge known to common law of Ireland—Whether creation of a new offence—Criminal Law Act 1976, s. 12. **DPP (Vizzard) v Carew** [1981] 91, HC.

PUBLIC MORALS
Offence
Conspiracy to corrupt public morals
Whether offence established—Non-directive counselling regarding abortion. **Attorney General (SPUC) v Open Door Counselling** [1987] 477, HC.

PUBLIC PLACE
Accident occurring in grounds of country house
Whether a 'public place'. See MOTOR INSURANCE (Liability of insurer—Whether accident in a "public place").

PUBLIC POLICY
Restraint of trade. *See* RESTRAINT OF TRADE (Reasonableness—Public policy).

PUBLIC RIGHT
Attorney General as guardian of public right. *See* ATTORNEY GENERAL.

Locus standi
Private citizen. See CONSTITUTION (Locus standi—Public right).

PUBLIC RIGHT OF WAY *See* EASEMENT (Right of way—Public right of way).

PUBLICATION
Breach of confidence
Injunction application to restrain publication. See CONFIDENTIALITY (Breach—Publication—book written by deceased member of British intelligence service).

Contempt of court (Criminal contempt—Newspaper publication).

Contract
Claim in quasi-contract
Discussion concerning publication of an encyclopedia—Publishing company expending money on project—Claim for indemnity against money expended and damages for breach of contract—Whether contract agreed as to publication—Whether interest on sum payable allowed—Whether inflation to be taken into account. **Folens & Co Ltd v Minister for Education** [1984] 265, HC.

Defamation
Libel. See DEFAMATION (Libel).

Freedom of the press. *See* PRESS (Freedom).

PURCHASE NOTICE *See* PLANNING (Purchase notice).

PURCHASER
Lien. *See* SALE OF LAND (Lien—Purchaser).

Protection clause. *See* SALE OF LAND (Contract—Purchasers protection clause).

QUALIFIED PRIVILEGE. *See* DEFAMATION (Libel—Qualified privilege).

QUARRY
Nuisance. *See* NUISANCE (Quarry).
Planning permission
Whether unauthorised use of land. See PLANNING (Quarrying).

QUASI-CONTRACT
Damages
Assessment
Discussion concerning publication of an encyclopedia—Publishing company expending money on project—Claim for indemnity against money expended and damages for breach of contract—Whether contract agreed as to publication—Whether interest on sum payable allowed—Whether inflation to be taken into account. **Folens & Co Ltd v Minister for Education** [1984] 265, HC.

Restitution
Quantum meruit
Reasonable sum for services rendered—Whether relief possible where parties have entered into concluded agreement. **G F Galvin (Estates) Ltd v Hedigan** [1985] 295, HC.

QUESTION OF LAW
Arbitration
Case stated. See ARBITRATION (Case stated).

Revenue case. *See* REVENUE (Practice and procedure—Questions of law).

QUIA TIMET INJUNCTION *See* INJUNCTION (Quia timet).

QUIET ENJOYMENT
Covenant
Breach. See LANDLORD AND TENANT (Breach of covenant—Quiet enjoyment).

QUIT
Notice to quit. *See* LANDLORD AND TENANT (Ejectment—Notice to quit).

RADIO *See* BROADCASTING

RAILWAY BRIDGE
Vertical clearance
Mechanical digger colliding with overhead bridge—Derailment of train—Liability—Clearance betwen road surface and underside of the bridge less than the prescribed statutory dimension—Apportionment of fault—Whether breach of statutory duty by railway authority—Diminution in clearance due to road works carried out by local authority—Railway Clauses Consolidation Act 1845, ss. 46, 49, 52–57—Local Government Act 1925, Part III. **Coras Iompair Éireann v Carroll** [1983] 173, HC; [1986] 312, SC.

RAPE
Sentencing. *See* CRIMINAL LAW (Rape).

RATING AND VALUATION
Agricultural land
Validity

Constitution—Property rights—Valuation carried out between 1852 and 1866—No revaluation ever taking place—Whether an unjust attack on property rights—Whether arbitrary and unjust discrimination— Constitution of Ireland 1937, Articles 40.1, 40.3, 43—Valuation (Ireland) Act 1852, ss. 5, 11, 32, 33, 34—Local Government Act 1946, ss. 11, 12. **Brennan v Attorney General** [1983] 449, HC; [1984] 355, SC.

Annual value
Calculation

Reduction of valuation sought—Hotel—Basis upon which rateable valuation of premises may be reduced—Whether rateable valuation of premises could be reviewed solely on grounds that business no longer profitable—Rateable Valuation (Ireland) Act 1852, s. 11. **Rosses Point Hotel Co Ltd v The Commissioner of Valuation** [1987] 512, HC.

Assessment
Valuation

Whether owner of premises entitled to be furnished with evidence of valuation of similar premises in locality—Whether finding of fact that premises were separately valued previously—Evidence—Admissibility—Valuations of similar premises. **Munster & Leinster Bank Ltd v Commissioner of Valuation** [1979] 246, HC.

Exemption
Charitable or public purposes

Private fee paying school—Whether school of a public nature or used for charitable purposes—Basis of exemption—Poor Relief (Ireland) Act 1838, s. 63—Valuation (Ireland) Act 1854, s. 2. **Governors of Wesley College v Commissioner of Valuation** [1984] 117, SC.

Machinery

Brewery—Whether brewers' tanks and vessels rateable as being part of the rateable hereditament—Whether tanks machinery—Meaning of "machine"—Annual Revision of Rateable Property (Ireland) Act 1860, s. 7. **Beamish & Crawford Ltd v Commissioner of Valuation** [1980] 149, SC.

Rateable property
Newly created hereditaments

Land reclaimed from sea. *See* Reclaimed land (*below*).

Reclaimed land
Valuation

Whether such land may be valued by the Commissioner—Valuation of two adjoining properties held under separate titles as a single unit—Whether ultra vires—Statute—Interpretation—Valuation (Ireland) Act 1852, ss. 11, 20, 23—Valuation (Ireland) Amendment Act 1854, s. 4—Annual Revision of Rateable Property Act 1860, s. 6—Harbour Act 1946, s. 55. **Coal Distributors Ltd v Commissioner of Valuation** [1990] 172, HC.

Relief
Municipal rate

Whether relief extends only to hereditaments occupied by ratepayer at time statute enacted—Whether relief extends to hereditaments subsequently acquired by ratepayer—Interpretation of legislation—Local Government (Dublin) Act 1930, s. 69, 2nd Schedule. **Dublin Corporation v Trinity College Dublin** [1984] 84, HC; [1985] 283, SC.

RECEIVERSHIP *See* COMPANY (Receivership).

RECEIVING STOLEN GOODS *See* (CRIMINAL LAW—Larceny—Offence—Receiving stolen goods).

REAL PROPERTY
Adverse possession. *See* ADVERSE POSSESSION.

Easement
Right of way. *See* EASEMENT (Right of way).

Ejectment
Trespasser
Action for possession—Plaintiff's lands built on by defendants—Court's exercise of equitable jurisdiction to refuse order for possession. **McMahon v Kerry Co Council** [1981] 419, HC.

Fishing rights
Interference
Lakes and rivers—Outdoor education centre—Canoeing—Ownership of bed and soil of lake and river—Whether plaintiff entitled only to profit a prendre—Injunction application. **Tennent v Clancy** [1988] 214, HC.

Incumbrance
Charge
Deed of charge—Registered land—Possession—Entitlement—Whether owner of deed of charge entitled to possession without order of court—Deed conferring power of possession—Whether contractual licence to enter lands only created. **Gale v First National Building Society** [1987] 30, HC.

Deed of charge—Registered land—Extent of property mortgaged—Receiver—Whether entitled to appropriate all income from land—Whether receiver entitled to portion of proceeds of land—Conveyancing and Law of Property Act 1881, s. 24. **Donohoe v Agricultural Credit Corporation** [1987] 26, HC.

Lis pendens
Registration—Effect of proceedings establishing equitable interest in property on mortgage executed subsequent to registration of *lis pendens*—Whether equitable interest entitled to priority over mortgagee's interest—Whether mortgage valid. **In re Kelly's Carpetdrome Ltd; Byrne v UDT Bank Ltd** [1984] 418, HC.

Mortgage. See MORTGAGE.

Inhibition
Registered land
Whether affected parties must be given notice of entry of inhibition—*See* REGISTRATION OF TITLE (Inhibition).

Partition
Order for sale in lieu of partition. See JOINT TENANCY (Partition).

Transfer of land
Deed
Reservation of right of residence, care and support—Application to cancel transfer—Whether undue influence—Whether deed improvident. **Leonard v Leonard** [1988] 245, HC.

REASONABLE EXPECTATION *See* LEGITIMATE EXPECTATION.

RECLAIMED LAND
Valuation
Whether such land may be valued by Commissioner of Valuation. See RATING AND VALUATION (Reclaimed land).

RECREATIONAL DEVELOPMENT
Compulsory purchase powers
Local authority. See COMPULSORY PURCHASE (Powers—Local authority—Residential and recreational development).

REDUNDANCY. *See* EMPLOYMENT (Redundancy).

REGISTERED DESIGN
Copyright. *See* COPYRIGHT (Infringement—Registered design).

REGISTERED LAND
Charge
Possession
 Whether owner of deed of charge entitled to possession without order of court. *See* REAL PROPERTY (Incumbrance—Charge—Registered land).

Inhibition
Notice
 Whether affected parties must be given notice of entry of inhibition. *See* REGISTRATION OF TITLE (Inhibition).

REGISTRAR OF FRIENDLY SOCIETIES
Function and jurisdiction
Industrial and provident societies
 Amendment to rules—Registration—Credit union. *See* INDUSTRIAL AND PROVIDENT SOCIETY (Credit union—Amendment to rules).

 Registration of rules. *See* INDUSTRIAL AND PROVIDENT SOCIETY (Rules—Registration).

REGISTRATION OF BIRTHS
Paternity of child
Evidence admissible to prove paternity
 Evidence of wife that child not the child of the marriage—Whether admissible. *See* CHILD (Paternity).

REGISTRATION OF TITLE
Inhibition
Entry in register
 Whether affected parties must be given notice of entry of inhibition—Whether power to be exercised in judicial manner—Registration of Title Act 1964, s. 121. **State (Philpott) v Registrar of Titles** [1986] 499, HC.

Registered land
Incumbrance. See REAL PROPERTY (Incumbrance).

RELATOR ACTION. *See* PRACTICE (Relator proceedings).

RELIGION, MINISTER OF *See* PRIEST.

RELIGIOUS DENOMINATION
Right to manage its own affairs
Seminary. See RELIGIOUS DISCRIMINATION (Seminary—Employment—Dismissal of teacher).

RELIGIOUS DISCRIMINATION
Seminary
Employment
 Dismissal of teacher—Teacher also priest—Whether discrimination in dismissing teacher—Seminary fund-aided by State as recognised college of university—Whether primarily seminary or university—Rights of religious denomination to manage its own affairs—Constitution of Ireland, Articles 44.2.3, 44.2.5—Maynooth College Establishment Act 1795, s. 3—Irish Universities Act 1908, s. 2(4)—Higher Education Authority Act 1971, s. 1(4). **McGrath and O Ruairc v Maynooth College** [1979] 166, SC.

RELIGIOUS SCHOOL
Convent secondary school
Dismissal of teacher
Pregnancy. *See* EDUCATION (Teacher—Dismissal—Pregnancy).

REMOTENESS
Damages. *See* DAMAGES (Remoteness).

RENT *See* LANDLORD AND TENANT (Rent).

REPEAL
Statute. *See* STATUTE (Repeal).

REPRESENTATION
Reliance
Estoppel. See ESTOPPEL (Representation).

REPUDIATION OF CONTRACT
Sale of land. *See* SALE OF LAND (Contract—Repudiation).

RES JUDICATA
Estoppel. *See* ESTOPPEL (Res judicata).

RESCISSION OF CONTRACT
Generally. *See* CONTRACT (Rescission).

Sale of land. *See* SALE OF LAND (Contract—Rescission).

RESERVATION OF TITLE *See* SALE OF GOODS (Retention of title clause).

RESIDENCE *See* DOMICILE; DWELLING.

RESIDENTIAL PROPERTY TAX. *See* REVENUE (Residential property tax).

RESTAURANT LICENCE. *See* LICENSING ACTS (Restaurant certificate).

RESTITUTION
Mistake
Money paid under a mistake of law
Money paid voluntarily—Whether recoverable—Housing Act 1966, s. 99. **Rogers v Louth County Council** [1981] 144, SC.

Payment induced by fraud
Infant plaintiff sustaining serious injury in the course of employment—Lodgment of money into court—Mistaken assumption of liability induced by fraud—RSC 1962, O 22, rr 4, 10, 13. **Carey v Ryan Ltd** [1982] 121, SC.

Quasi-contract
Quantum meruit
Reasonable sum for services rendered—Whether relief possible where parties have entered into concluded agreement. **G F Galvin (Estates) Ltd v Hedigan** [1985] 295, HC.

RESTRAINT OF TRADE
Contract
Employment
Restraint of trade clause—Contract prohibiting employment with competitor for two years after termination—Injunction—Balance of convenience—Valid interest to be protected. **European Chemical Industries Ltd v Bell** [1981] 345, HC.

Lease
Exclusive trading covenant—Oil company leasing land to proprietor of petrol filling

RESTRAINT OF TRADE
Contract
Lease continued
station—Exclusive purchase covenant—Breach—Whether enforceable—Whether common law doctrine of restraint of trade applicable to restrictions in leases—Injunction—enforcement of negative covenants—Whether plaintiff disentitled to relief by reason of delay—Balance of convenience—Jurisdiction of court to grant mandatory injunction on interlocutory application. **Irish Shell Ltd v Elm Motors Ltd** [1982] 519, HC; [1984] 595, SC.

Sale of business
Restrictive covenant—Enforceability of restraint clauses—Whether restraint reasonable. **John Orr Ltd v Orr** [1987] 702, HC.

Employment contract
Application for interlocutory injunction
Whether onus on employer to establish the reasonableness of the restraint—Power of court to modify agreement—Injunction application. **European Chemical Industries Ltd v Bell** [1981] 345, HC.

Industrial and provident society
Rules
Whether rules of an industrial and provident society which benefit members who trade with that society over those who prefer not to do so are in restraint of trade. **Kerry Co-Operative Creameries v An Bord Bainne** [1990] 664.

Reasonableness
Public policy—Equestrian rule-making body—Prohibition on use of non-Irish horses by Irish showjumpers in international competitions—Whether unreasonable restraint on individual showjumpers' trade. **Macken v O'Reilly** [1979] 79, HC, SC.

RESTRICTIVE COVENANT
Lease. *See* LANDLORD AND TENANT (Covenant—Restriction as to user).

RESTRICTIVE PRACTICES
European Communities
Abuse of a dominant position
Treaty of Rome, Article 86. **Cadbury Ireland Ltd v Kerry Co-Operative Creameries Ltd** [1982] 77, HC.

Prices regulation
Retail prices
Advertising—Prohibition on advertising goods at cost less than 'net invoice price'—Whether meaning of prohibition clear—Whether injunction appropriate remedy—Restrictive Practices Act 1972, s. 19—Restrictive Practices (Groceries) (Amendment) (No 2) Order 1978, Art 5. **Irish Association of Distributive Trades v Three Guys** [1979] 269, HC.

RETENTION OF TITLE
Contract for sale of goods. *See* SALE OF GOODS (Retention of title clause).

RETROSPECTIVE LEGISLATION. *See* STATUTE (Retrospectivity).

RETURN FOR TRIAL *See* CRIMINAL LAW (Return for trial).

REVENUE
Advance rulings
Revenue Commissioners answering certain queries
Whether inspector of taxes bound by such rulings—Finance Act 1973, s. 34—

REVENUE
Advance rulings
Revenue Commissioners answering certain queries continued

Corporation Tax Act 1976, s. 10—Rules of The Superior Courts 1986, O 84, r 18(2). **Pandion Haliaetus Ltd v Revenue Commissioners** [1988] 419, HC.

Capital acquisitions tax
Relief

Nephew or niece—Gift of farm to niece—Whether niece worked substantially full time on the farm—Whether supervision of another's cattle under a letting agreement constituted a business—Capital Acquisitions Tax Act 1976, 2nd Schedule, part 1, para 9. **AE v Revenue Commissioners** [1984] 301, CC.

Capital gains tax
Company

Winding up—Liquidator selling property and incurring liability for Capital Gains Tax—Whether tax payable 'an expense incurred in the realisation of an asset'—Whether tax payable 'a necessary disbursement' of the liquidator—Companies Act 1963, s. 285 (2)—Capital Gains Tax Act 1975, Schedule 4, Clause 15—Corporation Tax Act 1976, ss. 6(2), 13(5)—Winding Up Rules 0 74 r 129. In re Van Hool McArdle Ltd [1982] 340, HC.

Tax avoidance

Whether transactions intended merely to avoid incidence of tax—Function of courts—Whether courts empowered to invalidate tax avoidance schemes in general—Whether fiscal reality to be considered—Capital Gains Tax Act 1975, ss. 5(1), 33(5)—Corporation Tax Act 1976, s. 102. **McGrath v McDermott (Inspector of Taxes)** [1988] 181, HC; [1988] 647, SC.

Corporation profits tax
Liability

Whether taxpayer is corporate body precluded by its constitution from distributing profits among its members—Meaning of company for corporation profits tax purposes—Meaning of profits—Nature of what is distributed in a winding up—Finance Act 1932, s. 47—Finance Act 1954, s. 21—Companies Act 1963, s. 275. **Wilson v Dunnes Stores Ltd** [1982] 444, HC.

Corporation tax
Appeal

Questions of law—Statutory provision requiring expressions of dissatisfaction to be made immediately after the determination—Whether "immediately" to be interpreted strictly. *See* Practice and Procedure—Questions of law—Corporation tax appeal (*below*).

Assessment

Capital or revenue transaction—Settlement of action for nuisance—Whether expenditure on settling the claim to be regarded as capital or revenue transaction. **Insulation Products Ltd v Inspector of Taxes** [1984] 610, CC.

Training grants—Whether capital or revenue receipts—Industrial Development Act 1969, s. 239. **Jacob International Ltd Inc v O Cleirigh** (Inspector of Taxes) 1985] 651, SC.

Calculation of profits

Accounting conventions—Whether current cost accounting system acceptable. Carroll Industries plc (formerly **P.J. Carroll and Co. Ltd) v O Culachain, Inspector of Taxes** [1989] 552, HC.

Distributions

Company in voluntary liquidation—Distributable income exceeding amount of distributions—Whether additional surcharge of tax payable—Definition of distributions of a company—Whether literal interpretation would lead to absurd or unjust results—

REVENUE
Corporation tax
Distributions continued
Income Tax Act 1967, s. 428—Corporation Tax Act 1976, ss. 84, 100, 101, 146.
Rahinstown Estates Co v Hughes, Inspector of Taxes [1987] 599, HC.

Dividends
Company receiving dividends—Dividends derived from sale of capital assets—Whether dividend liable to be assessed for tax—Finance Act 1920, ss. 52, 53(2)—Corporation Tax Act 1976, s. 164, 3rd Schedule. **Kellystown Co v Hogan, Inspector of Taxes** [1985] 200, SC.

Double taxation agreement
Interest payable to non-resident—Effect of alteration in domestic fiscal system on the practice followed under a prior international agreement—Income Tax Act 1967, ss. 361(1), 434(5)(a)—Finance Act 1974 s. 31(2)—Corporation Tax Act 1976, ss. 83, 84, 151—Double Taxation Agreement with Japan 1974, Article 12(2). **Murphy v Asahi Synthetic Fibres** [1986] 24, HC.

Export sales relief
Goods manufactured within the State—Ripening of bananas imported into the State—Whether processing of bananas by heating amounts to manufacturing—Whether relief may be granted only in respect of material produced within the State—Statute—Interpretation—Provision of taxation legislation creating relief from taxation—Corporation Tax Act 1976, s. 54(1), (2). **McCann v O'Culachain** [1986] 229, HC.

Calculation—Method of calculating export sales relief where company entitled to claim other relief—Meaning of the words 'total income brought into charge to Corporation Tax'—Corporation Tax Act 1976, s. 58(3). **Cronin (Inspector of Taxes) v Youghal Carpets (Yarns) Ltd** [1985] 666, HC, SC.

Loss relief
Change of ownership of company which ceased to slaughter and to manufacture meat products and continued to distribute products of new owner—Whether permanent cessation—Whether change in nature or conduct of trade—Whether scale of activities became small or negligible—Corporation Tax Act 1976, ss. 16(1), 27, 182, 184. **Cronin v Lunham Brothers Ltd** [1986] 415, HC.

Small companies relief
Reduced rate of tax where company has "associated companies"—Whether non-resident company associated company—Statute—Interpretation—Context of words—Corporation Tax Act 1976, ss. 1(5), 28(4). **Bairead v Maxwells of Donegal Ltd** [1986] 508, HC.

Stock relief
Whether company carrying on trade—Whether company engaged in the manufacture of goods—Statute—Interpretation—Whether ordinary meaning be given—Finance Act 1975, s. 31. **Irish Agricultural Machinery Ltd v O Culachain, Inspector of Taxes** [1989] 478, SC.

Winding up
Deposit interest—Liability to tax—Interest accruing on monies placed on deposit by liquidator—*See* COMPANY (Winding up—Deposit interest—Liability to tax).

Winding up—Sale of properties—Liability incurred for corporation tax—Whether such tax an expense incurred in the realisation of an asset—Whether such tax a necessary disbursement of the liquidator—Companies Act 1963, s. 285 (2)(ii)—Winding up Rules O 77, r 129—Capital Gains Tax Act 1975. **Revenue Commissioners v Donnelly** [1983] 329, SC.

Customs and excise. *See* CUSTOMS AND EXCISE.

REVENUE *continued*
Disclosure of information
Accountants
Anti-avoidance law—Notice served by Revenue Commissioners requiring information—
Judicial review—Whether notice *ultra vires*—Whether notice unduly burdensome and
oppressive—Finance Act 1974, s. 59. **Warnock v Revenue Commissioners** [1986] 37, HC.

Banker
Application for an order directing a bank to furnish particulars of an account—Extent
of information which bank may be required to furnish—Bankers' Books Evidence
Act 1959—Income Tax Act 1967, ss. 169, 172, 174—Finance Act 1983, s. 16. **O'C v D
and Anor** [1985] 123, HC, SC.

Particulars sought by Revenue Commissioners—Exemption—Scope of exemption—
Finance Act 1974, s. 59. **Royal Trust Co (Ireland) Ltd v Revenue Commissioners** [1982]
459, HC.

Excise duty. *See* CUSTOMS AND EXCISE.

Farm tax
Discontinuance
Termination of appointment of farm tax inspectors—Judicial review—Whether
inspectors having legitimate expectation of permanent appointment. *See* JUDICIAL
REVIEW (Farm tax office—Discontinuance of farm tax).

Income tax
Arrears of tax
Collection—Statute enacted in consequence of decision that portion of income tax
legislation unconstitutional—Whether lawful for State to collect arrears of tax due
under unconstitutional provisions—Constitution of Ireland 1937, Articles 40.2, 40.3,
41—Finance Act 1980, s. 21. **Muckley v Ireland** [1986] 364, HC, SC.

Assessment
Compromise of appealed assessment—Whether a fresh assessment permissible—Whether
compromise final and conclusive—Income Tax Act 1967, ss. 186, 416. **Hammond Lane
Metal Company Ltd v O Culachain** [1990] 249, HC.

Husband and wife—Former provision authorising aggregation of earned incomes
declared invalid—New legislation purporting to authorise collection of arrears of tax
due under the unconstitutional provisions—Constitutional validity. *See* Income tax—
Arrears of tax (*above*).

Occupier of land—Profits arising from activities carried on by taxpayers on part of a
military aerodrome—Determination of who should be assessed as the occupier of
land—Whether military use intended to be predominant—Whether liability to income
tax decided on actual or intended user—Income Tax Act 1918, Schedule B r 4—
Income Tax Act 1967, s. 32—Finance Act 1969, s. 18. **O'Conail v Shakleton & Sons
Ltd** [1982] 451, SC.

Avoidance
Commissioner's power to require particulars—Transfer of assets abroad in such a
manner as to retain the power to enjoy the income thereof—Whether transaction
carried out in the ordinary course as banking business—Finance Act 1974, s. 59.
Royal Trust Co (Ireland) Ltd v Revenue Commissioners [1982] 459, HC.

Capital allowances
Plant—Barrister's expenditure on law reports and legal textbooks—Whether 'plant'
qualifying for allowances—Income Tax Act 1967, s. 241—Finance Act 1971, s. 26.
Breathnach v McCann [1984] 679, HC.

Plant—Limited partnership—Claim by partners for initial allowances in respect of the
purchase of plant—Close relationship between the partners and a hotel company to

REVENUE
Income tax
Capital allowances continued

which the plant was leased—Whether colourable transaction—Limited Partnerships Act 1907, ss. 4, 5, 8—Income Tax Act 1967, ss. 241(5), 252, 282, 296, 307. **MacCarthaigh v Daly** [1986] 116, HC.

Plant—Plant and machinery used in designated area—Whether plant to be used exclusively in designated area—Whether allowance applies to plant and machinery used in pursuance of a hire contract—Finance Act 1971, s. 22. **McNally v O'Maoldhomhnaigh** [1989] 688, HC.

Statute—Interpretation—Whether rule that singular includes plural applicable—Income Tax Act 1967, ss. 218, 220—Finance Act 1975, s. 33. **Irish Agricultural Wholesale Society Ltd v McDermot** [1982] 457, HC.

Deductions

Expenses—Director of company obliged to incur expenses of travelling—Whether necessary to identify the individual expenses—Whether sufficient evidence before appeal commissioner—Income Tax Act 1967, Schedule 2, para 3. **MacDaibheid v Carroll** [1978] 14; [1982] 430, HC.

Expenses of management—Rental income—Auctioneer's commission and solicitor's costs—Whether expense of a capital nature—Income Tax Act 1967, ss. 81(5)(d), 81(6)(a)(i)—Finance Act 1969, s. 22. **Stephen Court Ltd v Browne** [1984] 231, HC.

Default provisions

Employer—Default in making PAYE returns—Enforcement procedure—Computer-based programme—Enforcement procedure activated—Payment due received before enforcement notice issued—Whether procedure involved the administration of justice—Whether operated unfairly—Whether publication of enforcement notice a libel—Whether invasion of plaintiff's constitutional rights—Constitution of Ireland 1937, Articles 34, 40.3—Income Tax Act 1967, ss. 131, 485—Finance Act 1968, ss. 7, 8—Income Tax (Employment) Regulations 1960. **Kennedy v Hearne** [1988] 52, HC; [1988] 531, SC.

Recovery by sheriff or county registrar—Delay in levying assessed sums by seizure—Whether delay invalidates power to seize goods—Statute—Interpretation—Whether interpretation consistent with overall scheme of legislation—Income Tax Act 1967, s. 485(2). **Weekes v Revenue Commissioners** [1989] 165, HC.

Estimation of tax liability

Default provisions—Whether s. 485 Certificate issued ultra vires—Whether invasion of plaintiff's constitutional rights. **Kennedy v Hearne** [1988] 52, HC; [1988] 531.

Exemption

Club to promote athletic or amateur games or sports—Whether legitimate avoidance of payment of tax—Funds provided by one person—Total control in two trustees—Whether bona fide club—Whether established for sole purpose of 'promoting sport'—Whether two persons can constitute a 'body of persons'—Income Tax Act 1967, ss. 1(1), 349. **Revenue Commissioners v O'Reilly** [1983] 34, HC; [1984] 406, SC.

Farming—Animal husbandry—Partnership—Fattening of pigs in purpose-built housing—Whether farming—Whether exempt from taxation—Whether trade or profession—Finance Act 1974, s. 13(1), (3)—Finance Act 1969, s. 18(1). **Knockhall Piggeries v Kerrane** (Inspector of Taxes) [1985] 655, HC.

Liability

Purchase of premises for investment purposes—Sale—Whether constituted a business of 'dealing in or developing land'—Whether the profit accrued from a trade—Extent of judicial review of findings of fact by Appeal Commissioner—Nature of case

REVENUE
Income tax
Liability continued

stated—Income Tax Act 1967, s. 1, Schedule D—Finance (Miscellaneous Provisions) Act 1968, s. 17. **Mara v Hummingbird Ltd** [1982] 421, HC, SC.

Married couple
Statute with retrospective effect. *See* CONSTITUTION (Marriage—Married couple—Income tax).

Patent
Income from qualifying patent—Payment of royalties under licence—Whether of revenue nature—Revenue Commissioners answering certain queries—Whether inspector of taxes bound by such rulings—Whether scheme had commercial reality—Finance Act 1973, s. 34—Corporation Tax Act 1976, s. 10—RSC 1986, O 84, r 18(2). **Pandion Haliaetus Ltd v Revenue Commissioners** [1988] 419, HC.

Penalty
Recovery—Whether criminal proceeding—Purpose of section imposing penalty—Whether creates a form of civil liability—Income Tax Act 1967, s. 128. **Downes v DPP** [1987] 665, HC.

Relief
Deduction from trading profits—Increase in stock values—Company having a number of activities—Whether activities can be assessed separately—Whether decision one of fact—Finance Act 1975, ss. 31(1), 31(9)—Finance Act 1977, s. 43. **In re P McElligott & Sons Ltd** [1985] 210, HC.

Mining profits—Termination of relief—Assessment basis—Option to have tax assessed by relation to income—Period to which calculation relates—Avoidance of retrospective imposition of tax—Intentions of legislators—Finance (Taxation of Profits of Certain Mines) Act 1974, ss. 15, 16—Income Tax Act 1967, s. 386 Corporation Tax Act 1976, s. 174. **Mogul of Ireland v O'Riain** [1979] 75, HC.

Returns
Employer—Default—Enforcement provisions. *See* Income tax—Default provisions—Employer—Default in making PAYE returns (*above*).

Employer—Failure to send returns—Whether contract of service or partnership existed—Fishermen—Captain of vessel engaging crew at commencement of each separate voyage—Remuneration of crew based on custom and agreement—Whether element of control by captain outweighed by other factors—Whether arrangement in reality partnership—Income Tax (Employments) Regulations 1960—Social Welfare (Collection of Employment Contributions by the Collector General) Regulations 1979. **DPP v McLoughlin** [1986] 493, HC.

Statute
Interpretation—Taxpayer's principal activity intensive pig production—Whether by reason of such business taxpayer was 'dealer in cattle'—Whether court should presume that the legislature was aware of and endorsed judicial decisions concerning previous statutory use of the same expression in the same context—Criticism of delay in signing case stated—Income Tax Act 1918, Schedule D—Income Tax Act 1967, s. 78. **Inspector of Taxes v Kiernan** [1981] 157, HC; [1982] 13, SC.

Validity—Statute with retrospective affect—Statute enacted in consequence of decision that portion of income tax legislation unconstitutional—Whether lawful for State to collect arrears of tax due under the unconstitutional provisions—Constitution of Ireland 1937, Articles 40.2, 40.3, 41—Finance Act 1980, s. 21. **Muckley v Ireland** [1986] 364, HC, SC.

REVENUE

Income tax *continued*

Tax avoidance

Computation of profits—Deduction by lessee of premium payable on entry into lease—Premium payable in instalments—Whether lessee entitled to deduct whole of premium in computing annual profits—Income Tax Act 1967, ss. 61, 80, 81, 83, 81. **Hammond Lane Metal Company Ltd v O Culachain** [1990] 249, HC.

Limited partnership—Claim by partners for initial allowances in respect of the purchase of plant—Close relationship between the partners and a hotel company to which the plant was leased—Whether partnership existed as a matter of law—Whether colourable transaction—Limited Partnerships Act 1907, ss. 4, 5, 8—Income Tax Act 1967, ss. 241(5), 252, 282, 296, 307. **MacCarthaigh v Daly** [1986] 116, HC.

Trade of dealing in or developing land—Valuation of stock in trade—Merger of leasehold and freehold interests—Actual legal consequences and effects of scheme—Finance (Miscellaneous Provisions) Act 1968, s. 18. **Belvedere Estates Ltd v O Connlain** [1990] 100, SC.

Trading stock

Trade of dealing in or developing land—Farm land—Formation of company—Land zoned for development—Whether land trading stock of company—Finance (Miscellaneous Provisions) Act 1968, s. 17. **O'hArgain v Beechpark Estates Ltd** [1979] 57, HC.

Information Disclosure. *See* Disclosure of information (*above*).

Liability to tax

Winding up

Deposit interest—*see* COMPANY (Winding up—Deposit interest—Liability to tax).

Offence

Excise offence. See CUSTOMS AND EXCISE (Offence)

Penalty

Income tax—Payment of penalties in default of income tax returns—Whether penalties imposition of punishment—Whether criminal matter—Constitution of Ireland 1937, Article 34—Income Tax Act 1967, s. 500. **McLoughlin v Tuite** [1986] 304, HC.

Recovery—Income tax—Whether recovery of a penalty under s. 128 of the Income Tax Act 1967 is a criminal proceeding—Purpose of section imposing penalty—Whether creates a form of civil liability—Income Tax Act 1967, s. 128. **Downes v DPP** [1987] 665, HC.

Penalty for offence. *See* Offence—Penalty (*above*).

Practice and procedure

Advance rulings. See Advance rulings (*above*).

Anti-avoidance law

Notice served by Revenue Commissioners requiring information—Judicial review—Whether notice *ultra vires*—Whether notice unduly burdensome and oppressive—Finance Act 1974, s. 59. **Warnock v Revenue Commissioners** [1986] 37, HC.

Collector General

Whether decision reviewable. *See* Tax clearance certificate (*below*).

Questions of law

Corporation tax appeal—Questions of law arising before Circuit Court—Statutory provision requiring expression of dissatisfaction on a point of law to be made "immediately after the determination "—Prosecutor not expressing dissatisfaction with the judge's determination at the end of the hearing—Prosecutor subsequently wishing to express dissatisfaction—Judge refusing to state case to the High Court on the basis

REVENUE

Practice and procedure

Questions of law continued

that dissatisfaction had not been expressed 'immediately' after the determination—Meaning of 'immediately'—Whether mandatory requirement—Income Tax Act 1967, ss. 428. **State (Multiprint Label Systems Ltd) v Neylon** [1984] 545, HC.

Tax clearance certificate. See Tax clearance certificate (*below*).

Residential property tax

Constitutional validity

Residential property tax levied on properties over certain value—Whether unjust attack on property and family rights—Whether constituting invidious discrimination—Presumption of constitutionality in taxation matters—Constitution of Ireland 1937, Articles 40.1, 40.3, 41, 43—Finance Act 1983. **Madigan v Attorney General** [1986] 136, HC, SC.

Stamp duty

Exemption

Conveyance of house upon erection—Exempt from stamp duty—Whether applicable to the first purchaser of a house anytime after erection—Whether 'erection' and 'completion' synonymous—Stamp Act 1891, s. 13—Finance Act 1969, s. 49 (1). **Dunne v Revenue Commissioners** [1982] 438, HC.

Statute

Interpretation. See STATUTORY INTERPRETATION (Taxing statute).

Validity. See CONSTITUTION (Statute—Validity—Taxing statute).

Tax clearance certificate

Mandamus

Requirement of tax clearance certificate with tenders for Government contracts—Refusal to issue by Collector General—Mandamus application—Whether Revenue Commissioners can have regard to tax default of previous "connected" company—Whether Collector General's decision amenable to judicial review—Duty to act judicially—Requirement not based on statutory provisions. **State (Melbarien Enterprises Ltd) v Revenue Commissioners** [1986] 476, HC.

Tax inspectors

Advance rulings

Whether inspector of taxes bound by opinion given to taxpayer by Revenue Commissioners. **Pandion Haliaetus Ltd v Revenue Commissioners** [1988] 419, HC.

Farm tax

Termination of appointment of farm tax inspectors—Discontinuance of farm tax—Judicial review—Whether inspectors having legitimate expectation of permanent appointment. *See* JUDICIAL REVIEW (Farm tax office—Discontinuance of farm tax).

Value added tax

Rate of VAT

"Fixtures'—Television aerials installed on the roofs of private houses—Whether "fixtures"—Value Added Tax Act 1972, s. 10(8). **Maye v Revenue Commissioners** [1986] 377, HC.

RIGHT OF WAY. *See* EASEMENT (Right of way).

ROAD

Accidents. *See* ROAD TRAFFIC ACCIDENTS.

Authority. *See* HIGHWAY (Highway authority).

Generally. *See* HIGHWAY.

ROAD *continued*
Maintenance. *See* HIGHWAY (Maintenance).

ROAD TRAFFIC ACCIDENTS
Cattle straying onto main road
Driver colliding with cattle ·
Whether cattle constituted a public nuisance—Whether defendants negligent—Whether under a duty to prevent cattle straying onto public road. **Gillick v O'Reilly** [1984] 402, HC.

Duty to take care
Driver of motor vehicle
Infant plaintiff—Whether finding of negligence justifiable—Apportionment of fault—Assessment of damages. **Brennan v Savage Smith & Co Ltd** [1982] 223, SC.

Failure to wear seat belt
Apportionment of fault
Damages. **Sinnott v Quinnsworth Ltd** [1984] 523, SC.

Insurance. *See* MOTOR INSURANCE.

Personal injuries
Damages. See DAMAGES (Personal injuries).

Victims
Medical services
Regulations rendering victims of road traffic accidents ineligible for free medical services—Validity. *See* HEALTH SERVICES (Regulations—Validity—Whether *ultra vires*—Legislation empowering Minister to make regulations).

ROAD TRAFFIC OFFENCES
Arrest
Drunken driving
Arrest without warrant—Arrest taking place in driver's driveway—Whether garda trespassing—Whether arrest lawful if garda effecting it a trespasser—Constitution of Ireland 1937, Article 40.5—Road Traffic Act 1961, s. 49(2), (3), (6)—Road Traffic (Amendment) Act 1978, ss. 10, 13. **DPP v Corrigan** [1987] 575, HC.

Arrest without warrant—Breathalyser test—Whether opinion of garda justified arrest without warrant—Road Traffic Act 1961, s. 49—Road Traffic (Amendment) Act 1978, ss. 10, 12. **DPP v Gilmore** [1981] 102, SC.

Conviction—Appeal—Whether gardai entitled to require accused to take a breath test and subsequently arrest accused in a place that was not a public place—Road Traffic (Amendment) Act 1978, s. 12, 49(2), 49(4)(a). **DPP v Joyce** [1985] 206, SC.

Opinion of garda—Whether garda entitled from observation alone to form an opinion that the driver was drunk—Matters to be taken into account—Whether taking of a breath test a condition precedent—Road Traffic Act 1961, s. 49(1), (2), (3), (6)—Road Traffic (Amendment) Act 1978, s. 10. **DPP v Donoghue** [1987] 129, HC.

Opinion of garda that accused person had committed offence—Whether statement that accused person was being arrested for offence under relevant section sufficient to support conviction—Road Traffic Act 1961, s. 49—Road Traffic (Amendment) Act 1978, s. 10. **DPP v O'Connor** [1985] 333, SC.

Whether gardai entitled to require accused to take a breath test and subsequently arrest accused in a place that was not a public place—Road Traffic (Amendment) Act 1978, s. 12, 49(2), 49(4)(a). **DPP v Joyce** [1985] 206, SC

Whether necessary that accused be brought to garda station as an arrested person—Road Traffic Act 1961, ss. 12, 49(2), 49(4)(a), 49(6)—Road Traffic (Amendment) Act 1978, ss. 10, 12(3), 13(1), 17(1), 17(4), 21, 23. **DPP v Greeley** [1985] 320, HC.

ROAD TRAFFIC OFFENCES
Arrest
Drunken driving continued
Whether removal to a second garda station made arrest unlawful—Reason for removal—Carrying out of statutory procedures—Offences against the State Act 1939—Intepretation Act 1937, s. 11(a)—Road Traffic (Amendment) Act 1978, s. 13. **DPP v Sheehy** [1987] 138, HC.

Place of arrest
Dwelling of citizen—Arrest made inside accused's home—No invitation to enter—Whether absence of order to leave could be construed as implied invitation—Whether gardai empowered to enter a private dwelling without permission of occupant—Whether arrest illegal. **DPP v Gaffney** [1986] 657, HC; [1988] 39, SC.

Disqualification from driving
Judicial review
Whether factors to be considered taken into account in judicial manner—Whether necessary to reconsider evidence presented to convict—Road Traffic Act 1961, s. 106. **Joyce v Circuit Court Judge for the Western Circuit** [1987] 316, HC.

Driving without insurance. *See* Insurance (*below*).

Drunken driving
Arrest
Legality. *See* Arrest—Drunken driving (*above*).

Blood specimen
Driver electing to provide urine sample—Inability to provide such sample—Specimen of blood taken—Whether taken in compliance with statutory requirements—Road Traffic Act 1961, s. 49 (6)—Road Traffic (Amendment) Act 1978, ss. 10, 13(1), 13(3), 19, 21, 33. **Connolly v Salinger** [1982] 482, SC.

Sample given to designated medical practitioner—Whether specimen analysed as soon as practicable—Certificate issued showing excessive quantity of alcohol in body—Whether certificate forwarded to garda as soon as practicable—Obligations of Medical Bureau of Road Safety—Road Traffic Act 1961, s. 49(2)—Road Traffic (Amendment) Act 1978, ss. 10, 22(1), 22(3), 23(2). **DPP v Corrigan** [1980] 145, HC.

Certificate of Medical Bureau of Road Safety. *See* Drunken driving—Evidence (*below*).

Conviction
Validity—Statute—Interpretation—New regulations providing for breathalyser—Authorising legislation enacted but not yet operative—Whether regulations necessary or expedient for implementation of legislation when operative—Road Traffic Act Regulations 1978—Interpretation Act 1937, s. 10(1)(b). **State (McColgan) v DPP** [1980] 75, SC.

Evidence
Admissibility—Medical certificate—Correct legal procedure culminating in issue of certificate not followed—Absence of power to require defendant to furnish blood specimen—Road Traffic Act 1961, ss. 12, 49(2), 49(4)(a), 49(6)—Road Traffic (Amendment) Act 1978, ss. 10, 12(3), 13(1), 17(1), 17(4), 21, 23. **DPP v Greeley** [1985] 320, HC.

Certificate of Medical Bureau of Road Safety—Accused not receiving copy of certificate of analysis of a blood specimen until just before the trial—Conviction—Whether District Court order be quashed—Road Traffic Act 1962, s. 49 (2)—Road Traffic (Amendment) Act 1978, s. 10. **State (O'Regan) v Plunkett** [1984] 347, HC.

Certificate of Medical Bureau of Road Safety—Copy of certificate sent to accused but returned 'uncollected'—Whether Bureau under an obligation to ensure accused received a copy—Road Traffic (Amendment) Act 1978, s. 22(3). **DPP v Walsh** [1985] 243, HC.

ROAD TRAFFIC OFFENCES
Drunken driving
Evidence continued

Certificate of Medical Bureau of Road Safety—Excessive concentration of alcohol shown—Whether certificate evidence of concentration of alcohol at any time other than when the sample was analysed—Road Traffic Act 1961, s. 49—Road Traffic (Amendment) Act 1978, ss. 2, 23(2). **DPP v Smyth** [1987] 570, HC.

Certificate of Medical Bureau of Road Safety—Typographical error—Whether affects the certificate—Road Traffic (Amendment) Act 1978, s. 23(2). **DPP v Flahive** [1988] 133, SC.

Certificate of Medical Bureau of Road Safety—Whether statutory requirements to be strictly complied with—Road Traffic (Amendment) Act 1978, ss. 22, 23(2). **Connolly v Sweeney** [1988] 35, HC; [1988] 483, SC.

Medical certificate—Refusal of prosecution to supply copy of the certificate completed by designated registered medical practitioner—Whether obligation to supply copy of documentary evidence in advance of the hearing—Mandamus application—Road Traffic Act 1961, s. 10—Road Traffic (Amendment) Act 1978, ss. 21(1), 21(4), 22(3). **State (Higgins) v Reid** [1983] 310, HC.

Medical certificate—Whether sufficient evidence—Misdescription—Whether accused the person named on the certificate—Road Traffic Act 1961, ss. 49(2), 49(4)(a)—Road Traffic (Amendment) Act 1978, s. 10. **DPP v McPartland** [1983] 411, HC.

Validity—Validity of form signed by doctor—Validity of certificate—Defendant convicted of driving in a public place when the concentration of alcohol in his blood exceeded the permitted maximum—Whether form signed by the designated medical practitioner duly completed in the statutory manner—Evidential onus of proof—Whether Medical Bureau of Road Safety analysed the sample as soon as practicable—Whether legibility the hallmark of an effective signature—Documentary Evidence Act 1925, s. 4(1)—Road Traffic Act 1961, s. 49—Road Traffic (Amendment) Act 1978, ss. 10, 21, 22, 23—Road Traffic (Amendment) Act Regulations 1978, Part III. **DPP v Collins** [1981] 447, SC.

Prosecution

Matters which prosecution are required to prove—Whether sufficient justification for arrest without warrant—Observation of accused's behaviour—Whether Garda can rely on result of breathalyser—Road Traffic Act 1961, s. 49—Road Traffic (Amendment) Act 1978, ss. 10, 12, 13, 22, 23. **DPP v Gilmore** [1981] 102, SC.

Refusal to provide blood or urine specimen

Caution—Whether caution prescribed by the regulation fell short of what was required by statute—Whether requirement that caution be given as to the possible consequences of such a refusal—Road Traffic Act 1968, s. 36(1)(b)—Road Traffic Act 1968 (Part V) Regulations 1969. **Grogan v Byrne** [1976–7] 68, SC.

Whether proof of time of driving or time of requirement to provide specimen required—Road Traffic (Amendment) Act 1978, s. 13(3). **DPP v Clinton** [1984] 127, HC.

Insurance
Driving without insurance

Approved policy of insurance in force in respect of vehicle—Defendant not covered by policy—Conviction—Appeal—Limitation of cover permitted by regulations—Jurisdiction of Circuit Court to rule on whether the regulations were *ultra vires*—Whether regulations *ultra vires* scheme of compulsory insurance—Whether Court's duty to safeguard the position of third parties—Road Traffic Act 1961, s. 56—Road Traffic (Compulsory Insurance) Regulations 1962—Courts of Justice Act 1947, s. 16. **Greaney v Scully** [1981] 340, SC.

ROAD TRAFFIC OFFENCES
Insurance
Driving without insurance continued
Conviction—Validity—Certiorari—Whether necessary that the statutory period in which to produce insurance had expired before prosecutor can be found guilty—Malicious Damage Act 1861, s. 51—Road Traffic Act, 1961, s. 56 (1)—Criminal Justice Act 1961, s. 2—Offences Against the State Act 1939, s.45 (2)—Offences against the State (Scheduled Offences) Order 1972. **State (McDonagh) v Sheerin** [1981] 149, HC.

Parking
Breach of regulations
Statute authorising regulations making parking in a particular manner a criminal offence—General regulations prohibiting parking in contravention of parking sign—Parking sign prohibiting parking by reference to weight of vehicle—No particular regulations prohibiting parking by reference to weight—Limerick Traffic and Parking Bye-laws 1978, reg 18—Road Traffic Act 1961, ss. 89(2)(m), 89(7), 90(2), 90(9). **DPP v Clancy** [1986] 268, HC.

Street trading
Breaches of bye-laws made for the control of traffic
Street traders using motor vehicles as mobile shops—Whether vehicles being used in connection with the sale of goods in a lawful market—Presumption of immemorial usage from which a lost grant presumed—Constitution of Ireland 1937, Article 40.3—Road Traffic Act 1961, ss. 89(1), 89(7), 90(1), 92. **DPP (Long) v McDonald** [1983] 223, SC.

Summons
Delay in serving summons
Date of issue altered—Whether summons invalid—Road Traffic (Amendment) Act 1978, ss. 12(2), 13(3). **DPP v Clein** [1983] 76, SC.

ROMALPA CLAUSE
Contract for sale of goods. *See* SALE OF GOODS (Retention of title clause).

ROYAL PREROGATIVE
Treasure trove
Whether carried over into Irish law
Constitution of Ireland 1937, Articles 5, 10. **Webb v Ireland** [1988] 565, HC, SC.

ROYALTIES
Income from qualifying patent. *See* REVENUE (Income tax—Patent—Income from qualifying patent).

RUBBISH *See* WASTE DISPOSAL.

RULES OF COURT
District Court. *See* DISTRICT COURT RULES.

Superior Courts
Validity of rule
Whether rule *ultra vires* rule-making committee—Discovery—Non-party discovery—Whether rule related to practice and procedure. *See* DISCOVERY (Non-party discovery—Rules of court).

SAFETY *See* HEALTH AND SAFETY.

SAFETY AT WORK
Employer's duty of care. *See* NEGLIGENCE (Employer).

SALE OF GOODS
Casual trading licence. *See* CASUAL TRADING.

Contract
Breach
Claim for damages—Whether contract void for illegality—Onus of proof—Sale of Goods Act 1893, s. 51. **Whitecross Potatoes (International) Ltd v Coyle** [1978] 31, HC.

Claim for damages—Exclusion clause. *See* Contract—Exclusion clause (*below*).

Exclusion clause
Distributor agreement—Motor vehicles—Claim for damages for breach of agreement—Negotiations between parties and Department of Industry and Commerce—Document drawn up—Whether new agreement reached—Whether unfairness of original agreement a matter with which the court is concerned—Whether claim defeated by exclusion clause. **British Leyland Exports Ltd v Brittain Group Sales Ltd** [1982] 359, HC.

Mistake
Both parties contracting on assumption which proved false—Supply of seed potatoes—Crop failure—Whether contract rendered void—Whether implied obligations remaining. **Western potato Co-Operative Ltd v Durnan** [1985] 5, CC.

Retention of title clause. See Retention of title clause (*below*).

Terms
Letters of credit—Time within which credits to be opened—Whether parties *ad idem*—Whether statutory requirements complied with—Whether implied term necessary to give business efficacy to agreement—Sale of Goods Act 1893, s. 4. **Tradax (Ireland) Ltd v Irish Grain Board Ltd** [1984] 471, SC.

Dealing as consumer
Drink dispensing machine
Defects manifesting themselves—Whether purchaser entitled to refund of monies paid and damages for loss of profit—Whether purchaser 'dealing as a consumer'—Sale of Goods and Supply of Services Act 1980, s. 3 (1). **O'Callaghan v Hamilton Leasing (Ireland) Ltd** [1984] 146, HC.

Defective product
Whether purchaser entitled to refund of monies paid and damages for loss of profit
Whether purchaser 'dealing as a consumer'. *See* Dealing as consumer (*above*).

Hire-purchase agreement. *See* HIRE-PURCHASE AGREEMENT.

Price
Letters of credit
Time within which credits to be opened. *See* Contract—Terms—Letters of credit (*above*).

Retention of title clause
Legal effect
Whether binding—Whether reasonable notice given of the contents of the standard conditions. **Sugar Distributors Ltd v Monaghan Cash and Carry Ltd** [1982] 399, HC.

Liquidation
Suppliers entering into a leasing contract of plant machinery with bank—Purchasing company going into liquidation—Application by liquidator for directions as to the rights of the three parties—Whether plant, by reason of being affixed to the land, became part of the land—Whether plant merely tenant's fixtures—No express provision in agreement of sale empowering suppliers to repossess in the event of default—Whether such term to be implied and whether purchasing company to bear cost of removal of plant—Whether charge created by retention of title clause—Companies Act 1963, s. 99. **In re Galway Concrete Ltd** [1983] 402, HC.

SALE OF GOODS
Retention of title clause *continued*
Passing of property
Whether clause effective to reserve title—Whether a bill of sale of stock—Whether valid—Agricultural Credit Act 1978, s. 36—Bills of Sale (Ireland) Act 1879, s. 3—Sale of Goods Act 1893, ss. 1, 17. **Somers v James Allen (Ireland) Ltd** [1984] 437, HC; [1985] 624, SC.

Receivership
Priority of creditors—Whether clause a term of the contract—Nature of interest created—Whether clause enforceable for want of registration as a charge—Bills of Sale (Ireland) Act 1879, s. 4—Companies Act 1963, ss. 99(2)(c), 100. **Fried Krupp Huttenwerke AG v Quitmann Products Ltd** [1982] 551, HC.

Refrigerating equipment—Whether property in the equipment passed—Whether clause void. **Frigoscandia Ltd v Continental Irish Meat Ltd** [1982] 396, HC.

Suppliers claiming to be entitled to trace the proceeds of their goods—Whether reservation of title clause effective. **In re Stokes & McKiernan** [1978] 240, HC.

Rights of vendor in respect of the proceeds of sale of the goods in question
Whether charge created—Companies Act 1963, s. 99. **Carroll Group Distributors Ltd v G and J F Bourke Ltd** [1990] 285, HC.

Whether clause waived
Intention of parties. **S. A Foundries du Lion MV v International Factors (Ireland) Ltd** [1985] 66, HC.

Street trading
Casual trading licence. See CASUAL TRADING.

Motor vehicles used as mobile shops
Traders convicted for breach of byelaws made for the control of traffic—Whether vehicles being used in connection with the sale of goods in a lawful market—Presumption of immemorial usage from which a lost grant presumed—Road Traffic Act 1961, ss. 89(1), 89(7), 90(1), 92—Constitution of Ireland 1937, Article 40. **DPP (Long) v McDonald** [1983] 223, SC.

SALE OF LAND
Auction
Licensed premises
Agent for vendor bidding—Whether contract rendered illegal—Sale of Land by Auction Act 1867, s. 3. **Airlie v Fallon** [1976–7] 1, HC.

Auctioneer. *See* AUCTIONEER.

Contract
Breach
Action for specific performance. *See* Specific performance (*below*).

Damages for failure to complete. *See* DAMAGES (Breach of contract—Sale of land—Damages for failure to complete).

Damages in lieu of specific performance. *See* DAMAGES (Breach of contract—Sale of land—Damages in lieu of specific performance).

Condition
Building society loan approval—Approval granted subject to conditions—Conditions not fulfilled—Deposit forfeited—Claim for return of deposit—Claim that conditions unreasonable—Onus of proof—Absence of "purchasers protection clause". **Draisey v Fitzpatrick** [1981] 219, HC.

Interest—Failure to complete by agreed date—Requirement that purchaser may pay interest in certain circumstances—Whether circumstances envisaged had occurred—

SALE OF LAND
  Contract
    Condition continued
      Period for which interest payable—Duties owed by vendor and purchaser—Liability to pay interest—Vendor and Purchaser Act 1874. **Northern Bank Ltd v Duffy** [1981] 308, HC.

      Land Commission approval—Lands earmarked for compulsory purchase—Whether prospective purchaser has standing to object to compulsory acquisition of the land—Land Act 1923, s. 40(6), **State (Callaghan) v Irish land Commission** [1978] 201, SC.

      Objections or requisitions on title to be sent within ten days after delivery of title deeds—Time made of the essence—Plaintiff seeking to rely upon this condition and rescind the sale and retain the deposit—Whether defendant's objection went to the root of title. **Coyle v Central Trust Investment Society Ltd** [1978] 211, HC.

      Planning permission—Agreement subject to obtaining planning permission—Non-refundable deposit paid—Delays—Contract not completed within time specified by vendor—Vendor specifying new date—Time agreed to be of essence—Planning permission not obtained—Purchaser not waiving permission requirement—Vendor treating contract as repudiated—Whether vendor entitled to rescind—Whether vendor entitled to retain deposit. **Sepia Ltd v M & P Hanlon Ltd** [1979] 11, HC.

      Planning permission—Contract further providing that if permission obtained purchaser might pay a higher price at his own discretion—Whether void for uncertainty—Enforceability of contract—Statute of Frauds 1695, s. 2. **O'Mullane v Riordan** [1978] 73, HC.

      Planning permission—Requirement that purchaser obtain permission by specified date—Permission not obtained—Vendor withdrawing from sale—Purchaser purporting to waive requirement—Whether waiver effective—Whether vendor obliged to complete—Whether contract discharged by failure to obtain permission—Whether term to be implied for discharge—Whether for mutual benefit of parties—Whether capable of unilateral waiver. **Maloney v Elf Investments** [1979] 253, HC.

      Planning permission—Permission within specified time—Specific performance—Meaning of month—Meaning of 'full planning permission '—Waiver—Whether term for the exclusive benefit of person waiving it—Local Government (Planning and Development) Act 1963, s. 36. **Tiernan Homes Ltd v Sheridan** [1981] 191, SC.

      Subject to building society loan approval. *See* Contract—Condition—Building society loan approval (*above*).

      Subject to option to purchase—Pre-condition to contract—Option exercised by third party—Whether purchaser can maintain action against vendor. **O'Hara v Flint** [1979] 156, SC.

      Subject to vendor remedying any possible defects in title before closing date—Vendor unable to comply—Purchaser deciding not to proceed—Claim for return of deposit—Interpretation of agreement—Whether time of the essence. **Crean v Drinan** [1983] 82, HC.

      Waiver—Express condition requiring exchange of contracts—Contract signed but not exchanged—Whether plaintiff purchaser entitled to specific performance. **Kelly v Irish Nursery and Landscape Co Ltd** [1981] 433, SC.

      Waiver—Purchaser purporting to waive requirement—Whether waiver effective—Whether vendor obliged to complete—Whether term capable of unilateral waiver. **Maloney v Elf Investments** [1979] 253, HC.

    Delay in completion
      Whether explained—Whether specific performance be granted. **Horgan v Deasy** [1979] 71, HC.

SALE OF LAND
Contract *continued*
Formation

Oral agreement—Contract for the sale of a site—Vacant possession guaranteed—
Terms inserted into formal contract which were not agreed to at initial meeting—
Break down of arrangements—Whether concluded oral agreement—Whether sufficient
note or memorandum—Whether agent authority to sign memorandum—Laches—
Statute of Frauds 1695. **Guardian Builders Ltd v Kelly** [1981] 127, HC.

"Subject to contract"—Express condition requiring exchange of contracts—Contract
signed but not exchanged—Waiver—Whether plaintiff purchaser entitled to specific
performance. **Kelly v Irish Nursery and Landscape Co Ltd** [1981] 433, SC.

"Subject to contract"—Prior to formal contract being executed property sold to another
purchaser—Whether letter, posted before second agreement but arriving after, constitutes a sufficient note or memorandum—Title of vendor—Defendant not sole owner
of property—Meaning of 'subject to contract'—Statute of Frauds 1695. **Carthy v
O'Neill** [1981] 443, SC.

"Subject to contract"—Written agreement on terms of contract—Subsequent correspondence describing negotiations as "subject to contract"—Whether agreement deprived
of binding effect—Sufficiency of memorandum of agreement—Specific performance—
Statute of Frauds 1695, s. 2. **McInerney Properties v Roper** [1979] 119, HC.

General Conditions of Sale

Compensation—Misdescription—Claim by purchaser for compensation for misdescription—Whether purchasers obliged to complete sale pending resolution of such
claim by arbitration—Equity. **Keating v Bank of Ireland** [1983] 295, HC.

Illegality

Auction—Agent for vendor bidding—Whether contract rendered illegal—Sale of Land
by Auction Act 1867, s. 3. **Airlie v Fallon** [1976-7] 1, HC.

Mistake

Deposit paid—Purchaser seeking to withdraw—Whether vendor entitled to forfeit
deposit—Whether deposit paid under mistake of fact. **Siebel and Seum v Kent** [1976–7]
127, HC.

Purchasers protection clause

Advisability of including such a clause—Contract subject to building society loan
approval—Approval granted subject to conditions—Conditions not fulfilled—Deposit
forfeited—Purchaser claiming conditions unreasonable—Onus of proof—Absence of
purchasers protection clause. **Draisey v Fitzpatrick** [1981] 219, HC.

Repudiation

Delay in completion—Whether delay unreasonable—Whether delay entitled parties
to treat agreement as repudiated. **Taylor v Smith** [1990] 377, HC.

Deposit—Retention—Agreement subject to obtaining planning permission—Non-
refundable deposit paid—Contract not completed within time specified—Planning
permission not obtained—Purchaser not waiving permission requirement—Vendor
treating contract as repudiated—Whether vendor entitled to rescind—Whether vendor
entitled to retain deposit. **Sepia Ltd v M & P Hanlon Ltd** [1979] 11, HC.

Rescission

Default of plaintiffs—Deposit—Forfeiture—Land resold at a profit—Whether vendor
entitled to keep deposit. **Doyle v Ryan** [1981] 374, CC.

Illegality—Auction—Licensed premises—Whether representation as to turnover—
Conflict of evidence—Agent for vendor bidding—Whether contract rendered illegal—
Sale of Land by Auction Act 1867, s. 3. **Airlie v Fallon** [1976–7] 1, HC.

SALE OF LAND
Contract
Rescission continued

Property in fee simple subject to lease—Lease originally subject to a trust—Condition that any objections or requisitions on title should be sent within ten days after delivery of title deeds—Time made of the essence—Plaintiff seeking to rely upon this condition and rescind the sale and retain the deposit—Whether defendant's objection went to the root of title—Whether trust disclosed on the conveyance of the freehood—Freehold interest purchased by trustee of trusts of the leasehold interest—Whether fee simple interest taken upon same trusts. **Coyle v Central Trust Investment Society Ltd** [1978] 211, HC.

Terms

Rescission clause—Contract for the sale of premises—Lost title deeds—Inability to obtain release of mortgage—Mortgage statute barred—Whether vendor entitled to rely on rescission clause—Whether rights under rescission clause lawfully and reasonably exercised—Title deeds found—Vendor's duties to purchaser. **Kennedy v Wrenne** [1981] 81, HC.

Waiver—Waiver of clause conferring benefit only on the party waiving—Whether effective. **Tiernan Homes Ltd v Sheridan** [1981] 191, SC.

Waiver—Waiver of term by purchaser—Whether waiver effective—Whether vendor obliged to complete—Whether term capable of unilateral waiver—Sale subject to obtaining planning permission—Permission not obtained. **Maloney v Elf Investments** [1979] 253, HC.

Validity

Family home—Agreement to sell prior to enactment of protective legislation—Existing rights—Whether affected by enactment—Presumption against retroaction—Constitution of Ireland 1937, Articles 40.3.2, 43—Interpretation Act 1937, s. 21(1)—Family Home Protection Act 1976, ss. 2, 3, 4. **Dunne v Hamilton; Hamilton v Hamilton and Dunne** [1982] 290, SC.

Conveyance
False declaration

Husband purchasing property in name of wife—Presumption of the advancement rebutted—Husband procuring wife to make false declaration in conveyance—Husband subsequently invoking court's aid to enforce trust—Whether husband entitled to relief in equity—Clean hands doctrine—Finance (No 2) Act 1947, s. 13(1), (4) and (5)—Finance Act 1951, s. 17—Land Act 1965, ss. 45(2)(a), 45(3)—Finance Act 1965, s. 66(6). **Parkes v Parkes** [1980] 137, HC.

Family home. See Family home (*below*).

Negligence

Solicitor. *See* SOLICITOR (Negligence—Sale of land).

Requisitions on title

No special condition relating to planning permission—Standard form warranty—Purchaser put an enquiry as to unauthorised use—Whether purchaser entitled to raise the matter by way of requisition—Whether certificate of discharge of capital acquisitions tax required to be furnished. **Meagher v Blount** [1984] 671, CC.

Damages
Breach of contract. See DAMAGES (Breach of contract—Sale of land).

Interest

Negligence—Solicitor—Booking deposit—Date from which interest to run. **Desmond v Brophy** [1986] 547, HC.

SALE OF LAND *continued*
Default
Liability to pay interest
Vendor and Purchaser Act 1874. **Northern Bank Ltd v Duffy** [1981] 308, HC.

Deposit
Forfeiture
Contract—Mistake—Purchaser seeking to withdraw—Whether vendor entitled to forfeit deposit—Whether deposit paid under mistake of fact. Siebel and **Seum v Kent** [1976–7] 127, HC.

Contract—Rescission—Default of plaintiffs—Deposit forfeited—Land resold at a profit—Whether vendor entitled to keep deposit. **Doyle v Ryan** [1981] 374, CC.

Contract subject to building society loan approval—Approval granted subject to conditions—Conditions not fulfilled—Deposit forfeited—Claim for order directing the return of deposit—Whether plaintiff entitled to refuse to complete the sale on the grounds that the conditions were unreasonable—Implied terms—Absence of purchaser's protection clause—Onus of proving compliance with implied terms of contract. **Draisey v Fitzpatrick** [1981] 219, HC.

Loss
Booking deposit—Solicitor—Stakeholder—Whether solicitor negligent because of failure to communicate specifically to builder's solicitors that deposits to be held by them as stakeholders. **Desmond and Boyle v Brophy** [1986] 547, HC.

Retention
Contract—Repudiation—Contract not completed within time specified—Contract subject to obtaining planning permission—Permission not obtained—Vendor treating contract as repudiated—Whether vendor entitled to rescind—Whether vendor entitled to retain deposit. **Sepia Ltd v M & P Hanlon Ltd** [1979] 11, HC.

Family home
Consent of spouse
Application for order dispensing with consent—Time for making. **H and L v s.** [1979] 105, HC.

Conveyance of family home without consent of wife—Purchaser taking up residence—Supreme Court declaring conveyance void—Application by wife for possession—Whether Supreme Court order vested leasehold interest in wife—Family Home Protection Act 1976, ss. 3(1), 4(1), 5. **Weir v Somers** [1983] 343, SC.

Statutory declaration—Consent of spouse not obtained—Purchaser making no inquiries—Vendor spouse making statutory declaration that house not a family home—Whether purchaser deemed to have notice—Whether declaration avoids necessity to obtain consent to sale—Family Home Protection Act 1976, ss. 3, 4. **H and L v s.** [1979] 105, HC.

Statutory declaration—Declaration by vendor that premises were not a 'family home'—Purchaser not prepared to accept this—Purchaser wanting either consent of vendor's wife or joint declaration from vendor and wife—Delay on completion—Whether declaration by vendor adequate evidence—Whether vendor in default—Family Home Protection Act 1976, s. 3. **Reynolds v Waters** [1982] 335, HC.

Contract
Validity—Agreement to sell prior to enactment of legislation rendering conveyance of the family home void if executed without prior notice to the wife—Failure to complete—Statute—Interpretation—Presumption against retroaction—Pre-existing contractual rights—Purchaser entitled to specific performance—Constitution of Ireland 1937, Articles 40.3.2, 43—Interpretation Act 1937, s. 21(1)—Family Home Protection Act 1976, ss. 2, 3, 4. **Dunne v Hamilton: Hamilton v Hamilton** [1982] 290, SC.

SALE OF LAND *continued*
Lien
Purchaser
'Booking deposit'—Proposed development—Building company—Winding up—Whether a person who has paid a 'booking deposit' but entered into no contract with the builder is entitled to a purchaser's lien or to rank as a secured creditor in the liquidation of the building company. **In re Barrett Apartments Ltd** [1985] 679, HC, SC.

Misdescription
Compensation
General Conditions of Sale—Claim by purchaser for compensation for misdescription—Whether purchasers obliged to complete sale pending resolution of such claim by arbitration—Equity. **Keating v Bank of Ireland** [1983] 295, HC.

Misrepresentation
Auctioneers
Pre-contractual representation—Plaintiff relying on representation—Claim for damages for loss suffered. **Stafford v Mahony** [1980] 53, HC.

Mistake. *See* Contract—Mistake (*above*).

Negligence
Solicitor. See SOLICITOR (Negligence—Sale of land).

Specific performance
Completion notice
Validity—Purchaser refusing to complete—Whether vendor good marketable title—Purchaser claiming to sign contract as agent—Whether purchaser acting in a representative capacity. **Dublin Laundry Company Ltd (In Liquidation) v Clarke** [1989] 29, HC.

Consecutive contracts for the sale of land
Second contract taking effect in event of first becoming void—Whether first contract void because of no compliance with conditions attached to the agreement—Planning permission—Meaning of month—Meaning of 'full planning permission '—Waiver—Whether term for the exclusive benefit of person waiving it—Local Government (Planning and Development) Act 1963, s. 36. **Tiernan Homes Ltd v Sheridan** [1981] 191, SC.

Delay in completion
Land Commission serving notice of inspection subsequent to agreement for sale—Purchaser obtaining consent to registration as owner—Whether consent sufficient to enable completion of sale—Delay—Whether explained—Land Act 1965, s. 13. **Horgan v Deasy** [1979] 71, HC.

Discretionary remedy
Hardship—Failure to complete due to issuance of proceedings by third party—Increase in value of property—Whether to order completion at the contract price would cause excessive hardship—Whether rule applicable. **Roberts v O'Neill** [1981] 403, HC; [1983] 206, SC.

Enforceability of contract
Agreement by receiver in possession to sell factory—Performance of agreement delayed by the court—Allegation that the alleged price an undervalue—Whether contract enforceable. **McCarter & Co. Ltd v Roughan** [1986] 447, HC.

Contract subject to planning permission being obtained—Contract further providing that if permission obtained purchaser might pay a higher price at his own discretion—Whether void for uncertainty—Subsequent agreement as to wayleave—Whether material part of contract—Whether sufficient note or memorandum—Statute of Frauds 1695, s. 2. **O'Mullane v Riordan** [1978] 73, HC.

Licensed premises—Verbal agreement—Written memorandum containing no express terms as to licence—Vendor claiming incapacity—Whether enforceable agreement that

SALE OF LAND
Specific performance
Enforceability of contract continued
existing licence was to pass with premises—Laches—Whether decree of specific performance be granted—Whether damages appropriate remedy—Statute of Frauds 1695. **White v McCooey** [1976-7] 72, HC.

Negotiations with two potential purchasers for sale of licensed premises
Formal contract drawn up with second potential purchaser—First potential purchaser alleging existence of prior enforceable agreement—Institution of proceedings for specific performance—Claim dismissed—Second potential purchaser now seeking to complete sale—Whether appropriate to order specific performance. **Roberts v O'Neill** [1981] 403, HC; [1983] 206, SC.

Oral agreement
memorandum—Authority of agent—Laches—Statute of Frauds 1695. **Guardian Builders Ltd v Kelly** [1981] 127, HC.

Order not complied with
Court dissolving order—Damages for breach of contract—Measure of damages. **Vandeleur v Dargan** [1981] 75, HC.

Title
Personal representative
Leasehold interest in property—Interest bequeathed to testatrix's executor upon trust for sale—Delay—Upon executor's death letters of administration de bonis non then obtained by testatrix's two daughters—Contract for the sale of the interest—Purchaser refusing to accept title from administratices—Whether vendor, selling as personal representative, must satisfy the purchaser that he has power to sell as such—Whether assent to the establishment of a trust for sale should be inferred—Succession Act 1965, s. 51(1). **Crowley v Flynn** [1983] 513, HC.

Waiver
Condition. Se Contract—Condition—Waiver (*above*).

Terms. See Contract—Terms—Waiver (*above*).

SALMON
Unlawful possession. *See* FISHERIES (Offence—Unlawful possession of salmon).

SANITARY SERVICES *See* LOCAL GOVERNMENT (Sanitary services).

SCHEDULED OFFENCE
Arrest
Questioning in respect of non-scheduled offence. See ARREST (Legality—Motive).

SCHOOL
Admission of students. *See* EDUCATION (School—Admission of students).

Discipline *See* EDUCATION (School—Discipline).

Industrial *See* INDUSTRIAL SCHOOL

Law school
System of entry. See SOLICITOR (Entry to profession).

Teacher. *See* EDUCATION (Teacher).

SEA FISHING LICENCE. *See* FISHERIES (Licence—Offshore fishing).

SEARCH WARRANT. *See* CRIMINAL LAW (Search warrant).

SECONDARY LEGISLATION *See* DELEGATED LEGISLATION.

SECRECY
Oath
Central Bank officers. See CENTRAL BANK (Privilege—Oath of secrecy).

SECRET INFORMATION *See* CONFIDENTIALITY.

SECURITY FOR COSTS. *See* COSTS (Security for costs).

SEMINARY
Employment
Dismissal of teacher
Teacher also priest—Whether discrimination in dismissing teacher—Seminary fund-aided by State as recognised college of university—Whether primarily seminary or university—Rights of religious denomination to manage its own affairs. *See* RELIGIOUS DISCRIMINATION (Seminary).

SENTENCE. *See* CRIMINAL LAW (Sentence).

SEPARATION AGREEMENT *See* MARRIAGE (Separation agreement).

SEPARATION OF POWERS. *See* CONSTITUTION (Separation of powers).

SERVICE CHARGES
Local authority. *See* LOCAL GOVERNMENT (Service charges).

SET OFF *See* PRACTICE (Set off).

SETTLEMENT
Marriage. *See* MARRIAGE SETTLEMENT.

SETTLEMENT OF ACTION
Generally. *See* ACTION (Compromise).

Mistake
Whether mistake making agreement a nullity. See MISTAKE (Agreement—Settlement of action).

SEWERAGE. *See* PUBLIC HEALTH (Sewerage).

SEX DISCRIMINATION
Employment. *See* EMPLOYMENT (Equality of treatment).

Irish nationality and citizenship
Differentiation between alien men and women
Whether breach of guarantee of equality—Interests of the common good—Irish Nationality and Citizenship Act 1956, ss. 8, 15, 16. **Somjee v Minister for Justice** [1981] 324, HC.

Pay. *See* EMPLOYMENT (Equal pay).

Social welfare. *See* SOCIAL WELFARE (Equal treatment).

SEXUAL OFFENCES
Rape. *See* CRIMINAL LAW (Rape).

SHAREHOLDER
Industrial and provident society
Property rights. See INDUSTRIAL AND PROVIDENT SOCIETY (Shareholder—Property rights).

Oppression of minority. *See* COMPANY (Oppression of minority).

Reduction in shareholding
Breach of European Community competition rules
Shareholder allegedly suffering damage by reason of reduction in share value—

SHAREHOLDER
Reduction in shareholding
Breach of European Community competition rules continued
Whether such claim subject to national limitations. *See* EUROPEAN COMMUNITY (Competition—Breach of competition rules alleged).

SHARES *See* COMPANY (Shares).

SHIPPING
Canal
Lack of maintenance
Breach of statutory duty—Negligence. *See* NEGLIGENCE (Statutory duty—Canal).

Explosion at sea
French registered ship in Irish waters
Fatal damages claim—Jurisdiction of Irish courts—Victims French nationals employed under French contracts of service—RSC 1962, O 12, r 26. **O'Daly v Gulf Oil Terminals Ltd** [1983] 163, HC.

Ferry service
Suspension
Ferry service from Ireland to Wales—Suspension of service by decision of British government minister. *See* CONTRACT (Statutory duty—Substitution by agreement of parties for statutory obligations).

SHOP
Larceny
Department store
Accused arrested before leaving store—Whether offence of larceny complete. **DPP v Keating** [1989] 561, HC.

Shoplifting
Conviction
Plea of guilty—Whether voluntary—Certiorari. *See* CRIMINAL LAW (Trial—Plea of guilty—Whether voluntary—Shoplifting).

Shopping centre units
Restrictive covenant as to user. See LANDLORD AND TENANT (Covenant—Restriction as to user).

Supermarket. *See* SUPERMARKET.

SINGLE EUROPEAN ACT
Ratification of treaty
Challenge. See CONSTITUTION (International relations—Treaty—Ratification)

SLAUGHTER-HOUSE. *See* ABATTOIR.

SLOT MACHINES *See* GAMING AND LOTTERIES (Gaming machine).

SOCIAL WELFARE
Appeals officer
Decision
Judicial review—Refusal of old age pension—Certiorari—Whether decision of appeals officer bad in law—Whether error within jurisdiction—Social Welfare Act 1952, s. 43. **State (Power) v Moran** [1976–7] 20, HC.

Judicial review—Widow's contributory pension—Disqualification on ground of cohabitation. *See* Pensions—Widow's contributory pension (*below*).

SOCIAL WELFARE *continued*
Benefits
Deduction from award
Compensation—Criminal injuries. *See* MALICIOUS INJURIES (Compensation—Deduction).

Damages. *See* DAMAGES (Personal injuries—Deduction from award).

Employment contributions
Company
Winding up—Preferential debts—Wages due to employees—Such wages having preferential status—Employment contributions under social welfare legislation in respect of such wages due—Whether 'employer's contribution' having similar preferential status—Companies Act 1963, s. 285(2)(e)—Social Welfare (Consolidation) Act 1981, ss. 9(1)(a), 10(1)(b). **In re Castlemahon Poultry Products Ltd** [1987] 222, SC.

Insurability of employment
Rate of contribution—Whether ordinary or special rate of contribution applied—Whether board a public authority—Health Act 1970, ss. 11, 18, 20, 27, 28, 31(1), 33, 58(1), 59(1). **General Medical Services (Payments) Board v Minister for Social Welfare** [1976–7] 210, HC.

Equal treatment
European directive
Failure to fully implement directive—Whether directive has direct effect—Whether directive sufficiently unconditional and precise—Whether in the absence of implementing measures, women entitled to the benefits under the same condition as men—Council Directive 79/7EEC, Article 4(1)—Social Welfare (No. 2) Act 1985, ss. 2, 6(c). **McDermott and Cotter v Minister for Social Welfare** [1987] 324, ECJ.

Implementation—Implementation effected in such a way that certain married couples adversely treated—Whether failure on the part of the State to vindicate the institution of marriage—Constitution of Ireland 1937, Article 41.3.1—Council Directive 79/7—Social Welfare (No 2) Act 1985, s. 12(4). **Hyland v Minister for Social Welfare** [1989] 196, HC; [1990] 213, SC.

European Community directive
Equal treatment. See Equal treatment (*above*).

Offence
False statements
Unemployment benefit—Minor offence—Number of similar offences charged in the one summons—District Court—Jurisdiction. **State (Wilson) v Neilan** [1987] 118, HC.

Overlapping benefits
Regulations
Validity—Appellant prevented from receiving both blind and widow's pension—Whether regulations *ultra vires* and invalid—Whether blind pension accelerated old age pension—Old Age Pensions Act 1932, s. 6—Social Welfare Act 1979, s. 7—Social Welfare (Consolidation) Act 1981, s. 175—Social Welfare (Overlapping Benefits) Regulations 1953—Social Welfare (Overlapping Benefits) (Amendment) Regulations 1979. **Harvey v Minister for Social Welfare** [1990] 185, SC.

Pensions
Old age pension
Refusal—Certiorari—Whether decision of appeals officer bad in law—Whether error within jurisdiction—Social Welfare Act 1952, s. 43. **State (Power) v Moran** [1976–7] 20, HC.

Overlapping benefits
Blind pension—Widow's pension—Regulations—Validity—Appellant prevented from receiving both blind and widow's pension. *See* Overlapping benefits (*above*).

SOCIAL WELFARE
Pensions *continued*
Widow's contributory pension
Disqualification on ground of cohabitation—Meaning thereof—Whether required financial dependance of the woman upon the man with whom she was living—Whether dependants had legitimate expectation that the benefit would continue to be paid—Social Welfare (Consolidation) Act 1981, s. 92(3). **Foley v Moulton** [1989] 169, HC.

Regulations
Validity
Overlapping benefits—Appellant prevented from receiving both blind and widow's pension—Whether regulations *ultra vires* and invalid. *See* Overlapping benefits (*above*).

Returns
Employer
Contract of service or partnership—Fishing vessel—Whether arrangement in reality partnership—Income Tax (Employments) Regulations 1960—Social Welfare (Collection of Employment Contributions by the Collector General) Regulations 1979. **DPP v McLoughlin** [1986] 493, HC.

Supplementary welfare allowance
Fuel allowance
Regulations providing for payment of allowance on means test—Departmental circular excluding from scheme persons on short term social welfare—Whether circular *ultra vires* the Minister for Social Welfare—Social Welfare (Consolidation) Act 1981, ss. 209, 312—Social Welfare (Supplementary Welfare Allowances) Act 1975, s. 11—Social Welfare (Supplementary Welfare Allowances) Regulations 1977, Art 6. **State (Kershaw) v Eastern Health Board** [1985] 235, HC.

SOLDIER
Injury
UN action. See DEFENCE FORCES (Negligence—Duty of care—UN service—Injury to soldier).

SOLICITOR
Access
Accused person
Right of access to solicitor while in detention—Whether such right a constitutional right—Constitution of Ireland 1937, Article 40 3. **People (DPP) v Conroy** [1988] 4, CCA, SC.

Right of access to solicitor while in detention—Whether delay by Gardai in permitting access by solicitor to client constituted a denial of right of access—Whether right of reasonable access to solicitor was a constitutional right—Constitution of Ireland 1937, Article 40 3. **DPP v Healy** [1990] 313, SC.

Prisoner
Prison regulations—Exclusion of certain solicitors—Validity of rule depriving prisoner of his free choice of legal adviser—Whether regulations unconstitutional—Whether *ultra vires*—General Prisons (Ireland) Act 1877, ss. 12, 13(2)—Rules for the Government of Prisons 1976. **Incorporated Law Society v Minister for Justice** [1978] 112, HC.

Appearance
Presumption that counsel and solicitor appear on express instruction of the client— **L'Henryenat v Ireland** [1984] 249, SC.

Conveyancing
Negligence. See Negligence—Sale of land (*below*).

Costs
Lien. See Lien (*below*).

SOLICITOR

Costs *continued*
Taxation. See COSTS (Taxation).

Duty of care
Breach. See Negligence (*below*).

Entry to profession
Examination
Student unsuccessful—Whether student reached standard required to pass examination—Whether Law Society agreed to award a certain number of places irrespective of standard achieved—Whether student entitled to enter the society's law school—Solicitors Act 1954 and 1960 (Apprenticeship and Education) Regulations 1975, regs. 6, 7, 10, 18, 28—Solicitors Act 1954, ss. 40, 73(i). **Gilmer v Incorporated Law Society of Ireland** [1989] 590, HC.

System of entry
Law Society—Whether limit on numbers imposed—Examination—Compensation rules—Whether Education Committee acted arbitrarily—Solicitors Act 1954 (Apprenticeship and Education) (Amendment No 1) Regulations 1974—Solicitors Acts 1954 and 1960 (Apprenticeship and Education) Regulation 1975. **MacGabhann v Incorporated Law Society of Ireland** [1989] 854, HC.

Legal aid
Choice of solicitor. See CRIMINAL LAW (Legal aid—Choice of solicitor).

Lien
Costs
Solicitors arranging auction of mortgaged property—Solicitors receiving title deeds on foot of an accountable receipt—Receipt providing that documents to be held in trust—Whether lien created. In re Galdan Properties Ltd [1988] 559, SC.

Whether lien arises where charging order for costs not obtained or applied for—Priority of solicitor's claim. **Fitzpatrick v DAF Sales Ltd and Allied Irish Finance Company Ltd** [1989] 777, HC.

Misconduct
Dishonesty
Law Society Compensation Fund—Solicitor dishonestly obtaining a loan—Creditor suffering loss—Whether creditor entitled to claim compensation—Whether dishonest act done in connection with his solicitor's practice. **Trustee Savings Bank v Incorporated Law Society of Ireland** [1988] 541, HC; [1989] 665, SC.

Negligence
Conveyancing
Building contract followed by lease—Stage payments—Building company—Charge by deposit of title deeds created—No search made in Companies' Office—Mortgage not discovered—Building company going into liquidation—Whether solicitors negligent. **Roche v Peilow** [1986] 189, SC.

Delay in institution of proceedings
Agreement—Option—Failure to exercise option on behalf of client—Failure to notify client—Whether breach of duty of care—Whether loss suffered by client attributable to breach of duty—Whether client entitled to damage. **McCarthy v Moloney** [1979] 39, HC.

Sale of land
Damages—Booking deposit—Interest—Date from which interest to run. **Desmond v Brophy** [1986] 547, HC.

Purchaser successfully seeking recission of contract—Whether vendor's solicitor negligent. **Fallon v Gannon** [1988] 193, SC.

SOLICITOR
Negligence
Sale of land continued

Solicitor acting for vendor—Vendor becoming involved in two legal actions and incurring financial loss—Whether solicitor in breach of duty of care. Park **Hall School Ltd v Overend** [1987] 345, HC.

Stakeholder—Booking deposit—Clients being prospective purchasers—Building society requiring payments of deposits by intending purchasers of flats to be built— Plaintiffs wishing to become purchasers but unwilling to accept risk of paying booking deposit to builder—Plaintiffs consulting defendant solicitor—Defendant submitting plaintiffs' deposits to builder's solicitors—Deposits forwarded to builder by his solicitors— Flats not built—Insolvency of builder—Loss of deposits—Whether solicitor negligent because of failure to communicate specifically to builder's solicitors that deposits to be held by them as stakeholders. **Desmond and Boyle v Brophy** [1986] 547, HC.

Will

Preparation—Carelessness—Resulting financial loss to a legatee—Whether solicitor owing a duty of care to legatee—Extent of liability—Interest—Succession Act 1965, s. 78. **Wall v Hegarty** [1980] 124, HC.

Privilege. *See* DISCOVERY (Privilege—Legal professional privilege).

Settlement of action
Authority

Consent order—Settlement not in writing—Consent not drawn up—Denial by plaintiffs that action settled. **Barrett v W J Lenehan & Co Ltd** [1981] 206, HC.

Mistake

Whether unilateral mistake rendering agreement a nullity. **Reen v Bank of Ireland Finance Ltd.** [1983] 507, HC.

Town agent
Taxation of costs

Whether taxing master entitled to disallow claim. *See* COSTS (Taxation—Review— Town agent's charges).

Watching brief
Validity of concept of "representation without prejudice". **State (O'Leary) v Neilan** [1984] 35, HC.

SOLUS AGREEMENT
Licence or lease
Agreement to allow occupation and user of premises

Termination of agreement—Agreement held to constitute tenancy—Continued occupation and user—Whether constituted licence or tenancy—Intention of parties. **Irish Shell & BP Ltd v John Costello Ltd** [1985] 554, SC.

SPECIAL CRIMINAL COURT
Independence. *See* CONSTITUTION (Courts—Judicial independence.

Procedure
Warrant

Accused before the court on a warrant for a scheduled offence charged with a non-scheduled offence—Whether separate warrant or summons required in respect of each offence charged—Offences Against the State Acts 1939–1972 (Special Criminal Court) Rules 1975—Offences Against the State Act 1939, ss. 43 and 47. **McElhinney v Special Criminal Court and DPP** [1989] 411, SC.

SPECIFIC PERFORMANCE
Building contract. *See* BUILDING CONTRACT (Specific performance).

Contract. *See* CONTRACT (Specific performance).

Sale of land. *See* SALE OF LAND (Specific performance).

SPORTING ACTIVITIES
Athletics
Suspension of athlete
Natural justice—Dope testing procedure—Failure of athlete to undergo test. *See* NATURAL AND CONSTITUTIONAL JUSTICE (Athletic body).

Racing
Bookmaker
Course betting permit. *See* BOOKMAKER (Course betting permit).

Showjumping
Rule-making body
Prohibition on use of non-Irish horses by Irish showjumpers in international competitions—Whether unreasonable restraint of trade. *See* RESTRAINT OF TRADE (Reasonableness— Public policy—Equestrian rule-making body).

SPOUSE
Surviving spouse. *See* SUCCESSION (Legal right).

STAFF ASSOCIATION
Civil service. *See* CIVIL SERVICE (Staff association).

Garda Síochána
Right of freedom of association for members of Garda Síochána
Limitations on extent to which members of the Force may organise. *See* CONSTITUTION (Personal rights—Freedom of association—Garda Síochána)

Negotiation licence
Public interest
Application for declaration—Staff association disaffiliating from a trade union—Association unable to carry on negotiations for the fixing of wages and other conditions of employment without a licence—Refusal by Minister to confer 'excepted body' status—Statutory conditions for the grant of licence not satisfied—Whether granting of licence against the public interest—Trade Union Act 1941, ss. 6, 7—Trade Union Act 1971, ss. 2, 3. **Irish Aviation Executive Staff Association v Minister for Labour** [1981] 350, HC.

STAKEHOLDER
Sale of land. *See* SOLICITOR (Negligence—Sale of land—Stakeholder—Booking deposit).

STAMP DUTY *See* REVENUE (Stamp duty).

STARE DECISIS *See* PRECEDENT.

STATE
Constitutional obligations
Breach
Infringement of personal rights—Damages—Telephone tapping—Breach of right to privacy—Conscious and deliberate violation—Whether plaintiffs entitled to punitive or aggravated damages—Constitution of Ireland 1937, Article 40 3—Civil Liability Act 1961, ss. 7(2), 14(4). **Kennedy v Ireland** [1988] 472, HC.

Liability—Garda Síochána—Discipline—Invalid inquiry—Whether plaintiff entitled to costs and expenses of his representation and attendance at the inquiry. **McHugh v Commissioner of Garda Síochána** [1987] 181, SC.

STATE *continued*
Fundamental rights
Constitution
Interest of the common good—Control of activities of aliens—Restriction on personal right to liberty. **Osheku v Ireland** [1987] 330, HC.

Immunity from suit
Defence forces
Injury to soldier—UN service—Whether soldier owed duty of care by superior officers—Whether State enjoys common law immunity from suit during armed conflict or hostilities—Whether sufficient case for jury—Constitution of Ireland 1937, Articles 28, 40 3 1 and 40 3 2—Defence Act 1954, s. 111—Defence (Amendment) Act 1960, s. 4. **Ryan v Ireland** [1989] 544, SC.

Liability
Breach of constitutional obligations. See Constitutional obligations—Breach (*above*).

Vicarious liability
Acts of servant—Breach of constitutional rights—Unjustified infringement—Whether tort—Whether damages may be granted—Right to communicate—Convicted prisoner—Interception of letter—Whether loss suffered—Whether nominal damages appropriate. **Kearney v Minister for Justice** [1987] 52, HC.

Name
Correct name of State. **Ellis v O'Dea** [1990] 87, SC

Prerogative
Immunity from suit. See Immunity from suit (*above*).

Treasure trove
Whether Royal prerogative of treasure trove carried over into Irish law—Whether such prerogative a necessary ingredient of soveriegnty—Constitution of Ireland 1937, Articles 5, 10. **Webb v Ireland** [1988] 565, HC, SC.

Privilege
Discovery of documents
Public interest—Factors to be taken into consideration—Injustice to applicant or potential damage to public service. **Incorporated Law Society v Minister for Justice** [1987] 42, HC.

Sovereignty
Constitution
Treasure trove—Whether necessary ingredient of sovereignty—Constitution of Ireland 1937, Articles 5, 10. **Webb v Ireland** [1988] 565, HC, SC.

Vicarious liability. *See* Liability (*above*).

STATE SIDE *See* HABEAS CORPUS; JUDICIAL REVIEW.

STATEMENT
Accused
Admissibility in evidence. See CRIMINAL LAW (Evidence—Statement by accused).

False statement. *See* FALSE STATEMENT.

Minister
Reliance. See MINISTER (Statement in Dáil Éireann—Reliance).

STATION BAIL *See* CRIMINAL LAW (Bail—Station bail).

STATUTE
Amendment
Interpretation
Whether new offence created. *See* STATUTORY INTERPRETATION (Amendment).

STATUTE *continued*
Avoidance of provisions
Landlord and tenant
Rent review clause—Multiplier clause restricting application of statutory provisions—
Validity. *See* LANDLORD AND TENANT (Lease—Rent review clause—Validity).

Breach
Remedy
Injunction—Restrictive practices regulations—Whether injunction appropriate remedy—
Restrictive Practices (Groceries) (Amendment No 2) Order 1978, art 5. **Irish Asso-
ciation of Distributive Trades v Three Guys Ltd** [1979] 269, HC.

Constitutional validity
Review by courts. See CONSTITUTION (Statute—Validity).

Construction. *See* STATUTORY INTERPRETATION.

Delegated legislation
Retrospectivity
Whether unjust. *See* Retrospectivity—Delegated legislation (*below*).

Status
Constitution—Whether statutory instrument a "law". *See* DELEGATED LEGISLATION
(Status).

Validity
Constitution. *See* CONSTITUTION (Statute—Validity—Delegated legislation).

Whether *ultra vires*. *See* DELEGATED LEGISLATION (Validity).

Discretionary power
Exercise. See STATUTORY POWER (Exercise—Discretion).

Duty. *See* STATUTORY DUTY.

Enforcement
Injunction
Private individual seeking injunction to enforce statutory provisions—Whether statute
passed for benefit of small class of persons—Constitution—Right to earn livelihood—
Whether breach of right requires enforcement through injunction—Constitution of
Ireland 1937, Articles 40 3, 45—Road Transport Act 1932—Road Transport Act
1933. **Parsons v Kavanagh** [1990] 560, HC.

Invalidity
Constitution. See CONSTITUTION (Statute—Validity).

Effect
Whether operates retrospectively—Compulsory acquisition—Assessment of compensation—Property at valuation date subject to rent control—Subsequent declaration
of invalidity of rent control legislation—Whether operates retrospectively to affect the
assessment of compensation—Legislation void *ab initio*—Acquisition of Land (Assessment of Compensation) Act 1919, s. 2—Rent Restrictions Act 1960, Parts II and IV.
Reid v Limerick Corporation [1984] 366, HC; [1987] 83, SC

Mistake
Draftsman's error
Defective clause in penal provision—Validity—Whether provision inoperable—Whether
obvious error could be rectified by judicial intervention—Finance Act 1926, s. 25 (2)—
Betting Duty (Certified Returns) Regulations 1934, regs 26, 27, 29. **State (Rollinson) v
Kelly** [1984] 625, SC.

STATUTE *continued*
Operation
Postponement
Governmental discretion to bring section into operation—Whether failure to do so reviewable—Civil Liability Act 1961, s. 60. **State (Sheehan) v Ireland** [1988] 437, SC.

Power. *See* STATUTORY POWER.

Repeal
Effect on rights acquired under repealed legislation
Presumption against retrospective effect—Whether contrary intention shown—Interpretation Act 1937, s. 21(1)—Landord and Tenant (Amendment) Act 1980, ss. 23(5), 29. **Caulfield v D H Bourke & Son Ltd** [1980] 223, HC.

Implication
Construction of statute—Test to be applied—Penal statute—Excise Management Act 1827, s. 78—Criminal Justice Act 1951, s. 8. **DPP v Gray** [1987] 4, SC.

Statute law revision
Effect of legislation—Partition of land—Right of joint tenant to order for sale in lieu of partition—Whether jurisdiction to make order extant—Repeal of statutory power—Whether right existed prior to statutory power—Purpose of statute—Protection of existing principles or rules of law—Act for Joint Tenants 1542—Statute law Revision (Pre-Union Irish Statutes) Act 1962, s. 2(1). **F F v C F.** [1987] 1, HC.

Effect of legislation—Whether repeal nominal or substantive—Criminal Law (Ireland) Act 1928, s. 20—Statute Law Revision Act 1983, s. 2. **State (Dixon) v Martin** [1985] 240, HC.

Retrospectivity
Declaration of invalidity. See Invalidity—Effect—Whether operates retrospectively (*above*).

Delegated legislation
Presumption against retrospectivity—Agriculture—Levy on livestock—Imposition of Duties (No 239) Agricultural Produce (Cattle and Milk) Order 1979—Agricultural Produce (Cattle and Milk) Regulations 1979. **Doyle v An Taoiseach** [1986] 693, HC.

Whether unjust—Regulations giving effect to EC milk levy—Whether unjustified infringement with property rights—Whether necessitated by membership for the European Community—Commission Regulation 1371/84—European Communities (Milk Levy) Regulations 1985, regs 4, 12—Constitution of Ireland 1937, Articles 29 4 3, 40 3 2, 43. **Lawlor v Minister for Agriculture** [1988] 400, HC.

Intention
Whether legislative intent to off-set and frustrate pre-Act contractual rights—Whether such constitutionally permissible—Proceedings for the specific performance of a pre-Act agreement—Conveyance of family home—Constitution of Ireland 1937, Art 40 3 2, 43—Interpretation Act 1937, s. 21(1)—Family Home Protection Act 1976, ss. 2, 3, 4. **Dunne v Hamilton** [1982] 290, HC.

Repeal
Effect on rights acquired under repealed legislation—Presumption against retrospective effect—Whether contrary intention shown—Interpretation Act 1937, s. 21(1)—Landord and Tenant (Amendment) Act 1980, ss. 23(5), 29. **Caulfield v D H Bourke & Son Ltd** [1980] 223, HC.

Rules of Court
Validity
Whether *ultra vires. See* DELEGATED LEGISLATION (Validity—Rules of Court).

Severance
Levy orders
Bonus scheme paid to bacon exporters by plaintiffs—Bonus scheme financed from

STATUTE
Severance
Levy orders continued

levies—Part of levies scheme condemned by the Court of Justice—Severability of levy orders by the court—Pigs and Bacon (Amendment) Act 1939, ss. 34, 38. **Pigs and Bacon Commission v McCarren** [1981] 237, SC.

Taxing statute
Constitutional validity. See CONSTITUTION (Statute—Validity—Taxing statute).

Validity
Constitution. See CONSTITUTION (Statute—Validity).

STATUTE OF FRAUDS
Contract for sale of land
Whether sufficient note or memorandum. See SALE OF LAND (Contract—Formation—"Subject to contract").

STATUTE OF LIMITATIONS *See* LIMITATION OF ACTIONS.

STATUTORY DEFINITIONS *See* WORDS AND PHRASES.

STATUTORY DUTY
Breach
Negligence. See NEGLIGENCE (Statutory duty).

Right of individual to bring common law action

Whether statute passed for benefit of limited class of persons—Whether private individual entitled to enforce legislation through injunction—Constitution—Right to earn livelihood—Unlawful infringement of right—Constitution of Ireland 1937, Articles 40 3, 45—Road Transport Act 1932—Road Transport Act 1933. **Parsons v Kavanagh** [1990] 560, HC.

Duration
Contract providing for alternative basis for parties concerned

Whether parties to contract estopped from reverting to position prior to contract—Provision of ferry service—Fishguard and Rosslare Railways and Harbour Act 1898, s. 70. **Waterford Harbour Commrs v British Railways Board** [1979] 296, HC, SC.

Interpretation
Extent of duty

Housing authority—Duty to prepare and adopt a building programme—Whether statutory duty to provide serviced halting sites for travelling community—Whether duty to include in its building programme proposals for provision of such sites—Whether statutory duty to review programme already adopted so as to include such proposals—Constitution of Ireland 1937—Housing Act 1966, ss. 53, 54, 56, 58, 60, 111. **O'Reilly v Limerick Corporation** [1989] 181, HC.

Performance
Enforcement

Mandamus—Locus standi of applicant—Test to be applied—Sufficient interest—Failure of government to make order bringing section of statute into operation. **State (Sheehan) v Ireland** [1988] 437, SC.

STATUTORY INTERPRETATION
Amendment
Whether new offence created

Gaming and Lotteries Act 1956, s. 4(1)(c) as amended by Gaming and Lotteries Act 1979, s. 1. **DPP (McGrath) v Murphy** [1982] 143, HC.

STATUTORY INTERPRETATION *continued*
Application
Housing authority
Statutory duty to allocate houses in accordance with scheme of priorities—Allocation to persons residing outside functional area—Whether authority acting *ultra vires*—Housing Act 1966, ss. 53, 60, 109. **McNamee v Buncrana UDC** [1984] 77, HC.

Limitation of actions
Operative date of amending legislation—Statute of Limitations 1957, s. 45 as amended by the Succession Act 1965, s. 126—Date upon s. 126 came into operation—Applicability of s. 126 to claim of a personal representative to recover assets of the deceased from a person holding adversely to the estate. **Drohan v Drohan** [1981] 473, HC.

Penal statute
Excise offences—Imposition of penalty—Whether other offences may be taken into consideration—Whether statute to be construed liberally—Criminal Justice Act 1951, s. 8(1). **DPP v Gray** [1987] 4, SC.

Conclusive evidence clause
Companies Act 1963, s. 104. **Lombard & Ulster Banking v Amurec Ltd** [1976–7] 222, HC.

Context of words
"Issue"
Succession law—Provision for intestate succession—Whether "issue" includes illegitimate child of deceased—Absence of definition in Act—Intention of legislature—Presumption of constitutionality—Constitution of Ireland 1937, Articles 40 1 and 3, 43 1 2—Succession Act 1965, ss. 67, 69, 110. **In re Walker: O'Brien v s.** [1982] 327, HC; [1985] 86, SC.

Revenue
Small companies relief—Reduced rate of tax where company has "associated companies"—Whether non-resident company associated company—Meaning of "associated company"—Corporation Tax Act 1976, ss. 1(5), 28(4). **Bairead v Maxwells of Donegal Ltd** [1986] 508, HC.

Crime against property damaged
Burglary
Malicious injuries code—Test to be applied—Malicious Injuries Act 1981, ss. 5(1), (2)(d)—Larceny Act 1916, s. 23. **Shennick Lodge v Monaghan Co Council** [1986] 273, SC.

Discretionary power
Exercise
Condition precedent—Whether fulfilled. *See* STATUTORY POWER (Exercise—Discretion—Condition precedent—Whether fulfilled).

Draftsman's error
Defective clause in penal provision
Validity—Whether provision inoperable. *See* Mistake—Draftsman's error (*below*).

Ejusdem generis rule
Landlord and tenant
Ejectment proceedings—Application for new tenancy under new Act—Whether deliberate omission from new benefits of tenant ejected by court order—Words "or otherwise"—Landlord and Tenant (Amendment) Act 1980, s. 29. **Kenny v Quinn** [1981] 385, CC.

Ordinary and natural meaning of words
Revenue—Corporation Tax Act 1976, s. 27. **Cronin v Lunham Brothers Ltd** [1986] 415, HC.

STATUTORY INTERPRETATION

Ejusdem generis rule *continued*

Whether applicable

Revenue—Excise duties—Ice pops—Whether 'table waters'—Whether product something intended to be drunk—Finance (New Duties) Act 1916, ss. 4(1)(2), 6(3)—Table Waters Duties Regulations 1916, reg 6. **Attorney General v Palmer Products Ltd and Attorney General v Leaf Ltd** [1982] 441, HC.

Employment

Equal pay

"Like work"—National legislation providing for entitlement to equal pay where employes engaged in work of equal value—Whether inlcudes work higher in value—Compatibility with European Community law—Anti-Discrimination (Pay) Act 1974, ss. 2, 3—Treaty of Rome, Article 119. **Murphy v Bord Telecom Éireann** [1986] 483, HC; [1989] 53, ECJ, HC.

Enabling or mandatory power

Law reform provision

Section to come into operation "on such day . . . as may be fixed" by government order—No such order made—Whether discretion limited as to time—Civil Liability Act 1961, s. 60(7). **State (Sheehan) v Ireland** [1988] 437, HC, SC.

European Community law

Compatibility

Whether purposive or literal approach to be adopted—Provisions of national law in apparent conflict with Community law—Primacy of Community law—Anti-Discrimination (Pay) Act 1974, ss. 2, 3—Treaty of Rome, Article 119. **Murphy v Bord Telecom Éireann** [1986] 483, HC; [1989] 53, ECJ, HC.

Exercise of statutory power

Condition precedent

Whether fulfilled. *See* STATUTORY POWER (Exercise—Discretion—Condition precedent—Whether fulfilled).

Incongruity

Garda compensation

Assessment—Fatal injury—Whether compensation shall be reduced to take into account the value of special pensions and allowances payable on death or injury—Uncertainty—Apparent incongruity of provisions—Amending legislation—Garda Síochána (Compensation) Act 1941, s. 9. **McLoughlin v Minister for Public Service** [1986] 28, SC.

Intent of legislature. *See* Legislative intent (*below*).

Irish language

Use in court

"So far as may be practicable"—Whether District Justice obliged to hear case without an interpreter—Courts of Justice Act 1924, s. 71. **Ó Monacháin v An Taoiseach** [1986] 660, SC.

"Issue"

Succession Act

Intestate succession—Whether "issue" includes illegitimate child of deceased. *See* Interpretation—Context of words—"Issue" (*above*).

Legislation lacuna

Failure to make provision for contingency arising

Planning—Purchase notice—Failure of planning authority to reply—Consequences unprovided for—Whether default procedure to be implied—Alternative remedy available—Function of courts in interpreting legislation where lacuna exists—Local Government (Planning and Development) Act 1963, ss. 2, 29. **State (McInerney & Co Ltd) v Dublin Co Council** [1985] 513, HC.

STATUTORY INTERPRETATION

Legislation lacuna *continued*

Legislature not addressing point now arising
Whether court may impute intention of legislature—Anti-Discrimination (Pay) Act 1974, ss. 2, 3. **Murphy v Bord Telecom Éireann** [1986] 483, HC.

Legislative intent

Literal interpretation giving result plainly contrary to the legislative intent
Taxing statute—Company receiving dividends—Dividend derived from sale of capital assets—Whether dividend liable to be assessed for corporation profits tax—Finance Act 1920, s. 53(2). **Kellystown Co v Hogan, Inspector of Taxes** [1985] 200, SC.

Patent appeal
Decision of Controller—Appeal to the High Court—Whether further appeal to the Supreme Court—Regulation by law of Supreme Court's appellate jurisdiction—Object of achievement of uniformity in patent decisions—Patents Act 1964, ss. 15, 75(7). **Beechams Group Ltd v Bristol Myers** [1983] 500, SC.

Long title

Whether words of statute uncertain or ambiguous
Whether long title may be used—Whether relevant—Criminal law—Arrest—Offences Against the State Act 1939, Long title, ss. 30, 36. **People (DPP) v Quilligan** [1987] 606, CCC.

Mandatory or directory

Arbitration
Question of law—Refusal of arbitrator to state case—Whether misconduct—Whether statutory provision mandatory—Arbitration Act 1954, s. 35(1). **Stillorgan Orchard Ltd v McLoughlin and Harvey** [1978] 128, HC.

Planning appeal regulations
Requirement to state grounds of appeal in written notice of appeal—Whether requirement mandatory or directory—Local Government (Planning and Development) Regulations 1977, art 36. **State (Elm Developments Ltd) v An Bord Pleanála** [1981] 108, SC.

Planning application regulations
Requirement that application comply with regulations—Whether regulations mandatory or directory—Purpose of Act—Extent of obligation to comply—Local Government (Planning and Development) Act 1963, s. 26(4)—Local Government (Planning and Development) Regulations 1977, arts 14, 15, 17. **Monaghan UDC v Alf-a-Bet Promotions Ltd** [1980] 64, SC.

Revenue appeal
Statutory provision requiring expression of dissatisfaction on point of law to be made "immediately after the determination"—Whether "immediately" to be interpreted strictly—Whether provision directory or mandatory—Income Tax Act 1967, ss. 428, 430. **State (Multiprint Label Systems Ltd) v Neylon** [1984] 545, HC.

Ordinary meaning

Clear and unambiguous language
Whether liberal interpretation produces unjust results—Road Traffic (Amendment) Act 1978, s. 13 (3). **DPP v Clinton** [1984] 127, HC.

Employment equality—Statutory time-bar for reference of 'disputes'—Employment Equality Agency making a reference—Statute providing that such reference be 'dealt with as if it were a reference' of a dispute—Whether time-bar applicable to such reference—Duty of courts in interpreting the statute—Employment Equality Act 1977, ss. 19, 20. **State (Aer Lingus) v Labour Court** [1987] 373, HC, SC.

Fair practice regulation
Particular meaning within the relevant trade—Admissibility—Whether ambiguity in expression. **Irish Association of Distributive Trades v Three Guys** [1979] 269, HC.

STATUTORY INTERPRETATION

Ordinary meaning *continued*

Revenue

Income tax—"Cattle"—Whether pigs included—Intensive pig production—Whether by reason of such business taxpayer was 'dealer in cattle'—Whether court should presume that the legislature was aware of and endorsed judicial decisions concerning previous statutory use of the same expression in the same context—Income Tax Act 1918, Schedule D—Income Tax Act 1967, s. 78. **Inspector of Taxes v Kiernan** [1981] 157, HC; [1982] 13, SC.

Relief—"Manufacture of goods"—Meaning of "manufacture"—Process of ripening bananas—Whether process constitutes manufacturing—Corporation Tax Act 1976, s. 54(1), (2). **McCann v O'Culachain** [1986] 229, HC.

Relief—"Manufacture of goods"—Whether ordinary meaning be given—Finance Act 1975, s. 31. **Irish Agricultural Machinery Ltd v O Culachain, Inspector of Taxes** [1989] 478, SC.

Tax avoidance scheme—Capital gains—Whether transactions intended merely to avoid incidence of tax—Function of courts—Whether empowered to invalidate tax avoidance schemes in general—Capital Gains Tax Act 1975, ss. 5(1), 33(5)—Corporation Tax Act 1976, s. 102. **McGrath v McDermott** [1988] 647, SC.

Whether words uncertain or ambiguous

Whether long title may be used—Whether relevant—Criminal law—Arrest—Offences Against the State Act 1939. Long title, ss. 30, 36. **People (DPP) v Quilligan** [1987] 606, CCC.

Penal statute

Motor vehicle insurance regulations

Information—Duty of insurers to give information to Garda Síochána—Whether regulations valid—Whether natural rights of insured invaded—*Uberrima fides*—Road Traffic Act 1961, s. 75—Road Traffic (Compulsory Insurance) Regulations 1962, arts 7, 9. **Murphy v PMPA Insurance Co** [1978] 25, HC.

Principles applicable

Strict construction of word or expression. **Inspector of Taxes v Kiernan** [1981] 157, HC; [1982] 13, SC.

Whether statute to be construed liberally—Imposition of penalty—Whether other offences may be taken into account—Criminal Justice Act 1951, s. 8. **DPP v Gray** [1987] 4, SC.

Presumption

Constitutionality

Succession law—Intestate succession—Meaning of "issue"—Whether includes illegitimate child of deceased—Absence of definition in Act—Constitution of Ireland 1937, Articles 40 1 and 3, 43 1 2—Succession Act 1965, ss. 67, 69, 110. In re Walker: **O'Brien v s.** [1982] 327, HC; [1985] 86, SC.

Legislative endorsement of judicial decisions

Qualification of principle—Meaning of word or expression—Whether court should presume that the legislature was aware of and endorsed judicial decisions concerning previous statutory use of the same expression in the same context—Income Tax Act 1918, Schedule D—Income Tax Act 1967, s. 78. **Inspector of Taxes v Kiernan** [1981] 157, HC; [1982] 13, SC.

Qualification of principle—Whether court also entitled to interpret legislation by reference to report of English Royal Commission which led to similar English statute—Income Tax Act 1967, s. 241—Finance Act 1971, s. 26. **Breathnach v McCann** [1984] 679, HC.

STATUTORY INTERPRETATION *continued*
Purposive approach
Affiliation proceedings
Legislation conferring jurisdiction on High Court but contemplating the making of
rules as to relevant procedures to be followed—No such rules of Court made—Whether
High Court inherent jurisdiction—Purpose of Act—Effect of literal interpretation—
Illegitimate Children (Affiliation Orders) Act 1930—Courts Act 1971, s. 19. **O'B v W**
[1982] 234, SC.

Building society
"Prior mortgage"—Building Societies Act 1976, s. 80. **Rafferty v Crowley** [1984] 350,
HC.

European Community law
Compatibility of national law—Anti-Discrimination (Pay) Act 1974, ss. 2, 3—Treaty
of Rome, Article 119. **Murphy v An Bord Telecom** [1986] 483, HC; [1989] 53, ECJ, HC.

Rate relief
Municipal rate
Whether relief extends only to hereditaments occupied at time statute enacted—
Whether relief extends to hereditaments subsequently acquired—Intention of statute—
Local Government (Dublin) Act 1930, s. 69 and 2nd Schedule. **Dublin Corporation v
Trinity College Dublin** [1984] 84, HC; [1985] 283, SC.

Repeal
Effect on rights acquired under repealed legislation. See STATUTE (Repeal—Effect on rights
acquired under repealed legislation).

Repeal by implication
Test to be applied
Penal statute—Excise Management Act 1827, s. 78—Criminal Justice Act 1951, s. 8.
DPP v Gray [1987] 4, SC.

Singular and plural rule
Casual trading
Whether individual trader could constitute a "concourse of buyers and sellers"—
Interpretation Act 1937, s. 11(a)—Casual Trading Act 1980, s. 1. **Skibbereen UDC v
Quill** [1986] 170, HC.

Income Tax Act
Capital allowance—Whether rule that the singular includes the plural applicable—
Income Tax Act 1967, ss. 218, 220 (5). **Irish Agricultural Wholesale Society Ltd v
McDermot** [1982] 457, HC.

Whether rule that singular includes plural applicable—Purpose of statutory provision—
Arrest under s. 30—Whether detention in successive Garda stations permitted—
Offences Against the State Act 1939, ss. 30(3)—Interpretation Act 1937, s. 11(c). **DPP
v Kelly** [1983] 271, SC.

Taxing statute
Corporation profits
Company dividends—Dividend derived from sale of capital assets—Literal interpretation giving result plainly contrary to the legislative intent—Finance Act 1920, s.
53(2). **Kellystown Co v Hogan** [1985] 200, HC.

Principles applicable
Fiscal nullity—Tax avoidance scheme—Whether court must adopt new approach in
construction of taxing statute—Capital Gains Tax Act 1975, ss. 5(1), 33(5)—Corporation Tax Act 1976, s. 102. **McGrath v McDermott** [1988] 647, SC.

Strict construction of word or expression. **Inspector of Taxes v Kiernan** [1981] 157,
HC; [1982] 13, SC.

STATUTORY INTERPRETATION

Taxing statute *continued*

Stamp duty exemption

Conveyance of house upon erection—Whether 'erection' and 'completion' synonymous—Stamp Act 1891, s. 13—Finance Act 1969, s. 49 (1). **Dunne v Revenue Commissioners** [1982] 438, HC.

Whether interpretation consistent with overall scheme of legislation

Income Tax Act 1967, s. 485(2). **Weekes v Revenue Commissioners** [1989] 165, HC.

Teleological approach. *See* Purposive approach (*above*).

Testacy

Meaning

Succession Act—Sole executrix and universal legatee predeceasing testator—Will inoperative—Whether deceased dying intestate—Succession Act 1965, ss. 3, 109, 117. **G v G** [1980] 225, HC.

Time

Computation

Time for giving notice of decision—Time expiring on a Sunday—Whether extra day given for giving notice of decision—Planning decision—Intepretation Act 1937, ss. 11(h), 18—Sunday Observance Act 1695—Statute Law Revision (Pre-Union Irish Statutes) Act 1962, s. 1—RSC, O 108 rr 2, 3—Local Government (Planning and Development) Act 1963, ss. 7, 26(4)(a), 82(3a)—Local Government (Planning and Development) Act 1976, s. 27—Housing Act 1969, ss. 3, 4(6)(b), 10. **Freeney v Bray UDC** [1982] 29, HC.

Time limit

Extension

Malicious injuries claim—Whether court power to extend time—Malicious Injuries Act 1981, ss. 8, 14, 23. **Dublin Corporation v Murdon Ltd** [1988] 86, HC.

Succession Act 1965—Infants—Family provision—Jurisdiction of court —Statutory provision allowing for extension of limitation period in cases of disability— Whether such provision applicable to applications under s. 117—Succession Act 1965, ss. 117, 121, 127. **D v D** [1981] 179, HC.

Words and phrases. *See* WORDS AND PHRASES.

STATUTORY MONOPOLY

Postal service

Monopoly in respect of the conveying of "letters"

Private courier service—Whether trading in breach of the monopoly. *See* POST OFFICE (Monopoly).

STATUTORY POWERS

Condition precedent

Whether fulfilled. See Exercise—Discretion—Condition precedent (*below*).

Whether statutory provisions workable. See Exercise—Impossibility—Condition precedent—Whether statutory provisions workable (*below*).

Exercise

Discretion

Condition precedent—Whether fulfilled—Revenue—Application for an order directing a bank to furnish particulars of an account—Whether conditions precedent to the right to apply for such order fulfilled—Whether conditions precedent to exercise by court of its discretion to grant an order fulfilled—Extent of information which bank may be required to furnish—Bankers' Books Evidence Act 1959—Finance Act 1983, s. 18. **O'C v D** [1985] 123, HC, SC.

STATUTORY POWERS
Exercise
Discretion continued
Notice—Registrar of Titles—Registration of inhibition—Whether affected parties be given notice—Whether registration must be made in judicial manner—Opportunity to object to registration of inhibition—Registration of Title Act 1964, s. 121. **State (Philpott) v Registrar of Titles** [1986] 499, HC.

Duty to act judicially
Decision of tribunal—Whether reasons must be furnished—Guarantee of fair procedures. **Anheuser Busch Inc v Controller of Patents** [1988] 247, HC.

Impossibility
Condition precedent—Whether statutory provisions workable—County Registrar— Purchase of fee simple—Fixing of price in absence of agreement—Landlord and Tenant (Ground Rents) Act 1967, s. 18. **Gilsenan v Foundary House Investments Ltd** [1980] 273, SC.

Injunction application to restrain. See INJUNCTION (Interlocutory—Statutory power Exercise).

Natural justice
Fair procedures. *See* NATURAL AND CONSTITUTIONAL JUSTICE.

Presumption of conformity with Constitution
Minister—Decision-making power affecting personal rights—Whether reviewable by courts—Constitution of Ireland 1937, Article 40 6 1—Broadcasting Authority Act 1960, s. 31 (No 2) Order 1982. **State (Lynch) v Cooney** [1982] 190, HC; [1983] 89, SC.

Reasonableness
Contract of adhesion—Supply of electricity—Disconnection of supply to customer— Whether supply may be disconnected without notice—Electricity (Supply) Act 1927, s. 99. **McCord v ESB** [1980] 153, SC.

Validity
Arrest—Legality. *See* ARREST (Legality).

Constitution—Whether administration of justice. *See* CONSTITUTION (Administration of justice).

Whether *ultra vires*—Minister. *See* MINISTER (*Ultra vires*—Exercise of powers).

Interpretation
Scope of power
Registrar of Building Societies—Orderly and proper regulation of building society business—Whether Registrar's powers authorise him to interfere with legitimate discretion of directors of building society—Interest rates offered to shareholders— Building Societies Act 1976, s. 19. **Ireland Benefit Building Society v Registrar of Building Societies** [1981] 73, HC.

Whether discretionary
Whether duty imposed—Section providing for radical law reform—Section to come into operation on day fixed by governmental order—Application for order of man- damus requiring government to make such order—Whether government has discretion to bring section into operation—Civil Liability Act 1961, s. 60. **State (Sheehan) v Ireland** [1988] 437, SC.

STATUTORY PRIVILEGE
Central Bank
Evidence
Disclosure of information—Subpoena *duces tecum* issued requiring officer to produce documents—Oath of secrecy—Central Bank Act 1942, ss. 6(1), 31. **Cully v Northern Bank Finance Corporation** [1984] 683, HC.

STATUTORY RIGHTS
Infringement
Damages. See DAMAGES (Statutory rights).

STATUTORY TENANCY
Death of tenant intestate. *See* LANDLORD AND TENANT (Statutory tenancy).

STAY OF ACTION. *See* PRACTICE (Stay of action).

STOCK RELIEF. *See* REVENUE (Corporation tax—Stock relief).

STOLEN PROPERTY
Receiving. *See* CRIMINAL LAW (Larceny—Receiving stolen property).

STREET AND HOUSE-TO-HOUSE COLLECTIONS
Appeal procedure
Validity
Opinion that proceeds of collection would benefit an unlawful organisation—Appeal to District Court—Review of opinion excluded—Whether appeal procedure constitutionally invalid—Constitution of Ireland 1937, Article 34—Street and House-to-House Collections Act 1962, s. 13(4). **State (McEldowney) v Kelleher and Attorney General** [1982] 568, HC; [1985] 10, SC.

STREET TRADING
Casual trading licence *See* CASUAL TRADING.

Offences
Convictions for breaches of bye-laws made for the control of traffic. See ROAD TRAFFIC OFFENCES (Street trading).

STRIKING OUT
Charge. *See* CRIMINAL LAW (Procedure— Striking out of charge—District Court).

STUDENT
Discipline. *See* UNIVERSITY (Committee of discipline—Charge of plagiarism).

STUDENTS' UNION
Abortion information
Publication of information about abortion clinics outside the State
Whether right to give such information under European Community law. *See* ABORTION (Information—Publication—Students' groups).

SUBORDINATE LEGISLATION *See* DELEGATED LEGISLATION.

SUCCESSION
Administration
Adverse possession
Administrator seeking to recover possession of land—Limitation period—Statute of Limitations 1957, s. 45, as amended by Succession Act 1965, s. 126—Operative date of s. 126—Applicability to claim of a personal representative to recover assets of deceased. **Drohan v Drohan** [1981] 472, HC.

Joint tenants—Next-of-kin of deceased owner remaining in possession—Whether interest of other next-of-kin defeated by adverse possession—Whether shares of those excluded from possession acquired as joint tenants or as tenants in common—Administration of Estates Act 1959, ss. 13, 22—Succession Act 1965, s. 125(1). **Maher v Maher** [1987] 582, HC.

SUCCESSION
Administration *continued*
Appropriation
Dwelling—Widow's legal right—Application to appropriate dwelling in part satisfaction—Whether 5-acre field "occupied with the dwelling"—Widow dying after application—Whether her executor could enforce appropriation—Succession Act 1965, s. 56. **In re Hamilton: Hamilton v Armstrong** [1984] 306, HC.

Ascertainment of next-of-kin
Insufficiency of evidence—Refusal of examiner's certificate—Application for order presuming the deaths of certain persons and giving administrator leave to distribute assets—Benjamin order. **Baker v Cohn-Vossen, In re Mieth** [1986] 175, HC.

Expenses of personal representative
Will—Executor commencing proceedings in Ireland and defending foreign proceedings—Delay in distributing assets—Whether executor entitled to retain costs and expenses and to be indemnified out of the assets. **In the goods of Rowan (deceased): Rowan v Rowan** [1989] 625, SC.

Sale of land by personal representative
Title—Leasehold interest in property—Interest bequeathed to executor upon trust for sale—Delay—Death of executor—Letters of administration *de bonis non* then obtained by testatrix's two daughters—Contract for the sale of the interest—Purchaser refusing to accept title from administratices—Whether vendor, selling as personal representative, must satisfy the purchaser that he has power to sell as such—Whether assent to the establishment of a trust for sale should be inferred—Succession Act 1965, s. 51(1). **Crowley v Flynn** [1983] 513, HC.

Claim
Initiation
Unfair dismissal claim—Death of employer—Whether claim should proceed against the personal representatives of the employer—Civil Liability Act 1961, s. 8(1)—Succesion Act 1965, s. 8—Unfair Dismissals Act 1977, ss. 1, 15. **Hutton v Philippi** [1982] 578, EAT.

Family provision
Moral duty of testator
Bulk of estate left to testator's grandchild—Whether testator failed in his moral duty to make proper provision for his children—Whether court empowered to create a discretionary trust—Succession Act 1965, ss. 90, 117. **H L v Governor and Company of the Bank of Ireland** [1978] 160, HC.

Claim by son abandoned by mother testatrix at birth—Succession Act 1965, s. 117. **O'H v R** [1986] 563, HC.

Devise of farm to nephew—Charges in favour of daughter and testator's sister—Moral duty to daughter—Other moral obligations of the testator—Succession Act 1965, s. 117. **L v L** [1984] 607, HC.

Duty to provide for children—Testator failing to make provision for three of his children—Children having independent incomes—Factors to be considered—Succession Act 1965, s. 117. **MacNaughton v Walker** [1976–7] 106, HC.

Limitation period. *See* Limitation period—Family provision (*below*).

Objective nature of factors to be considered—Effect on legal right share of widow—Whether court precluded from reviewing will which would interfere with legal right share—Succession Act 1965, ss. 111, 117, **J R v J R** [1979] 236, HC.

Testator's estate valued at £40,000—Legacies of £1,000 to each of his two children—Whether testator failed to make proper provision for his children—Succession Act 1965, s. 117. **J H v Allied Irish Banks Ltd** [1978] 203, HC.

SUCCESSION
Family provision
Moral duty of testator continued
Whether testator failed to make proper provision for his children—Succession Act
1965, s. 117. **M H v N M** [1983] 519, HC.

Whether testatrix failed in moral duty to make proper provision for children—Onus
of proof—Succession Act 1965, s. 117. In the Estate of I A C Deceased; **C and F v W
C and T C** [1989] 815, SC.

Will—Failure—Prior death of sole executrix and universal legatee—Will inoperative—
Application under s. 117—Whether deceased dying intestate—Merits of s. 117 application—Succession Act 1965, ss. 3, 109, 117. **R G v P** s. **G** [1980] 225, HC.

Illegitimate child
Intestate succession. See Intestacy—Illegitimate child (*below*).

Intestacy
Illegitimate child
Right of illegitimate child to intestate succession to father's estate—Whether 'issue'
included illegitimate issue—Whether to confine right to intestate succession to legitimate children repugnant to the Constitution—Whether statutory discrimination between
child born inside and outside marriage invalid—European Convention on Human
Rights and Fundamental Freedoms—Whether part of Irish Law—Whether any constitutional right to inherit property—Constitution of Ireland 1937, Arts, 40, 41, 43—
Succession Act 1965, ss. 67(2), 69(1), 110. **In re Walker: O'Brien v s.** [1982] 327, HC;
[1985] 86, SC.

Non-statutory tenant
Death of tenant—Whether dependent entitled to tenancy—Whether rights under Rent
Restrictions Act 1960 can accrue to a member of such tenant's family—Landlord and
Tenant Act 1931, Part III—Rent Restrictions Act 1960, ss. 2(1), 31(3)—Rent Restrictions
(Amendment) Act 1967, ss. 2(4), 13(2). **Byrne v O'Neill** [1979] 47, SC.

Legal right
Appropriation
Widow—Application to appropriate dwelling in part satisfaction—Whether 5-acre
field "occupied with the dwelling"—Widow dying after application—Whether her
executor could enforce appropriation—Succession Act 1965, s. 56. **In re Hamilton;
Hamilton v Armstrong** [1984] 306, HC.

Exercise
Surviving spouse unaware of will made by husband—Death of surviving spouse—
Whether knowledge of will essential prerequisite to imputed exercise of legal right by
surviving spouse—Whether exercise personal to surviving spouse—Whether legal right
becomes exerciseable by surviving spouse's executor in default of exercise—Succession
Act 1965, s. 113. **Reilly v McEntee** [1984] 572, HC.

Limitation period
Family provision
Testator having two families—Separation agreement providing maintenance etc for
wife and children—Testator subsequently purchasing house as family home—Transfer
into the joint names of testator and defendant—Testator dying one year later—Whether
transfer of disposition made for purpose of defeating or diminishing wife's share—
Whether application in respect of a diminished share dependent on wife having been
served with notice of her right to elect—Whether defendant estopped from pleading
time limit—Application in respect of children—Whether dependent on success of s. 117
application—Extension of time limit in case of infancy—Interpretation of statu-tory
provisions—Whether obligations of testator under separation agreement continue after
his death—Moral obligations of testator toward defendant and her children—Succession
Act 1965, ss. 115, 117, 121, 127. **In re E D deceased; M P D v M D** [1981] 179, HC.

SUCCESSION *continued*
Personal representative
Expenses. See Administration—Expenses of personal representative (*above*).

Sale of land
Title. *See* Administration—Sale of land by personal representative (*above*).

Recovery of land
Adverse possession
Administrator seeking to recover possession of land—Limitation period. *See* Administration—Adverse possession (*above*).

Will. *See* WILL.

SUICIDE
Inquest verdict
Whether permissible. See INQUEST (Verdict—Suicide).

SUMMARY JURISDICTION *See* DISTRICT COURT.

SUMMONS *See also* CRIMINAL LAW (Summons).
Delay in serving. *See* CRIMINAL LAW (Summons—Delay in issuing)

Date of issue altered
Whether invalid—Road Traffic (Amendment) Act 1978, ss. 12(2), 13(3). **DPP v Clein** [1983] 76, SC.

Renewal
Plenary summons issued but not served
Limitation period expiring—Appication to renew—Whether defendant prejudiced by lapse of time—RSC 1962, O 8 r 1. **Walshe v CIE** [1985] 180, HC.

Service out of jurisdiction. *See* PRACTICE (Service out of jurisdiction).

Sufficiency
Signature
District Court clerk affixing signature by use of rubber stamp—Conviction—Certiorari—Whether open to prosecutor to challenge sufficiency of summons. **State (O'Leary) v Neilan** [1984] 35, HC.

Validity. *See* CRIMINAL LAW (Summons—Validity).

SUNDAY
Time limit expiring on a Sunday
Notice of decision
Whether extra day given for giving notice of decision. *See* STATUTORY INTERPRETATION (Time—Computation—Time for giving notice of decision).

SUPERIOR COURT RULES COMMITTEE
Rules of court
Discovery
Non-party discovery—Whether *ultra vires*—Whether discovery a matter of practice and procedure. *See* DISCOVERY (Non-party discovery—Rule of court).

SUPERMARKET
Licensing
On-licence application
Procedure for acquiring off-licence not available—Application for a certificate that the entire food department would be "fit and convenient" for sale for consumption on the premises—Licensing (Ireland) Act 1902, s. 2—Intoxicating Liquor Act 1927, ss. 61, 62—Intoxicating Liquor Act 1960, s. 15. **In re Powers Supermarkets Ltd** [1981] 270, HC.

SUPPLEMENTARY WELFARE ALLOWANCE
Fuel allowance *See* SOCIAL WELFARE (Supplementary welfare allowance).

SUPPLY OF SERVICES
False statements. *See* CONSUMER PROTECTION (Offence—False statements).

SUPREME COURT
Appeal
Acquittal
> Jurisdiction. *See* Appeal—Jurisdiction—Acquittal (*below*).

Damages award
> Assessment and award of damages in first instance. **Bahkt v Medical Council** [1990] 840, SC.

> Review—Jurisdiction—Whether Supreme Court may substitute its own assessment of damages for those made by a jury in the High Court—Constitution of Ireland 1937, Article 34.4.3—Courts of Justice Act 1924, s. 96. **Holohan v Donoghue** [1986] 250, SC.

> Review—Matters to be considered. **Reddy v Bates** [1984] 197, SC.

Evidence
> Findings of fact—Whether disturbable on appeal—Adoption—Consent of mother—Finding of fact by trial judge that consent not free and informed—Whether such finding could be disturbed on appeal. **In re M; J M and G M v An Bord Uchtala** [1988] 203, SC.

Function of court
> Primary and secondary facts—Whether Supreme Court empowered to reach different conclusions to those of trial court in relation to inferences from primary facts. **Hanrahan v Merck Sharp & Dohme (Ireland) Ltd** [1988] 629, SC.

Grounds
> New arguments—Argument raised in Supreme Court not made in High Court—Whether appropriate to address issue—Whether basis in fact for making finding. **K E D (otherwise KC) v M C** [1987] 189, HC, SC.

Jurisdiction. *See* Jurisdiction—Appeal (*below*).

Occupier's liability
> Case tried in High Court on basis of duty owed to licensee—Whether appropriate for Supreme Court to decide case on basis of a different duty. **Rooney v Connolly** [1987] 768, SC.

Case stated
Jurisdiction. *See* Jurisdiction—Case stated (*below*).

Damages award
Appeal. *See* Appeal—Damages award (*above*).

Jurisdiction
Appeal
> Acquittal—Not guilty verdict in Central Criminal Court—Whether jurisdiction to hear appeal against acquittal—Constitution of Ireland 1937, Articles 34.3.1, 34.4.3, 38.1, 38.5, 38.6—Courts of Justice Act 1924, ss. 31, 63. **People (DPP) v O'Shea** (No 1) [1983] 549, SC.

> Central Criminal Court—Conviction of murder—Appeal direct to Supreme Court—Constitution of Ireland 1937, Article 34.4.3. **DPP v Lynch** [1981] 389, SC.

> Central Criminal Court—Not guilty verdict. *See* Jurisdiction—Appeal—Acquittal (*above*).

SUPREME COURT
Jurisdiction
Appeal continued
Damages—Whether Supreme Court may substitute its own assessment of damages for those made by a jury in the High Court—Constitution of Ireland 1937, Article 34.4.3—Courts of Justice Act 1924, s. 96. **Holohan v Donoghue** [1986] 250, SC.

Discretionary order—High Court judge—Whether judgment only to be set aside if judge had erred in principle. **Jack O'Toole Ltd v MacEoin Kelly Associates** [1987] 269, SC.

High Court decision—"From all decisions of the High Court"—Interpretation—Whether includes jurisdiction to hear appeal against acquittal—Constitution of Ireland 1937, Article 34.4.3. **People (DPP) v O'Shea (No 1)** [1983] 549, SC.

High Court decision—Whether decision in existence—Interlocutory injunction proceedings—High Court deciding to refer certain questions to Court of Justice—Whether decision by the High Court declining to grant an injunction constitutes a decision appealable to the Supreme Court. **SPUC Ireland Ltd v Grogan** [1990] 350, SC.

Malicious injuries—Application for compensation—Application dismissed on appeal by High Court—Whether substantive appeal lies to Supreme Court—Courts of Justice Act 1936, ss. 38, 39—Malicious Injuries Act 1981, ss. 17, 18—Constitution of Ireland 1937, Article 34 4 3. **W J Prendergast & Son Ltd v Carlow Co Council** [1990] 749, SC.

Patent appeal—Decision of Controller—Appeal to the High Court—Whether further appeal to the Supreme Court—Statute—Interpretation—Object and intent of achievement of uniformity in patent decisions—Patents Act 1964, ss. 15, 75(7). **Beechams Group Ltd v Bristol Myers** [1983] 500, SC.

Re-trial—Appeal against acquittal—Appeal allowed—Whether Supreme Court empowered to order re-trial—Whether consistent with principle of *autrefois acquit*—Whether re-trial would result in arbitrary discrimination—Constitution of Ireland 1937, Articles 34 4, 40 1—Criminal Procedure Act 1967, s. 34(1)—RSC 1986, O 87. **People (DPP) v Quilligan (No 2)** [1989] 245, SC.

Time limit—Extension—Appeal from High Court—Whether Supreme Court has same powers as High Court to extend time for appeal—RSC 1962, O 58 r 8, O 108 r 7, O 111 r 1. **Hughes v O'Rourke** [1986] 538, SC.

Case stated
Case stated from High Court—Landlord and tenant—Compensation award—Appeal—Function of Supreme Court in answering case stated. **Aherne v Southern Metropole Hotel** [1989] 693, SC.

Case stated under Article 40.4.3 of the Constitution—Extradition—Order extending Part II of the 1965 Act to the USA—Whether such order a 'law' within the meaning of Article 40.4.3, so as to allow High Court to state a case to the Supreme Court—Whether 'one judgment' rule applied—Constitution of Ireland 1937, Articles 15 2 1, 29 5 2, 34 4 5, 40 4 3—Extradition Act 1965, ss. 4, 8(1)—Extradition Act 1965 (Part II) Order 1984. **State (Gilliland) v Governor of Mountjoy Prison** [1987] 278, SC.

Consultative case stated from Circuit Court to Supreme Court—Evidence not completed in Circuit Court—Whether Supreme Court prevented from answering the question raised in the case stated—Courts of Justice Act 1947,s 16. **Doyle v Hearne** [1988] 318, SC.

Precedent
Stare decisis
Decision not followed—Reconsideration of ratio decidendi. **Costello v DPP** [1984] 413, SC.

Earlier decision overruled where legal principle incorrectly applied. **Finucane v McMahon** [1990] 505, SC.

SUPREME COURT
Precedent
Stare decisis continued
Previous decision of Supreme Court on issue of when case stated lies—Interpretation of relevant statutory provision—Whether compelling reasons for departing from court's previous interpretation—Status of three-judge court decisions. **Doyle v Hearne** [1988] 318, SC.

Reference to European Court of Justice
Issue arising for first time—Consideration of mandatory reference—Treaty of Rome 1957, Art. 177. **Macken v O'Reilly** [1979] 79, HC, SC.

SURETY
Charge to bank to secure loan to company
Associated company acting as surety
Directors also guaranteeing loan—Default in repayments—Proceedings against corporate surety—Decree—Appeal pending—Proceedings also instituted against directors—Whether doctrine of marshalling applicable. **Lombard & Ulster Banking Ltd v Murray** [1987] 522, HC.

Deed of bond
Deferred payment of excise duty
Whether necessary for creditor to have resort to securities received by the creditor from the principal before proceedings against the surety—Excise Collection and Management Act 1841, s. 24. **Attorney General v Sun Alliance and London Insurances Ltd** [1985] 522, SC.

SURGEON *See* MEDICAL PRACTITIONER (Surgeon).

SURVIVAL OF CAUSE OF ACTION
Death of respondent
Whether claim should proceed against the personal representatives. See ACTION (Cause—Survival).

SUSPENSION
Employee. *See* EMPLOYMENT (Suspension).

Garda Síochána. *See* GARDA SÍOCHÁNA (Discipline—Suspension).

Pupil. *See* EDUCATION (School—Discipline).

TAOISEACH
Dissolution of Dáil Éireann
Constitutional duty to advise President
Whether courts can prevent the Taoiseach from advising the President to dissolve Dáil Éireann—Constitution of Ireland 1937, Articles 13.2.1, 13.2.2, 13.8.1, 16.3.1. **O'Malley v An Taoiseach** [1990] 461, HC.

TAPE RECORDINGS
Evidence
Admissibility
Telephone calls—whether defect in quality affects admissibility—Whether recording of telephone call made to person not then on trial admissible if part of a transaction as a whole. **People (DPP) v Prunty** [1986] 716, CCA.

TAXATION *See* REVENUE.
Costs. *See* COSTS (Taxation).

TAXATION *continued*
Local. *See* RATING AND VALUATION

TEACHER
Appointment. *See* EDUCATION (Teacher—Appointment).

Dismissal. *See* EDUCATION (Teacher—Dismissal).

TELEPHONE CALLS
Tape recording
Evidence
Admissibility—Hearsay. *See* TAPE RECORDINGS.

Tapping
Right to privacy
Breach—Damages—Whether plaintiffs entitled to punitive or aggravated damages—
Constitution of Ireland 1937, Article 40 3—Civil Liability Act 1961, ss. 7(2), 14(4).
Kennedy v Ireland [1988] 472, HC.

TELEVISION *See* BROADCASTING.

TEMPORARY DWELLINGS
Caravan site
Unauthorised use
Area zoned as agricultural land in development plan—Use of land to store caravans
and fuel oils—Whether intensification or abandonment of use—Whether exempted
development. **Furlong v A F & G W McConnell Ltd** [1990] 48, HC.

Unlicensed caravan site
County Council prohibiting the erection or retention of any temporary dwellings on
the site—Whether order void—Natural justice. *See* LOCAL GOVERNMENT (Sanitary
services—Temporary dwellings).

Travelling community
Serviced halting sites
Whether housing authority under a statutory duty to provide serviced sites for
plaintiffs. *See* HOUSING (Travelling community).

TENANCY AT WILL
Occupation of lands with consent of owner
Occupation continuing
Whether tenancy at will created. *See* LIMITATION OF ACTIONS (Land—Adverse pos-
session—Occupation of lands with approval and consent of owner).

TENANCY *See* LANDLORD AND TENANT.

TESTAMENTARY SUCCESSION *See* WILL

TESTATOR
Moral duty
Family provision. *See* SUCCESSION (Family provision).

THEATRE
Rent
Quantum
New tenancy application. **Olympia Productions Ltd v Olympia Theatres Ltd** [1981]
424, HC.

New tenancy application. **Eamonn Andrews Productions Ltd v Gaiety Theatre (Dublin)
Ltd** [1976–7] 119, HC.

TIME
Computation. *See also* TIME LIMIT (Computation of time).
"Week"
Redundancy compensation—Continuity of employment—Meaning of "week".
Gormley v McCartin Brothers (Engineering) Ltd [1982] 215, EAT.

TIME LIMIT *See also* DELAY.
Case stated
District Justice signing case stated after expiration of six month period
Whether High Court jurisdiction to hear appeal—District Court Rules 1955, r 17.
McMahon v McClafferty [1990] 32, HC.

Computation of time
Service of notice
Statute—Interpretation—Planning decision—Planning authority required to make and give notice of their decision within five weeks of final determination—Time expiring on a Sunday—Registered letter containing notice of refusal received after expiry of period—Whether notice given within period. *See* PLANNING (Decision—Time for giving—Computation of period).

Extension
Appeal
Appeal against conviction—Criteria to be considered—Whether documents served out of time irregular or void—RSC 1962, O 86 rr 5, 8, 40. **People (DPP) v Kelly** [1982] 1, SC.

Appeal from High Court to Supreme Court—Whether Supreme Court has same powers as High Court to extend time for appeal—RSC 1962, O 58 r 8, O 108 r 70, O 111, r 1. **Hughes v O'Rourke** [1986] 538, SC.

Arbitration
Agreement to refer disputes to arbitration—Time limit—Whether undue hardship caused by refusal to extend time—Arbitration Act 1954, ss. 3(1), 42, 45. **Walsh v Shield Insurance Co Ltd** [1976–7] 218, HC.

Certiorari. See CERTIORARI (Time limit).

Statement of claim
Proceedings instituted on behalf of infant sixteen years after cause of action accrued—Whether delay unreasonable—Statute of Limitations 1957, s. 49—Convention for the Protection of Human Rights and Fundamental Freedoms (1950) Art 6(1). **O'Domhnaill v Merrick** [1985] 40, SC.

Initiation of claim
Unfair dismissal claim
Notice in writing—Whether mandatory requirement on employee to notify employer within six months of date of dismissal—Statute—Interpretation—Unfair Dismissals Act 1977, s. 8. **IBM (Ireland) Ltd v Feeney** [1983] 50, CC.

Statute
Interpretation
Malicious injuries claim—Proceedings commenced outside statutory period—Whether court power to extend time—Malicious Injuries Act 1981, ss. 8, 14, 23. **Dublin Corporation v Murdon Ltd** [1988] 86, HC.

Planning decision—Time for goving notice of decision—Computation of period. *See* PLANNING (Decision—time for giving—Computation of period).

TITLE
Goods
Contract for sale of goods
Retention of title clause. *See* SALE OF GOODS (Retention of title clause).

TITLE *continued*
Land. *See* REGISTRATION OF TITLE.

TORT
Assault
Arrest. See FALSE IMPRISONMENT (Arrest).

False imprisonment
Person of unsound mind. *See* FALSE IMPRISONMENT (Person of unsound mind).

Breach of confidence
Injunction sought to restrain publication
Book written by deceased member of British intelligence service—Whether different criteria applied to government information—Constitution of Ireland 1937, Article 40 6 1. **Attorney General for England and Wales v Brandon Book Publishers Ltd** [1987] 135, HC.

Conspiracy
Inducement of breach of contract
Contract of employment. *See* Inducement of breach of contract—Conspiracy—Employment (*below*).

Constitutional right
Infringement
Whether tort. **Kearney v Minister for Justice** [1987] 52, HC.

Interference
Claim for damages—Whether such claim a claim in tort. **Hayes v Ireland** [1987] 651, HC.

Constitutional tort
Constitutional obligations of the State
Breach—Invalid inquiry—Garda Síochána disciplinary investigation—Whether plaintiff entitled to costs and expenses of his representation and attendance at the inquiry—Appropriate defendant—Constitution of Ireland 1937—Garda Síochána (Discipline) Regulations 1971, reg 8. **McHugh v Commissioner of An Garda Síochána** [1987] 181, SC.

Conversion
Damages for conversion
Assessment—Copyright—Infringement—Whether plaintiff entitled to damages for conversion under s. 24 in addition to damages for infringement under s. 22—Copyright Act 1963, ss. 22, 24. **Allibert s. A v O'Connor** [1982] 40, HC.

Damages. *See* DAMAGES.

Defamation. *See* DEFAMATION.

Employer's liability. *See* NEGLIGENCE (Employer).

False imprisonment. *See* FALE IMPRISONMENT.

Inducement of breach of contract
Collateral contract
Whether contract in existence—Whether injunction lies—Balance of convenience—Relevance of foreign arbitration clause. **Mitchelstown Co-operative Society Ltd v Societe des Produits Nestle SA** [1989] 582, SC.

Conspiracy
Employment—Plaintiff offered position as principal of a primary school—Pressure exerted on manager to cancel appointment—Plaintiff not member of trade union—Appointment subsequently cancelled—Whether manager in breach of contract—Whether defendants induced such breach—Whether defendants engaged in an actionable conspiracy. **Cotter v Ahern** [1976–7] 248, HC.

TORT
Inducement of breach of contract
Conspiracy continued
Employment—Trade dispute—Whether contract of employment in existence—Sub-contractor—Trade union in dispute with employer of sub-contractor—Contract terminated—Application for interlocutory injunction—Whether appropriate to grant injunction in respect of continuing picketing. **J Bradbury Ltd v Duffy** [1979] 51, HC.

Exclusive supply contract
Purchaser subsequently entering into similar contract with another supplier—Whether inducement of breach of contract—Position of person who innocently enters into contract without knowledge of prior inconsistent contract—Whether under duty to cease supplies. **Flogas Ltd v Ergas Ltd** [1985] 221, HC.

Supplier subsequently terminating contract and entering into agreement with another purchaser—Application for interlocutory injunction—Whether fair *prima facie* case—Whether damages adequate remedy. **Reno Engrais et Produits Chemiques s. A v Irish Agricultural Wholesale Society Ltd** [1976–7] 179, HC.

Intimidation. *See* INTIMIDATION.

Liability for animals. *See* ANIMALS (Negligence—Liability of owner).

Libel. *See* DEFAMATION.

Limitation of actions. *See* LIMITATION OF ACTIONS (Negligence).

Malicious abuse of process of the courts
Claim for damages
Whether such action lay in respect of instituting a civil action—Ingredients of such tort—Meaning of malice—Proof of damage—Cause of loss. **Dorene Ltd v Suedes (Ireland) Ltd** [1982] 126, HC.

Negligence. *See* NEGLIGENCE.

Nuisance. *See* NUISANCE.

Passing off. *See* PASSING OFF.

Personal injury
Damages. See DAMAGES (Personal injuries).

Road traffic accident. *See* NEGLIGENCE (Road traffic accidents).

Trespass. *See* TRESPASS.

Unlawful interference with economic interests
Mandatory interlocutory injunction sought
Principles on which such injunctions granted. **Bula Ltd v Tara Mines Ltd** [1988] 157, HC.

Vicarious liability. *See* NEGLIGENCE (Vicarious liability).

TOUR OPERATOR
Licence
Breach of condition
Decision to revoke—Appeal to High Court—Whether applicant fit and proper to carry on business—Power of High Court on appeal—Transport (Tour Operators and Travel Agents) Act 1982, ss. 8(2)(b), 9(2), (3), (4)—RSC O 102. **Balkan Tours Ltd v Minister for Communications** [1988] 101, HC.

TOWN AGENT
Costs
Taxation
Whether taxing master entitled to disallow claim. *See* COSTS (Taxation—Review—Town agent's charges).

TOWN AND COUNTRY PLANNING *See* PLANNING.

TRACING
Money paid in error
Claim for repayment
Whether tracing available. In re Irish Shipping Ltd [1986] 518, HC.

TRADE
Casual trading. *See* CASUAL TRADING.

Conditions of trade
Exemption clause
Whether reasonable notice given of the conditions of trade—Whether parties competent to include exemption clause. **Western Meats Ltd v National Ice and Cold Storage Co Ltd** [1982] 99, HC.

Markets and fairs
Casual trading licence
Franchise to carry on market and fair—Failure to hold market or fair—Legislation regulating carrying on of markets and fairs by licence—Whether franchise survived legislation even though not in use—Statute—Interpretation—Singular including plural—Interpretation Act 1937, s. 11(a)—Casual Trading Act 1980, ss. 1, 2(2)(h), 3, 5, 9. **Skibbereen UDC v Quill** [1986] 170, HC.

Restraint. *See* RESTRAINT OF TRADE.

Restrictive practices. *See* RESTRICTIVE PRACTICES.

TRADE DISPUTE
Connection with employer
Non-employment
Meaning—Refusal of employer to employ some but not all members of trade union—Trade Disputes Act 1906, ss. 3, 5. **J Bradbury Ltd v Duffy and Whelan** [1979] 51, HC.

Constitutional right
Interference
Right to free primary education—Action for damages—Whether such claim a claim in tort—Constitution of Ireland 1937, Article 42 2—Trade Disputes Act 1906, s. 4. **Hayes v Ireland** [1987] 651, HC.

Contempt of court
Factory occupation
Injunction—Deliberate disobedience—No serious effort to purge contempt—Nature of court's jurisdiction—Whether defendants be committed to prison—Prohibition of Forcible Entry and Occupation Act 1971. **Ross Co Ltd v Swan** [1981] 416, HC.

Contract of employment
Whether contract in existence
Sub-contractor—Trade union in dispute with employer of sub-contractor—Whether protection of legislation available—Trade Disputes Act 1906, s. 3. **J Bradbury Ltd v Duffy and Whelan** [1979] 51, HC.

Occupation of factory premises
Unlawful occupation. See Contempt of court (*above*).

Picketing
Injunction
Dispute over termination of contract—Whether picketing entitled to statutory protection—Contractual relationship—Whether picketer an employee of the plaintiff—Whether plaintiff the employer of the picketer—Trade Disputes Act 1906, ss. 2, 5(3)—Constitution of Ireland 1937, Art 40. **Lamb Bros Dublin Ltd v Davidson** [1978] 226, HC.

TRADE DISPUTE
Picketing
Injunction continued
Whether contract in existence—Whether appropriate to grant injunction in respect of continuing picketing. **J Bradbury Ltd v Duffy** [1979] 51, HC.

TRADE EFFLUENT. *See* LOCAL GOVERNMENT (Public health—Sewer)

TRADE MARK
Decision of Controller
Whether Controller required to give reasons for his decision
Applicant wishing to appeal—Trade Marks Act 1963, ss. 25, 26, 34, 56—RSC O 94 r 46—Trade Marks Rules 1963, rr 43, 70. **Anheuser Busch Inc v Controller of Patents** [1988] 247, HC.

Infringement
Innocent user of registered trade mark
Campaign to help members of the public give up smoking—Whether actionable—Campaign built around imitation pack of cigarettes—Whether mark used 'in relation to' cigarettes—Whether mark used 'in the course of trade'—Trade Marks Act 1963, s. 12. **Gallaher Ltd v Health Education Bureau** [1982] 240, HC.

Similar goods with similar marks
Whether likelihood of direct confusion—Trade Marks Act 1963, ss. 12(1), 20(1). **Industrie Buitoni Perugina s. P A v Dowdall O'Mahony & Co** [1978] ILRM 116, HC.

Soft drink
"Tango"—Marketing of product ceasing—Application for removal of mark from register—Use resumed shortly before application—Whether resumed user bona fide—Trade Marks Act 1963, s. 34(1)(3)—Trade Marks Rules 1963, Schedule 2 class 32. **Beecham Group Ltd v Goodalls of Ireland Ltd** [1978] 106, HC.

Passing off. *See* PASSING OFF.

Patents. *See* PATENTS.

Registration
"Bubble Up"
Non-alcoholic beverage—Opposition by owners of registered mark "7-Up" and "Seven-Up"—Whether proposed mark capable of distinguishing—Whether mark likely to deceive or cause confusion—Trade Marks Act 1963, ss. 18(1) and (2), 19, 20. **Seven-Up Co v Bubble Up Co Inc** [1990] 204, HC.

"Crocodile"
Refusal—Distinctiveness—Whether mark inherently capable of distinguishing the goods—Whether mark likely to deceive—Trade Marks Act 1963, ss. 17, 18, 19. **La Chemise Lacoste s. A v Controller of Patents** [1978] 8, SC.

"Dent"
Rare surname—Refusal—Whether evidence of distinctiveness—Whether mark inherently capable of distinguishing the goods—Trade Marks Act 1963, ss. 17, 18. **A Dent & Co Ltd v Controller of Patents** [1978] 12, HC.

"Durex"
Refusal—Appeal—Extent to which controller entitled to seek information from applicant—Whether mark's use would be deceptive or confusing. **LRS International Ltd v Controller of Patents, Designs and Trade Marks** [1976–7] 164, HC.

"Golden pages"
Refusal—Classified telephone directories—Whether directories constitute goods—Whether 'connection in the course of trade' necessitates sale—Whether words descriptive of the goods produced—Trade Marks Act 1963, ss. 2(1), 17. **ITT World Directories Inc v Controller of Patents, Designs and Trade Marks** [1985] 30, SC.

TRADE MARK
Registration *continued*
"High life"
Refusal—Distinctiveness—Whether capable of distinguishing applicant's goods—Trade Marks Act 1963, ss. 17(1), 18. **Miller Brewing Co v Controller of Patents** [1988] 259, SC.

"Kiku"
Refusal—Perfumes and toiletries—Whether mark direct reference to character of the goods—Foreign words—Whether word apt to distinguish—Trade Marks Act 1963, s. 17—Trade Marks Rules 1963, r 19(4). **Faberge Inc v The Controller of Patents, Designs and Trade Marks** [1976–7] 335, HC, SC.

"SAF"
Refusal—Whether mark a collection of letters or an invented word—Registration under Part A or B—Extent to which mark distinctive—Trade Marks 1963, s. 17 (1) (c). **Soudure Autogene Francaise v Controller of Patents** [1982] 207, HC.

"Waterford"
Refusal—Distinctiveness—Geographical name—Mark factually distinctive of goods—Whether 'inherently capable of distinguishing'—Trade Marks Act 1963, ss. 17, 18(2)(b), 58(3). **Waterford Glass Ltd v Controller of Patents, Designs and Trade Marks** [1981] 91, HC; [1984] 565, SC.

Removal from register
Application refused
Whether controller required to give reasons—Applicant wishing to appeal—Trade Marks Act 1963, ss. 25, 26, 34, 56—RSC O 94 r 46—Trade Marks Rules 1963, rr 43, 70. **Anheuser Busch Inc v Controller of Patents** [1988] 247, HC.

TRADE NAMES AND DESIGNS
Passing off. *See* PASSING OFF.

TRADE UNION
Collective agreement
Equal pay
Agreement providing for the implementation of a unisex salary structure—Whether agreement binding on all members of the union. **PMPA v 15 Insurance Officials** [1982] 367, LC.

Discipline
Irish Congress of Trade Unions
Disciplinary powers—Complaint to ICTU executive council—Whether injunction be granted restraining executive council from considering a resolution to impose any sanction on union—ICTU Constitution, cl. 41. **Irish Distributive & Administrative Trade Union v Carroll** [1988] 713, HC.

Dispute
Interference with constitutional right
Right to free primary education—Action for damages—Whether such claim a claim in tort—Constitution of Ireland 1937, Article 42 2—Trade Disputes Act 1906, s. 4. **Hayes v Ireland** [1987] 651, HC.

Freedom of association
Constitution
Garda Síochána—Statute—Validity—Rights of members of Garda Representative Association and Association of Garda Sergeants and Inspectors—Limitation of ranks within the Garda Síochána—Rights of freedom of association for members of Garda Síochána—Limitation on extent to which members of the force may organize—Garda Síochána Act 1977, s. 1—Constitution of Ireland 1937, Article 40 6 1(iii). **Aughey v Attorney General** [1986] 206, HC; [1989] 87, SC.

TRADE UNION
Freedom of association
Constitution continued
Right to dissociate—Teacher—Appointment—Teacher not member of trade union—Pressure exerted to cancel appointment—Appointment cancelled—Whether defendants engaged in actionable conspiracy to cause plaintiff to abandon his constitutional right to dissociate. **Cotter v Ahern** [1976–7] 248, HC.

Meeting
Resolution
Validity—Resolution for introduction of a compulsory retirement scheme—Resolution passed—Plaintiff not present when vote taken—Whether resolution valid—Whether natural justice infringed—Whether infringement of plaintiff's right to work—Constitution of Ireland 1937, Arts 40 3 1, 45. **Rogers v Irish Transport and General Workers' Union** [1978] 51, HC.

Negotiation licence
Public interest
Application for declaration—Opportunity for other trade unions to give evidence—Whether reasonable notice given of application—Trade Union Act 1971, s. 3. **Post Office Workers Union v Minister for Labour** [1981] 355, HC.

Application for declaration—Staff association disaffiliating from a trade union—Association unable to carry on negotiations for the fixing of wages and other conditions of employment without a licence—Refusal by Minister to confer 'excepted body' status—Statutory conditions for the grant of licence not satisfied—Whether granting of licence against the public interest—Trade Union Act 1941, ss. 6, 7—Trade Union Act 1971, ss. 2, 3. **Irish Aviation Executive Staff Association v Minister for Labour** [1981] 350, HC.

Staff association. *See* STAFF ASSOCIATIONS.

TRAFFIC ACCIDENTS *See* ROAD TRAFFIC ACCIDENTS.

TRAFFIC OFFENCES *See* ROAD TRAFFIC OFFENCES.

TRANSPORT
Canal
Lack of maintenance
Breach of statutory duty—Negligence. *See* CANAL.

Ferry service
Suspension
Ferry service from Ireland to Wales—Suspension of service by decision of British government minister. *See* CONTRACT (Statutory duty—Substitution by agreement of parties for statutory obligations).

Tour operator
Licence
Breach of condition—Decision to revoke—Appeal to High Court—Whether applicant fit and proper to carry on business. *See* TOUR OPERATOR (Licence).

TRAVEL
Right to travel
Injunction application to restrain travel abroad
Irish rugby football tour of South Africa—Whether tour in breach of plaintiff's constitutional rights—Whether injunction be granted—Constitutional rights to travel and play rugby abroad. **Lennon v Ganly** [1981] 84, HC.

TRAVEL AGENT *See* TOUR OPERATOR.

TRAVELLING COMMUNITY
Housing
Halting sites
Whether housing authority under a statutory duty to provide serviced sites for plaintiffs—Whether State under a constitutional duty to provide such sites—Claim for damages for alleged breach of constitutional duty by State. *See* HOUSING (Travelling community).

TREASURE TROVE
Chattel found in land
Finder trespassing
Chattel part of ancient hoard—Whether finder entitled to reward—Factors to be taken into consideration—National Monuments Act 1930, ss. 8, 14(1), 26. **Webb v Ireland** [1988] 565, HC, SC.

Royal prerogative
Whether such prerogative carried over into Irish law
Whether necessary ingredient of sovereignty—Constitution of Ireland 1937, Articles 5, 10. **Webb v Ireland** [1988] 565, HC, SC.

TREATY
Validity
Constitution. See CONSTITUTION (International relations—Treaty).

TRESPASS
Animals
Cattle wandering onto cemetery
Cattle poisoned by eating yew leaves—Wall between pastureland and cemetery damaged—Whether local authority negligent or in breach of statutory duty in not having wall repaired—Duty of care. **Walsh v Kilkenny Co Council** [1978] 1, HC.

Criminal offence
Entering premises as trespasser and stealing therein
Evidence of owner—Whether offence established—Whether accused entered as trespasser—Distinction between breaking and entering—Larceny Act 1916, s. 23—Criminal Law (Jurisdiction) Act 1976, s. 6. **Travers v Ryan** [1985] 343, HC.

Defence
Entitlement
Right of way—Trespasser claiming right of way—Absence of defined path—Evidence of user—Whether use of the way over the land sufficient in extent and regularity—Whether knowledge of such user to be imputed to the owner of the land. **Flanagan v Mulhall** [1985] 134, HC.

Ejectment
Action for possession
Conveyance of family home without consent of wife—Purchaser taking up residence—Supreme Court declaring conveyance void—Application by wife for possession—Whether Supreme Court order vested leasehold interest in wife—Family Home Protection Act 1976, ss. 3(1), 4(1), 5. **Weir v Somers** [1983] 343, SC.

Plaintiff's lands built on by defendants—Court's exercise of equitable jurisdiction to refuse order for possession. **McMahon v Kerry Co Council** [1981] 419, HC.

Factory occupation
Trade dispute
Prohibition of Foreceable Entry and Occupation Act 1971 —Injunction—Deliberate disobedience—Contempt of court. **Ross Co Ltd v Swan** [1981] 416, HC.

TRESPASS *continued*
Injury to trespasser
Occupier's liability
Contribution—Architects—Foreseeability. *See* NEGLIGENCE (Occupier—Contribution—Foreseeability).

Landlord
Intimidation
Quiet and peaceable enjoyment—Interference—Damages—Whether aggravated damages be awarded. **Whelan v Madigan** [1978] 136, HC.

TRIAL
Action. *See* ACTION.

Adjournment. *See* ADJOURNMENT.

Costs. *See* COSTS.

Courts. *See* COURTS.

Criminal trial. *See* CONSTITUTION (Trial of offences); CRIMINAL LAW (Trial).

Evidence. *See* EVIDENCE.

Judge. *See* JUDGE.

Jury. *See* JURY.

Practice. *See* PRACTICE (Trial)

TRIBUNAL
Army Pensions Board
Natural justice
Application for widow's allowance rejected—Denial of oral hearing—Refusal to furnish evidence on which decision based—Whether in breach of natural justice. *See* NATURAL AND CONSTITUTIONAL JUSTICE (Defence Forces—Army Pensions Board).

Decision
Error in law
Rent tribunal—Application to fix gross rent—Dispute over landlord's income—Tribunal refusing tenant's request for more information as to landlord's means—Whether tribunal erred in law—Housing (Private Rented Dwellings) Act 1982, s. 13. **Quirke v Folio Homes Ltd** [1988] 496, SC.

Judicial review
Certiorari (*generally*). *See* CERTIORARI.

Criminal Injuries Compensation Tribunal—Compensation award—Whether decision subject to judicial review—Whether Tribunal acted contrary to natural justice. **State (Hayes) v Criminal Injuries Compensation Tribunal** [1982] 210, HC.

Reasonableness
Whether decision at variance with reason and common sense—Test of irrationality—Purpose of remedy of judicial review—Function of court. **State (Keegan) v Stardust Victims Compensation Tribunal** [1987] 202, HC, SC.

Whether decision at variance with reason and common sense—Whether inference from facts open to tribunal—Whether tribunal obliged to give reasons for decision—Certiorari—Scheme of Compensation for Personal Injuries Criminally Inflicted 1974, rule 4(d). **State (Creedon) v Criminal Injuries Compensation Tribunal** [1989] 104, SC.

Certiorari—Whether at variance with reason and common sense—Whether inference from facts open to tribunal—Whether tribunal obliged to give reasons for decision—Scheme of Compensation for Personal Injuries Criminally Inflicted 1974, rule 4(d). **State (Creedon) v Criminal Injuries Compensation Tribunal** [1989] 104, SC.

TRIBUNAL
Decision
Reasons continued
Whether obligation to furnish reasons for decision—Trade marks—Decision of Controller. *See* TRADE MARK (Decision of Controller—Whether Controller required to give reasons for his decision).

Whether obligation to furnish reasons for decision. **State (Creedon) v Criminal Injuries Compensation Tribunal** [1989] 104, SC.

Validity
Employment—Appointment—Teacher—Appeal Board ruling appointee ineligible—Whether appointment valid—Whether tribunal acted improperly. **Ahern v de Hora** [1980] 203, HC.

Disciplinary powers
Exercise
Natural justice—Garda Síochána. *See* GARDA SIOCHÁNA (Discipline).

Natural justice—Trade unions—Irish Congress of Trade Unions. *See* TRADE UNION (Discipline).

Dismissal
Requirements of natural justice. See NATURAL AND CONSTITUTIONAL JUSTICE (Employment—Dismissal).

Validity
Bias—Predisposition to dismiss—Whether such affects validity of dismissal—Judicial review—Function of court—Whether court entitled to review exercise of discretion where tribunal acted honestly and reasonably. **McGrath v Maynooth College** [1979] 166, SC.

Garda probationer—Previous breaches of of discipline as basis for dismissal—Pending inquiry into breach of discipline discontinued—Whether dismissal *ultra vires*—Garda Síochána (Appointments) Regulations 1945, arts 8, 9. **State (Burke) v Garvey** [1979] 232, SC.

Employment appeals. *See* EMPLOYMENT APPEALS TRIBUNAL.

Fair procedures
Duty to act judicially
Whether obligation to furnish reasons for decision. *See* TRADE MARK (Decision of Controller—Whether Controller required to give reasons for his decision).

Land Commission
Acquisition of lands—Objectors' application for sight of certain documents refused—Whether procedure adopted fair and in accordance with natural justice—Land Act 1965, ss. 12, 45. **State (Hussey) v Irish Land Commission** [1983] 407, HC.

Prison
Temporary release scheme—Revocation. *See* PRISONS (Temporary release scheme—Revocation of order).

Racing Board
Revocation of course betting permit—Whether valid—Whether Racing Board administering justice—Whether hearing contrary to natural justice—Racing Board and Racecourses Act 1945, s. 24—Constitution of Ireland 1937, Articles 37, 40. **McCann v Attorney General** [1983] 67, HC.

Industrial tribunals. *See* EMPLOYMENT APPEALS TRIBUNAL; LABOUR COURT.

Natural justice (generally). *See* NATURAL AND CONSTITUTIONAL JUSTICE.

Planning appeals board. *See* Planning (Appeal).

TRIBUNAL *continued*
  Powers
  Exercise
  Natural justice—Bord na Mona—Power to compulsorily acquire bogland—Whether power of judicial nature—Whether statutory provisions invalid—Absence of right of appeal—Whether procedures adopted in breach of natural justice—Constitution of Ireland 1937, Articles 40 3, 43—Turf Development Act 1946, ss. 17, 28, 30–36. **O'Brien v Bord na Mona** [1983] 314, HC.

TRUST
  Charitable trusts. *See* CHARITY (Cy-pres).

  Construction
  Marriage settlement
  Original deed of settlement destroyed by fire—Whether secondary evidence of the contents of the deed admissible—Construction of admitted document—Whether parties take trust property in equal shares or whether they enjoy life interests only. **Savage v Nolan** [1978] 151, HC.

  Will trust
  Power of appointment—No disposition in default of appointment—Executor unable to carry out the trusts in the manner directed by the testator. **Tuite v Tuite** [1978] 197, HC.

  Constructive trust
  Money paid in error
  Claim for repayment—Whether tracing available—Mixed fund—Whether money held in trust—Whether subject to set off—Purpose of constructive trust. **In re Irish Shipping Ltd** [1986] 518, HC.

  Whether breach
  Effect of proceedings establishing equitable interest in property on mortgage executed subsequent to registration of lis pendens—Whether equitable interest entitled to priority over mortgagee's interest. **In re Kelly's Carpetdrome Ltd: Byrne v UDT Bank Ltd** [1984] 418, SC.

  Contractual rights
  Agreement for the supply of milk
  Sale of supplier's creameries—Undertaking in contract of sale as to no diminution on the supply—No collateral agreement between purchaser and new owner—Dispute over requirements and prices—Whether new owner under any obligation to supply a specified quantity of milk—Whether a trust of contractual rights created—Estoppel. **Cadbury Ireland Ltd v Kerry Cooperative Creameries Ltd** [1982] 77, HC.

  Creation
  Company
  Insurance policy—Benefits stated to be payable to company—Whether intention to pay benefits to employees—Whether company holding benefits in trust for beneficiaries. **McCann v Irish Board Mills Ltd** [1980] 216, HC.

  Resulting trust
  Beneficial interest. *See* Resulting trust (*below*).

  Will
  Construction—Devise subject to condition—Whether words imperative—Whether subject certain—Whether trust created. **In re Sweeney: Hillary v Sweeney** [1976–7] 88, HC.

  Enforcement
  Clean hands doctrine
  Husband purchasing property in name of wife—Presumption of advancement rebutted—Husband procuring wife to make false declarations in conveyance—Husband

TRUST
Enforcement
Clean hands doctrine continued
subsequently invoking court's aid to enforce trust—Whether husband entitled to relief in equity—Finance (No 2)Act 1947, s. 13(1),(4) and (5), Finance Act 1951, s. 17, Land Act 1965, ss. 45(2)(a), 45(3)(b), Finance Act 1965, s. 66(6). **Parkes v Parkes** [1980] 137, HC.

Fiduciary duty
Property in fee simple subject to lease
Lease originally subject to a trust—Whether trust disclosed on the conveyance of the freehold—Freehold interest purchased by trustee of trusts for the leasehold interest—Whether fee simple interest taken upon same trusts. **Coyle v Central Trust Investment Society Ltd** [1978] 211, HC.

Marriage settlement
Construction. See Construction—Marriage settlement (*above*).

Matrimonial property
Beneficial interest
Resulting trust. *See* Resulting trust—Beneficial interest (*below*).

Powers
Alteration of objects of association
Whether *ultra vires* the deed of trust—Whether application by trustees of certain moneys a breach of trust. **McMillan v McMillan** [1976–7] 45, HC.

Resulting trust
Beneficial interest
House purchased in sole name of husband—Wife's application for declaration of her interest—Contribution by wife to family finances—Mortgage payments not met directly out of family finances—Whether wife contributed to the acquisition of the equity of redemption—Computation of beneficial share. **G v G** [1982] 155, HC.

Matrimonial home. *See* FAMILY LAW (Property—Beneficial interest).

Purchase of house by unmarried couple—Conveyance solely in man's name—Joint contribution to purchase price—Whether resulting trust to be inferred. **Power v Conroy** [1980] 31, HC.

Trust for sale
Whether created. *See* Will trust—Trust for sale (*below*).

Trustee Savings Bank
Trustee's agreement to purchase loan portfolio of commercial bank
Consent of Minister ultra vires his powers—Agreement in breach of statute—Whether rights acquired by trustees under agreement enforceable—Trustee Savings Bank Act 1863, s. 15—Trustee Savings Bank Act 1965, s. 3(1)—Trustee Savings Bank Act 1979, s. 1. **Hortensius Ltd and Durack v Bishop** [1989] 294, HC.

Will trust
Charitable gift
Cy-pres. *See* CHARITY (Cy-pres—Charitable gift—Will trusts).

Construction. See Construction—Will trust (*above*).

Trust for sale
Leasehold interest in property—Delay of over 20 years—Death of executor—Purchaser refusing to accept title from administrators de bonis non—Whether vendor, selling as personal representative, must satisfy purchaser that he has power to sell as such—Whether assent to establishment of trust should be inferred—Succession Act 1965, s. 51. **Crowley v Flynn** [1983] 513, HC.

TURF DEVELOPMENT
Compulsory purchase powers
Bord na Móna
Power to compulsorily acquire bogland—Whether power of judicial nature—Absence
of right of appeal—Whether statutory provisions invalid—Whether procedures adopted
in breach of natural justice—Constitution of Ireland 1937, Articles 40.3, 43—Turf
Development Act 1946, ss. 17, 28, 30–36. **O'Brien v Bord na Móna** [1983] 314, SC.

UBERRIMA FIDES
Insurance contract. *See* INSURANCE (Contract—Uberrima fides).

ULTRA VIRES
Administrative body
Regulation in restraint of trade
Equestrian Federation—Prohibition of use of non-Irish horses by Irish showjumpers
in international competitions. **Macken v O'Reilly** [1979] 79, HC, SC.

Administrative tribunal
Exercise of discretion
Judicial review—Whether court entitled to review exercise of discretion where tribunal
acted honestly and reasonably. **McGrath v Maynooth College** [1979] 166, SC.

Company
Commercial transation
Guarantee and mortgage—Transaction ultra vires powers of company—Notice—
Whether creditor had actual note of guarantee being *ultra vires*. *See* COMPANY (Ultra
vires).

Departmental circular
Social welfare
Fuel allowances—Departmental circular excluding persons on short term social
welfare—Whether *ultra vires* Minister for Social Welfare—Social Welfare (Supple-
mentary Welfare Allowances) Regulations 1977, art 6. **State (Kershaw) v Eastern
Health Board** [1985] 235, HC.

Director of Public Prosecutions
Delegation of carriage of case. See DIRECTOR OF PUBLIC PROSECUTIONS (Powers—
Delegation—Whether ultra vires).

District Court Rules. *See* DISTRICT COURT RULES (Validity).

Farm tax office
Discontinuance of farm tax
Termination of appointment of farm tax inspectors—Whether *ultra vires*—Judicial
review. *See* JUDICIAL REVIEW (Farm tax office—Discontinuance of farm tax).

Garda Síochána
Dismissal
Garda probationer—Previous breaches of discipline as basis for dismissal—Pending
inquiry into breach of discipline discontinued—Garda Síochána (Appointments)
Regulations 1945, arts 8, 9. **State (Burke) v Garvey** [1979] 232, SC.

Health board
General medical services scheme
Complaints of abuse of scheme—Referral of matter to Minister—Failure to inform
fully of nature of complaint—Whether referral *ultra vires*—Certiorari—Declaration—
Health Act 1970, s. 58. **O'Flynn v Mid-Western Health Board** [1990] 149, HC.

ULTRA VIRES *continued*

Health Service Regulations

Free general medical services

"Choice of doctor" scheme—Provision for investigation—Hearing—Whether natural justice disregarded. **State (Boyle) v General Medical Services (Payments) Board** [1981] 14, HC.

Housing authority

Allocation of houses

Allocation to person residing outside authority's functional area. **McNamee v Buncrana UDC** [1984] 77, HC, SC.

Local authority standing orders

Vacancy in county council. **McNelis v Donegal Co Council** [1978] 230, HC.

Minister. *See* MINISTER (*Ultra vires*).

Motor insurance regulations

Jurisdiction of Circuit Court to decide validity

Criminal appeal—Road Traffic Act 1961, s. 56—Road Traffic (Compulsory Insurance) Regulations 1962—Courts of Justice Act 1947, s. 16. **Greaney v Scully** [1981] 340, SC.

Planning authority

Agent representing that development exempt

Whether authority estopped from denying the development exempt—Whether representation *ultra vires* as being in breach of statutory provisions. **Dublin Corporation v McGrath** [1978] 208, HC.

Refusal of extension of planning permission

Whether irrelevant factors considered by planning authority. **State (McCoy) v Dun Laoghaire Corporation** [1985] 533, HC.

Preservation order

National monument. See NATIONAL MONUMENT (Preservation order).

Prison regulations

Access to legal advisers

Regulations excluding certain solicitors. *See* PRISONS (Regulations—Validity).

Revenue Commissioners

Notice requiring information

Whether notice ultra vires—Whether notice unduly burdensome and oppressive—Finance Act 1974, s. 59. **Warnock v Revenue Commissioners** [1986] 37, HC.

Rules of Court

District Court. See DISTRICT COURT RULES (Validity).

Superior Courts Rules Committee

Non-party discovery—Power of court to order discovery against third party. *See* DISCOVERY (Non-party discovery—Rule of court).

Social welfare regulations. *See* SOCIAL WELFARE (Regulations—Validity).

Trust

Powers

Alteration of objects of association—Whether *ultra vires* the deed of trust—Whether application by trustees of certain moneys a breach of trust. **McMillan v McMillan** [1976–7] 45, HC.

Trustee Savings Bank

Trustee's agreement to purchase loan portfolio of commercial bank

Consent of Minister *ultra vires* his powers. *See* TRUST (Trustee Savings Bank).

UNAUTHORISED DEVELOPMENT
Enforcement of planning control. *See* PLANNING (Enforcement—Unauthorised development).

UNBORN, RIGHT TO LIFE OF. *See* CONSTITUTION (Personal rights—Right to life of unborn).

UNDUE INFLUENCE
Deed
Transfer of land
Reservation of right of residence, care and support—Application to cancel transfer—Whether undue influence—Whether deed improvident. **Leonard v Leonard** [1988] 245, HC.

Duress
Marriage
Nullity proceedings. *See* MARRIAGE (Nullity—Duress).

Practice
Particulars
Probate application—Claim that the making of the will was procured by undue influence—Whether full particulars of undue influence required—RSC O 19 r 5, O 111. **In re Rutledge: Hanly v Finnerty** [1981] 198, HC.

Will. *See* WILL (Validity—Undue influence).

UNEMPLOYMENT BENEFIT
Offence
False statements
Minor offence—Number of similar offences charged in the one summons—District Court—Jurisdiction. **State (Wilson) v Neilan** [1987] 118, HC.

UNFAIR DISMISSALS. *See* EMPLOYMENT (Unfair dismissal).

UNIONS *See* TRADE UNION.

UNITED NATIONS SERVICE
Injury to Irish soldier. *See* DEFENCE FORCES (Negligence—Duty of care—UN service—Injury to soldier).

UNIVERSITY
Committee of discipline
Charge of plagiarism
Natural justice—Whether fair procedures followed—Whether committee required to act judicially. **Flanagan v University College Dublin** [1989] 469, HC.

Pontifical university
Seminary
Dismissal of teacher—Whether discrimination in dismissing teacher—Teacher also priest—Seminary obtaining funds from State—Funds applied for lay purposes as recognised college of university—Whether primarily seminary or university—Natural justice. Constitution of Ireland 1937, Articles 44.2.3, 44.2.5—Maynooth College Establishment Act 1795, s. 3—Irish Universities Act 1908, s. 2(4)—Higher Education Authority Act 1971, s. 1(c). **McGrath and O'Ruairc v Maynooth College** [1979] 166, SC.

Whether rules of pontifical university part of canon law—Whether recognisable in court of law. **McGrath v Maynooth College** [1979] 166, SC.

Teacher
Terms of office
Teacher accepting post on basis of adhering to college statutes—Certain statutes in disuse—Whether affecting validity of dismissal under other provisions of statutes—Whether statutes inimical of academic freedom—College also pontifical university—

UNIVERSITY
Teacher
Terms of office continued
Whether rules of pontifical university part of canon law—Whether recognisable in court of law. **McGrath v Maynooth College** [1979] 166, SC.

UNJUST ENRICHMENT
Action for possession
Plaintiff's lands built on by defendants
Court's exercise of equitable jurisdiction to refuse order for possession. **McMahon v Kerry Co Council** [1981] 419, HC.

Copyright
Infringement
Compilation—Reliance on copyright owner's compilation—Unfair benefit—Compensation—Whether for breach of copyright or unjust enrichment. **Allied Discount Card Ltd v Bord Fáilte Éireann** [1990] 811, HC.

UNLAWFUL INTERFERENCE
Eonomic interests
Tort
Mandatory interlocutory injunction sought. **Bula Ltd v Tara Mines Ltd** [1988] 157, HC.

UNMARRIED COUPLE
Purchase of house
Conveyance solely in man's name
Joint contribution to purchase price—Whether resulting trust to be inferred. **Power v Conroy** [1980] 31, HC.

VALUATION *See* RATING AND VALUATION.

VALUE ADDED TAX *See* REVENUE (Value added tax).

VENDOR AND PURCHASER *See* SALE OF LAND.

VICARIOUS LIABILITY
Employer. *See* NEGLIGENCE (Employer—Vicarious liability).

Generally. *See* NEGLIGENCE (Vicarious liability).

State
Wrongful actions of its servants
Prison officers—Non-delivery of correspondence to prisoner. Kearney v Minister for Justice [1987] 52, HC.

VICTIMS OF CRIME
Compensation. *See* MALICIOUS INJURIES.

VOIR DIRE
Evidence
Admissibility
Effect on subsequent trial. *See* CRIMINAL LAW (Trial—Voir dire).

VOLUNTARY WINDING UP. *See* COMPANY (Winding up—Voluntary winding up).

VOTING
National and local elections. *See* ELECTORAL LAW.

WAGES
Statutory minimum wage. *See* EMPLOYMENT (Pay—Minimum wage).

WAIVER
Condition in contract. *See* CONTRACT (Condition—Waiver).

Sale of land. See SALE OF LAND (Contract—Condition—Waiver).

Terms of contract
Contract for sale of land. See SALE OF LAND (Contract—Terms—Waiver).

WANT OF PROSECUTION
See PRACTICE (Dismissal for want of prosecution).

WARD OF COURT
Child. *See* CHILD (Ward of court).

Mentally retarded girl
Application for an inquiry as to her soundness of mind
Whether condition precedent for the jurisdiction to bring persons of unsound mind into
the wardship of the court that they be entitled to property which requires manage-
ment or protection—Constitution of Ireland 1937, Articles 40.3.2, 40.4.2—Lunacy
Regulations (Ireland) Act 1871—Mental Treatment Act 1945—Courts (Supplementary
Provisions) Act 1961, s. 9. **In re Midland Health Board** [1988] 251, SC.

Senile patient
Nursing care
Geriatric institution—Chargeability of services—Whether ward receiving in-patient
services—Whether receiving more than shelter and maintenance. **In re McInerney**
[1976–7] 229, SC.

WARRANT
Arrest warrant. *See* CRIMINAL LAW (Arrest warrant).

Extradition. *See* EXTRADITION (Warrant).

Search warrant. *See* CRIMINAL LAW (Search warrant).

WASTE DISPOSAL
Asbestos waste
Grant of permission
for use of site for disposal of asbestos waste—Appeal against decision—Whether due
consideration given to evidence as to danger of health arising from proposed user.
See PLANNING (Appeal—Grant of permission—Use of site for disposal of asbestos
waste).

Refuse dump proposal
National monument on lands. See PLANNING (Development plan—Contravention—National
monument on lands—Refuse dump proposal).

WATER SUPPLY
Service charges. See LOCAL GOVERNMENT (Service charges—Water supply).

WATERWAYS *See also* LAKES AND RIVERS
Canal
Lack of maintenance. See CANAL.

WELFARE
See SOCIAL WELFARE.

WIDOW
Legal right. *See* SUCCESSION (Legal right).

Pension
Army pension
Application for widow's allowance rejected. *See* DEFENCE FORCES (Pensions—Army Pensions Board—Application for widow's allowance rejected).

Disqualification on ground of cohabitation. See SOCIAL WELFARE (Pensions—Widow's contributory pension).

WIDOWER
Adoption
Statutory exclusion
Legislation providing that, whereas a widow could obtain an adoption order, widower could not—Constitution—Validity. *See* ADOPTION (Eligibility to adopt—Exclusion—Widower).

WIFE
Matrimonial property
Application for declaration of interest. See FAMILY LAW (Property—Beneficial interest).

Sole executrix in testator's will
Wife predeceasing testator
failure of will. *See* WILL (Failure).

Widow. *See* WIDOW.

WILL
Charitable gifts
Cy-près. See CHARITY (Cy-pres).

Construction
Condition
Bequest of leasehold property—Settled Land Acts—Condition as to residence—Whether void for uncertainty—Whether inconsistent with widow's power of sale and lease—Testator's intention—Whether fee tail created—Whether widow's estate extinguished by running of time—Conveyancing Act 1881, s. 65—Settled Land Act 1882, ss 51, 58(1)—Statute of Limitations 1957, ss 13(2), 18. **Atkins v Atkins** [1976–7] 62, HC.

Devise subsequent to a condition—Whether words imperative—Whether subject certain—Whether trust created. **In re Sweeney: Hillary v Sweeney** [1976–7] 88, HC.

Extrinsic evidence
Admissibility—Testator making elaborate provisions in the event of his wife surviving him—No provision made for the case of the wife predeceasing husband—Wife predeceasing husband—Whether intestacy—Whether court power to transpose words within a will—Whether extrinsic evidence admissible—Succession Act 1965, s. 90. **Fitzpatrick v Collins** [1978] 244, HC.

Admissibility—Whether will sufficiently certain to enable effect to be given to it. **In re Clinton: O'Sullivan v Dunne** [1988] 80, HC.

Foreign will
Testator domiciled abroad—Distribution of immovables—Proper law—Intention of testator—Identity of beneficiary. **In re Bonnet: Johnston v Langheld** [1983] 359, HC.

Specific and residuary bequests
Testator and wife owning shares in the company used to run their business—Wife predeceasing testator—Her estate left unadministered—Testator leaving 'all my shares and interests in the business' to two of his children—Residue of the estate left to his

WILL

Construction

Specific and residuary bequests continued

remaining four children—Whether testator's proportion of the shares in the company held by his wife, which would have passed to him on completion of the administration of her estate, passed under the specific bequest to his two children or under the residuary bequest to his remaining children—Whether testator failed to make proper provision for his children—Succession Act 1965, s. 117. **M H v N M** [1983] 519, HC.

Trust

Power of appointment—No disposition in default of appointment—Executor unable to carry out the trusts in the manner directed by the testator—Direction of the court as to the proper application of the proceeds—Whether should pass under the residuary clause. **Tuite v Tuite** [1978] 197, HC.

Execution

Negligence

Solicitor—Carelessness in preparation—Resulting financial loss to legatee—Whether duty of care owed to legatee—Extent of liability—Interest—Succesion Act 1965, s. 78. **Wall v Hegarty** [1980] 124, HC.

Failure

Prior death of sole executrix and universal legatee

Testator's wife appointed sole executrix—Wife predeceasing testator—Will inoperative—Application under s. 117—Whether deceased dying intestate—Merits of s. 117 application—Succession Act 1965, ss 3, 109, 117. **R G v P s. G** [1980] 225, HC.

Family provision

Moral duty of testator. See SUCCESSION (Family provision).

Revocation

Marriage

Application for letter of administration—Will made in 1971—Deceased going through ceremony of marriage in 1977—Whether will revoked by this marriage—Whether deceased free to marry in 1977—Previous marriage annulled in 1968—Whether such order would be recognised—Domicile of deceased—Succession Act 1965, ss 27(4), 85. **In re Fleming** [1987] 638, HC.

Two wills

Purported revocation of second will—Intention of testatrix to revive first will—Intention ineffective—Dependent relative revocation—Whether revocation of second will effective—Whether court to give effect to intention of testatrix—Whether photocopy of second will should be admitted to probate—Succession Act 1965, ss 78, 85(2), 87, 89. **In re Hogan** [1980] 24, HC.

Trust

Charitable gifts. See CHARITY (Cy-pres).

Construction. See TRUST (Construction—Will trust).

Creation. See TRUST (Creation—Will).

Trust for sale. See TRUST (Will trust—Trust for sale).

Two wills. *See* Revocation—Two wills—Purported revocation of second will (*above*).

Undue influence. *See* Validity—Undue influence. (*below*).

Validity

Capacity of testator

Application to condemn a will—Deceased suffering a stroke—Subsequent to attack deceased executing a document—Whether document purporting to be a will represented

WILL
Validity
Capacity of testator continued
the testamentary wishes of the deceased—Whether deceased had capacity to know and appreciate contents of executed document—Succession Act 1965, s. 78. **Glynn v Glynn** [1987] 589, HC.

Testator suffering serious illness—Whether testator of sound disposing mind—Whether testator knew and approved of contents of the will—Onus of proof—Succession Act 1965. **O'Connor v O'Connor** [1978] 247, HC.

Undue influence
Application to have will admitted to probate—Claim that will procured by undue influence—Whether full particulars of undue influence required—RSC 1962, O 19 r 5, O 111. In re Rutledge: **Hanly v Finnerty** [1981] 198, HC.

Person instrumental in having will prepared taking a benefit under it—Whether will be condemned—Whether testator knew and approved of its contents. **In re Kavanagh: Healy v MacGillicudy** [1978] 175, HC.

WINDING UP
Company. *See* COMPANY (Winding up).

WIRELESS TELEGRAPHY
Unlicensed possession and use of apparatus
Seizure of apparatus. See BROADCASTING (Radio station—Unlicensed possession and use of apparatus for wireless telegraphy).

WITNESS
Expenses
Taxation. See COSTS (Taxation—Review—Witnesses' expenses).

WOMEN
Equality of treatment
Employment. See EMPLOYMENT (Equality of treatment).

Pay. See EMPLOYMENT (Equal pay).

Social welfare. See SOCIAL WELFARE (Equal treatment).

WORDS AND PHRASES *See separate table.*

WORK *See* EMPLOYMENT.
Accidents at work. *See* NEGLIGENCE (Employer).

Right to earn livelihood. *See* CONSTITUTION (Personal rights—Right to earn livelihood).

Right to work
Compulsory retirement scheme
Trade union resolution—Whether introduction of compulsory retirement scheme with pension rights an infringement of constitutional right to work—Constitution of Ireland 1937, Articles 40.3.1, 45. **Rodgers v ITGWU** [1978] 51, HC.

WRONGFUL DISMISSAL
Damages. *See* DAMAGES (Wrongful dismissal).

NOT TO BE REMOVED
FROM LIBRARY

YACHT
  Company charge
  Registration
  Whether yacht a ship for the purpose of company law—Companies Act, 1963, s. 99—
  Bills of Sale (Ireland) Act 1879, s. 4. **Barber v Burke** [1980] 186, SC.

YOUNG OFFENDER. *See* CRIMINAL LAW (Young offender).

YOUNG PERSON *See* CHILD; INFANT

Cases Considered

A v A (1887) 19 LR Ir 403 **Referred to** [1982] 263

A v B (1868) LR IP & D 559 **Applied** [1984] 173

ACEC (Ireland) Ltd, In re [1962] IR 201 **Dictum explained** [1982] 207

Abbot v Refuge Assurance Co Ltd [1962] 1 QB 432 **Followed** [1982] 126

Abbot-Smith v The Governors of the University of Toronto (1975) 45 DLR
    (3d) 672 **Referred to** [1986] 627

Abbots Park Estates (No 2), In re [1972] 1 WLR 1597 **Dictum approved** [1984] 350

Abbott v Sullivan [1952] 1 KB 189; [1952] 1 All ER 226 **Considered** [1987] 747

Abdelkefi v Minister for Justice [1984] ILRM 138 **Referred to** [1987] 330

Abels v Bedrijfsvereniging voor de Metaalindustrie (Case 135/83) [1985] ECR 469 **Considered**
    [1989] 844

Aberdeen Glen Line Steamship Co v Macken [1899] 2 IR 1; 32 ILTR 230 **Referred to** [1987]
    669

Aberfoyle Plantations Ltd v Cheng [1960] AC 115 **Referred to** [1979] 11, 253; **Applied** [1983]
    82; **Distinguished** [1978] 73

Acciairie San Michele SpA v High Authority [1967] ECR 1 **Considered** [1987] 400

Adams In re: Bank of Ireland Trustee Co Ltd v Adams [1967] IR 424 **Referred to** [1982] 217;
    [1983] 359; [1988] 67

Adams v Southerden: In re Southerden [1925] P 177 **Followed** [1980] 24

Adamson v Jarvis (1827) 4 Bing 66 **Referred to** [1984] 523

Addis v Gramophone Co Ltd [1909] AC 488 **Applied** [1979] 266

Adidas Sportschuhfabriken v Charles O'Neill & Co Ltd High Court, unreported, 20 May 1980
    affirmed [1983] 112

Administration des Douanes v Gondrand Freres SA (Case 169/80) [1981] ECR 1931 **Considered**
    [1990] 466

Adoiu v Belgium [1982] ECR 1665; [1982] 3 CMLR 631 **Referred to** [1987] 400

Adoption (No 2) Bill 1987, In re [1989] ILRM 266 **Considered** [1990] 767

Aer Lingus Teo v Labour Court [1989] 1 CMLR 857 **Considered** [1990] 193

Aga Khan v Times Publishing Co [1924] 1 KB 675 **Approved** [1985] 673

Ageret v A & K Construction Ltd [1976] AC 167 **Referred to** [1984] 583

Agra Trading Ltd v Minister for Agriculture High Court, unreported, 19 May 1983 **Applied**
    [1989] 783

Agricultural Credit Corporation v Vale [1935] IR 631 **Dictum approved** [1982] 421

Ainsworth v Wilding [1896] 1 Ch 673 **Referred to** [1986] 624

Airey v Ireland (1979–80) 2 EHRR 305 **Considered** [1982] 497

Ajit v Sammy [1967] 1 AC 255 **Referred to** [1979] 11

Alain Bernadin et Cie v Pavilion Properties Ltd [1967] RPC 581 **Referred to** [1983] 112

Allcock v Hall (1891) 1 QB 444 **Considered** [1986] 250

Allen v Sir Alfred McAlpine & Sons Ltd [1968] 2 QB 229 **Referred to** [1985] 41

Allied Irish Banks Ltd v Glynn [1973] IR 188 **Referred to** [1988] 480; [1990] 106

Allied Stores of Ohio Inc v Bowers [1959] 358 US 522 **Referred to** [1983] 449

Allsopp v Day (1861) 7 H & N 457; 158 ER 552 **Referred to** [1985] 624

Alma v Dublin Corporation (1876) IR 10 CL 476 **Followed** [1990] 172

Aluminium Industrie Vaassen BV v Romalpa Aluminium Ltd [1976] 1 WLR 679; [1976] 2 All ER 552 **Referred to** [1982] 399, [1985] 624; **Considered** [1982] 396, [1982] 551; **Applied** [1978] 240; **Principles adopted** [1985] 66

Amalgamated Investment & Property Co Ltd v Texas Commerce Investment Bank [1982] QB 84 **Applied** [1988] 565

American Cyanamid Co v Ethicon Ltd [1975] AC 396 **Referred to** [1983] 541; **Applied** [1979] 277; [1983] 258; dicta approved [1984] 45, 161, 595; **Distinguished** [1987] 702; not **Followed** [1982] 349

Amies v Inner London Education Authority [1977] ICR 308 **Distinguished** [1990] 485

Amministrazione della Finanze dello Stato v Simmenthal SpA (Case 106/77) [1978] ECR 629 **Referred to** [1984] 45, [1987] 400; **Followed** [1989] 53

Anderson v Bank of British Columbia (1876) 2 ChD 644 **Referred to** [1989] 257; **Dictum adopted** [1990] 588

Anderson v Fitzgerald (1853) 4 HLC 484 **Dictum approved** [1990] 110

Anderson v Nobels Explosive Co (1906) 12 OLR 644 **Not followed** [1986] 627

Anisminic Ltd v Foreign Compensation Commission [1969] 2 AC 147; [1969] 2 WLR 163 **Referred to** [1981] 242; **Dicta approved** [1981] 62

Annesley, In re; Davidson v Annesley [1926] Ch 692 **Referred to** [1982] 433

Anns v London Borough of Merton [1978] AC 728; [1977] 2 All ER 492 **Referred to** [1983] 156; [1990] 658; **Considered** [1981] 21; [1989] 373; **Dictum approved** [1989] 400; **Applied** [1986] 43

Archer v Fleming High Court, unreported, 21 January 1980 **Followed** [1990] 648

Argyle v Arglye [1967] 1 Ch 302 **Distinguished** [1987] 135

Aristoc Ltd v Rysta Ltd [1945] AC 68; 62 RPC 65 **Referred to** [1982] 240; **Considered** [1990] 204

Armagas Ltd v Mundogas SA [1985] 3 All ER 795 **Dictum approved** [1987] 364

Armagh Shoes Ltd, In re [1982] NI 59 **Dicta applied** [1985] 254 **Referred to** [1985] 641

Armory v Delamarie (1722) 1 Strange 505 **Considered** [1988] 565

Arnold Tours Inc v Kamp (1970) 400 US 45 **Referred to** [1981] 244

Arnold v Veale [1979] IR 342n **Referred to** [1979] 119

Aro Road and Land Vehicles Ltd v Insurance Corporation of Ireland Ltd [1986] IR 403 **Referred to** [1990] 110

Artificial Coal Co v Minister for Finance [1928] IR 238 **Considered** [1985] 249, 269

Ashby v White (1703) 2 Ld Raym 928 **Considered** [1982] 48

Ashmark Ltd, In re (No 1) [1990] ILRM 330 **Referred to** [1990] 455

Assaf v Fuwa [1955] AC 215 **Referred to** [1979] 156

Associated Provincial Picture Houses Ltd v Wednesbury Corporation [1948] 1 KB 223; [1947] 2 All ER 680 **Referred to** [1990] 36; **Considered** [1987] 202; **Dictum doubted** [1989] 565

Association of Data Processing Organisations v Kamp (1970) 397 US 150 **Referred to** [1981] 242

Athlumney, In re [1898] 2 QB 551 **Followed** [1982] 290

Atkins v Atkins [1942] 2 All ER 637 **Referred to** [1981] 361

Attenborough (George) & Son v Solomon [1913] AC 76 **Referred to** [1983] 513

Attorney General v Able [1984] QB 795; [1984] 1 All ER 277 **Considered** [1987] 477

Attorney General v Best's Stores Ltd [1970] IR 225 **Explained** [1990] 391

Attorney General v Blogh [1958] IR 91 **Considered** [1976–7] 305

Attorney General v Bruen and Kelly [1935] IR 615 **Referred to** [1987] 65

Attorney General v Burke [1955] IR 30 **Referred to** [1986] 690, [1987] 65; **Followed** [1987] 316; **Distinguished** [1978] 18

Attorney General v Callaghan [1937] IR 386 **Referred to** [1987] 65

Attorney General v Casey [1930] IR 163 **Applied** [1986] 304

Attorney General v Chaudry [1971] 1 WLR 1614; [1971] 3 All ER 938 **Referred to** [1990] ILRM 560; **Dictum approved** [1984] 373

Attorney General v Cunningham High Court, unreported, 6 December 1976 **Doubted** [1984] 39

Attorney General v Dublin United Tramways Co Ltd [1939] IR 590; 74 ILTR 46 **Followed** [1984] 45

Attorney General v Farrell Court of Criminal Appeal, unreported, 23 July 1935 **Distinguished** [1982] 1

Attorney General v Great Eastern Railway Co (1880) 5 App Cas 473 **Referred to** [1979] 221

Attorney General v Harris [1961] 1 QB 74 **Referred to** [1984] 373

Attorney General v Healy [1928] IR 460 **Referred to** [1987] 65

Attorney General v Hurley 71 ILTR 29 **Considered** [1986] 716

Attorney General v Jameson [1904] 2 IR 644 **Applied** [1990] 664

Attorney General v Linehan [1929] IR 19; 63 ILTR 30, 100 **Referred to** [1990] 780

Attorney General v Logan [1891] 2 QB 100 **Referred to** [1987] 477

Attorney General v McCabe [1927] IR 129 **Referred to** [1988] 4, 666

Attorney General v Mallen [1957] IR 344 **Referred to** [1983] 549; **Considered** [1984] 99

Attorney General v Metropolitan Water Board [1928] 1 KB 833; [1927] All ER 526 **Referred to** [1985] 666

Attorney General v Northern Petroleum Tank Co Ltd [1936] IR 450; 70 ILTR 205 **Followed** [1984] 45

Attorney General v Paperlink Ltd [1984] ILRM 373 **Followed** [1985] 542, [1986] 177, [1987] 52, [1990] 560

Attorney General v Premier Line Ltd [1932] 1 Ch 303 **Referred to** [1984] 373

Attorney General v Ryan's Car Hire Ltd [1965] IR 642; 101 ILTR 57 **Referred to** [1984] 595; **Considered** [1988] 318, [1989] 544, [1990] 505; **Principle applied** [1983] 89

Attorney General v Sharp [1931] 1 Ch 121 **Referred to** [1984] 373

Attorney General v Simpson [1959] IR 105 **Not followed** [1984] 149

Attorney General v Smith [1927] IR 564 **Considered** [1989] 245

Attorney General v Southern Industrial Trust Ltd 94 ILTR 161 **Referred to** [1981] 60, [1983] 391; [1986] 304; **Considered** [1986] 136; **Dictum approved** [1981] 34; **Distinguished** [1978] 12

Attorney General v Thornton (1824) 13 Price 805 **Applied** [1980] 21

Attorney General v Times Newspapers Ltd [1973] QB 710 **Distinguished** [1984] 577

Attorney General v Tynan; In re Tynan [1964] Ir Jur Rep 28 **Referred to** [1983] 549

Attorney General v Vernazza [1960] AC 965 **Referred to** [1982] 290; **Dictum approved** [1981] 385

Attorney General v Westminster City Council [1924] 2 Ch 416 **Applied** [1981] 365

Attorney General (Doherty) v Gilsenan High Court, unreported, 5 July 1963 **Applied** [1983] 41

Attorney General (Fahy) v Breen [1936] IR 750; 70 ILTR 247 **Referred to** [1983] 549

Attorney General (Humphries) v Governors of Erasmus Smith Schools [1910] 1 IR 325 **Dictum approved** [1983] 254

Attorney General (Lambe) v Fitzgerald [1973] IR 195 **Referred to** [1983] 17; **Considered** [1981] 47

Attorney General (McDonnell) v Higgins [1964] IR 374 **Referred to** [1987] 65; **Distinguished** [1990] 850; **Followed** [1986] 565, [1987] 309

Attorney General (McGrath) v Healy [1972] IR 393 **Followed** [1990] 391

Attorney General (O'Connor) v Jordan 107 ILTR 112 **Overruled in part** [1976–7] 68

Attorney General (O'Connor) v O'Reilly High Court, unreported, 29 November 1976 **Referred to** [1981] 17

Attorney General (O'Duffy) v Appleton [1907] 1 IR 252 **Approved** [1984] 373

Attorney General (Pickfords Ltd) v Great Northern Railway Co [1916] 2 AC 356 **Dictum approved** [1983] 173

Attorney General (ex rel SPUC (Irl) Ltd) v Open Door Counselling Ltd [1987] ILRM 477; [1988] IR 593 **Affirmed (with order varied)** [1989] 19; **Followed** [1990] 70, 350

Attorney General (ex rel SPUC (Irl) Ltd) v Open Door Counselling Ltd [1989] ILRM 19 **Referred to** [1989] 526

Attorney General for Alberta v Attorney General for Canada [1974] AC 503 **Considered** [1985] 61

Attorney General for Alberta v Huggard Assets Ltd [1953] AC 420 **Referred to** [1983] 350

Attorney General for Hong Kong v Kwok-a-Sing LR 5 PC 179 **Followed** [1981] 120

Attorney General for Northern Ireland's Reference (No 1 of 1975) [1977] AC 105 **Referred to** [1990] 505

Attorney General of England and Wales v The Observer Ltd and Guardian Newspapers Ltd, The Times, 26 July 1986 **Distinguished** [1987] 135

Attorney General of Ontario v Mercer (1882) 8 App Cas 767 **Considered** [1988] 565

Attorney General of St Christopher, Nevis and Anguilla v Reynolds [1980] AC 637 **Considered** [1982] 190

Attorney General's Reference (No 1 of 1975) [1975] QB 773; [1975] 1 All ER 684 **Considered** [1987] 477

Australian Newspaper Co v Bennett [1894] AC 284 **Referred to** [1986] 601

B v An Bord Uchtála High Court, unreported, 18 February 1983 **Referred to** [1985] 302

B (N) v An Bord Uchtála Supreme Court, unreported, 28 May 1984 **Referred to** [1988] 203

B v B High Court, unreported, 20 June 1973 **Followed** [1982] 277; **Considered** [1986] 75

B (L) v B (H) [1980] ILRM 257 **Followed** [1988] 456

BSC Footwear Ltd v Ridgway [1972] AC 544 **Considered** [1989] 552

Back v Daniels [1925] 1 KB 526 **Dictum Considered** [1982] 451

Baglin v Cusenier (1910) 221 US 580 **Referred to** [1984] 565

Baily v de Crespigny (1869) LR 4 QB 180 **Referred to** [1982] 290

Baily & Co v Clark Son & Morland [1938] AC 557 **Dictum Applied** [1976–7] 335

Bain v Fothergill (1874–5) LR 7 HL 158 rule **Applied** [1981] 403

Bains v Tweddle [1959] Ch 679 **Applied** [1981] 81

Baker v Willoughby [1970] AC 467 **Referred to** [1982] 317

Balgownie Land Trust Ltd v Inland Revenue Commissioners 1929 SC 790 **Referred to** [1982] 421

Banbury v Montreal [1918] AC 626 **Referred to** [1986] 250

Bank of America National Trust & Savings Association's Trade Mark [1977] FSR 7 **Disapproved** [1985] 30

Bank of Ireland v Caffin [1971] IR 123 **Referred to** [1982] 217; [1987] 287

Bank of Ireland v Purcell [1988] ILRM 480 **Affirmed** [1990] 106

Bank of Ireland Finance Ltd v D J Daly Ltd [1978] IR 79 **Referred to** [1984] 418

Bank of Ireland Finance Ltd v Rockfield Ltd [1979] IR 21 **Referred to** [1979] 221

Bank of Ireland Trustee Co Ltd v Adams; In re Adams [1967] IR 424 **Referred to** [1982] 217; [1983] 359; [1988] 67

Bank of Syria, In re: Owen and Ashworth's claim [1961] 1 Ch 115 **Followed** [1982] 57

Bannerton, In re application of [1984] ILRM 662 **Affirmed** [1986] 471

Barber v Burke High Court, unreported, 20 November 1979 **Affirmed** [1980] 186

Barclay-Johnson v Yuill [1980] 1 WLR 1259 **Dictum approved** [1983] 541

Barclay's Bank Plc v Bank of England [1985] 1 All ER 385 **Considered** [1987] 142

Barclay's Bank Ltd v Levin Brothers (Bradford) Ltd [1977] QB 270 **Dicta adopted** [1976–7] 335

Barentz v Whiting [1965] 1 WLR 433 **Referred to** [1988] 333

Barlow v Collins (1970) 397 US 159 **Referred to** [1981] 242

Barrett Bros (Taxis) Ltd v Davies [1966] 1 WLR 1354 **Not followed** [1985] 109

Barrett v Flynn [1916] 2 IR 1 **Dictum approved** [1990] 391

Barrington's Hospital v Commissioners of Valuation [1957] IR 299; 92 ILTR 156 **Referred to** [1982] 457

Barry v Buckley [1981] IR 306 **Distinguished** [1984] 24; **Considered** [1982] 126

Bartlett v Smith (1843) 11 M & W 483 **Referred to** [1988] 4

Barton v Gainer (1858) 3 H & N 387 **Distinguished** [1980] 131

Barton v Harten [1925] 2 IR 37 **Referred to** [1979] 51

Bateman v Green (1868) IR 2 CL 166 **Referred to** [1990] 285

Bater v Bater [1906] P 209 **Referred to** [1980] 257

Bater v Bater [1951] P 35; [1950] 2 All ER 458 doubted [1987] 669

Battle v Irish Art Promotion Centre Ltd [1968] IR 252 **Distinguished** [1983] 7

Batty v Metropolitan Property Realisations Ltd [1978] QB 554 **Considered** [1980] 33

Baulk v Irish National Insurance Co Ltd [1969] IR 66 **Followed** [1985] 180

Baxter v Baxter [1948] AC 274; [1947] 2 All ER 886 **Dictum adopted** [1986] 515

Bayley-Worthington and Cohen's Contract, In re [1909] 1 Ch 648 **Dictum approved** [1981] 308

Beamish & Crawford Ltd v Commissioner of Valuation High Court, unreported, 8 May 1978 **Affirmed** [1980] 149

Beamish & Crawford Ltd v Crowley [1969] IR 142 **Considered** [1989] 757

Beaudesert Shine Council v Smith (1969) 120 CLR 145 **Referred to** [1987] 747

Beauforte (Jon) (London) Ltd, In re [1953] Ch 131 **Referred to** [1979] 221

Becker v Riebold (1913) 30 TLR 142 **Approved** [1983] 402

Beddoe, In re [1893] 1 Ch 547 **Referred to** [1989] 625

Beer v Bowden [1981] WLR 522 **Considered** [1982] 77

Begley v McHugh [1939] IR 475 **Considered** [1978] 247

Behrens v Bertram Mills Circus Ltd [1957] 2 QB 1 **Approved** [1987] 306

Behrens v Richards [1905] 2 Ch 614 **Referred to** [1981] 365

Belgische Radio en Televisie v SV SABAM (Case 127/73) [1974] ECR 51 **Considered** [1990] 534

Bell v Director of Public Prosecutions [1985] AC 937; [1985] 2 All ER 585 **Discussed** [1986] 639

Bell v Lever Bros Ltd [1932] AC 161 **Applied** [1985] 5

Bell Brothers Pty Ltd v Shire of Serpentine-Jarrahdale (1969–70) 121 CLR 137 **Referred to** [1981] 144

Bellew v Bellew [1982] IR 447; [1983] ILRM 128 **Affirmed** [1983] 128; **Considered** [1985] 554

Belshaw v Bush (1851) 11 CB 191 **Referred to** [1988] 526

Belvedere Fish Guano Co Ltd v Rainham Chemical Works Ltd [1920] 2 KB 487 **Followed** [1976–7] 287

Belvoir Finance Co Ltd v Stapleton [1971] 1 QB 210 **Referred to** [1989] 294

Beni-Felkai Mining Co Ltd, In re [1934] 1 Ch 406 **Considered** [1989] 155

Benjamin, In re; Neville v Benjamin [1902] 1 Ch 723 **Applied** [1986] 175

Benjamin v Stone (1874) Lr 9 CP 400 **Dictum approved** [1981] 365

Benmax v Austin Motor Co Ltd [1955] AC 370 **Referred to** [1988] 203

Bennett v Griffin Finance [1967] 2 QB 46 **Followed** [1984] 613

Bennitt v Whitehouse (1860) Beav 119 **Considered** [1988] 149

Benson v Northern Ireland Road Transport Board [1942] AC 520 **Considered** [1981] 389

Bentley (Henry) & Co and the Yorkshire Breweries Ltd, In re; ex parte Harrison (1893) 69 LT 204 **Followed** [1989] 452

Benton v Maryland (1969) 395 US 784 **Referred to** [1983] 549

Benzine en Petroleum Handelsmaatchappij BV v Commission of the European Communities [1978] ECR 1513 **Dictum Considered** [1982] 77

Bernadin (Alain) et Cie v Pavilion Properties Ltd [1967] RPC 581 **Referred to** [1983] 112

Berry v Irish Times Ltd [1973] IR 368; 108 ILTR 22 **Considered** [1986] 601

Bibby (James) Ltd v Woods and Howard [1949] 2 KB 449; [1949] 2 All ER 1 **Followed** [1989] 777

Biddle v Bond (1865) 6 B & s. 225 **Referred to** [1988] 565

Birch, In re (1892) 29 LR Ir 274 **Followed** [1988] 251

Birch v Cropper (1889) 14 App Cas 525 **Considered** [1982] 444

Birch v Delaney [1936] IR 517 **Referred to** [1982] 421

Birkett v James [1978] AC 297 **Referred to** [1985] 41

Birmingham Corp v Barnes [1935] AC 292; 19 TC 195 **Referred to** [1985] 651

Biscoe v Jackson (1857) 35 Ch D 460 **Referred to** [1990] 835

Bishop (Thomas) Ltd v Helmville Ltd [1972] 1 QB 464 **Referred to** [1982] 29

Bismag v Amblins Chemists Ltd (1937) 57 RPC 205 **Followed** [1982] 240

Black-Clawson Ltd v Papierwerke AG [1975] AC 591; [1975] 1 All ER 810 **Considered** [1987] 606

Blacklock (H) & Co Ltd v C Arthur Pearson Ltd [1915] 2 Ch 376 **Considered** [1990] 534

Blagrave v Bristol Waterworks Co (1856) 1 H & N 369 **Distinguished** [1981] 365

Blake v Attorney General High Court, unreported, 18 April 1980 **Affirmed** [1981] 34

Blake v Attorney General [1981] ILRM 34; [1982] IR 117 **Referred to** [1982] 290; [1983] 449; [1984] 373; [1985] 364; [1987] 83; [1988] 400, 497; [1989] 670; **Applied** [1984] 366; **Considered** [1983] 246; [1986] 136; **Distinguished** [1983] 391; [1986] 177

Blisset v Daniel (1853) 10 Hare 493 **Referred to** [1979] 141

Bloom (Kosher) & Sons Ltd v Tower Hamlets London Borough Council (1977) 247 EG 1091 **Not followed** [1983] 56

Blue Paraffin Trade Mark (1960) 77 RP 473 **Considered** [1982] 91

Board of Education v Rice [1911] AC 179 **Referred to** [1981] 62

Bock v Comission [1971] ECR 897 **Referred to** [1988] 400

Boguslawski v Gdynia Ameryka Lines [1951] 2 KB 328 **Considered** [1988] 490

Bohane v Driscoll [1929] IR 428 **Considered** [1987] 768

Boissevain v Weil [1950] AC 327 **Considered** [1988] 1

Bolam v Friern Hospital Management Committee [1957] 1 WLR 582; [1957] 2 All ER 118 **Followed** [1986] 43

Boland v An Taoiseach [1974] IR 338; 109 ILTR 13 **Referred to** [1986] 381; [1988] 333; [1990] 70; **Considered** [1987] 400; [1988] 437; [1989] 209; **Dictum approved** [1990] 441

Bolger v Doherty [1970] IR 233 **Followed** [1990] 391

Bolton (Engineering) Co Ltd v T J Graham & Sons Ltd [1957] 1 QB 159 **Referred to** [1980] 216

Bolton v Stone [1951] AC 850 **Considered** [1989] 437

Bond Worth Ltd, In re [1980] Ch 228 **Referred to** [1983] 402; **Considered** [1982] 396, [1982] 551 **Distinguished** [1982] 399

Dr Bonham's case (1610) 8 Coke Rep 107a **Referred to** [1982] 290

Booth & Co International Ltd v National Enterprise Board [1978] 3 All ER 624 **Considered** [1981] 242

Boots' Pure Drug Company's Trade Mark Application [1938] Ch 54 **Referred to** [1976–7] 335

Borden (UK) Ltd v Scottish Timber Products Ltd [1981] Ch 25 **Referred to** [1983] 402; **Considered** [1982] 551; [1984] 437

Borrowes, In re [1900] 2 IR 593 **Referred to** [1985] 269

Boslock's Settlement, In re [1921] 2 Ch 469 **Distinguished** [1978] 151

Bottomley v Bannister [1932] 1 KB 458 not **Followed** [1986] 43

Boughton v Bray Urban District Council [1964] Ir Jur Rep 57 **Considered** [1987] 768

Bourgoin SA v Ministry of Agriculture [1986] QB 716; [1985] 3 All ER 585 **Referred to** [1987] 747

Bourke v Attorney General [1972] IR 36; 107 ILTR 33 **Referred to** [1985] 422; [1988] 333; [1990] 505, 780; **Considered** [1985] 410; [1986] 401; [1988] 75; **Distinguished** [1988] 738; dicta adopted [1985] 385 **Followed** [1985] 410

Bowie v Liverpool Royal Infirmary [1930] AC 588 **Referred to** [1982] 433

Bowman v Secular Society [1917] AC 406 **Followed** [1980] 103

Boyce v Paddington Borough Council [1903] 2 Ch 556 **Referred to** [1981] 365

Boylan v Dublin Corporation [1949] IR 60 **Referred to** [1987] 768; **Considered** [1984] 595

Boyne v Rossborough (1854) 6 HLC 48 **Considered** [1978] 175

Bradley v Córas Iompair Éireann [1976] IR 217 **Considered** [1989] 117; **Followed** [1987] 768

Bradshaw v McMullan [1920] 2 IR 47, 412, 490; 53 ILTR 185; 54 ILTR 109, 169; 56 ILTR 93 **Referred to** [1980] 94

Brady v Donegal County Council [1989] ILRM 282 **Followed** [1989] 309

Brandao v Barnett (1846) 12 Cl & Fin 787 **Applied** [1980] 132

Bray v Bray, High Court, unreported, 25 February 1977 **Referred to** [1978] 203

Breathnach v Ireland [1989] IR 478 **Referred to** [1990] 817

Bremer Vulkan Schiffbau und Maschinenfabrik v South India Shipping Corp Ltd [1981] AC 909 **Applied** [1990] 277; **Considered** [1988] 129

Brennan v Attorney General High Court 1980/1067P **Referred to** [1984] 45

Brennan v Attorney General [1983] ILRM 449 **Reversed in part** [1984] 355; **Referred to** [1988] 400; **Applied** [1986] 157; [1989] 196; **Considered** [1986] 177; **Dictum approved** [1986] 136;

Brennan v Bank of Ireland High Court, unreported, 23 May 1985 **Considered** [1987] 142

Brennan v Dorney (1888) 21 LR Ir 353 **Applied** [1979] 113

Brennan v Lockyer [1932] IR 100 **Referred to** [1986] 627

Brennan v Savage Smyth & Co Ltd High Court, unreported, 4 March 1981 **Appeal allowed in part** [1982] 223

Brewer Street Investments Ltd v Barclay's Woollen Co Ltd [1954] 1 QB 428 **Principles applied** [1984] 265; **Considered** [1985] 295

Brice v Brown [1984] 1 All ER 997 **Referred to** [1987] 202

Bridges v Hawkesworth (1851) 21 LJQB 75 **Referred to** [1988] 565

Bridgewater Navigation Co, In re [1891] 2 Ch 317 **Distinguished** [1982] 444

Bridgman v Powell [1937] IR 584 **Considered** [1976–7] 14

Briggs v Morgan (1820) 3 Phill Ecc 325 **Referred to** [1976–7] 156

Bright v Bright [1954] P 270 **Distinguished** [1984] 173

Brighton Marine & Pier Ltd v Woodhouse [1893] 2 Ch 486 **Followed** [1982] 324

Brindley v Woodhouse (1845) 1 C & K 647 **Referred to** [1978] 151

British Broadcasting Co v Wireless League Gazette Publishing Co [1926] 1 Ch 433 **Considered** [1990] 534

British Insulated and Helsby Cables v Atherton [1926] AC 205 **Applied** [1984] 610

British Traders Insurance Co Ltd v Monson (1964) 111 CLR 86 **Dictum approved** [1984] 507

British Transport Commission v Gourley [1956] AC 185 **Referred to** [1980] 107

British Wagon Co Ltd v Shortt [1961] IR 164 **Referred to** [1988] 565

Broken Hill Pty Co Ltd v Commissioners of Taxation (1967) 41 ALJR 377 **Referred to** [1984] 679

Brooks and Burton Ltd v Secretary of State for the Environment [1977] 1 WLR 1294 **Referred to** [1980] 1; **Dicta applied** [1978] 85; **Dictum approved** [1983] 268; **Followed** [1982] 534

Broome v Agar (1928) 138 LT 698; 44 TLR 339 **Dictum Applied** [1986] 601

Broome v Cassell & Co Ltd [1972] AC 1027; [1972] 1 All ER 801 **Referred to** [1979] 266; **Dictum applied** [1986] 601

Broomfield v Minister for Justice, High Court, unreported, 10 April 1981 **Not followed** [1988] 173

Brown, In re [1894] 2 IR 363 **Followed** [1983] 45

Brown v Donegal County Council [1980] IR 132 **Referred to** [1982] 13

Brown v Dyerson [1969] 1 QB 45 **Referred to** [1988] 333

Brown v Gould [1972] Ch 53 **Considered** [1982] 77

Brown v Harrison (1947) 63 TLR 484 **Referred to** [1990] 857

Brown v Norton [1954] IR 34 **Referred to** [1985] 189; **Applied** [1976-7] 93

Brown & Co v T & J Harrison 96 LJ KB 1025; (1927) 43 TLR 394 **Referred to** [1985] 109

Browne v Dowie 93 ILTR 179 **Referred to** [1981] 365

Browning v Morris (1778) 2 Cowp 790 **Referred to** [1985] 283

Browns Transport Ltd v Kropp (1958) 100 CLR 263 **Considered** [1986] 693

Bryanstone Finances Ltd v de Vries (No 2) [1976] Ch 63 **Referred to** [1979] 141

Buchanan v Motor Insurers' Bureau [1955] 1 WLR 488; [1955] 1 All ER 607 **Referred to** [1985] 290

Buchanan (James) & Co. Ltd v Babco Forwarding and Shipping (UK) Ltd [1977] QB 208, [1978] AC 141 **Considered** [1988] 400

Buckland v Buckland [1968] P 296 **Considered** [1982] 277

Buckley & Ors (Sinn Fein) v Attorney General [1950] IR 67 **Referred to** [1984] 657; [1986] 123; [1987] 555, 747; [1988] 333; **Principles applied** [1985] 11; **Considered** [1982] 290; [1983] 489; [1987] 400; **Dictum Applied** [1989] 209 **Distinguished** [1982] 568; [1984] 224; [1989] 670;

Buckley v Gross (1863) 3 B & s. 566 **Considered** [1981] 469

Buckley v Holland Clyde High Court, unreported (date unavailable) **Referred to** [1979] 273

Buckley's Stores Ltd v National Employers Mutual General Insurance Association Ltd [1978] IR 351 **Referred to** [1984] 523

Bugge v Taylor [1941] 1 KB 198 **Referred to** [1985] 290

Bugle Press Ltd, In re [1961] Ch 270 **Distinguished** [1978] 191

Bula Ltd v Tara Mines Ltd [1987] IR 494 **Dictum endorsed** [1990] 266

Bula Ltd v Tara Mines Ltd [1988] ILRM 149 **Referred to** [1988] 501

Bula Ltd v Tara Mines Ltd, Irish Times Law Report, August 20, 1990 **Followed** [1990] 756

Burdett v Abbott (1811) 14 East 1 **Considered** [1987] 575

Burgess (Thomas), In re (1888) 23 LR Ir 5 **Considered** [1989] 501

Burgess v Cox [1951] Ch 383 **Referred to** [1976–7] 72; **Not followed** [1978] 73

Burke v Minister for Labour [1979] IR 354 **Referred to** [1983] 449; **Dictum Applied** [1988] 400

Burma Steamship Co Ltd v Commissioners of Inland Revenue 1931 SC 156 **Referred to** [1980] 107

Burmah Oil Co Ltd v Governor and Company of the Bank of England [1980] AC 1090 **Referred to** [1988] 707

Burman v Burman 1930 SC 262 **Considered** [1984] 66

Burman v Thorn Domestic Appliances (Electrical) Ltd [1982] STC 179 **Referred to** [1985] 651

Burns v Attorney General High Court, unreported, 4 February 1974 **Referred to** [1985] 385; [1988] 333; [1990] 505; **Explained** [1985] 422

Burns v Hearne [1987] ILRM 508 **Affirmed** [1989] 155

Burt v Claude Cousins & Co [1971] 2 QB 426; [1971] 2 All ER 611 **Distinguished** [1986] 547

Butler, Application of [1960] IR 45 **Referred to** [1980] 145

Buttegeig v Universal Terminal and Stevedoring Corp [1972] VR 626 **Referred to** [1986] 627

Butterly v United Dominion Trust (General) Ltd: Larkin and Matthews Third party, 95 ILTR 66 **Distinguished** [1985] 1

Butterworth v Supplementary Benefits Commission [1982] 1 All ER 498 **Considered** [1989] 169

Buttes Gas & Oil Co v Hammer (No 3) [1981] QB 223; [1980] 3 All ER 475 **Followed** [1989] 257

Buxton, Ex parte; In re Miller (1880) 15 Ch D 289 **Considered** [1984] 273

Byrne v Dublin County Council [1983] ILRM 213 **Approved** [1987] 733

Byrne v Grey [1988] IR 31 **Approved** [1990] 569

Byrne v Ireland [1972] IR 241 **Referred to** [1983] 449; [1984] 45; [1986] 99; [1987] 52, 477; **Applied** [1987] 181; **Considered** [1990] 560; **Dicta applied** [1986] 318; **Followed** [1988] 565

Byrne v Limerick Steamship Co Ltd [1946] IR 138; 80 ILTR 142 **Referred to** [1976–7] 327

Byrne v Loftus [1978] IR 211; 113 ILTR 17 **Referred to** [1980] 107; **Considered** [1978] 82; [1981] 197; **Distinguished** [1980] 273

Byrne v Triumph Engineering Ltd, High Court, unreported, 23 June 1980 **Affirmed** [1982] 317

Byrne v Allied Irish Banks, In re Kum Tong Restaurant (Dublin) Ltd [1978] IR 446 **Considered** [1989] 777

C v C [1921] P 399 **Followed** [1976-7] 156

C v C [1976] IR 254; 111 ILTR 133 **Applied** [1979] 1; [1980] 31; [1981] 202; **Considered** [1989] 528; [1985] 153; [1986] 1

C & A Modes v C & A (Waterford) Ltd [1976] IR 198 **Referred to** [1983] 112; [1984] 393

Cadbury Ireland Ltd v Kerry Co-Operative Creameries Ltd [1982] ILRM 77 **Considered** [1988] 157

Cadbury-Schweppes Ltd v Pub Squash Co Pty Ltd [1981] 1 WLR 193 **Approved** [1983] 112

Cadwell v Labour Court [1988] IR 280 **Approved**[1990] 21

Caffin (deceased), In re [1971] IR 123 **Referred to** [1980] 257

Cahill v Governor of the Military Detention Barracks, Curragh Camp High Court, unreported, 31 July 1980 **Distinguished** [1981] 86

Cahill v Sutton [1980] IR 269 **Referred to** [1985] 86, 465; [1989] 670; [1990] 70, 403, 441; **Applied** [1983] 67; [1989] 710; [1990] 14; **Considered** [1981] 242; [1983] 89; [1984] 208; [1987] 400; [1988] 437; [1989] 209, 282; **Followed** [1982] 497; [1984] 249; [1986] 136, 428

Caldwell v Pagham Harbour Reclamation Co (1876) 2 Ch D 221 **Referred to** [1987] 477

Caldwell v Stuart (1984) 15 DLR (4th) 1 **Considered** [1985] 336

Caldwell v Sumpter [1972] Ch 478; [1972] 2 WLR 412 **Distinguished** [1988] 559

Calero-Toledo v Pearson Yacht Leasing Co (1974) 416 US 663 **Considered** [1989] 670

Camilla Cotton Oil Co v Granedex SA [1976] 2 Lloyd's Rep 10 **Considered** [1990] 159

Caminer v Northern and London Investment Trust Ltd [1951] AC 88 **Principles applied** [1990] 857

Campbell College Belfast (Governors) v Commissioner of Valuation Northern Ireland [1964] 1 WLR 912 **Referred to** [1984] 117

Campbell v Wallsend Shipping & Engineering Co Ltd [1977] Crim LR 351 **Referred to** [1988] 294

Campus Oil Ltd v Minister for Industry and Energy [1983] ILRM 258 **Referred to** [1984] 45; [1988] 149

Campus Oil Ltd v Minister for Industry and Energy [1983] IR 88; [1984] ILRM 45 **Referred to** [1983] 595; [1984] 373; [1986] 68; **Followed** [1987] 400; [1989] 582; [1990] 350; **Considered** [1988] 157, 221; [1990] 350; **Applied** [1986] 10

Canning v Donegal Co Council [1961] Ir Jur Rep 7 **Considered** [1986] 627

Capital & National Trust v Golder [1949] 2 All ER 956 **Doubted** [1984] 231

Cappelloni v Pelkmans (Case 119/84) [1985] ECR 3147 **Considered** [1989] 162

Carl Zeiss Stiftung v Rayner and Keeler Ltd (No 2) [1967] 1 AC 853; [1966] 2 All ER 536 **Dictum Applied** [1986] 318

Carpenter v Carpenter (1827) Milward's Reports 159 **Approved** [1981] 361

Carrick Furniture House Ltd v General Accident 1978 SLT 65 **Referred to** [1984] 501

Carrington, In re [1932] 2 Ch 1 **Referred to** [1978] 197

Carritt v Real and Personal Advance Co Ltd (1889) 42 Ch D 263 **Referred to** [1978] 211

Carroll v Clare County Council [1975] IR 221 **Referred to** [1986] 43; **Applied** [1978] 85; [1980] 153

Carroll v Kildare County Council [1950] IR 258 **Distinguished** [1990] 403; **Followed** [1987] 603

Carroll v McManus Supreme Court, unreported, 15 April 1964 **Dictum Applied** [1986] 538

Carroll (PJ) & Co Ltd v Philip Morris Inc [1970] IR 115 **Referred to** [1978] 106, 116

Carron v Germany (Case 198/85) [1986] ECR 2437 **Applied** [1990] 825; **Considered** [1989] 659

Carter v Wadman & Sons Ltd (1946) 28 TC 41 **Referred to** [1980] 107

Carthy v O'Neill High Court, unreported, 1 October 1979 **Reversed** [1981] 443

Cartledge v E Jopling & Sons Ltd [1963] AC 758 **Referred to** [1990] 403; **Doubted** [1983] 156

Carvalho v Hull, Blyth (Angola) Ltd [1975] 1 WLR 1228 **Referred to** [1988] 501

Casdagli v Casdagli [1919] AC 145 **Referred to** [1982] 433

Casey v Irish Intercontinental Bank [1979] IR 393; 114 ILTR 18 **Considered** [1983] 517; [1987] 345

Cassella (Leopold) & Co, In re [1910] 2 Ch 240 **Applied** [1976-7] 335

Cassells v Dublin Corporation [1963] IR 193 **Referred to** [1981] 242

Cassidy v Goodman Ltd [1975] IRLR 86 **Referred to** [1985] 336

Cassidy v Minister for Industry and Commerce [1978] IR 297 **Followed** [1988] 693; **Applied** [1984] 854; [1986] 693; **Distinguished** [1981] 237; [1989] 629;

Castellain v Preston (1883) 11 QBD 380 **Referred to** [1984] 501

Castioni, In re [1891] 1 QB 149 **Referred to** [1988] 333; **Considered** [1985] 385, 422

Castree v ER Squibb & Sons Ltd [1980] 1 WLR 1248; [1980] 2 All ER 589 **Considered** [1986] 627

Caulfield v D H Bourke & Son Ltd High Court, unreported, 13 November 1980 **Distinguished** [1981] 203

Cavalier v Pope [1906] AC 428 **Considered** [1986] 43

Cavan Central Co-operative Society Ltd, In re [1917] 2 IR 594; 12 TC 1 **Dicta applied** [1985] 655

Cavendish Ltd v Dublin Corporation [1974] IR 171 **Applied** [1989] 46; **Principles adopted** [1985] 249

Cavern Systems Ltd v Clontarf Residents Association [1984] ILRM 24 **Referred to** [1989] 282

Cawthorne v H M Advocate [1968] JC 32; 1968 SLT 330 **Considered** [1985] 25

Caxton Publishing Co Ltd v Sutherland Publishing Co Ltd [1939] AC 178 **Applied** [1982] 40

Cement Ltd v Commissioners of Valuation [1960] IR 283 **Dictum approved** [1980] 149

Cenlon Finance Co Ltd v Ellwood [1962] AC 782 **Distinguished** [1990] 249

Central Asbestos Co Ltd v Dodd [1973] AC 518 **Referred to** [1990] 403

Central Dublin Development Association Ltd v Attorney General 109 ILTR 69 **Referred to** [1983] 449; **Approved** [1984] 88; **Followed** [1983] 391

Central London Property Trust Ltd v High Trees House Ltd [1947] 1 KB 130 **Referred to** [1982] 367; [1985] 173; **Distinguished** [1984] 265

Ceylon University v Fernando [1960] 1 WLR 223 **Referred to** [1980] 46; [1989] 469

Chaine-Nickson v Bank of Ireland [1976] IR 393 **Considered** [1983] 517

Chambers v Cork Corporation 93 ILTR 45 **Considered** [1986] 43

Chaparral, The [1968] 2 Lloyd's Rep 315 **Referred to** [1988] 501

Chaplin v Boys [1971] AC 356 **Doubted** [1986] 627

Chariot Inns Ltd v Assicurazioni Generali SPA High Court, unreported, 23 January 1980 **Reversed** [1981] 173

Chariot Inns Ltd v Assicurazioni Generali Spa [1981] IR 199; [1981] ILRM 173 **Referred to** [1990] 110

Charleston Federal Savings & Loan Association v Alderson 324 US 182 **Referred to** [1983] 449; [1986] 136

Charlton v Ireland [1984] ILRM 39 **Followed** [1987] 118

Charterbridge Corp Ltd v Lloyd's Bank Ltd [1970] Ch 62 **Referred to** [1979] 221

Chase Manhattan Bank NA v Israel-British Bank (London) Ltd [1981] Ch 105; [1979] 3 All ER 1025 **Followed** [1986] 518

Chelmsford RDC v Powell [1963] 1 WLR 123 **Approved** [1981] 108

Cheshire v Bailey [1905] 1 KB 237 **Doubted** [1986] 559

Chettiar v Chettiar [1962] AC 294 **Referred to** [1980] 137

Chibbett v J Robinson & Sons Ltd (1924) 9 TC 48 **Referred to** [1980] 107

Chief Constable of North Wales Police v Evans [1982] 1 WLR 1155; [1982] 3 All ER 141 **Dictum Applied** [1987] 202

Child v Edwards [1909] 2 KB 75 **Referred to** [1982] 29

Chillingworth v Esche [1924] 1 Ch 97 **Followed** [1981] 433

Chinn v Collins [1981] AC 533 **Referred to** [1988] 181

Christie, The [1975] 2 Lloyd's Rep 100 **Dictum approved** [1986] 677

Christie v Christie [1917] 1 IR 17 **Referred to** [1987] 582

Christie v Leachinsky [1947] AC 573 **Distinguished** [1978] 122

Chung Che Cheung v R [1938] 4 All ER 786 **Applied** [1983] 163

Churchill v Siggers (1854) 3 E & B 929 **Dictum approved** [1982] 126

Churchward v Churchward [1895] P 7 **Applied** [1985] 35

City Life Assurance Co Ltd, In re [1926] Ch 191 **Referred to** [1985] 254

City of Chicago v Atchinson, Topeka and Santa Fe Railway Co (1958) 357 US 76 **Referred to** [1981] 242

City of Kamloops v Nielsen (1984) 10 DLR (4th) 641 **Considered** [1989] 400

City of London v Wood (1710) 12 Mod 687 **Referred to** [1982] 290

Cityview Press Ltd v An Comhairle Oiliúna [1980] IR 381 **Applied** [1984] 208; [1989] 342;

Considered [1986] 136; [1987] 278; **Followed** [1983] 429; [1986] 3, 381;

Clapham v National Assistance Board [1961] 2 QB 77 **Referred to** [1988] 333

Clarke, In re (1887) 36 Ch D 348 **Referred to** [1985] 641

Clarke, In re ; ex parte East & West India Dock Co (1881) 17 Ch D 759 **Considered** [1984] 273

Clarke, In re [1950] IR 235; 85 ILTR 119 **Referred to** [1983] 186

Clarke v Maguire [1990] 2 IR 681 **Followed** [1990] 220

Clarke v Ulster Bank [1950] NI 132 **Considered** [1986] 518

Clayton's case (1816) 1 Mer 572 **Referred to** [1980] 171; [1986] 518; [1990] 285

Clegg v Metcalfe [1914] 1 Ch 808 **Considered** [1989] 706

Cleveland Petroleum Co Ltd v Dartstone Ltd [1969] 1 WLR 116 **Followed** [1982] 519

Clinch v Inland Revenue Commissioners [1974] 1 QB 76; [1973] 1 All ER 977 **Followed** [1986] 37

Clonmel Foods Ltd v Eire Continental Trading Co Ltd [1955] IR 170; 87 ILTR 35 **Followed** [1989] 519

Clune v Director of Public Prosecutions; [1981] ILRM 17 **Referred to** [1984] 39; [1989] 71; **Considered** [1983] 311; **Dictum approved** [1983] 241, 285; [1984] 249

Cobb v Lane [1952] 1 All ER 1199 **Approved** [1983] 128

Coca Cola Co v F Cade & Sons Ltd [1957] IR 196 **Referred to** [1978] 106, 116; **Considered** [1990] 204

Cohane v Cohane [1968] IR 176 **Applied** [1982] 176

Coleman v Innes; In re Harwood [1936] Ch 285 **Referred to** [1990] 835

Coleman's Depositories Ltd, In re [1907] 2 KB 798 **Considered** [1985] 109; **Dictum approved** [1984] 545

Colgan v Connolly Construction Co (Ireland) Ltd [1980] ILRM 33 **Not followed** [1986] 43

Collco Dealings Ltd v Inland Revenue Commissioners [1962] AC 1; [1961] 1 All ER 762 **Considered** [1986] 24

Collins v Doyle [1982] ILRM 495 **Referred to** [1987] 255

Colonial Sugar Refining Co v Irving [1905] AC 318 **Referred to** [1982] 290

Colonial Trust Corp, In re (1880) 15 Ch D 465 **Referred to** [1985] 641

Combe v Combe [1951] 2 KB 215 **Referred to** [1985] 173; **Dictum approved** [1982] 367

Combe v Lord Swaythling [1947] 1 Ch 625 **Considered** [1985] 679

Comhlucht Paipear Riomhaireachta Teo v Údaras na Gaeltachta [1987] IR 684 **Referred to** [1989] 461; **Appeal allowed** [1990] 266

Commercial Plastics Ltd v Vincent [1965] 1 QB 623 **Considered** [1981] 345

Commission v Belgium (Case 102/79) [1980] ECR 1473 **Applied** [1989] 865

Commission v Belgium (Case 239/85) [1988] 1 CMLR 248 **Applied** [1989] 865

Commission v Germany (Case 29/84) [1985] ECR 166 **Considered** [1989] 865 Commission v Germany (Case 205/84) [1986] ECR 3755 **Considered** [1990] 466

Commission v Italy [1982] ECR 2187 **Referred to** [1984] 45

Commission v Italy (Case 145/82) [1983] ECR 711 **Applied** [1989] 865

Commissioner of Police of the Metropolis v Carron [1976] 1 WLR 87 **Distinguished** [1984] 127

Commissioners of Inland Revenue v Cock Russel & Co Ltd [1949] 2 All ER 889 **Referred to** [1989] 552

Commonwealth of Australia v John Farfax & Sons Ltd (1980) 147 CLR 39 **Dictum approved** [1987] 135

Company, A, In re [1894] 2 Ch 394 **Referred to** [1979] 141

Conaty v Tipperary (NR) County Council Circuit Court, unreported, 6 February 1987 **Approved** [1988] 86

Conlon v Mohamed [1987] ILRM 172 **Affirmed** [1989] 523

Connelly v Director of Public Prosecutions [1964] AC 1254; [1964] 2 All ER 401 **Considered** [1986] 639
Connolly v Salinger High Court, unreported, 3 November 1980 **Affirmed** [1982] 482
Connolly v Sweeney [1988] ILRM 35 **Reversed** [1988] 483
Connor v Potts [1897] 1 IR 534 **Followed** [1983] 295
Connors v Delap [1989] ILRM 93 **Followed** [1989] 110
Conole v Redbank Oyster Co Ltd [1976] IR 191 **Followed** [1988] 225
Conroy v Attorney General [1965] IR 411; **Referred to** [1981] 17; [1984] 39, 625; **Applied** [1981] 469; [1984] 249; **Considered** [1978] 12; **Dictum applied** [1987] 316; **Dictum approved** [1989] 149; **Distinguished** [1986] 343; **Followed** [1982] 249, 512; [1988] 430
Conroy v Tullamore Motor Works Ltd High Court, unreported, 27 July 1983 **Referred to** [1985] 100
Const v Harris (1824) Tar & Rus 496 **Referred to** [1979] 141
Constantine v Imperial Hotel Ltd [1944] KB 693 **Considered** [1982] 48
Constantine Line v Imperial Smelting Corp [1942] AC 154 **Referred to** [1976-7] 327
Containercare (Ir) Ltd v Wycherley [1982] IR 143 **Followed** [1983] 380
Contract Corporation, In re (1871) LR 5 Ch App 112 **Considered** [1989] 501
Conway v Ni Mhainnin High Court, unreported, 20 March 1980 **Referred to** [1984] 555; [1990] 617
Conway v Rimmer [1968] AC 910 **Considered** [1948] 149
Cook, In re [1986] 1 NIJB 43 **Applied** [1988] 392
Cook v Bath Corporation (1868) LR 6 Eq 177 **Referred to** [1981] 365
Cook v Carroll [1945] IR 515; 79 ILTR 116 **Considered** [1981] 125
Cook v Mayor and Corporation of Bath (1868) LR 6 Ex 177 **Principles applied** [1984] 451
Cook v Swinfen [1967] 1 WLR 457 **Considered** [1982] 48
Cooke v Midland Great Western Railway of Ireland Ltd [1909] AC 229 **Referred to** [1987] 768
Cooke v Walsh [1983] ILRM 429 **Reversed** [1984] 208
Cooke v Walsh [1984] ILRM 208 **Referred to** [1984] 523; **Discussed** [1985] 582; **Followed** [1989] 735
Cooke v Walsh [1989] ILRM 322 **Considered** [1989] 785
Coope v Rideout [1921] 1 Ch 291 **Referred to** [1979] 119
Cooper v Cooper (1874) LR 7 HL 53 **Referred to** [1987] 582; **Applied** [1983] 519
Cooper v Ince Hall Co [1876] WN 24 **Considered** [1988] 149
Cooper v Millea [1938] IR 749 **Referred to** [1988] 157
Cooper (Gerald) Chemicals Ltd, In re [1978] Ch 262 **Referred to** [1985] 76
Córas Iompair Éireann v Carroll [1983] ILRM 173 **Reversed** [1986] 312
Córas Iompair Éireann v Carroll High Court, unreported, 24 June 1988 **Referred to** [1990] 617
Corbett v Fagan; In re Joyce [1946] IR 277; 80 ILTR 158 **Followed** [1987] 606; **Dictum approved** [1982] 217; **Applied** [1980] 257
Corboy, In re: Leahy v Corboy [1969] IR 148 **Applied** [1978] 175, 247
Corby v Morrison [1980] ICR 564 **Applied** [1983] 363
Cordingly v Cheeseborough (1862) 31 LJ Ch (ns) 617 **Referred to** [1983] 295
Cordova Land Ltd v Victor Brothers Inc [1966] 1 WLR 793 **Considered** [1986] 627
Cork Corporation v O'Connell High Court, unreported, 19 October 1981 **Affirmed** [1982] 505
Cork Corporation v O'Connell [1982] ILRM 505 **Discussed** [1985] 325
Cork Corporation v Rooney (1881) 7 LR Ir 191 **Referred to** [1979] 277

Corley v Gill [1975] IR 313 not **Followed** [1988] 318

Corrigan v Irish Land Commission [1977] IR 317 **Considered** [1982] 568; **Distinguished** [1989] 865

Cosgrove v Ireland [1982] ILRM 48 **Considered** [1989] 810; **Followed** [1987] 651

Costa v ENEL [1964] ECR 585; [1964] CMLR 425 **Referred to** [1987] 400

Costello v Bofin High Court, unreported, 20 March 1979 **Overruled** [1980] 233

Costello v Director of Public Prosecutions [1983] ILRM 489; [1984] IR 436; **Referred to** [1986] 123; [1987] 65; **Distinguished** [1989] 309, 325; **Reversed** [1984] 413

Costello v Director of Public Prosecutions [1984] ILRM 413 **Followed** [1987] 320

Costello v Riordan High Court, unreported, 19 October 1988 **Referred to** [1989] 777

Cottin v Blane (1795) 2 Anstr 544; 145 ER 962 **Distinguished** [1985] 522

Cottrill v Steyning and Littlehampton Building Society [1966] 1 WLR 753 **Referred to** [1982] 201

Coughlan v Cumberland [1898] 1 Ch 704 **Referred to** [1987] 669

Coulson, In re; Mullen v Brady 87 ILTR 93 **Followed** [1976-7] 88

Council of Civil Service Unions v Minister for the Civil Service [1985] 1 AC 374; [1984] 3 All ER 935 **Referred to** [1988] 693; [1989] 1; **Dictum approved** [1987] 202; **Considered** [1989] 710; [1990] 293; **Followed** [1989] 710

County of Gloucester Bank v Rudry Merthyr Steam and House Coal Colliery Co [1895] 1 Ch 629 **Applied** [1982] 57

Courtney v Courtney [1923] 2 IR 31 **Considered** [1990] 886

Courtney & Fairbairn Ltd v Tolaini Bros (Hotels) Ltd [1975] 1 WLR 297 **Referred to** [1988] 157

Coveney v Persse [1910] 1 IR 194 **Referred to** [1985] 641

Cowley v Higginson (1838) 4M & W 245 principles **Applied** [1984] 451

Cox v Glue (1848) 5 CH 533 **Dictum approved** [1982] 451; **Distinguished** [1982] 451

Cox v Hakes (1890) 15 App Cas 506 **Considered** [1983] 549

Cox v Massey [1969] IR 243 **Referred to** [1985] 100

Cox v Phillips Industries Ltd [1976] 1 WLR 638 **Considered** [1979] 266

Coyle v McFadden [1901] 1 IR 298 **Followed** [1987] 582

Crabb v Arun District Council [1976] 6 Ch 179; [1975] 2 All ER 865 **Applied** [1976-7] 266; **Approved** [1983] 300

Craig v Lamoureux [1920] AC 349 **Referred to** [1978] 175

Crake v Supplementary Benefits Commission [1982] 1 All ER 498 **Considered** [1989] 169

Crane v Naughton [1912] 2 IR 318 **Dictum approved** [1981] 328

Creedon v Dublin Corporation High Court, unreported, 3 July 1981 **Affirmed** [1983] 339

Creedon v Dublin Corporation [1984] IR 428; [1983] ILRM 339; **Applied** [1985] 513; **Distinguished** [1990] 633

Cricklewood Property Trust Ltd v Leighton Investment Trust Ltd [1945] AC 221 **Applied** [1976–7] 327

Crighton v Law Car and General Insurance Corp [1910] 2 KB 738 **Dictum doubted** [1990] 277

Criminal Law (Jurisdiction) Bill 1975, In re [1977] IR 129; 110 ILTR 69 **Referred to** [1981] 113; [1989] 333; **Considered** [1984] 224, 539; [1986] 639; [1989] 209; [1990] 441; **Followed** [1989] 266

Crippen, In re [1911] P 108 **Referred to** [1986] 318

Cripps Warburg Ltd v Cologne Investment Co Ltd [1980] IR 321 **Referred to** [1986] 167; **Applied** [1982] 551

Crodaun Homes Ltd v Kildare County Council High Court, unreported **Reversed** [1983] 1

Crodaun Homes Ltd v Kildare County Council [1983] ILRM 1 **Referred to** [1989] 282, 865; **Applied** [1985] 494

Crompton v Customs and Excise Commissioners [1974] AC 405; [1973] 2 All ER 1169 **Dictum adopted** [1987] 516

Cronin v Cork & County Property Co Ltd [1986] IR 559 **Referred to** [1990] 100; **Dictum Applied** [1989] 552

Cronin v Strand Dairy Ltd High Court, unreported, 18 December 1985 **Approved** [1989] 478

Crosfield & Son's Application [1910] 1 Ch 130 **Referred to** [1990] 204; **Considered** [1982] 91; [1984] 565

Crossley v Lightowler (1867) 2 Ch App 478 **Principles applied** [1984] 451

Crossley Bros Ltd v Lee [1908] 1 KB 86 **Followed** [1983] 402

Crotty v An Taoiseach [1987] IR 713; [1987] ILRM 400 **Referred to** [1988] 333; [1990] 70, 617; **Considered** [1989] 209; **Dicta applied** [1989] 710; **Followed** [1989] 53; **Distinguished** [1990] 441

Crowe v Crowe [1937] 2 All ER 723 **Referred to** [1980] 257

Crowe (W & L) Ltd v Dublin Port and Docks Board [1962] IR 294 **Considered** [1976-7] 311

Crowley v Ireland [1980] IR 102 **Referred to** [1987] 651

Crump v Lambert (1867) LR 3 Eq 409 **Considered** [1976-7] 28

Cullen v Attorney General [1979] IR 394 **Referred to** [1982] 249; [1982] 512

Cullen v Clein [1970] IR 146 **Referred to** [1986] 235

Cullen v Cullen [1962] IR 268 **Considered** [1981] 419

Cullinane v British Rema Manufacturing Co Ltd [1954] 1 QB 292 **Distinguished** [1979] 296

Cumper v Pothecary [1941] 2 KB 58 **Dictum approved** [1982] 121

Cunliffe v Goodman [1950] 2 KB 237 **Considered** [1985] 25

Cunliffe-Owen, In re [1953] 1 Ch 545 **Referred to** [1987] 582

Cunningham v MacGrath Brothers [1964] IR 209; 99 ILTR 183 **Followed** [1984] 402

Cunningham v Whelan 52 ILTR 67 **Referred to** [1984] 402

Cunningham-Howie v F W Dimbleby & Sons Ltd [1951] 1 KB 360; [1950] 2 All ER 882 **Dicta approved** [1985] 673

Cunningham-Reid v Buchanan-Jardine [1988] 1 WLR 678 **Applied** [1990] 159

Curran v Northern Ireland Co-Ownership Housing Association Ltd [1987] AC 718 **Considered** 400

Currie and Niagara Escarpment Commission, In re [1984] 10 DLR (4th) 113 **Referred to** [1986] 343

Currie v Fairy Hill Ltd [1968] IR 232 **Referred to** [1985] 41

Curtis v The Marquis of Buckingham (1814) 3 Ves & B 168 **Applied** [1979] 156

Cutler v Wandsworth Stadium Ltd [1949] AC 398 **Considered** [1990] 560

Cyona Distributors Ltd, In re [1967] Ch 889 **Considered** [1985] 75

Cyril Lord Carpets Ltd v Schofield [1966] NI 178; 42 TC 637 **Referred to** [1985] 651

Czarnikow (C) Ltd v Koufos, The Heron II [1969] 1 AC 350 **Referred to** [1979] 240, 296; **Applied** [1980] 107

D v C [1984] ILRM 173 **Referred to** [1986] 618; **Approved** [1985] 383; **Considered** [1985] 35; **Followed** [1987] 58

D v D High Court, unreported, 16 December 1981 **Followed** [1983] 380

D (E) v D (F) High Court, unreported, 23 October 1980 **Considered** [1983] 387

D (H) v D (J) High Court, unreported, 31 July 1981 **Referred to** [1989] 528

D (H) v D(P) Supreme Court, unreported, 8 May 1978 **Distinguished** [1982] 562

DHN Food Distributors Ltd v Tower Hamlets London Borough Council [1976] 1 WLR 852; [1976] 3 All ER 462 **Distinguished** [1985] 513

Daiguiri Rum Trade Mark (1966) RPC 582 **Referred to** [1982] 240

Daily Mirror Newspapers Ltd v Gardiner [1968] 2 QB 762 **Referred to** [1988] 157

Dallaway, In re [1982] 1 WLR 756 **Referred to** [1989] 625

Damen v O'Shea High Court, unreported, 25 May 1977 **Referred to** [1986] 167

Danchevsky v Danchevsky [1975] Fam 17 **Considered** [1981] 416

Dandridge v William (1970) 397 US 471 **Referred to** [1983] 449

Daniels v Heskin [1954] IR 73; 86 ILTR 141; 87 ILTR 189 **Referred to** [1986] 189; [1989] 735

Daphne v Shaw (1926) 11 TC 256 **Not followed** [1984] 679

Data Products (Memories) Ltd v Simpson (EP 20/1978: DEP 1/1979) **Distinguished** [1982] 367; [1985] 173

Daulia Ltd v Four Millbank Nominees Ltd [1978] Ch 231 **Referred to** [1979] 119

Davidson v Annesley; In re Annesley [1926] Ch 692 **Referred to** [1982] 433

Day v Savadge (1614) Hob 47 **Referred to** [1982] 290

Davidson v Lloyd Aircraft Services Ltd [1974] 1 WLR 1042 **Referred to** [1987] 790

Davies v Sweet [1962] 2 QB 300 **Referred to** [1986] 447

Davis v Inland Revenue Commissioners [1922] 2 KB 805; 8 TC 341 **Observations applied** [1985] 666

Davis v M [1947] IR 145; 80 ILTR 57; 81 ILTR 157 **Distinguished** [1984] 610

Davis v Mater Misercordiae Hospital [1933] IR 480 **Referred to** [1985] 210

Davis & Co v Stribolt & Co (1889) 6 RPC 207 **Considered** [1976-7] 335

Davis Contractors Ltd v Fareham UDC [1956] AC 696 **Considered** [1976-7] 327; [1990] 601

Dawes v Hawkins (1860) 8 CB (ns) 848 **Principles applied** [1984] 451

Dawkins v Antobus (1879) 17 Ch D 615 **Referred to** [1979] 166

Dawkins v Lord Paulet (1869) LR 5 QB 94 **Considered** [1989] 544

Dawnays Ltd v F G Minter & Co Ltd [1971] 1 WLR 1205 **Dictum disapproved** [1976-7] 204

de Burca v Attorney General [1976] IR 38 **Referred to** [1983] 549; [1990] 767; **Considered** [1983] 449; [1985] 86; [1989] 528; **Distinguished** [1982] 108

de Francesco v Barnum (1890) 45 Ch D 430 **Referred to** [1985] 221

Deansrath Investments, In re [1974] IR 228 **Considered** [1976-7] 343

Dearle v Hull (1828) 3 Russ. 1 **Referred to** [1985] 254

Deaton v Attorney General [1963] IR 170; 98 ILTR 99 **Referred to** [1980] 242; [1983] 489; **Considered** [1986] 428

Debtor, A (No 24 of 1971), In re: ex parte Marley v Trustee of the Property of the Debtor [1976] 1 WLR 952; [1976] 2 All ER 1010 **Distinguished** [1987] 522

Defrenne v SABENA (No 2) (Case 43/75) [1976] ECR 455 **Referred to** [1989] 196; **Followed** [1989] 53; **Considered** [1986] 483

Defries (N) & Co Ltd, In re [1904] 1 Ch 366 **Referred to** [1976-7] 222

Deighan v Hearne [1986] IR 603 **Referred to** [1988] 52

Delenville v Delenville [1948] P 100 **Doubted** [1984] 667

Dennehy v Minister for Social Welfare High Court, unreported, 26 July 1984 **Distinguished** [1989] 196

Denny, Mott and Dickson Ltd v Fraser & Co Ltd [1944] AC 265 **Referred to** [1976-7] 327

Dent v Dent (1865) 13 LT 252 **Followed** [1989] 528

Dental Manufacturing Co Ltd v de Troy [1912] 3 KB 76 **Distinguished** [1976-7] 144

Derry v Peek (1889) 14 App Cas 337 **Considered** [1980] 53

Devenport Corporation v Tozer [1903] 1 Ch 759 **Referred to** [1981] 365

Dewhurst (John) & Sons Ltd's Trade Mark [1896] 2 Ch 137 **Considered** [1976-7] 335

Diamond v Campbell-Jones [1961] Ch 22 **Referred to** [1982] 201

Dickinson v North Eastern Railway Co (1863) 33 LJ Ex 91 **Approved** [1982] 327

Dillane v Attorney General [1980] ILRM 167 **Applied** [1985] 349; **Considered** [1984] 443

Dillon v O'Brien (1887) 20 LR Ir 300 **Followed** [1989] 71

Dillon-Leetch v Calleary Supreme Court, unreported, 25 July 1973, 31 July 1974; 25 February 1975 **Referred to** [1979] 281

Diment v N H Foot Ltd [1974] 2 All ER 785 **Not followed** [1985] 134

Dinan Dowdall & Co Ltd v Dublin Corporation [1954] IR 230 **Referred to** [1985] 249

Dingle v Associated Newspapers [1964] AC 371; [1962] 2 All ER 737 **Referred to** [1986] 601

Diplock In re: Diplock v Wintle [1941] Ch 253; [1948] Ch 465 **Considered** [1985] 109; **Dictum approved** [1981] 473

Director of Public Prosecutions v Bradfute & Associates Ltd [1967] 2 QB 291 **Referred to** [1990] 301

Director of Public Prosecutions v Brady 2 Frewen 16 **Considered** [1984] 461

Director of Public Prosecutions v Clein [1981] ILRM 465 **Affirmed** [1983] 76

Director of Public Prosecutions v Clein [1983] ILRM 76 **Referred to** [1987] 65; **Followed** [1987] 316; **Applied** [1984] 35; [1989] 495; **Considered** [1986] 565

Director of Public Prosecutions v Closkey High Court, unreported 6 February 1984 **Followed** [1986] 657; **Distinguished** [1987] 575; [1988] 39

Director of Public Prosecutions v Collins [1981] ILRM 447 **Dictum Applied** [1987] 570

Director of Public Prosecutions v Corrigan [1980] ILRM 145 **Approved** [1981] 447

Director of Public Prosecutions v Corrigan Special Criminal Court, unreported, 23 June 1982 **Distinguished** [1984] 461

Director of Public Prosecutions v Flanagan [1979] IR 265; 114 ILTR 34 **Referred to** [1986] 177; **Considered** [1982] 143; **Dictum Applied** [1986] 483

Director of Public Prosecutions v Gaffney [1986] ILRM 657 **Distinguished** [1987] 575; reversed [1988] 39

Director of Public Prosecutions v Gannon Supreme Court, unreported, 3 June 1986 **Referred to** [1988] 318

Director of Public Prosecutions v Gill [1980] IR 263 **Referred to** [1987] 65; [1988] 623; **Applied** [1986] 565, 597; **Dictum Applied** [1988] 720; **Distinguished** [1981] 465; [1983] 76

Director of Public Prosecutions v Gilmore [1981] ILRM 102 **Distinguished** [1985] 206; **Followed** [1987] 129

Director of Public Prosecutions v Grey [1986] IR 317; [1987] ILRM 4 **Referred to** [1989] 113

Director of Public Prosecutions v Healy [1990] ILRM 313 **Referred to** [1990] 569

Director of Public Prosecutions v Humphreys [1977] AC 1; [1976] 2 All ER 497 **Considered** [1986] 318

Director of Public Prosecutions v Irish Press Ltd High Court, unreported, 15 December 1976 **Followed** [1984] 577

Director of Public Prosecutions v Joyce [1985] ILRM 206 **Principles adopted** [1985] 465; **Distinguished** [1987] 575

Director of Public Prosecutions v Kelly. *See* People (Director of Public Prosecutions) v Kelly

Director of Public Prosecutions v Kennedy, High Court, unreported, 11 July 1985 **Applied** [1988] 243

Director of Public Prosecutions v Luft [1976] 3 WLR 32 **Cited** [1983] 34

Director of Public Prosecutions v McGarrigle Supreme Court, unreported, 22 June 1987 **Referred to** [1988] 483

Director of Public Prosecutions v McGuoy High Court, unreported, 25 July 1983 **Dictum approved** [1985] 243

Director of Public Prosecutions v McMahon, Supreme Court, unreported, 20 June 1986 **Referred to** [1988] 39

Director of Public Prosecutions v McNally and Breathnach, Court of Criminal Appeal, unreported, 16 February 1981 **Referred to** [1982] 1

Director of Public Prosecutions v McQuaid High Court, unreported 26 October 1984 **Distinguished** [1986] 565, 597

Director of Public Prosecutions v Morrissey [1982] ILRM 487 **Applied** [1989] 561

Director of Public Prosecutions v Nangle [1984] ILRM 171 **Distinguished** [1990] 220

Director of Public Prosecutions v O'Neill, Supreme Court, unreported, 13 July 1982 **Referred to** [1988] 483

Director of Public Prosecutions v Ping Lin [1976] AC 574 **Referred to** [1988] 666

Director of Public Prosecutions v Roche [1989] ILRM 39 **Applied** [1989] 498

Director of Public Prosecutions v Sheeran [1986] ILRM 579 **Followed** [1986] 588

Director of Public Prosecutions v Walsh [1985] ILRM 243 **Referred to** [1988] 483

Director of Public Prosecutions v Walsh and Conneely. *See* State (Director of Public Prosecutions) v Walsh and Conneely

Director of Public Prosecutions (Hurlihy) v Hannon Supreme Court, unreported, 4 March 1981 **Dictum Applied** [1982] 143

Director of Public Prosecutions (Nagle) v Flynn [1987] IR 535 **Referred to** [1989] 491

Director of Public Prosecutions for Northern Ireland v Lynch [1975] AC 653; [1975] 1 All ER 913 **Referred to** [1986] 80

Distillers Co Biochemicals Ltd v Thompson [1971] AC 458; [1971] 1 All ER 694 **Not followed** [1986] 627

Dixon v Wells (1890) 25 QBD 249 **Dictum approved** [1986] 565

Dodd Properties (Kent) Ltd v Canterbury City Council [1980] 1 WLR 433; [1980] 1 All ER 928 **Referred to** [1984] 265; **Approved** [1985] 189

Doe v Bridges (1831) 1 B & Ad 847 **Considered** [1990] 560

Doe v Chamberlain (1839) 5 M & W 14 **Referred to** [1983] 128

Doherty v Allman (1878) 3 App Cas 709 **Considered** [1984] 595; **Followed** [1982] 519

Doherty v Bowaters Irish Wallboard Mills Ltd [1968] IR 277 **Followed** [1989] 735

Dolan v Corn Exchange [1975] IR 315 **Not followed** [1988] 318

Dolan v County Councils of Louth and Meath and the Corporation of Drogheda [1957] Ir Jur Rep 53 **Considered** [1985] 269

Dolan v Neligan [1967] IR 247; 103 ILTR 46 **Referred to** [1981] 144; **Approved** [1985] 283; **Dictum approved** [1984] 366

Dominion of Canada Plumbago Co, In re (1884) 27 Ch D 33 **Referred to** [1990] 266

Domvilles Estate, In re [1930] IR 640 **Referred to** [1983] 549

Doncaster Amalgamated Collieries Ltd v Bean [1946] 1 All ER 642 **Distinguished** [1984] 610

Donnelly v Adams [1905] IR 154 **Distinguished** [1985] 134

Donnelly v Browne Supreme Court, unreported, 15th May 1982 **Followed** [1983] 429

Donoghue v Stevenson [1932] AC 562; [1932] All ER 1 **Referred to** [1986] 627; [1988] 610; **Applied** [1980] 33, 124; [1986] 43; **Dictum Applied** [1987] 768

Donohoe v Browne [1986] IR 90 **Distinguished** [1989] 133 **Considered** [1989] 342

Doran v Thomas Thompson & Sons Ltd [1978] IR 223; 113 ILTR 93 **Referred to** [1981] 179; **Followed** [1983] 156; [1987] 95

Dorrian v McHugh [1907] 2 IR 564 **Distinguished** [1981] 213

Dorset Yacht Co Ltd v Home Office [1970] AC 1004 **Referred to** [1988] 610; [1990] 658

Dowd v Kerry County Council [1970] IR 27 **Referred to** [1985] 41

Dowse, In re; Walsh v AIB Ltd, High Court, unreported, 2 March 1977 **Referred to** [1978] 203

Dowsett, In re [1901] Ch 398 **Considered** [1978] 197

Doyle v An Taoiseach [1986] ILRM 693 **Considered** [1989] 342

Doyle v Ireland [1981] ECR 735 **Referred to** [1986] 693

Doyle v Wicklow Co Council [1974] IR 55 **Followed** [1986] 244

Drake v Chief Adjudication Officer [1986] 3 CMLR 43; [1986] 3 All ER 65 **Dictum applied** [1987] 324

Drane v Evangelou [1978] 1 WLR 455 **Considered** [1978] 136

Draper v Attorney General [1984] IR 277; [1984] ILRM 643 **Considered** [1987] 290

Draper v Trist [1939] 3 All ER 513 **Followed** [1976–7] 144

Draper & Son Ltd v Edward Turner & Son Ltd [1965] 1 QB 424 **Referred to** [1983] 350

Dreher v Irish Land Commission (1980) 4 JISEL 72 **Affirmed** [1984] 94

Dreher v Irish Land Commission [1984] ILRM 94 **Referred to** [1985] 86, 685; [1988] 400; **Considered** [1985] 364; [1989] 670; principles **Applied** [1985] 494

Dronfield Silkstone Coal Co (No 2), In re (1883) 23 Ch D 511 **Referred to** [1990] 266

Drury v Defontain (1808) 1 Taunt 131 **Referred to** [1982] 29

Du Cros v Ryall (1935) 19 TC 444 **Referred to** [1980] 107

Dublin Corporation v Flynn [1980] IR 357 **Referred to** [1990] 817; **Considered** [1986] 318, 428

Dublin Corporation v Garland [1982] ILRM 104 **Approved** [1990] 48

Dublin Corporation v Moore High Court, unreported, 20 April 1982 reversed [1984] 339

Dublin Corporation v Mulligan High Court, unreported, 6 May 1980 **Followed** [1982] 104

Dublin Corporation v Trinity College Dublin [1984] ILRM 84 **Referred to** [1985] 283

Dublin County Council v Crampton Builders High Court, unreported, 10 March 1980 **Referred to** [1984] 297

Dublin County Council v Elton Homes Ltd [1984] ILRM 297; **Distinguished** [1986] 104; **Considered** [1989] 235

Dublin County Council v O'Riordan [1985] IR 159; [1986] ILRM 104 **Considered** [1989] 235

Dublin County Council v Sellwood Quarries Ltd [1981] ILRM 23 **Followed** [1987] 564

Dublin County Council v Shortt [1982] ILRM 117 **Affirmed** [1983] 377

Dublin County Council v Shortt [1983] ILRM 377 **Considered** [1984] 313; **Followed** [1984] 616

Dublin County Council v Tallaght Block Co Ltd [1982] ILRM 534 **Followed** [1988] 274

Dublin County Council v Tallaght Block Co Ltd Supreme Court, unreported, 17 May 1983 **Considered** [1985] 325; **Followed** [1987] 564

Dublin Port and Docks Board v Bank of Ireland [1976] IR 118 **Considered** [1987] 142

Dublin Port and Docks Board v Brittania Dredging Co [1968] IR 136 **Distinguished** [1982] 349; [1983] 258; **Followed** [1982] 519; **Considered** [1984] 595

Duchess of Kingston's Case 20 How St Tr 355 **Referred to** [1980] 257

Duck v Tower Galvanising Co [1901] 2 KB 314 **Followed** [1982] 57

Duckett v Williams (1834) 2 Cr & M 348 **Considered** [1990] 110

Duffy v Doyle High Court, unreported, 9 May 1979 **Considered** [1990] 835

Duncan v Cammell Laird & Co [1942] AC 624 **Referred to** [1984] 149

Duncan Stephenson MacMillan and Jervois v Carey High Court, unreported, 8 February 1980; **Appeal allowed** [1982] 121

Dunlop v Dunlop Rubber Co [1921] 1 AC 367; [1921] 1 IR 173 **Considered** [1986] 627

Dunlop v Woollahra Municipal Council [1982] AC 158; [1981] 1 All ER 1202 **Considered** [1987] 747; **Followed** [1989] 416

Dunne, In re [1968] IR 312 **Referred to** [1983] 331

Dunne v Clinton [1930] IR 366 **Referred to** [1989] 821; **Followed** [1987] 727

Dunne v Hamilton High Court, unreported, 14 February 1980 **Appeal allowed** [1982] 290

Dunne v Hamilton; Hamilton v Hamilton [1982] IR 466; [1982] ILRM 290 **Referred to** [1988] 400; **Applied** [1990] 641; **Considered** [1986] 37; **Dictum Considered** [1988] 318; **Followed** [1986] 693

Dunne v National Maternity Hospital [1989] ILRM 735 **Followed** [1990] 110

Dunne v O'Neill [1974] IR 180; 109 ILTR 101 **Referred to** [1990] 617; **Applied** [1987] 555; principles **Applied** [1984] 555; **Followed** [1976–7] 50; [1978] 63

Dunne (Brendan) Ltd v Fitzpatrick [1958] IR 29 **Referred to** [1984] 373

Dunne (Frank) Ltd v Dublin County Council [1974] IR 45 **Referred to** [1983] 141; **Distinguished** [1980] 64

Durant v Durant (1826) 1 Hagg Ecc 733 **Followed** [1989] 528

Dutton v Bognor Regis UDC [1972] 1 QB 373; [1972] 1 All ER 462 **Referred to** [1990] 658; **Applied** [1986] 43; **Considered** [1980] 33

Dyott v Reade 10 ILTR 110 **Dictum approved** [1976–7] 50

Dyson v Attorney General [1911] 1 KB 410 **Dicta applied** [1979] 273

East & West India Dock Co, Ex parte; In re Clarke (1881) 17 Ch D 759 **Considered** [1984] 273

East Barnet UDC v British Transport Commission [1962] 2 WLR 134; [1962] 2 QB 484 **Dictum approved** [1987] 564

East Cork Foods Ltd v O'Dwyer Steel Co Ltd [1978] IR 103 **Followed** [1981] 10; **Dictum Applied** [1984] 265

East Donegal Co-Operative Livestock Marts Ltd v Attorney General [1970] IR 317; 104 ILTR 81 **Referred to** [1980] 208; [1981] 242, 456; [1982] 290; [1984] 88, 224; [1985] 11, 410; [1986] 693; [1988] 52, 545; [1989] 854; [1990] 70; **Applied** [1976–7] 184; [1983] 67, 89, 314, 429; [1985] 302; [1986] 343, 499; [1990] 185; **Dictum applied** [1981] 324; [1982] 190; [1987] 606; **Considered** [1985] 86; [1986] 136; **Distinguished** [1989] 209; **Followed** [1981] 324; [1986] 3; [1987] 36, 477; [1989] 266

East Realty Investment Co v Schneider Granite Co (1916) 240 US 55 **Referred to** [1986] 136

Eastern Health Board v 79 Psychiatric Nurses DEE 5/1984 **Doubted** [1990] 485

Eastham Corporation v Bernard Sunley & Sons Ltd [1906] AC 406 **Referred to** [1976–7] 93

Eastman Photographic Materials Co v Comptroller General of Patents [1898] AC 571 **Dictum Applied** [1976–7] 335

Eastmans Ltd v Shaw (1928) 14 TC 218 **Considered** [1984] 231

Ebrahimi v Westbourne Galleries Ltd [1973] AC 360; [1972] 2 All ER 492 **Referred to** [1986] 239; **Applied** [1979] 141

EC Commission. *See* Commission

Eccles v Bryant and Pollock [1948] Ch 93 **Referred to** [1979] 119; **Followed** [1981] 433

Echliff v Baldwin (1809) 16 Ves Jun 167 **Applied** [1979] 156

Editor of Sunday Express, In re (1953), Times Newspaper, 25 February 1953 **Referred to** [1985] 183

Educational Co of Ireland Ltd v Fallon Bros [1919] 1 IR 62; 53 ILTR 41 **Distinguished** [1990] 534; **Followed** [1990] 811

Educational Co of Ireland Ltd v Fitzpatrick [1961] IR 323; 97 ILTR 16 **Referred to** [1978] 51; [1986] 68; **Applied** [1979] 277; **Considered** [1987] 477; **Dictum applied** [1982] 327; **Dictum approved** [1981] 84; explained [1984] 45, 595; **Explained and Applied** [1983] 258; principles **Applied** [1982] 349

Edwards v Bairstow [1956] AC 14 **Principles applied** [1985] 210

Edwards v Skyways Ltd [1964] 1 WLR 349 **Referred to** [1982] 367; **Approved** [1984] 587

Fachini v Brysin (1951) 1 TLR 1386 **Referred to** [1983] 128

Factortame Ltd v Secretary of State for Transport. *See* R. v Secretary of State for Transport, ex parte Factortame Ltd

Farah Manufacturing Co v Controller of Patents [1978] FSR 239 **Referred to** [1976–7] 335

Farrell v Alexander [1976] QB 345 **Dictum approved** [1982] 13

Farrell v Barron [1938] Ir Jur Rep 19 **Referred to** [1976–7] 119

Farrell v Federated Employers Insurance Association Ltd [1970] 1 All ER 360 **Not followed** [1985] 109

Farrell v Halal Meat Packers (Ballyhaunis) Ltd UD 672/1986 **Referred to** [1990] 293

Fehmarn, The [1958] 1 WLR 159 **Considered** [1988] 1, 501

Fenton v Thorley & Co Ltd [1903] AC 443 **Referred to** [1988] 373

Feres v United States of America (1950) 340 US 135 **Considered** [1989] 544

Ferguson, Ex parte (1871) LR 6 QB 280 **Referred to** [1980] 186

Ferguson v Weaving [1951] 1 KB 814; [1951] 1 All ER 412 **Considered** [1987] 477

Fermanagh County Council v Board of Education of Donegal Presbytery [1923] 2 IR 184 **Considered** [1986] 627

Fermanagh County Council v Farrendon [1923] 1 IR 180 **Considered** [1986] 627

Field v Megaw (1869) LR 4 CP 660 **Considered** [1989] 777

Fielding v Preston (1857) 1 De G & J 438 **Considered** [1976–7] 106

Fine Industrial Commodities Ltd, In re [1956] Ch 256 **Considered** [1990] 42

Finlay v Murtagh [1979] IR 249 **Referred to** [1985] 41; [1988] 373; [1990] 588; **Applied** [1980] 124; **Followed** [1986] 189

Finley, In re (1888) 21 QBD 475 **Applied** [1984] 273

Finn v Attorney General [1983] IR 154 **Referred to** [1987] 400

Finucane v McMahon [1990] ILRM 505 **Applied** [1990] 648, 802

Firma P v Firma K (Case 179/83) [1984] ECR 3033 **Referred to** [1989] 162 Fisher v Irish Land Commission [1948] IR 3; 82 ILTR 50 **Referred to** [1983] 314; **Considered** [1983] 391

Fishington v Higgs and Hill Ltd 153 LT 128 **Considered** [1988] 157

Fitzgerald v Limerick Corporation [1985] ILRM 445 **Discussed and Explained** [1986] 273

Fitzleet Estates Ltd v Cherry [1977] 1 WLR 1345 **Referred to** [1988] 318

Fitzpatrick v Behan; In re Moore's Estates [1944] IR 295; 78 ILTR 187 **Referred to** [1981] 328

Flast v Cohen (1968) 392 US 82 **Referred to** [1981] 242

Fleming v Cavan County Council [1974] IR 159 **Referred to** [1985] 249, 269; **Applied** [1989] 46

Fleming's Patent, In re (1919) 36 RPC 55 principles **Applied** [1984] 393

Fletcher v Auto and Transporters Ltd [1968] 2 QB 322 **Dictum approved** [1983] 429

Flood's Estate, In re; Rooney v Salaman (1864–66) 17 Ir Ch Rep 116 **Dictum approved** [1982] 113

Florence Land and Public Works Co, In re (1879) 10 Ch D 530 **Referred to** [1985] 641

Fluharty v Fluharty (1937) 193 ALT 858 **Dictum disapproved** [1982] 277

Flynn, In re [1968] 1 WLR 103 **Referred to** [1982] 433

Flynn v Buckley [1980] IR 423 **Referred to** [1982] 126

Flynn v Director of Public Prosecutions [1986] ILRM 290 **Referred to** [1989] 735

Flynn v Rivers 86 ILTR 85 **Referred to** [1982] 495

Folens & Co Ltd v Minister for Education [1981] ILRM 21 **Referred to** [1984] 149; **Referred to** [1987] 42

Folens & Co Ltd v Minister for Education [1984] ILRM 265 **Distinguished** [1985] 295

Foley v Classique Coaches Ltd [1936] 2 KB 1 **Considered** [1982] 77

Foley v Galvin [1932] IR 339; 66 ILTR 169 **Applied** [1981] 370

Foley v Irish Land Commission [1952] IR 118; 86 ILTR 44 **Referred to** [1981] 60; [1983] 449; [1984] 94; [1985] 685

Foley v Musgrave Cash & Carry Ltd Supreme Court, unreported, 20 December 1985 **Considered** [1987] 768

Foley v Thermocement Products Ltd 90 ILTR 92 **Referred to** [1984] 197, 208; [1986] 250

Fong Foo v United States (1962) 369 US 141 **Referred to** [1983] 549

Football League Ltd v Littlewoods Pools Ltd [1959] Ch 637 **Considered** [1990] 534

Ford Motor Co Ltd v Amalgamated Union of Engineering and Foundry Workers [1969] 2 QB 303 **Considered** [1984] 587

Ford's Hotel Co v Bartlett [1898] AC 1 **Distinguished** [1982] 324

Formosa v Formosa; Gray (Otherwise Formosa) v Formosa [1963] P 259 **Considered** [1980] 257

Fosberry v Waterford and Limerick Railway Co (1862) 13 ICLR 494 **Considered** [1983] 173

Foss v Harbottle (1843) 2 Hare 461 rule **Applied** [1990] 140

Foster v British Gas plc [1988] ICR 584 **Considered** [1989] 865

Fox v Chief Constable of Gwent [1985] 3 All ER 392 **Distinguished** [1987] 575

Foyle Fisheries Commission v Gallen [1960] Ir Jur Rep 35 **Followed** [1989] 485

Francis, In re 97 ILTR 151 **Considered** [1985] 465

Fraser v BN Furman (Productions) Ltd [1967] 3 All ER 57; [1967] 1 WLR 898 **Followed** [1986] 669

Fraser v Mudge [1975] 1 WLR 1132 **Referred to** [1980] 46

Freaney v Bank of Ireland [1975] IR 376 **Referred to** [1986] 518

Freedman v Opdeheyde [1945] Ir Jur Rep 22 **Referred to** [1983] 163

Freeman & Lockyer v Buckhurst Properties (Mangal) Ltd [1964] 2 QB 480 **Referred to** [1987] 364

Freeney v Bray Urban District Council [1982] ILRM 29 **Referred to** [1990] 633

Frescati Estates Ltd v Walker [1975] IR 177 **Referred to** [1979] 11; [1980] 64; **Followed** [1987] 733

Fried Krupp Huttenwerke AG v Quitman Products [1982] ILRM 551 **Referred to** [1984] 437

Frigoscandia (Contracting) Ltd v Continental Irish Meats Ltd [1982] ILRM 396 **Referred to** [1982] 399; [1983] 402; **Considered** [1985] 66; **Dictum approved** [1990] 285

Fromancais SA v FORMA (Case 66/82) [1983] ECR 393 **Considered** [1990] 466

Fry v Inland Revenue Commissioners [1959] Ch 86 **Considered** [1985] 200

Fullam v Associated Newspapers [1955–56] Ir Jur Rep 45 **Referred to** [1986] 601

Fulton v Andrews (1875) LR 7 HL 445 **Applied** [1978] 247

Fung Kai Sun v Chan Fui Hing [1951] AC 489 **Referred to** [1981] 419

Furey v Eagle Star and British Dominions Insurance Co Ltd 56 ILTR 112 **Referred to** [1987] 255

Furniss v Dawson [1984] AC 374; [1984] 1 All ER 530 **Considered** [1988] 419; **Not followed** [1988] 181, 647

G v An Bord Uchtála [1980] IR 32; 113 ILTR 25 **Referred to** [1984] 237; [1985] 302; [1988] 203; [1990] 121; **Applied** [1982] 159; [1983] 228; **Considered** [1982] 327; **Dictum applied** [1987] 477; **Dictum approved** [1982] 164

G v G [1984] IR 368 **Approved** [1987] 297

G v M (1875) 10 App Cas 171 **Referred to** [1982] 545; **Applied** [1984] 173

Gaffney v Gaffney [1975] IR 133 **Referred to** [1984] 173, 595; [1987] 189, 297; **Applied** [1982] 217; **Followed** [1980] 257; [1987] 638; [1988] 462

Gagner v Scarpelli (1972) 411 US 778 **Followed** [1982] 475

101; **Followed** [1982] 404; **Distinguished** [1982] 568

Glover v BLN Ltd (No 2) [1973] IR 432 **Distinguished and explained** [1980] 107

Glynn v Keele University [1971] 1 WLR 487; [1971] 2 All ER 89 **Referred to** [1980 46]; [1989] 469

Godfrey, In re (1892) 29 LR Ir 278 **Followed** [1988] 251

Godley v Power 95 ILTR 135 **Followed** [1981] 127

Golder v United Kingdom [1975] 1 EHRR 524 **Referred to** [1987] 52

Goldfarb v Williams & Co Ltd [1945] IR 433 **Considered** [1978] 85

Goldrick v Dublin Corporation (1987) 6 JISLL 156 **Not followed** [1989] 1

Goldstein v Commissioner of Internal Revenue (1966) 364 F 2d 734 **Referred to** [1988] 647

Gollins v Gollins [1964] AC 644 **Approved** [1981] 361

Gomez v Perez (1973) 409 U S 535 **Considered** [1985] 86

Good v Parry [1963] 2 QB 418 **Dictum approved** [1983] 300

Goodman v Whyte & Co 83 ILTR 159 **Referred to** [1982] 121

Goodright v Moss (1777) 2 Cowp 591 **Referred to** [1984] 66

Goodwin v Grey (1874) 22 WR 312 **Considered** [1989] 652

Gordon v Gordon [1951] IR 301; 88 ILTR 6 **Distinguished** [1981] 206

Gordon & Blair Ltd v Commissioners of Inland Revenue (1962) 40 TC 358 **Distinguished** [1986] 415

Gorman, In re [1971] IR 1; 105 ILTR 93 **Referred to** [1981] 279; **Followed** [1982] 182

Gotobed v Pridmore (1970) 115 SJ 78 **Principles applied** [1984] 451

Goulding Chemicals Ltd v Bolger [1977] IR 211 **Referred to** [1979] 51; [1983] 541; [1984] 487; **Followed** [1982] 367

Gouriet v Union of Post Office Workers [1978] AC 435 **Referred to** [1981] 242; [1984] 373; [1990] 70; **Discussed** [1979] 273

Government of Denmark v Nielson [1984] 2 All ER 81 **Considered** [1985] 465

Grange Developments Ltd v Dublin County Council High Court, unreported, 28 February 1984 **Overruled** [1987] 245

Grange Developments Ltd v Dublin County Council [1987] ILRM 245 **Referred to** [1987] 659

Grange Developments Ltd v Dublin County Council [1987] ILRM 733 **Affirmed** [1989] 145

Grangeford Structures Ltd v SH Ltd [1988] ILRM 129 **Affirmed** [1990] 277

Grant v Aston Ltd 103 ILTR 39 **Referred to** [1984] 273; [1988] 751

Grant v Dawkins [1973] 1 WLR 1406 **Referred to** [1983] 295

Granville Building Co Ltd v Oxby (1954]) 35 TC 245 **Referred to** [1982] 421

Gray (Otherwise Formosa) v Formosa [1963] P 259 **Considered** [1980] 257

Gray v Morrison [1954] JC 31 **Considered** [1981] 91

Gray v Tiley (1944) 26 TC 80 **Considered** [1982] 421

Gray's Inn Construction Co Ltd, In re [1980] 1 WLR 711 **Dictum approved** [1990] 330, 441; **Followed** [1981] 51

Grealy v Bank of Nova Scotia Supreme Court, unreported, 11 April 1975 **Followed** [1987] 541

Great Southern and Western Railway Co v Gooding [1908] 2 429 **Referred to** [1983] 549

Greaves v Greaves (1872) LR 2 P&D 423 **Considered** [1985] 691

Greaves & Co v Baynham Meikle & Partners [1975] 1 WLR 195; [1975] 3 All ER 99 **Approved** [1986] 43

Green v Bailey (1847) 15 Sim 542 **Referred to** [1978] 151

Green v Rozen [1955] 2 All ER 797 **Referred to** [1990] 377

Green v Russell [1959] 1 QB 28 **Followed** [1980] 216

Greendale Building Co Ltd, In re [1977] IR 256 **Followed** [1978] 208; [1989] 639

Greene v Louisville and Interurban Railway Co (1917) 244 US 499 **Referred to** [1983] 449; [1986] 136

Greenough v Gaskill (1833) 1 My & K 98 **Considered** [1990] 588

Greenwood v Bennett [1973] QB 195 **Followed** [1988] 565

Greenwood v Metcalfe (1873) LR 16 Eq 288 **Not followed** [1989] 706

Grehan v Medical Incorporated [1986] IR 528; [1986] ILRM 627 **Referred to** [1988] 501

Grehan v Mount Elm Construction Ltd Supreme Court, unreported, 19 April 1985 **Referred to** [1988] 47

Greig v Insole [1978] 1 WLR 302 **Considered** [1981] 345

Grierson, Oldham & Adams Ltd, In re [1968] 1 Ch 17 **Followed** [1978] 191

Griffith v Griffith [1944] IR 35; 78 ILTR 95 **Referred to** [1986] 80; **Dictum explained** [1982] 263; **Dictum not followed** [1982] 277

Griffiths v Owen (1844) 13 M & W 58 **Referred to** [1988] 56

Griffiths v Young [1970] 1 Ch 675; [1970] 3 All ER 601 **Referred to** [1979] 119; [1987] 345

Grimes v Owners of SS Bangor Bay [1948] IR 350; 83 ILTR 69 **Referred to** [1987] 535; **Considered** [1986] 337

Groome v Fodhla Printing Co [1943] IR 380; 77 ILTR 198 **Applied** [1978] 136

Grosvenor Hotel London Ltd, In re (No 2) [1965] Ch 1210 **Dictum approved** [1988] 707

Groves v Lord Winborne [1898] 2 QB 402 **Referred to** [1990] 560

Guardian Builders Ltd v Kelly [1981] ILRM 127 **Referred to** [1987] 345

Guardians of Waterford Union v Barton [1896] 2 IR 538 **Considered** [1984] 117

Guckian v Brennan High Court, unreported, 3 March 1980 **Followed** [1982] 113

Guildford RDC v Fortescue [1959] 2 QB 112 **Referred to** [1980] 1; **Dicta applied** [1978] 85

Guiney, In re, 75 ILTR 110 **Considered** [1981] 315; **Dictum approved** [1982] 182

Guinness (Arthur) Son & Co Ltd v Federated Workers' Union of Ireland DEP 11/1983 **Referred to** [1986] 483

Guinness (Arthur) Son & Co Ltd v Inland Revenue Commissioners [1923] 2 IR 186; 1 ITC 1 **Referred to** [1985] 651

Gunston v Winox [1921] 1 Ch 664 **Referred to** [1989] 124

Gunton v Richmond-upon-Thames London Borough Council [1981] Ch 448 **Followed** [1984] 15

H (J), In re [1985] IR 375; [1986] ILRM 65 **Referred to** [1988] 263

H (H) v Forbes Irish Tax Cases, Leaflet No 113 **Referred to** [1985] 210

H v H High Court, unreported, 2 March 1983 **Applied** [1983] 519

H & G Kinemas Ltd v Cook (1933) 18 TC 116 **Referred to** [1985] 210

H H Realisations Ltd, In re (1975) 31 P 7 CR 249 **Applied** [1984] 273

Hadley v Baxendale (1854) 9 Exch 341 **Referred to** [1979] 296; **Applied** [1976-7] 93, 239; [1980] 107; **Rule applied** [1982] 201

Halfdan Grieg & Co v Sterling Coal & Navigation Co [1973] QB 843; [1973] 2 WLR 904 **Considered** [1987] 17

Halifax Banking Co Ltd v Woods [1898] WN 62, 174 **Considered** [1978] 151

Hall v Hall (1868) LR 1 P & D 481 **Referred to** [1978] 175

Hall v Wightman [1926] NI 72 **Referred to** [1984] 402

Hallett's Estate, In re; Knatchbull v Hallett (1880) 13 ChD 696 **Referred to** [1990] 285; **Applied** [1982] 551; [1986] 518

Halpin v Tara Mines Ltd [1976-7] ILRM 28 **Approved** [1988] 631; **Distinguished** [1978] 85

Hambly v Trott (1776) 1 Cowp 371 **Applied** [1982] 578

Hamilton Cosco Incorporated, In re [1966] IR 266 **Referred to** [1982] 207; **Dictum applied** [1976–7] 164

Hamilton v Hamilton; Dunne v Hamilton [1982] IR 466; [1982] ILRM 290 **Referred to** [1988] 400; **Applied** [1990] 641; **Considered** [1986] 37; **Dictum considered** [1988] 318; **Followed** [1986] 693

Hamilton v West Sussex County Council [1958] 2 QB 286 **Referred to** [1983] 268

Hampstead Garden Suburbs Trust Ltd, In re [1962] Ch 806 **Referred to** [1988] 333

Hampton (JW) & Co v United States (1927) 276 US 394 **Referred to** [1986] 381

Handelmaatschappij Pesch & Co B V v Hoofproducktschap voor Akkerbouwprodukten [1980] ECR 2705 **Applied** [1983] 503; **Distinguished** [1981] 161

Handelskwekerij G J Bier BV v Mines de Potasse d'Alsace SA [1976] ECR 1735 **Discussed** [1986] 627

Handyside v Durbridge [1971] Ch 277 **Applied** [1983] 519

Hanlon, In re estate of 71 ILTR 160 **Not followed** [1985] 685

Hanlon v Fleming [1981] IR 489; [1982] ILRM 69 **Referred to** [1985] 385, 422; **Dictum Applied** [1986] 235; **Followed** [1988] 70

Hanlon v Garvey High Court, unreported, 6 October 1980 **Affirmed** [1982] 69

Hannah v Peel [1965] KB 509 **Referred to** [1988] 565

Hanratty v Hardy [1967] Ir Jur Rep 42 **Applied** [1981] 370

Harbutt's Plasticine Ltd v Wayne Tank and Pump Co Ltd [1970] 1 QB 447 **Referred to** [1979] 3; [1982] 359; [1983] 458; [1984] 501

Harding v Preece (1882) 9 QBD 281 **Principles applied** [1984] 273

Harris v Director of Public Prosecutions [1952] AC 694 **Referred to** [1981] 389

Harris v James (1876) 45 LJ QB 545 **Followed** [1978] 85

Harrison v Battye [1975] 1 WLR 58 **Referred to** [1979] 119

Harrison v Creswick (1852) 13 CB 399 **Considered** [1978] 128

Harrison v Hill 1932 SC (J) 13 **Applied** [1985] 290

Hartley v Minister for Housing and Local Government [1970] 1 QB 413 **Referred to** [1988] 274; **Followed** [1982] 534

Harvey v Cawlcott (1952) TC 245 **Referred to** [1982] 421

Harvey v Crawley Development Corporation [1957] 1 QB 485 **Considered** [1976–7] 343; [1983] 56

Harvey v R G O'Dell Ltd [1958] 2 QB 78 **Doubted** [1984] 523

Harwood, In re; Coleman v Innes [1936] Ch 285 **Referred to** [1990] 835

Harz v Deutsche Tradax GmbH (Case 19/83) [1984] ECR 1921 **Referred to** [1990] 485

Haughey, In re, [1971] IR 217 **Referred to** [1980] 46; [1982] 249; [1982] 512; [1983] 449; [1984] 333, 625; [1987] 107, 290; [1988] 52; [1990] 313; **Applied** [1981] 17; **Considered** [1978] 12; [1981] 113; **Dictum applied** [1984] 66; **Distinguished** [1981] 14; [1982] 568; [1989] 670; **Followed** [1990] 293

Hauptzollamt Bremerhaven v Massey-Ferguson GmBH [1973] ECR 897 **Referred to** [1987] 400

Hawkins v Price [1947] Ch 645 **Referred to** [1976–7] 72

Hayes v Criminal Injuries Compensation Tribunal. *See* State (Hayes) v Criminal Injuries Compensation Tribunal

Hayes, Conyngham and Robinson Ltd v Kilbride [1963] IR 185 **Considered** [1976–7] 14

Hayward v Hayward [1961] P 152 **Distinguished** [1984] 173

Hazell v Hazell 1 WLR 301 **Explained** [1981] 377

Healey v Wright [1912] 3 KB 249 **Distinguished** [1981] 465

Healy v Bray Urban District Council [1962–63] Ir Jur Rep 9 **Overruled** [1989] 437

Healy v Commissioners of Internal Revenue (1953) 345 US 278 **Dictum approved** [1986] 518

Healy v Healy Homes Ltd [1973] IR 309 **Referred to** [1978] 73; [1979] 253; **Considered** [1981] 191

Heaney v Malocca [1958] IR 111; 92 ILTR 117 **Applied** [1982] 495

Heath's Garage Ltd v Hodges [1916] 2 KB 370 **Referred to** [1984] 402

Heather v PE Consulting Group Ltd [1973] Ch 189; [1972] 3 WLR 883 **Followed** [1989] 349

Heaven and Kesterton Ltd v Establishment Francois Albrae and Co [1956] 2 Lloyd's Rep 316 **Referred to** [1987] 17

Heavey v Heavey 111 ILTR 1 **Applied** [1981] 202; **Followed** [1985] 153

Hebditch v MacIlwaine [1894] 2 QB 54 **Followed** [1989] 349

Hedley Byrne & Co Ltd v Heller & Partners Ltd [1964] AC 465 **Applied** [1980] 53 **Considered** [1980] 124; [1987] 142; [1989] 698; **Dicta applied** [1989] 373

Heffernan v Heffernan High Court, unreported, 12 December 1974 **Referred to** [1984] 555

Hegarty v O'Loughran [1987] IR 135; [1987] ILRM 603 **On different grounds** [1990] 403

Hegarty (PJ) & Sons Ltd v Royal Liver Friendly Society [1985] IR 524 **Not followed** [1989] 777

Helbert Wagg & Co Ltd, In re [1956] Ch 323 **Considered** [1988] 1

Henderson v Henderson [1976] P 77 **Referred to** [1988] 456

Henley v Murray [1980] 1 All ER 908 **Referred to** [1980] 107

Henry Coxon, The (1878) 3 PD 156 **Referred to** [1978] 247

Hepenstall v Wicklow County Council [1921] 2 IR 165 **Referred to** [1980] 38

Herne Bay Steam Boat Co v Hutton [1903] 2 KB 683 **Referred to** [1990] 601

Heron II, The. *See* Czarnikow (C) Ltd v Koufos

Heron Garage Properties Ltd v Moss [1974] 1 WLR 148 **Referred to** [1979] 253; **Considered** [1981] 191; **Discussed** [1979] 11

Heslop v Burns [1974] 1 WLR 1241; [1974] 3 All ER 406 **Referred to** [1983] 128; **Followed** [1985] 554

Hewitt's Contract, In re [1963] 3 All ER 419 **Referred to** [1979] 240

Heywood v Wellers [1976] QB 446 **Considered** [1982] 48

Hibernian Transport Companies Ltd, In re [1984] ILRM 583 **Considered** [1987] 508

Hickey v Norwich Union High Court, unreported, 23 October 1987 **Referred to** [1989] 400

Hickey & Co Ltd v Roches Stores [1980] ILRM 107 **Referred to** [1979] 296; [1984] 265

Hide, In re (1871) 7 Ch App 28 **Referred to** [1988] 751

Hill v Chief Constable of West Yorkshire [1988] QB 60 **Referred to** [1989] 400

Hill v East & West India Dock Co (1884) 9 App Cas 448 **Principles applied** [1984] 273

Hill (Christopher) Ltd v Ashington Piggeries Ltd [1972] AC 441 **Referred to** [1984] 471

Hillas & Co v Arcos Ltd (1932) 147 LT 503 **Referred to** [1988] 157

Hilton v Ankesson (1872) 29 LT 519 **Referred to** [1978] 1

Hilton v Guyot (1895) 159 US 113 **Referred to** [1988] 501

Hirani v Hirani (1982) 4 FLR 232 **Considered** [1986] 80

Hitchcock v Way (1837) 6 A & E 943 **Referred to** [1982] 290

Hoare & Co Ltd, In re (1933) 150 LT 374 **Followed** [1978] 191

Hoare (Charles) and Co v Hove Bungalows Ltd (1912) 56 SJ 686 **Followed** [1987] 26

Hobbs v Hurley High Court, unreported, 10 June 1980 **Approved** [1981] 447; **Doubted** [1981] 102; **Followed** [1980] 145; [1987] 129

Hobson v Bass (1871) LR 6 Ch App 722 **Considered** [1989] 652

Hoffman La Roche v Centrafarm Vertriebgesellschaft Pharmazeutischer Erzeugnisse mbH [1977] ECR 957 **Referred to** [1984] 45

Hoffman La Roche & Co AG v EC Commission (Case 85/76) [1979] ECR 461 **Referred to**
[1990] 664

Hogan v Minister for Justice High Court, unreported, 8 September 1976 **Referred to** [1987] 107

Holden v Holden [1986] NI 7 **Referred to** [1988] 456

Holdsworth (Harold) & Co (Wakefield) Ltd v Caddies [1955] 1 WLR 352, [1955] 1 All ER 725
Referred to [1985] 513

Hole v Garnsey [1930] AC 472 **Considered** [1990] 664

Holland v Hodgson (1872) LR 7 CP 328 **Considered** [1986] 377

Holliday v Overton (1852) 15 Beav 480 **Considered** [1978] 151

Hollington v F Hewthorn & Co [1943] KB 587 **Referred to** [1986] 318

Holloway v Belenos Publications Ltd [1987] IR 405; [1987] ILRM 790 **Referred to** [1988] 685

Holme v Brunskill (1878) 3 QBD 495 **Followed** [1980] 171

Holmes (Eric) Property Ltd, In re [1965] Ch 1052 **Referred to** [1976–7] 175; **Followed** [1976–7]
222

Holohan v Donohue [1986] IR 45; [1986] ILRM 250 **Referred to** [1989] 245

Holohan v Friends Provident & Century Life Office [1966] IR 1 **Referred to** [1986] 447

Holstead v Commissioner of Taxation [1926] AC 155 **Referred to** [1984] 173

Home Investment Society, In re, (1880) 14 ChD 167 **Considered** [1990] 266

Home Office v Dorset Yacht Co Ltd [1970] AC 1004; [1970] 2 All ER 294 **Referred to** [1986] 43

Hong Kong Fir Shipping Co Ltd v Kawaski Kisen Kaisha Ltd [1962] 2 QB 26 **Applied** [1990] 377

Hordean v Hordean [1910] AC 465 **Referred to** [1980] 237

Horn v Sunderland Corporation [1941] 2 KB 26 **Applied** [1983] 56

Hosie v Lawless [1927] IR 464 **Referred to** [1987] 535

Hospital World Trade Mark (1967) RPC 595 **Referred to** [1982] 240

Hounslow London Borough Council v Twickenham Garden Development Ltd [1971] Ch 233
Referred to [1979] 277; [1984] 45

House of Spring Gardens Ltd v Point Blank Ltd [1984] IR 611 **Distinguished** [1987] 135

Housing (Private Rented Dwellings) Bill 1981, In re, [1983] IR 181; [1983] ILRM 246
Referred to [1984] 366; **Considered** [1988] 400, 490

Howard v Bodington [1877] 2 PD 203 **Applied** [1983] 50

Howard v Secretary of State for the Environment [1975] QB 235 **Approved** [1981] 108

Howe, In re, ex parte Brett (1871) 6 Ch App 838 **Referred to** [1985] 522

Howe v Smith (1884) 27 Ch D 89 **Applied** [1981] 374

Hoystead v Commissioner of Taxation [1926] AC 155 **Referred to** [1986] 318

Hubert v Groves (1794) 1 Esp 14 **Referred to** [1981] 365

Hughes v Griffin [1969] 1 WLR 23 **Referred to** [1983] 128

Humber Ironworks & Shipbuilding Co, In re (1869) LR 4 Ch App 643 **Considered** [1989] 501;
Followed [1990] 42

Humblet v Belgium [1960] ECR 559 **Referred to** [1987] 400

Hummerstone v Leary [1921] 2 KB 664 **Referred to** [1982] 317

Humphrey's Estate, In re [1916] IR 21 **Applied** [1976–7] 88

Hunt v Roscommon County Council High Court, unreported, 1 May 1981 **Referred to** [1984]
149

Hunter v Chief Constable of West Midlands [1982] AC 529; [1981] 3 All ER 727 **Considered**
[1986] 318

Hunter v Manchester City Council [1975] 1 QB 877 **Distinguished** [1983] 56

Hurley v Wimbush; In re Sillar [1956] IR 344 **Referred to** [1982] 217, 433; [1983] 359; **Applied**
[1988] 67, 456; **Dictum applied** [1980] 257; [1987] 189; **Followed** [1987] 638

Hutchman v Jauncey [1950] 1 KB 576 **Referred to** [1982] 290

Hutton v West Cork Railway Co (1883) 23 Ch D 654 **Dicta mentioned** [1979] 221

Hyland v Minister for Social Welfare [1989] ILRM 196 **Affirmed** [1990] 213; **Referred to** [1990] 364

Hynes v Garvey [1978] IR 174 **Considered** [1988] 173

I (P) v Ireland High Court, unreported, 18 August 1988 **Affirmed** [1989] 810

IBM (Ireland) Ltd v Feeney [1983] ILRM 50 **Disapproved in part** [1984] 31

ICI Ltd v EC Commission (Case 48/69) [1972] ECR 619 **Dictum applied** [1990] 534

Ibraham v R [1914] AC 599 **Dictum applied** [1988] 666

Illingworth v Houldsworth [1904] AC 355 **Referred to** [1985] 641; **Applied** [1985] 641; **Dicta applied** [1985] 254

Imperial Land Company of Marseilles, In re (1871) LR 11 Eq 478 **Considered** [1989] 501

Imperial Tobacco Ltd v Attorney General [1981] AC 718 **Referred to** [1990] 391

Independent Television Publications Ltd v Time Out Ltd [1984] FSR 64 **Considered** [1990] 534

Industrial Development Consultants Ltd v Cooley [1972] 1 WLR 443 **Referred to** [1978] 211

Industrials Finance Syndicate Ltd v Lind [1915] 2 Ch 345 **Referred to** [1985] 254

Indyka v Indyka [1969] AC 33 **Distinguished** [1987] 189

Infabrics Ltd v Jaytex Ltd [1982] AC 1 **Applied** [1982] 40

Ingle v O'Brien 109 ILTR 7 **Referred to** [1986] 499; **Distinguished** [1983] 413; **Followed** [1978] 167

Inglefield (George) Ltd, In re [1933] Ch 1 **Applied** [1990] 285

Ingram (FG) & Son Ltd v Callaghan [1969] 1 WLR 456; [1969] 1All ER 433 **Distinguished** [1986] 415

Inland Revenue Commissioners v Blott [1902] 2 KB 657 **Dictum approved** [1982] 444

Inland Revenue Commissioners v Burmah Oil Co Ltd [1982] STC 30 **Referred to** [1988] 181

Inland Revenue Commissioners v Burrell [1924] 2 KB 52 **Applied** [1982] 444

Inland Revenue Commissioners v Clay [1914] 3 KB 466 **Considered** [1978] 82

Inland Revenue Commissioners v Duke of Westminster [1936] AC 1 **Followed** [1988] 181 **Referred to** [1988] 647

Inland Revenue Commissioners v Fraser (1952) SC 493 **Approved** [1985] 210

Inland Revenue Commissioners v Hyland Investment Co Ltd (1929) 14 TC 694 **Referred to** [1982] 421

Inland Revenue Commissioners v Land Securities Investment Trust Ltd [1969] 1 WLR 712 **Distinguished** [1984] 231

Inland Revenue Commissioners v Livingston (1924) 11 TC 538 **Referred to** [1982] 421

Inland Revenue Commissioners v Mascoe [1919] 1 KB 647 **Referred to** [1985] 210

Inland Revenue Commissioners v National Federation of Self Employed and Small Businesses Ltd [1982] AC 617 **Referred to** [1988] 437; **Applied** [1989] 710

Inland Revenue Commissioners v Newcastle Breweries Ltd (1927) 12 TC 927 **Referred to** [1985] 651

Inland Revenue Commissioners v Plummer [1980] AC 896 **Referred to** [1988] 181

Inland Revenue Commissioners v Reinhold (1953) SC 49 **Referred to** [1982] 421

Inland Revenue Commissioners v Scottish & Newcastle Breweries Ltd [1982] 1 WLR 322 **Referred to** [1984] 679

Inland Revenue Commissioners v Toll Property Co Ltd (1953) 34 TC 13 **Referred to** [1982] 421

Inland Revenue Commissioners v William Ranson & Son Ltd [1918] 2 KB 709 **Referred to** [1985] 210

Inspector of Taxes v Kiernan [1981] ILRM 157 **affirmed** [1982] 13

Inspector of Taxes v Kiernan [1981] IR 117; [1982] ILRM 13 **Referred to** [1985] 655; **Applied** [1986] 229; **Considered** [1985] 200; **Dictum Applied** [1984] 679; [1989] 478; **Followed** [1988] 647

Inspector of Taxes Association v Minister for the Public Service High Court, unreported, 24 March 1983 affirmed [1986] 296; **Distinguished** [1986] 206

Insurance Corporation of Ireland Ltd v 8 female staff DEP 6/1977 **Distinguished** [1982] 367

International Alltex Corp v Lawlor Creations Ltd [1965] IR 264 **Followed** [1988] 501

International Securities Ltd v Portmarnock Estates Ltd High Court, unreported, 9 April 1975 **Applied** [1981] 374

Internationale Handelsgesellschaft GmbH v EVSt (Case 11/70) [1970] ECR 1125 **Referred to** [1987] 400; **Considered** [1990] 466

Interstate Commerce Commission v Goodrich Transit Co (1911) 224 US 194 **Referred to** [1986] 381

Interview Ltd, In re [1975] IR 382 **Referred to** [1978] 215; **Dictum applied** [1982] 551; **Considered** [1990] 285

Inverclyde v Inverclyde [1951] P 29 doubted [1984] 667

Investment Co Institute v Camp (1971) 401 US 617 **Referred to** [1981] 242

Investors in Industry Ltd v South Bedfordshire DC [1986] QB 1034 **Referred to** [1990] 658

Irish Agricultural Machinery Ltd v O Culachain [1987] IR 458 appeal allowed [1989] 478

Irish Amusements Ltd v Carey [1968] IR 121 **Referred to** [1986] 177

Irish Aviation Executive Staff Assocation v Minister for Labour [1981] ILRM 350 **Dictum approved** [1981] 355

Irish Cinemas Ltd, In re 106 ILTR 17 **Followed** [1990] 228

Irish Civil Service Building Society v Registrar of Friendly Societies [1985] IR 167 **Followed** [1990] 664

Irish Employers Mutual Insurance Association Ltd, In re [1955] IR 176 **Considered** [1988] 565

Irish Family Planning Association Ltd v Ryan [1979] IR 295 **Considered** [1981] 456

Irish Industrial Building Society v O'Brien [1941] IR 1 **Referred to** [1979] 113; **Considered** [1976–7] 72

Irish Insurance Commissioners v Trench [1914] 2 IR 172; 47 ILTR 115 **Followed** [1986] 565; [1987] 309

Irish Land Commission v Dolan [1930] IR 235 **Followed** [1982] 290

Irish Permanent Building Society v Registrar of Building Societies [1981] ILRM 242 **Applied** [1983] 34

Irish Permanent Building Society v Ryan [1950] IR 12 **Referred to** [1987] 477

Irish Shell Ltd v Elm Motors Ltd [1982] ILRM 519 **Appeal allowed in principle** [1984] 595

Irish Shell Ltd v Elm Motors Ltd [1984] IR 200; [1984] ILRM 595 **Referred to** [1986] 68

Irish Shell and BP Ltd v John Costello Ltd High Court, unreported, 18 March 1980 **Affirmed** [1981] 66

Irish Shell and BP Ltd v Ryan [1966] IR 75 not **Followed** [1982] 519

Irish Transport and General Workers Union v Green [1936] IR 471 **Referred to** [1981] 242

Irish Trust Bank Ltd v Central Bank of Ireland [1976–7] ILRM 50 **Referred to** [1990] 617; **Followed** [1978] 63

Irvine, In bonis [1919] 2 IR 485 **Followed** [1980] 24

Irving's Yeast Vite Ltd v Horsenail (1934) 51 RPC 110 **Not followed** [1982] 240

Island Records Ltd, ex parte [1978] Ch 122 **Considered** [1990] 560

Italy v The Commission [1963] ECR 165 **Referred to** [1983] 449

J (An infant), In re [1966] IR 295 **Referred to** [1984] 292; **Followed** [1985] 302

J v C [1970] AC 669 **Referred to** [1985] 302

J v D Supreme Court, unreported, 22 June 1977 **Dicta explained** [1985] 302

J (RS) v J (JS) [1982] ILRM 263 **Referred to** [1986] 618; **Considered** [1985] 35; **Dictum approved** [1987] 58; **Followed** [1984] 173

JEB Fasteners Ltd v Marks, Bloom & Co [1981] 3 All ER 289 **Dicta applied** [1989] 373

Jack O'Toole Ltd v MacEoin Kelly Associates [1986] IR 277 **Referred to** [1987] 504; [1990] 266

Jackson v Denno (1964) 378 US 268 **Considered** [1988] 4

Jackson and Haden's Contract [1906] 1 Ch 412 **Applied** [1981] 81

Jaques v Millar (1877) 6 Ch D 153 **Referred to** [1979] 240

Jameson v McGovern [1934] IR 758 **Applied** [1978] 151

Jarvis v Swan Tours Ltd [1973] QB 233 **Considered** [1976–7] 93

Jefford v Gee [1970] 2 QB 130 **Considered** [1987] 390

Jenkins v Kingsgate (Clothing Productions) Ltd (Case 96/80) [1981] ECR 911 **Applied** [1990] 21

Jennings Motors Ltd v Secretary of State for the Environment [1982] QB 541 **Referred to** [1983] 268

Jennings v Quinn [1968] IR 305 **Applied** [1984] 249

Jenoure v Delmege [1891] AC 73 **Referred to** [1989] 349

Jermyn Street Turkish Baths Ltd, In re [1971] 1 WLR 1042 **Considered** [1980] 94

Jiminez v Winberger (1974) 417 U S. 628 **Considered** [1985] 86

Jobling v Associated Dairies Ltd [1981] 3 WLR 155 **Referred to** [1982] 317

Joel v Law Union and Crown Insurance Co [1908] 2 K B 863 **Considered** [1990] 110

John v Humphreys [1955] 1 WLR 325 **Considered** [1981] 213

Johnson v Agnew [1980] AC 367 **Followed** [1981] 75

Johnson v Longleat Properties Ltd [1976–7] ILRM 93 **Followed** [1976–7] 314

Johnston v Chief Constable of the RUC (Case 222/84) [1986] ECR 1651 **Referred to** [1989] 196; [1990] 485

Johnston v Langheld [1983] ILRM 359 **Referred to** [1990] 835

Joint Stock Discount Company, In re (1869) LR 5 Ch App 86 **Considered** [1989] 501

Jones v Bailey [1910] 1 IR 110 **Referred to** [1978] 197

Jones v Gardiner [1902] 1 Ch 191 **Referred to** [1979] 240

Jones v Nuttall (1926) 10 TC 346 **Not followed** [1985] 655

Jones v Rosenberg [1950] 2 K B 52 **Referred to** [1982] 290

Jones v Secretary of State for Social Services [1972] AC 944 **Referred to** [1988] 318

Joplin Brewery Co Ltd, In re [1902] 1 Ch 79 **Referred to** [1978] 215

Joyce, In re; Corbet v Fagan [1946] IR 277; 80 ILTR 158 **Referred to** [1988] 67, 456; **Applied** [1980] 257; **Dictum approved** [1982] 217

Joynt v M'Crum [1899] 1 IR 217 **Referred to** [1986] 627

Judge v Leonard [1941] Ir Jur Rep 39 **Dictum approved** [1985] 290

Junior Books Ltd v Veitchi Ltd [1983] 1 AC 520; [1982] 3 All ER 201 **Applied** [1986] 43

K v K High Court, unreported, 16 February 1971 **Referred to** [1986] 80

K v K [1973] Fam 39 **Considered** [1989] 322

K v K [1977] 1 All ER 576 **Considered** [1987] 390

K (R) v K (M) High Court, unreported, 24 October 1978 **Referred to** [1989] 528

K (M) v McC [1982] ILRM 277 **Distinguished** [1986] 75 **Followed** [1986] 80

K (J) v W (K) [1990] ILRM 121 **Considered** [1990] 749; **Principles applied** [1990] 791

Karak Rubber Co v Burden (No 2) [1972] 1 WLR 602 **Considered** [1980] 171

Katherine et Cie, In re [1932] 1 Ch 70 **Disapproved** [1984] 273

Kaufhof AG v European Commission [1976] ECR 431 **Referred to** [1988] 400

Kayford Ltd, In re [1975] 1 WLR 279 **Referred to** [1980] 216

Keady v Commissioner of an Garda Siochána High Court, unreported, 1 December 1988 **Referred to** [1990] 5

Kearney v Kearney [1911] 1 IR 137 **Referred to** [1981] 62

Keating v New Ireland Assurance Co plc, Irish Times Law Report, 17 April 1989 **Affirmed** [1990] 110

Keech v Sandford (1726) Sel Cas Ch 61 **Followed** [1978] 211

Keegan v de Burca [1973] IR 223 **Referred to** [1981] 416; [1983] 355

Keelan v Garvey [1925] 1 IR 1 **Distinguished** [1981] 477

Keir v Gillespie (1919) 7 TC 473; [1920] SC 67 **Considered** [1985] 655

Kelly v Breen [1978] ILRM 63 **Applied** [1987] 555; **Approved** [1984] 555; **Followed** [1990] 617

Kelly v Crowley High Court, unreported, 5 March 1985 **Approved** [1986] 189

Kelly v Hoey High Court, unreported, 18 December 1973 **Referred to** [1978] 63; approved [1984] 555

Kelly v Ireland [1986] ILRM 318 **Referred to** [1989] 466; **Considered** [1990] 817; **Distinguished** [1988] 274

Kelly v Irish Landscape and Nursery Co Ltd High Court, unreported, 16 May 1980 **Affirmed** [1981] 433

Kelly v Kelly (1868/9) LR 2 P & M 59 **Dictum approved** [1981] 361

Kelly v Montague (1891) 29 LR Ir 429 **Referred to** [1979] 113; [1982] 342; **Considered** [1976–7] 72

Kelly v Park Hall School [1979] IR 340; 113 ILTR 9 **Referred to** [1979] 119; [1986] 447; **Distinguished** [1981] 443

Kellystown Co v Hogan [1985] ILRM 200 **Dictum Applied** [1989] 165

Kemlin v Gardiner [1967] 2 QB 510; [1966] 3 All ER 931 **Considered** [1986] 111

Kennedy and McCann, In re [1976] IR 382 **Distinguished** [1984] 577

Kennelly v Clonmel Corporation 89 ILTR 164 **Referred to** [1985] 249

Kenny v Preen [1963] 1 QB 449 **Referred to** [1978] 136

Kent and Sussex Sawmills Ltd, In re [1947] Ch 177 **Referred to** [1990) 285

Kerins v Davoren (1861) 12 Ir Ch R 352 **Referred to** [1978] 151

Kerr v Browne Northern Ireland Court of Appeal, unreported, 1944 **Not followed** [1981] 198

Kerr v Hill (1936) SC (J) 71 **Considered** [1981] 91

Kiely v Minister for Social Welfare [1971] IR 21 **Referred to** [1979] 134

Kiely v Minister for Social Welfare [1977] IR 267 **Referred to** [1987] 107; **Applied** [1983] 331, [1983] 407; **Discussed** [1979] 273; **Distinguished** [1981] 14

Kilburn v Kilburn (1845) 13 M & W 671 **Referred to** [1978] 128

King and Duveen's Arbitration, In re [1913] 2 KB 32 **Followed** [1982] 550

King v Attorney General [1981] IR 233 **Considered** [1985] 61, 86; **Followed** [1986] 136

King v Director of Public Prosecutions High Court, unreported, 24 October 1978 **Referred to** [1984] 461

King v Director of Public Prosecutions Supreme Court, unreported, 31 July 1980 **Referred to** [1981] 34

King v King [1953] AC 124 **Referred to** [1981] 361

King v Long 53 ILTR 60 **Referred to** [1990] 835

King v Victor Parsons & Co [1978] 1 WLR 29 **Followed** [1983] 156

Kingston v Irish Dunlop Co Ltd [1969] IR 233 **Considered** [1988] 501

Kinsella v Russel Kinsella Pty Ltd (1986) 4 NSWLR 722 **Referred to** [1990] 341

Kiriri Cotton Co Ltd v Dewani [1960] AC 192 approved [1981] 144; **Considered** [1985] 283; **Dictum considered** [1982] 121

Kirkwood Hackett v Tierney [1952] IR 185; 88 ILTR 17 **Considered** [1989] 349

Kitchen v Royal Air Force Assoc [1958] 1 WLR 563 **Followed** [1983] 156

Kitton v Hewitt [1904] WN 21 **Referred to** [1985] 679

Klensch v Secretaire d'Etat a l'Agriculture et a la Viticulture (Joined Cases 201 and 202/85) [1986] ECR 3477 **Considered** [1990] 466

Klopfer v North Carolina (1967) 386 US 213 **Considered** [1986] 639

Knapp v Railway Executive [1949] 2 All ER 508 **Referred to** [1983] 173

Knatchbull v Hallett; In re Hallett's Estate (1880) ChD 696 **Applied** [1982] 551

Knetsch v United States (1960) 364 US 361 **Referred to** [1988] 647

Knuller v Director of Public Prosecutions [1973] AC 435; [1972] 2 All ER 898 **Considered** [1987] 477

Kok Hoong v Keong Cheong Kweng Mines Ltd [1964] AC 993 **Referred to** [1980] 94

Kostan v Ireland [1978] ILRM 12 **Referred to** [1981] 17; [1982] 512; [1990] 441; **Approved but distinguished** [1984] 249; **Distinguished** [1981] 469

Koufos v Czarnickow Ltd [1969] 1 AC 880 **Applied** [1981] 63

Kowalczuk v Kowalczuk [1973] 1 WLR 930 **Explained** [1981] 377

Krell v Henry [1903] 2 KB 740 **Applied** [1990] 601

Kreuzer v Controller of Patents [1978] FSR 239 **Referred to** [1976–7] 335; **Distinguished** [1978] 172

Krock v Rossell [1937] 1 All ER 725 **Referred to** [1986] 627

Kum Tong Restaurant (Dublin) Ltd, In re [1978] IR 446 **Considered** [1989] 777

Kuruma v The Queen [1955] AC 197 **Referred to** [1981] 389

Kutchera v Buckingham International Holdings Ltd [1988] ILRM 1 **Affirmed** [1988] 501

L v L [1978] IR 288 **Referred to** [1982] 327; **Applied** [1978] 203; **Approved** [1981] 179

L v L High Court, unreported, 21 December 1979 **Applied** [1980] 31

L'Henryenat v Ireland [1984] ILRM 249 **Referred to** [1988] 430

Labine v Vincent (1970) 401 US 532 **Considered** [1982] 327; [1985] 86

Lacey (William) (Hounslow) Ltd v Davis [1957] 1 WLR 932 **Considered** [1985] 295; **Principles applied** [1984] 265

Lalli v Lalli (1978) 439 US 259 **Considered** [1985] 86

Lally v Meath County Council [1985] ILRM 269 **Referred to** [1985] 249

Lambert v Lambert [1987] ILRM 390 **Dictum endorsed** [1989] 322

Landers v Attorney General 109 ILTR 1 **Referred to** [1983] 449; **Followed** [1984] 373

Lane v Hope [1970] Ch 94 **Approved** [1981] 374

Lansdowne v Lansdowne (1820) 2 Bligh PC 60 **Followed** [1986] 167

Latchford & Sons Ltd v Minister for Industry and Commerce [1950] IR 33 **Referred to** [1989] 639; **Considered** [1988] 693

Launock v Brown (1819) 2 B & Ald 593 **Considered** [1987] 575

Lavan v Walsh [1964] IR 87; 99 ILTR 147 **Approved** [1983] 186; **Cited** [1981] 403; **Followed** [1989] 29

Lavan v Walsh (No 2) [1967] IR 129 **Referred to** [1976–7] 50; [1990] 617; **Followed** [1978] 63

Lavender v Diamints Ltd [1949] 1 KB 535 **Followed** [1980] 153

Law v Jones Ltd [1974] Ch 112; [1973] 2 All ER 437 **Referred to** [1979] 119; [1987] 345

Law v Minister for Local Government, Circuit Court, unreported, 30 May 1974 **Followed** [1988] 545

Law v Robert Roberts & Co [1964] IR 292 **Referred to** [1979] 119; [1981] 443; **Considered** [1987] 345

Lawes v Bennett (1785) 1 Cox 167 **Referred to** [1978] 197

Lawlor v Minister for Agriculture [1988] ILRM 400 **Followed** [1990] 364, 466

Lawrence v Jenkins (1873) LR 8 QB 274 **Referred to** [1978] 1

Lawrie v Muir (1950) SC (J) 19 **Referred to** [1981] 389

Lawritzer's Application (1931) 48 RPC 352 **Referred to** [1984] 565

Leahy v Corboy; In re Corboy [1969] IR 148 **Applied** [1978] 175, 247

Lean and Dickson v Ball (1925) 10 TC 341; [1926] SC 15 **Obiter adopted** [1985] 655

Leary v National Union of Vehicle Builders [1971] 1 Ch 34; [1970] 2 All ER 713 **Referred to** [1980] 46; [1986] 499

Leather Cloth Co v Lorsont (1869) LR 9 Eq 345 **Dictum Considered** [1981] 345

Lee, Behrens & Co, In re [1932] 2 Ch 46 **Doubted** [1979] 221

Lee-Parker v Izzet [1971] 1 WLR 1638 **Dictum approved** [1981] 219

Lee-Parker v Izzet (No 2) [1972] 1 WLR 775 **Dictum doubted** [1981] 219

Leemac Overseas Investments Ltd v Harvey [1973] IR 160 **Dictum applied** [1986] 547

Le Mesurier v Le Mesurier [1895] AC 517 **Referred to** [1982] 217; [1987] 189

Leeson v General Council of Medical Education & Registration (1889) 43 Ch D 366 **Referred to** [1979] 166

Leigh's Wills Trusts, In re; Handyside v Durbridge [1971] Ch 277 **Applied** [1983] 519

Leitch (William) Bros Ltd, In re [1932] 2 Ch 71 **Considered** [1985] 75

Lemon v Sergeant [1972] 1 WLR 72 **Referred to** [1981] 137

Leopold Cassella & Co, In re [1910] 2 Ch 240 **Applied** [1976–7] 335

Leslie Engineers Co Ltd, In re [1976] 1 WLR 292 **Referred to** [1990] 330; **Dictum approved** [1981] 51

Lett v Lett [1906] 1 IR 618 **Referred to** [1988] 501

Lever v Goodwin (1887) 36 ChD 1 **Considered** [1976–7] 144

Lever Brothers v Beddingfield (1898) 16 RPC 453 **Referred to** [1983] 112

Lever Finance Ltd v Westminster (City) London Borough Council [1971] 1 QB 222 **Considered** [1978] 208; **Distinguished** [1984] 265

Levy (Holdings) Ltd, In re [1964] Ch 19 **Referred to** [1990] 330

Levy v Louisiana (1968) 391 US 68 **Considered** [1985] 86

Lewis v Lewis [1940] IR 42; 74 ILTR 170 **Referred to** [1982] 562

Leydon v Clare County Council [1942] IR Jur Rep 79 **Referred to** [1985] 249

Lickless v Milestone Motor Policies at Lloyds [1966] 2 All ER 972 **Not followed** [1985] 109

Liddington In re: Liddington v Thomas [1940] 1 Ch 345 **Approved** [1981] 179

Liesbosch, The [1933] AC 449 **Applied** [1984] 156; **Distinguished** [1985] 189

Linders (Chapelizod) Ltd v Syme [1975] IR 161 **Applied** [1976–7] 14

Lines Bros Ltd, In re [1984] BCLC 215 **Distinguished** [1990] 42

Lines Bros Ltd (No 2), In re [1984] BCLR 227 **Referred to** [1990] 42

Linford v Fitzroy (1849) 13 QB 240 **Referred to** [1990] 14

Linson Ltd v Association of Scientific, Technical and Managerial Staffs DEP 2/1977 **Followed** [1982] 367

Lister v Lane [1893] 2 QB 212 **Applied** [1978] 136

Lister v Romford Ice and Cold Storage Co Ltd [1957] AC 555 **Referred to** [1984] 523

Lister & Co v Stubbs (1890) 45 Ch D 1 **Considered** [1983] 541; [1984] 123

Listowel Urban District Council v McDonagh [1968] IR 312 **Referred to** [1983] 339; [1985] 513; [1989] 565; **Followed** [1981] 340; **Reasoning doubted** [1981] 340

Littlewood v George Wimpy & Co [1953] 2 QB 501 **Referred to** [1976–7] 210

Littlewoods Organisation v Harris [1977] 1 WLR 1472 **Considered** [1981] 345

Liverpool Cable Co's Application (1928) 46 RPC 99 **Doubted** [1984] 565

Liverpool Electric Cable Co Ltd, In re application of (1929) 46 RPC 99 **Referred to** [1982] 91

Liversidge v Anderson [1942] AC 206 **Considered** [1982] 190

Livingstone v Rawyards Coal Co (1880) 5 App Cas 25 **Referred to** [1980] 107

Lloyd v Grace Smith & Co [1912] AC 716 **Considered** [1986] 559

Lloyd v Sullivan High Court, unreported, 6 March 1981 **Approved** [1982] 113

Lloyds Bank Ltd v Peake [1970] 1 All ER 1057 **Considered** [1978] 247

Lloyd's v Harper (1880–1) 16 Ch D 290 **Dictum approved** [1982] 77

Llynvi Coal and Iron Co, Ex parte; In re Hide (1871) Ch App 28 **Referred to** [1988] 751

Lock v Abercester Ltd [1939] Ch 861 **Principles applied** [1984] 451

Lockhart v Harrison (1928) 139 LT 521; 44 TLR 794 **Followed** [1986] 601

Loftus v Attorney General [1979] IR 221 **Referred to** [1983] 89, 314; [1985] 86; **Followed** [1987] 36

Lohan v Fusco [1967] IR 11; 102 ILTR 129 **Referred to** [1982] 512

London and Counties Assets Co v Brighton Grand Concert Hall and Picture Palace Ltd [1915] 2 QB 493 **Referred to** [1978] 219

London and County Banking Co v Terry (1884) 25 Ch D 692 **Followed** [1980] 171

London and Globe Finance Corp Ltd, In re [1903] 1 Ch 728 **Considered** [1987] 260

London Armoury Co v Ever Ready Co (Great Britain) Ltd [1941] 1 KB 742 **Distinguished** [1981] 242

London Association for Protection of Trade v Greenlands Ltd [1916] 2 AC 15 **Distinguished** [1989] 349

London City Corp v Appleyard [1963] 1 WLR 982 **Referred to** [1988] 565

London County Council v Attorney General [1902] AC 165 **Applied** [1981] 365

London County Council v Aylesbury Co [1898] 1 QB 106 **Dictum Applied** [1978] 25

London Investment and Mortgage Co Ltd v Worthington [1959] AC 199; [1958] 2 All ER 230; 38 TC 86 **Referred to** [1985] 651

London Metallurgical Co, In re [1895] 1 Ch 758 **Considered** [1990] 266

London, Windsor & Greenwich Hotels Co, In re [1892] 1 Ch 638 **Considered** [1989] 501

Long v O'Brien and Cronin Ltd Supreme Court, unreported, 24 March 1972 **Followed** [1983] 429

Long v Saorstat and Continental Steamship Co Ltd 93 ILTR 137 **Referred to** [1987] 768

Longford (Earl of) v Purden (1877) 1 LR Ir 75 **Referred to** [1978] 175

Lonhro Ltd v Shell Petroleum Co Ltd (No 2) [1982] AC 173 **Considered** [1988] 157; **Distinguished** [1990] 560

Louisville Gas and Electric Co v Coleman (1928) 277 US 32 **Referred to** [1986] 136

Lowe v Inland Revenue Commissioners [1983] NZLR 416 **Considered** [1989] 552

Lucey, In re application of [1972] IR 347 **Dictum approved** [1983] 17

Luipaard's Vlei Estate and Gold Mining Co Ltd v Inland Revenue Commissioners [1930] 1 KB 593; [1930] All ER 688 **Referred to** [1985] 666

Luke v Inland Revenue Commissioners [1963] AC 557 **Referred to** [1988] 501; **Dictum applied** [1989] 342; **Dictum approved** [1984] 350

Lumley v Gye (1853) 2 E & B 216; 22 LJQB 463 **Referred to** [1985] 221; [1988] 157

Lundie Bros Ltd, In re [1965] WLR 1051 **Referred to** [1979] 141

Lupton v Cadogan Gardens Developments Ltd [1971] 3 All ER 460 **Dictum approved** [1986] 116

Lupton v F A and A B Ltd [1972] AC 634 **Considered** [1986] 116

Lurcott v Wakely [1911] 1 KB 903 **Applied** [1978] 136

Lushington v Sewell (1827) 1 Sim 435 **Referred to** [1983] 359

Luxor (Eastbourne) Ltd v Cooper [1941] AC 108 **Applied** [1976–7] 269; **Considered** [1985] 295

Lynch v Limerick County Council [1925] IR 61 **Referred to** [1987] 535

Lynes v Snaith [1899] 1 QB 486 **Referred to** [1983] 128

Lynham v Butler (No 2) [1933] IR 74; 67 ILTR 75 **Referred to** [1984] 657; **Considered** [1983] 489; [1989] 309

Lyons v Kilkenny Corporation High Court, unreported, 13 February 1987 **Applied** [1987] 595

Lyons (J) & Co Ltd, In re application of (1959) RPC 120 **Considered** [1978] 120

M, In re [1946] IR 341 **Referred to** [1982] 327

M (G), In re 106 ILTR 82. *See* M (F) v M (T), In re GM

M (J) v An Bord Uchtála [1977] IR 287 **Referred to** [1985] 302

M v An Bord Uchtála [1988] ILRM 203 **Referred to** [1988] 203; **Dicta applied** [1988] 629

M (F) v M (T), In re GM 106 ILTR 82 **Referred to** [1979] 236; **Dictum approved** [1989] 815; **Followed** [1978] 203

M (B) v M (R) 107 ILTR 1 **Referred to** [1979] 236

M v O High Court, unreported, 24 January 1984 **Referred to** [1987] 58

MCB (Galway) Ltd v Industrial Development Authority High Court, unreported, 4 May 1979 **Affirmed** [1981] 58

McAllister, In re [1973] IR 238 **Referred to** [1984] 657

MacAlpine v MacAlpine [1958] P 35 **Referred to** [1980] 257

MacAndrew's Will Trusts, In re [1964] Ch 704; [1963] 3 WLR 822 **Considered** [1978] 244

Macauley v Minister for Posts and Telegraphs [1966] IR 345 **Referred to** [1980] 82; [1982] 497; [1984] 66; **Considered** [1982] 568; **Dicta doubted** [1990] 70; **Followed** [1984] 66

McC v An Bord Uchtála [1982] ILRM 159 **Referred to** [1985] 302; [1988] 203; **Distinguished** [1983] 228

McC (D) v McC (M) [1986] ILRM 1 **Considered** [1989] 528

McCabe v Harding Investments Ltd High Court, unreported, 1 March 1982 **Affirmed** [1984] 105

McCabe v Harding Investments Ltd [1984] ILRM 105 **Considered** [1987] 733; **Distinguished** [1984] 24; **Followed** [1990] 633

McCabe v Joynt [1901] 2 IR 115 **Referred to** [1990] 364

McCabe v Lisney and Son [1981] ILRM 289 **Followed** [1982] 390

McCabe v McGonigle [1956] IR 162 **Applied** [1981] 370

McCann (Charles) Ltd v O Culachain [1986] IR 196; [1986] ILRM 229 **Applied** [1989] 165, 478

McCarry v Attorney General High Court, unreported, 15 January 1976 **Referred to** [1990] 505

McCarthy v Johnson [1988] IR 24 **Affirmed** [1989] 706

McCarthy v Limerick Corporation, Circuit Court, unreported, 25 November 1986 **Approved** [1988] 86

McCarthy v McCarthy 70 ILTR 79 **Referred to** [1990] 886

McCarthys Ltd v Smith [1979] 1 WLR 1189; [1979] 3 All ER 325 **Referred to** [1986] 483

M'Cartie v McCarthy [1904] 1 IR 100; 38 ILTR 3 **Dictum applied** [1987] 477

McCausland v Ministry of Commerce [1956] NI 36 **Applied** [1989] 478; **Considered** [1986] 229

McCheane v Gyles [1902] 1 Ch 287 not **Followed** [1989] 788

McComiskey v McDermott [1974] IR 75 **Dictum applied** [1987] 768

McCooey v Minister for Finance [1971] IR 159 **Followed** [1985] 180

McCrea v Knight [1896] 2 IR 619 **Referred to** [1986] 627

McCrumlish v Minister for Agriculture High Court, unreported, 28 May 1975 **Referred to** [1983] 300

McCullagh v Irish Free State 57 ILTR 171 **Considered** [1986] 627

MacCurtain, In re [1941] IR 83 **Referred to** [1986] 343; **Considered** [1984] 224; **Dictum Considered** [1982] 385

McD v O'R High Court, unreported, 26 January 1984 **Referred to** [1986] 618

McDermott and Cotter v Minister for Social Welfare (Case 286/85) [1987] ECR 1453, [1987] ILRM 324 **Considered** [1989] 865

McDonald v Bord na gCon [1964] IR 350; 100 ILTR 11 **Referred to** [1983] 314, 449; **Applied** [1983] 89; **Followed** [1983] 67, 429

McDonald v Bord na gCon (No. 2) [1965] IR 217; 100 ILTR 89 **Referred to** [1982] 290; [1985] 86, 410; [1986] 304; [1987] 107; **Applied** [1985] 302; [1988] 52; **Considered** [1989] 309; **Followed** [1981] 324

McDonald v Córas Iompair Éireann 105 ILTR 13 **Approved** [1982] 223

McDonald v Feeley Supreme Court, unreported, 23 July 1980 **Distinguished** [1989] 181; **Explained** [1984] 77

McDonald v Law Union Fire & Life Insurance Co (1874) LR 9 QB 328 **Referred to** [1990] 110

McDonnell v McGuinness [1939] IR 223; 73 ILTR 80 **Distinguished** [1981] 403

McEllistrim v Ballymacelligott Co-operative Agricultural and Dairy Society [1919] AC 548 **Referred to** [1981] 345; **Considered** [1990] 664

McEntire v Crossley Bros [1895] AC 457 **Referred to** [1982] 396; [1990] 285

McEvoy v Belfast Banking Co Ltd [1934] NI 67 **Considered** [1980] 137

McEvoy (William) Ltd v James Calder & Co Ltd 55 ILTR 121 **Considered** [1986] 250

McF v G [1983] ILRM 220 **Referred to** [1985] 302; [1988] 203

McFadden, Ex parte [1903] Exch Div Judgements of the Superior Court of Ireland 168 **Considered** [1983] 17

MacEnroe v Allied Irish Banks Ltd High Court, unreported, 12 December 1979 **Overruled** [1980] 171

MacFoy v United Africa Co Ltd [1962] AC 152 **Followed** [1982] 1

McGee v Attorney General [1974] IR 284; 109 ILTR 29 **Referred to** [1976–7] 164; [1980] 82; [1982] 327; [1985] 86; [1988] 472; **Dictum applied** [1983] 449; [1987] 477; **Dictum approved** [1982] 164; **Distinguished** [1985] 542

McGill v Snodgrass [1979] IR 283 **Applied** [1981] 202

McGimpsey v Ireland [1988] IR 567; [1989] ILRM 209 **Affirmed** [1990] 441

McGlinchey v Wren [1982] IR 54; [1983] ILRM 169 **Referred to** [1985] 422]; [1988] 70; [1990] 780; **Applied** [1985] 385, 410; [1988] 75; **Approved** [1985] 410; **Followed** [1990] 505; **Reversed in part** [1983] 314

McGovern v His Majesty's Advocate (1950) SC (J) 33 **Referred to** [1981] 389

McGowan v Carville [1960] IR 330; 95 ILTR 41 **Distinguished** [1981] 213

McGowan v Harrison [1941] IR 331; 75 ILTR 163 **Not followed** [1986] 43

McGowan v Maryland (1961) 366 US 420 **Referred to** [1983] 449

McGrath and Harte, In re [1941] IR 68 **Considered** [1987] 606

McGrath v Bourne (1876) IR 10 CL 160 **Referred to** [1984] 197; [1986] 250

McGrath v Commissioner of an Garda Síochána [1990] ILRM 5 **Affirmed** [1990] 817

McGrath v McDermott [1988] ILRM 181 **Affirmed** [1988] 467

McGrath v McDermott [1988] IR 258; [1988] ILRM 647 **Referred to** [1990] 100

McGreene v Hibernian Taxi Company [1931] IR 319 **Not followed** [1989] 735

McGuire v Pacific Steam Navigation Supreme Court, unreported, 26 May 1965 **Referred to** [1987] 768

McHenry Brothers Ltd v Carey High Court, unreported, 19 November 1976 **Referred to** [1979] 51

McIlkenny v Chief Constable of West Midlands [1980] QB 283; [1980] 3 All ER 227 **Considered** [1986] 318

McInerney v Clareman Printing and Publishing Co Ltd [1903] 2 IR 347 **Considered** [1986] 601

McK v McK [1936] IR 177 **Referred to** [1986] 80

MacKalley's case (1611) 9 Co Rep 656 **Referred to** [1982] 29

Mackintosh v McGlinchey (1921) SC 75 **Referred to** [1989] 333

Macklin v Greacen & Co Ltd [1983] IR 61; [1982] ILRM 182; [1981] ILRM 315; **Referred to** [1979] 113; **Affirmed on different grounds** [1982] 182

McKeon, In re [1965] Ir Jur Rep 24 **Followed** [1990] 84

MacLain v Gatty [1921] AC 376 **Dictum approved** [1984] 15

McLaughlin v Florida (1961) 379 US 222 **Referred to** [1983] 449

McLellan, Rawson & Co Ltd v Newell (1955) 36 TC 117 **Referred to** [1982] 421

McLeod v Earl of Shrewsbury; In re Shrewsbury [1922] P 112 **Dictum approved** [1981] 198

McLoughlin v Attorney General High Court, unreported, 20 December 1974 **Referred to** [1990] 505

McLoughlin v Minister for Social Welfare [1958] IR 1; 93 ILTR 73 **Applied** [1985] 349; **Considered** [1988] 231

McLoughlin v O'Brian [1983] 1 AC 410; [1982] 2 All ER 298 **Referred to** [1988] 300; [1989] 400; **Discussed** [1987] 202

McLoughlin v Tuite [1986] IR 235; [1986] ILRM 304 **Followed** [1987] 665

McM v McM [1936] IR 177 **Referred to** [1982] 243; [1984] 173

McMahon v Attorney General [1972] IR 69; 106 ILTR 89 **Referred to** [1984] 643; [1990] 767

McMahon v Leahy [1984] IR 525; [1985] ILRM 422 **Referred to** [1987] 202; [1988] 333; [1990] 505; **Distinguished** [1988] 70; **Followed** [1985] 385; [1988] 75

McMahon v Murtagh Properties Ltd [1982] ILRM 342 **Followed** [1984] 134

McMahon Ltd v Dunne 99 ILTR 45 **Referred to** [1985] 221

McManus v Attorney General High Court, unreported, 23 March 1977 **Referred to** [1990] 505

McMillan v Le Roi Mining Co [1900] 1 Ch 331 **Referred to** [1981] 242

McMorrow v Knott Supreme Court, unreported, 21 December 1859 **Referred to** [1983] 429

McNamara v Electricity Supply Board [1975] IR 1 **Applied** [1978] 244; **Considered** [1987] 768; **Dictum Applied** [1987] 575

McNamara & Son v The Owner of the SS. Hatteras [1933] IR 675 **Referred to** [1988] 501

McNamee v Buncrana Urban District Council [1983] IR 213; [1984] ILRM 77 **Considered** [1989] 181

McQueen v McCann (1945) SC 151 **Referred to** [1980] 21

Magill v Magill [1914] 2 IR 533 **Referred to** [1985] 100

Maguire v Keane [1986] ILRM 235 **Referred to** [1990] 505

Maher v Attorney General [1973] IR 140; 108 ILTR 41 **Referred to** [1985] 266; [1989] 670; **Applied** [1981] 34; **Distinguished** [1982] 568; **Principles applied** [1985] 11

Mahony v Liquidator of East Holyford Mining Co Ltd (1874–5) LR 7 HL 869 **Followed** [1982] 57

Maidstone Buildings Promotions Ltd, In re [1971] 1 WLR 1085 **Referred to** [1985] 75

Mair v Woods 1948 SLT 326 **Distinguished** [1986] 493

Malhotra v Choudhury [1980] Ch 52; [1978] 3 WLR 825 **Distinguished** [1981] 403; **Followed** [1982] 201

Mallet v Staveley Coal and Iron Co [1928] 2 KB 405 **Referred to** [1984] 610

Maloney v Elf Investments Ltd [1979] ILRM 253 **Referred to** [1983] 82

Maltglade Ltd v St Albans RDC [1972] 1 WLR 1230 **Referred to** [1982] 29

Mann v Goldstein [1968] 1 WLR 1091 **Referred to** [1979] 141

Mannix v Pluck [1975] IR 169 **Referred to** [1987] 269

Manprop Ltd v O'Dell [1969] 2 Ch 378 **Referred to** [1990] 377

Manuel v Attorney General [1983] Ch 77; [1982] 2 All ER 822 **Dictum approved** [1987] 606

Mapp v Ohio (1961) 367 US 643 **Referred to** [1981] 389

Mara v Hummingbird Ltd [1982] ILRM 421 **Referred to** [1979] 57; [1985] 210; **Applied** [1986] 116

Marckx v Belgium (1979–80) 2 EHRR 330 **Considered** [1982] 327; **Distinguished** [1985] 86

Marcroft Wagons Ltd v Smith [1951] 2 KB 496; [1951] 2 All ER 271 **Referred to** [1985] 554

Marene Knitting Mills Pty Ltd v Greater Pacific General Insurance Ltd [1976] 2 Lloyd's Rep 631 **Followed** [1981] 173

Mareva Compania Naveriera SA v International Bulkcarriers SA [1975] 2 Lloyd's Rep 509 **Approved** [1983] 541

Marginson v Blackburn Borough Council [1939] 1 All ER 273 **Followed** [1989] 133

Mark Fishing Co Ltd v United Fishermen & Allied Workers' Union (1972) 24 DLR (3d) 585 **Considered** [1986] 493

Marreco v Richardson [1908] 2 KB 584 **Considered** [1988] 526

Marshall v Southampton and Southwest Hampshire Area Health Authority (Case 152/84) [1986] ECR 723 **Considered** [1989] 865

Martin v Kearney 36 ILTR 117 **Not followed** [1987] 582

Martin v Puttick [1968] 2 QB 82 **Considered** [1982] 487

Martin v Pyecroft (1852) 3 de G, M & G 785 **Referred to** [1978] 73

Martin v Quinn [1980] IR 244 **Applied** [1981] 270; **Followed** [1988] 294

Martin v Spalding [1979] 1 WLR 1164 **Referred to** [1981] 137

Mason v Mason [1944] NI 134 **Dictum approved** [1984] 667

Mason v New South Wales (1959–60) 102 CLR 108 **Referred to** [1985] 283; **Dictum approved** [1981] 144

Massereene (Viscount) v Bellew (1889) 24 LR Ir 420 **Considered** [1990] 220

Matthews v Chicory Marketing Board (1938) 60 CLR 263 **Referred to** [1986] 693

Maunsell v Minister for Education [1940] IR 213; 73 ILTR 36 **Referred to** [1987] 107

Mayne Nickless Ltd v Pegler [1974] 1 NSWLR 228 **Dictum approved** [1981] 173

Mayo-Perrott v Mayo-Perrott [1958] IR 336 **Referred to** [1982] 217; [1987] 189, 477; **Dicta applied** [1982] 418; **Distinguished** [1987] 297; **Followed** [1980] 257

Meade v Cork County Council Supreme Court, unreported, 31 July 1974 **Referred to** [1981] 144

Meagher v Meagher [1961] IR 96 **Referred to** [1980] 237

Mechanisations (Eaglescliffe) Ltd, In re [1966] Ch 20 **Referred to** [1976–7] 222

Mediline AG, In re [1970] IR 169 **Dictum approved** [1978] 116

Melling v O Mathgamhna [1962] IR 1; 97 ILTR 60 **Referred to** [1982] 512; [1983] 449; **Applied** [1981] 469; [1984] 39, 625; [1986] 304; **Considered** [1978] 12; **Followed** [1982] 249

Mertens v Home Freeholds Co [1921] 2 KB 526 **Referred to** [1976–7] 93

Mesco Properties Ltd, In re [1979] 1 WLR 558; [1979] 1 All ER 302 **Referred to** [1987] 508; **Approved** [1982] 340; **Dictum not followed** [1982] 340

Meskell v Córas Iompair Éireann [1973] IR 121 **Referred to** [1985] 494; [1986] 99; [1988] 631; **Applied** [1976–7] 248; [1990] 364; **Considered** [1982] 48; [1987] 477; **Dictum applied** [1987] 651; **Followed** [1988] 472

Metropolitan Board of Works v McCarthy (1874) LR 7 HL 243 **Considered** [1976–7] 343

Metropolitan Coal Consumers' Association, In re (1890) 45 ChD 606 **Referred to** [1988] 490

Meunier, In re [1894] 2 QB 415 **Considered** [1985] 385

Meyer (NV Arnold Otto) v Anne [1939] 3 All ER 168 **Applied** [1984] 616

Middleton v Magnay (1864) 2 H & M 233; 71 ER 452 **Referred to** [1985] 679

Middleton v Middleton (1967) P 62 **Applied** [1980] 257

Midland Bank Trust Co Ltd v Hett Stubbs & Kemp [1978] Ch 384 **Referred to** [1980] 124

Midland Railway Company, In re 38 ILTR 52 **Distinguished** [1989] 46

Miley v Carty [1927] IR 541 **Referred to** [1978] 197

Miliangos v George Frank (Textiles) Ltd [1976] AC 443 **Considered** and **Distinguished** [1976–7] 275

Millar v Toulmin (1886) 17 QBD 603 **Considered** [1986] 250

Miller v Jackson [1977] 1 QB 966 **Considered** [1978] 85

Miller v Karlinski (1945) 62 TLR 85 **Considered** [1983] 464

Mills v Hableutzel (1982) 456 U S. 91 **Considered** [1985] 86

Milnes v Gery (1807) 14 Ves 400 **Followed** [1976–7] 149

Minister for Agriculture v Kelly [1953] NI 151 **Referred to** [1980] 145

Minister for Agriculture v Norgro Ltd [1980] IR 155 **Applied** [1986] 565, 579; [1989] 498; **Followed** [1984] 35; [1987] 309; [1989] 65

Minister for Finance v O'Brien [1949] IR 91; 84 ILTR 95 **Referred to** [1984] 595

Minister for Home Affairs v Fischer [1980] AC 319 **Considered** [1982] 190

Minister for Housing and Local Government v Hartnell [1963] AC 1 **Referred to** [1988] 333

Minister for Industry and Commerce v Hales [1967] IR 50; 102 ILTR 109 **Dictum applied** [1987] 606

Minister for Industry, Commerce and Energy v Quinn Supreme Court, unreported, 23 January 1981 **Followed** [1981] 302

Minister of National Revenue v Anaconda American Brass Ltd [1956] AC 85 **Considered** 552

Ministere Public Luxembourg v Miller [1971] ECR 723 **Referred to** [1983] 258

Ministry of Health v Simpson [1951] AC 251 **Considered** [1981] 473

Minter v Priest [1929] 1 KB 655; [1930] AC 558 **Referred to** [1988] 4; **Considered** [1990] 588

Minto v Cahill [1940] IR 302 **Followed** [1982] 269

Mixnam's Properties Ltd v Chertsey Urban District Council [1965] AC 735; [1964] 1 QB 214 **Referred to** [1988] 693; **Applied** [1989] 854

Mogul of Ireland Ltd v Tipperary (NR) County Council [1976] IR 260 **Referred to** [1990] 505; **Considered** [1988] 318; **Dictum applied** [1989] 865; principle **Applied** [1983] 89

Molloy v Gray (1889–90) 24 LR lr 258 **Applied** [1982] 117

Molton Finance Ltd, In re [1966] Ch 325 **Followed** [1980] 131

Molyneaux v White (1884) 15 LR Ir 383 **Followed** [1983] 513

Monaghan UDC v Alf-a-Bet Promotions Ltd [1980] ILRM 64 **Referred to** [1988] 47; [1989] 865; **Applied** [1985] 593; **Dictum applied** [1984] 105; [1990] 603; **Distinguished** [1981] 108; **Followed** [1982] 160

Monaghan v Swan Co Ltd (1961) 96 ILTSJ 93 **Discussed** [1986] 627

Monk v Warbey [1935] 1 KB 75 **Applied** [1978] 1

Monmouthshire County Council v British Transport Commissioner [1957] 1 WLR 1146 **Considered** [1983] 173

Monolithic Building Co, In re [1915] 1 Ch 643 **Distinguished** [1978] 215

Monro (George) Ltd v American Cyanamid & Chemical Corporation [1944] KB 432 not **Followed** [1986] 627

Montagu v Earl of Sandwich (1886) 32 Ch D 525 **Referred to** [1976–7] 50

Mullen v Brady, In re Coulson 87 ILTR 93 **Followed** [1976–7] 88

Mullins v Howell (1879) 11 Ch 763 **Referred to** [1986] 624; [1987] 504

Mulloy v Minister for Education [1975] IR 88 **Referred to** [1979] 166; **Considered** [1986] 136

Mulock, In bonis [1933] IR 171 **Referred to** [1980] 24

Multinational Gas and Petrochemical Co v Multinational Gas and Petrochemical Services Ltd [1983] Ch 258; [1983] 2 All ER 563 **Referred to** [1986] 627

Mulvey v Kennedy and Fox (1989) 7 ILR (n s) 28 **Referred to** [1990] 293

Mulvihill v Limerick Co Council (1951) 87 ILTR 63 **Referred to** [1986] 250

Munby v Furlong [1977] Ch 359 **Applied** [1984] 679

Munnelly v Calcon Ltd [1978] IR 387 **Referred to** [1980] 38; **Applied** [1976–7] 287; [1978] 85; **Dicta applied** [1984] 501; **Distinguished** [1980] 107

Munro v Wilmott [1948] 2 All ER 983; [1949] 1 KB 295 **Followed** [1988] 565

Murdoch v Workman & Co 28 ILTR 39 **Referred to** [1986] 250

Murphy v Attorney General [1982] IR 241 **Referred to** [1983] 449; [1984] 45; [1987] 83, 290; [1988] 333; **Applied** [1988] 456; [1989] 196; [1990] 213; **Considered** [1985] 86; [1989] 93, 110; **Followed** [1986] 136, 364; [1990] 364

Murphy v Bord Telecom Éireann [1986] ILRM 483 **Reevaluated** [1989] 53

Murphy v Dublin Corporation [1972] IR 215; 107 ILTR 65 **Applied** [1981] 21; [1982] 169; **Referred to** [1987] 516; [1988] 707; **Considered** [1976–7] 343; [1984] 149; **Dicta approved** [1990] 588; **Explained** [1983] 314; **Followed** [1987] 42

Murphy v Minister for Social Welfare [1987] IR 295 **Referred to** [1988] 693

Murphy v Murphy [1962–63] Ir Jur Rep 77 **Followed** [1989] 528

Murphy v Murphy [1980] IR 183 **Considered** [1983] 128

Murphy v Roche [1987] IR 106 **Followed** [1989] 282

Murphy v Stewart [1973] IR 97; 107 ILTR 117 **Referred to** [1984] 373; **Applied** [1978] 51; **Considered** [1990] 560

Murphy v Wexford County Council [1921] 2 IR 230 **Referred to** [1980] 38; **Referred to** [1984] 501

Murphy Buckley and Keogh Ltd v Pye (Ireland) Ltd [1971] IR 57 **Discussed** [1985] 295

Murphy (James) & Co Ltd v Crean [1915] 1 IR 11 **Followed** [1976–7] 72

Murray v Ireland and Attorney General [1985] IR 532; [1985] ILRM 542 **Dictum approved** [1986] 80; **Followed** [1987] 52

Murtagh Properties Ltd v Cleary [1972] IR 330 **Considered** [1978] 51; [1983] 449; [1990] 560; **Followed** [1984] 373; [1986] 136

Mutter v Eastern and Midlands Railway Co (1888) 38 Ch D 92 **Followed** [1989] 13

Mutual Life Insurance Co of New York v Rank Organisation Ltd [1985] BCLC 11 **Considered** [1990] 664

Myers v Director of Public Prosecutions [1965] AC 1001; [1964] 2 All ER 81 **Considered** [1986] 716; **Discussed** [1985] 18

N (Infants), In re [1967] Ch 512 **Referred to** [1982] 29

Nagle v Feilden [1966] 2 QB 633 **Referred to** [1979] 79

Nally v Nally [1953] IR 19 **Referred to** [1978] 151

Napier v Napier [1915] P 184 **Referred to** [1976–7] 156; **Considered** [1984] 173

Nash v Halifax Building Society [1979] Ch 584 **Referred to** [1984] 350

National Anti-Vivisection Society v Inland Revenue Commissioners [1948] AC 31 **Followed** [1980] 103

National Bank of Greece v Metlis [1958] AC 509 **Referred to** [1979] 296

National Bank of Nigeria v Awolesi [1964] 1 WLR 1311 **Distinguished** [1980] 171

National Bank of Wales, In re [1902] 2 Ch 412 **Referred to** [1990] 97

National Bank v Hegarty (1901) 1 NIJR 13 **Considered and Explained** [1987] 30

National Building & Land Investment Co, In re (1885) 15 LR Ir 47 **Considered** [1990] 266

National Carriers Ltd v Panalpina (Northern) Ltd [1981] AC 675 **Referred to** [1990] 601

National Provincial & Union Bank Ltd v Charnley [1924] 1 KB 431 **Referred to** [1976–7] 222

National Provincial Bank Ltd v Ainsworth [1965] AC 1175 **Considered** [1982] 113

National Provincial Bank Ltd v Liddiard [1941] Ch 158 **Referred to** [1989] 652

National Provincial Bank of England v United Electric Theatres Ltd [1916] 1 Ch 132 **Referred to** [1985] 641

National Research Development Corporation's Patent [1972] RPC 829 **Referred to** [1984] 393

National Sporting Club Ltd v Cope (1900) 82 LT 352 **Distinguished** [1984] 246

National Union of Railwaymen v Sullivan [1947] IR 77; 81 ILTR 55 **Referred to** [1984] 161; **Distinguished** [1986] 206; [1989] 87

Nebbia v New York (1933) 291 US 502 **Referred to** [1983] 449

Nederlandsche Banden—Industrie Michelin NV v EC Commission (Case 322/81) [1983] ECR 3641 **Referred to** [1990] 664

Nelson v Larholt [1948] 1 KB 359 **Applied** [1982] 121

Nestor v Murphy [1979] IR 326 **Referred to** [1982] 290; [1988] 400, 545; [1989] 342; **Distinguished** [1982] 113; [1984] 350; [1986] 483

Netherlands v Federatie Nederlands Vakbeweging [1987] 3 CMLR 767 **Followed** [1987] 324

New Windsor (Mayor of) v Stovell (1882) 27 Ch D 665 **Followed** [1984] 326

Newbold v Attorney General [1931] P 75 **Considered** [1984] 667

Newcastle City Council v Royal Newcastle Hospital [1959] AC 248 **Applied** [1982] 451

Newington Local Board v Cottingham Local Board (1879) 12 Ch D 725 **Followed** [1984] 326

Newland v Simons & Willer (Hairdressers) Ltd [1981] ICR 521 **Followed** [1983] 363

Newlin v Woods (1965) 42 TC 649 **Referred to** [1978] 16; [1982] 430

Newman v Alarmco Ltd [1976] IRLR 45 **Referred to** [1985] 336

Niedersachsen, The [1983] 1 WLR 1412; [1984] 1 All ER 398 **Applied** [1986] 10

Nixon v Commissioner of Valuation [1980] IR 340 **Distinguished** [1985] 655

Nixon v Nixon [1969] 1 WLR 1676 **Followed** [1982] 155

Noble v Harrison [1926] 2 KB 332 **Referred to** [1990] 857

Nolan v Irish Land Commission [1981] IR 23 **Considered** [1981] 456; **Followed** [1983]407

Nold (J) KG v Commission [1974] ECR 491; [1974] 2 CMLR 338 **Referred to** [1987] 400

Noor Mohamed v The King [1949] AC 182 **Referred to** [1981] 389

Nordenfelt v Maxim—Nordenfelt Guns & Ammunition Co Ltd [1894] AC 535 **Referred to** [1979] 79; **Considered** [1981] 345

Norris v Attorney General [1984] IR 36 **Referred to** [1989] 282; dicta **Applied** [1987] 477; [1988] 472; **Dictum approved** [1984] 373

North Carolina v Pearce (1969) 395 US 711 **Referred to** [1984] 333

North Western Health Board v Martyn [1985] ILRM 226 **Reversed** [1988] 519

Northampton County Council v ABF [1982] ILRM 164 **Referred to** [1986] 99; **Distinguished** [1984] 292

Northern Bank Co v Devlin [1924] 1 IR 90 **Followed** [1987] 30

Northern Bank Ltd v Duffy [1981] ILRM 308 **Referred to** [1983] 295; **Followed** [1984] 671

Northern Bank Finance Corp Ltd v Charlton [1979] IR 149 **Referred to** [1983] 271; [1987] 255; [1990] 780; **Considered** [1984] 461; **Dictum applied** [1986] 235; **Dictum explained** [1986] 250; **Distinguished** [1981] 75; **Followed** [1981] 173, 447; [1987] 669; [1988] 203; [1989] 735

Norwood and Blake's Contract, In re [1917] 1 IR 472 **Referred to** [1983] 513; **Not followed** [1982] 1

Nottinghamshire County Council v Bowly [1978] IRLR 252 **Referred to** [1985] 336

Nova Media Services Ltd v Minister for Posts and Telegraphs [1984] ILRM 161 **Followed** [1984] 170

Noyek & Sons Ltd, In re [1988] IR 772; [1987] ILRM 508 **Affirmed** [1989] 155

Nye (CL) Ltd, In re [1971] Ch 474 **Followed** [1976–7] 222

Oakes v Lynch Supreme Court, unreported, 27 November 1953 **Followed** [1987] 255

Oakey Abattoir Pty Ltd v Federal Commissioner of Taxes (1984) 84 ATC 4718 **Referred to** [1988] 181

Oaks Pitts Colliery Ltd, In re (1882) 21 ChD 322 **Referred to** [1988] 751

O'B v O'B High Court, unreported, 23 June 1982 **Reversed** [1984] 1

O'B v W High Court, unreported, 13 November 1974 **Appeal allowed** [1982] 234

O'Brien (a bankrupt), In re (1883) 11 LR Ir 213 **Referred to** [1979] 113

O'Brien v Bord na Mona, High Court, unreported, 18 March 1981 **Considered** [1982] 568; **Reversed in part** [1983] 314

O'Brien v Bord na Mona [1983] IR 255; [1983] ILRM 314 **Referred to** [1988] 52, 545; [1989] 98; **Applied** [1986] 296; **Followed** [1987] 36

O'Brien v Keogh [1972] IR 144 **Referred to** [1981] 179, 324; [1982] 327, 497; [1983] 449; **Considered** [1990] 70; **Dicta explained** [1986] 136; **Discussed** [1985] 41; **Followed** [1981] 60; [1984] 66; [1985] 86

O'Brien v Manufacturing Engineering Co Ltd [1973] IR 334; 108 ILTR 105 **Referred to** [1981] 60; [1984] 657; **Considered** [1984] 643; **Dictum explained** [1983] 449; **Followed** [1986] 136

O'Byrne v Minister for Finance [1959] IR 1; 94 ILTR 11 **Referred to** [1983] 449; [1986] 343; **Considered** [1986] 136

O'Byrne's Estate, In re (1885) 15 LR Ir 373 **Distinguished** [1988] 480

O'Callaghan v Commissioners for Public Works [1985] ILRM 364 **Referred to** [1988] 400; [1989] 670

O'Callaghan v O'Sullivan [1925] 1 IR 90 **Referred to** [1988] 501

O'Carroll Kent Ltd, In re 89 ILTR 72 **Referred to** [1980] 131

O'Conail v Shakleton High Court, unreported, 8 November 1974 **Appeal allowed** [1982] 451

O'Connell, In re Supreme Court, unreported, 21 June 1976 **Followed** [1990] 84

O'Connor, In re [1952] Ir Jur Rep 51 **Followed** [1976–7] 199

O'Connor v Director of Public Prosecutions [1987] ILRM 723 **Referred to** [1989] 71

O Croinin v Brennan [1939] IR 274 **Referred to** [1986] 304

O'D v O'D High Court, unreported, 18 November 1983 **Considered** [1987] 1

O'Daly v Gulf Oil Terminals (Ireland) Ltd [1983] ILRM 163 **Referred to** [1986] 627

Odeon Associated Theatres Ltd v Jones [1971] 1 WLR 442; [1971] 2 All ER 407 **Applied** [1989] 552

O'Doherty v Attorney General [1941] IR 569 **Referred to** [1981] 242

O'Donoghue v Green [1967] IR 40 **Referred to** [1987] 768

O'Donoghue v Veterinary Council [1975] IR 398 **Considered** [1982] 568; [1986] 225; **Distinguished** [1983] 67

O'Donovan v Attorney General [1961] IR 114; 96 ILTR 121 **Referred to** [1980] 145; [1981] 242; **Followed** [1986] 381

O'Donovan v Cork County Council [1967] IR 173; 102 ILTR 157 **Referred to** [1987] 768; **Followed** [1986] 189; [1989] 437, 735

O'Sullivan v Hartnett [1983] ILRM 79 **Dictum approved** [1984] 39

O'Sullivan v Noonan and Transit Ltd Supreme Court, unreported, 28 July 1972 **Referred to** [1983] 595

O'Sullivan v P Ltd (1962) 3 ITC 355 **Followed** [1988] 181, 647

O'Toole (Jack) Ltd v MacEoin Kelly Associates [1986] IR 277; [1987] ILRM 269 **Referred to** [1987] 504; [1990] 266

Otto v Bolton and Norris [1936] 2 KB 46; [1936] 1 All ER 960 **Not followed** [1986] 43

Overseas Commodities Ltd v Style [1958] 1 Lloyds Rep 546 **Dictum approved** [1986] 677

Overseas Food Importers & Distributors v Brandt (1978) 93 DLR (3d) 317 **Referred to** [1988] 501

Overseas Tankship (UK) Ltd v Morts Dock & Engineering Co Ltd; The Wagon Mound (No 1) [1961] AC 388; [1961] 1 All ER 404; [1961] 2 WLR 126 **Referred to** [1979] 3; **Applied** [1979] 3; [1986] 283

Owen and Ashworth's claim, In re Bank of Syria [1961] 1 Ch 115 **Followed** [1982] 57

Owenabue Ltd v Dublin County Council [1982] ILRM 150 **Dicta approved** [1983] 213

Owners of Dredger Liebosch v Owners of SS. Edison [1933] AC 499 **Disapproved** [1979] 3

P v P [1916] 2 IR 400 **Considered** [1984] 667

P (C) v P (D) [1983] ILRM 380 **Applied** [1983] 387

P (H) v P (W) [1985] ILRM 527 **Followed** [1986] 3

PMPS Ltd v Attorney General High Court, unreported, 15 July 1981 **Affirmed** [1984] 88

PMPS Ltd v Attorney General [1983] IR 339; [1984] ILRM 88 **Referred to** [1990] 234; **Applied** [1986] 177; **Distinguished** [1984] 373

Pacific Coast Syndicate Ltd, In re [1913] 2 Ch 26 **Considered** [1990] 266

Padfield v Minister of Agriculture, Fisheries and Food [1968] AC 997 **Referred to** [1988] 437

Pais v Pais [1970] 3 WLR 830 **Approved** [1981] 125

Palermo, The (1883) 9 PD 6 **Doubted** [1989] 257

Palmer v Day & Son [1895] 2 QB 618 **Distinguished** [1986] 518

Palser v Grinling Property Holding Co Ltd [1948] AC 291 **Applied** [1984] 301

Panama, New Zealand & Australian Royal Mail Co, In re (1870) LR 5 Ch App 318 **Considered** [1985] 641

Paquin v Beauclerk [1906] AC 148 **Referred to** [1986] 250

Parfitt v Lawless (1872) LR 2 P & D 462 **Referred to** [1978] 175

Paris v Stepney Borough Council [1951] AC 367 **Referred to** [1989] 117

Park v Park [1946] NI 151 **Not followed** [1984] 66

Parke v Daily News Ltd [1962] 1 Ch 927 **Followed** [1981] 408

Parke Davis & Co v Controller of Patents, High Court, unreported, 13 December 1971, **Considered** [1976–7] 164

Parker v British Airways Board [1982] QB 1004 **Referred to** [1988] 565

Parker v Commonwealth of Australia (1964) 112 CLR 295 **Considered** [1989] 544

Parker v Walker 1961 SLT 252 **Distinguished** [1986] 493

Parkinson v Watson [1956] NI 1 not **Followed** [1981] 198

Parkinson (Sir Lindsay) & Co Ltd v Commissioners of Works [1949] 2 KB 632 **Referred to** [1990] 601

Parkinson (Sir Lindsay) & Co Ltd v Triplan Ltd [1973] QB 609 **Referred to** [1987] 255

Parmiter v Coupland (1840) 3 M & W 105 **Dictum Applied** [1986] 601

Parojcic v Parojcic [1958] 1 WLR 1280 **Considered** [1982] 277

Partington v Attorney General (1869) LR 4 HL 100 **Dictum cited** [1988] 181 **Referred to** [1988] 647

Pat Ruth Ltd, In re [1981] ILRM 51 **Referred to** [1990] 330, 441

Paton v British Pregnancy Advisory Trustees [1979] 1 QB 276; [1978] 2 All ER 987 **Referred to** [1987] 477

Patrick v Broadstone Mills Ltd [1954] 1 WLR 158 **Considered** [1989] 552

Patrick & Lyon Ltd, In re [1933] Ch 786 **Followed** [1978] 219

Patterson v Murphy High Court, unreported, 4 May 1978 **Considered** [1983] 268; **Followed** [1980] 1; [1982] 534; [1987] 564

Paul v Rendell (1981) 55 ALJR 371 **Referred to** [1984] 208; **Dictum approved** [1983] 429

Pavia & Co SPA v Thurmann-Neilsen [1952] 2 QB 84 **Considered** [1984] 471

Payzu Ltd v Saunders [1919] 2 KB 581 **Referred to** [1980] 153

Peables v Crosthwaite (1897) 13 TLR 198 **Referred to** [1982] 373

Peabody Donation Fund (Governor of) v Sir Lindsay Parkinson & Co Ltd [1985] AC 210; [1984] 3 All ER 529 **Referred to** [1988] 300; [1990] 658; **Applied** [1986] 43; **Considered** [1989] 400

Pearce v Woodall Duckham Ltd [1978] 1 WLR 832 **Referred to** [1989] 245

Pearlman v Keepers and Governors of Harrow School [1979] QB 56 **Referred to** [1981] 242

Pearlberg v Varly [1972] 1 WLR 534 **Dictum approved** [1990] 485

Peat v Gresham Trust Ltd [1934] 252 **Referred to** [1976-7] 175

Pedro v Diss [1981] 2 All ER 59 **Considered** [1986] 111

Pemberton v Hughes [1899] 1 Ch 781 **Referred to** [1980] 257

Pembroke Urban District Council v Commissioners of Valuation [1904] 2 IR 429 **Distinguished** [1984] 117

Penhas v Eng [1953] AC 304 **Considered** [1987] 172

People (Attorney General) v Ainscough [1960] IR 136 **Referred to** [1988] 4

People (Attorney General) v Bell [1969] IR 24; 105 ILTR 41 **Referred to** [1980] 167; [1983] 549; [1984] 657

People (Attorney General) v Berber and Levey [1944] IR 405 **Dictum approved** [1982] 69

People (Attorney General) v Boggan [1958] IR 67 **Referred to** [1983] 489; [1985] 19; [1987] 65

People (Attorney General) v Boylan [1963] IR 238 **Considered** [1986] 455

People (Attorney General) v Casey (No 2) [1963] IR 33 **Referred to** [1983] 2; **Considered** [1990] 780

People (Attorney General) v Conmey [1975] IR 341 **Referred to** [1981] 389; [1987] 535; [1990] 749; **Considered** [1983] 549; [1989] 245; [1990] 350; **Dictum applied** [1986] 250; **Distinguished** [1983] 449

People (Attorney General) v Cradden [1955] IR 130 **Referred to** [1990] 780; cited [1981] 389

People (Attorney General) v Cronin [1972] IR 159 **Referred to** [1983] 549

People (Attorney General) v Cullen [1969] IR 24 **Referred to** [1983] 549

People (Attorney General) v Cummins [1972] IR 312; 108 ILTR 5 **Referred to** [1988] 666

People (Attorney General) v Doyle 101 ILTR 136 **Referred to** [1988] 318

People (Attorney General) v Earls [1969] IR 414 **Distinguished** [1983] 17

People (Attorney General) v Fennell (No 2) [1940] IR 453; 75 ILTR 183 **Considered** [1983] 549

People (Attorney General) v Galvin [1964] IR 325 **Referred to** [1981] 389; **Approved** [1983] 271

People (Attorney General) v Giles [1974] IR 422; 110 ILTR 33 **Referred to** [1988] 4

People (Attorney General) v Griffin [1974] IR 416; 108 ILTR 81 **Referred to** [1981] 447; **Considered** [1989] 245; **Followed** [1985] 18

People (Attorney General) v Kennedy [1946] IR 517; 81 ILTR 73 **Referred to** [1981] 447; [1983] 549

People (Attorney General) v Kerins [1945] IR 339; 79 ILTR 75 **Referred to** [1990] 780

People (Attorney General) v Kervick Supreme Court, unreported, 29 July 1971 **Referred to** [1989] 333

People (Attorney General) v McDermott (1974) 2 Frewen 211 **Disapproved** [1987] 606

People (Attorney General) v McGlynn [1967] IR 232 **Referred to** [1988] 4, 318; [1989] 485

People (Attorney General) v Martin [1956] IR 22 **Applied** [1985] 18

People (Attorney General) v Mills (1955) 1 Frewen 153 **Not followed** [1990] 310

People (Attorney General) v O'Brien [1963] IR 65 **Referred to** [1983] 549

People (Attorney General) v O'Brien [1965] IR 142 **Referred to** [1988] 4; **Affirmed** [1981] 389; **Considered** [1986] 433; [1987] 575; [1988] 39; [1990] 313, 569; **Followed** [1985] 465; [1987] 87

People (Attorney General) v O'Callaghan [1966] IR 501; 102 ILTR 45 **Dictum applied** [1988] 333; **Followed** [1984] 249; [1986] 357; [1989] 333

People (Attorney General) v O'Donoghue Supreme Court, unreported, 1970 **Referred to** [1982] 1

People (Attorney General) v O'Driscoll (1972) 1 Frewen 351 **Referred to** [1989] 149; **Dictum applied** [1988] 333; [1989] 139

People (Attorney General) v Poyning [1972] IR 402 **Referred to** [1987] 316; **Dictum applied** [1989] 139

People (Attorney General) v Ruttledge (1946) 1 Frewen 20 75 **Considered** [1986] 716

People (Attorney General) v Williams [1940] IR 195 **Dictum Applied** [1990] 780

People (Director of Public Prosecutions) v Byrne [1987] IR 363 **Followed** [1989] 629

People (Director of Public Prosecutions) v Campbell (1983) 2 Frewen 20, 148 **Referred to** [1988] 117; **Considered** [1986] 716

People (Director of Public Prosecutions) v Conroy [1986] IR 460; [1988] ILRM 4 **Considered** [1990] 313

People (Director of Public Prosecutions) v Egan (1989) 3 Frewen 20 **Referred to** [1990] 780

People (Director of Public Prosecutions) v Eccles Court of Criminal Appeal, unreported, 10 February 1986 **Referred to** [1987] 606

People (Director of Public Prosecutions) v F 114 ILTR 110 **Applied** [1985] 343

People (Director of Public Prosecutions) v Farrell [1978] IR 13 **Referred to** [1985] 465; [1988] 4; [1990] 569; **Considered** [1990] 313; **Distinguished** [1988] 294; **Followed** [1978] 122

People (Director of Public Prosecutions) v Ferris, Court of Criminal Appeal, unreported, 15 December 1986 **Referred to** [1989] 613

People (Director of Public Prosecutions) v Kehoe [1985] IR 444; [1986] ILRM 690 **Followed** [1987] 316

People (Director of Public Prosecutions) v Kelly Court of Criminal Appeal, unreported, 2 April 1982 **Affirmed** [1983] 271

People (Director of Public Prosecutions) v Kelly (No. 2) [1983] IR 1; [1983] ILRM 271 **Referred to** [1987] 606; [1990] 780; **Considered** [1984] 461; **Dictum applied** [1987] 138; **Followed** [1989] 629

People (Director of Public Prosecutions) v Kenny, Irish Times Law Report, March 19, 1990 **Reversed** [1990] 569

People (Director of Public Prosecutions) v Lawless, Court of Criminal Appeal, unreported, 18 November 1985 **Referred to** [1987] 87

People (Director of Public Prosecutions) v Lynch [1982] IR 64; [1981] ILRM 389 **Referred to** [1983] 549; [1990] 313, 569, 780; **Considered** [1988] 4; [1990] 850; **Dictum applied** [1987] 727; **Followed** [1985] 465; [1986] 428

People (Director of Public Prosecutions) v McGuinness [1978] IR 189 **Referred to** [1988] 448

People (Director of Public Prosecutions) v Madden [1977] IR 336; 111 ILTR 117 **Referred to** [1981] 389; [1984] 461; [1987] 606; [1989] 821; [1990] 569; **Approved** [1983] 271; **Considered** [1990] 313; **Followed** [1985] 465

Pett v Greyhound Racing Assocation (No 2) [1970] 1 QB 46 **Referred to** [1980] 46

Pettit v Pettit [1963] P 177 **Dictum approved** [1982] 545

Petty v Daniel (1887) 34 Ch D 172 **Followed** [1982] 1

Phelan v Laois Vocational Education Committee High Court, unreported, 28 February 1977 **Referred to** [1989] 342

Philips Trade Mark (1969) RPC 78 **Referred to** [1978] 106

Phillipart v William Whiteley Ltd [1908] 2 Ch 274 **Dictum approved** [1976–7] 335

Phillips v Bourne [1947] KB 533; 27 TC 498 **Referred to** [1985] 655; **Not followed** [1981] 157; [1982] 13

Phillips v Britannia Hygienic Laundry Co Ltd [1923] 2 KB 832 **Considered** [1990] 560; **Dictum Applied** [1978] 1; **Doubted** [1981] 242

Phillips v Eyre (1870) LR 6 QB 1 **Disapproved** [1986] 627

Phillips v Lamdin [1949] 2 KB 33 **Referred to** [1979] 240

Phillips v Ward [1956] 1 WLR 471 **Referred to** [1976–7] 287

Phipps v Boardman [1967] 2 AC 46 **Followed** [1978] 211

Phipps v Earl of Anglesea (1721) 1 P Wms 696 **Followed** [1986] 167

Photo Productions Ltd v Securicor Transport Ltd [1980] AC 827 **Considered** [1982] 359 **Followed** [1982] 99

Pianotist Co Ltd, In re (1906) 23 RPC 774 **Referred to** [1978] 116; **Considered** [1990] 204

Pigs and Bacon Commission v McCarren & Co High Court, unreported, 24 June 1980 **Reversed** [1981] 237

Pigs Marketing Board v Donnelly (Dublin) Ltd [1939] IR 413 **Referred to** [1983] 391; **Applied** [1989] 342; **Considered** [1986] 136; [1987] 278

Pike v Waldrum [1952] 1 Lloyds Rep 431 **Followed** [1982] 126

Pine Valley Developments Ltd v Minister for the Environment [1987] IR 23; [1987] ILRM 747 **Referred to** [1988] 610; **Considered** [1990] 403

Pioneer Aggregates (UK) Ltd v Secretary of State for the Environment [1985] AC 132; [1984] 3 WLR 32 **Referred to** [1985] 41; **Distinguished** [1988] 274

Pirelli General Cable Works Ltd v Oscar Faber & Partners [1983] 2 AC 1 **Referred to** [1990] 403; **Not followed** [1983] 156

Pittortou (A bankrupt) In re, ex parte Trustee of the Property of the Bankrupt [1985] 1 WLR 58; [1985] 1 All ER 285 **Distinguished** [1987] 522

Pok Sum Shum v Ireland [1986] ILRM 593 **Distinguished** [1990] 234; **Followed** [1987] 330

Ponting v Noakes [1894] 2 QB 281 **Referred to** [1978] 1

Portland Estates Ltd v Limerick Corporation High Court, unreported, 31 July 1979 **Reversed** [1980] 77

Pott's Executors v Commissioners of Inland Revenue [1951] AC 443 **Referred to** [1988] 181

Poulett Peerage, The [1903] AC 395 **Referred to** [1984] 66

Power Securities Ltd v Daly High Court, unreported, 27 February 1984 **Referred to** [1987] 17

Power Supermarkets Ltd, In re [1988] IR 206 **Considered** [1990] 228, 877

Premier Confectionery Ltd v London Commercial Sale Rooms Ltd [1933] 1 Ch 904 **Considered** [1976–7] 311

Prendergast v Porter [1961] IR 440 **Followed** [1990] 32

Prenn v Simmonds [1971] 1 WLR 1381 **Dictum approved** [1982] 359

Prestcold (Central) Ltd v Minister of Labour [1969] 1 WLR 89 **Dictum applied** [1989] 478

Price v Civil Service Commission [1977] 1 WLR 1417; [1978] ICR 27; [1978] 1 All ER 1228, EAT **Considered** [1985] 226

Pride of Derby and Derbyshire Angling Association Ltd v British Celanese Ltd [1953] Ch 149 **Dictum approved** [1981] 84

Private Motorists Provident Society Ltd v Attorney General. *See* PMPS v Attorney General (above)

Proc and Minister of Community and Social Services, Re (1978) 53 DLR (3d) 512 **Considered** [1989] 169

Procunier v Martinez (1973) 416 US 296 **Considered** [1987] 52

Procureur du Roi v Dassonville [1974] ECR 837 **Referred to** [1984] 45; **Considered** [1983] 258

Procureur du Roi v Royer (Case 48/75) [1976] ECR 497 **Referred to** [1990] 364

Property and Bloodstock Ltd v Emerton [1967] 2 All ER 839 **Distinguished** [1983] 82

Proudman v Dayman [1941] 67 CLR 536 **Dictum approved** [1984] 329

Provincial Building Society v Brown [1950] NI 163 **Referred to** [1984] 350

Pulsford v Devinish [1903] 2 Ch 625 **Referred to** [1979] 296

Purcell v Trigell Ltd [1971] 1 QB 358; [1970] 3 All ER 671 **Dictum applied** [1986] 624; [1987] 504

Purtill v Athlone Urban District Council [1968] IR 205 **Applied** [1978] 1

Pyke v Hibernian Bank [1950] IR 195; 85 ILTR 149 **Dictum applied** [1986] 601

Quartz Hill Consolidated Gold Mining Co v Eyre (1882–83) 11 QBD 674 **Dictum affirmed** [1982] 126

Quigley v Beirne [1955] IR 65 **Referred to** [1979] 51

Quigley v Creation Ltd [1971] IR 269; 108 ILTR 1 **Dictum approved** [1986] 601

Quigley v Fanning High Court, unreported, 22 July 1980 **Referred to** [1990] 505

Quilter v Mapleson (1881–2) 9 QBD 672 **Distinguished** [1981] 203

Quinn v Leathem [1901] AC 495 **Referred to** [1988] 157

Quinn v Quality Homes Ltd High Court, unreported, 21 November 1977 **Referred to** [1979] 3; **Distinguished** [1980] 107

Quinn v Scott [1965] 1 WLR 1004 **Approved** [1990] 857

Quinn v Wren [1985] IR 322; [1985] ILRM 410 **Referred to** [1990] 780; **Applied** [1986] 401; [1988] 333; approved [1990] 505; **Followed** [1986] 235; [1988] 75

Quinn's Supermarket Ltd v Attorney General [1972] IR 1 **Referred to** [1982] 327; [1985] 86; [1987] 278, 290; **Applied** [1985] 606; **Considered** [1983] 449; [1990] 364; **Dictum approved** [1984] 355, [1984] 657; **Followed** [1986] 136

R v Adams (1968) 52 Cr App Rep 588 not **Followed** [1989] 370

R v Algar [1954] 1 QB 279 **Doubted** [1984] 667

R v Ashford, Kent Justices, ex parte Richley [1955] 1 WLR 562 **Referred to** [1989] 159

R v Bailey [1956] NI 15 **Dictum approved** [1981] 91

R v Barnado [1891] 1 QB 194 **Considered** [1989] 277

R v Baslo (1954) 91 CLR 628 **Referred to** [1988] 4

R v Bateson (1969) 54 Cr App Rep 373 **Referred to** [1989] 370

R v Belfon [1976] 1 WLR 741 **Applied** [1985] 25

R v Berry [1969] QB 73 **Referred to** [1980] 21

R v Billam [1986] 1 WLR 349; [1986] 1 All ER 985 **Referred to** [1989] 149

R v Blundeston Prison Board of Visitors, ex parte Fox-Taylor [1982] 1 All ER 646 **Referred to** [1989] 71

R v Board of Inland Revenue, ex parte Goldberg [1989] QB 267 **Not followed** [1989] 257

R v Bourne [1939] 1 KB 687 **Referred to** [1987] 477

R v Bow Road Domestic Proceedings Court, Ex parte Adedigba [1968] 2 QB 572; [1968] 2 All ER 89 **Dictum approved** [1982] 13

R v Bow Street Magistrates, Ex parte Mackeson (1981) 75 Cr. App. R. 24 **Considered** [1985] 465

R v Brailsford [1905] 2 KB 730 **Followed** [1985] 465

R v Brentwood Superintendent Registrar of Marriages [1968] 2 QB 956 **Considered** [1987] 189

R v Briggs [1977] 1 All ER 475 **Referred to** [1985] 249

R v Brighton Justices ex parte Robinson [1973] 1 WLR 69 **Referred to** [1981] 54

R v Brinkley [1984] NI 48 **Referred to** [1988] 4

R v Brixton Prison Governor, ex parte Armah [1968] AC 192; [1966] 3 WLR 828; [1966] 3 All ER 177 **Referred to** [1988] 333; **Principles adopted** [1985] 385

R v Brixton Prison Governor, ex parte Kolcyzki [1955] 1 QB 540; [1955] 2 WLR 116; [1955] 1 All ER 31 **Considered** [1985] 385 **Referred to** [1985] 422

R v Brixton Prison Governor, ex parte Schtraks [1963] 1 QB 55; [1962] 2 WLR 976; [1962] 2 All ER 176. *Appeal to House of Lords reported sub nom* Schtraks v Government of Israel [1964] AC 556; [1952] 3 WLR 1013; [1962] 3 All ER 529 **Referred to** [1988] 333; **Considered** [1985] 385, 422

R v Brixton Prison Governor, ex parte Stallman [1912] 3 KB 424 **Followed** [1981] 120

R v Burns [1988] 7 NIJB **Referred to** [1990] 505

R v Byrne [1960] 2 QB 396; [1960] 3 All ER 1 **Not followed** [1986] 244

R v Cameron (1982) 6 WWR 270 **Referred to** [1986] 639

R v Cardiff City Coroner, ex parte Thomas [1970] 1 WLR 1475; [1970] 3 All ER 469 **Dictum approved** [1986] 133

R v Chan Wee-Keung [1967] 2 AC 160 **Referred to** [1988] 4

R v Chapple (1804) Russ & Ry 77 **Referred to** [1981] 157

R v Chorley (1848) 1 QB 515 **Principles applied** [1984] 451

R v Clarke (1857) 7 E & B 186 **Considered** [1989] 277

R v Cooper [1969] 1 QB 267 **Doubted** [1983] 271; **Not followed** [1990] 780

R v Coroner for the City of London, ex parte Barber [1975] 1 WLR 1310; [1975] 3 All ER 538 **Dictum approved** [1986] 133

R v Coroner of Margate (1865) 1 ILT 707 **Approved** [1980] 233

R v Cotham [1898] 1 QB 802 **Referred to** [1986] 476

R v Criminal Injuries Compensation Board, ex parte Lain [1967] 2 QB 864; [1967] 2 All ER 770 **Principles applied** [1986] 476

R v Cunningham [1957] 2 All ER 412 **Referred to** [1985] 249

R v Daily Mirror, ex parte Smith [1927] 1 KB 845 **Referred to** [1985] 183

R v Davies, ex parte Delbert-Evans [1945] KB 435 **Dicta applied** [1984] 577

R v Diggines, ex parte Rahmani [1985] QB 1109 **Referred to** [1989] 71

R v Edwards [1975] QB 27 **Considered** [1981] 213

R v Evening Standard Company [1954] 1 QB 578 **Referred to** [1983] 355

R v Faulkner (1877) IR 11 CL 8 **Referred to** [1985] 269

R v Federal Steam Navigation Co Ltd [1974] 1 WLR 505; [1974] 2 All ER 97 **Principles applied** [1985] 109

R v Fegan [1972] NI 80 **Dicta approved** [1984] 329

R v Furnished Houses Rent Tribunal for Paddington and St Marylebone, ex parte Kendal Hotels Ltd [1947] 1 All ER 448 **Considered** [1988] 117

R v Gaming Board of Great Britain, ex parte Benaim [1970] 2 QB 417 **Considered** [1981] 456

R v Gateshead Justices, ex parte Tesco Stores Ltd [1981] QB 470; [1981] 1 All ER 1027 **Referred to** [1986] 565; [1987] 309

R v Governor of Brixton Prison. *See* R v Brixton Prison Governor (above)

R v Greater London Council, ex parte Blackburn [1976] 1 WLR 550 **Referred to** [1983] 89

R v Greenberg [1943] 1 KB 381 **Referred to** [1985] 577

R v Grossman (1981) 73 CAR 302 **Followed** [1983] 350

R v H M Treasury, ex parte Smedley [1985] QB 657; [1985] 1 All ER 589 **Referred to** [1987] 400

R v Hamilton (1969) 113 SJ 546 **Referred to** [1988] 448

R v Hartley [1978] 2 NZLR 199 **Considered** [1985] 465

R v Henn [1979] ECR 3795; [1981] AC 850 **Referred to** [1987] 400

R v Herrod, ex parte Leeds City Council [1976] QB 540 **Considered** [1989] 113; **Dicta not approved** [1988] 89

R v Hillingdon Borough Council ex parte Royco Homes Ltd [1974] QB 720 **Referred to** [1981] 54; **Considered** [1982] 590

R v Hopkins [1893] 1 QB 621 **Followed** [1983] 45

R v Hughes (1879) 4 QBD 614 **Referred to** [1986] 690

R v Huntbach, ex parte Lockley [1944] 1 KB 606; [1944] 2 All ER 453 **Dictum applied** [1986] 133

R v Hyam [1975] AC 55 **Considered** [1985] 25

R v Inland Revenue Commissioners ex parte National Federation of Self Employed and Small Businesses Ltd [1980] QB 407 **Considered** [1981] 242

R v Inland Revenue Commissioners, ex parte National Federation of Self-Employed and Small Businesses Ltd [1982] AC 617; [1981] 2 WLR 722 **Referred to** [1983 89

R v Inland Revenue Commissioners, ex parte Preston [1985] AC 835; [1985] 2 All ER 372 **Distinguished** [1986] 37

R v Inns (1974) 60 Cr App Rep 231 **Dictum approved** [1981] 47

R v Inspector of Taxes, ex parte Clarke [1974] QB 220 **Followed** [1984] 545

R v Johnson (1865) 15 ICLR 60 **Considered** [1983] 271

R v Jones (1895) 59 JP 87 **Considered** [1982] 342

R v Jones (Robert) (No. 2) [1972] 1 WLR 1485 **Not followed** [1982] 1

R v Jones [1978] 1 WLR 195; [1978] 2 All ER 718 **Followed** [1985] 123

R v Lawrence [1982] AC 510; [1981] 1 All ER 974 **Dictum approved** [1986] 639

R v Leach, ex parte Fritchley [1913] 3 KB 40 **Followed** [1983] 45

R v Leyland Justices, ex parte Hawthorn [1979] QB 283 **Referred to** [1989] 71

R v Lushington, ex parte Otto [1894] 2 QB 423 **Followed** [1989] 71

R v Lyon (1898) 14 TLR 357 **Considered** [1982] 342

R v McAloon [1959] OR 441 **Referred to** [1988] 4

R v McCormack Crimes Act Cases 244 **Referred to** [1984] 149

R v McLaren [1949] 2 DLR 682 **Referred to** [1988] 4

R v Manchester Stipendiary Magistrate, ex parte Hill [1983] 1 AC 328; [1982] 2 All ER 963 **Referred to** [1987] 309; **Not followed** [1986] 565

R v Manley [1933] 1KB 529 **Applied** [1981] 91

R v Martin (1881) 8 QBD 54 **Referred to** [1985] 269

R v Maxwell [1978] 1 WLR 1350 **Approved** [1985] 385

R v Millis (1844) 10 Cl and Fin 534 **Referred to** [1976-7] 156; [1987] 172

R v Milne [1978] NI 110 **Referred to** [1985] 449

R v Minister for Health [1939] 1 KB 232 **Referred to** [1988] 117

R v Minister of Town and County Planning [1951] 1 KB 1 **Referred to** [1980] 75

R v Mohan [1976] QB 1 **Referred to** [1985] 25

R v Murphy [1921] 1 IR 190 **Considered** [1988] 117

R v Murray [1951] 1 KB 391 **Referred to** [1988] 4

R v Newcastle-under-Lyme, ex parte Whitehouse [1952] 2 All ER 351n **Referred to** [1983] 17

R v Newland [1954] 1 QB 158 **Considered** [1981] 91

R v Ng Chun-Kwan [1974] HKLR 319 **Referred to** [1988] 4

R v Norfolk Quarter Sessions, ex parte Brunson [1953] 1 QB 503 **Considered** [1988] 117

R v Oakes [1959] 2 QB 350 **Referred to** [1985] 109

R v Ottewell [1970] AC 642 **Dictum approved** [1982] 13

R v Oxford Justices, ex parte Smith [1982] RTR 201 **Followed** [1988] 720

R v Parke [1903] 2 KB 432 **Referred to** [1985] 183

R v Parket [1977] 2 All ER 37 **Referred to** [1985] 249

R v Patents Appeal Tribunal, ex parte Swift & Co [1962] 2 QB 647 **Referred to** [1988] 333

R v Pembleton (1874) 43 LJ (MC) 91 **Referred to** [1985] 249, 269

R v Pentonville Prison Governor, ex parte Budlong [1980] 1 WLR 1110; [1980] 1 All ER 701 **Considered** [1985] 385

R v Pentonville Prison Governor, ex parte Cheng [1973] 1 All ER 935; [1973] 2 WLR 746. *Appeal to House of Lords reported sub nom* Cheng v Governor of Pentonville Prison [1973] AC 931; [1973] 2 WLR 746; [1976] 2 All ER 204 **Referred to** [1985] 422; [1988] 333; **Considered** [1985] 385; **Dictum adopted** [1986] 401

R v Perter Dadson (1983) 77 Cr App Rep 91 **Followed** [1985] 123

R v Pillington (1958) 42 CR App Rep 233 **Referred to** [1986] 547

R v Poor Law Commissioners 6 AD & EL 1 **Referred to** [1987] 4

R v Puru [1984] 1 NZLR 248 **Referred to** [1989] 149

R v R [1984] IR 296 **Referred to** [1986] 337; **Considered** [1988] 52; **Distinguished** [1984] 657

R v R High Court, unreported, 21 December 1984 **Referred to** [1987] 58

R (E) v R (J) [1981] ILRM 125 **Considered** [1985] 186

R v Rennie [1982] 1 WLR 64 **Dictum Applied** [1988] 666

R v Russell (1854) 3 El & Bl 942 **Referred to** [1983] 549

R v Sang [1980] AC 402; [1979] 2 All ER 46 **Considered** [1986] 433

R v Savandrayanagan and Walker [1968] 3 All ER 439 **Dicta not followed** [1985] 183

R v Secretary of State for the Home Department, ex parte Khan [1984] 1 WLR 1337 **Distinguished** [1989] 639

R v Secretary of State for the Home Department, ex parte Ruddock [1987] 1 WLR 1482 **Distinguished** [1989] 639

R v Secretary of State for Transport, ex parte Factortame Ltd [1990] 2 AC 857 **Considered** [1990] 350

R v Simons [1953] 1 WLR 1014 **Referred to** [1987] 4

R v Smith [1961] AC 290 **Considered** [1985] 25

R v Smith [1975] AC 476 **Referred to** [1982] 69

R v Smyth [1982] NI 271 **Considered** [1985] 385

R v Southampton Income Tax Commissioners, ex parte Singer [1966] 2 KB 249 **Referred to** [1982] 290

R v Sparks [1964] AC 964 **Referred to** [1988] 4

R v Stapleton [1979] 2 All ER 1198 **Referred to** [1985] 249

R v Tolson (1889) 23 QBD 168 **Dictum approved** [1984] 329

R v Turnbull [1976] 3 WLR 445 **Referred to** [1983] 271

R v W High Court, unreported, 1 February 1980 **Distinguished** [1986] 489

R v Ward (1872) LR ICCR 356 **Referred to** [1985] 269

R v Watford Justices, ex parte Outrim [1983] RTR 26 **Followed** [1988] 720

R v Welch (1875) 1 QBD 23 **Referred to** [1985] 269

R v Whitney (1842) 1 Mood CC3 **Referred to** [1981] 157

R v Whybrow (1951) 35 Cr App Rep 141 **Referred to** [1985] 25

R v Winson Green Prison Governor, ex parte Littlejohn [1975] 1 WLR 893; [1975] 3 All ER 208 **Considered** [1985] 385

R v Wong Kam-Ming [1980] AC 247 **Referred to** [1988] 4

R (Blakeney) v Justices for County Roscommon [1894] 2 IR 158 **Followed** [1988] 117

R (Bowden) v Belfast Justices [1952] NI 91 **Distinguished** [1981] 213

R (Bridges) v Armagh JJ [1897] 2 IR 236 **Referred to** [1986] 565

R (Bridgman) v Drury [1894] 2 IR 489 **Considered** [1983] 89

R (Collins) v Donegal JJ [1903] 2 IR 533 **Considered** [1990] 857

R (Cottingham) v Justices of County Cork [1906] 2 IR 415 **Approved** [1982] 342; **Dicta approved** [1984] 134

R (Cox) v Recorder of Dublin (1885/6) 16 LR Ir 424 **Considered** [1981] 279

R (Doris) v Ministry for Health [1954] NI 79 **Referred to** [1976–7] 305

R (Dudgeon) v Antrim County Court Judge 56 ILTR 124 **Not followed** [1981] 279

R (Futter) v Justices of County Cork [1917] 2 IR 430 **Considered** [1986] 565; **Followed** [1987] 309

R (Geraghty) v Dublin Justices 35 ILTR 136 **Distinguished** [1981] 213

R (Giant's Causeway Tramway Co) v Antrim Justices [1895] 2 IR 603 **Referred to** [1983] 549; **Distinguished** [1981] 47

R (Hastings) v Justices of Galway [1906] 2 IR 499; 43 ILTR 185 **Referred to** [1983] 549; **Followed** [1988] 117

R (Henderson) v Louth Justices [1911] 2 IR 312 **Considered** [1990] 857

R (IUDWC) v Rathmines UDC [1928] IR 260 **Considered** [1988] 437

R (Kane) v Tyrone Justices (1906) 40 ILTR 181 **Considered** [1981] 389

R (Kildare County Council) v Commissioners of Valuation [1901] 2 IR 215 **Distinguished** [1989] 865

R (Lambe) v Armagh Justices [1897] 2 IR 57 **Applied** [1981] 279

R (Marshall) v Tyrone Justices [1895] 2 IR 174 **Referred to** [1981] 270

R (Martin) v Mahony [1910] 2 IR 695 **Dictum Applied** [1987] 202

R (McGrath) v Chairman and Justices of Clare [1905] 2 IR 510 **Referred to** [1983] 549

R (Morell) v Antrim Justices [1900] 2 IR 692 **Considered** [1981] 279

R (Murphy) v Recorder and Justices of Cork [1895] 2 IR 104 **Dictum approved** [1981] 2

R (O'Neill) v Tyrone Justices [1917] 2 IR 96 **Approved** [1981] 333

R (O'Reilly) v Divisional Justices of Dublin 37 ILTR 200 **Followed** [1982] 290

R (Roe) v Roscommon Justices [1905] 2 IR 101 **Applied** [1981] 279

R (Sheehan) v Cork Justices [1907] 2 IR 5 **Followed** [1981] 213

R (Wexford County Council) v Local Government Board [1902] 2 IR 349; 35 ILTR 87 **Considered** [1988] 52, 531; **Dictum applied** [1986] 499

RCA Corporation v Pollard [1983] Ch 135; [1982] 3 All ER 771 **Referred to** [1985] 221; **Distinguished** [1990] 560

Racal Communications Ltd, In re [1981] AC 374 **Referred to** [1981] 242; **Followed** [1982] 590

Racke v Mainz [1979] ECR 69 **Referred to** [1988] 400

Radford v de Froberville [1977] 1 WLR 1262; [1978] 1 All ER 33 **Principles adopted** [1985] 189

Radio Telefís Éireann v Magill TV Guide Ltd [1988] IR 97; [1989] IR 554 **Followed** [1990] 811

Radnall's Registered Design (1934) 51 RPC 164 **Followed** [1989] 124

Rahill v Brady [1971] IR 69 **Dictum approved** [1981] 157 **Referred to** [1981] 137

Rahman v Abu-Taha [1980] 1 WLR 1268 **Dictum approved** [1983] 541

Raineri v Miles [1981] AC 1050 **Referred to** [1984] 156

Rainey v Delap [1988] ILRM 620 **Referred to** [1988] 689

Rainsford v Limerick Corporation [1984] IR 152n **Principles adopted** [1985] 41

Ramsay v Liverpool Royal Infirmary [1930] AC 588 **Referred to** [1988] 67

Ramsay v Margrett [1894] 2 QB 18 **Referred to** [1985] 624

Ramsay (WT) Ltd v Inland Revenue Commissioners [1982] AC 300; [1981] 2 WLR 449 **Not followed** [1988] 181, 647

Ramsden v Dyson (1866) LR 1 HL 129 **Dictum Considered** [1981] 419 **Distinguished** [1981] 419

Ranelaugh (Earl) v Hayes (1683) 1 Vern 189; 23 ER 405 **Referred to** [1985] 522

Ranks Hovis McDougall Ltd v Controller of Patents [1979] IR 142 **Considered** [1988] 231

Ransom v Higgs [1974] 1 WLR 1594 **Dictum Considered** [1988] 181

Rasu Maritima SA v Perusahaan Pertambangan Minyak Dan Gas Bumi Negera [1978] QB 644 **Referred to** [1983] 541

Rawlins v Rickards (1860) 28 Beau 370 **Referred to** [1978] 247

Rawson v Peters (1972) 116 SJ 884 **Considered** [1988] 214

Raynor v Paskell (1948) 152 EG 270 **Referred to** [1986] 547

Read v Browne (1888) 22 QBD 128 **Referred to** [1990] 463

Readers Digest Association Ltd v Williams [1976] 1 WLR 1109 **Considered** [1990] 391

Readymix (Eire) Ltd v Dublin County Council, Supreme Court, unreported, 30 July 1974 **Referred to** [1980] 64; **Considered** [1978] 85; [1983] 268; **Followed** [1989] 602

Realisations (HH) Ltd, In re (1975) 31 P & CR 249 **Referred to** [1988] 751

Reardon Smith Ltd v Yngvar Hansen-Tangen [1976] 1 WLR 989 **Dictum applied** [1988] 373

Redbreast Preserving Co (Ireland) Ltd, In re [1958] IR 234; 91 ILTR 12 **Considered** [1990] 266; **Dictum disapproved** [1989] 757

Reddy v Bates [1983] IR 141; [1984] ILRM 197; [1990] 36; **Dictum Applied** [1984] 208, 523; discussed [1985] 582; **Followed** [1988] 268; [1989] 735

Reed v Ingham (1854) 23 LJMC 156 **Applied** [1989] 416

Reeves v Carthy [1984] IR 348 **Referred to** [1989] 735

Registrar of Trade Marks v W and G Du Cross Ltd [1913] AC 624 **Referred to** [1976–7] 335; **Distinguished** [1982] 207

Reid v Limerick Corporation [1984] ILRM 366 **Affirmed** [1987] 83

Reid v Reid (1886) 31 Ch D 402 **Followed** [1982] 290

Reid & Co v Employers Accident (1898) SC 1031 **Referred to** [1990] 110

Reigate v Union Manufacturing Co Ltd [1918] 1 KB 592 **Referred to** [1984] 471

Reilly v Gill 85 ILTR 165 **Referred to** [1989] 349

Reno Engrais et Produits Chemiques SA v Irish Agriculture Wholesale Society and Anor; High Court, unreported, 8 September 1976 **Referred to** [1985] 221

Representative Church Body v Barry [1918] 1 IR 402 **Principles applied** [1984] 451

Revenue Commissioners v Donnelly, In re Van Hool McArdle Ltd [1983] ILRM 329 **Distinguished** [1987] 508; [1989] 155; **Followed** [1984] 583

Revenue Commissioners v Doorley [1933] IR 750 **Dictum applied** [1988] 181 **Followed** [1988] 647

Revenue Commissioners v Iveagh [1930] IR 356, 431; 63 ILTR 89 **Referred to** [1982] 433

Revenue Commissioners v Moroney [1972] IR 372 **Referred to** [1986] 529

Revenue Commissioners v Muller & Co's Margarine Ltd [1901] AC 217 **Dictum approved** [1983] 112

Revenue Commissioners v N 101 ILTR 196 **Discussed** [1985] 655

Revenue Commissioners v O'Reilly [1983] ILRM 406 **Affirmed** [1984] 406

Rewe Handelsgesellschaft v Hauptzollamt Kiel (Case 158/80) [1981] ECR 1805 **Applied** [1990] 140

Rex Pet Foods Ltd v Lamb Bros (Dublin) Ltd High Court, unreported, 26 August 1982 **Approved** [1984] 45

Reynolds v Phoenix Assurance Co Ltd [1978] 2 Lloyd's Rep 440 **Referred to** [1984] 501

Rhatigan v Textiles y Confecciones Europeas SA [1989] ILRM 659 **Affirmed** [1990] 825

Rice v Dublin Corporation [1947] IR 425 **Considered** [1976–7] 311

Richardson v London County Council [1957] 1 WLR 751 **Dictum approved** [1983] 186

Ricket v Metropolitan Railway Co (1867) LR 2 HL 175 **Referred to** [1983] 56

Ridge v Baldwin [1964] AC 40 **Followed** [1976–7] 184

Ridley, In re [1950] Ch 415 **Referred to** [1976–7] 106

Riggs, In re [1901] 2 KB 16 **Followed** [1985] 442

Riordan, In re [1981] ILRM 2 **Distinguished** [1986] 471

Riordan v Butler [1940] IR 347; 74 ILTR 152 **Referred to** [1988] 157

Riordan's Travel Ltd v Acres & Co Ltd [1979] ILRM 3 **Referred to** [1984] 156; **Followed** [1981] 364

River Estates v Director General of Inland Revenue (1984) STC 60 **Referred to** [1985] 210

Riverstone Meat Co Ltd v Lancashire Shipping Co Ltd [1960] 1 QB 536; [1960] 1 All ER 193 **Followed** [1986] 669

Roadstone Ltd v Commissioners of Valuation [1961] IR 239; 96 ILTR 148 **Referred to** [1979] 246; [1990] 172; **Followed** [1987] 512

Robb v Connor (1875) IR 9 Eq 373 **Referred to** [1976–7] 50; [1987] 555

Roberts v Humphries (1873) 8 QB 483 **Followed** [1981] 213

Roberts v O'Neill High Court, unreported, 3 July 1981 **Affirmed** [1983] 206

Robertson v Fleming (1861) 4 Macq 465 **Not followed** [1980] 124

Robertson v Minister of Pensions [1949] 1 KB 227 **Referred to** [1978] 208; **Distinguished** [1984] 265

Robinson v Dolan [1935] IR 509; 1 ITC 25 **Referred to** [1985] 651

Robinson v Moore [1962–3] Ir Jur Rep 29 **Applied** [1978] 197

Robson v Hallet [1967] 2 QB 939 **Referred to** [1988] 39

Robson v Secretary of State for Social Services [1982] 3 Fam Law Rep 332 **Referred to** [1989] 169

Roche v Peilow [1985] IR 232; [1986] ILRM 189 **Referred to** [1987] 768; [1989] 735

Rogers v Ingham (1876) 3 Ch D 351 **Referred to** [1985] 283

Rogers v Irish Transport and General Workers' Union High Court, unreported, 15 March 1978 **Distinguished** [1980] 206

Rogers v Louth County Council [1981] IR 265; [1981] ILRM 144 **Considered** [1985] 283

Rogers Sons & Co v Lambert & Co [1891] 1 QB 318 **Considered** [1988] 565

Rohan Construction Ltd v Insurance Corp of Ireland plc [1986] ILRM 419 **Reversed** [1988] 373

Rolley v Murphy [1964] 2 QB 43 **Referred to** [1988] 333

Rolls v Miller (1884) 27 Ch D 71 **Dictum approved** [1984] 301

Rolls Royce Ltd, In re [1974] 1 WLR 1584 **Considered** [1990] 42

Ronayne v Ronayne [1970] IR 15 **Followed** [1976–7] 41

Rondel v Worsley [1969] 1 AC 191 **Referred to** [1989] 400

Rookes v Barnard [1964] AC 1129; [1964] 2 WLR 269 **Referred to** [1976–7] 41; [1978] 136; [1979] 266; [1987] 52; [1988] 159, 472

Rooney v Byrne [1933] IR 609 **Dictum approved** [1981] 219

Rooney v Connolly [1987] ILRM 768; [1986] IR 572 **Referred to** [1988] 39

Roscoe v Winder [1915] 1 Ch 62 **Referred to** [1990] 285

Rose v Watson (1864) 10 HL Cas 672; 11 ER 1187 **Considered** [1985] 679

Ross v Bradshaw (1761) 1 Wm Bl 312 **Dictum approved** [1990] 110

Ross v Caunters [1980] Ch 297 **Followed** [1980] 124

Ross v Helm [1913] 3 KB 42 **Referred to** [1988] 294

Ross and Boal Ltd, In re [1924] 1 IR 129 **Distinguished** [1986] 377

Ross Smith v Ross Smith [1963] AC 280; [1962] 1 All ER 344 **Considered** [1987] 606

Rossiter v Miller (1878) 3 App Cas 1124 **Referred to** [1979] 119; [1987] 345

Rowan, In re [1988] ILRM 65 **Considered** [1988] 456

Rowe v Law [1978] IR 55; 114 ILTR 86 **Referred to** [1978] 160; **Applied** [1978] 244; [1988] 80

Royal Bank of Canada v Inland Revenue Commissioners [1972] 1 Ch 665; [1972] 1 All ER 225 **Followed** [1986] 37

Royal Bank of Ireland Ltd v O'Rourke [1962] IR 159; 97 ILTR 112 **Considered** [1987] 142

Royal British Permanent Building Society v Bomash (1887) 35 Ch d 390 **Referred to** [1979] 240

Royster Guano Co v Virginia (1920) 253 US 412 **Referred to** [1983] 449; **Considered** [1986] 136

Rummens v Hare (1876) 1 Ex Div 169 **Distinguished** [1980] 131

Rushforth v Hadfield (1805) 6 East 519 **Referred to** [1988] 559

Russell, Ex parte (1882) 19 Ch D 588 **Followed** [1978] 269

Russell v Duke of Norfolk [1949] 1 All ER 109 **Dictum approved** [1981] 14

Russell v Fanning [1986] ILRM 401 **Affirmed** [1988] 333

Russell v Fanning [1988] IR 505; [1988] ILRM 333 **Referred to** [1990] 87, 648, 780; **Considered** [1989] 209; **Dictum approved** [1990] 441; **Not followed** [1990] 505

Russell v Le Bert [1896] 1 IR 334 **Dictum approved** [1986] 627

Russell v Russell (1888) 14 Ch D 471 **Considered** [1990] 159

Russell v Russell [1924] AC 687 **Disapproved** [1984] 66

Ruth (Pat) Ltd, In re [1981] ILRM 51 **Referred to** [1990] 330, 441

Rutili v Ministre de l'Interieur [1975] ECR 1219; [1976] 1 CMLR 140 **Referred to** [1987] 400

Ryan v Attorney General [1965] IR 294 **Referred to** [1980] 182; [1981] 242; [1983] 246; [1985] 542; [1990] 560; **Dictum applied** [1983] 449; [1988] 472; **Dictum approved** [1988] 300

Rylands v Fletcher (1866) LR 1 Ex 265; (1868) LR 3 HL 330 **Considered** [1988] 631

S v Eastern Health Board High Court, unreported, 28 February 1979 **Referred to** [1988] 203; **Applied** [1983] 228; **Followed** [1982] 159

S v S High Court, unreported, 10 November 1978 **Considered** [1982] 277; [1986] 75

S v S Supreme Court, unreported, 1 July 1976 **Referred to** [1985] 631, 637; **Approved** [1985] 383; dicta approved [1982] 263; [1984] 173; **Distinguished** [1986] 489 **Followed** [1986] 618

SEE Co Ltd v Public Lighting Services Ltd [1987] ILRM 255 **Referred to** [1990] 266; **Followed** [1987] 269; [1989] 461

Sachs v Standard Chartered Bank (Ireland) Ltd High Court, unreported, 30 July 1985 **Affirmed** [1987] 297

St John Shipping Corporation v Joseph Rank Ltd [1957] 1 QB 267 **Distinguished** [1983] 156

Salisbury v Nugent (1884) 9 PD 23 **Not followed** [1981] 198

Salmon v Mathews (1841) 8 M & W 827 **Followed** [1987] 26

Salomon v Salomon & Co [1895] 2 Ch 323; [1897] AC 22 **Referred to** [1984] 373; **Applied** [1981] 242; **Dictum considered** [1981] 242

Salsbury v Woodland [1970] 1 QB 324 **Considered** [1976–7] 287

San Antonio Independent School District v Rodriguez (1973) 411 US 1 **Referred to** [1983] 449

Sanderson v Mayor of Berwick Upon Tweed (1889) 13 QBD 574 **Referred to** [1978] 136

Sandwell Park Colliery Co, In re [1929] 1 Ch 277 **Referred to** [1983] 82

Sarflax Ltd, In re [1979] Ch 592 **Referred to** [1985] 75

Sass, In re; ex parte National Provincial Bank of England Ltd [1896] 2 QB 12 **Considered** [1989] 652

Savage v Director of Public Prosecutions [1982] ILRM 385 **Applied** [1987] 225; **Distinguished** [1980] 208; **Followed** [1984] 224

Savile v Roberts (1698) 1 Ld Raym 374 **Followed** [1982] 126

Sayce v Coupe [1953] 1 QB 1 **Referred to** [1980] 21

Scales v Thompson (1927) 13 TC 83 **Referred to** [1985] 210

Scanlon v Browne & Carolan Ltd High Court, unreported, 14 May 1979 **Followed** [1982] 260

Scaptrade, The [1981] 2 Lloyd's Rep 425 **Referred to** [1988] 157

Schneider v Dawson [1960] 2 QB 106 **Referred to** [1980] 21

Schofield v Hall [1975] NI 12 **Referred to** [1984] 679

School Attendance Bill 1942, In re [1943] IR 334; 77 ILTR 96 **Followed** [1989] 277

Schroeder Music Publishing Co Ltd v Macaulay [1974] 1 WLR 1308 **Referred to** [1990] 664

Schweppes Ltd v Gibbons (1905) 22 RPC 601 **Referred to** [1983] 112

Scott v Bradley [1971] Ch 850 **Referred to** [1976–7] 72; **Approved** [1978] 73

Scott v Sebright 12 PD 21 **Considered** [1982] 27; **Followed** [1986] 80

Scott Group Ltd v McFarlane [1978] 1 NZLR 553 **Referred to** [1989] 373

Scottish Co-operative Wholesale Society Ltd v Meyer [1959] AC 324 **Dictum approved** [1980] 94

Scottish Insurance Corporation Ltd v Wilson [1949] AC 462 **Referred to** [1982] 444

Seaham Harbour Dock Board v Crook (1930) 16 TC 333 **Referred to** [1985] 651

Searle v Wallbank [1947] AC 341 **Doubted** [1984] 402

Searose Ltd v Seatrain UK Ltd [1981] QB 923 **Referred to** [1983] 541

Secretan v Hart [1969] 1 WLR 1599 **Referred to** [1989] 552

Secretary of State for Education and Science v Metropolitan Borough of Tameside [1977] AC 1014 **Considered** [1982] 190

Secretary of State for Ireland v Studdert [1902] IR 240 **Considered** [1976–7] 41

Securities Trust Ltd v Hugh Moore and Alexander Ltd [1964] IR 417 **Applied** [1980] 53; **Considered** [1989] 698

Semaine's Case (1604) 5 Co Rep 196 **Referred to** [1987] 575

Senior v Holdsworth, Ex parte Independent Television News Ltd [1976] QB 23 **Dictum adopted** [1984] 683

Sepia Ltd v M & P Hanlon Ltd [1979] ILRM 11 **Referred to** [1979] 253

Serjeant v Nash, Field & Co [1903] 2 KB 304 **Referred to** [1985] 442

Sexton v Kelly (1903) 3 NIJR 60 **Referred to** [1984] 273

Shadford v Fairweather & Co Ltd (1966) 43 TC 291 **Referred to** [1982] 42

Shand v McCrabbe (1962) 96 ILTR 197 **Considered** [1986] 538

Shannon v Attorney General and Ireland [1984] IR 548; [1985] ILRM 449 **Referred to** [1990] 505; **Dictum followed** [1986] 401

Shannon v Fanning [1984] IR 569; [1985] ILRM 385 **Referred to** [1988] 75, 333; [1990] 87; **Followed** [1985] 410

Sharkey v Wernher [1956] AC 58; [1955] 3 All ER 494 **Considered** [1986] 116

Sharp v Wakefield [1891] AC 173 **Referred to** [1981] 137

Shaw v Applegate [1977] 1 WLR 970 **Distinguished** [1978] 222

Shaw v Director of Public Prosecutions [1962] AC 220; [1961] 2 All ER 446 **Referred to** [1987] 477; **Dictum approved** [1981] 91

Shaw v Director of Public Prosecutions [1982] IR 1. *See* People (Director of Public Prosecutions) v Shaw

Shaw v Groom [1970] 2 QB 504 **Referred to** [1983] 363

Shaw v Sloan [1982] NI 393 **Dictum approved** [1989] 133

Shaw v Tati Concessions Ltd [1913] 1 Ch 292 **Referred to** [1981] 242

Shaw Savill & Albion Co Ltd v Commonwealth of Australia (1940) 66 CLR 344 **Considered** [1989] 544

Sheddon v Patrick (1854) 1 Macq 396 **Applied** [1980] 257; **Considered** [1980] 257

Sheehan v Amond [1982] IR 235 **Referred to** [1985] 41

Sheikh Bros Ltd v Ochsner [1957] AC 136 **Followed** [1985] 5

Shelfer v City of London Electric Co (1875) 1 Ch 287 **Referred to** [1978] 85

Shell-Mex and BP Ltd v Manchester Garages Ltd [1971] 1 WLR 612 **Dictum approved** [1981] 66; [1983] 128

Shelton v Creane High Court, unreported, 17 December 1987 **Referred to** [1989] 400

Shepherd Homes Ltd v Sandham [1971] Ch 340; [1970] 3 All ER 402 **Applied** [1982] 519; **Considered** [1984] 45; [1988] 157

Sheppard v Hong Kong & Shanghai Banking Corp (1872) 20 WR 459 **Not followed** [1976–7] 311

Sheridan v Higgins [1971] IR 291 **Considered** [1981] 308

Sheriff v McMullen [1952] IR 236 **Referred to** [1988] 157

Sherry-Brennan, In re [1979] ILRM 114 **Referred to** [1982] 512

Shipsey v British & South American Steam Navigation Co Ltd [1936] IR 65 **Referred to** [1989] 788; **Considered** [1986] 627

Shirlaw v Southern Foundries Ltd [1939] 2 KB 206 **Applied** [1984] 471

Shrewsbury In re: McLeod v Shrewsbury [1922] P 112 **Dictum approved** [1981] 198

Siebe Gorman & Co Ltd v Barclays Bank Ltd [1979] 2 Lloyd's Rep 142 **Approved** [1985] 641 not **Followed** [1985] 254

Sifton v Sifton [1938] AC 656 **Distinguished** [1976–7] 62

Sillar, In re; Hurley v Wimbush [1956] IR 344 **Referred to** [1982] 217, 433; [1983] 359; **Applied** [1988] 67, 456; **Dictum Applied** [1987] 189; **Followed** [1987] 638

Silver v United Kingdom (1983) 5 EHRR 347 **Referred to** [1987] 52

Simmons v Pennington & Son [1955] 1 WLR 183; [1955] 1 All ER 240 **Distinguished** [1986] 189

Sinason-Teicher Inter-American Grain Corp v Oilcakes & Oilseeds Trading Co Ltd [1954] 1 WLR 935 **Considered** [1984] 471

Siney v Dublin Corporation [1980] IR 400 **Referred to** [1980] 33; **Applied** [1986] 43; **Distinguished** [1990] 658; **Followed** [1989] 400

Singer, In re (No. 2) 98 ILTR 112 **Considered** [1985] 465; **Followed** [1981] 120; [1986] 639, 653; not **Followed** [1985] 606

Singh v Ali [1960] AC 167 **Followed** [1989] 294

Singh v Singh [1971] P 226; [1971] 2 All ER 828 **Referred to** [1986] 80; **Followed** [1982] 277

Sinnott v Quinnsworth Ltd [1984] ILRM 523 **Referred to** [1985] 41; **Discussed** [1985] 582; **Followed** [1989] 735

Sisk & Sons Ltd v Lawter Products BV [1976–7] ILRM 204 **Followed** [1989] 783

Siskina, The [1979] AC 210; [1977] 3 All ER 803 **Dicta disapproved** [1986] 18 **Distinguished** [1986] 10 **Followed** [1986] 18

Sligo Corporation v Gilbride [1929] IR 351; 63 ILTR 105 **Referred to** [1987] 535; **Considered** [1990] 560

Smart v Lincolnshire Sugar Co [1937] AC 697 1 All ER 413; 20 TC 643 **Referred to** [1985] 651

Smelter Corporation v O'Driscoll [1977] IR 305 **Referred to** [1978] 73

Smith v Buller (1875) LR 19 Eq 475 **Applied** [1976–7] 50

Smith v Butler [1900] 1 QB 694 **Referred to** [1979] 11

Smith v East Elloe Rural District Council [1956] AC 736 **Considered** [1989] 565

Smith v Hughes (1871) LR 6 QB 597 **Applied** [1983] 507

Smith v Inner London Education Authority [1978] 1 All ER 411 **Referred to** [1989] 77

Smith v Morgan [1971] 1 WLR 803 **Applied** [1988] 80

Smith v Savage [1906] 1 IR 469 not **Followed** [1987] 582

Smith v Scott [1973] 1 Ch 314 **Considered** [1978] 85

Smith—Bird v Blower [1939] 2 All ER 406 **Referred to** [1990] 588

Smith Kline & French Laboratories Ltd v Sterling Winthrop Group Ltd [1975] 1 WLR 914 **Referred to** [1982] 91

Smith, Stone and Knight Ltd v Birmingham Corporation [1939] 4 All ER 116 **Not followed** [1985] 513

Smurfit Paribas Bank Ltd v AAB Export Finances Ltd [1990] ILRM 588 **Considered** [1990] 756

Smyth v Smyth [1948] NI 181 **Referred to** [1984] 66

Snook v London and West Riding Investments Ltd [1967] 2 QB 786 **Considered** [1984] 613

Society for the Protection of Unborn Children (Ireland) Ltd v Coogan [1989] ILRM 526 **Reversed** [1990] 70

Society for the Protection of Unborn Children (Ireland) Ltd v Coogan [1990] ILRM 70 **Applied** [1990] 350

Solicitors Act 1954, In re [1960] IR 239 **Followed** [1983] 67

Solle v Butcher [1950] 1 KB 671 **Referred to** [1985] 5

Solomons v Gertzerstein Ltd [1952] 2 QB 243 **Dictum Applied** [1978] 1

Solosky v The Queen [1980] 1 SCR 821; 105 DLR (3rd) 745 **Considered** [1987] 52

Somers v Weir [1979] IR 94 **Referred to** [1982] 290; [1983] 513; **Applied** [1979] 105; **Explained** [1982] 335; [1983] 343

Somjee v Minister for Justice [1981] ILRM 324 **Considered** [1984] 643

Somma v Hazlehurst [1978] 2 All ER 1011 **Referred to** [1981] 66

Sorrell v Finch [1977] AC 728; [1976} 2 All ER 371 **Distinguished** [1986] 547

Sorrell v Smith [1925] AC 700 **Referred to** [1988] 157

South East Asia Fire Bricks Sdn Bnd v Non-Metallic Mineral Products Manufacturing Employees' Union [1981] AC 363 **Followed** [1982] 590

South Staffordshire Water Co v Sharman [1896] 2 QB 44 **Followed** [1988] 565

Southend-on-Sea Corporation v Hodgson Ltd [1962] 1 QB 416 **Considered** [1978] 208

Southerden, In re [1925] P 177 **Followed** [1980] 24

Southerland Publishing Co Ltd v Caxton Publishing Ltd [1938] Ch 174 **Referred to** [1985] 109

Southern v Aldwych Property Trust Ltd [1940] 2 KB 266 **Considered** [1984] 231

Southern v Borax Consolidated Ltd [1941] 1 KB 111 **Referred to** [1984] 610

Spa Estates Ltd v O hArgain High Court, unreported, 20 June 1975 **Referred to** [1982] 421

Spackman, ex parte (1849) 1 Mac and G 170 **Referred to** [1979] 141

Spanish Prospecting Co Ltd, In re [1911] 1 Ch 92 **Considered** [1982] 44

State (Boyd) v An Bord Pleanála High Court, unreported, 18 February 1983 **Referred to** [1989] 98

State (Boylan) v Governor of St Patrick's Institution High Court, unreported, 13 December 1982 **Approved** [1984] 555

State (Brennan) v Conlon High Court, unreported, 17 June 1986 **Referred to** [1990] 62

State (Brennan) v Governor of Mountjoy Prison High Court, unreported 7 May 1975 **Referred to** [1983] 17; **Followed** [1981] 169

State (Brennan) v Mahon High Court, unreported, 13 February 1978 **Referred to** [1981] 25; [1983] 17

State (Browne) v Feran [1967] IR 147 **Referred to** [1983] 52; [1984] 657; [1986] 250; [1987] 535; [1990] 749; **Considered** [1983] 549; [1987] 278; **Followed** [1981] 333

State (Burke) v Garvey [1979] ILRM 232 **Distinguished** [1988] 173

State (Burke) v Lennon [1940] IR 136; 74 ILTR 36, 131 **Referred to** [1983] 52, 449; **Considered** [1982] 190; [1983] 549; **Considered and explained** [1983] 89

State (C) v Frawley [1976] IR 365 **Considered** [1980] 82

State (C) v Minister for Justice [1967] IR 106; 102 ILTR 177 **Referred to** [1984] 413; **Applied** [1985] 11; **Considered** [1983] 489; **Dictum applied** [1990] 200; **Followed** [1985] 196

State (Cahill) v President of Circuit Court [1954] IR 128 **Referred to** [1988] 318

State (Cannon) v Kavanagh [1978] IR 131 **Referred to** [1980] 82

State (Clancy) v Wine [1980] IR 228 **Referred to** [1981] 17; [1983] 241; **Considered** [1989] 881

State (Clarke) v Roche [1986] ILRM 565 **Affirmed** [1987] 309

State (Clarke) v Roche [1986] IR 619; [1987] ILRM 309 **Referred to** [1987] 316; [1988] 456; [1989] 821; **Considered** [1989] 93, 110, 491; **Followed** [1988] 623; [1989] 65

State (Clune) v Clifford [1981] ILRM 17. *See* Clune v Director of Public Prosecutions

State (Collins) v Kelleher [1983] ILRM 388 **Referred to** [1987] 129

State (Collins) v Ruane [1984] IR 105; [1985] ILRM 349 **Referred to** [1987] 225

State (Commins) v McRann [1977] IR 78 **Referred to** [1981] 416

State (Conlon Construction Ltd) v Cork Co Council High Court, unreported, 31 July 1975 **Referred to** [1979] 249

State (Córas Iompair Éireann) v An Bord Pleanála, Supreme Court, unreported, 12 December 1984 **Followed** [1988] 545

State (Creedon) v Criminal Injuries Compensation Tribunal [1988] IR 51 **Applied** [1990] 36

State (Cronin) v Circuit Court Judge of the Western Circuit [1937] IR 34; 70 ILTR 145 **Referred to** [1980] 167; [1985] 349; **Dictum approved** [1984] 443

State (Crowley) v Irish Land Commission [1951] IR 250; 85 ILTR 26 **Referred to** [1986] 499

State (Cussen) v Brennan [1981] IR 181 **Referred to** [1985] 141; **Considered** [1982] 475; **Distinguished** [1988] 89; **Followed** [1989] 113

State (D) v G [1990] ILRM 10 dicta emphasised [1990] 767 **Referred to** [1990] 243

State (Dillon) v Kelly [1970] 174 **Followed** [1981] 333

State (Director of Public Prosecutions) v Esmonde, High Court, unreported, 30 July 1984 **Referred to** [1988] 720

State (Director of Public Prosecutions) v Walsh and Conneely [1981] IR 412 **Referred to** [1983] 549; **Considered** [1983] 355; [1984] 424

State (Divito) v Arklow UDC High Court, unreported, 1983 **Affirmed** [1986] 123

State (Donnelly) v Minister for Defence High Court, unreported, 8 October 1979 **Referred to** [1987] 107

State (Dowling) v Kingston (No 2) [1937] 699 **Considered** [1981] 120

State (Doyle) v Carr [1970] IR 87 **Referred to** [1982] 590; **Applied** [1981] 242

State (Duffy) v Minister for Defence [1979] ILRM 65 **Referred to** [1983] 67; [1987] 107;

Considered [1982] 475; **Distinguished** [1985] 141; [1988] 89; **Followed** [1983] 413

State (Elm Developments Ltd) v An Bord Pleanála High Court, unreported, 14 July 1980 **Affirmed** [1981] 108

State (Elm Developments Ltd) v An Bord Pleanála [1981] ILRM 108 **Referred to** [1988] 483; **Applied** [1983] 112

State (Ennis) v Farrell [1966] IR 107 **Applied** [1985] 349; **Considered** [1990] 70

State (Fagan) v Governor of Mountjoy Prison High Court, unreported, 6 March 1978 **Referred to** [1981] 86

State (Finglas Industrial Estates Ltd) v Dublin County Council, Supreme Court, unreported, 17 February 1983, **Considered** [1988] 47

State (Fitzsimons) v Kearney [1981] IR 406 **Referred to** [1989] 159; **Considered** [1986] 218; **Distinguished** [1983] 125

State (Freeman) v Connellan [1986] IR 433; [1987] ILRM 470 **Considered** [1989] 367

State (Furey) v Minister for Defence [1988] ILRM 89 **Distinguished** [1989] 491

State (Furlong) v Kelly [1971] IR 132 **Referred to** [1990] 87; **Considered** [1982] 69; [1985] 465; **Distinguished** [1986] 381

State (Gallagher Shatter & Co) v de Valera High Court, unreported, 9 December 1983 **Reversed** [1986] 3

State (Gallagher Shatter & Co) v De Valera [1986] ILRM 3 **Considered** [1989] 865

State (Gallagher Shatter & Co) v de Valera [1987] IR 55; [1987] ILRM 555 **Referred to** [1990] 617

State (Genport Ltd) v An Bord Pleanála [1983] ILRM 12 **Referred to** [1989] 98

State (Gettins) v Fawsitt [1945] IR 183 **Referred to** [1982] 249

State (Gilliland) v Governor of Mountjoy Prison [1987] IR 201; [1987] ILRM 278 **Referred to** [1987] 400; [1989] 209

State (Gilsenan) v McMorrow [1978] IR 360 **Referred to** [1989] 209

State (Gleeson) v Minister for Defence [1976] IR 280 **Referred to** [1980] 46; [1981] 113; [1987] 107, 290; **Considered** [1978] 25, 167; **Dictum applied** [1976–7] 184; **Distinguished** [1979] 65; **Followed** [1988] 89

State (Gleeson) v Minister for Defence High Court, unreported, 23 June 1980 **Referred to** [1984] 555; [1990] 617

State (Harkin) v O'Malley [1978] IR 269 **Referred to** [1988] 318

State (Harrington) v Commissioner of an Garda Siochána High Court, unreported, 14 December 1976 **Followed** [1990] 313

State (Hartley) v Governor of Mountjoy Prison Supreme Court, unreported, 21 December 1967 **Referred to** [1985] 86; **Followed** [1983] 449

State (Hayes) v Criminal Injuries Compensation Tribunal [1982] ILRM 210 **Referred to** [1988] 693; **Followed** [1987] 202

State (Healy) v Ballagh, High Court, unreported, 22 April 1983 **Considered** [1988] 117

State (Healy) v Donoghue [1976] IR 325; 110 ILTR 9; 112 ILTR 37 **Referred to** [1979] 243; [1983] 489; [1984] 249, 333, 461; [1987] 555, 723; [1988] 4; **Applied** [1981] 17; [1986] 639; [1989] 690; [1990] 257; **Approved** [1985] 349; **Considered** [1981] 47; [1985] 196; [1989] 93; **Dictum considered** [1981] 113; **Distinguished** [1982] 568; [1986] 343; [1987] 202; **Followed** [1987] 470; [1988] 448; [1989] 71

State (Hennessy) v Commons [1976] IR 238 **Dictum Referred to** [1982] 342; **Followed** [1984] 134

State (Hogan) v Carroll High Court, unreported, 4 April 1979 **Affirmed** [1981] 25

State (Hogan) v Carroll [1981] ILRM 25 **Referred to** [1983] 285

State (Holland) v Kennedy [1977] IR 193 **Distinguished** [1989] 303; **Followed** [1986] 31

State (Holmes) v Furlong [1967] IR 210 **Approved** [1981] 113, 120

State (Modern Homes Ltd) v Dublin Corporation [1953] IR 202; 88 ILTR 79 **Considered** [1988] 437

State (Murphy) v Dublin County Council [1970] IR 253 **Referred to** [1990] 633; **Followed** [1985] 593; not **Followed** [1982] 29

State (Murphy) v Johnson [1983] IR 235 **Referred to** [1988] 483; **Followed** [1984] 625

State (Murphy) v Kielt [1984] IR 458; [1985] ILRM 141 **Applied** [1987] 33

State (Murray) v McRann [1979] IR 133; 112 ILTR 33 **Referred to** [1990] 5

State (Nevin) v Tormey [1976] IR 1 **Referred to** [1981] 17; [1983] 241

State (Nicolaou) v An Bord Uchtála [1966] IR 567; 102 ILTR 1 **Referred to** [1982] 164; [1983] 89; [1986] 136; [1987] 290; [1990] 121, 441; **Considered** [1982] 327; [1985] 86; **Dictum referred to** [1981] 324; **Followed** [1982] 568; [1983] 449

State (O) v Daly [1977] IR 312 **Referred to** [1981] 113

State (O'Callaghan) v O hUadhaigh [1977] IR 42 **Referred to** [1981] 113; [1987] 723; **Applied** [1986] 290; **Considered** [1983] 489; [1986] 639; **Distinguished** [1982] 284; [1989] 245, 466; **Followed** [1982] 568; [1988] 744; [1989] 71

State (O'Connell) v Fawsitt [1986] IR 364; [1986] ILRM 639 **Considered** [1990] 62; **Followed** [1986] 653; [1988] 166

State (O'Flaherty) v O Floinn [1954] IR 295; 90 ILTR 179 **Referred to** [1989] 159, 245; **Dictum applied** [1988] 623, 689; [1990] 767; **Followed** [1987] 65

State (O'Leary) v Neilan [1984] ILRM 35 **Followed** [1986] 565; [1987] 309

State (O'Regan) v Plunkett [1984] ILRM 347 **Referred to** [1985] 243

State (O'Rourke) v Kelly [1983] IR 58 **Dictum Applied** [1982] 568; **Distinguished** [1985] 11

State (O'Sullivan) v Buckley 101 ILTR 152 **Considered** [1986] 218

State (Pheasantry Ltd) v Donnelly [1982] ILRM 512 **Referred to** [1988] 430

State (Pine Valley Developments Ltd) v Dublin County Council High Court, unreported, 27 may 1981 appeal allowed [1982] 169; **Dictum approved** [1982] 29

State (Pine Valley Developments Ltd) v Dublin County Council [1984] IR 407; [1982] ILRM 169 **Referred to** [1987] 747; **Followed** [1985] 494

State (Prendergast) v Rochford Supreme Court, unreported, 1 July 1952 **Followed** [1990] 1

State (Quinn) v Mangan [1945] IR 532 **Referred to** [1976–7] 305

State (Quinn) v Ryan [1965] IR 70; 100 ILTR 105 **Referred to** [1981] 113; [1983] 391, 449; [1984] 595; [1985] 385, 465; [1988] 333; [1990] 767; **Considered** [1988] 318; [1990] 505; **Dictum approved** [1989] 19

State (Reddy) v Johnson High Court, unreported, 31 July 1980 **Followed** [1981] 2

State (Redmond) v Wexford Corporation [1946] IR 409 **Referred to** [1976–7] 305

State (Richardson) v Governor of Mountjoy Prison [1980] ILRM 82 **Referred to** [1980] 191, 242; **Considered** [1980] 208; **Explained** [1981] 86

State (Roche) v Delap [1980] IR 170 **Referred to** [1987] 118; [1988] 448; [1989] 65; **Considered** [1981] 47; **Distinguished** [1982] 512

State (Rogers) v Galvin High Court, unreported, 18 October 1980 **Reversed** [1983] 149

State (Rollinson) v Kelly [1982] ILRM 249 affirmed [1984] 625; **Dictum approved** [1984] 39

State (Rollinson) v Kelly [1984] IR 248; [1984] ILRM 625 **Referred to** [1987] 4, 118; **Considered** [1988] 430

State (Royle) v Kelly [1974] IR 259 **Dictum approved** [1983] 17; **Discussed** [1986] 95; **Followed** [1987] 470

State (Shanahan) v Attorney General [1964] IR 239 **Referred to** [1985] 196; **Considered** [1983] 489; [1989] 309; **Dictum applied** [1984] 224; **Followed** [1983] 489; **Not followed** [1984] 413

State (Shannon) v O hUadhaigh [1975] IR 98 **Followed** [1981] 25

State (Sharkey) v McArdle Supreme Court, unreported, 4 June 1981 **Dictum approved** [1987] 470

State (Sheehan) v Government of Ireland [1987] IR 550; [1988] ILRM 437 **Dictum applied** [1989] 639

State (Sheerin) v Kennedy [1966] IR 379 **Referred to** [1980] 242; [1982] 249; [1983] 449; [1986] 381, 455; [1989] 485; [1990] 767; **Applied** [1981] 469; **Considered** [1984] 625; **Distinguished** [1987] 278

State (Smullen) v Duffy [1980] ILRM 46 **Referred to** [1989] 469

State (Stanford) v Dun Laoghaire Corporation Supreme Court, unreported, 20 February 1981 **Referred to** [1988] 545; **Applied** [1987] 245

State (Taylor) v Circuit Court Judge for County Wicklow [1951] IR 311; 87 ILTR 105 approved [1981] 447

State (Tern Houses (Brennanstown) Ltd) v An Bord Pleanála [1985] IR 725 **Referred to** [1989] 98

State (Toft) v Galway Corporation High Court, unreported, 28 April 1980 **Affirmed** [1981] 439

State (Toft) v Galway Corporation [1981] ILRM 439 **Referred to** [1982] 590; **Considered** [1988] 47

State (Trimbole) v Governor of Mountjoy Prison [1985] IR 550; [1985] ILRM 465 **Referred to** [1987] 606; [1989] 821; **Approved** [1989] 629; **Considered** [1990] 850; **Distinguished** [1988] 724; **Followed** [1986] 381

State (Tynan) v Keane [1968] IR 348 **Considered** [1990] 62

State (Vozza) v O Floinn [1957] IR 227 **Referred to** [1981] 54; **Distinguished** [1982] 590

State (Walsh) v An Bord Pleanála, High Court, unreported, 19 November 1980 **Approved** [1981] 108

State (Walsh) v Lennon [1942] IR 112; 76 ILTR 207 **Dictum approved** [1982] 284

State (Walsh) v Maguire [1979] IR 372 **Referred to** [1981] 2, 25; [1983] 52; **Applied** [1985] 577; **Dictum disapproved** [1986] 690

State (Walshe) v Murphy [1981] IR 275 **Considered** [1989] 71; **Dictum approved** [1984] 347; **Distinguished** [1985] 243

State (White) v Martin 111 ILTR 21 **Applied** [1986] 455; **Dicta not followed** [1985] 66; **Distinguished** [1988] 243

State (Williams) v Army Pensions Board [1981] ILRM 379 **Reversed** [1983] 331

State (Williams) v Director of Public Prosecutions and Kelleher [1983] ILRM 285 **Reversed** [1983] 537

State (Williams) v Director of Public Prosecutions and Kelleher [1983] IR 112; [1983] ILRM 537 **Referred to** [1988] 117

State (Williams) v Kelly (No 2) [1970] IR 271 **Applied** [1985] 602

State (Williams) v Markey [1940] IR 421; 74 ILTR 237 **Referred to** [1985] 302

State (Wilson) v Governor of Portlaoise Prison Supreme Court, unreported, 11 July 1968 **Referred to** [1983] 17

State (Wilson) v Governor of Portlaoise Prison Supreme Court, unreported, 29 July 1969 **Referred to** [1983] 17

State (Woods) v Kelly [1969] IR 269 **Referred to** [1983] 149

State Board of Tax Commissioners of the State of Indiana v Jackson (1931) 283 US 527 **Referred to** [1983] 449; **Dictum applied** [1980] 136

Staunton v Counihan 92 ILTR 32 **Distinguished** [1983] 350

Stave Falls Lumber Co Ltd v Westminster Trust Co Ltd [1940] 4 WWR 382 **Considered** [1985] 254 **Referred to** [1985] 641

Stenhouse Australia Ltd v Phillips [1974] AC 391 **Referred to** [1990] 664

Stevenson, In re [1902] 1 IR 23; [1903] 1 IR 403 **Referred to** [1976–7] 222

Stevenson (Hugh) & Sons Ltd v AG fur Carton-Hagen-Industrie [1918] AC 239 **Considered** [1980] 237

Stevenson Jordan and Harrison Ltd v McDonald and Evan [1952] 1 TLR 101 **Dictum approved** [1982] 260

Stewart v Garnett (1830) 3 Sim 358 **Referred to** [1983] 359

Stickney v Keeble [1915] AC 386 **Referred to** [1979] 11

Stillorgan Orchard Ltd v McLoughlin & Harvey Ltd [1978] IRM 128 **Applied** [1987] 47

Stokes and McKiernan Ltd, In re [1978] ILRM 240 **Referred to** [1982] 396; **Followed** [1982] 399

Stokiewicz and Filas, Re (1979) 92 DLR (3d) 129 **Considered** [1989] 169

Stonegate Securities Ltd v Gregory [1980] 3 WLR 168 **Approved** [1983] 510

Stoner v California (1964) 376 US 483 **Referred to** [1985] 465

Strunk v United States (1973) 412 US 434 **Considered** [1986] 639

Stubart Investment Ltd v The Queen (1984) 10 DLR (4th) 1 **Dictum approved** [1988] 181

Sudeley (Lord) v Attorney General [1897] AC 11 **Referred to** [1987] 582

Suisse Atlantique Societe d'Armement Maritime SA v NV Rotterdemsche Kolen Centrale [1967] 1 AC 361 **Referred to** [1982] 359

Sun Life Assurance Society v Davidson [1956] Ch 524 **Considered** [1984] 231

Sutherland Publishing Co Ltd v Caxton Publishing Co Ltd [1936] 1 Ch 323 **Applied** [1982] 40

Sutherland Shire Council v Heyman (1985) 157 CLR 424 **Considered** [1989] 400

Swaine v C [1964] IR 423; 100 ILTR 21 **Referred to** [1982] 421

Swallow Raincoats Ltd, In re application of (1947) 64 RPC 92 **Considered** [1978] 172

Swanley Coal Co v Denton [1906] 2 KB 673 **Referred to** [1980] 131

Sweet v Parsley [1970] AC 132 **Referred to** [1984] 329

Swiss Bank Corporation v Lloyds Bank Ltd [1979] Ch 548 **Referred to** [1985] 221

Switzer & Co v Commissioner of Valuation [1902] 2 IR 275 **Followed** [1990] 172

Swords v Attorney General High Court, unreported, 22 December 1977 **Referred to** [1990] 505

Swords v St Patrick's Copper Mines [1965] Ir Jur Rep 63 **Referred to** [1983] 429

Symington v Symington's Quarries Ltd (1905) 8 F 121 **Referred to** [1979] 141

Syred v Carruthers (1858) El, Bl & El 469 **Followed** [1990] 220

Szechter v Szechter [1971] P 286; [1970] 3 All ER 905 **Referred to** [1986] 80; **Considered** [1982] 277

T v T [1983] IR 29; [1982] ILRM 217 **Dictum Applied** [1987] 189 **Followed** [1987] 638; [1988] 456

TMG Group Ltd v Al Babtain [1982] ILRM 349 **Referred to** [1984] 595

Tailby v Official Receiver (1888) 12 App Cas 523 **Referred to** [1985] 641

Taisce, An, v Dublin Corporation High Court, unreported, 31 January 1973 **Considered** [1989] 768

Taverner Rutledge v Specters Ltd (1959) RPC 355 **Considered** [1976–7] 144

Taylor v Ryan High Court, unreported, 10 March 1983 **Approved** [1986] 189

Taylor (CR) (Wholesale) Ltd v Hepworths Ltd [1977] 1 WLR 659 **Referred to** [1980] 38

Teddington UDC v Vile (1906) 70 JP 381 **Considered** [1990] 220

Tehidy Minerals Ltd v Norman [1971] 2 QB 528 **Principles applied** [1984] 451

Tempany v Hynes [1976] IR 101 **Applied** [1985] 679; [1987] 733; **Distinguished** [1982] 290

Tempany v Royal Liver Trustees Ltd [1984] ILRM 273 **Followed** [1988] 751

Tempest v Snowden [1952] 1 KB 130 **Followed** [1982] 126

Templeton v Tyree (1872) LR 2 P&D 420 **Considered** [1985] 691

Teofani & Co's Trade Mark, In re [1913] 2 Ch 545 **Dictum approved** [1978] 172

Terry v Ohio (1968) 392 US 1 **Referred to** [1981] 389; [1985] 255; **Principles adopted** [1985] 465

Trimbole v Governor of Mountjoy Prison. *See* State (Trimbole) v Governor of Mountjoy Prison

Trinidad Petroleum Development Co Ltd v Inland Revenue Commissioners [1937] 1 KB 408; [1936] 3 All ER 801 **Referred to** [1985] 666

Trustee Savings Bank v Incorporated Law Society of Ireland [1987] IR 430; [1988] ILRM 541 **Affirmed** [1989] 665

Trustees of Magee College v Commissioner of Valuation (1870) IR 4 CL 438 **Considered** [1984] 717

Tryka Ltd v Newell (1963) 41 TC 146 **Distinguished** [1986] 415

Tuck and Sons v Priester (1887) 19 QBD 629 **Dictum approved** [1982] 13

Tulsk Co-operative Livestock Mart Ltd v Ulster Bank Ltd High Court, unreported, 13 May 1983 **Considered** [1987] 142

Turner v Last (1965) 42 TC 517 **Referred to** [1982] 421

Turner v Metro-Goldwyn-Mayer Pictures Ltd [1950] 1 All ER 449 **Dictum Applied** [1989] 349

Turner v Ringwood Highway Board (1870) LR 9 Eq 418 **Principles applied** [1984] 451

Tweddel v Henderson [1975] 1 WLR 1496 **Referred to** [1976–7] 72

Tynan, In re; Attorney General v Tynan [1964] Ir Jur Rep 28 **Referred to** [1983] 549

Tynan, In re [1969] IR 1 **Referred to** [1987] 65; **Followed** [1987] 316

Tzortzis v Monark Line [1968] 1 WLR 406 **Considered** [1988] 1

Union Bank of Australia Ltd v Murray-Aynsley [1898] AC 693 **Considered** [1986] 518

Unione Sterainerie Lanza v Wieney [1917] 2 KB 558 **Referred to** [1990] 277

United Molasses Co Ltd v Commissioner for Valuation [1972] RA 242 **Dictum referred to** [1980] 149

United Railways of Havana and Regla Warehouses Ltd, In re [1961] AC 1007 **Not followed** [1976–7] 275

United States v Kubrick (1979) 444 US 111 **Referred to** [1990] 403

United States v Leon (1983) 468 US 897 **Considered** [1990] 569

United States v Salerno (1987) 107 S Ct 2095 **Considered** [1989] 333

University College Cork v Commissioner of Valuation [1911] 2 IR 593 **Distinguished** [1984] 117

Unwin v Hanson [1891] 2 QB 115 **Referred to** [1979] 269; **Dictum applied** 1982 13

Urie v Thompson (1949) 337 US 163 **Referred to** [1990] 403

Urquhart, In re [1974] IR 201 principle **Applied** [1984] 572

Usher v Barlow [1952] Ch 255 **Referred to** [1980] 75

Ussher v Ussher [1912] 2 IR 445; 46 ILTR 109 **Referred to** [1976–7] 156; [1986] 80; **Considered** [1987] 172

V (D) v C (A) [1981] ILRM 357 **Referred to** [1982] 502

Van Gend en Loos NV v Nederlandes Belastingadministratie [1963] ECr 12; [1963] CMLR 105 **Referred to** [1987] 400

Van Hool McArdle Ltd, In re [1982] ILRM 340 **Affirmed** [1983] 329

Van Hool McArdle Ltd, In re: Revenue Commissioners v Donnelly [1983] ILRM 329 **Distinguished** [1987] 508; [1989] 155

Vance v Foster (1841) IR Cir Rep 47 **Dictum approved** [1984] 501

Vanneck v Benham [1917] 1 Ch 60 **Applied** [1983] 519

Vella v Morelli, In bonis Morelli [1968] IR 11 **Referred to** [1983] 549; [1986] 250; [1990] 749; **Applied** [1987] 269

Vera Cruz, The (1884) 10 App Cas 59 **Dictum approved** [1987] 4

Vernon v Madden [1973] 1 WLR 663 **Considered** [1976–7] 305

Vervaeke v Smith [1983] 1 AC 145 **Distinguished** [1984] 173

Vesey v Elwood (1843) 3 Dr and War 74 **Dictum approved** [1987] 733

Vestey's (Lord) Executors v Commissioners of Inland Revenue [1949] 1 All ER 1108 **Referred to** [1988] 181

Victoria Laundry (Windsor) Ltd v Newman Industries Ltd [1949] 2 KB 528 **Referred to** [1979] 296; **Applied** [1980] 107

Vidal's Patent [1981] FSR 493 **Referred to** [1984] 393

Villiers v Holmes [1917] 1 IR 165 **Applied** [1983] 519

Viscount Securities Ltd, In re 112 ILTR 17 **Considered** [1978] 197

Viscount Securities Ltd v Kennedy Supreme Court, unreported, 6 May 1986 **Considered** [1989] 29

Vita Food Products Inc v Unus Shipping Co Ltd [1939] AC 277 **Considered** [1988] 1

Von Hatzfeldt-Wildenburg v Alexander [1912] 1 Ch 284 **Referred to** [1987] 345

Vone Securities Ltd v Cooke [1979] IR 59 **Referred to** [1981] 191

Vyse v Foster (1874) LR 7 HL 318 **Referred to** [1980] 237

W v Inspector of Taxes High Court, unreported, 22 October 1974 **Followed** [1990] 249

W v P High Court, unreported, 7 June 1984 **Referred to** [1987] 58

W v Somers [1983] IR 122 **Considered** [1989] 528

W v W [1952] P 152; [1952] 1 All ER 858 **Applied** [1982] 545

W v W [1967] 1 WLR 1554; [1967] 3 All ER 178 **Referred to** [1986] 515

W v W [1981] ILRM 202 **Referred to** [1989] 528; **Applied** [1985] 153; **Followed** [1985] 302

Wachauf v Bundesamt fur Ernahrung und Forstwirkshaft (Case 5/88) 13 July 1989 not yet reported, **Followed** [1990] 466

Wagon Mound (No. 1) The [1961] AC 388; [1961] 2 WLR 126 *See* Overseas Tankship (UK) Ltd v Morts Dock & Engineering Co

Waldy v Gray (1875) 20 LR Eq 238 **Considered** [1978] 151

Walker, In re; Walker v Lutyens (1887) 2 Ch 238 approved [1982] 327

Walker, In re; O'Brien v M S and the Attorney General [1984] IR 316; [1985] ILRM 86 **Followed** [1985] 61

Walker D Wallet, The [1893] P 202 **Approved** [1982] 125

Wallace v McDowell [1920] 2 IR 194 **Not followed** [1981] 198

Wallers v Woodbridge (1878) 7 Ch D 504 **Referred to** [1989] 625

Wallersteiner v Moir (No 2) [1975] QB 373 **Dicta approved** [1980] 237

Wallis v Hirsch (1856) 1 CB (ns) 316 **Considered** [1990] 159

Walsh, In re 96 ILTR 173 **Applied** [1986] 555

Walsh v Allied Irish Banks Ltd, High Court, unreported, 2 March 1977 **Referred to** [1978] 203

Walton, Ex parte; In re Levy (1881) 17 Ch D 746 **Referred to** [1984] 273

Ward v Kenehan Electrical Ltd High Court, unreported, 21 December 1979 **Followed** [1984] 657

Ward v Kirkland [1967] Ch 194 **Referred to** [1981] 419

Ward v McMaster [1986] ILRM 43; [1985] IR 29 **Appeal dismissed** [1989] 400

Ward v McMaster [1988] IR 337; [1989] ILRM 400 **Distinguished** [1990] 658

Ward v National Bank of New Zealand Ltd (1883) 8 App Cas 755 **Principles applied** [1980] 171

Ward v Spivack Ltd [1957] IR 40 **Referred to** [1984] 471

Ward v Ward (1852) 7 Ex 838 **Principles applied** [1984] 451

Waring v McCaldin (1873) IR 7 CL 282 **Dictum doubted** [1989] 349

Warner v Minister for Industry and Commerce [1929] IR 582 **Considered** [1983] 549

Warnford Investments Ltd v Duckworth [1979] Ch 127 **Dictum approved** [1984] 273

Warnink (Erven) BV v Townend Sons (Hull) Ltd (No 2) [1982] 3 All ER 312 **Considered** [1987] 390; [1989] 322

Warren, In re [1938] 1 Ch 725 **Considered** [1989] 777

Waterford and Limerick Railway Co v Kearney (1860) 12 ICLR 224 **Considered** [1983] 173

Waterford Glass Ltd v Controller of Patents [1984] ILRM 565 **Referred to** [1990] 204

Waterford Glass Ltd v Registrar of Trade Marks (1972) 89 RPC 149 **Not followed** [1982] 91

Watling (NC) & Co Ltd v Richardson [1978] ICR 1049 **Dictum approved** [1982] 404

Watson v Cammell Laird & Co Ltd [1959] 1 WLR 702 **Referred to** [1989] 257

Watson v Duff, Morgan and Vermont Holdings Ltd [1974] 1 WLR 450 **Applied** [1978] 215

Watson and Belmann [1976] ECR 1185 **Referred to** [1988] 400

Waugh v British Railways Board [1980] AC 521; [1979] 2 All ER 1169 **Considered** [1989] 257l; **Dictum adoped** [1987] 516

Webb v Ireland [1988] IR 353; [1988] ILRM 565 **Considered** [1989] 710; **Distinguished** [1989] 639; **Followed** [1989] 1

Webb v Minister of Housing and Local Government [1965] 1 WLR 755 **Distinguished** [1989] 629

Weber v Aetna Casualty and Surety Co (1972) 406 U S 164 **Referred to** [1985] 86

Wedick v Osmond & Son [1935] IR 820; 71 ILTR 9 **Referred to** [1980] 167; [1985] 349; **Considered** [1984] 443

Weeks v Hackett (1908) 71 Atl Rep 858 **Referred to** [1988] 565

Weeks v United States (1913) 232 US 383 **Referred to** [1981] 389

Weir v Dun Laoghaire Corporation High Court, unreported, **Affirmed** [1984] 113

Weir v Fermanagh County Council [1913] 1 IR 193 **Referred to** [1981] 287

Welby v Parker [1916] 2 Ch 1 **Referred to** [1982] 290

Welch v Bowmaker (Ireland) Ltd [1980] IR 251 **Discussed** [1985] 254

Weldmesh Trade Mark (1965) 82 RPC 920 **Dictum considered** [1982] 91

Wells v Minister for Housing and Local Government [1967] 1 WLR 1000 **Considered** [1978] 208

Wells v Secretary of State for Northern Ireland [1981] NIJB 3 **Discussed** [1986] 627

Wendelboe v LJ Music Ap S (Case 19/83) [1985] ECR 457 **Considered** [1989] 844

West (Richard) and Partners (Inverness) Ltd v Dick [1969] 2 Ch 424 **Referred to** [1981] 219

West Ham Churchwardens v Fourth City Mutual Building Society [1892] 1 QB 654 **Dictum approved** [1987] 4

West Mercia Safetyware Ltd v Dodd [1988] BCLC 250 **Distinguished** [1990] 341

West Midland Baptist (Trust) Association Inc v Birmingham Corporation [1970] AC 874 **Referred to** [1980] 38, 78; **Applied** [1983] 56

West v Phillips (1959) 38 TC 203 **Referred to** [1982] 421

West Wake Price & Co v Ching [1957] 1 WLR 45 **Distinguished** [1988] 373

Westbourne Galleries Ltd, In re [1970] 1 WLR 1378 **Referred to** [1980] 94

Westcombe v Hadnock Quarries Ltd (1931) 16 TC 137 **Referred to** [1985] 651

Western Meats Ltd v National Ice and Cold Storage Ltd [1982] ILRM 99 **Distinguished** [1982] 399

Wexford Timber Co Ltd v Wexford Corporation 88 ILTR 137 **Considered** [1985] 269; [1988] 318; **Followed** [1985] 249; [1989] 46

Wheatley v Silkstone & Haigh Moor Coal Co (1885) 29 Ch D 715 **Referred to** [1985] 641

Whelan v Madigan [1978] ILRM 136 **Dictum approved** [1986] 377

Wormald v Cole [1955] 1 QB 614 **Dictum approved** [1987] 306

Wright v Atkyns (1823) T & R 143 **Applied** [1976–7] 88

Wroth v Tyler [1974] Ch 30; [1973] 1 All ER 897 **Referred to** [1979] 71; [1982] 201

Wyatt v McLoughlin [1974] IR 378 **Referred to** [1990] 87; **Considered** [1982] 69; [1985] 449, 465; **Distinguished** [1986] 381

Wykes, In re [1961] Ch 229 **Referred to** [1987] 229; **Dictum Applied** [1987] 373

Wythes v Lee (1855) 3 Drew 396; 61 ER 954 **Referred to** [1985] 679

Yagar v Musa [1961] 2 QB 214 **Considered** [1981] 416

Yarmouth v France (1887) 19 QBD 647 **Considered** [1984] 679

Yeates v Minister for Posts and Telegraphs [1978] ILRM 22 **Considered** [1990] 560

Yenidje Tobacco Co Ltd, In re [1916] 2 Ch 426 **Referred to** [1979] 141; **Followed** [1986] 239

Yianni v Edwin Evans & Sons [1982] QB 438; [1981] 3 All ER 529 **Referred to** [1986] 43

Yolland Husson & Birkett Ltd, In re [1908] 1 Ch 152 **Referred to** [1976–7] 222

York Trade Mark, In re (1981) 7 FSR 33 **Considered** [1982] 91

York Trailer Holdings Ltd, In re [1982] 1 WLR 195 **Not followed** [1984] 565

Yorkshire Copper Works Ltd v Registrar of Trade Marks [1954] 1 WLR 554 **Considered** [1982] 91

Yorkshire Woolcombers Assocation Ltd, In re [1903] 2 Ch 284; *sub nom* Illingsworth v Houldsworth [1904] AC 355 **Applied** [1985] 641 **Dicta applied** [1985] 254

Young and Harston's Contract In re (1885) 31 Ch D 168 **Dictum approved** [1981] 308

Yuen Kun-Yeu v Attorney General of Hong Kong [1988] AC 175; [1987] 3 WLR 776 **Referred to** [1989] 400; **Followed** [1988] 610

Z Ltd v A-Z and AA-LL [1982] QB 558 **Referred to** [1983] 541

Zamil bin Hashim v Government of Malaysia [1980] AC 734 **Referred to** [1982] 290

Zurich General Accident and Liability Insurance Co Ltd v Morrison [1942] 2 KB 53; [1942] 1 All ER 529 **Referred to** [1990] 110; **Dictum approved** [1981] 173

Zwann, In re, High Court, unreported, 9 December 1980 **Reversed** [1981] 333

Zwann, In re [1981] IR 395; [1981] ILRM 333 **Followed** [1983] 149

NOT TO BE REMOVED
FROM LIBRARY

Statutes etc. Considered

1. IRISH AND BRITISH STATUTES

Acquisition of Land (Assessment of Compensation) Act 1919
Generally	[1987] 733
s. 2	[1983] 56, 377
	[1987] 83
s. 2 r. 2	[1984] 313, 366
	[1984] 616
s. 2 r. 16	[1984] 313

Act for Joint Tenants 1542
Generally	[1987] 1

Adaptation of Enactments Act 1922
s. 5	[1979] 297

Administration of Estates Act 1959
s. 13	[1987] 582
s. 22	[1987] 582

Adoption Act 1952
Generally	[1988] 203
s. 13(1)	[1985] 61
s. 40	[1982] 48

Adoption Act 1964
s. 2	[1985] 302
s. 3	[1985] 302

Adoption Act 1974
s. 3	[1982] 150
	[1983] 228
	[1985] 302
	[1988] 203
s. 5(1)	[1985] 61

Adoption Act 1976
s. 3(1)	[1985] 302
s. 8	[1985] 186

Agricultural Credit Act 1978
s. 23(1)	[1984] 437
s. 36	[1985] 624
s. 36(1)	[1984] 437

Aliens Act 1935
Generally	[1990] 234
s. 4	[1987] 330
s. 5	[1987] 330
s. 12	[1987] 330

Annual Revision of Rateable Property (Ireland) Act 1860
s. 6	[1990] 172
s. 7	[1980] 149

Anti-Discrimination (Pay) Act 1974
Generally	[1989] 53
s. 2	[1986] 483
s. 2(1)	[1985] 173
	[1990] 21
s. 2(3)	[1990] 21
s. 3	[1990] 21
s. 3(c)	[1986] 483
s. 4	[1982] 367
	[1985] 173
s. 5	[1982] 367
	[1985] 173
s. 7	[1985] 173
	[1987] 357
s. 7(3)	[1990] 21
s. 8	[1982] 367

Arbitration Act 1954
s. 2	[1990] 739
s. 3(1)	[1976–7] 218
s. 12	[1990] 159
s. 12(1)	[1990] 739
s. 18	[1976–7] 149
s. 19(1)	[1990] 277
s. 35(1)	[1978] 128
	[1980] 38
	[1987] 17
	[1984] 616
s. 36	[1978] 128
s. 36(1)	[1978] 128
s. 38(1)	[1978] 128
s. 39	[1990] 159
s. 41	[1988] 129

Farm Tax Act 1985
s. 4	[1989] 710
s. 9	[1989] 710
s. 14	[1989] 710

Finance Act 1920
s. 52	[1985] 200
s. 53(2)	[1982] 200

Finance Act 1926
s. 24	[1984] 39
s. 25	[1984] 39
s. 25(2)	[1982] 249
	[1984] 625
	[1987] 4
s. 42	[1982] 249
s. 43	[1982] 249

Finance Act 1932
s. 38	[1980] 21
s. 45	[1980] 21

Finance Act 1951
s. 17	[1980] 137

Finance Act 1954
s. 21	[1982] 444

Finance Act 1963
s. 34	[1986] 428

Finance Act 1965
s. 66(6)	[1980] 137

Finance Act 1966
s. 15(2)(d)	[1986] 693

Finance Act 1968
s. 7	[1988] 52, 531
s. 8	[1988] 52, 531

Finance Act 1969
s. 18	[1982] 451
s. 18(1)	[1985] 655
s. 22	[1984] 231
s. 49	[1982] 438

Finance Act 1971
s. 22	[1989] 688

Finance Act 1973
s. 34	[1988] 419

Finance Act 1974
s. 13(1)(3)	[1985] 655
s. 31(2)	[1986] 24
s. 57	[1986] 37
s. 58	[1986] 37
s. 59	[1982] 459
	[1986] 37

Finance Act 1975
s. 31	[1989] 478
s. 31(1)	[1985] 210
s. 31(9)	[1985] 210
s. 43	[1987] 320

Finance Act 1976
s. 44	[1986] 428
s. 46	[1989] 342

Finance Act 1977
s. 43	[1985] 210

Finance Act 1980
s. 21	[1986] 364
s. 79	[1986] 693

Finance Act 1981
s. 26	[1984] 679

Finance Act 1982
s. 69(1)(b)	[1987] 4
s. 70	[1987] 4

Finance Act 1983
s. 16	[1985] 123
s. 18	[1985] 123
s. 56	[1984] 583
s. 95	[1980] 136
s. 96	[1986] 136
s. 97	[1986] 136
s. 98	[1986] 136
s. 99	[1986] 136
s. 100	[1986] 136
s. 101	[1986] 136
s. 102	[1986] 136
s. 108	[1986] 136
s. 109	[1986] 136

Finance (Excise Duty on Tobacco Products) Act 1977
s. 11	[1986] 693

Finance (Miscellaneous Provisions) Act 1956 [1986] 164

Finance (Miscellaneous Provisions) Act 1968
s. 17	[1979] 57
	[1982] 421
s. 18	[1990] 100

Finance (New Duties) Act 1916
s. 4(1)	[1982] 441
s. 4(2)	[1982] 441
s. 6(3)	[1982] 441

Finance (No 2) Act 1947
s. 13(1)	[1980] 137

Licensing (Ireland) Act 1872
s. 51(4)   [1981] 213

Licensing (Ireland) Act 1874
s. 23   [1987] 87

Licensing (Ireland) Act 1902
s. 2   [1981] 2
s. 2(ii)   [1984] 662
s. 2(2)   [1986] 471
    [1989] 806

Limited Partnerships Act 1907
s. 4   [1986] 116
s. 5   [1986] 116
s. 8   [1986] 116

Local Elections (Petitions and Disqualifications) Act 1974
s. 4(4)   [1979] 281
s. 5(1)   [1979] 281
s. 5(2)   [1979] 281
s. 7   [1979] 281
s. 8   [1979] 281

Local Government Act 1955
s. 66   [1983] 413

Local Government (Dublin) Act 1930
s. 69   [1985] 283
s. 69(1)   [1984] 84

Local Government (Financial Provisions) (No 2) Act 1983
s. 1(3)   [1986] 277
s. 2   [1990] 864
s. 2(1)   [1986] 277
s. 4   [1986] 277
s. 8   [1986] 277

Local Government (Ireland) Act 1898
Generally   [1989] 46
s. 5(7)   [1984] 688
s. 10   [1976–7] 236
    [1984] 605

Local Government (No 2) Act 1960
s. 10   [1976–7] 236
    [1984] 605
s. 10(1)   [1980] 77
s. 11   [1976–7] 236
    [1984] 605

Local Government (Planning and Development Act) 1963
Generally   [1989] 565
s. 1   [1990] 48
s. 1(1)   [1981] 23
s. 2   [1982] 534

    [1983] 339
    [1984] 605
    [1989] 602
s. 2(1)   [1986] 465
s. 3   [1978] 85
    [1982] 505, 534
    [1987] 564
    [1990] 48
s. 3(1)   [1981] 23
s. 4   [1990] 48
s. 4(1)   [1982] 505, 534
s. 4(1)(g)   [1986] 465
s. 4(2)   [1982] 505
    [1982] 534
s. 5   [1978] 85
    [1982] 505
    [1982] 534
s. 8   [1981] 439
    [1988] 47
s. 19   [1989] 98, 768
s. 19(1)   [1982] 469
s. 19(7)   [1987] 733
    [1989] 145
s. 21   [1982] 469
s. 24   [1982] 104, 505
    [1988] 274
s. 24(1)   [1978] 85, 208
s. 25   [1990] 48
s. 26   [1978] 78
    [1979] 35
    [1981] 54, 108, 439
    [1982] 590
    [1987] 747
    [1990] 48, 658
s. 26(1)   [1983] 339
    [1989] 98
s. 26(2)   [1983] 339
    [1989] 98
s. 26(3)   [1982] 169
    [1983] 339
    [1989] 145
s. 26(4)   [1980] 64
    [1982] 29, 169, 534
    [1983] 141, 145, 339
    [1990] 633
s. 26(5)   [1981] 108, 191
    [1982] 169
    [1983] 141, 339
    [1989] 98
s. 26(6)   [1982] 169
s. 26(9)   [1981] 191
s. 27   [1982] 590
s. 28   [1990] 658

Prisons (Ireland) Act 1877
s. 12 [1981] 86
s. 13 [1981] 86

Prisons Act 1972
s. 2 [1976–7] 13
s. 2(3) [1980] 208, 242
s. 2(4) [1980] 242
s. 2(9) [1980] 242
s. 2(10) [1980] 242
s. 4 [1976–7] 13

Prohibition of Forcible Entry Act 1971
s. 3 [1981] 416
s. 9 [1981] 416

Property Values (Arbitrations and Appeals) Act 1960
Generally [1987] 733

Prosecution of Offences Act 1974
[1986] 318
s. 1 [1983] 489
s. 2 [1983] 489
s. 2(4) [1984] 413
s. 3 [1980] 167
[1982] 385
[1983] 489
[1984] 224, 413, 443
[1985] 349
s. 3(1) [1979] 281
s. 4 [1986] 290
s. 7 [1986] 290

Protection of Employees (Employers' Insolvency) Act 1984
s. 6(1) [1990] 180
s. 6(2) [1990] 180

Public Health (Ireland) Act 1878
s. 23 [1983] 377
[1990] 864
s. 24 [1984] 313
s. 28 [1982] 117
s. 65A [1986] 277
s. 160 [1989] 706
s. 174 [1989] 706
s. 216 [1984] 313
s. 217 [1984] 313

Racing Board and Racecourses Act 1945
s. 24 [1983] 67

Railway and Canal Traffic Act 1854
s. 2 [1979] 296
s. 3 [1979] 296

Railway and Canal Traffic Act 1888
s. 7 [1979] 296
s. 8 [1979] 296
s. 12 [1979] 296

Railways Act 1924
[1979] 296

Rateable Valuation (Ireland) Act 1852
s. 11 [1987] 512

Redundancy Payments Act 1967
s. 2(1) [1982] 215
s. 7(2) [1981] 289
s. 11 [1984] 15
s. 13 [1984] 15

Redundancy Payments Act 1971
s. 4 [1981] 289
s. 11 [1984] 15

Registration of Births and Deaths (Ireland) Act 1863
[1984] 66

Registration of Clubs (Ireland) Act 1904
s. 4 [1984] 246

Registration of Title Act 1964
s. 52 [1982] 113
s. 71(4) [1982] 113
s. 72 [1982] 113
s. 98 [1986] 499
s. 120 [1986] 499
s. 121 [1986] 499

Rent Restrictions Act 1960
s. 2(1) [1979] 47
s. 2(d) [1981] 370
s. 3(2) [1981] 34
s. 7 [1981] 34
s. 8(1)(a) [1981] 34
s. 9 [1981] 34
s. 10 [1981] 34
s. 11 [1981] 34
s. 31 [1981] 34
s. 31(3) [1979] 47
s. 32 [1981] 34
s. 54 [1981] 34

Rent Restrictions (Amendment) Act 1967
s. 2(4) [1979] 47
s. 4(3) [1981] 34
s. 13(2) [1979] 47
s. 13(3) [1979] 47

Restrictive Practices Act 1972
s. 19 [1979] 269

548   ILRM INDEX, 1976-1990

Road Traffic Act 1961

s. 3	[1985] 290
s. 4(1)	[1981] 102, 447
s. 4(2)	[1981] 102
s. 4(3)	[1981] 102
s. 4(5)	[1981] 102
s. 4(6)	[1981] 102
s. 10	[1983] 310
s. 12	[1985] 320
s. 49	[1985] 333
	[1988] 720
s. 49(1)	[1987] 129, 570, 575
s. 49(2)	[1980] 145
	[1981] 447
	[1983] 45, 411
	[1984] 347
	[1985] 243, 320
	[1987] 129, 570, 575
s. 49(3)	[1987] 129, 570, 575
s. 49(4)	[1988] 39
s. 49(4)(a)	[1983] 45, 411
	[1985] 320
s. 49(6)	[1982] 482
	[1985] 320
	[1987] 129, 570, 575
s. 54(1)	[1981] 149, 340
s. 54(4)	[1981] 149
s. 56	[1985] 290
s. 56(4)	[1981] 149
s. 60	[1981] 340
s. 62	[1981] 340
s. 69	[1981] 149
s. 75	[1978] 25
s. 76	[1985] 290
s. 89(1)	[1983] 223
s. 89(7)	[1983] 223
s. 89(2)(m)	[1986] 268
s. 89(7)	[1986] 268
s. 90(1)	[1983] 223
s. 90(2)	[1986] 268
s. 90(9)	[1986] 268
s. 92	[1983] 223
s. 106	[1987] 316
s. 107	[1988] 39
s. 107	[1986] 657
s. 112(1)	[1985] 445
s. 118	[1984] 523

Road Traffic Act 1968

s. 6	[1983] 223
s. 65	[1985] 445

Road Traffic (Amendment) Act 1978

s. 2	[1987] 570
s. 10	[1980] 145
	[1981] 102, 447
	[1983] 411
	[1984] 347
	[1985] 320, 333
	[1987] 129, 575
s. 10(4)(a)	[1983] 45
s. 12	[1985] 206, 320
s. 12(1)	[1981] 102
s. 12(2)	[1983] 76
s. 12(4)	[1981] 102
s. 13	[1981] 102
	[1987] 138, 575
s. 13(1)	[1982] 482
	[1985] 320
s. 13(3)	[1982] 482
	[1983] 76
	[1984] 127
s. 17(1)	[1985] 320
s. 17(4)	[1985] 320
s. 19	[1982] 482
s. 21	[1981] 102, 447
	[1982] 482
	[1981] 447
	[1985] 320
s. 21(1)	[1983] 310
s. 21(4)	[1983] 310
s. 22	[1980] 145
	[1982] 482
	[1988] 35, 483
s. 22(3)	[1983] 310
	[1985] 243
s. 23	[1980] 145
	[1981] 102, 447
	[1985] 320
s. 23(2)	[1987] 570
	[1988] 35, 133, 483
s. 49(2)	[1985] 206
s. 49(4)(a)	[1985] 206

Road Transport Act 1932

Generally	[1990] 561

Road Transport Act 1933

Generally	[1990] 561

Sale of Goods Act 1893

s. 1	[1984] 437
s. 4	[1984] 471
s. 14	[1985] 217
s. 17	[1984] 437
s. 51	[1978] 31

2. CONSTITUTION OF IRELAND

Constitution of Ireland 1937 (contd.)

Art 10	[1988] 565
Art 11	[1986] 381
Art 12 2	[1984] 539
Art 12 4 1	[1984] 539
Art 13 2 1	[1990] 461
Art 13 2 2	[1990] 461
Art 13 8 1	[1990] 461
Art 15	[1986] 693
Art 15 1	[1989] 1
Art 15 2	[1987] 477
	[1990] 185
Art 15 2 1	[1987] 278
	[1989] 342, 710
Art 15 4 1	[1985] 422
Art 16	[1982] 190
	[1987] 290
Art 16 1	[1984] 539, 643
Art 16 2	[1990] 461
Art 16 3 1	[1990] 461
Art 16 7	[1984] 539, 643
Art 26	[1983] 246
	[1984] 539
	[1989] 266
Art 27 4 1	[1987] 278, 400
Art 28	[1989] 209, 544
	[1990] 441
Art 28 2	[1989] 544
Art 29	[1986] 24
	[1990] 441
Art 29 4	[1989] 209
Art 29 4 1	[1987] 400
	[1990] 86
Art 29 4 3	[1986] 68
	[1987] 400
	[1988] 400
	[1990] 364
Art 29 5	[1987] 278
Art 29 5 2	[1985] 465
	[1986] 129, 381
	[1987] 278
Art 30	[1984] 443
	[1987] 400
Art 30 3	[1986] 318
	[1989] 209
Art 34	[1978] 147
	[1982] 568
	[1983] 489
	[1984] 413
	[1985] 10
	[1986] 136, 304, 343
	[1988] 52, 531, 620
	[1989] 309, 757
	[1990] 200

Art 34 1	
Art 34 2	
Art 34 3	
Art 34 3 1	
Art 34 3 2	
Art 34 3 4	
Art 34 4 3	
Art 34 4 4	
Art 34 4 5	
Art 34 5	
Art 35	
Art 36 (iii)	
Art 37	
Art 38	
Art 38 1	
Art 38 2	
Art 38 3	
Art 38 3 1	
Art 38 5	
Art 38 6	
Art 40	
Art 40 1	

[1984] 66
[1985] 449
[1990] 14
[1984] 657
[1985] 375
[1985] 375
[1983] 549
[1984] 657
[1989] 485
[1986] 428
[1987] 535
[1981] 389
[1983] 549
[1986] 250, 538
[1987] 255, 316
[1990] 749
[1981] 389
[1989] 245
[1987] 278
[1981] 389
[1982] 568
[1986] 343
[1985] 375
[1986] 337
[1983] 67
[1988] 620
[1978] 12
[1981] 469
[1984] 161, 373
[1984] 66, 249
[1986] 401, 428, 639, 653
[1987] 723
[1988] 4
[1982] 249, 512
[1984] 39, 625
[1986] 428
[1988] 430
[1986] 343
[1982] 385
[1983] 549
[1984] 625
[1986] 428
[1988] 4
[1983] 549
[1986] 343
[1978] 226
[1981] 86, 389
[1982] 327
[1984] 292
[1987] 330
[1989] 266, 277
[1990] 234, 802
[1979] 134
[1980] 167
[1981] 34, 246, 391, 449

Constitution of Ireland 1937 (contd.)

	[1984] 355, 643, 657		[1984] 237
			[1986] 95, 129
	[1985] 61, 86, 302, 422, 494, 542, 606		[1987] 45
			[1989] 229, 670
			[1990] 850
		Art 40 4 3	[1986] 381
	[1986] 136, 164, 364		[1987] 278
		Art 40 5	[1986] 657
	[1987] 290, 606		[1987] 575
	[1988] 456		[1988] 39
	[1990] 441	Art 40 6	[1983] 89
Art 40 3	[1979] 134		[1984] 577
	[1980] 82, 167	Art 40 6 1	[1982] 190
	[1981] 14, 34, 113, 242, 273		[1987] 135
			[1989] 19, 349
	[1982] 512	Art 40 6 1(i)	[1984] 161
	[1983] 67, 223, 314, 391, 449		[1987] 52
		Art 40 6 1(ii)	[1984] 88
	[1984] 66, 88, 94, 138, 249, 355, 373, 643	Art 40 6 1(iii)	[1986] 206
			[1989] 87
		Art 41	[1981] 125
	[1985] 86, 494, 542		[1982] 164, 327
			[1984] 292
	[1986] 136, 177, 364		[1985] 542
			[1986] 65, 98, 136, 364, 593
	[1987] 52, 290, 723		[1987] 330
			[1988] 300, 456
	[1988] 4, 52, 251, 400, 456, 472, 531, 629		[1989] 266, 528
			[1990] 234, 364
	[1990] 313, 505, 560, 561, 648	Art 41 1	[1984] 138
		Art 41 2 2	[1989] 196
Art 40 3 1	[1978] 51	Art 41 3	[1984] 667
	[1982] 568	Art 41 3 1	[1989] 196
	[1985] 61, 465		[1990] 213
	[1987] 747	Art 41 3 3	[1987] 189
	[1989] 333, 349	Art 42	[1984] 292
	[1990]		[1986] 65, 98, 593
Art 40 3 2	[1982] 290		
	[1986] 601		[1987] 330
	[1987] 747		[1988] 300
	[1989] 282, 349, 544		[1989] 266, 277
			[1990] 234
Art 40 3 3	[1987] 477	Art 42 2	[1987] 651
	[1989] 19	Art 42 5	[1985] 302
	[1990] 70, 350	Art 43	[1982] 290, 327
Art 40 4	[1980] 82		[1983] 314, 391, 449
	[1983] 17, 52, 149		[1984] 94
			[1985] 494
	[1985] 542		[1986] 136
	[1988] 251, 724		[1988] 400
	[1990] 505, 648		[1989] 266, 670
Art 40 4 1	[1984] 249	Art 43 1	[1981] 34
Art 40 4 2	[1978] 195	Art 43 1 2	[1985] 86
	[1980] 191	Art 43 2	[1981] 34
	[1981] 333		

3. STATUTORY INSTRUMENTS

Prisons Act 1972 (Military Custody) Regulations 1972 (SI No 138 of 1972)

reg 8	[1980] 191
reg 16	[1980] 191
reg 19	[1980] 191
reg 34	[1980] 191
reg 35(1)	[1982] 491
reg 39	[1980] 191
reg 40	[1980] 191
reg 50	[1980] 191
reg 51	[1980] 191
reg 62	[1980] 191
reg 134	[1980] 191

Redundancy Appeals Tribunal Regulations 1968 (SI No 24 of 1968)

reg 23	[1990] 293

Restrictive Practices (Groceries) (Amendment) (No 2) Order 1978 (SI No 336 of 1978)

Art 5	[1979] 269

Retail Price (Beverages in Licensed Premises) Display Order 1976 (SI No 146 of 1976)

	[1979] 302

Road Traffic Act 1968 (Part V) Regulations 1969 (SI No 196 of 1969)

Generally	[1976–7] 68

Road Traffic (Amendment) Act 1978 Regulations (SI No 193 of 1978)

	[1980] 75
	[1981] 447

Road Traffic (Compulsory Insurance) Regulations 1962 (SI No 14 of 1962)

art 5	[1981] 340
arts 7, 9	[1978] 25

Rules for the Government of Prisons 1947 (S R & O No 320 of 1947)

Generally	[1980] 242
	[1981] 86
r 34	[1980] 82
r 46	[1980] 82
r 59	[1987] 45
r 60	[1987] 45
r 63	[1987] 45
r 108	[1980] 82
r 172	[1980] 82

Rules for the Government of Prisons 1976 (SI No 30 of 1976)

O 99 rr 37, 38	[1978] 63

Rules of the Superior Courts. *See* **Rules of Court** (Table 4).

Sea Fisheries (Control of Catches) Order 1985 (SI No 163 of 1985)

Generally	[1989] 411

Social Welfare (Collection of Employment Contributions by the Collector General) Regulations 1979 (SI No 77 of 1979)

Generally	[1986] 493

Social Welfare (Modification of Insurance) Regulations 1956 (SI No 236 of 1956)

art 5 (1)(c)	[1976–7] 210

Social Welfare (Overlapping Benefits) Regulations 1953 (SI No 14 of 1953)

Generally	[1990] 185

Solicitors Act 1954 (Apprenticeship and Education) (Amendment No 1) Regulations 1974 (SI No 138 of 1974)

Generally	[1989] 854

Solicitors Acts 1954 and 1960 (Apprenticeship and Education) Regulations 1975 (SI No 66 of 1975)

Generally	[1989] 854
reg 6	[1989] 590
reg 7	[1989] 590
reg 10	[1989] 590
reg 18	[1989] 590
reg 28	[1989] 590

Summary Jurisdiction Rules 1909 (S R & O No 952 of 1909)

r 6	[1990] 243
r 12	[1990] 243

Supreme Court and High Court (Fees) Order 1984 (SI No 19 of 1984)

Generally	[1989] 501

Table Water Duties Regulations 1916 (S R & O No 708)

reg 6	[1982] 441

Trade Mark Rules 1963 (SI No 268 of 1963)

r 19 (4)	[1976–7] 335
r 43	[1988] 247
r 70	[1988] 247

Trade Mark Rules 1963–1977 (SI Nos 268 of 1963, 265 of 1977)

r 24	[1982] 91
r 26	[1982] 91

Trustee (Authorised Investments) Order
1977 (SI No 41 of 1977)
[1983] 429

Trustee (Authorised Investments) (No 2)
Order 1977 (SI No 344 of 1977)
[1983] 429

Unfair Dismissals (Claims and Appeals)
Regulations 1977 (SI No 286 of 1977)
reg 5   [1990] 293
reg 9   [1990] 293
reg 10   [1990] 293

Winding Up Rules 1966 (Rules of the
Superior Courts 1966, SI No 28 of 1966)
O 74 r 129   [1982] 340
                   [1983] 329
                   [1984] 583

4. RULES OF COURT

District Court Rules 1948 (S R & O No
431 of 1947)
r 4   [1990] 761
r 25   [1987] 118
r 29   [1986] 579
                   [1988] 620
r 30   [1987] 309
                   [1988] 620
r 44   [1986] 565
                   [1987] 118
r 48   [1986] 565
r 64(5)   [1990] 761
r 66   [1986] 565
r 67   [1980] 167
r 190   [1981] 169
r 197   [1981] 169
r 201   [1984] 171

District Court Rules 1955 (SI No 83 of
1966)
r 17   [1990] 32

District Court (Criminal Procedure Act
1967) Rules 1967 (SI No 181 of 1967)
Generally   [1982] 108
r 5   [1983] 285
                   [1986] 653
r 65   [1983] 45
r 84   [1983] 525
r 85   [1983] 525

District Court (Criminal Procedure Act
1967) Rules 1985 (SI No 23 of 1985)
Generally   [1987] 65

Rules of the Circuit Court 1950 (SI No 179
of 1950)
O 30 r 11   [1985] 100

Rules of the Superior Courts 1962 (SI No
72 of 1962)
O 4 r 2   [1986] 10
O 8 r 1   [1985] 180

O 11 r 1(f)   [1986] 627
O 11 r 1(g)   [1986] 10
O 12 r 26   [1983] 163
                   [1986] 10
O 16 r 7   [1985] 1
O 16 r 11   [1985] 1
O 18 r 1   [1982] 317
O 18 r 8   [1982] 317
O 19 r 5   [1981] 198
O 19 r 6   [1981] 198
O 19 r 6(1)   [1985] 673
O 19 r 27   [1984] 24
O 19 r 28   [1979] 273
                   [1981] 242
                   [1984] 24, 105
O 19 r 29   [1986] 136
O 22 r 4   [1982] 121
O 22 r 10   [1982] 121
O 22 r 13   [1982] 121
O 31 r 9   [1987] 790
O 31 r 12   [1976–7] 50
O 31 r 24   [1976–7] 50
O 39 r 1   [1985] 449
O 52 r 2   [1986] 218
O 52 r 17(5)   [1976–7] 50
O 56 r 4   [1987] 47
O 58 r 3   [1986] 538
O 58 r 8   [1986] 538
O 58 r 10   [1986] 538
O 58 r 13   [1986] 538
O 58 r 19   [1986] 538
O 58 r 20   [1986] 538
O 60 r 1   [1982] 568
                   [1986] 164
O 61 r 12   [1984] 555
O 62 r 5   [1984] 171
O 70 r 54   [1982] 562
O 70 r 55   [1982] 562
O 81 r 10   [1981] 439
O 84 r 2   [1981] 333
                   [1983] 149

5. STATUTORY SCHEMES

6. INTERNATIONAL TREATIES AND CONVENTIONS

7. EUROPEAN COMMUNITY LEGISLATION

8. MISCELLANEOUS CONSTITUTIONS ETC.

Words and Phrases Considered

"abuse . . . of a dominant position" Adoption of rules by farmers' co-operative — Treaty of Rome, Article 86. [1990] 664, HC.

"accident" Insurance policy. [1988] 373, SC.

"acting reasonably". [1979] 3.

"active service" Defence (Amendment) Act 1960, s. 4. [1989] 544, SC.

"adaptation or modification of a statute" Courts of Justice Act 1924, s. 91. [1987] 65, SC; [1988] 620, HC, SC.

"administration of justice" Constitution of Ireland 1937, Article 34. [1988] 531, SC.

"all costs, charges and expenses properly incurred" Whether Corporation tax a liability properly incurred — Companies Act 1963, s. 281. [1987] 508, HC; [1989] 155, SC.

"all matters and questions" Constitution of Ireland 1937, Article 34 3 1. [1984] 657, HC; [1985] 375, SC.

"all royalties" Constitution of Ireland 1937, Article 10. [1988] 565, HC, SC.

"all the income of the property" Conveyancing and Law of Property Act 1881, s. 24. [1987] 26, HC.

"allotment of alimony" RSC 1962 O 70 r 55. [1982] 562, HC.

"amount chargeable" Income Tax Act 1967, s. 91. [1990] 249, HC.

"amounts due in respect of contributions payable during the 12 months next before the relevant date" Companies Act 1963, s. 285(2). [1987] 222, SC.

"annual percentage rate of charge" Consumer Information (Consumer Credit) Order 1987, Art 3. [1990] 743, HC.

"any Act of the Oireachtas" Courts (Supplemental Provisions) Act 1961, s. 34(2). [1989] 757, SC.

"any benefit" Arterial Drainage Act 1945, s. 17. [1980] 38, HC.

"any person" Solicitors (Amendment) Act 1960, s. 21(4). [1989] 665, SC.

"any property" Garda Siochana (Compensation) Act 1941, s. 10(1). [1986] 28, SC.

"arrangements for providing services therein" Health Act 1970, s. 38(2). [1985] 616, SC.

"as if it were a reference under s. 19 of a dispute" Employment Equality Act 1977, s. 20. [1987] 373, HC, SC.

"as may be fixed" Civil Liability Act 1961, s. 60(7). [1988] 437, SC.

"as soon as may be"   Fisheries (Consolidation) Act 1959, s. 233A. [1989] 821, HC.

"as soon as practicable"   Road Traffic (Amendment) Act 1978, ss. 22(1),22(3). [1980] 145, HC.

"associated company"   Corporation Tax Act 1976, ss. 1(5), 28(4). [1986] 508, HC.

"at a price to be agreed"   Will — Construction. [1988] 80, HC.

"at least two hours for deliberation"   Jury — Minimum time limit for deliberation — Criminal Justice Act 1984, s. 25(3). [1989] 370, CCA.

"bankers books"   [1985] 123, HC, SC.

"bill of sale"   Bills of Sale (Ireland) Act 1879. [1985] 624, SC.

"body of persons"   Whether two persons can constitute a "body of persons" — Income Tax Act 1967, s. 349. [1983] 34, HC, [1984] 406, SC.

"bona fide concern and interest"   Locus standi to seek enforcement of Constitutional provision. [1990] 70, SC.

"brought into charge to tax"   [1985] 666, HC, SC.

"burial ground"   Public Health (Ireland) Act 1878, s. 174 — Local Government (Sanitary Services) Act 1948, s. 44. [1989] 706, SC.

"capable of distinguishing"   Trade Marks Act 1963. s. 18. [1984] 565, SC; [1988] 259, SC; [1990] 204, HC.

"capital allowance"   Whether rule that singular includes plural applicable — Income Tax Act 1967, ss. 218, 220 — Finance Act 1975, s. 33. [1982] 457, HC.

"cattle"   Dealer in cattle — Whether "cattle" includes pigs. Income Tax Act 1918, Schedule D — Income Tax Act 1967, s. 78. [1982] 13, SC.

"caused"   Malicious Injuries Act 1981, s. 5(2). [1985] 269, HC.

"character of the structure"   Local Government (Planning and Development) Act 1963, s. 4(1)(g). [1986] 465, SC.

"charge   [on public funds] — Constitution of Ireland 1937, Article 29 5 2. [1986] 129, HC.

"charges and expenses"   Companies Act 1963, s. 281. [1987] 508, HC; [1989] 155, SC.

"close confinement"   Prisons Act, 1972 (Military Custody) Regulations 1972, regs 66, 68. [1980] 242, HC, SC.

"cohabiting as man and wife"   Social Welfare (Consolidation) Act 1981, s. 92(3). [1989] 169, HC.

"committed within the jurisdiction"   RSC O 11 r 1(f). [1986] 627, SC.

"compilation"   Copyright Act 1963, s. 2(1). [1990] 534, HC.

"concerted practice"   Treaty of Rome 1957, Article 85. [1990] 554, HC.

"concourse of buyers and sellers"   Casual Trading Act 1980, s. 1. [1986] 170, HC.

"confirmed"   Finance Act 1976, s. 46. [1989] 342, HC.

"connected with a political offence"   Extradition Act 1965, s. 50. [1990] 802, SC.

"connection in the course of trade"   Trade Marks Act 1963, s. 2(1). [1985] 30, SC.

"conscious and deliberate violation"   See "Deliberate and conscious violation".

"consent"   Adoption Act 1974, s. 3. [1988] 203, SC.

"consent"   Marriage. [1986] 75, HC, SC.

"contract of employment"   Trade Disputes Act 1906, s. 3. [1979] 51, HC.

"control of staff"   Delegation of power — Whether control includes power to dismiss staff. [1986] 225, HC.

"costs, charges and expenses properly incurred"   Companies Act 1963, s. 281. [1987] 508, HC; [1989] 155, SC; [1990] 97, HC.

"course of trade"   Trade Marks Act 1963, s. 2(1). [1985] 30, SC.

"crime against the property damaged"   Malicious Injuries Act 1981, s. 5(2)(d). [1985] 445, SC; [1986] 273, SC.

"criminal charge"   [1986] 304, HC.

"criminal offence"   [1986] 304, HC.

"customary overhauling"   Marine insurance policy. [1986] 669, HC, SC.

"customs duty"   [1986] 693, HC, SC.

"date on which the action is first listed for hearing"   RSC O 22 r 1(2). [1988] 654, HC.

"dealer in cattle"   Whether "cattle" includes pigs. Income Tax Act 1918, Schedule D — Income Tax Act 1967, s. 78. [1982] 13, SC.

"dealing as a consumer"   Sale of Goods and Supply of Services Act 1980, s. 3(1). [1984] 146, HC.

"debt"   Protection of Employees (Employers' Insolvency) Act 1984, s. 6(2)(a)(i). [1990] 180, HC.

"deliberate and conscious violation"   [1990] 313, SC; [1990] 569, SC.

"decision by the High Court"   Whether declining to grant an injunction constitutes a decision appealable to the Supreme Court. [1990] 350, SC.

"detention"   Overt surveillance — Whether amounts to continuing detention. [1988] 724, HC, SC.

"development"   Local Government (Planning and Development) Act 1963, s. 3. See PLANNING (Development).

"direct reference"   Trade Marks Act 1963. [1988] 259, SC.

"discovery"   Inspector of Taxes — Income Tax Act 1967, s. 186. [1990] 249, HC.

"discrimination"   Employment Equality Act 1977, ss. 2, 3 — Council Directive 76/207/EEC, Article 2.1. [1990] 485, HC, SC.

"discrimination based on sex"   Anti-Discrimination (Pay) Act 1974. [1990] 21, HC.

"dispute"   Public Health (Ireland) Act 1878, s. 24. [1984] 313, HC.

"due course of law"   Constitution of Ireland 1937, Article 38.1. [1986] 343, HC, SC.

"due diligence"   Marine insurance policy. [1986] 669, HC, SC.

"duress"   Contract of marriage — Nullity petition. [1986] 75, HC, SC.

"dwelling"   Succession Act 1965, s. 56. [1984] 306, HC.

"employee"   Unfair Dismissals Act 1977, s. 1. [1982] 260, EAT.

"employer"   Income Tax (Employments) Regulations 1960 — Social Welfare (Collection of Employment Contributions by the Collector General) Regulations 1979. [1986] 493, HC.

"employer"   Whether includes personal representative of employer — Unfair Dismissals Act 1977, s. 1. [1982] 578, EAT.

"enactment"   Local Government (Financial Provisions) (No 2) Act 1983, s. 1(3). [1986] 277, SC.

"excepted letters"   Post Office Act 1908, s. 34(2). [1984] 373, HC.

"exceptional circumstances"   Criminal Justice (Legal Aid) Act 1962, s. 2. [1979] 243, HC.

"excise duty"   [1986] 693, HC, SC.

"exempted development"   Local Government (Planning and Development) Act 1963, s. 4(1)(g). [1986] 465, SC.

"exempted development"   Use of land to store caravans and fuel oils — Local Government (Planning and Development) Act 1963, s. 4(2). [1990] 48, HC.

"failed in his moral duty to make proper provision for the child in accordance with his means"   Succession Act 1965, s. 117(1). [1989] 815, SC.

"family"   Constitution of Ireland 1937, Article 41. [1985] 86, SC.

"family"   Constitution of Ireland 1937, Articles 41, 42. [1984] 292, HC.

"family home"   Family Home Protection Act 1976, s. 2. [1980] 257, HC.

"farming"   Fattening of pigs in purpose-built housing — Finance Act 1974, s. 13(1). [1985] 655, HC.

"fit and convenient"   Intoxicating Liquor Act 1960, s. 15. [1981] 270, HC.

"fit person"   Whether Health Board qualified to be a "fit person" — Children Act 1908, s. 24(1). [1990] 130, SC.

"fixed charge"   Company. [1985] 641, SC.

"fixtures"   Television aerials on roofs of private houses — Value Added Tax Act 1972, s. 10(8). [1986] 377, HC.

"floating charge"   Company. [1985] 641, SC.

"forthwith enquire"   Constitution of Ireland 1937, Article 40 4 2. [1983] 52, HC.

"fraud"   Statute of Limitations 1957, s. 71(1). [1983] 156.

"fraudulent preference"   Companies Act 1963, s. 286. [1990] 341, HC.

"from all decisions of the High Court"   Constitution of Ireland 1937, Article 34 4 3. [1983] 549, SC.

"full particulars of all accounts maintained"   Finance Act 1983, s. 18. [1985] 123, HC, SC.

"gaming"   Gaming and Lotteries Act 1956, s. 2. [1982] 143, HC.

"goods manufactured within the State"   Tax relief — Whether ripened bananas included in definition — Corporation Tax Act 1976, s. 54(2). [1986] 229, HC.

"government of the State"   Offences Against the State Act 1939, s. 7(1). [1983] 237, CCA.

"gravity of the charge" Criminal Justice (Legal Aid) Act 1962, s. 2. [1979] 243, HC.

"grounds other than sex" Anti-Discrimination (Pay) Act 1974, s. 2(3). [1990] 21, HC.

"hearing of the proceedings" Companies Act 1963, s. 205(7). [1989] 757, SC.

"hereditaments and tenements occupied" Whether applicable only to premises occupied at date of passing of Act — Local Government (Dublin) Act 1930, s. 69(1). [1984] 84, HC; [1985] 283, SC.

"holding" Council Regulation 857/84/EEC (Quota Regulations) — Council Regulation 764/89/EEC (Mulder Regulations). [1990] 466, HC.

"husbandry" Fattening of pigs in purpose-built housing — Finance Act 1974, s. 13(1). [1985] 655, HC.

"immediately" Income tax default — Recovery by sheriff — Income Tax Act 1967, s. 485(2). [1989] 165, HC.

"immediately" Revenue appeal — Whether mandatory requirement — Income Tax Act 1967, s. 428. [1984] 545, HC.

"improper inducement by threat" [1988] 666, SC.

"in accordance with law" Constitution of Ireland 1937, Article 40 4 2. [1983] 17, SC; [1986] 95, HC.

"in connection with that solicitor's practice as a solicitor" Solicitors (Amendment) Act 1960, s. 21(4). [1989] 665, SC.

"in like manner" Children Act 1908, s. 24(1). [1990] 130, SC.

"in the immediate vicinity" Intoxicating Liquor Act 1960, s. 14. [1990] 228, HC.

"income" Conveyancing and Law of Property Act 1881, s. 24. [1987] 26, HC.

"income brought into charge" Corporation Tax Act 1976, s. 58(3). [1985] 666, HC, SC.

"inducement" Statement admitting responsibility for crime — Whether admission induced by Gardai — Test to be applied. [1988] 666, SC.

"injustice done" Constitution of Ireland 1937, Article 40 3 2. [1987] 747, HC, SC.

"inpatient services" Health Act 1970, s. 51. [1976–7] 229, HC, SC.

"institutional assistance" Health Act 1953, s. 54. [1976–7] 229, HC, SC.

"intention" Family Home Protection Act 1976, s. 5(1). [1983] 380, HC; [1983] 387.

"is hereby amended" Succession Act 1965, s. 126. [1981] 473, HC.

"is of opinion" Broadcasting Authority Act 1960, s. 31(1), as amended. [1983] 89, SC.

"issue" Whether includes illegitimate issue — Succession Act 1965, ss. 67, 69. [1982] 327, HC; [1985] 86, SC.

"judge of the High Court" — Courts Act 1981, s. 22. [1983] 152, HC.

"judicial authority" Extradition Act 1965, ss. 54(1), 55(1). [1988] 333, SC.

"judicial function" [1988] 531, SC.

"law" Government order applying provisions of Extradition Act 1965 to the United States — Whether order a "law" within meaning of Articles 34 4 5 and 40 4 3 of the Constitution of Ireland 1937. [1987] 278, SC.

"occupied" Relief against municipal rate — Whether applied only to premises occupied at date of passing of Act — Local Government (Dublin) Act 1930, s. 69(1). [1984] 84, HC; [1985] 283, SC.

"occupied with the dwelling" Succession Act 1965, s. 56. [1984] 306, HC.

"opinion" Broadcasting Authority Act 1960, s. 31(1), as amended. [1983] 89, SC.

"or" Whether conjunctive or disjunctive — Employer's liability insurance contract. [1985] 109, HC.

"or otherwise" Landlord and Tenant (Amendment) Act 1980, s. 29. [1981] 385, CC.

"orderly and proper regulation of building society business" Building Societies Act 1976, s. 19. [1981] 73, HC.

"original literary work" Copyright Act 1963, ss. 2(1), 8(1). [1990] 534, HC.

"other proceedings" Companies Act 1963, s. 245(4). [1984] 399, HC.

"owner" Local Government (Planning and Development) Act 1963, ss. 2, 29. [1985] 513, HC.

"partly testate" Succession Act 1965, s. 109(1). [1980] 225, HC.

"payable" Companies Act 1963, s. 285(2). [1987] 222, SC.

"person concerned" EEC Regulation 1380/75, Art 14. [1981] 10, HC.

"philanthropic" Gaming and Lotteries Act 1956, s. 28. [1980] 103, SC.

"plant" Whether barrister's books "plant" qualifying for allowances — Income Tax Act 1967, s. 241 — Finance Act 1971, s. 26. [1984] 679, HC.

"political offence" Extradition Act 1965, s. 50. [1983] 169; [1985] 385, HC, SC; [1985] 410, SC; [1988] 75, HC; [1988] 333, SC; [1990] 505, SC; [1990] 802, SC.

"practice and procedure" Rules of court — Orders of discovery and inspection — RSC O 31 r 29. [1988] 685, HC.

"practice and procedure" Rules of court — Orders of discovery and inspection — RSC O 31 rr 29, 32. [1988] 707, HC.

"practice and procedure of the District Court generally" Rules of court — Courts of Justice Act 1924, s. 91. [1987] 65, SC; [1988] 620, HC, SC.

"practice as a solicitor" Solicitors (Amendment) Act 1960, s. 21(4). [1989] 665, SC.

"prior mortgage" Charge to secure apportioned part of a leasehold rent — Building Societies Act 1976, s. 80. [1984] 350, HC.

"profits" [1989] 552, HC.

"provide and maintain" Hospital — Health Act 1947, s. 10(1) — Health Act 1970, s. 38(1). [1985] 616, SC.

"provided for use in any designated area" Finance Act 1971, s. 22. [1989] 688, HC.

"provides" Landlord and Tenant (Amendment) Act 1980, s. 85. [1989] 452, HC.

"public interest" Freedom of association — Regulation and control — Constitution of Ireland 1937, Article 40 6 1(iii). [1989] 87, SC.

"public place" Road Traffic Act 1961, s. 3. [1985] 290, HC.

"purchase of house upon erection thereof" Finance Act 1969, s. 49(1). [1982] 438, HC.

"purchaser's lien"   [1985] 679, SC.

"rank"   Garda Siochana Act 1977, s. 1. [1989] 87, SC.

"reciprocal"   Extradition Act 1965, s. 8(1). [1985] 465, HC, SC.

"reference under this section"   Employment Equality Act 1977, s. 19(5). [1987] 373, HC, SC.

"regulation and control in the public interest"   Freedom of association — Constitution of Ireland 1937, Article 40 6 1(iii). [1989] 87, SC.

"render such appearance inconsistent with the character of the structure"   Local Government (Planning and Development) Act 1963, s. 4(1)(g). [1986] 465, SC.

"required for the provision of services"   Health Act 1970, s. 38(1). [1985] 616, SC.

"sa mhéid gur feidir é agus gach ní a bhaineann leis an scéal d'áireamh"   Courts of Justice Act 1924, s. 71. [1986] 660, SC.

"safety"   Family Law (maintenance of Spouses and Children) Act 1981, s. 2. [1984] 1, SC.

"satisfied"   Mental Treatment Act 1945, s. 260(1). [1983] 186.

"scheduled offences"   Offences Against the State Act 1939, ss. 30, 36(1). [1988] 137, CCC, CCA, SC.

"separate confinement"   Prisons Act, 1972 (Military Custody) Regulations 1972, regs 6, 66, 68. [1980] 242, HC, SC.

"servant"   Health Act 1970, s. 14. [1982] 390, HC.

"shall"   Unfair Dismissals Act 1977, s. 8. [1983] 50.

"shall"   Whether mandatory or directory — Local Government (Planning and Development) Regulations 1977, arts 14, 15, 17, 18. [1980] 64, SC.

"shall be in camera"   Companies Act 1963, s. 205(7). [1989] 757, SC.

"shall come into operation on such day . . . as may be fixed"   Civil Liability Act 1961, s. 60(7). [1988] 437, SC.

"shall indicate the matters"   Consumer Information Act 1978, s. 16(2). [1985] 273, SC.

"shall proceed"   Income Tax Act 1967, s. 485(2). [1989] 165, HC.

"ship"   Companies Act 1963, s. 99(1). [1980] 186, SC.

"so far as may be practicable having regard to all relevant circumstances"   [Irish text]   Courts of Justice Act 1924, s. 71. O [1986] 660, SC.

"special occasion"   Intoxicating Liquor Act 1927, s. 5 — Intoxicating Liquor Act 1960, s. 12. [1981] 137, SC.

"spouse"   Foreign divorce proceedings initiated — Family Law (Maintenance of Spouses and Children) Act 1976, s. 5. [1988] 262, HC.

"statutory conditions of employment"   Industrial Relations Act 1946, s. 45. [1989] 485, HC.

"substantial grounds"   Mental Treatment Act 1945, s. 260(1). [1983] 186, SC.

"substantial grounds justifying dismissal"   Unfair Dismissals Act 1977, s. 6(1). [1985] 336, HC.

"substantially on a full-time basis"   Capital Acquisitions Tax Act 1976, 2nd Sched, Part 1. [1984] 301, CC.

"table water" Finance (New Duties) Act 1916, s. 4. [1982] 441, HC.

"take into account" Garda Siochana (Compensation) Act 1941, s. 10(1). [1986] 28, SC.

"testator" Succession Act 1965, s. 17. [1980] 225, HC.

"textile design" Industrial and Commercial Property (Protection) Act 1927, s. 72. [1989] 124, HC.

"tort committed within the jurisdiction" RSC O 11 r 1(f). [1986] 627, SC.

"total cost of credit" Consumer Information (Consumer Credit) Order 1987, Art 3. [1990] 743, HC.

"total income brought into charge to Corporation Tax" Corporation Tax Act 1976, s. 58(3). [1985] 666, HC, SC.

"unauthorised use" Resumption of abandoned use — Local Government (Planning and Development) Act 1963, s. 24. [1988] 274, HC.

"unjust attack on property rights" Constitution of Ireland 1937, Articles 40 3 1, 40 3 2. [1987] 747, HC, SC.

"unreasonably witholding its consent" Landlord and tenant. [1986] 451, HC.

"want of due diligence" Marine insurance policy. [1986] 669, HC, SC.

"wanton act" Malicious injury code. [1985] 269, HC.

"week" Redundancy Payments Act 1967, s. 2(1). [1982] 215, EAT.

"welfare" Family Law (maintenance of Spouses and Children) Act 1981, s. 2. [1984] 1, SC.

"wrongful act" Malicious Injuries Act 1981, s. 5(2). [1985] 269, HC.

Subject Matter Titles

Main heading under which cases are indexed

Abandonment of Trial
Abattoir
Abortion
Abuse of Process
Access to Courts, Right of
Accident
Accountant
Accused
Acquittal
Action
Adjournment
Administration of Company
Administration of Estates *See* Succession
Administration of Justice *See* Constitution
Administrative Circular
Administrative Tribunal
Administrative Scheme
Admissibility of Evidence
Admission by Accused
Adoption
Adultery
Adverse Possession
Advertisement
Affidavit
Affiliation Order
Age Limit
Agency
Agreement
Agricultural land
Agriculture
Alien
Alimony
Allowance
Amusement Halls
Anglo-Irish Agreement 1985
Animals
Apartheid
Appeal
Aquaculture
Arbitration
Architect
Army *See* Defence forces
Arrest
Arterial Drainage
Asbestos Waste

Athletics
Attachment
Attorney General
Auction
Auctioneer
Auditor
Authorised Officers

Bail
Bailment
Bank
Bankruptcy
Barrister
Beneficial Interest
Benjamin Order
Betting *See* Bookmaker
Bias
Bill of Exchange
Bill of Sale
Birth
Birth Control
Blood
Bodily Integrity, Right to
Bog Land
Bookmaker
Books
Bord na Móna
Brain Damage
Breach of Confidence
Breach of Contract
Breach of Injunction
Bread
Brewery
Bridge
Broadcasting
Broker
Building
Building Company
Building Contract
Building Society
Bunreacht
Burglary
Burial Ground
Bye-Laws

Defective Premises
Defective Products
Defence
Defence Forces
Delay
Delegated Legislation
Demolition Work
Dependant
Deportation Order See Alien
Deposit
Design
Designated Area
Detention
Detinue
Development See Planning
Diminished Responsibility
Directive See European Community
Director of Public Prosecutions
Disabled Person
Disadvantaged Areas See Agriculture
Discipline
Disclaimer
Disclosure of Information
Discovery
Discrimination
Disease
Diseases of Animals
Dismissal
Dispute See Trade Dispute
Dissolution
District Court
District Court Rules
Distributions
Disturbance
Dividends
Divorce See Marriage
Doctor See Medical Practitioner
Documents
Dog
Domicile
Double Taxation Agreement See Revenue
Drainage Scheme See Arterial Drainage
Drugs See Criminal Law
Drunken Driving See Road Traffic Offences
Duress
Duty of Care See Negligence
Dwelling

Easement
Education
Ejectment
Electoral Law
Electricity Supply Board
Emergency Powers Act 1976
Employer's Liability
Employment

Employment Appeals Tribunal
Enforcement
Entertainment
Entry on Premises
Environment
Environmental Impact Assessment See
    Planning
Equal Pay See Employment
Equality before the law
Equality of Treatment
Equity
Error See Mistake
Error of Law See Certiorari
Escape from Custody
Estoppel
European Community
European Convention on Human Rights
Evidence
Excise Duty See Customs and Excise
Exclusive Supply Contract
Executive Privilege
Exemption Clause
Exploration Work
Export Levies See Agriculture
Export Sales Relief See Revenue
Expression, Freedom of
Extra-Territorial Offence
Extradition
Extrinsic Evidence

Factory
Fair procedures
Fair Trading See Restrictive practice
Fairs and markets See Markets
False Imprisonment
False Statement
Family Law
Family Provision See Succession
Farm Tax Office
Farming See Agriculture
Fatal Injury
Ferry Service
Finance
Finance Company
Fire
Fiscal Nullity
Fisheries
Fishing Rights
Fit Person Order See Child
Fixtures
Force
Forcible Entry
Foreign Currency
Foreign Divorce
Foreign Domicile
Foreign Fishing Vessel

Joint Tenancy
Judge
Judge's Rules
Judgment
Judgment Mortgage
Judicial Function
Judicial Independence
Judicial Notice
Judicial Review
Jurisdiction
Jurisdictional Error *See* Certiorari
Jury
Juvenile Offender *See* Criminal Law

Labour Court
Labour Injunction
Labour Law *See* Employment
Laches *See* Equity
Lakes and Rivers
Land
Land Acts
Land Commission
Landlord and Tenant
Larceny *See* Criminal Law
Law Society *See* Incorporated Law
  Society
Legal Advice
Legal Aid
Legal Costs *See* Costs
Legal Profession
Legal Right
Legislation
Legitimate Expectation
Letters
Letters of Credit
Levy *See* Agriculture
Libel *See* Defamation
Liberty, Right to
Licence
Licensed Premises
Licensing Acts
Licensor and Licensee
Lien
Life Insurance
Life of Unborn
Limitation of Actions
Liquidation *See* Company
Lis Pendens
Livelihood, Right to Earn
Loan
Local Elections
Local Government
Local Taxation *See* Rating and Valuation
Locus Standi
Lottery *See* Gaming and Lotteries

Machine
Machinery
Mail
Maintenance
Malice
Malicious Abuse of Process
Malicious Injuries
Mandamus
Mandatory Injunction
Mandatory Provision
Manslaughter
Manufacture of Goods
Mareva Injunction
Marine Insurance
Marital Status
Markets and Fairs
Marriage
Marriage Settlement
Married Woman
Master of the High Court
Material Change of Use *See* Planning
Material Fact
Maternity Protection Legislation
Matrimonial Proceedings
Matrimonial Property *See* Family Law
Maynooth College
Medical Bureau of Road Safety
Medical Certificate
Medical Council
Medical Practitioner
Memorandum
Memorandum of Association
Men and Women
Mens Rea
Mental Capacity
Mental Handicap
Mental Hospital
Mental Illness
Mental Injury
Mental Treatment
Military Custody
Milk *See* Agriculture
Mines
Minimum Notice *See* Employment
Minister
Minor Offence
Minor
Minority Shareholder
Misconduct
Misdescription
Misrepresentation
Mistake
Misuse of Drugs *See* Criminal Law
Money
Monopoly
Mortgage

Professions
Profit à Prendre
Prohibition
Promissory Estoppel
Proper Law *See* Private International Law
Property
Property Rights
Proprietary Estoppel
Prosecution of Offences
Psychiatric Illness
Psychiatric Nurse
Psychiatrist
Public Authority
Public Finance
Public Funds
Public Health
Public Housing *See* Housing
Public Interest
Public International Law
Public Mischief
Public Morals
Public Place
Public Policy
Public Right
Public Right of Way
Publication
Purchase Notice
Purchaser

Qualified Privilege
Quarry
Quasi-Contract
Question of Law
Quia Timet Injunction
Quiet Enjoyment
Quit

Radio *See* Broadcasting
Railway Bridge
Rape
Rating and Valuation
Receivership
Receiving Stolen Goods
Real Property
Reasonable Expectation *See* Legitimate
    Expectation
Reclaimed Land
Recreational Development
Redundancy *See* Employment
Registered Design
Registered Land
Registrar of Friendly Societies
Registration of Births
Registration of Title
Relator Action *See* Practice
Religion, Minister of

Religious Denomination
Religious Discrimination
Religious School
Rent *See* Landlord and Tenant
Res Judicata *See* Estoppel
Residence
Residential Property Tax
Restaurant Licence
Restitution
Restraint of Trade
Restrictive Covenant
Restrictive Practices
Retention of Title *See* Sale of Goods
Retrospective Legislation *See* Statute
Return for Trial *See* Criminal Law
Revenue
Right of Way *See* Easement
Road
Road Traffic Accidents
Road Traffic Offences
Romalpa Clause
Royal Prerogative
Royalties
Rules of Court

Safety *See* Health and Safety
Safety at Work
Sale of Goods
Sale of Land
Salmon
Sanitary Services
Scheduled Offence
School
Sea Fishing *See* Fisheries
Search Warrant
Secondary Legislation *See* Delegated
    Legislation
Secrecy
Secret Information
Security for Costs *See* Costs
Seminary
Sentence *See* Crimial Law
Separation of Powers
Service Charges
Set Off *See* Practice
Settlement of Action *See* Action
Sewerage *See* Public Health
Sex Discrimination
Sexual Offences
Shareholder
Shares
Shipping
Shop
Single European Act
Slot Machines *See* Gaming and Lotteries
Social Welfare

Widower
Wife
Will
Winding up *See* Company
Wireless Telegraphy
Witness
Women

Words and Phrases
Work
Wrongful Dismissal

Yacht
Young Offender *See* Criminal law
Young Person *See* Child

NOT TO BE REMOVED
FROM LIBRARY